GOLDY & MAX SMITH LIBRARY
FRANCES & JOSEPH PALLER
REFERENCE COLLECTION

honoring recovery of

PRESENTED BY

27575 SHAKER BOULEVARD, PEPPER PIKE, OHIO 44124

RABBI MEIR OF ROTHENBURG

HIS LIFE AND HIS WORKS AS SOURCES FOR THE RELIGIOUS,
LEGAL, AND SOCIAL HISTORY OF THE JEWS OF GERMANY
IN THE THIRTEENTH CENTURY

The publication of this book has been made
possible through the generosity of the renowned
Maecenas of Talmudic-Rabbinic Culture

MR. HARRY FISCHEL

whose unique patronage of true Hebrew learning
and passionate devotion to numerous philanthro-
pic endeavors have gained for him the love and
admiration of Jewry throughout the world.

TWO VOLUMES IN ONE

RABBI MEIR
OF ROTHENBURG

HIS LIFE AND HIS WORKS AS SOURCES FOR
THE RELIGIOUS, LEGAL, AND SOCIAL HISTORY
OF THE JEWS OF GERMANY IN THE
THIRTEENTH CENTURY

By

IRVING A. AGUS, Ph. D.

SECOND EDITION
WITH APPENDIX
Jewish Community Self-Rule

VOLUME ONE

KTAV PUBLISHING HOUSE, INC.
NEW YORK
1970

DEDICATED TO

MY DEAR PARENTS

ה"ר יהודה ליב שליט"א

מרת בילה דבורה שתחיה

TABLE OF CONTENTS

VOLUME I

VOLUME II

PREFACE

The second half of the thirteenth century comprises one of the most critical periods in the history of European Jewry, for in that half century the policy of degradation and humiliation of the Jew, that had been so relentlessly pursued by the Church for a thousand years, also received powerful support from the highest authorities of the state, and thus fully attained its objectives. The personal subjugation and political enslavement of the Jew began in this period thus inaugurating the dark age of the fourteenth, fifteenth and sixteenth centuries.

The Jews did not passively submit to this policy of complete humiliation. They fought steadfastly and valiantly for their honor and their freedom. A veritable war for independence ensued during which the Jews combatted the Emperors of Germany with every means at their command, enlisting the aid of the local rulers, the princes of the church, and the rising power of the municipalities. Rabbi Meir of Rothenburg was one of the principal figures in this bitter struggle which decided the fate of the Jews for over half a millennium; he was the very hub of the powerful resistance movement, and the first tragic victim of its failure.

The Responsa of R. Meir, therefore, being so closely linked with his own activities and bound up with the struggles of many individuals and communities, constitute an invaluable source of information on the cultural, social, economic, and political life of the Jews of Germany immediately before their complete subjugation. They afford us a glimpse of the free, bold, and enterprising Jew before he was broken in spirit and body

by the confining atmosphere of the Ghetto. The life of the Jews
in Germany from the ninth to the end of the thirteenth century
is not only shrouded in obscurity, but has often been misrepre-
sented by historians who have failed to see the all-embracing,
radical change that took place at the end of this period. The
last quarter of the thirteenth century witnessed a veritable
metamorphosis in Jewish life and marked the close of a heroic
era that had lasted for five hundred years. The Responsa
of R. Meir throw considerable light on this fateful period
in Jewish history and, therefore, deserve detailed study.

The Responsa of a great Rabbi, a leader of his generation,
however, do not form merely a collection of highly valuable
historical documents, or a mine of various bits of information
of greater or lesser importance, but are rather the very embodi-
ment of the spirit of the age, the product of the interplay
of dynamic forces — social, religious, cultural and economic —
which mold and fashion the group-life of a people. A Responsum, therefore, is not merely a mirror of life; it is also an integral
part of life itself, and cannot be fully comprehended and correctly evaluated without a clear understanding of the life that
created it. In the several chapters of the first part of the
book an attempt is, therefore, made to describe and analyze
the milieu in which the Responsa of R. Meir were composed.
An account is given of the legal and religious attitudes of the
people; of the role played by the talmudic scholar; of the
organization, function, and power of the community government; of the political ideas of the age; and of the acute crisis
in the relationship of the Jews to Emperor Rudolf of Habsburg
which caused the sudden exodus of many Jews from Germany
and the tragic end of R. Meir. The life, character, and position
of the author are also set forth. In composing the digest of
the Responsa Text, I have sought to retain as much as possible

all the elements of each query and response that might be of interest to the student of history, sociology, economics, government, or law; but above all I endeavored to maintain the unity and the spirit of the Responsum as a clear and definitive literary creation.

It is now my pleasant duty to express my appreciation and thankfulness to those who have made possible the successful completion of this work. I am profoundly grateful to Mr. Harry Fischel, the great patron of Hebrew learning who has dedicated his life and fortune to the dissemination of true scholarship and who is now devoting all his time and energy to the founding and nurturing of great talmudical schools in America and in the Holy Land. A very generous grant by the Harry Fischel Foundation made possible the publication of this work. I am greatly indebted to my beloved teacher and friend, Professor Solomon Zeitlin, for his valuable advice and constant encouragement, and for having instilled within me a love and respect for original sources, taught me to assume a critical attitude to superficial studies, and to probe deeply beneath the surface, and aroused in me an intense interest in the powerful forces governing communal organizations. My gratitude is extended to Professor Abraham A. Neuman, president of the Dropsie College, who was always ready to discuss with me various aspects of my work and helped me with many suggestions and criticisms. Professor Joseph Reider, librarian of the Dropsie College, assisted me greatly in procuring many rare books and manuscripts. I am indebted to the officials of the Library of the Jewish Theological Seminary and the New York Public Library, who very generously assisted me with unfailing courtesy. I am greatly indebted to Mr. Albert Mordell who went over the entire manuscript, painstakingly read the proofs, and offered invaluable suggestions for many improvements in style and diction; and to my dear brother, Dr. Haim Agus, who read the proofs with great care. Above all I must mention my dear wife, Tema Agus, who gave me every assistance possible in the preparation of the manuscript for the printer and in the reading of the proofs. All of these persons as well as others unnamed have given me generously of their time and their advice. Their help to me was great and my gratitude to them is profound.

IRVING A. AGUS

Cedarhurst, L.I.

INTRODUCTION

A Responsum is a written answer by an outstanding talmudic scholar to a query of a legal or religious nature put to
him in writing. A distinction must be drawn between the academic query and the practical. The former arose as a matter
of speculation during the pursuit of one's studies, while the latter was occasioned by an actual problem for which the inquirer
was earnestly seeking a solution. A Responsum to an academic
query is of minor importance to the historian since the specula-
tions and methods of study of medieval thinkers were often
far removed from reality. The Responsum to a practical query,
on the other hand, is of extreme importance as an historic
source for the following reasons:

a) Since the practical query was occasioned by a real problem, it thus represented part of the realities of life.

b) The problem was a serious one, for the inquirer spent
money and exerted effort in obtaining the parchment on which
to write the question, and in hiring a messenger to carry the letter to the scholar.

c) The inquirer stated his problem very carefully in all its
details. In cases of litigation the inquirers were usually the
judges of the courts before which the cases were brought. These
judges closely examined all the evidence and took the testimony of witnesses before presenting the query. Thus the question put to the talmudic scholar was not the product of mere
rumor, speculation, or hearsay, but was a part of real life, the
facts of which had been ascertained by a court.

d) The talmudic scholar considered the problem seriously
and circumspectly. He resorted to neither sophistry nor idle

speculation. He was deeply conscious of the fact that he was dispensing justice and therefore carefully considered every argument he used and every proof he adduced in answer to the query.

This type of Responsum, therefore, is highly trustworthy and furnishes very accurate historical data. The majority of the Responsa included in this work were written as answers to practical queries, and therefore deserve serious consideration.

In order to appreciate fully, however, the great value of Responsa as historical documents, it is necessary to have a clear understanding of the religious and legal circumstances that gave rise to this type of literature, of the authority and jurisdiction of the talmudic scholar who was the author of the Responsa, and of the degree to which talmudic law dominated and controlled the life of the individual and that of the group.

Let us first consider, therefore, the role the Responsum played in the life of the Jews in the Middle Ages, and the particular need that led to the creation of this type of literature. The most important consideration, of course, is the fact that the Talmud dominated the life of the German Jews of this period and served as the supreme authority in law and religion, custom and ritual, group organization and business activities. How did the Talmud become the supreme and only authority in Jewish life?

During the talmudic and geonic periods there were three distinct sources of authority in Jewish life: a) *Books*. The Pentateuch, the Mishna, certain collections of *Baraitot*, and later on, the Talmud were invested with considerable authority and served as guides to life. b) *Living tradition*. Talmudic law was an outgrowth of Jewish life. The customs and ceremonies, legal principles and standards of justice, embodied in the Talmud, originated and reached a high degree of development among the people; they were a product of the moral and religious ideas and attitudes of the early Israelites. These customs, ceremonies and legal principles, collectively called the *halakah*, were developed and expanded by the later generations and were handed down as a living tradition from father to son and from judges and leaders of one generation to those of the next generation. During this period the *halakah* developed in a natural way through the interpretation of new experiences in the light of the old traditions, and through the modification of the old customs to fit the new conditions. When the Jews, however, were forced to move away from their country and disperse, the living tradition lost a great part of its natural force and the continuity of natural development was broken. In a new, strange, and often hostile environment the Jew had to rebuild his life and adopt new ways and methods of gaining a livelihood. During this process of readjustment and of readaptation to the new circumstances, he often lost actual contact with his old, traditional way of life. c) *Authority inherent in certain persons.* During the talmudic period, a central authority in Jewish life still existed: the Patriarch and his court for Palestine, and the Exilarch with his appointed judges, for the diaspora. They derived their authority from their official position. Their decisions in law and ritual were final and binding not only because they were the greatest scholars of their generation, or because their decisions were based on the *halakah*, but chiefly because they acquired the legal power "to bind and to loosen, to permit and prohibit" through ordination or inheritance (from the family of David).

After the talmudic period, the Gaonate was the central authority for the Jews of Babylonia, and for a large portion of the diaspora. But after the extinction of the Gaonate and the dispersion of the Jews throughout Europe and northern Africa, there was no central authority in Jewish life, no organized body of men possessing any coercive powers over the Jews.

During the Middle Ages, therefore, there remained to the Jews but a single source of authority. The book, viz. the Bible and the Talmud, reigned supreme as the only guide to life.

Personal memories of customs and ceremonies, strongly in-
grained habits of conduct and life, could rarely be drawn upon
when a question of law or ritual arose. The book became the
source from which a conception of justice and of proper Jewish
conduct was derived. There were no ordained judges, no central authority, no superior courts who could decide merely by
virtue of their position problems of law and ritual. The Talmud remained the only authority in Jewish life.

The talmudic scholars, the custodians of the *halakah* and
its best interpreters, being well equipped to find in the Talmud
the proper answers to dubious questions in law and ritual, often
acquired authority in Jewish life. But that authority was vested
in them out of respect for their knowledge, and the Jews accepted their decisions because these were ingeniously derived
from the Talmud. The scholar, personally, however, possessed
no legal powers to enforce the acceptance of his decision. Consequently, a written decision emanating from a talmudic scholar
regarding a dubious question in law or ritual, submitted to him
by an inquirer, had to be accompanied by a detailed explanation and discussion of the underlying talmudic principles, and
by convincing proof that the decision was in complete accord
with talmudic law.[1]

Ever since the Jews had come to Germany, they tried to
live according to the laws of conduct and the principles of justice embodied in the Talmud. Business arrangements and contracts were entered into with the implied understanding, by
all parties concerned, that their agreements were to be inter-

---

[1] See Am II, 46: צריך אני לדקדק ולחלק על כל אנפי הדין צדדי' וצידי צדדים שלא
לתן פתחון פה לבעל הדין לחלוק. It is important to note as a general rule that the
length of a Responsum was usually inversely proportional to the official authority
of the scholar. Thus the Responsa of the early Geonim are very brief and contain but few references to the Talmud. The Responsa of the later Geonim, especially those written to inquirers in European countries or North Africa (far away
from the Babylonian center), are quite elaborately written and contain detailed
discussions of the relevant talmudic passages.

preted in accordance with talmudic law. The life of the Jews of Medieval Germany was thus based on the civil as well as on the ritual law of the Talmud.

No organized life, however, is possible if it is based only on a body of law without some organized power to enforce that law. To bring law and order in Jewish life and to enforce the rulings of the Talmud, therefore, the communities organized themselves into corporate bodies with coercive powers over their members. The communities established courts of justice for their members and enforced the rulings of these courts (see chapter IV). Many disputes and litigations, however, arose between communities and their members, between members of different communities and among the communities themselves, which could not be settled by the community courts and had to depend for solution on the great talmudic scholars of the age. Moreover, the Jews of Germany met with new conditions and circumstances out of which problems arose which could not be settled by direct reference to the Talmud and could not be solved by the local judges appointed by the community. Such problems were sent to the leading scholars of the age and the answers usually took the form of the Responsa. Thus the great talmudic scholars of each age gained prime importance in Jewish life, and the Responsum became the medium through which the amorphous and unwieldy mass of legal matter in the Talmud was sought out and sifted, analyzed and interpreted, to fit the new conditions and to become a living and potent force in Jewish life. Through the Responsum, Jewish life was shaped and molded into that pattern which the scholars of that day believed to be the talmudic ideal.

One must keep in mind, however, that a Responsum was merely an opinion of a scholar regarding talmudic law, not a court decision; it was not necessarily binding upon the inquirer. The recipient of a Responsum might accept the decision it contained, or might reject it on the ground that the proof cited was not convincing. He might even send the question to another authority, and, in case the two decisions conflicted, use his own judgment in selecting the one more convincingly in accord with talmudic law.[2]

The Responsa literature thus came into being because of the desire of the Jews to live in accordance with the Talmud, because of the lack of an ordained group of men whose opinion would be final on account of their position, and because of the great need of the Jews for a supreme arbiter in ritual, legal, and community matters. It was the product of an active and creative life permeated by deep religious feeling; and it was the result of a yearning for complete religious freedom, for self government and group autonomy in the midst of a foreign and often hostile environment.

On the other hand, since the Responsa literature was the product of a particular kind of life, it may serve as an excellent mirror to reflect this very life. Thus it throws abundant light on the establishment and development of new sources of authority in Jewish life, on the founding and financing of institutions to take care of communal and religious needs, on the relation of the Jews to their Gentile neighbors and to their overlords, on their reaction to the law of the land, and on their opinion concerning their own status and the limitation of the power of the secular authorities over them. The Responsa are also a mine of information on the social and economic life of the Jews, on their family life and the position of women, on their methods of business and sources of income, on their profits, risks, and losses, and on their taxation and security. Thus the Responsa literature registers their struggles, trials and tribulations, and reflects the ideas and opinions of the various classes of Jews.

---

[2] Thus we find that the same query was sent to several authorities; see: L. 108; Mord. B. B. 482; R. Hayyim Or Zarua, *Responsa*, 222; Am II, 41–2, and *Text*, 271; Am II, 63.

In order to understand the life of the Jews in the first centuries of their settlement in Germany, their process of adaptation, and the method they used in transplanting their age-old
heritage to their new habitation; in order to comprehend the
problems that were vital to them, and to evaluate correctly the
circumstances and ideas that were instrumental in producing the
characteristic medieval institutions, one must make a thorough
study of the Responsa literature of that period, and try to discover the social, economic, political and religious forces which
went into forming the woof and web of Jewish life in the Middle
Ages.

A mere description no matter how able and correct of the
life of a particular age based on the Responsa of that period
is insufficient; for such a description represents but a single
point of view, that of the author, and must necessarily be
one-sided. Furthermore, a Responsum is a multiform and complex document lending itself to so many various interpretations,
depending on the point of view, and is as irreducible to a description as life itself. An historical survey of a particular collection
of Responsa, no matter how comprehensive, can barely uncover
the mine of information contained therein and can never take
the place of the Responsa themselves.

The archaic language, cryptic style, and complicated discussions, of the Responsa, however, render them sealed books
to many historians.[3] In many cases the author of the Respon-

---

[3] See Excursus III. A comparison of the Responsa of R. Meir translated by
Moses Hoffman in his *Der Geldhandel der deutschen Juden während des Mittelalters*
(Leipzig, 1910), with our digest, will prove that in many instances Hoffman mis-
interpreted the texts treated. As a typical example may also serve the following note
of Berthold Altmann in his article in the *Proceedings of the American Academy for
Jewish Research*, vol. X (1940), p. 45: "In a Responsum probably written in 1146
Rabbenu Tam states that the Jews would not be treated by the royal officers in a
harder way than the Christians: והם לא ימירו משפטם [של היהודים] לרשעה מן הכותים
Altmann, ".מרדכי ב"ק קע"ט; לקצוב על אחד יותר ממה שיש לו כי שארית ישראל לא יעשו עולה
however, did not realize that the word והם does not refer to the royal officers, but
to the Jews, the community officers charged with the apportioning of the tax; for

sum has failed to reproduce the full text of the question. Since
a Responsum was often written on the same piece of parchment
as the question, the answer to such a question contained but
cryptic references to the case under discussion. The collectors
of the Responsa, being interested only in the legal discussions,
left out the questions entirely and preserved only the answers
of the scholar. To reconstruct the original question, therefore,
a thorough and painstaking study of the answer is necessary,
requiring an intimate and thorough knowledge of talmudic law
and rabbinic style. These considerations may explain why the
Responsa, the richest sources for Jewish history, have been so
scantily utilized by historians.

The purpose of the present work, therefore, is to digest the
Responsa of Rabbi Meir b. Baruch of Rothenburg; to state
in brief and concise form the questions presented and the decisions rendered; and, by eliminating the complicated legal discussions, make the historical material of these Responsa more
easily accessible to the historian.

---

the clause כי שארית ישראל לא יעשו עולה is an admonition to these community officers
not to deal with their brothers more harshly than the royal officers deal with the
individual Gentiles. I find it necessary to point out this misinterpretation in order
to eradicate the wrong impression that the royal officers assessed the king's tax
upon every individual Jew; for the clause והם לא ימירו משפטם לרשעה מן הכותים לקצוב
על אחד יותר ממה שיש לו, would imply just that, if the word והם referred to the royal
officers. Altmann also misinterpreted the statement of Rabbi Samuel b. Meir in
the latter's commentary to B. B. 54b, s. v. דינא דמלכותא דינא: דינא דמלכותא וארנוניות כל מכים
ומנהגות של משפטי מלכים שרגילין להנהיג במלכותם דינא הוא [.] שכל בני המלכות מקבלין עליהם
מרצונם חוקי המלך ומשפטיו והילכך דין גמור הוא. This comment of R. Samuel is in complete agreement with the opinion current during that time that voluntary consent
was the only legal basis of government (see views of Rabbenu Tam and Rabbi
Eliezer b. Nathan discussed in detail in the chapter on Community Government).
Altmann, however, translates it thus: "There is a legal rule that all inhabitants
of the kingdom *should* voluntarily *submit* (italics mine) to the king's laws and
decrees (ibid. p. 11)." Here Altmann put the comma in the wrong place; instead
of putting it after דינא הוא, he put it after במלכותם, and combined דינא הוא שכל בני
המלכות, without realizing that this would make the tense of מקבלים completely
incongruous. Rabbi Samuel's habitual redundancy contributed to Altmann's
confusion.

THE SOURCES

At the time of R. Meir of Rothenburg (1215?–1293), Responsa literature had already reached a high stage of development. Many collections of Geonic Responsa were often drawn upon when a solution to a problem in law or ritual was sought.[1] The Responsa of German and French scholars were also collected, and were used as sources for practical decisions.[2] Scholars and teachers had private collections of Responsa, as well as of *halakic* discussions and novellae of the Geonim and the German and French authorities, and many scholars included this material in their works.[3]

R. Meir, too, had a rich collection of Responsa by earlier scholars,[4] and to this he added his own store of answers to inquiries. He kept copies of his Responsa for future reference, for the benefit of his students, and for the purpose of sending them to other inquirers on similar topics.[5] He later included

[1] See Hag. Maim. to *Talmud Torah*, 5,3: עוד הורה מורי רבינו שכל פסק שאדם רואה וכן מצאתי בתשוב' רב :Pr. 493 בפירוש בספר מספרי הגאונים יכול להורות אפילו בימי רבו ושוב מצאתי כדברי בתשו' הגאונים :Pr. 996; נטורנאי ב"ר הילאי דאסמכתא קני' במילי דצדקה כי הקרה השם לפני ובאו לידי תשו' שהובאו מדינת אפדיקא ספר גדול מתשו' חכמי :Am II, 99 אפריקה ששאלו מגאוני בבל והשיבום, ובראש התשו' כתב רב נטורנאי בר מר רב נהילאי ריש מתיבתא דמתא מחסיא למרי ורבנא יהודה ברי' דרבינו שאול זצ"ל והתשו' מוחזקת יותר מקונטרס גדול מכמה שאלות ששאלוהו

[2] See L. 386: אצל מורי ה"ר שמואל בר שלמה . . . ומורי היה חולה באותה שעה ולא היה ותשו' רבי' יואל :Am II, 41; יכול לכתוב והראה לי תשובת ר"ת וצוה לי להעתיקה להם וחתם עליה הלוי זצ"ל בידי על מעשה . . . ותשובתו אצוה להעתיק לך למען תשכיל כי אין בדברינו עקש ופתלתל Pr 941; 996: כי רבינו שמשון זצ"ל כתב בתשו'.

[3] See R. Eliezer b. Nathan, *Sefer Rabn*, passim; R. Eliezer b. Joel, *Sefer Rabiah*, passim; especially Aptowitzer's *Mabo l'Sefer Rabiah*, chaps. 5, 6, and 7; R. Isaac b. Moses ha-Levi, of Vienna, *Or Zarua*, passim.

[4] See Pr. 976: ושוב מצאתי בתשו' ר' פלטוי גאון ; ibid. 988: יש בידי תשו' ר' צמח גאון ; נם בתשובה הגאונים כתוב להיתר, אמנם בתשובה הגאונים שלי כתובה תשובת ר' נתן מאפריקה: L. 193 ל"ז; Am II, 41.

[5] See L. 436; P. 477: וגם בתשובות רבינו ראיתי שכתב בפשיטות בסימן קמ"נ. This was written to R. Meir by his pupil, R. Hayyim b. Makir, and the Responsum referred

xxiii

these Responsa in his *halakic* works.[6] His students also compiled collections of their own. They copied his Responsa before
they were dispatched to the inquirers, as well as old ones of his
authorship, and added important Responsa and decisions by
other authorities taken from his collection.[7] Each student had
his individual method of arranging his material. Some grouped
the Responsa in topical order, while others copied for their private use every scrap of *halakic* material they could find. Thus
they included novellae to isolated talmudic passages, collections of laws for certain occasions, *takkanot* of the communities,
Responsa of the Tosaphists and contemporary scholars, and
they often wrote down decisions on cases about which they had
heard or on matters they had witnessed.

Most of the collections of R. Meir's Responsa that we possess, therefore, do not contain Responsa material exclusively,
nor do they contain only material written by R. Meir. They
are mostly collections of *halakic* material gathered by his stu-

---

to is found in the Prague edition, no. 151. By this time, therefore, R. Meir must
have had a standardized collection of many of his Responsa to which his students
could refer by number. This was probably the collection that was later printed
together with many additions in Prague. Some additions were made after his
death, see Pr. 840; 952; 1022. Assuming that the original Prague collection was
made by R. Meir himself, we can well understand why this particular collection
contains so many Responsa belonging to Rabbi Judah ha-Kohen, Rabbenu
Gershom, Rashi, the Tosaphists and Rabbi Eliezer b. Nathan. It is surprising,
however, that the various collections of R. Meir's Responsa do not contain any
large groups of Responsa that should appear as a group in two or more collections. This fact seems to prove that R. Meir kept his Responsa in a loose form,
unnumbered and unbound, and gave them to his students to copy whenever a
particular question of law or ritual was discussed, but in no specific order. It is
also possible that R. Meir numbered his collection in later life, while in his younger
days they were used in a loose form.

[6] See Hag. Maim. to Shabb. 19,4: ושוב קבע תשובה זו במגדל אינזינשהיים בחדושיו;
Tesh. Maim. to *Ishut*, 30: תשובת מורי רבי' למה"ר אשר ממגדל אינזינשהיים וקבעה מורי;
ibid. to *Mishpatim*, 60: תשובת מורי רבינו למה"ר אשר ממגדל רבי' בחדושיו בכתב ידו;
אינזישהיי"ם וקבעה בחדושיו.

[7] See *Tashbetz* 90; Tesh. Maim. to *Maakalot Asurot*, 13: הועתק מנימוקי ה"ר יעקב;
מקורסן תלמידו של רבינו שמשון וקיבץ תשובות והוראות לפניו וכתבן על ספר. This was probably also the method used by the students of R. Meir.

dents in which his Responsa are included. As they were compiled by various students and collectors, therefore, some of the
same material is often found in the various collections.

Let us list below the printed editions, manuscripts, and
other sources, that were utilized in the present work.

1) A collection of R. Meir's Responsa was first printed in
Cremona, in 1557, and was often referred to as מאיר] ר' ותשובות
הקצרות in contradistinction to the Prague edition called
הארוכות. There are three hundred and fifteen Responsa in
this collection. It contains very little extraneous material, very
few Responsa by other scholars; it preserves in many cases the
introductory greetings and remarks, and it gives the names of
the inquirer or inquirers, as well as the name of the author.
Consequently it is a very reliable collection. Responsa by the
following scholars are also included in this collection:

R. Eliezer b. Joel ha-Levi (nos. 77, 165);
R. Isaac b. Abraham (nos. 147, 175, 176, 226);
R. Jacob b. Solomon (no. 79);
Rashi (nos. 90, 135);
R. Samuel b. Meir (no. 152);
R. Samuel b. Menahem (no. 80);
R. Samuel b. Baruch (nos. 73, 74, 143);
R. Simha b. Samuel (no. 148);
R. Jacob Tam (nos. 73, 78, 93);
R. Yakar ha-Levi (nos. 153-5).

2) A collection of R. Meir's Responsa, often referred to as
ותשובות ר' מאיר] הארוכות, was printed in Prague in 1608, then
reprinted without change, in Sdilkow, in 1835, and was later
edited by Moses Bloch and printed in Budapest, in 1895. It
contains one thousand and twenty-two numbered items, but
only about four hundred Responsa of R. Meir. The collector
left out most of the introductory greetings, and the names of
inquirers, and did not pay attention to R. Meir's signature. One

must consult the other collections, therefore, in order to identify the author of most of the Responsa of this collection. Lists of the *takkanot* of R. Gershom, R. Tam, and the Rhine communities, are included in this collection, together with a number of legal decisions, collections of laws on individual topics, novellae to certain talmudic passages and even several Responsa regarding an inquiry written in the year 1375 (Pr. 1022). Responsa by the following scholars are also included in this collection:

R. Abigdor ha-Kohen (nos. 55–6);

R. Asher b. Yehiel (no. 537);

R. Baruch b. Samuel (nos. 486, 560, 576, 578, 591, 618, 704, 727, 739, 810, 849, 867, 872, 933);

R. David b. Kalonymus (no. 872);

R. Eliezer b. Joel ha-Levi (nos. 559, 577, 585, 600, 798, 929);

R. Eliezer b. Nathan (nos. 328–9, 393–6, 403–19, 580–1, 650, 663–6, 668–73, 679, 681, 684–8, 714, 736, 738, 740, 756–93, 802, 806–8);

Rabbenu Gershom b. Judah (nos. 5, 261, 264, 815, 816, 826, 847, 850, 865, 869, 928);

R. Hayyim b. Yehiel Hefez Zahav (nos. 188–9, 209, 241, 249, 296–8, 339–41, 355–6, 382–3, 461–3);

R. Isaac b. Abraham (nos. 6, 9, 16, 157, 181, 289, 319, 452, 458, 494, 866, 991);

R. Isaac b. Judah (no. 195);

R. Isaac b. Menahem (no. 922);

R. Isaac b. Moses (no. 753);

R. Isaac b. Samuel (nos. 152, 170, 220, 311, 316, 346, 357, 360, 369, 370, 474, 477, 484, 795);

R. Jacob b. Solomon (no. 870);

R. Joel ha-Levi (nos. 12, 44);

R. Joseph Tub Elem (nos. 940–1);

R. Judah ha-Kohen (nos. 451, 874–913);

R. Moses Azriel b. Eleazar ha-Darshan (no. 965);

R. Moses b. Hisdai (no. 601);

Rashi (nos. 173, 456, 580, 660, 800, 851, 853–4);

R. Samson b. Abraham (nos. 3–4, 19, 22, 113, 174, 194, 200–1, 203, 287, 310, 318, 320, 385–7, 479–81, 502, 752, 797, 840);

R. Samuel b. Salomo (no. 250);

R. Samuel b. Baruch (nos. 690, 726, 743, 750, 755);

R. Samuel Judah b. Menahem ha-Levi (nos. 509, 533);

R. Simha b. Samuel (nos. 927, 931–2);

Rabbenu Tam (nos. 10, 153, 156, 185–7, 192, 205, 221–3, 240, 268, 270, 275, 283, 303–4, 315, 335, 373, 473, 570, 584, 642, 701, 796, 403–4, 934);

R. Yehiel b. Jacob ha-Levi (no. 251).

There are also included several court decisions (nos. 501, 576, 611, 917); portions of the *Mishna Torah* of Maimonides (nos. 550–5, 640–1, 659, 662); and excerpts from the *Sefer ha-Hokmah* (nos. 571, 712); from the *Sefer Yereim* of R. Eliezer of Metz (no. 624); from the *Sefer ha-Terumah* of R. Baruch b. Samuel of Mayence (no. 629); and from the *Sefer Hefetz*, a geonic work, (no. 852).

3) A third collection was printed by Rabbi Nathan Rabbinowitz, in Lemberg, in 1860. It contains five hundred and seven numbered items. The manuscript used by Rabbinowitz was incomplete, a number of leaves missing at the beginning, and several leaves in the middle, with the result that this edition begins with number fifty-seven, and lacks numbers eighty-eight to ninety-nine inclusive. The collection was probably compiled by R. Hayyim b. Makir,[8] a student of R. Meir

---

[8] See L. 425: חיים ב'ר מכיר . . . מאיר רבי' למורי כתבתי אשר וזה. This collection contains but few complete questions. Usually the answer alone is preserved. The several Responsa written to R. Hayyim, however, are given in great detail without omitting a single flourish of the introductory remarks. This leads us to believe that R. Hayyim was the compiler of this collection.

after the year 1291. It also includes Responsa by the following scholars:

R. Abigdor b. Elijah ha-Kohen (nos. 500, P. 528);

R. Abigdor b. Menahem (nos. 175, 491);

R. Abraham b. Isaac (nos. 396–7);

R. Baruch b. Samuel (nos. 199, 204, 502);

R. Dan b. Joseph (no. 424);

R. Eliezer b. Isaac of Bohemia (no. 112);

R. Eliezer b. Joel ha-Levi (nos. 57–65, 67, 69–86, 100–103, 315, 451–3, 455, 495, P. 3, P. 52–53, P. 55–64, P. 66–7, P. 69–70, P. 88–9, P. 96);

R. Eliezer b. Nathan (nos. 66, 68, 87, 492, 497, P. 66, P. 68);

Rabbenu Gershom b. Judah (nos. 498, P. 100);

R. Eliezer b. Solomon (no. 476);

R. Ephraim b. Jacob (nos. 318–9);

R. Hayyim (no. 311);

R. Hayyim b. Isaac (P. 52);

R. Hayyim Paltiel (nos. 130–6; 157, 161, 164, 177, 424, 476, P. 51, P. 53, P. 132);

R. Hezekiah b. Jacob (no. 200);

R. Isaac b. Abraham (nos. 121, 391, 401, 471, 505);

R. Isaac b. Asher ha-Levi (no. 107);

R. Isaac b. Baruch (P. 512);

R. Isaac b. Moses (nos. 109, 113, 118–9, 152–3, 165–6, 169, 478, 486, P. 19–47, P. 516, P. 520);

R. Isaac b. Samuel (nos. 162–3, 167, 421–2, 427–8, 493);

R. Israel Jonathan b. Jacob (no. 506);

R. Jacob b. Solomon (no. 450);

R. Joel ha-Levi (nos. 157, 419, P. 52);

R. Jonathan (no. 496);

R. Joseph b. Baruch (no. 155);

R. Joseph Tub-Elem (no. 423, P. 94);

R. Judah b. Moses ha-Kohen (no. 173, P. 2);

R. Meshulam b. Jacob (no. 225);
R. Moses b. Hisdai (nos. 110–11, 114);
Rashi (nos. 103–4, 201);
R. Samuel b. Isaac (no. 120);
R. Samuel b. Salomo of Falaise (nos. 473, 489, P. 509);
R. Samson b. Abraham (nos. 155, 390–1, 410–11, 472, 475);
R. Shabbatai b. Samuel (no. 504);
R. Simha b. Samuel (nos. 316–7, 402);
R. Simon of Spiers (no. 414);
Rabbenu Tam (nos. 162, 168, 180, 210, 320);
R. Yehiel b. Joseph (no. 137).

4) In 1891–2 R. Moses Bloch published in Berlin those portions of several manuscripts not included in the older editions. For this edition Bloch used three manuscripts. The first manuscript, that of Parma, contained the collection printed by Rabbinowitz, but without the omissions mentioned above, plus some additional material. The second manuscript, that of Amsterdam, contained a collection in which the Responsa on related topics were grouped together. It was divided into two parts: the first part, Am. I, contained one hundred and nine Responsa which dealt mainly with ritual problems; the second part, Am. II, contained two hundred and sixty-four Responsa which dealt mainly with civil law and the laws of marriage, divorce, and the purity of women. This collection contains a number of Responsa addressed to R. Asher b. Yehiel, and was probably compiled by him or one of his sons. It contains very little extraneous material. The third manuscript, that of Prague, contained very few Responsa that were not included in the other editions.

5) *Mordecai*, a great work of encyclopedic proportions composed by R. Mordecai b. Hillel, a student of R. Meir, contained a large number of the master's Responsa. The author discussed the laws of the Talmud, in the order of their appearance, in an

effort to establish the accepted norm of each law in actual practice. He quoted a large number of Responsa, discussions, and
decisions, of French and German authorities, as well as dwelling
on the customs and practices current in Germany and France. In
its original composition the *Mordecai* was an enormous work,
perhaps as large as the Talmud itself. It was therefore unwieldy
and impracticable for purposes of study, while copying it in its
entirety constituted an heroic feat. Moreover, whenever a
Responsum dealt with two distinct laws which were treated in
different tractates of the Talmud, it was copied by R. Mordecai in its entirety in each tractate in its appropriate place.[9]
Thus the *Mordecai* contained a number of repetitions and dup-
lications which unnecessarily increased its size. Several abridge-
ments of the *Mordecai*, therefore, were prepared, and were
current in the later centuries. One such abridgement was printed
in Riva di Trani, in 1559; another was later included in the Rom
edition of the *Alfasi*. All references to the *Mordecai* in this work
are to the Rom edition, and refer both to the *Mordecai* proper
and to the *Hagahot Mordecai*. Since the *Mordecai* carefully
records the name of the author of each Responsum it cites, it
is a very valuable source enabling us to identify many of the
anonymous Responsa of the other collections.

6) A very fine recension of the *Mordecai* was acquired several years ago by the library of the Jewish Theological Seminary (acc. no. 0838). This manuscript is referred to in the
notes as the *Mordecai Hagadol*, although it is not the complete
Mordecai, but merely a longer recension thereof. In addition
to the usual material this recension contains a collection of
Responsa arranged in topical order, some belonging to the order
"Damages" and some to the order "Women." This separate
collection of Responsa constitutes a unique feature among the

---

[9] The *Mordecai Hagadol*, Goldschmidt manuscript, now in the Jewish Theological Seminary library, contains many such repetitions.

various recensions of the *Mordecai*. R. Joseph Kolon refers to
a *Mordecai* constructed along similar lines. Thus Kolon writes:
כתב המרדכי בתשובות, also כמו שכתב המרדכי בתשובה מסדר נשים
השייכות לסדר נשים.[10] The Responsa cited by Kolon, however,
are not found in the Seminary manuscript, nor in the printed
editions. This fact leads us to believe that the Seminary manuscript is also but an abbreviation of the original *Mordecai*.
On the other hand, R. Judah Minz (*Responsa*, 11) cites a rare
Responsum of R. Meir, which, to my knowledge, is found in no
other place but in the Seminary manuscript (p. 212d, and *Text*
no. 271) and gives the *Mordecai Hagadol* as his source (cf. also
Judah Minz, op. cit. 14, 15). This does not prove, however, that
Minz used the present recension. The Seminary manuscript
contains a number of R. Meir's Responsa not found in any other
collection.

7) The *Teshubot Maimuniot*, printed at the end of several
books of the *Mishne Torah* of Maimonides, consists of a collection of Responsa compiled by R. Meir ha-Kohen of Rothenburg, a student of R. Meir, and the author of the *Hagahot
Maimuniot*. It contains a number of R. Meir's Responsa, interspersed with those of many German and French authorities,

---

[10] See Joseph Kolon, *Responsa* 1; ibid. 160. Dr. Samuel Cohen in his biography of Rabbi Mordecai b. Hillel (reprinted in *Sinai*, vol. VI, p. 60), tries to prove
that R. Mordecai was the author of the *Teshubot Maimuniot*, since the *Mordecai*
does not contain any תשובות השייכות. Thus he writes: והנה מציין ר' יוסף קולון דבר —
שער כמה שידיעותי מגיעות עוד לא העירו על כך — חוזר ומציין הוא את ר' מרדכי שלנו כמחבר של
התשובות למיימונו. הוראה כה ברורה, מאת אישיות בת סמך, שחיתה כ150 שנה אחר ר' מרדכי ראויה
עיין בתשובותיו [של ר' יוסף קולון] א' .כמו שכתב. In his note he explains: לתשומת לב
המרדכי בתשובה מסדר נשים', וסמוך לכך: .המרדכי ... בתשובות השייכות לסדר נשים'; שם ק"ס
נאמר .כתב המרדכי בתשובות השייכות לסדר נשים'. והנה כידוע לא כתב ר' מרדכי בספרו תשובות
לסדרים .לעומת זה התשובות למיימוני מסודרות באמת לסדרים. Now, aside from the fact
that both the Goldschmidt manuscript of the *Mordecai Hagadol*, and the מרדכי
דבני ריינוס (also in the J. Th. S.), contain special Responsa collections at the end of
the *Sedarim* of *Nashim* and *Nezikin* that are labeled תשובות השייכות לסדר, the
Teshubot Maimuniot are not designated as שייכות לסדר, since Maimonides did not
divide his *Mishna Torah* into *Sedarim* but into *Sefarim*. There is no doubt, therefore, that Rabbi Joseph Kolon referred to a certain recension of the *Mordecai
Hagadol*, and not at all to the *Teshubot Maimuniot*.

and arranged according to the topics discussed by Maimomides.
R. Meir ha-Kohen had copied his material with great care and
had preserved most of the introductory remarks, the names of
the inquirers and of the authors of the Responsa. The *Teshubot
Maimuniot*, therefore, constitutes a very valuable collection.

8) In the text of his *Hagahot Maimuniot*, R. Meir ha-Kohen
also included a number of R. Meir's Responsa.

9) The compiler of the material found in the first volume
of שאלות ותשובות הרשב״א (*The Responsa of R. Solomon b. Adret*),
included a large number of R. Meir's Responsa. The compiler
was probably a student of R. Meir who later moved to Spain
and became a student of R. Solomon b. Adret.

10) R. Samson b. Zadok, a student of R. Meir, followed
him in Boswellian fashion and wrote down in minute detail,
in his work *Tashbetz*, the master's comments and observations,
and referred to his observances, his religious life, his manner of
recitation of blessings, and of conducting public prayers. This
material, interspersed with a number of R. Meir's Responsa, was
arranged in topical order, and the arrangement of the topics
followed more or less consistently the arrangement of the *Mishne
Torah*. The *Tashbetz* was very popular in the succeeding centuries and, though small in compass, has exerted a more profound
influence on the *Ashkenazic* ritual than the vastly more volumi-
nous works of the other students of R. Meir.

11) In 1941, Dr. I. Z. Cahana began to publish the Oppenheim manuscript (Ad. Newbauer, Cat. of Hebrew Mss. in Bodl.
Libr., no. 844) of the Responsa of R. Isaac Or Zarua and R.
Meir of Rothenburg, in the monthly *Sinai*, in Jerusalem.
Because of the war many issues of *Sinai* never reached this
country. The writer, therefore, has utilized this source but
scantily.

In the present digest all extraneous material found in the
sources enumerated above, such as *halakic* discussions, novellae
to talmudic passages, court decisions, codified law, and collec-

tions of community ordinances, were omitted. An effort was made to eliminate all non-Responsa material, and all Responsa not written by R. Meir. Many Responsa of doubtful authorship are included; however, since a number of these may be properly assigned to R. Meir, though no proof of his authorship can be adduced at present. Such doubtful cases bear the mark "D". Most Responsa are divided into two parts: the first, marked Q., contains the question which was usually reconstructed from the answer, since in most cases only the answer is contained in the sources; the second, marked A., contains a brief digest of the answer. Some Responsa, however, did not lend themselves to such treatment and therefore were given in the same form as the original. No attempt was made at direct translation, since conciseness was sought. The legal principles underlying the decisions were usually included in the digest (in the answer), though the method of deriving these principles from the Talmud, the Geonic Responsa or earlier codes, discussed in considerable length by R. Meir, was usually omitted. The arrangement of the digested material follo   ..i the main, the four divisions of the *Tur*.

THE LIFE AND WORK OF
RABBI MEIR

CHAPTER I

R. Meir's Early Life, Family, Teachers, and Home.

Rabbi Meir b. Baruch of Rothenburg, the greatest talmudic authority in Germany in the second half of the thirteenth century, came from a family of scholars and community leaders. In his Responsa he mentions two uncles and twelve other relatives bearing the title הרב,[1] a title reserved for talmudic scholars

[1] In R. Meir's Responsa as well as in the works of his students we find references to the following relatives of R. Meir who were talmudic scholars:

a) His uncle Rabbi Joseph b. Meir to whom he refers as ומורי דודי הרב ר' יוסף ב"ר מאיר זצ"ל. (See *Hagahot Maimuniot, Hilkot Ebel,* 5, 1; cf. Zunz, *Literaturgeschichte,* p. 487; Samuel Back, *R. Meir ben Baruch aus Rothenburg,* Frankfurt A.M. 1895, p. 17; J. Wellescz, "Méir b. Baruch de Rothenbourg", *Revue Des Etudes Juives,* LVIII (1909), p. 229; cf. Cr. 144.)

b) His uncle, Rabbi Nathan, whom he addresses: מורי דודי ה"ר נתן; (see Cr. 18; Pr. 637; *Tashbetz* 23; cf. Cr. 20; Back *op. cit.* p. 17; Wellescz, ibid. p. 229).

c) Rabbi Samuel b. Baruch of Bamberg to whom he often refers as מורי קרובי הרב. (See Cr. 8; ibid. 205; Pr. 957; Am II, 17; ibid, 209; Mord. *Gittin* 393; Tesh Maim. to *Mishpatim* 7; cf. Wellescz ibid. pp. 234-5. Rabbi Samuel was a scholar of note, to whom queries were sent regarding law and ritual. Some of his Responsa are still extant. See Pr. 690; 726; 743; 750; 755; Cr. 73, 74, 143; *Mordecai Hagadol* p. 148d. See V. Aptowitzer, *Sefer Rabiah, Mabo,* Jerusalem 1938, pp. 408-9; see also *Tashbetz,* 117; 356; 536.)

d) Rabbi Yakar b. Samuel ha-Levi whom he addresses as מורי קרובי הרב. (See Cr. 76, 125, 160; cf. Cr. 180, 155; Back op. cit. p. 18; R. Hoeniger and M. Stern, *Das Judenschreinbuch der Laurenzpfarre zu Köln,* Berlin 1898, documents of years 1266-91. A Responsum of his is included in the Responsa of Rabbi Asher b. Yehiel, 101, 1; see also Aptowitzer op. cit. p. 214 f.)

e) Rabbi Judah b. Moses ha-Kohen of Mayence, referred to as מורי קרובי הרב, who was R. Meir's teacher for a considerable time. (See Cr. 95; Pr. 95; L. 179, 213; Hag. Maim. to *Zizit* 1, 40; ibid. *Shebuot* 12, 3; cf. literature quoted by Wellescz op. cit. p. 232; ibid. pp. 235-6. One of his Responsa was quoted by *Rabiah,* see

3

of high standing, and possibly only for heads of *yeshiboth* (talmudic colleges).[2] R. Meir addresses most of his relatives with

P. 2; Responsum L. 173 also bears his signature, but *Mord. Pesachim* 558-10
ascribes this Responsum to Rabbi Yehiel of Paris. See also R. Hayyim Or Zarua,
Responsa, 221.)

f) Rabbi Jacob b. Uri of Lüneburg. (See *Mordecai Hagadol* p. 326d: אלופי
קרובי ה"ר יעקב בר אורי ושאר כנותו קהל לינפורק. Cf. note to Pr. 974, and Cr. 288; also
Pr. 988.)

g) Rabbi Menahem b. Natronai of Würzburg, addressed as: מורי קרובי הרב.
(See Pr. 34; L. 343; cf. Cr. 17; *Mordecai Hagadol* p. 328c: כאשר פסק מורי קרובי
הר"ר מאיר כן נראה לי והנני אחריו לקיים דבריו. מנחם ב"ר נטרונאי, אפרים ב"ר נתן, מנחם ב"ר דוד,
כאשר כתב ה"ר מאיר שי' כן גם דעתי נוטה . . . מנחם ב"ר נטרונאי :108 .L; הילל ב"ר עזריאל
ישיע"מ; *Mordecai Hagadol* p. 179 margin: וכן פסקו ה"ר מנחם בר נטרונאי ואביו של רבי'
מאיר. Cf. Back p. 19 note 2; Wellescz *op. cit.* p. 232. Rabbi Menahem was the
teacher of R. Hayyim Or Zarua, see the latter's *Responsa* 110.)

h) Rabbi Joel. (See *Mordecai Hagadol* p. 159c: אלופי ה"ר יצחק עמיתי וקרובי הר"ר
קרובי ה"ר יואל :367a .ibid. p; יואל וה"ר אפרים.)

i) Rabbi Samuel of Eisenach, addressed as מורי קרובי הרב; also מורי
לימדתני מורי. (See Cr. 14; Am. I, 75.)

j) Rabbi Baruch b. Urshraga ha-Kohen of Cologne, addressed as קרובי הרב
ר' ברוך. (See Am II, 49; cf. Back p. 19 note 3; Wellescz *op. cit.* p. 231; Michael,
Or ha-Hayyim no. 641; Moses Frank, קהלות אשכנו ובתי דיניהם p. 148.)

k) Rabbi Elijah, addressed as: אלופי ומיודעי קרובי הר' אליהו (see Am II, 19).

l) Rabbi Eliezer, addressed as: וקרובי חביבי ה"ר אליעזר בנן דמוריין בר אבהן ובר
אורייו (See Pr. 698, 1008).

m) Rabbi Joseph Ha-Kohen, addressed: אלופי מיודעי מלמדי קרובי הר"ר יוסף הכהן
וה"ר יעקב שיחיו (See Pr. 974 note 1).

n) Rabbi Asher, addressed: מורי קרובי הרב אשר. (See Am II, 107; cf. H. J.
Zimmels, *Beiträge zur Geschichte der Juden in Deutschland*, Vienna, 1926, p. 75,
note 23.)

[2] See Cr. 6: מ"ו הר' משה אדוני שאל . . . ושלום מ"ו ושלום ישיבתו ושלום תורתו :ibid. 8, 12;
ibid. 15 and 16: הלא עמכם ארון הברית והפליתי ואת האורים והתומים מורי הר' אבינדור
מ"ו הר"ר אליעזר ב"ר :30 .ibid; מ"ו הר' אבינדור . . . ושלום מ"ו רבי' ושלום תורתו ושלום ישיבתו
תתחזק והתאשר מורי הר"ר :34 ,Am II; אפרים . . . ושלום מ"ו ושלום תורתו ושלום כל כנותך
מתניתא דמר תנינא :52 .ibid; אשר שיחי' . . . ואתה שלום ותורתך שלום וכל ביתך וכל כנותך
אלופי :78 .ibid; ושליחותי' קא עבידנא ורשותא דריש גלותא והרמנא דמרנא ורבנא הר"ר יקותיאל
אם יהיו :123 ,99 .ibid; ומיודעי ה"ר יצחק וה"ר יקותיאל הלוי . . . ואתם ותורתכם וכל כנותכם שלום
כל חכמי ישראל בכף מאזנים ומורינו ה"ר אליעזר שי' בכף שנייה יכריע המצו"ן . . . ושלום מורינו
מה אשיב לאדוני מורי מורי הר"ר אליקים כהן :141 .ibid; רבינו ושלום כל ביתו ושלום כל החבורה
אפוטרופוס :564 *Kiddushin* .Hag. Mord; צדק שיחי' . . . ושלום תורתך ושלום כל כנותך
,ed. Asher, מסעות ר' בנימין מטולידה; see also ראובן תובע עלובן הרב שנתפס הוא ובחוריו
p. 60: ושם בעיר עשר ישיבות וראש הישיבה הגדולה הרב רבי שמואל בן עלי ראש ישיבת גאון יעקב.

the title of deference מורי, "my teacher".[3] He credits them with great learning and treats their opinions with profound respect.[4] He often quotes their opinions and legal decisions in order to bolster his own rulings; hence they must have been well known and greatly esteemed.[5] A detailed study reveals that members of his family held key positions as leaders and judges in many important communities of Germany.[6]

His father, R. Baruch, was credited with a wide knowledge of talmudic lore.[7] Questions of ritual law were occasionally referred to him in the city of Worms, where he lived.[8] He was probably a member of the rabbinical collegium of Worms, and was often chosen to act as judge.[9] We even find *halakic* decisions recorded in his name.[10] He was greatly honored and loved as a teacher, and he was chiefly occupied in study

---

[3] See Cr. 8, 14, 17, 76, 95, 125, 160, 205; Pr. 34, 95, 637, 957; L. 179, 213, 343; Am I, 75; Am II, 17, 107, 209; Hag. Maim, *Ebel* 5, 1; *Tashbetz* 23.

[4] See Cr. 8, 160; Pr. 34; L. 213; Am II, 49; *Tashbetz*, 117, 356, 536.

[5] See Mord. *Gittin* 393; Hag. Maim. *Ebel* 5, 1; Pr. 95, 957; Cr. 95; L. 179.

[6] We find R. Meir's relatives in leading positions in the following communities: In Würzburg, R. Nathan, and R. Menahem b. Natronai; in Cologne, R. Yakar b. Samuel, and R. Baruch b. Urshraga ha-Kohen; in Bamberg, R. Samuel b. Baruch; in Eisenach, R. Samuel; in Mayence, R. Judah ha-Kohen; in Lüneburg, R. Joel b. Uri; and in Worms, his father R. Baruch (see below). See the sources and the literature quoted in note 1 under each name. Cf. also Pr. 983: דעו כי זה קרובי ר' אברהם בא אלי בשליחות קהלו וקובלים על מקצת בני קהלכם. For other relatives of R. Meir, see Am II, 19, 20, 107; L. 229; perhaps also B. p. 294 no. 372.

[7] See his epitaph in Lewysohn, נפשות צדיקים, no. 16: ותלמודו בפיו ערוך; *Shalshelet hakabbalah*, ed. Warsaw, p. 25b; *Kore ha-Dorot*, ed. Cassel p. 20b.

[8] See Am II, 54: בצרפת זכרוני ששאל מורי אבי זלה"ה את מורי הרב זצ"ל אם ימי [בהיותי טוהר נוהגים בזמן הזה. This question was probably asked of R. Baruch, and he in turn sent the query to R. Meir's teacher in France. Cf. Mord. *Niddah* 738.

[9] See Cr. 21: כי גם הוא ישב עמהם בדין . . . שלח לו אביו; Pr. 50: והוא כמו דיין שם; cf. Back pp. 7-9; Wellscz op. cit. p. 228, for a more detailed discussion.

[10] See *Mordecai Hagadol* p. 179 margin: וכן פסקו ה"ר מנחם בר נטרונאי ואביו של רבי' מאיר; *Tashbetz* 110-1: מרבי ברוך הוא זה. Cf. *Sinai* VI (1943) 13, no. 475: והרב רבינו ברוך אבי; Mord. B. M. 346: ושמעתי ממורי אבי שי' שקבל מרבותיו בשם ר' תם והגיד בשם אביו ה"ר ברוך שאמר בשם רבי' שמחה; L. 430: ר' מאיר הביא ראיה מספר.

and communal activities.[11] He is often referred to as הרב ר' ברוך.[12]

R. Meir had a brother, Abraham,[13] who was the author of a talmudic work, סיני, which is still extant in manuscript.[14]

R. Meir is referred to in rabbinic literature as ר' מאיר ב"ר מאיר מרוטנבורק,[15] רמנ"ע,[16] מהר"ם,[17] and simply ר' ברוך,[18]

---

[11] We reprint here his epitaph, Lewysohn, ibid.:

זוכר צדיק לברכה, ציון זה נערכה, עלי מעשיו הישרים
הוא הכה את הארי, ביום שלג כלי, נשא לע.רה צור בנבורים
ותלמודו בפיו ערוך, הוא הרב ר' ברוך, במז"ל צדיק ראש הרים
נבר חכם בעז עלה, במסילה העולה, ליושבי גנים חברים
בשם טוב בא להתקרב, עבודתו עדי ערב, ערב ובקר הטרים
והיה אמונה עתו, מראשיתו עד אחריתו, אשר קבע בכל שחרים
נבר ישיש ותחכמוני, יפה עין ואדמוני, היה אדיר באדירים
והוא נאסף אל ה א ה ה ל, למחנה טוב אור יהל, עם משכילים מזהירים
ומצא חן ושכל טוב, בשיבתו כנן רטב, כמו בימי הנעורים
בני דורו היה מכלכל, בדעו מוסר השכל, בשפתי חן היקרים
פרי צדיק מקור חיים, פרץ מעין לכל איים, מפיק נפך וספירים
ארזים לא עממוהו, כאלו חי במותו הוא, קם בנו תחתיו לשרים
ויהי בחדש הראשון, אשר נכבה מאור אישון, ונס לחיו מפארים
יהא שלום מנוחתו, צרור חיים רפידתו עם צדיקים אבירים
אמן א'א סלה.

[12] See Pr. 50: מורי אבי הר'ר ברוך; Mord. Shabb. 451: ושמעתי ממורי אבי הר'ב; שקיבל מרבותיו, which statement is out of context here, but belongs to Shabb. 228, where R. Meir discusses the problem. Cf. also Asher, *Responsa*, 108, 27: ורבינו מאיר בן ה"ר ברוך; note 10 above; Zunz, *Literaturgeschichte*, p. 361 note 4: וזה היוצר יסד הרב ר' מאיר מרוטנבורג בן הרב ר' ברוך מנרמשא.

[13] See Mord. *Gittin* 404: עוד מצאתי שכתב רבי' אברהם בשם הר'ם אחיו. The Corrections of Wellescz *op. cit.* p. 229 note 2, are unwarranted.

[14] See Zunz, *Ritus*, p. 199; ibid. *Zur Geschichte u. Literatur* p. 162; ibid. *Literaturgeschichte* p. 491; Michael *op. cit.* no. 68; Neubauer, *R.E.J.* XII. p. 92.

[15] See R. Asher, *Responsa* 18, 6; ibid. 108, 27. R. Meir signed his Responsa מאיר ב'ר ברוך.

[16] See R. Asher, *Responsa* 13, 8; 20, 25; 31, 10; 53, 2; 78, 4; 107, 6; Asheri to *Kiddushin* 1, 57. That R. Meir of Rothenburg and R. Meir b. Baruch are the same person, may be seen from R. Asher's quotations in the name of the former, which are also found in R. Meir's Responsa bearing the signature Meir b. Baruch. See R. Asher, *Responsa* 13, 8, and L. 478; *Responsa* 53, 2, and Pr. 864; Asheri B. M. 1, 3, and Pr. 954; cf. also Asher, *Responsa* 20, 25, and *Tashbetz* 343; *Responsa* 31, 10, and *Tashbetz* 483; R. Perez, Novellae to *Semak* (ed. Cremona) 146: הר'ם ז'ל מרוטנבורק אומר במקום שיש מנין ויש יחידים שאינם יכולים לבא לבית הכנסת . . . אינם קוראים which statement is recorded in *Tashbetz*, 207. See also *Tur Hoshen Mishpat* 183: תשובה להר'ם מרוטנבורק, which is a quotation of Pr. 326; *Tur Hoshen Mishpat* 243

ר.בנא מאיר or רבנא מאיר.[19] We do not know the date nor the place
of his birth. He was probably born in Worms about the year
1215.[20] He received his early talmudic education in Würzburg
under R. Isaac b. Moses of Vienna, the author of the *Or Zarua*.[21]
He studied under R. Isaac while R. Eliezer b. Joel ha-Levi was
still alive and active in Würzburg.[22] Since R. Eliezer died about

---

quotes P. 287 in the name of R. Meir of Rothenburg; cf. also *Tur Eben Haezer* 71
with Am II 242–4. See *Tur Orah Hayyim* 128; ibid. 165; ibid. 202–3, and compare with *Tashbetz*.

[17] See *Orhot Hayyim* II, pp. 21, 46, 59, 126, 222, 244, 245; *Kol Bo* chapters
4, 20, 96.

[18] Maharil, *Responsa* 17, 37, 156, 171; Weil, *Responsa* 8, 10, 22, 28, 30, 38, 40;
Kol Bo ch. 104; *Tashbetz*, passim.

[19] R. Asher, *Responsa* 1, 8; 3, 13; 12, 3; 13, 2; 17, 3; 18, 7; 19, 1; 20, 3; 23, 4;
29, 2; 30, 4; *Mordecai*, passim; Alexander Süsslein, *Sefer Agudah*, passim.

[20] R. Meir was probably born in Worms since his father lived there. He was
also buried there (see below). For the date of his birth, see Back op. cit. p. 79;
Wellescz op. cit. p. 227, where the opinions of scholars are cited and discussed.
However, the calculations of these scholars were based mainly on the assumption
of H. Gross (*Eliezer b. Joel ha-Levi*, Krotoschin, 1885; *Gallia Judaica* p. 348) that
R. Eliezer b. Joel died in 1235. V. Aptowitzer, *Mabo to Rabiah* pp. 4–6, however,
throws doubt on Gross' assumption, proving that R. Eliezer was born about 1140,
and it is quite improbable that he lived to be ninety-five without anyone mentioning this unusual age. Rabbi Eliezer, however, was still alive in 1223, for he
was present at the synod of the communities in Speier (see old Prague edition,
p. 112c; L. Finkelstein, *Jewish Self-Government in the Middle Ages*, New York,
1924, Part II, ch. 7) and probably lived two or three years longer. R. Meir,
therefore, must have studied in Würzburg under R. Isaac about the year 1225.
Since R. Isaac of Vienne was not an elementary school teacher of Talmud, we
must assume that R. Meir was about ten or twelve years of age when he joined
the school of R. Isaac. Consequently he was not born later than 1215.

[21] Mord. *Moed Katan* 925: ומיהו זכורני כשהייתי תינוק והייתי בוורצבורק בהציקותי מים
על ידי הרר"י מווין; cf. Mord. B. K. 31; P. 289; Mord. B. B. 538; ibid. M. K. 886;
Hag. Maim. *Taanit* 5; ibid. *Hametz u-Matzah* 8, 6; Asheri, *Taanit* 4, 32.

[22] Mord. *Moed Katan* 925: בהציקותי מים על ידי הרר"י מווין באה אלינו נכרית אחת
H. Tykocinsky. אמרה לה"ר יוסף אחיו של ה"ר יונתן שנפטרה אחותו ושאלו לראבי"ה כדת מה לעשות
"Die Schüler des Isaak Or Zarua" *MGWJ*, 1919, p. 334 f., also *Germania Judaica*
p. 404, ascribes this statement to Mordecai b. Hillel, the author of the *Mordecai*
V. Aptowitzer, *op. cit.* p. 31, has pointed out, however, the statements of Asheri,
M. K. 3, 32, and Hag. Maim *Abel* 7, 6, reporting the entire legal discussion in
the name of R. Meir, which undoubtedly negates the assumption of Tykocinsky.
Moreover the *Mordecai* concludes the passage with the words עד כאן לשון רבינו מאיר;
a study of the *Mordecai* will show that such conclusions usually embrace complete

1225, R. Meir must have joined the school of R. Isaac about the year 1225.[23] He refers to that period with the words בהיותי תינוק "while I was a mere child." R. Meir, therefore, must have been at that time about ten or twelve years of age. Under the tutelage of R. Isaac of Vienna, however, R. Meir must have reached a certain degree of maturity, for he later recalled discussions with this teacher regarding intricate questions of law. On one occasion R. Meir had rejected his teacher's explanation of an involved legal principle and had offered a brilliant suggestion of his own;[24] and on another occasion R. Isaac had listened without protest to R. Meir's expounding of a legal decision in direct opposition to his own opinion.[25] In later life R. Meir concluded that his teacher R. Isaac had agreed with his reasoning and logic and had accepted his opinions.[26] The study of the Talmud was very difficult in those days, without the help of commentaries and cross references, without the use of standardized texts and codes (such as the *Tur* and the *Shulhan Aruh*) amply provided with detailed discussions of the sources relevant

discussions, and not short statements of opinions. Furthermore the statement of Tykocinsky (ibid.) that Mord. B. B. 538: ושוב בלומדי בב"ק לפני ה"ר יצחק מוינא הייתי רוצה לדקדק, does not belong to R. Meir is also untenable since the entire portion, beginning with אומר רבינו מאיר and including the statement quoted, forms a single thought without a break. Tykocinsky must have thought that R. Meir's words ended with וכו', an impossible assumption.

[23] Cf. note 20 above.

[24] Mord. B. K. 30–1: כתב רבינו מאיר וז"ל אמר לי ה"ר יצחק מוינא בשם רבינו יונתן מדלא מחייב ליה מדרבי נתן ... ואמרתי למורי דהכא מיירי. In this discussion R. Meir reveals considerable knowledge of talmudic argumentation; his keen analysis displayed therein is worthy of a mature scholar.

[25] Am II, 55: וכן דנתי משכבר לפני הר"ר יצחק מוינא כשישבנו בבויי שבויר, וא' מן החבורה התחיל לדבר בדברים הללו וחזיתי לדעתי שהי' אומר ודנתי דכל לבעלה חול הוא ושתק. ושוב שמע מבחורי ממנטובא שמכבר שלח דבריו לאסור אל רבינו ישעי' מברנניא זצ"ל והשיב לו להיתר כדברי וכמדומה אני ששמעתי ממהר"ר יצחק מוינא שהיה אוסר, אמנם P. 289: ;ועל דא אנא סמיך, ושלום שוב נשאתי ונתתי לפניו בדבר להתירו ולא כתר את דברי ובקוצר נראה בעיני היתר גמור. ושוב מצאתי בשם רבי' ישעיה מטרנא ז"ל שהתיר הדבר כמו כן.

[26] R. Isaac of Vienna moved from Würzburg before 1240. See J. Wellescz, *Jahrbuch d. Jüdisch-Literarischen Geselschaft*, IV (1906) p. 75 f.; Tykocinsky "Lebenszeit und Heimat des Isaak Or Zarua" *MGWJ*, 1911. These discussions, therefore, took place at the time when R. Meir was a student of R. Isaac.

to each law.[27] A young student would hardly dare contradict a renowned scholar of the caliber of R. Isaac Or Zarua in arriving at the final *halakah*, especially in advocating a lenient view in ritual law, unless he was well versed in talmudic lore and was well acquainted with contemporary rabbinic literature. R. Meir, therefore, must have been about eighteen at the time of the above-mentioned discussions with R. Isaac.

While in Würzburg R. Meir also came under the influence of Rabbi Samuel b. Menahem, to whom he refers as מורי הר"ר שמואל בר מנחם.[28] Subsequently he studied under his relative Rabbi Judah b. Moses ha-Kohen of Mayence, whose opinions and decisions he quoted with great deference.[29] He then went to France and pursued his studies under R. Samuel b. Salomo of Falaise, also known as Sir Morel of Falaise, and R. Yehiel of Paris.[30] Although when R. Meir speaks of his studies in France he mentions his teachers in the plural רבותי שבצרפת,[31] and explicitly refers to R. Yehiel of Paris as מורי ה"ר יחיאל מפריז, he does not refer to any personal contact with R. Yehiel;[32] nor

---

[27] Thus we find that in those days some students required private instruction when they were thirty years of age, see Pr. 245.

[28] Hag. Maim. *Shabbat* 29, 20: כתב מהר"ם בשם רבו הר"ר שמואל בר מנחם; *Tosaphot Yuma* 40b, s. v. מה: הקשה מורי הר"ר שמואל בר מנחם: cf. Back op. cit. p. 23, note 4; Wellescz, op. cit. p. 234; *Germania Judaica* pp. 483-4. Cf. also *Tashbetz* 165: אמנם מהר"ם ז"ל אומר משם הר' שמואל מוויירצבורק שרבינו אבי העזרי אוסר לקנות חדשים בחול המועד, ולא אמר לו רבו שום ראיה

[29] Hag. Maim. *Zizit* 1, 40: דנתי לפני מורי קרובי הר' יהודה זצ"ל . . . עד כאן לשון מורי; ibid. *Shebuot* 12, 3: אמר לי מורי הרי"ך זצ"ל: בחדרושיו; *Tosaphot Yuma*, 7b, s. v. אם: הקשה מורי קרובי הכהן ה"ר יהודה: ibid. p. 63b, s. v. זריקת: ומורי ה"ר יהודה ממיץ; *Hagahot R. Perez* to *Semak* 82: הרמז"ל למד מפי רבנו הרב רבי יהודה הכהן; Pr. 95: אמר לי קרובי: Cr. 95: מורי ה"ר יודא כהן. See note 1e above; *Germania Judaica* pp. 110, 203–4. His references to this teacher deal with community law, local custom and post-talmudic law, subjects reserved for the mature scholar.

[30] See Back op. cit. p. 23; Wellescz op. cit. p. 238–9.

[31] L. 365; Am II, 54.

[32] Pr. 594: וכן שמעתי שמורי הר' ר' יחיאל מפריז; Hag. Maim. *Berkot* 3, 3: וכן שמעתי; *Tosafot* to *Yuma* 18b, s. v. יהודי: שמה"ר יחיאל מפריש לא היה רגיל לאכול אפילו פרט"ש כי שמעתי בשם מורי הר' יחיאל מפריז.

does the Responsum of R. Solomon Luria which deals with the succession of French and German Rabbis recognize R. Yehiel as the teacher of R. Meir.[33] On the other hand, we have a number of references by R. Meir to personal contacts with R. Samuel b. Salomo.[34] We must therefore assume that R. Samuel b. Salomo was R. Meir's most important teacher while the latter was in France.

R. Meir was in France while his teachers, R. Samuel and R. Yehiel, took part in the famous controversy over the Talmud with Nicolas Donin, which took place in 1240.[35] He was there

[33] R. Solomon Luria, *Responsa* 29.

[34] See Back op. cit. p. 23; Wellescz op. cit. p. 238; *Gallia Judaica* pp. 478–80. R. Meir tells us that he was in the house of R. Samuel when the latter received a query from R. Meir's father; see Am II, 54. Although this Responsum is not signed, it belongs to R. Meir since very few Responsa of other scholars were included in this particular collection, and since Mord. *Hilkot Niddah* 738 reports this Responsum in the name of R. Meir. On another occasion R. Meir reports that he was in the house of R. Samuel when the latter was sick; see L. 386: מורי אצל ה"ר שמואל ב"ר שלמה . . . ומורי היה חולה באותה שעה ולא היה יכול לכתוב . . . וצוה לי להעתיקה להם. Cf. also Pr. 138; L. 157; Pr. 146; Cr. 57.

R. Meir mentions several other teachers: a) Rabbi Meborak, (see *Mordecai Hagadol* p. 213: כמו שכתב מורי הר' סבורך); b) Rabbi Simha, (see Mord. B. K. 196: שוב מצאתי שהוכיח מורי רבינו שמחה); c) A Rabbi of Spiers whom he does not mention by name. (See Am II 41: שמורי הר' משפירא; *Mordecai Hagadol* p. 213: ונגד מורי ראיתי כתבים שהוכיחו כי אני תלמידו הר' משפירא איני מקפיד); d) R. Asher (see Cr. 192: מ"ו ה"ר אשר על אשר נשתדל).

Rabbi Simha may be identified with R. Simha b. Samuel of Spiers who died about 1230 and perhaps even later, (see *Germania Judaica* pp. 344-6). The date of his death is unknown, but is calculated according to the citations of his name by his pupil R. Isaac of Vienna, in the *Or Zarua*. The dating of the various parts of the *Or Zarua*, however, is problematical; the greatest difficulty being that R. Meir never quotes the *Or Zarua*, nor do the collections of his Responsa contain any appreciable part thereof. R. Isaak, therefore, must have begun to write the *Or Zarua* after R. Meir left his school, that is after the year 1230. Since the early tractates of the *Or Zarua* mention R. Simha as a living person, he must have died several years thereafter and could have been teacher to R. Meir for a short period of time (see Pr. 928: ומורי רבי' שמחה בר שמואל אמר). We could not, however, identify מורי הר' משפירא with R. Simha, since the abovementioned Responsa were written after 1245, and it is difficult to believe that R. Simha was still living at that time.

[35] See Graetz *History* VII (2) p. 107, also note 5; on Nicolas Donin see also Solomon Grayzel, *The Church and the Jews in the XIIIth Century*, pp. 239–40.

during the burning of the Talmud, on which occasion he wrote his famous elegy שאלי שרופה באש (1242).[36]

R. Meir must have returned to Germany and settled in Rothenburg a few years after this sad occurrence. In a Responsum regarding a young man of Rothenburg who bethrothed the daughter of R. Judah of Düren, R. Samuel b. Salomo bewails his lack of books and deplores the burning of the Talmud.[37] This Responsum, therefore, was written shortly after 1242, and not later than 1250.[38] R. Meir's court-decision on this case was written six years after this betrothal, though it was written before the Responsum of R. Samuel. R. Meir tells us that during these years he wrote repeatedly to R. Judah of Düren about this matter.[39] R. Meir, therefore, must have settled in Rothenburg not later than 1245.[40] He remained in Rothenburg for

[36] Graetz, op. cit. note 5.

[37] Pr. 250: אזל רוחי ותש כוחי ואור עיני אין אתי מחמת המציק אשר גברה ידו עלינו במאד ונפש וסחמד עינינו לקח ואין בידינו ספר להשכיל ולהבין, שדי יקנא לעמו ויאמר לצרותינו די.

[38] The Talmud may have been committed to the flames again in the year 1244, the year given by R. Zedekiah, the author of the *Shibbale Haleket* (see Baber's Introduction, p. 3, note 23). This second burning could have been prompted by the letter of Pope Innocent IV to King Louis the Pious of France, see Graetz *op. cit.* note 5. The Responsum of R. Samuel b. Salomo was probably written about 1245–1250; for R. Samuel died about 1250, see Gross, *Gallia Judaica* p. 479.

[39] L. 386; R. Hayyim Or Zarua, *Responsa* 147; Tesh. Maim. to *Ishut*, 28: וכאשר היה אצלו שנה החזירו אצלי ולא ידעתי מה היה לו ולא פירס בשלום בני ובשלומי, ובני נתבטל טלמודו והוצרכתי לפרנסו בדוחק גדול זה ה' שנים ופללתי רבים לבקשו לתת לבני יציאותיו כאשר נדר, וגם אני החתום מעיד שכמה כתבים שלחתי לו לרחם על חתנו כי היה שרוי בעירום ובחוסר כל ולא השניח להשיב דבר.

[40] H. J. Zimmels (*Beiträge zur Geschichte der Juden in Deutschland im 13. Jahrhundert*, p. 1) concludes from the statement in Cr. 82: וראה שובתי עם זה הכתב שצויתי להעתיק לך שהשבתי בשכבר על נזירת ורנקפורט על מעשה כזה, that R. Meir was a renowned scholar in the year 1241, since this Responsum proves that shortly after the notorious massacre of Frankfurt, in 1241, a query was sent to R. Meir. As this Responsum, however, bears no signature, it is very unlikely that R. Meir was its author, since the Cremona collection usually records the signatures of R. Meir with care. Moreover, there is no indication that the Responsum referred to in the above cited quotation, concerning victims of the massacre in Frankfurt, was written shortly after the year 1241. Litigations were often brought to the courts many years after the cause for action arose (see Pr. 460, 994; Cr. 205).

over forty years, till 1286.[41] There he occupied a house of more than twenty-one rooms, some of which were occupied by the students of his talmudic school;[42] from there he sent his Responsa to all the communities of Germany and its surrounding countries;[43] and from there he made occasional visits to other towns for private or community business.[44] We even learn that R. Meir once took a boat trip that lasted several days.[45] His home, however, remained in Rothenburg.[46]

Furthermore, this Responsum deals with inheritance; litigations involving the laws of inheritance very often arose many years after the death of the inheritor (see Mord. B. B. 527; ibid. 547; Pr. 860; Cr. 260; Am II, 14; ibid. 17; L. 226; ibid. 384; Pr. 1017).

[41] The *Annales Colmarienses* for the year 1287 (edited by Böhmer in *Fontes Rerum Germanicarum*) reports the following: *Rex Rudolphus cepit de Rotwilre Judeum.* This refers to the imprisonment of R. Meir in 1286 (see below). The letter of Pope Nicolas IV to King Rudolph regarding R. Meir's release (Langlois, *Registres de Nicolas IV* no. 313) designates R. Meir as "Mehir de Rothenbourg." R. Meir, therefore, lived in Rothenburg until 1286. Cf. Alfred Freimann, *Jahrbuch der jüdisch-literarischen Gesellschaft*, 1918, p. 245.

[42] Cr. 108: ובבית שלנו סבורני שיש קרוב לכ'ד מזוזות עשיתי מזוזה לבית המדרש ואף לבית
החורף שלי, ולפתח הבית ולשער החצר הפתוח לרשות הרבים, ולפתח הבית הפתוח לחצר ולעליית
המקורה שאני אוכל בקיץ, ולכל חדר וחדר של כל בחור ובחור; cf. Asheri, *Hilkot Mezuzah*,
10; Mord. *halakot Ketanot*, 962.

[43] Cr. 241 תשובה לבני וינא והר'. Cr. 15-6: אבינדור עמהם; Cr. 15-6: תשובה לבני וינא
is addressed to Rabbi Eliezer, probably R. Eliezer of Tuch (see Back, op. cit. p. 41 note 4); Pr. 131 was addressed to the Jews of Bohemia and Moravia (see Excursus I). He even wrote a Responsum to R. Solomon Ibn Adret, to Spain, see *JQR* o.s. VIII (1895-6) pp. 228–38; *Text*, 779.

[44] Cf. Pr. 106: זה חזיתי ואספרה, זה נוהג בכל הקהילות שעברתי; Hag. Maim. to *Maakalot Assurot* 17, 3: והנה מהר'ם התירו להדיא בכל מקום היותו.

[45] See Hag. Maim. *Shabbat* 30, 20: וכן ראיתי במהר'ם כשהלכנו בספינה בשבת והתפלל
ביחיד תפלת המנחה ואח'כ אכלנו.

[46] A number of towns are mentioned by scholars as residences of R. Meir. Graetz cites: Rothenburg, Constance, Worms, and Mayence; Back adds Augsburg, Würzburg, and Nuremberg (see Graetz op. cit. p. 171, note 1; Back op. cit. pp. 24–41). These suppositions, however, are groundless. Expressions such as על מעשה שעשה בוויירמשא (Asher, *Responsa* 48, 1) or בהיותי בקונסטנצה (L. 328), do not prove that R. Meir resided in these towns; he may have been there on short visits. We have shown that R. Meir already resided in Rothenburg in the year 1245, and that he remained there till the year of his imprisonment, 1286. It is very unlikely that he left Rothenburg after 1245 and subsequently returned there. For a detailed refutation of the views of Graetz and Back, see Wellescz, *R.E.J.* vol. 59 (1910)

pp. 42–5. I only want to cite proof of the truth of Wellescz' assumption that
אישפרוקה in *Tashbetz*, 207, means Wasserbourg. The law cited in *Tashbetz*, 207, is
also mentioned by R. Perez in his *Hagahot* to *Semak* 146, 2. However, instead of
the reading of the *Tashbetz* וכן עשה כשהיה באישפרוקא R. Perez writes: וכן עשה הר'מ
כשהיה בבית הסהר. R. Meir, therefore, was in prison in אישפרוקא, which could only
mean Wasserbourg. On the other hand, Wellescz' assertion (ibid. pp. 44–5) that
the custom of the Jews of Würzburg in constructing the uprights of an *Erub* out
of gypsum, originated with *Rabiah*, is groundless. Wellescz bases this opinion on
Cr. 51: ועל השאלה ידעתי שכך נוהגים בווירצבורק על פי ספר אב'י העזר'י. This Responsum,
however, does not at all deal with the material ou. which the uprights were to be
constructed, but refers to *Rabiah* I p. 400: ופסקינן להלכה שאין צריך לינע הקנה על
נביהן; while Mord. *Erubim* 482, reports explicitly: וכתב רבינו מאיר דמה שעושין לחיים
מסיד מחוי או צורת הפתח, יפה עושים ומטני יצאו בכולן בתחילה בעיר וירצבורג לפי שהנכרים היו
באים לעקור אותם אמרתי לעשות כן דהא אמרינן בכל עושין לחיים, וסיד מחוי או גיפסים שמדבקין
אותן אצל החומה כעובי אצבע הוא הרבה חזק יותר מחוט הסרבל או קנה וכשהקורה על נביו יש לה
.כח לקבל קורה ואריח

CHAPTER II

R. Meir's Position and Influence.

R. Meir's fame as a great talmudic authority spread rapidly throughout Germany and its neighboring countries. In the year 1249, when Wenceslaus, the king of Bohemia, appointed his son Ottokar margrave of Moravia, and gave him the income from the Jews of that territory, a serious dispute arose between the communities of Bohemia and those of Moravia regarding the payment of taxes. Formerly the communities of Bohemia and Moravia had paid their taxes to the king collectively, each community contributing its due share; now, however, the communities of Moravia sought to discontinue their participation in the payment of the taxes to the king. In order to settle this dispute, the opinion of R. Meir was sought.[1] Thus at this early period questions regarding litigations which concerned many communities and involved large sums of money, were sent to R. Meir from a foreign country, for his opinions on community law. Already at this early period he was reputed to be the greatest scholar of his generation.[2]

Accordingly, for nearly half a century R. Meir acted as the supreme court of appeals for Germany and its surrounding countries.[3] Rabbis, judges, and members of courts of arbitra-

---

[1] Pr. 131: אשר שאלת מעניני המס שהורגלו היהודים בכל מלכות המלך לתת בשותפות וכך נהגו כמה שנים, והנה נתן המלך אח׳כ קצת מלכותו לבנו מעכשו ואינו לוקח מס מן היהודים הדרים בעיירות של בנו . . . עתה תובעים הקהילות מס מאותם היהודים הדרים בעיירות של בן המלך לתת עמהם כמשפט הראשון. As to the identity of the king, the country, and the date, see Excursus I.

[2] Am II, 81: וידעתי אף כי מורי גדול הדור לא יצוה לו לעבור על דברי זקנים, ואם ישלחו נזירתם יקשה לך לעבור עליה ולבטלה פן ירבו מחלוקת בישראל. This Responsum was written before 1250, see below.

[3] R. Meir died in 1293, see below.

14

tion, sent to R. Meir their questions regarding law and ritual.[4]
Individual complaints that the local courts decided contrary
to talmudic law were also sent to him.[5] He was the arbiter
between communities and their members, between settlements
and new settlers, and between various communities in their
mutual relationships;[6] they turned to him during their greatest
crises.[7]

R. Meir sent his Responsa to the communities of Germany,
Austria,[8] Bohemia,[9] and even France.[10] In his lucid style and
terse language he gave short, clear, and unequivocal answers
to his correspondents. Sometimes he complains of the large
number of Responsa he is forced to write,[11] apologizes for ab-
breviating the introductory greetings,[12] is impatient with long

---

[4] R. Meir's Responsa were sent exclusively to Rabbis, scholars, members of
courts of arbitration, and community leaders. He rarely answered the queries of
individual litigants. See Cr. 192; Am II, 46: שהרי בשכבר קבלו לי קרובי האלמנה
שהעבירו עליה הדרך ורצו שהייתי משתדל בדבר, וכתבתי להם שאיני רגיל להשיב בלתי לדיינים
ועל הדיינים ששאלתי איני משיב ליחיד השואל; Tashbetz 518: לבדם ולא לבעלי דינין ולקרוביהם
cf. Judah Minz, Responsa 6; Pr. 560: ;זולתי לדיינים שלא לעשות עצמי כעורכי הדיינים
הלכך ירונו בעירם ואם הדיינים יודעים הדין יפסקו להם ואם הוצרך הדבר לשאול, הדבר תלוי
בדיינים לשאול למי שירצו ואין זה הדבר תלוי בבע"ד כלל לשאול למי שהם רוצים. Many Responsa
are addressed to a court of three judges (Text nos. 190, 352, 432, 570, 581) or of
two judges (Text nos. 514, 518, 571, 572, 584, 588, 609, 701, 735, 739).

[5] Pr. 982; Cr. 230; Am II, 127.

[6] Cr. 6, 9, 10, 49, 53, 54, 111, 121, 156, 165, 167, 209, 222, 292; Pr. 131, 331,
359, 369, 716, 918, 995, 983, 968, 980, 992, 1012; L. 77-9, 108, 111, 120, 130-5,
213-7, 313, 351, 369, 371, 383, 476; Am II, 127, 128, 130, 140, 141, 244,

[7] Am II, 141: דעו כי מאד מאד הקשיתם לשאול לבקשני להכריע בדבר זה ובמרומים סהרי
כי בשביל ממון גדול לא הייתי משתדל אך אחרי שככה השבעתני והודעתני שאם אמשוך את ידי אז
יבא לידי קטטה גדולה, בטלתי רצוני מפני רצונכם. Cf. Am II, 128; Pr. 131; Berl. p. 320
no. 865; Pr. 941: בכל מלכותינו אין נותנים כלום מס מן הקרקעות ופעמים רצו בעלי כיסין לשנות
ובא המעשה לפנינו ולא הנחנום.

[8] Pr. 102; Cr. 15-6; Am II, 162.

[9] Pr. 131; see Excursus I.

[10] Pr. 980; Cr. 241, cf. Back op. cit. p. 41 n. 4; see especially L. 212: כבר
נשאלתי על זה מגדול אחד מצרפת, which refers to Am II, 99, addressed: "to my teacher
Rabbi Solomon". He even sent a Responsum to Spain; see Text 779.

[11] Am II, 181: מרוב כתיבות מרובות חבילות תשובות לכל סביבות לא מצאה ידי לכתוב את
כל אשר עם לבבי; Cr. 21, 24, 46.

[12] Cr. 7: חכם; ibid. 93: ושרא לי מורי אם לא כתבתי לך לפי כבודך כי לא היה לי פנאי
להאריך בשבחך אין פנאי; Pr. 34: חרשים ונבון לחשים ה"ר יצחק אל יקשה בעיניך אם דברי מעטים.

and drawn out questions,[13] occasionally displays genuine anger when a case is repeatedly brought up before him because of persistent litigants,[14] flares up in high spirited temper when a litigant threatens to apply to the secular court,[15] and allows his passion to rise to a crescendo when confronted with serious crime.[16]

R. Meir sometimes complained that those who addressed their queries to him overestimated his prerogatives as a talmudic scholar, and asked him to decide matters over which he had no jurisdiction.[17] He was often unwilling to answer queries dealing with taxation, since the laws of taxation depended principally on local custom and indigenous procedures.[18] He was very careful not to become involved in disputes and quarrels

[13] Cr. 15: הארכתם עלי דבריכם; ibid. 185: ומטיבותי דמר נרא' בעיני כי האריכו עלי בעלי דיניך; Am II, 24: הארכתם עלי רבותי החתומים מעבר; ביותר ומי יפנה להשיב על כל הדברים האלה; ibid. 19: לכבוד השם ולכבוד תורתו חשתי ולא התמהמהתי ושלא ירבו מחלוקת בישראל, ולולא זה; ibid. 123: ושאר אריכות בעלי דינים וקנטורין שלהם דברי תהו הם; לא נזקקתי לאורך דבריכם ואין צריך להשיב עליהם.

[14] Am II, 22: וטאד מאד הארכתם עלי רבותי והכבדתם זה וכלל כלל לא לא אוכל לסבול; ibid. 23: אכן; יותר שישאלו מדין זה עוד ... וטכאן ואילך אם יהיה דין לכם דייניהו אתם רבותי נודע הדבר אוי לאזנים, כל התחבולות האלה הם מעמיקים לדחות האלמנה שלא תנבה כתובתה, ולא אותה אתם מקניטים כי אם אותי אתם קובעים ומטריחים חנם.

[15] Pr. 247: ומה שמגזם אפי' אם הפטור אמו שרוצה לקבול עליה בפני הדוכוס ... ראו לנדותו על הדבר ולהבדילו מעדת ישראל ... כ"ש וכ"ש אם ילך בערכאות של גוים שיהא [בנדוינו] Cf. וגם אתם תבדילהו ותחרימו אותו ואת כל עוזריו ומסייעיו ומחזיקי ידיו ואנחנו וכל ישראל נקיים; Cr. 140: ואם היתומים יתנו כסף כורדת ניזלו בתר שבקייהו ועל כל ישראל חיים.

[16] Cr. 214: הנה לשלום מר לי מר, המרמר, וריחי נטר, ואתמרמר ומה אומר אחרי אשר הפך; ישראל עורף אל המוכר וטוב לרע הוטר ... ומה אשיב לכם רבותי על המקרה הרע הזה אין דינו מכור בידינו בלהי לד' לבדו ... ברזל תבא נפשו וילקה בהסר ויתר, ויתבזה בפוטבי ובהסתר, ובגלויות ובנע ונד ינהר עד יענה בפניו כהשו ובקלסתר, כולי האי ואולי יעתר, וביום חרון אף ה' יסתר, אף יעם באעם נפעו ועל פשעו יכפה פסכתר, וישהיר פניו בתעניות ובמעמדות שנה או שנתהים, ולכל מה על גזוי; L. 246: שתטעינוהו אתם רבותי יותר, דעתי מסכמת להוסיף ולא לנרוע. להיות כותר כטבעות אהרי השבעם שבועת נילוח שיש בו השחתה שתים שהם ארבע רעות, דל אינהו ודל שבועתייהו, הקצן ידם על טיבורם בפרוע פרעות, וכמה דמים נשפכו על ידי אלה ...

[17] Am II, 123: האי לאו דינא הוא אלא קנבא והני קנסות אנן לא דיינינן אלא אתה טורי' עד שנתגלגל; Mord. Yebamot, 23: וקהלך אם נראה שנענשה דבר מכוער כזה כמו שנראה לקנסו הדבר ו באו לביה דין ובררו ב"ד ועאלוני מה אני אומר בדבר זה, ודהיתים שישאלו מן הנדולים שבמלכות. See Cr. 304, Am II, 162; also next note.

[18] Pr. 995: Am II. למה אתם שואלים דיני מכים שמהלכות מדינא הם נהרא נהרא ופשטיה; 128: למה שאלתוני מעניני מכים שעיקרם מהלכות מדינה הם והכל לפי המנהג שנהגו מדינה ומדינה כמנהגה.

with the communities.[19] Nevertheless, his opinion was earnestly sought in matters involving community rights and taxes "in order to avoid the outbreak of a great quarrel."[20]

The type of question sent to R. Meir speaks eloquently of the position he held in the esteem of his contemporaries. While more than ninety per cent of Rashi's Responsa deal with ritual law and only a small percentage with civil cases,[21] the great majority of R. Meir's Responsa deal with business transactions, real estate, inheritance, marriage contracts, partnerships, agents, sureties, trustees, employees, informers, community government, community property, settling rights, and taxation.[22] It is true that the knowledge of the Talmud was more widespread

[19] Am II, 141: דעו כי מאד מאד הקשיתם לשאול לבקשני להכריע בדבר זה ;234 .ibid: כי לא עקר תלונת ראובן על שמעון כי אם על הקהל ואיני בא לפסוק הדין בינו ובין הקהל כי לא על ככה נשאלתי, ואם יצא דבר מפי אנב אורחא אשר ממנו יודע זכות לראובן נגד הקהל סמיכנא בשמא קדישא דברישך שאל יודע לראובן דלא לימרו הקהל קא מנמרו טענתא לאינשי ומפסדו להו. Nevertheless the answer dealt exclusively with the obligation of the community toward A, and thus could only serve as a subtle reminder to the community that it had acted unethically and therefore should compensate A for his loss; see *Text* no. 536.

[20] Am II, 19; ibid. 141: אך אחרי שככה השבעתני והודעתני שאם אמשוך את ידי אז יבא לידי קטטה גדולה ;Berl. p. 320 no. 865: על אשר שאלתם אם יש קטטה בין קהלכם ואינם יכולים להשוות דעתם לברור להם ראשים בהסכמת כולם זה אומר ככה וזה אומר ככה ומחמת חלוק בוטל התמיד ומדת הדין לוקה, ואין אמת ומשפט ושלום בעיר ולא בכל המלכות הנגררת אחריהם, איך יעשו ... Cf. also Pr. 131.

[21] Dr. Elfenbein, *Responsa Rashi*, New York, 1943, p. XXIV, discusses this problem but offers unsatisfactory explanations. Various reasons may be adduced for the great preponderance of questions on ritual law in Rashi's Responsa. There was a rarity of codes of law and of special collections of ritual laws, necessitating direct reference to the Talmud for the solution of even simple problems. Consequently a great many problems in ritual law required the decision of an outstanding scholar. Further before the commentary of Rashi and the discussions of the *Tosaphot* became widespread, very few attained mastery of talmudic law, and these few were trusted and obeyed without question in civil cases (see *Kol Bo* p. 108c וקטנים שבנו נשמעים לגדולים) and hence there were few appeals to a higher court. The communities were small, closely knit, and controlled by an oligarchic form of government which was implicitly obeyed. Moreover Rashi's fame did not spread till after his death, while an arbitrator in civil cases gained popularity only because of his well established reputation as the outstanding scholar of his generation.

[22] Thus this digest contains two hundred fourty-four Responsa regarding ritual law; and five hundred forty-six Responsa regarding civil law.

in the thirteenth century than in the eleventh century (the commentary of Rashi simplified the study of the Talmud and popularized its content) and that the existence of the several codes and collections of Responsa, such as the *Mahzor Vitri,* *Sefer Haorah, Sefer Issur Veheter, Sefer Hapardes, Siddur Rashi,* *Sefer Hayashar, Eben Haezer,* the numerous collections of *Tosaphot,* the *Sefer Yereim, Sefer Haterumah, Rabiah, Abiasaf,* the *Semag,* and the *Mishne Torah,* obviated the necessity on the part of many scholars of sending queries on questions of ritual. Nevertheless, the preponderence of queries regarding civil cases, and the abundance of such queries, is eloquent proof of the importance of R. Meir as the leader of his people, the father of his generation, and the supreme judge and arbitrator of German Jewry in the second half of the thirteenth century.

The question now arises as to what was R. Meir's official position in Germany. Did he hold the office of Chief Rabbi of the communities? Jost[23] and Graetz[24] believe that he was appointed Chief Rabbi of Germany by Rudolph I. This view, however, is untenable as R. Meir would never have consented to such an appointment, since he was always firm in his view that no overlord, bishop, duke, or the king himself had a right to interfere in internal Jewish affairs.[25] It is indeed possible

---

[23] *Geschichte d. Judenthums u. s. Secten, III.* p. 58.

[24] Op. cit. p. 170, note 4.

[25] See Cr. 190: לא טוב עשה להמנות ש״צ דרחמנא על פי הדוכוס, ובארצנו היו מקפידים מאד על כיוצא בזה... ולא קבל ממנו החזנות אע׳׳פ שתחלה קבל עליו. There is no essential difference between a Rabbi and a *hazzan*; R. Meir's reaction would have been the same to the one as to the other. To understand R. Meir's reaction to an appointment by the government, one must consider the strong spirit of independence displayed in all his Responsa dealing with the relation of the Jews to their overlords. Cf. Pr. 677, 813; Cr. 49; Am II, 122: ולאו כל כמיניה של השר לשנות מנהג שהנהיג. נם המלך או השר הבא לשנות את הדין אין שומעים לו Pr. 134: ; ליהודים בעירו R. Meir regarded talmudic law as the only law binding on the Jews. The King possessed no legal power over the life, property or conduct of the Jews (see chapter on community which develops this idea in considerable detail), and therefore could delegate no powers to a Chief Rabbi. The position of Chief Rabbi appointed by the king was possible only after the new conception of the *servi-camerae* relationship to the

that R. Meir's emigration from Germany in 1286 was caused by an attempt of Rudolph to appoint him Chief Rabbi of Germany; such action would be in perfect accord with R. Meir's character, and with the complicated political situation of the time. The sources, however, are silent on this score.[26]

Was R. Meir elected by the communities as their chief Rabbi or supreme judge? R. Meir's correspondents lavished praises upon him and addressed him with high sounding titles such as: "the Gaon",[27] "the chief",[28] "the light of exile",[29] "the father of the Rabbis",[30] and "the father of all Israel".[31] Meiri[32] and Isaac de Lattes[33] styled him the head of the *yeshibot* of (France)

king (to the effect that the property of the Jews belonged to the king) was finally forced upon the Jews. See the chapter on R. Meir's later life, where the strong opposition of the Jews to this new conception is described. In any event, R. Meir would never have accepted an appointment by Rudolph I in the face of the express prohibition of such a step by the *takkanah* of R. Tam and the communities; see Pr. p. 159c: ועוד גזרנו ונדינו והחרמנו בשמתא ובשם מיתה שלא יהא אדם רשאי ליטול שררה על חבירו לא ע"י מלך ולא ע"י שר ושופט כדי לענוש ולקנוס ולכוף חבירו לא בדברי הבאי ולא בדברי שמים; cf. Finkelstein, op. cit. pp. 154–7.

[26] In the later years a Chief Rabbi was usually appointed by the king in order to facilitate the collection of taxes from the Jews. The communities were never happy over such an appointment but rather took it as an additional harshness imposed upon them by the government. For this reason, rabbinic literature rarely mentions the office of Chief Rabbi or the name of the person who filled the office. In the Responsa of the fifteenth and sixteenth centuries we can find not a single reference to such an office. The difficulty Rudolph I encountered in collecting taxes from the Jews (see chapter on R. Meir's later life) might have prompted him to resort to the expedient of appointing R. Meir Chief Rabbi of Germany. The sources, however, neither confirm nor deny this view.

[27] Pr. 934: הגאון מ"ו מאיר; מורינו הגאון הרב ר' מאיר; ibid. 946c.

[28] Pr. 946c: כי אתה הראש.

[29] L. 338: מאיר עיני הגולה; Cr. 63: מורי ה"ר מאיר מאור הגולה.

[30] B. p. 318, no. 553: ושמעתי שהיו רגילים בבית ר' מאיר אבי הרבנים.

[31] *Mordecai Hagadol* p. 161b: מורינו המאור הגדול אני עבדו ותלמידו משתטח לפניו שימחול לי על הטורח שאני מטריח עליו והשעה צריכה לכך כי דין מורדת בא לפנינו . . . לכן התיר לו כי אתה אביהן של ישראל מלמטה, ועיני כל ישראל עליך לעשות להן תקנה אשר לא תתפרצנה בנות ישראל . . .

[32] See Introduction to *Abot*; Gudeman, *Geschichte d. Erziungswesen in Frankreich u. Deutschland*, p. 170 note 4.

[33] *Shaare Zion*, ed. Buber, p. 39: ואחריהם הגיע הזמן לרב ר' מאיר מרוטנבורק ראש ישיבה מכל ארץ צרפת והרביץ את התורה והגדיל עד מעלה מעלה; cf. Wellescz, *R.E.J.* 59 (1910) p. 47, where he suggests the substitution of צרפת for אשכנו.

[Germany]. Yet, these titles and appellations do not prove that R. Meir held any official position in the German communities.[34] A very reliable source for the clarification of this problem ought to be his Responsa. We should expect an elected or an appointed officer of the communities to reveal in his Responsa as well as by his deeds some measure of authority such as is not granted to a person whose only claim to authority is his talmudic scholarship. Let us therefore scrutinize this evidence.

R. Meir's Responsa may be divided into two groups: those written before 1275, and those after that date. The former group was written while his father was alive, and R. Meir always added the short prayer, ש"י, "his life be prolonged", after the mention of his father's name in his signature. The latter group was written after his father was dead,[35] when he added instead the short prayer for the dead זלה"ה. Thus we possess a clear demarcation line separating the Responsa R. Meir wrote early in his career from those he wrote in later life.

There is little doubt that in the first three decades of his stay in Rothenburg, R. Meir held no official position in the German communities. In a Responsum written before 1275 he asserted that he would not try to arbitrate, for any amount of money,

---

[34] Graetz ibid. adduces as proof of his contention that R. Meir was the Chief Rabbi of Germany, the following two sources: a) Hayyim Or Zarua, *Responsa* 191: ומה"ר אליעזר זצ"ל הנהיג בזה המלכות להחזיר כל הנדוניא אפילו תפס כאלפסי וכרבינו מאיר זצ"ל והוא היה ראש המלכות ומנהיגו. (However, a close examination of the text will show that the term ראש המלכות refers to R. Eliezer, probably R. Eliezer of Touque, since this epithet was necessary for the person who instituted the custom. Moreover, even if it referred to R. Meir it would not prove that he was officially recognized as the Chief Rabbi, since it refers to the person's spiritual, and not temporal, influence.) b) Israel Isserlein, *Pesakim*, 142: וממור'ם אין להביא ראיה שהיה מופלג ובקי ולא היה בדורו כמותו. (Needless to say that this description refers to R. Meir's greatness as a talmudic scholar, but not to any official position held by him.)

[35] R. Meir's father died about 1275; his epitaph includes the phrase: והוא נאסף אל ה ה א א ל, which probably stands for ה' אלפים ה'ל; cf. Back op. cit. p. 8; Wellescz, *R.E.J.* 58 (1909), p. 228. Thus L. 310, Tesh. Maim. to *Ishut* 25, which was written in 1272, bears the signature: מאיר ב'ר ברוך שי'.

in a community quarrel or undertake to decide in matters of taxation.[36] A Chief Rabbi would undoubtedly feel it his duty to act as judge and arbiter in litigations arising between a community and its individual members, or between two factions in a community.

In the last two decades of his life R. Meir took a more aggressive stand in his relation to the communities. He convoked a synod of the communities and urged them to adopt an ordinance to the effect that a rebellious wife should forfeit upon divorce her right to any part of her husband's possessions and should not even be entitled to collect her dowry from him.[37] He wrote to the Jews of Würzburg that they should change their customary procedure in the sale of real-estate, and the change was adopted in spite of the fact that some members were loath to abandon their age-old practice.[38] In a Responsum R. Meir wrote: "On many occasions have individuals, whose wealth consisted of ready cash, desired to transfer the burden of taxation to real-estate owners, but we did not permit them to do so".[39] The last clause might imply that in such cases R. Meir

---

[36] Am II, 141: דעו כי מאד מאד הקשיתם לשאול לבקשני להכריע בדבר זה ובמרומים סהדי. מאיר ב׳ר :This Resp. signed כי בשביל ממון גדול לא הייתי משתדל, אך אחרי שכבה השבעתני ברוך שי׳, was, therefore, written before 1275.

[37] Hayyim Or Zarua, op. cit. no. 155: וכן דן מורינו רבינו מאיר זצ׳ל כמה פעמים ולבסוף בהיותו בנורנבורג פירש לקהלות הקודש שבריינס שתקנו שאפילו מה שהכניסה לו לא תטול; ibid. 126: ורבו המורדות אז שלח למורי הר׳ר ידידיה שהיה בשפירא לשלשלת הקהלות להתועד יחד ולתקן שהמורדת תפסיד גם מה שהכניסה ותצא ריקנית. This ordinance was adopted at a synod of the communities in Würzburg, see *Mordecai Hagadol* p. 160d: ועוד דהקהלות תקנו בוירצבורק דכל כי האי גוונא שמורדת על ידי קרוביה שמסיתין אותה שהבעל נוטל הכל וכה בכל הנכסים ויזרוק לה נט על כרחה. Cf. Asheri, *Ketubot* 5, 35; *Hagahot Asheri, Kiddushin* 3, 16; *Kol Bo,* 75; Weil, *Responsa* 22; R. Asher, *Responsa,* 43, 8; *Tur Eben Haezer,* 77.

[38] Mord. B. M. 396: וכן כתבתי לרבותינו בוירצבורק והוקשה למקצתם תחילה לשנות מנהגם ואעפ׳כ קבלו, וכן דנים עכשו שמה בכל יום.

[39] Pr. 941; Mord. B. B. 481: בכל מלכותינו אין נותנים כלום מן הקרקעות ופעמים רבות רצו בעלי כיסין לשנות ובא המעשה לפנינו ולא הנחנום. This Responsum bears the simple signature מאיר ב׳ר ברוך, without indicating whether R. Baruch was then alive or dead. In this particular case, however, the distinction is not important.

exercized greater authority than that vested in a talmudic scholar.

Even in the last two decades of his life, however, R. Meir was not an official of the communities. He was highly respected, and in many cases his word was law; but he enjoyed this authority because of his scholarship, because many leaders of the German communities were his students who owed him respect and even obedience,[40] and because the Talmud was the "constitution" of the community government, and R. Meir, the greatest scholar of the land, its best and most authoritative interpreter. But in the almost eight hundred Responsa of R. Meir we can find no trace of evidence that he was either appointed, elected, or considered the Chief Rabbi or supreme judge of the German communities. On the other hand, we possess evidence to the effect that he held no such official position: 1) Thus, after R. Meir repeatedly sent Responsa regarding the *ketubah* of the widow of a wealthy man, he wrote: "You have protracted your case and have burdened me beyond endurance. I cannot tolerate your sending me any further inquiries regarding this case; for it is obvious that the trustees are interested only in causing annoyance, vexation and protraction. From now on judge any case that may come before you yourselves".[41] Had R. Meir been the Chief Rabbi of Germany he would not have written to local judges never again to trouble him with litigations that might come up before them. 2) In another Responsum R. Meir confessed ignorance of the ordinances that had been passed by the communities to regulate

---

[40] A student was always under obligation to obey his teacher; see *Mishne Torah, Talmud Torah* 5. When R. Meir vigorously denounced the threats hurled against him by the Rhine communities (*Mordecai Hagadol* p. 212d), he was careful to insert the phrase: ונגד מורי ה'ר משפירא איני מקפיד, כי אני תלמידו, for a teacher excercised authority over his pupil even after the pupil left his school.

[41] Am II, 22: ומאד מאד הארכתם עלי רבותי והכבדתם זה וכלל כלל לא אוכל לכבול יותר שישאלו מדין זה עוד כי רואה אני בכמה כי האפוטרופי' מתכונים לקנטר ולדחות הדבר ומכאן ואילך אם יה' לכם דין דיינוהו אתם רבותי.

the division of an estate between the childless widow and her
levir, or husband's brother.[42] The Chief Rabbi of the communities would have made a special study of the ordinances and
customs of the communities, especially those passed by the
synods of the communities. 3) The community of Stendal sent
a query to R. Meir regarding persons who refused to cooperate
with the policy of taxation in the community. R. Meir's answer
was followed by statements of scholars, community leaders,
and members of official courts, to the effect that they all subscribed to his opinion and indorsed his decision.[43] Had R. Meir
been the Chief Rabbi of the communities, such indorsements
would be superfluous. 4) Finally, even after 1286, when R. Meir
was already held a prisoner, he had to be assured that his decision would be accepted, before he would decide between two
conflicting courts.[44]

R. Meir himself based his authority on his knowledge of
talmudic law and on his intellectual attainments both of which

[42] Pr. 563; Mord. *Yebamot*, 23: על ריב אלמנה משפירא שנתעצמו בדין זה כמה ימים עד
שנתגלגל הדבר שבא לבית דין וברדו ב'ד ושאלוני מה אני אומר בדבר זה, ודחיתים שישאלו מ ן
ה ג ד ו ל י ם ש ב מ ל כ ו ת מה תקנות הקהילות בין אלמנה ליבמה וראיתי שכלם הושוו בזה לאחר
שיחלצו לה היבמין שיחלקו הממון שהניח המת חציו לה וחציו ליבמין ובדין תקנות הקהלות לא ידעתי.
אך כאשר כתבו רבותי. By the term הגדולים שבמלכות are probably meant the great
scholars of the country, the leaders of the older communities who were considered authorities on community law; cf. Pr. 934: ואם . . . . כי לא שמעתי מעולם תקנה
הלכה רפופה בידכם שלחו אל רבותינו קהל וורצפורק והם יגידו לכם . . . סוף דבר אין לנו בזה אלא
דברי רבותינו שבוויירצפורק והקהילות, ושלום מאיר ב'ר ברוך זלה"ה. This quotation again
proves that R. Meir did not consider himself an authority on community law; cf.
also Pr. 994.

[43] L. 108, signed: מאיר ב'ר ברוך זלה"ה.

[44] Tesh. Maim. to *Kinyan*, 32: והודיעני מה אתה דן בה ואין מצוה גדולה מזו להעמיד
העולם על הדין ועל האמת לכן התחל תשובתך מעבר הפסק דין ובאר לנו צדדים וצדי צדדים
ו צ ו ר י נ ו י ו צ י א ך מ כ ל א ך שלומך יאריך לעד . . . והפרנסים צוו לדיינים לכתוב הטענות
והפסק למען להעמיד כל אדם על חזקתו ועל הדין, ועליך אין לפקפק ולהרהר כי כל מה שתפסוק
פסוק וחתום. Thus even after the inquirer made it clear that this query was sent to
R. Meir at the direction of the community leaders, he still found it necessary
to assure R. Meir that his decision would be accepted — a very unnecessary
statement if made to a man appointed or elected Chief Rabbi of the communities.
Since this inquiry was sent to R. Meir in prison, it furnishes conclusive evidence
that he was never an official of the communities.

enabled him to arrive at a correct decision in questions of law
or ritual; he did not consider it to be dependent upon appointment, election or even ordination. Thus he once wrote in high-
spirited defiance: "You, the aforementioned community leaders
[of the Rhine communities], probably delude yourselves with the
idea that since your permission is required before a person may
divorce his wife, no scholar is permitted to render decisions in
ritual law unless he receives your authorization. No, this is
not true, for the Torah is free to anyone who is capable of arriving at a correct decision".[45] R. Meir, therefore, assumed only
those powers and rights with which the Talmud endows an
unordained בית דין, but none of those privileges and prerogatives which the community rightfully bestows upon its elected
judges and rabbis.[46] For this reason he was averse to answering queries regarding taxation, pointing out that these laws
depended on local custom and community law only, and not
on talmudic law.[47] On several occasions he reminded his correspondents that he lacked the power of imposing fines and
penalties, though community officials possessed that power.[48]

[45] *Mordecai Hagadol* p. 212d: ושמא מחמת שצריכים לכם להסכמת גיטין כמדומים אתם
שאין לכל אדם להורות אי לא נקט רשותא מינייכו. לא, כי התורה הפקר אך שיורה כהלכה.
[46] Cr. 304: ועל שעשה שלא כהוגן שקבל עליו לנוי, איני דן דין קנסות אמנם הקהל הרשות. Cf. also
מאיר ב"ר ברוך זלה"ה. The signature reads: בידם לקנוס ולענש על דבר מכוער
Am II, 123: ואטו משום דעבר על שבועתו קנסינן ליה להוציא הקרקע מידו, ולהחליטו ביד ראובן.
האי לאו דינא הוא אלא קנסא, והני קנסא אנן לא דיינינן אלא אתה מורי וקהלך אם נראה שנעשה דבר
מכוער כזה כמו שנראה לקונסו לתן לצדקה הנראה לכם. Thus R. Meir draws a clear distinction between his own authority, which is that of a talmudic scholar, and the
authority of a court elected or appointed by a community. He had no right to impose fines since he was not an official of the communities, but the community had
the right to impose fines on its own members. Similar statements by Rashi (see Joel
Mueller תשובות חכמי צרפת ולותיר, 22; ibid. 27; *Ozar Nehmad* II, p. 178) have been
taken by many scholars as a proof of his modesty. There was no question of
modesty, however, for talmudic law did not permit Rashi to exercise any coercive power over a member of another community.
[47] Pr. 995: למה אתם שואלים דיני מסים שמהלכות מדינה הם נהרא נהרא ופשטי' ורבו בהם
למה Am II, 128: חלוקי מנהגים, ומה צורך להודיעכם מנהג מקומינו, ושמא אין מקומכם כך
שאלתוני מעניני מסים שעיקרם מהלכות מדינה הם; see also Pr. 106.
[48] See note 46 above.

R. Meir, however, was a community official in Rothenburg. He held the combined post of Rabbi[49] and head of the talmudic school.[50] He occasionally acted as cantor on the holidays,[51] and even as public reader of the Torah.[52] His house in Rothenburg was probably provided for him by the community since it contained a *Beth Midrash* (study-hall) and rooms for his students.[53] He did not, however, completely depend on his salary for a livelihood, since we find that he made financial investments.[54]

In the thirteenth century, when the prayer-ritual was still in an unsettled state, scholarship was required of a cantor rather than pleasantness of voice.[55] The reason for this was that great

[49] Isserlein, *Pesakim*, 142: שלח לך הרב הכהן טופס אחד מועתק מטופס גט ישן שנכתב; cf. Back, על שם רוטנבורק וכתוב על הטופס ההוא שהוא מסודר מפי מור'ם מרי דאתר' הדי'. op. cit. pp. 34, 45; Wellescz, *R.E.J.* 59 (1910), pp. 45-6.

[50] See Isaac de Lattes, *Shaare Zion* ed. Buber, p. 39; L. 425: ומן השמים ישלו. וישקטו כבוד מורינו ותורתו וישיבתו עם כל הסרים אל משמעתו. *Annales Colmarienses*, ed. Böhmer, for year 1288: *cui schola Judeorum et honores divines impendere videbantur*; also Cr. 3: ואתה מורי וכל החבורות היושבים בשורות.

[51] *Tashbetz*, 101: מהר'ם ז'ל; ibid. 119: וכשהוא מתפלל לפני התיבה ביום ראשון של פסח מתפלל כל ברכה ראשונה עד למען שמו באהבה ואז מחתיל מסוד חכמים וכו' ... ובשני ימים טובים ובערב יום הכפורים קודם ; ibid. 131: של ר'ה מתפלל קדיש ראשון בנגון קדיש ראשון של שבת ואומר בכל נדרי מיום כפורים זה עד יום ; ibid. 134: שאומר כל נדרי אומר בישיבה של מעלה וכן היה נוהג הר'ם מרוטנבורק כשהיה הוא ש'ץ. *Tur Orah Hayyim*, 128: כפורים הבא עלינו. היה אומר או'א בלחש עם הכהנים, ואומר כהנים בקול רם It is possible, however, that R. Meir was never an official cantor, but that all the references to his having served in that capacity were due to the fact that, like other heads of *Yeshibot*, he conducted private services at his home for his students; his *Bet Midrash* was probably converted into a synagogue on such occasions. Cf. *Sefer Maharil*, p. 30a: אמר מהריל פעם אחת בשבת נחמו סיים הצבור תפלתם בבה'כ טרם סיים מהר'ם [הלוי] עם הבחורים בביתו.

[52] *Tashbetz*, 188: וכשקורים בשני ספרי תורות, כשנותנים לו השניה לקרות, אינו פותח ואינו מסיר המפה עד שיגללו הראשונה במפה. In this connection it is interesting to note that R. Meir was even on occasion a scribe; see Hag. Maim. *Megilah*, 12, 70: וכן כתב מהר'ם במגילת אסתר שכתב לעצמו.

[53] Cr. 108; Mord. *Halakot Ketanot*, 962; cf. Asheri, *hilkot Mezuzah*, 10: וכן בית מדרשו של מהר'ם מרוטנבורק היה בו מזוזה ואמר כשהיה ישן שינת צהרים בביה'ם היה רוח רעה מבעתו עד שתקן מזוזה.

[54] R. Asher, *Responsa* 23, 4: הר'ם היה מלוה למערופיא שלו בחול המועד בחנם; *Tashbetz*, 166: אמנם למערופיא שלו יכול להלוות בחנם אותה שבוע ... וכן היה רגיל מהר'ם; cf. *Kol Bo*, ed. Fiorda, p. 49c.

[55] Regarding cantors and other religious officials of the community see *Sefer Hassidim*, 1199; *Or Zarua* I, 114-5; L. 109-113. We also learn that a cantor had

erudition was necessary, on the High Holidays, in deciding upon
the proper wording and sequence of the prayers and the liturgy.[56]
Even the manner of blowing the *shofar*, and the particular in-
tonation of each prayer, raised problems requiring a wide
acquaintance with talmudic lore for proper solution.[57] R. Meir's
part in the arrangement and fixing of the *Ashkenazic* ritual can
hardly be overestimated. He established a fixed and stereo-
typed ritual which was based, to its minutest detail, on his wide
and thorough knowledge of the Talmud, geonic literature, the
novellae of the rabbis, and the customs of the German communities.[58] His students, who lived with him, carefully observed
his method of prayer and his arrangement of the liturgy. They
often inquired into the reason for certain ceremonies and customs and were interested in every detail. His students later
became leaders of the German communities.[59] They became
rabbis, judges and cantors, and helped to implant R. Meir's
usages, practices and order of service into the rituals of
the various communities.[60] Not all of his ideas were ac-

---

the power to inflict punishment on a member of his community. See Cr. 190;
Pr. 137: החזן . . . וסבורני שקינס את היהודי. In this Responsum R. Meir refers to the
cantor as הרב.

[56] See *Tashbetz*, 101, 102, 119, 120, 125, 131–5, 139, 140, 142–3, 149–51, 154–8,
175–7, 186–8, 191–4, 197–201, 204, 207, 209–28, 237–42, 245, 248–54, 258.

[57] Ibid. 119.

[58] See *Tashbetz*, 81, 86–7, 98, 101–2, 105, 116, 119, 131, 133–5, 140, 142–3,
149–50, 156, 158, 171, 176–7, 182–6, 188–99, 204–6, 209, 211, 213–4, 216–8, 220,
222–8, 230–58. It is very important to note that R. Perez, the famous French
tosaphist who wrote novellae to the *Tashbetz*, raised very few objections to these
divisions of the Tashbetz.

[59] See sources cited in previous note; also ibid. 243: ושאלתי למהר"ם למה תפלת
הדרך חותמת בברוך הואיל ואינה פותחת בברוך. See *Hagahot Maimuniot* to *Hilkot Keriat
Shema*, to *Hilkot Tefillah*, to *Nesiat Kapaim*, to *Hilkot Berakot*, to *Seder Tefillot*,
to *hilkot Shofar*, to *Hilkot Taaniot*, and to *Hilkot Megilah*; *Mordecai* to *Berakot*,
to *Pesahim*, and to *Halakot Ketanot*.

[60] Maharil, *Responsa*, 17; ibid. 171; ibid. 201: אך ברוב מקומות נוהגים כשיטת
מהר"ם ז"ל אשר רוב מנהגינו ובפרט; Judah Minz, *Responsa*, 7: התוספות ראבי"ה ומהר"ם.

cepted,[61] but a great part of the practices and ceremonials that today characterize the *Ashkenazic* ritual at home and in the synagogue can be traced directly to his influence.[62]

R. Meir instituted many customs that later became standard practice throughout Germany and the eastern countries not only in the prayer ritual, but in other domains of religious life. His students followed him wherever he was, at home, in school, or elsewhere, and even when he was in prison. They studied his behavior and recorded their observations in their *halakic* works together with his decisions on law and ritual.[63] One student in particular, R. Samson b. Zadok, was a veritable Boswell. In his book *Tashbetz*, he described in great detail R. Meir's customs, habits, and practices. The *Sefer Agudah* by R. Alexander Zusslein ha-Kohen, and the *Kol Bo* of unknown authorship (though based mainly on the *Orhot Hayyim* of R. Aaron ha-Kohen of Lunel), copied R. Meir's usages and practices from the *Tashbetz*, made them known throughout Germany, Austria and Bohemia, and led to their being incorporated into the later codes.[64]

מנהג האשכנזים יצ״ו לילך אחרי דעתו כי הוא היה מן האחרונים. See also R. Hayyim Or Zarua, *Responsa*, 213.

[61] See Novellae of R. Perez to *Tashbetz* 119, 142, 182; *Kol Bo* p. 35c; *Tur Orah Hayyim*, 187.

[62] We owe to R. Meir the customs of reciting *kiddush* first and then washing the hands for the meal (*Tashbetz* 16); of not reciting the blessing על נטילת ידים on the first washing of hands at the Passover *Seder* (ibid. 100); of refraining from putting on the phylacteries in the morning of the ninth day of Ab (ibid. 104); of preparing fruit of the new crop for the recitation of שהחינו on the evening of the second day of *Rosh ha-Shanah* (ibid. 121); of reciting ד' שפתי תפתח before the Eighteen Benedictions, and כי שם ד' אקרא before these Benedictions on *Musaf* and *Minhah* (ibid. 228); and many others. Cf. also Hag. Maim. *Tefillah*, 3, 5; ibid. *Berakot*, 5, 2; *Mordecai, Taanit* 637; Tesh. Maim. *Shoftim* 16, *Sefer Haparnes*, 314.

[63] See *Mordecai, Hagahot Maimuniot, Tashbetz*, and *Sefer Agudah*; also *Tur Orah Hayyim*, 128; *Shaare Dura*, 5: אכן ראיתי מהר״ם שהתירו בריעבד; ibid. 37.

[64] *Kol Bo* and *Sefer Agudah* quote R. Meir's decisions together with the objections raised by R. Perez in his Novellae to the *Tashbetz*. See *Kol Bo* p. 35c:

R. Meir often put his stamp of approval on various *halakic* works which therefore became very popular, and he thus exerted a great influence on succeeding generations. When his students once brought him a copy of the *Sefer Mitzvot Katan*, of R. Isaac of Corbeil, he recommended it highly to them after reading it, and urged them to copy it; this book has since been widely copied throughout Germany.[65]

Thus R. Meir's influence on the way of life of the Jews of the succeeding generations was exerted along three main channels: a) His students became the leaders of a number of communities in Germany, Austria, and Bohemia, and imprinted his views upon the life of the members of these communities and their surrounding territories.[66] b) The *Mordecai, Hagahot Maimuniot,* and *Tashbetz,* compiled by his students, formed a mine of information on his views and practices. These works were studied and consulted by the scholars of the succeeding generations, by authors of codes and Responsa, and especially

---

... והרמ׳ע כתב ... והר׳ף ז׳ל כתב וטיהו ...; ibid. p. 41b; ibid. p. 49d, cf. with *Tashbetz* 165. The *Sefer Maharil* also utilized the *Tashbetz* as well as the *Hagahot Maimuniot* and *Mordecai.* See ed. Warsaw, 1874, pp. 9b, 10a, 14a and b, 15b, 17a, 19b, 21a, 23b, 25b, 28b, 30a, 31b, 32a and b, 33a, 34b, 35b, 36b, 37b, 40b, 41a, 42b, 44a, 47b, 48a, and b, 51a, 52a, 53a, 60a, and b, 62a, 63a, 65b, 67a, and b, 82a. R. Moses Isserles in his *Darkei Mosheh* also utilized these three sources and quoted them on almost every page.

[65] Introduction to *Semak* ed. Konstantinopol, ca. 1510: זהו לשון ה׳ר מרדכי בן ה׳ר נתן בן ה׳ר אליקים בן הישיש הרב רבי יצחק האשכנזי משטרשפורק ע׳ה כתוב מה ששמעתי בצרפת בעיר קורביל מתלמידי׳ ותיקין של אבי זה הספר איך נתחבר זה הספר מתחלה ... ליומ הביאו התלמידים זה הספר לפני מורי הר׳מ מרוטנבורג וקרא בו ואמר שראוי לכל אדם לסמוך עליו כי כל מה שכתב אבי זה הספר שהוא אמת ויציב ונכון וקיים ובקש לתלמידיו שיעתיקו אותו ומאז והלאה העתיקו אותו אנשי אשכנז. ולפי שסמך אותו ה׳ר מאיר ז׳ל כתבנו בו כטפה מן הים מדברי הר׳מ.

[66] His students continued their contacts with their master even after they left his school, and consulted him often on various questions of law and ritual. A great part of the Responsa of R. Meir were written to his students; note the large number that were sent to R. Asher b. Yehiel, and other students. See especially: Pr. 92: מעת גלינו מעל שלחן מהר׳ם שוב אין לנו פה להשיב כי רבו מחלוקת בישראל ... לכן נמנינו לילך אחר ב׳ד יפה אחר מהר׳ם לרוטנבורג להאיר עינינו.

by R. Moses Isserles who incorporated many of these views in the *Shulhan Aruk*.[67] c) He had a profound influence on R. Asher and on the latter's son, R. Jacob, the author of the *Turim*, and thus directly affected the final *halakah* incorporated in the *Shulhan Aruk*.[68]

---

[67] The *Darkei Mosheh*, and the *Hagah*, cite hundreds of laws and customs taken directly from R. Meir's decisions, or from the *Maharil, Terumat ha-Deshen* or *Mahariv* who had originally based themselves on the decisions of R. Meir.

[68] Aside from the personal influence as a teacher, and the numerous Responsa addressed to R. Asher, which undoubtedly have moulded his opinions, R. Asher quotes his teacher on numerous occasions in his works, especially in his Responsa (see Asheri to *Berakot* ch. 2, 5; ch. 3, 2; to *Erubin* ch. 1, 14; ch. 4, 10; ch. 5, 9; to *Rosh ha-Shanah*, ch. 4, 14; to *Taanit*, ch. 3, 32; *Responsa* 1, 8; 23, 4; 30, 4; 32, 11; 58, 2; 74, 4; 84, 3; 98, 1) which quotations were often incorporated by his son in the *Turim*. See *Tur Orah Hayyim*, 128, 187, 199, 202–3, 216, 217, 582–3, 600; *Tur·Eben Haezer*, 13, 71, 73, 77; *Tur Hoshen Mishpat*, 99, 183, 248, 250, 388; cf. also Alfred Freimann "Asher b. Yechiel", *Jahrb. d. Jud. Lit. Gesel.* XII (1918) p. 273. Moreover the *Beth Joseph* of R. Joseph Caro often quotes the Responsa of R. Meir taken from the *Hagahot* and *Teshubot Maimuniot*.

CHAPTER III

R. Meir the Talmudist and Legalist.

A study of R. Meir's traits of character, an examination of the considerations that were uppermost in his mind whenever he was confronted by a legal or ritual problem, and an analysis of his method of arriving at a decision, reveal the main principles and attitudes directing and controlling his conduct, his utterances, and his decisions.

A. Reliance on Talmud, Use of First Sources.

R. Meir's decisions in ritual and legal matters, his quest for the proper usage, and his fixing of particular customs, were all dominated by the central idea that in every doubtful case the Talmud prescribed the exact ceremonial to the minutest detail. The Talmud was for him the master guide to all behavior.[1]

The Jews of Germany of the thirteenth century were disturbed by questions regarding minute details of ritual observance: How to cut the loaves of bread at the Sabbath meal;[2] whether first to wash one's hands and then to recite the *kiddush*, or vice versa;[3] whether one was permitted to open a window on the Sabbath;[4] and whether one might drink water on the afternoon of the fourteenth day of *Nissan*.[5] The thirteenth

---

[1] See *Tashbetz*, 1, 11, 15, 18, 27, 29, 33, 42, 44–7, 62, 66, 71, 75, and many others.

[2] Ibid. 18; Hag. Maim. *Berakot*, 8, 3.

[3] Ibid. 15.

[4] Ibid. 67.

[5] Ibid. 92. For other minutiae which absorbed the interest of R. Meir and his contemporaries, see ibid. 81, 100, 182, 209, 216, 218, 220, 247, 280, 293, 297–8.

century was the beginning of isolation for the Jews of Germany. The oppressive taxes of local rulers, the political chaos during the interregnum, and the rising power of the merchant guilds, drove the Jews from large-scale business and international trade, and forced them to confine themselves to petty trade and money-lending.[6] Their minds as well as their experiences, therefore, were considerably narrowed. The farming of usury afforded the Jews a great deal of leisure; they could devote long hours to study, and had time for extreme religious devotion. The strengthening of religion in general, and the growing veneration for saintliness in particular among the Christians over all Europe, was a great factor in focusing the attention of the Jews on details of their own behavior. Their religious leaders, especially, aspired to saintliness and were highly concerned that every act of theirs, every utterance of blessing or prayer, every mode of behavior, should be in perfect conformity with the requirements of talmudic law.[7]

R. Meir looked to the Talmud for answers to many new and

[6] In R. Meir's Responsa we find no mention of important business transactions that involved large quantities of merchandize, or considerable sums of money. While in the Responsa of R. Judah ha-Kohen (eleventh century, see Pr. 874–913) and of R. Eliezer b. Nathan (twelfth century, see *Eben Ha-Ezer* pp. 73, 94b) we find Jews engaging in the transport and sale of fish, wool and fur on a large-scale, in R. Meir's Responsa we see them engaged in petty trade only. See Pr. 102, 155, 325–6, 335, 547, 575, 579, 747, 828–31, 835, 842, 961, 1010; L. 207, 218, 312, 331, 379; P. 302, 322; Am II, 245; Cr. 16, 112, 254–5, 258, 302.

[7] It was very characteristic of R. Meir to write a detailed compendium of the proper blessings for each occasion (סדר ברכות מהר״ם), and a minute description of the laws and customs of burial and mourning (הלכות שמחות). Moreover, these two works of R. Meir were very popular with his students and were copied more zealously than his novellae to talmudic tractates, to the extent that while mere mention is made of the latter, we have several versions preserved of the former two. A study of any page of *Tashbetz* will reveal R. Meir's great piety and his scrupulous observance of all minute details of personal behavior. The great popularity of the *Tashbetz* (it is mentioned and quoted by every scholar of the subsequent two centuries) proves that this piety and scrupulousness was highly honored and consistently followed by his students and by the Rabbis of the subsequent generations.

perplexing problems of ritual observance. He drew on the Palestinian[8] as well as on the Babylonian Talmud, on the minor tractates,[9] and even resorted to *Gematriot*[10] and to interpretations of the *Masorah*.[11] Thus he based a great number of usages and customs directly on talmudic sources, without any mention of post-talmudic scholars, or of accepted practices.[12] In legal questions as well, he relied directly on the *Talmudim*, and often went beyond the traditional interpretation of a particular text in order to obviate a contradiction between two texts, or even between two diverse sources, such as the Palestinian Talmud and the *Tosephta*, thus to arrive at a proper solution of a pressing legal problem.[13]

---

[8] *Tashbeṭz* 45, 99, 112, 215, 320, 322, 370, 528; Pr. 97; Am II, 78; L. 386; R. Hayyim Or Zarua, *Responsa* 68.

[9] *Tashbeṭz*, 87, 99, 180.

[10] Ibid. 122, 135, 156, 251, 255, 258, 261, 444.

[11] Ibid. 156, 414–5.

[12] Ibid. passim. The fact that regarding so many questions of ritual R. Meir looks for guidance to talmudic sources, which in themselves are often of a nature unrelated to the subject, seems to prove that most of these problems have arisen but recently and have never troubled the pious of former generations.

[13] His stand in the dispute between R. Judah of Düren and the young man of Rothenburg (discussed below) was motivated by this very consideration; for he reconciled the views of the *Tosephta* and the *Yerushalmi* and thus arrived at the law that R. Judah could not force his son-in-law to come to live in France. R. Meir was so deeply convinced of the correctness of his method of arriving at this decision that he braved a storm of protests, the wrath of a rich and powerful man, and even ran the danger of facing excommunication; see L. 386: ולכאורא סתרן אהדדי התוספתא והירושלמי . . . . . ויש ליישב . . . והשתא לא סתרן אהדדי; also the whole controversy in *Text* no. 280. This characteristic of R. Meir was so well known that it was identified with his personality. Thus we read in the Responsa of R. Hayyim Or Zarua, no. 164: ופעם אחת שהיה לי ללמוד אותה נראה לי רבינו מאיר בחלום אחר פטירתו, אמרתי ללבי אפשר שנאון זה שלא זכיתי לראותו מעולם נראה לי בחלום והשבתי ללבי אולי יש לישב הגרסא שמחקו כי רבינו מאיר היה רגיל בכך, וסתרתי מכח קושית הגירסא חדשה וקימתי הישנה. R. Meir even tried to smooth out difficulties to which the Talmud itself had no solution. See Am II, p. 141 f.: ואע"ג דפריך עלה מדרבא . . . ומסיק מלתא דשמואל בקשיא. הרי ר"ח ור"י אלפסי פסקו כשמואל כיון דלא מסיק מלתיה בתיובתא אלא בקושיא לא בטלו דבריו, אלא דההוא לא אשכחן פירוקא למלתי'. ול"נ דלא קשיא דההוא דאפיק רבא זוזא . . .

B. Post-Talmudic Authorities.

R. Meir had a deep reverence for the great post-talmudic scholars who had incorporated their decisions in codes, novellae, epitomes and Responsa.[14] He realized that these authorities had a penetrating insight into talmudic problems,[15] that they were close to the source, and that they expounded the Talmud on a traditional basis.[16] He considered the interpretations and decisions of the Geonim, R. Hananel, Alfasi, Maimonides, Rashi, and the Tosaphists, highly authoritative;[17] he believed that scholars of subsequent generations could not contravene them unless they could produce indisputable evidence in support of their own views.[18] Thus when R. Meir was forced to

[14] See L. 386: ואחרי שרוב הגאונים פירשו כך דבכפיית האשה טיירי מי יעבר על דבריהם;
Am II, 4: אמנם מנהגינו לפסוק בכל דבר כדברי רבי' אלפס בדבר שלא נחלקו עליו התוספות,
R. Asher, Responsa, אמנם איני זוכר בשום דבר שהתוספות חלוקי' עליו כי כל דרכיו משפט צדק;
כי רבנא מאיר ז'ל היה תופס עיקר כל דברי ר' אלפס, וכמה פעמים כתב בתשובותיו שלא 3: ,24
וכן היה רבינו מאיר ז'ל דן כמה שנים ושוב חזר בו :2 ,58 .ibid; כתב ר' אלפס דבר שלא לצורך
תופסי ניטין אין בידי ולא ספרי :108 ,Am II; כי מצא בתוספות רבינו ברוך שפירש ככתוב למעלה
פסקים בארץ הנגב . . . ואם ימצא שהתוסף' וספרי הפסקים חולקים עלי בשום דבר, דעתי מבוטלת;
Tashbetz, 516: אמנם אם הנהבע אומר אדון בעירי אין הר'ם ז'ל רגיל לכופו לילך לב'ד הגדול
כי הוינא בדינא :946 .Pr; והוה פלונתא דה'נ ור'ת מי יוכל לכופו ולומר לב'ד הגדול קאוילנא
דמורדת לא מסקינן מינה אלא כדמסיק תעלא מבי כרבא כי רבו בה דינים, דינא דמתניתין ודינא
דגמרא ודינא דמתיבתא ועוד הציבו לה ציונין האחרונים, ואנו יתמי דיתמי לא ידעינן איך נפתח
לפניכם . . . הכי דיינינן אנו, אין אנו חוסמין אותה לפניו לדור עם הנחש בכפיפה גם אין אנו כופי';
On the other hand, see Mord. B. K. אותו להוציא כדברי הגאונים ורש"י, אחרי שר' תם אוסר
ואמרתי למורי שכן ראיתי ולא השגיח . . . ושוב מצאתי כן בספר המצות . . . ושוב הרצו הדבר :172
לפני רבנו מאיר שכן ראו בספר המצות ולא השגיח.

[15] L. 426: ואף אם מסברא בעלמא פסק רבינו [הרמב"ם] כן מי אנכי וסברת לבי כמלא נקב
סדקית לחלוק על סברת רבינו כפתה האולם.

[16] Cr. 81: כי כל; L. 426: אפילו הכי נרא' כדברי האלפסי שכל דבריו דברי קבלה הן;
דבריו [הרמב"ם] דברי קבלה; cf. also Am II, 46; Pr. 576; P. 281; comp. with R. Tam,
Sefer ha-Yashar, 45, 6: שלא הכל נכתב בתלמוד, שהרי כמה דברים קבלה בידינו כנון עבור.

[17] See note 14 above; see also Cr. 6: ואע'פ שרבינו שמואל פי' לשם פי' אחר כדאי ר'ח;
cf. Pr. 101, 576, 680; 698; 946, 948, 974; 976; 988; 996; 1004; לסמוך עליו בכל מקום;
L. 384, 386, 426; Am II, 29; 46; 67; 209.

[18] Pr. 996: כי רבינו שמשון ז'ל כתב בתשובה דלא [קנה] דאמירה לנבוה כמסירתו להדיוט
אבל טפי מסירה ממסירה לא הויא, ואני אומר [כמסירה] המועלת בהדיוט . . . הלכך לנבוה באמירה נרידתא
אעפ'י שר'י כתב בפ' זה בורר . . . לא :960 .Pr also .Cf קניא . . . ויש לי ראיות הרבה לדברי
נהירא לי מאי פריך בזה . . . ע'כ נראה לי בשאר תביעות איזה מהם שיאמר נלך לבית הועד כופין
אותו ודן בעירו . . . וכמו שפרשתי כן פסקתי בשכבר כי מעשה שנשאלתי מששוניא.

change his opinion on many a point of law after studying the *Mishne Torah*, he gave the following reasons for so doing: a) Maimonides might have obtained correct traditions regarding these laws; b) he, R. Meir, did not dare question the reasoning and judgment of the great master of logic; c) he was actually persuaded of the superiority of the view of Maimonides.[19] R. Meir's own analysis of the considerations that led him to adopt the views of Maimonides, in certain instances, clearly showed that his reverence for the post-talmudic authorities was not based on blind faith, but on a carefully considered method of approach.

C. Applications of Principles to New Situations.

R. Meir was often confronted with problems for which neither the Talmud nor its expounders and interpreters offered any solution. He therefore formulated three main principles of action which he resolutely and confidently applied in such cases.

1) The laws cited in the Talmud presume principles of justice which may be applied to new cases and situations.[20] Thus R. Meir pointed out that the rabbis of the Talmud always protected the interests of the public,[21] were apprehensive lest the seller suffer a loss,[22] and endeavored to protect a litigant against circumstances that might confuse him and might pre-

[19] L. 426: אמנם משבא לידי ספר רבי' משה בן מיימון זצ"ל נשאלתי מאת כבודך שאילה זו, אמרתי בלבי אשאל באורים ותומים ודבר מה יראני והגדתי לך, וכאשר מצאתי סברתו על סברתי חלוקה, חזרתי לדבריו כי כל דבריו דברי קבלה הם. ואף אם מסברא בעלמא פסק רבינו כן, מי אנכי וסברת לבי כמלא נקב סידקית לא לחלוק על סברת רבינו כפתח האולם . . . כך יש לי לפרש לפי סברת רבינו משה, ובודאי סברא אמיתית היא בלי ספק.

[20] Pr. 333: וחכמי התלמוד לא יכלו לכתוב ולברר כל הדברים הגורמים לסתום טענת הבעל דין אלא כתבו לנו קצת ותן לחכם ויחכם עוד; Am II, 122: ואנן טעמא דפירושי' ניקו ונפרש; Tesh. Maim. *Kinyan*, 29b.

[21] Pr. 106: ובכמה דוכתי אשכחן דחשו רבנן טובא להפסד דרבים דהא מצר שהחזיקו בו רבים אסור לקלקלו, כגון מי שהיתה דרך רשות הרבים עוברת בתוך שדהו ונטלה ונתן להם מן הצד וכיו"ב.

[22] Pr. 1011: א"כ מפסידו למוכר . . . ורבנן חשו טובא לפסידא דמוכר העני ומוכר מחמת דחקו ומשמע כן בשמעת"ת דמצרנות דהמוכר לא תקינו משום ועשית הישר והטוב, וכן היינו ציירי (ב"מ קח:) שכללו כלל [דאין] לנו לעשות שום תקנה שיבא המוכר בה לידי שום פסידא בעולם.

vent him from logically presenting his claims.[23] He, therefore, held that any decision that protects the interests of the public, prevents losses to the seller, or relieves a litigant from confusing circumstances, is inherently a correct decision even though not directly derived from the Talmud.

2) A talmudic law or a rabbinical decree must be interpreted in such a manner that the unscrupulous be unable to defeat its original purpose by subterfuge or trickery. Such a law or decree should be immediately suspended whenever it is suspected that resort is made to evasive measures.[24]

3) Laws and regulations, the absence of which would make life unbearable and would endanger the postion of the Jews among their neighbors, are binding upon the Jews even though no precedents for such laws are to be found in the Talmud.[25] "In such cases" R. Meir writes "one should be strict even without any support from the Talmud . . . or else it might prove a great stumbling block [for Israel]".[26]

Accepting these three principles as basically talmudic, R. Meir considered talmudic law as adequate to cope with any situation that might arise in the course of life among the Jewish people.[27]

---

[23] Pr. 333.

[24] Am II, 199: נמצא כל אחד מערים להפקיע תקנת חכמים ויעשו דבריהם כחוכא וטלולה
סוף דבר כל היכא דאיכא למימר מאומד :Mord. B. B. 649; וחזינן נמי דחשו חכמים להערמה
הדעת דאערומי קמערים לאפקועי תקנתא דרבנן לאו כל כמיניה . . . ואם יוכל כל אדם לבטל תקנתא
דאם כן מה הועילו חכמים בתקנתם :cf. also Pr. 228; דרבנן א"כ ניהו מילי דרבנן כחוכי ואיטלולי
; לפחות מכתובתה [של מורדה] והא כשמרדה עד כלות כתובתה יכולה לומר עושה אני מכאן ולהבא
ועוד דא"כ משוי להו למלתא דרבנן כי חוכא ואטלולא :Am II, 97.

[25] Pr. 277: אבל עתי שבועות שכתבתם אין אני רואה, דאם כן אין לך אדם שמעביר חבית
שמעתי דנין בכל אלו הקהלות :Am II, 239; ממקום למקום שכל שעה יטיל עליו תנאים וישביענו
אם אדם מוחל לחבירו בקנין וקודם לכן עשה מודעה בפני שנים לומר, דעו מה שא י עתיד למחול
היום או למחר בטל, הרי זה בטל . . . וחלילה וחלילה כי לא נעשה כפשט הזה מימי שפוט השופטים . . .
דא"כ לא שבקת חיי לכל בריה . . . לא תהא כזאת בישראל

[26] Am II, 122: ובדברים הללו ראוי להחמיר אפילו בלא ראיה מן התלמוד שאם היה כל
אחד יכול ליפרד מחבילה, כמה פעמים באים לידי תקלה גדולה.

[27] In the chapter on community government we shall discuss several other principles utilized by R. Meir in the construction of a legal system based on

D. Controversial Issues, Civil Cases.

R. Meir's reverence for the great post-talmudic authorities occasionally proved to be a source of difficulty. Thus whenever the opinions of various authorities clashed on a certain issue he was faced with the perplexing problem of how to steer clear of controversy and avoid being forced to decide in accordance with the view of one authority as against that of another.

In most civil cases R. Meir simply refused to render a decision that would be opposed to the opinion of an authority. He accepted the talmudic dictum that the burden of proof was upon the plaintiff; and thus he left it, as it were, to the litigant to prove that the law was in his favor.[28] He did not coerce a husband into divorcing his rebellious wife, even though the Geonim and Rashi had ruled that he should be so coerced, since R. Tam had ruled that no coercive measures should be used against the husband. Nor did he force the woman to remain with her husband. He simply decided that the two should live apart until either the husband would agree to divorce her, or she would agree to become reconciled to him.[29] He did not permit a bridegroom to be forced to move to a country where his bride lived and marry her there, since the majority of the Geonim had ruled against such coercion.[30] When a defendant insisted that his case be tried before the local court, R. Meir ruled that he must not be compelled to appear before a higher

talmudic law and capable of coping with any situation that might arise in a self-governing community.

[28] See Pr. 946; *Tashbetz* 201: והבא להוציא ;Pr. 952: ועכשו אין אנו יכולים להכריע; Cr. 159: צריך ראיה ברורה; דכיון דמספקינן אי כרש"י או כר"ת לא מפקינן ממונא מספיקא וכן R. Asher, *Responsa* 1, 8: כך קבלתי מפי רבנא מאיר ז"ל היכא דאיכא פסקנו כמה פעמים; Hayyim Or Zarua, *Responsa* 53: פלוגתא דרבוותא לא מפקינן מספק ומוקי ממון אחזקתיה; ואתה מורי ידעת שמורי רבינו מאיר זצ"ל היה רגיל לומר כל היכא דאיכא מחלוקת גאונים ממונא היכא דקאי ליקום.

[29] Pr. 946; see note 14 above.

[30] L. 386: ואחרי שרוב הגאונים פירשו כך דבכפיית האשה מיירי מי יעבור על דבריהם לכופו להוציאו, ודאי היכא דהבעל היה רוצה לכוף את האשה לא היינו כופין אותה הואיל ונפק מפומי' דר"ת.

court, of another town, since this would be contrary to the view
of the *Halakot Gedolot*.[31] This attitude of R. Meir in controversial
issues was faithfully recorded by his students and had a profound
influence on the scholars of subsequent generations.[32]

Even in civil cases, however, R. Meir was often compelled
to take a firmer stand and decide with one authority against
another. Thus in a Responsum to his relative Rabbi Joel regarding the partitioning of a house belonging to several partners, he first ruled that whatever person or persons succeeded
in forcefully taking possession of the eastern part of the house,
he should acquire title to it, since no other decision was possible
because Rashi and R. Tam had held conflicting views on the
issue involved. R. Joel, however, objected to permitting the
use of force in this case, as it might lead to serious quarrels,
and insisted that a definite decision was absolutely necessary.
R. Meir, then, decided in favor of one partner and added: "This
ruling is in accordance with the views of both Rashi and Maimonides. In the present case we may disregard the view of R.
Tam since it is contradicted by the two authorities mentioned
above and since their interpretation of the pertinent talmudic
source is more acceptable to our way of thinking".[33] It is significant to note that even in this case where R. Meir was forced
to choose the view of one authority against that of another,
he did not blindly follow the opinion of the majority. He preferred the opinion of Rashi and Maimonides not only because
they were the majority, but also because their opinion was more
acceptable to his way of thinking. In several other cases we

---

[31] *Tashbetz*, 516: אמנם אם הנתבע אומר אדון בעירי אין הר"ם ז"ל רגיל לכופו לילך לב"ד
הגדול והוה פלוגתא דה"ג ור"ת מי יוכל לכופו ולומר לבית דין הגדול קא אזלינא לפירוש ה"ג דוקא
נתבע ולפי' ר"ת אפילו תובע.

[32] See R. Asher, *Responsa*, 1, 8; ibid. 85, 11; R. Hayyim Or Zarua, *Responsa*,
53; *Tur Hoshen Mishpat*, 25; *Terumat Hadeshen*, 341; ibid. 352.

[33] See *Text* no. 520; *Mordecai Hagadol* p. 367a: ויש לדון כך דאין דברי ר"ת אחד
במקום שנים רש"י ורבי' משה', ועוד כי לבי נוטה הרבה אחר חילוק שחילקתי בין הנך תרי עובדי
כדפרי' לעיל.

find R. Meir taking a definite stand in controversial matters because the reasoning of one authority seemed to him more logical than that of the other.[34]

E. Controversial Issues, Ritual Cases.

In ritual matters, however, a clash of opinions among authorities is a very serious problem, for one must here give a definite decision. Thus R. Meir had to decide unequivocally where, when, and how, certain religious acts had to be performed. His great piety and deepseated respect for authority was put to a severe test in ritual problems, requiring his utmost ingenuity in order to steer clear of controversy. The manner in which he solved such dilemmas gives us a clear insight into his character, and affords us a glimpse of the inner recesses of his heart.

Thus, in cases where there existed a difference of opinion among scholars, R. Meir followed three distinct procedures in his effort to prevent the performance of a ritual act that would be considered sinful in the opinion of a certain scholar. 1) Whenever possible he accepted the more stringent view and thus made sure that he committed no sin in the opinion of either one of the opposing authorities.[35] 2) In cases where acting in ac-

---

[34] See Pr. 248: ואין לו לדיין אלא מה שעיניו רואות, נראה בעניותינו בעניינו דברי רב האי.
Cf. also Cr. 81, where R. Meir decides against the view of R. Zerahiah ha-Levi. See Am II, 196: והאלפסי פסק כרשב"ג דמסתבר טעמיה ור"ח פסק כת"ק במתנה . . . ואעפ"י שאיני כדאי להכריע נ"ל דהלכה כת"ק כיון . . . ולענין פסק הלכה אסברא דמעיקרא סמכי' והלכה כת"ק.

[35] See Berl. p. 294, no. 386: והמגיד כי אני הוריתי להיתר כיחש לך כי בכל דבר שהגדולים; Tesh. Maim. *Kinyan*, 5: חולקים אני מורה להחמיר לבד מהיתר פשוט שפשט היתירה עפ"י קמאי; Hag. Maim. *Berakot*, 7, 3: ומורי ר' מאיר שי' מחמיר ומצריך מעות ומשיכה לאפוקי נפשיה מפלונתא; *Tur Orah Hayyim*, 34: יניח שני זוגי תפילין . . . וכן היה נוהג; ובוצע לצאת ידי כולם; also mentioned in *Tashbetz*, 272; Mord. *Megillah*, 781: ור"מ א"א ז"ל ורבו רבינו מאיר. היה רגיל לומר זמן ביום בלחש . . . לאפוקי מיד כל רבוותא. This characteristic is not peculiar to R. Meir; it was quite a common practice among German scholars and one could point out many examples of it in *Sefer ha-Terumah*, *Semag*, and *Rabiah*; cf. especially Sabb. 61a: אמר ר' נחמן בר יצחק ירא שמים יוצא ידי שתיהם.

cordance with either view would be labeled a sin by the author
of the opposing view, R. Meir contrived to change the situation in such a manner that both opposing authorities would agree
on the religious procedure required by the new situation.[36] Thus
some scholars held the opinion that a person was not permitted
to recite the blessing שהחינו during his recitation of the *kiddush*
on the eve of the second day of *Rosh Ha-Shanah*, while other
scholars held that it should be recited. In this case acceptance
of the more stringent view would not solve the problem. R. Meir,
therefore, refrained from drinking the wine made from the most
recent vintage, till the eve of the second day of *Rosh Ha-Shanah*,
at which time he would recite the *kiddush* over such wine.
A person who drank the wine made from the most recent
vintage, for the first time, was required to recite the blessing שהחינו. Thus in reciting the *kiddush* over such wine on the
eve of the second day of *Rosh ha-Shanah*, he was required to
recite the blessing שהחינו even according to the authority who
held that at such time the blessing should not be recited.[37] The
present day custom of preparing rare fruit, or fruit from the
new crop, for the eve of the second day of *Rosh ha-Shanah*, is
an outgrowth of the procedure followed by R. Meir.[38] 3) In
many cases in which this artifice was impossible, R. Meir took

[36] This characteristic is clearly brought out in the following: Mord. *Pesahim*,
592: ועל אודות החררה קטנה שלוקחות הנשים מעיסה ורימזיל"ש ואופין אותה ומשימות אותה אצל
חייבת ורימזיל"ש דעיה ... כתבו שהתוספות לפי להן הורינו וכן עושין יפה חלה, ומפרשת עיסה
שקלה נפשך ממה ועכשו ... ביחד העסה ומן ממנה מעט חלה ולטול ולאפותה קטנה חררה לעשות
כדין חלה; cf. also Am II, 60: שיהיה כדי טענה מחמת לבא למדוה טענה מחמת באה אינה ואם
גמור בהיתר הדבר; *Tashbetz*, 292: אכילה קודם לחוץ קצת נוטל ... פירות של מוליאות ועל
העץ פרי בורא ומברך.

[37] *Tashbetz*, 120; Mord. *Sukkah*, 768: ויש הכוס, על זמן מברכין יש ר"ה של שני ובליל
הן אחת קדושה אמרי' דלא משום שמברכין זמן אותם וטעם היא, אחת דקדושה מטעם מברכין שאין
חדש יין לשתות שלא רגיל היה ור"מ לא, להקל אבל בזה אסורה שנולדה ביצה כגון להחמיר אלא
רבוותא כל י"ח לאפוקי כדי זמן ואומר ר"ה של שני ליל עד.

[38] See Asheri, *Rosh Hashanah*, 4, 14; *Tur Orah Hayyim*, 600: וטוב ז"ל א"א וכתב
נוהג היה וכן ספק ידי ויצא הפרי על גם דעתו ויהא שההיינו ויברך לפניו ויניחנה חדש פרי אדם שיקח
מרוטנבורק הר"מ.

great care to act in such a manner that no doubtful situations should arise.[39] Thus the Tosaphists were of the opinion that when two persons ate together and a third joined them in partaking of drink but not of food, all three must join in reciting common grace, called *zimmun*. Alfasi, on the other hand, was of the opinion that if the third person did not partake of any food, the three persons were not to join in common grace. Whenever confronted with such a situation R. Meir would ask the third person to eat something in order to necessitate their joining in common grace even according to Alfasi. If R. Meir could not, however, or did not wish to, impose on the third person, he would be very careful not to offer him a drink in order that the question should not arise whether or not they were required to join in common grace.[40] R. Meir must have learned this method of avoiding controversial issues from his French teachers since a similar attitude is recorded as being taken by R. Yehiel of Paris.[41]

---

[39] Cf. R. Perez, *Hagahot* to *Semak*, 2, 11; *Tashbetz* 225: וספק אם אמר משיב הרוח ומוריד הגשם, אמרינן בתוך ל' חוזר לראש, דודאי לא אמרו הואיל שאינו רגיל בו, אבל לאחר ל' יום אינו חוזר לראש שכבר רגיל בו ולא שכח לאמרו. אבל הר"ם ז"ל היה רגיל לאמרו בשמיני עצרת צ' פעמים אתה גבור לעולם... משיב הרוח ומוריד הגשם כנגד ל' יום שהיה צריך לאומרו בכל יום ג' פעמים, ועכשיו אם הוא מסופק אם אמר משיב הרוח אינו חוזר לראש כי בודאי אמרו Cf. Am II, 60; Pr. 952: לכן טוב שיעשו בקנין סודר מה שנודרים להם.

[40] *Tashbetz*, 307: והר"ם ז"ל כשהיה אוכל ואדם אחר עמו ובא אדם שלישי ונתן לו לשתות בקש ממנו שיאכל עמו מעט מעט לפי שכבר חייב בזימון לפירוש התוספות ואינו רוצה לזמן עליו ע"י שתייה לבד לפי שפסק רב אלפס שאין לזמן ע"י שתייה, ואם אדם חשוב הוא שאינו רוצה לזמן אותו לאכול שוב מצאתי Hag. Maim. *Berakot* 5, 7: עמו בדבר מועט מזמן אחר שיאכל עמו כזית פת... כתוב משמו שהיה נזהר כשהיה אוכל הוא ואחר עמו שלא היה נותן לאדם הבא אליהם לשתות אם לא R. Hayyim שהיה יכול להזקיקו ליטול ידיו ולאכול עמהם כזית דגן... לאפוקי נפשיה מפלונתא Or Zarua, *Responsa* 1: ואז היה מסתפק... והוי מפיק נפשיה מפלונתא כי כן היה דרכו.

[41] See B. p. 300, no. 594: וכן שמעתי שמורי הרב ר' יחיאל מפריש שלא היה רגיל לאכול This. אפי' פרטי"ש וזהו דוקא אכלו בתוך הסעודה שלא היה ברור לו אם יש לו תורייתא דנהמא characteristic attitude of R. Meir is responsible for his strange conduct in relation to his father, reported by Asheri *Kiddushin*, 1, 57: אמרו עליו על רבי' מאיר מרוטנבורג שמיום שעלה לגדולה לא הקביל פני אביו ולא רצה שאביו יבא אליו. This statement needs no corrections or emendations, nor does it need any apology. R. Meir's conduct in this matter was a direct result of his great piety and his general attitude to the *halakah*; it fits in perfectly with his consistent avoidance of a situation of doubt. Thus the Talmud (*Kiddushin*, 33b) raised two questions to which it offered no

F. Strictness and Leniency.

From the foregoing discussion, as well as from a great number of laws which deal with minute details of proper conduct, recorded in R. Meir's name in the *Tashbetz* and the *Hagahot Maimuniot*, one might be led to think that he was extremely strict in religious matters, and that his only concern was to make the laws of conduct more stringent and exacting. Such an opinion, however, would be far from the truth. On the contrary, R. Meir was quite lenient in ritual matters; and on one occasion protests with threats of excommunication were hurled against him because of his liberal attitude in respect to the laws of marriage and divorce.[42]

Many of his decisions regarding forbidden food, salting and preparing meat, and similar topics, begin with the words: "R. Meir permits...".[43] In some cases he even went counter the strict view of his predecessors, in deciding on a more lenient policy.[44]

definite answer: a) בנו והוא רבו מהו לעמוד לפני אביו ;and b) בנו והוא רבו מהו שיעמוד אביו מפניו. The Talmud (ibid.) further stated that anyone who failed to accord the proper respect to his teacher would suffer severe punishment: אמר ר' אלעזר כל ת"ח שאין עומד מפני רבו נקרא רשע ולא מאריך ימים ותלמודו משתכח. R. Meir was generally acknowledged as the greatest scholar of Germany, and even his father sent queries to him. In order to avoid a situation of doubt and obviate the possibility that either he or his father unknowingly infringe upon the laws of etiquette and suffer severe punishment, he refrained from meeting his father. Cf. Back op. cit. pp. 10–16; Wellescz ibid. Although the characteristics outlined thus far were not exclusive with R. Meir, they were nevertheless the guiding principles of his life and conduct and were highly significant to an evaluation of his character and religious attitude.

[42] See below. See R. Jacob Weil, *Responsa*, 54; ibid. 88.

[43] See *Kol Bo* pp. 83d, 84d, 88c, 89b, 89d, 90b, 98d; *Tashbetz* 334, 338–9, 340–3, 346, 350–1, 354, 361; R. Hayyim Or Zarua, *Responsa*, 81.

[44] Mord. *Pesahim*, 552: וכתב דכל הקדמונים השוו לאסור, מצאתי כתוב דמהר"ם ז"ל אינו ; cf. Hag. Maim. *Maakalot Asurot*, 17, 2: והנה מהר"ם ז"ל התירו ;אוסר אלא כדי קליפה; Mord. *Hullin*, 722; אמנם מורי רבי' שי' מתיר ;ibid. 6, 8: להדיא כל ימיו בכל מקום היותו ומדקדק ראבי"ה ;Mord. ibid. 602: ומהר"ם נוהג להתיר בצליה ;R. Asher, *Responsa*, 20, 25: והר"ם מרוטנבורק היה נוהג על ;Tur Yoreh Deah, 126: מפי' רש"י ואסר, ולא נראה לרבינו מאיר פי גדולי צרפת דבהפסד מרובה היה מתיר ניצוק.

At times he even displayed a sense of humor and poked fun at
the overstringent pietists.[45]

How, then, can we explain the strange contradiction that
the man who scrupulously observed hundreds of minute details
of ritual law in his personal conduct, who repeated on *Shemini
Azeret* the formula אתה רב להושיע משיב הרוח ומוריד הגשם
ninety times in order to make sure that he would not fail to
include the formula in his subsequent prayers,[46] who tied his
hat by a band to his girdle, on the Sabbath, in order to secure
it to his head and thus avoid the necessity of ever having to
pick it up on the street,[47]— that such a man should allow the
use of meat unsalted for three days,[48] should permit a married
woman, who obviously had illict relations with another man,
to resume her marital relations with her husband,[49] and should
grant a bride, who was betrothed in the presence of disqualified witnesses, the right to marry another man without the
necessity of previously obtaining a divorce?[50]

A careful study of R. Meir's decisions, however, reveals the
fact that he was very strict and exacting whenever a problem
arose whether or not a person should perform a certain act,
and if so, in what manner, but that he was quite lenient after the
act had already taken place. Thus he took great care in establishing the proper prayer ritual,[51] in determining the fitting blessing
for each occasion,[52] in deciding upon the safest method of bak-

---

[45] Pr. 615; L. 500; Mord. *Hullin*, 687: בימי חורפי הייתי מתלוצץ בבני אדם שהיו
עושי' כן.

[46] See note 39 above; *Tur Orah Hayyim*, 114.

[47] *Tashbetz*, 69.

[48] *Tashbetz*, 342–3; Mord. *Hullin* 722.

[49] Am II, 63; Pr. 98; Rashba I, 832–3; Tesh. Maim. *Ishut*, 8; cf. also L. 310;
see *Text*, nos. 242, 246.

[50] See *Text*, no. 271.

[51] See *Tashbetz*, 101–2, 119–20, 131, 133–4; 208–14; 220–60.

[52] The פסקי ברכות של רבי' מאיר have come down to us in several versions; see
Berl. pp. 298–310; *Tashbetz*, 294–323; and were published separately in Riva di
Trani, 1558, under the title: ס' ברכת מהר"ם.

ing *Matzah*,[53] and in avoiding a situation that might cause the breaking of the Sabbath laws.[54] He was lenient, however, after the forbidden deed was done, after the fly was already in the soup,[55] after the grain of wheat was found in the salted chicken on Passover,[56] after the meat was salted without having previously been soaked in water,[57] after the meat was already unsalted for three days,[58] and after the bride was already betrothed in the presence of disqualified witnesses.[59] He even permitted one to shake off a burning candle that fell on the table, on the Sabbath, even though this act is explicitly prohibited by the Palestinian Talmud.[60]

R. Moses Parnes, a student of R. Meir and a resident of Rothenburg, tells us that R. Meir once forgot to perform the ceremony of *Erub Tabshilin* on the eve of a holiday that fell on a Friday, and was consequently not permitted by law to cook or prepare food on the holiday for the Sabbath. When, however, he reminded himself on Friday morning of his failure to perform the above-mentioned ceremony, he resorted to various legal fictions, and finally the Sabbath food was cooked and "the pot was placed in the stove" as usual.[61] Thus his strictness asserted itself only in cases where an additional act, a particular procedure, or a slight loss of money, would remove even the

---

[53] *Tashbetz*, 100; cf. Pr. 322.

[54] *Tashbetz*, 69, 44; Pr. 92; Cr. 5.

[55] *Tashbetz*, 350.

[56] Mord. *Pesahim*, 552: אבל אם נמצא חטה על בשר מלוח אין אוסר אלא כדי קליפה, וכן כתב ר' שמואל מפלמיזה... ושוב כתב משום חכמי נרבונא ומשום רבינו יהודה לאסור, וכתב דכל הקדמונים הושוו לאסור, מצאתי כתוב דמהר"ם ז"ל אינו אוסר אלא כדי קליפה. Cf. Pr. 177, 379.

[57] *Shaare Dura* 3: אבל ראיתי מהר"ם שהתירו בדיעבד.

[58] *Tashbetz*, 342-3; Mord. *Hullin*, 722; *Shaare Dura*, 2: אבל מהר"ם ז"ל אומר ע"י צלייה מותר.

[59] Am II, 41-2.

[60] *Tashbetz*, 5; cf. Hag. Maim. *Shabbat*, 12, 4; see *Text*, 164.

[61] *Sefer ha-Parnes*, 315: פעם אדת שכח מהר"ם ולא הניח עירובי תבשילין בשמחת תורה שדיה בע"ש ולא נזכר עד יום הששי בביהכ"נ שחרית והוקשה זאת בעיניו וחזר על כל צידי צדדים למצוא אמתלאות היתר... ועוד שינויי דחיקא מצא עד לבסוף שבישלו ואפו והטמינו את החמין והדליקו כדרכן.

slightest possibility that he might be transgressing against the law. In this particular case, however, the comfort and happiness of a Sabbath day were involved, and R. Meir chose to be lenient.

This deep-seated psychological trait of R. Meir reveals itself especially in his decisions regarding women and divorce. Thus it happened in a drinking hall in Esslingen, where young men and young ladies were indulging in drink and merriment, that a young lady (Leah) jokingly asked a young man (A) to betroth her. The young man borrowed a ring, threw it in her lap, and pronounced the betrothal formula. The case was brought before R. Meir who pointed out several reasons why no divorce should be required, and added: "If my teachers agree with my decision, all will be well. But if they will not agree, I shall subscribe to whatever they decide to do. However, I would prefer not to be strict in this matter and not to require Leah to obtain a divorce, lest A become rebellious and refuse to divorce her, and lest he travel to a distant land and thus render it impossible for the unfortunate woman ever to marry again".[62] R. Meir knew that he was treading on very dangerous ground, that he was dealing with adultery, one of the gravest sins in the Jewish religion, and yet he chose to be lenient.[63]

On another occasion, a husband saw his wife seclude herself with another man. He listened behind a partition and heard their heavy breathing and other sounds which were clearly indicative of consummated sexual intercourse. Rabbi Hezekiah of Magdeburg, to whom the case was first submitted, ruled that the husband was forbidden to continue his marital relations with his wife. R. Meir, however, took issue with R. Hezekiah and argued that there was no ground for such action.[64]

---

[62] *Mordecai Hagadol*, p. 209c; Pr. 933: שיש להקל שלא להצריכה גט ... וטוב בעיני יש להקל שלא להצריכה גט ... וטוב בעיני שלא להחמיר ולהצריכה גט לחומרא, פן יתן המקדש כתף סוררת כדי לעגנה או ירחיק נדוד ונמצאת זאת העלובה [עגונה] כל ימיה.

[63] See the great storm of protests raised against R. Meir's decision in a similar case: *Text*, 271.

[64] Am II, 63; Pr. 98; Tesh. Maim. *Nashim*, 8.

On one occasion R. Meir even tried to vindicate an apparently wicked woman.[65] Thus we see that in important matters R. Meir showed strength of character and determination, and that when matters vitally important depended on his ruling, he used his utmost ingenuity in order to arrive at a lenient decision.[66]

G. Change of Attitude on Account of Age.

In making a character-study of a person one must take into consideration the great changes in his nature and attitude caused by the passing of time. Any analytical character-study of a person based upon a synthesis of the data found in the writings, statements, and activities of the person during a period of fifty years, without any attempt at a chronological classification of such data in order to discover some elements of development and change, must necessarily be false. A person undergoes considerable changes in a period of fifty years; what is true of his youth is not true of his old age. Some persons mellow with age and others grow bitter. Any generalization without connecting events with the periods of a person's life within which they fall, contains but little of the truth.

It is almost impossible, however, to arrange the sources which are relevant to a study of R. Meir's character in any chronological order, or even to group the sources into definite periods. His writings bear no dates of composition, and even the division of his Responsa into two groups, those written before 1275, and those after that date, is of very little help since his Responsa contain but few personal references and furnish but meager data for a psychological study. The most revealing reports are garnered from the writings of his students who faithfully describe his behavior, his habits, and his idiosyncrasies. These reports, however, bearing no dates, are usually of but

[65] L. 310; Tesh. Maim. *Nashim*, 25.
[66] See also Berl. p. 295, no. 389; *Mordecai Hagadol* p. 119b.

little use for a study of the effect of age on R. Meir's character.

Nevertheless, we do possess several indications that the passing of time brought about deep-seated psychological transformations in R. Meir, that his attitude to life and religion changed considerably with the passing of the years, and that his confinement in prison has had a still greater effect upon him.

Thus in his youth R. Meir would ridicule the overpious who refrained from eating meat for several hours after eating cheese. Years later, however, he changed his opinion and himself refrained from eating meat after cheese.[67] This tendency to stricter piety, revealed itself also when in later life he began consistently to fast on both days of *Rosh Hashanah*.[68] In his youth he was brave, self-reliant, and of an independent nature. He openly contradicted his teachers,[69] reversed a decision of R. Hezekiah of Magdeburg,[70] relied on his own interpretation of a talmudic source completely disregarding the views of outstanding authorities,[71] and bravely permitted the marriage of

---

[67] Pr. 615: ושאל אדוני ששמעת דאני נוהג שלא לאכול בשר בהמה וחיה אחר גבינה ומיקל בבשר עוף. בימי חורפי היית י מתלוצ ץ בבני אדם שהיו עושי' כן ואדרבה שרא לי מורי היה נראה בעיני כמו טינות . . . ; cf. L. 500b. See also P. 289 ושלום מאיר ב"ר ברוך זלה"ה where he relates that as a young student he took a more lenient stand than his teacher.

[68] *Tashbetz*, 113; ibid. 566: התענה בסוף ימיו שני ימים טובים של ר"ה; R. Hayyim Or Zarua, *Responsa*, 49: ועוד כתב ראיה ממורי רבינו מאיר זצ"ל שהיה מקדש על השולחן לבני ביתו בי"ט שני של ר"ה אעפ"י שהיה מתענה.

[69] See Mord. B. K. 30–1; P. 289: וכמדומה אני ששמעתי ממהר"ר יצחק מוינא שהיה אוסר אמנם שוב נשאתי ונתתי לפניו בדבר להתירו ולא סתר את דברי, ובקוצר נראה בעיני היתר גמור; cf. also Hag. Maim. *Taanit*, 5, 70; Mord. B. B. 538.

[70] See Am II, 63; Pr. 98. The former source bears the signature מאיר ב"ר ברוך זלה"ה; while the latter source מאיר ב"ר ברוך שיחי', ברוך שיחי'; however, both Tesh. Maim. to *Nashim*, 8, and Rashba I, 833 bear the signature מאיר ב"ר ברוך שיחיה, thus prov- ing that this Responsum was written in R. Meir's younger days.

[71] See Mord. B. K. 172: אומר ר"מ דה"ה לשכר שדכנים שאינו מחויב לתת לו כ"א שכר טורחו, אמנם ראיתי בספר א"ז שפסק משם רבינו שמחה שחייב לשדכן לתת כל מה שהתנה ליתן לו . . . והביא ראיה דמעשה בא לפני ר"י . . . ופסק ר"י לתת לו כל מה שהתנה . . . ואמרתי לפני מורי שכן ראיתי ולא השגיח, ושוב מצאתי כן בספר המצות משום רבינו יהודה . . . ושוב הרצו הדבר לפני רבינו מאיר ראו כן בספר המצות ולא השגיח. On the other hand, in L. 308, R. Meir modified his stand on this subject: אבל אם שדכן [הוא] וקרוב לודאי שהוא מרויח מצד אחר כל כך

a maiden who presumably had been betrothed to another man.[72] In his later life, however, he grew more cautious in his relations to other rabbis, his contemporaries;[73] he no longer put complete trust in his own logical deductions but reversed his decisions, in several instances, upon discovering that earlier authorities disagreed with his views.[74] He became much stricter in his decisions on ritual laws,[75] and completely changed his former liberal attitude toward rebellious wives.[76]

His detention in prison, on the other hand, seems to have mellowed him considerably; gone is his self-reliance, gone is his fearlessness in rendering judgment, and gone is even his over-punctilliousness in ritual observances. His decisions are qualified by a statement that since he is suffering from a lack of books one should not rely on his opinion;[77] he has to be coaxed,

---

אם לא מתעסק בשליחותו של זה, נ׳ל לדמותו [להא דסיפא] דנותן לו שכרו משלם. The incident reported by Mordecai must have preceded the writing of L. 308, and therefore occurred in R. Meir's younger days.

[72] Am II, 41–2; cf. *Text* no. 271, and discussion below.

[73] See Pr. 993: ואם יסכימו רבותי לדברי טוב, ואם לאו הנני נמשך ונגרר אחריהם לכל אשר חזרנו על כל צדדים וצדי צדדים ...יעשו; Tesh. Maim. to *Nashim* 9: מאיר ב׳ר ברוך זלה׳ה וכמדומה אנחנו דלית דין ולית דיין דאיתתא שריא לאינסובא ... ואני איני כדאי שתסמכו על דברי, אמנם אם יסכים מה׳ר אליעזר ואתם שאר רבותי אשר שם התירוה להנשא, ואם לאו דעתי מבוטלת להם; this Responsum was probably written after Am II, 63.

[74] R. Asher, *Responsa*, 58, 2: עדות צריכה תחלתו וסופו בכשרות ה׳מ אם הפסול מחמת הגוף ולא מחמת ממון וכן היה ר׳ מאיר דן כמה שנים, ושוב חזר בו כי מצא בתוספות רבינו ברוך שפירש; cf. Hag. Maim. ...אמנם משבא לידי ספר רמב׳ם חזרתי לדבריו; L. 426: ככתוב למעלה *Toen*, 6, 1.

[75] Hag. Mord. to *Hullin* ch. 6: כי ר׳מ מתיר אם נפלה הטיפה על הקדירה מבחוץ אצל האש כנגד הרוטב שאז הרוטב מסייע... ושוב חזר בו; compare with Mord. *Hullin*, 679.

[76] R. Hayyim Or Zarua, *Responsa*, 69: אבל אבא מארי זצ׳ל אמר לנו שמתחלה היה דן מהר׳ם זצ׳ל כן אבל בסוף ימיו פסק דקנסינן לה בכולה אפי׳ במה שהביאה עמה וכ׳כ לקהילות ואני ראיתי את מורי רבי׳ מאיר זצ׳ל שדן בו הלכה :126 ibid; לתקן... וכן אמר לתקן לקהילות למעשה שצוה לבעל לתן גט בלא כתובה וגם הוא לא יקח מכל אשר לה אלא מה שהכניס משלו, ורבו המורדות, אז שלח למורי הר׳ר ידידיה שהיה בשפירא ולשלשלת הקהילות להתועד יחד ולתקן שהמורדת וכן דן מורינו ר׳ מאיר כמה פעמים ולבסוף בהיותו :155 ibid; תפסיד גם מה שהכניסה ותצא ריקנית; בנורנבורג פירש לקהלות הקודש שבריינוס שתקנו שאפילו מה שהכניסה לו לא תטו .cf *Text* no. 309, and the sources quoted there.

[77] Am II, 108: תוספי גיטין אין בידי ולא ספרי פסקים בארץ הנגב, סבבתי כל אלא כאשר הראוני מן השמים ואם ימצא שהתוסף׳ וספרי הפוסקי׳ חולקים עלי בשום דבר, דעתי מבוטלת; לעני יודע יושב חושך וצלמות ולא כדרים זה ג׳ שנים ומחצה; cf. Pr. 119.

by an appeal to his sense of justice, into rendering a decision
on a matter involving the reputation of local judges, and he
has to be assured that his decision will be final, before rendering judgment.[78] In former years he had constructed an
enclosure for his stove which he kept locked on the Sabbath to
prevent his servant from stealthily warming his house on the
Sabbath.[79] While he was in prison, however, not only did he
fail to protest, but, on the contrary, showed great satisfaction,
when his keepers increased the fire in his compartment on the
Sabbath, even though they expressly told him that they were
doing it for his benefit.[80]

H. Serious Quarrels.

R. Meir's strength of character and deep conviction of
his mastery of talmudic lore involved him, in his younger days,
in violent quarrels. Thus on two occasions many scholars and
community leaders rose against him, voicing their indignation,
pronouncing the ban against his followers and supporters, and
hurling threats at R. Meir himself.[81]

The first quarrel broke out because of the betrothal of the
daughter of the rich magnate, R. Judah of Düren, to a poverty-
stricken youth of Rothenburg, Jacob son of R. Moses. At the
time of the betrothal R. Moses had agreed to have his son settle
in Düren and marry R. Judah's daughter there. He kept his
promise and sent his son to R. Judah. When the latter, how-

---

[78] Tesh. Maim. *Kinyan*, 32: והודיעני מה אתה דן בה ואין מצוה גדולה מזו להעמיד
העולם על הדין ועל האמת לכן התחל תשובתך מעבר הפסק דין ובאר לנו צדדים וצדי צדדים וצורנו
יוציאך מבלאך ... והפרנסים צוו לדיינים לכתוב הטענות והפסק למען להעמיד כל אדם על חזקתו
See also ibid. ועל הדין ועליך אין לפקפק ולהרהר כי כל מה שתפסוק פסוק וחתום ותו לא מידי
no. 31.

[79] Pr. 92.

[80] Hag. Maim. *Shabbat*, 6, 6: וזכורני כשהייתי אצל מורי במגדל וושבור'ק שבע'ש
עשינו מדורה ... באו העבדים ועשוה גדולה ואמרו בפירוש שעשאוה לנו לנחת רוח וישבו ואנחנו
אצלם ושמחנו בדבר.

[81] See *Text*, 280; ibid. 271.

71-485

ever, saw that Jacob was small in stature and unattractive in appearance, he was concerned about his daughter, and, believing that she might eventually despise him, sent him back to his father. Jacob felt deeply humiliated. He nursed his grievance for five years, suffering privation in his father's house, deeply hurt because he was utterly ignored by his intended father-in-law. Meanwhile his bride grew up and she found that her tie to the hated youth of Rothenburg was unbearable. R. Judah, then, demanded that Jacob either come to Düren and marry his daughter, or divorce her forthwith; while, at the same time, secret warnings were dispatched to the youth never to come to Düren lest the servants of R. Judah do him harm. Jacob, therefore, refused to go to Düren, nor would he grant the requested divorce. He demanded, on his part, that his bride come to live in Rothenburg where they would consummate their marriage.[82]

R. Meir was intimately acquainted with the case. He had written many letters to R. Judah on behalf of the poverty stricken youth, and had repeatedly received a cold rebuff from the rich magnate. R. Meir knew that R. Judah was not sincere in his demands that Jacob come to Düren to consummate the marriage; he knew that R. Judah had set his heart on divorce and was merely engaging in bluster in order to force Jacob to free his daughter. R. Meir's sense of justice was aroused. He would not permit the rich and powerful R. Judah to take advantage of the helpless youth. Talmudic law was the same for the rich as for the poor, and even the weak had their rights.[83]

R. Judah sought to move heaven and earth to his will. He wrote letters to the leading rabbis of France and Germany enlisting their aid and urging them to wield their most devas-

[82] See L. 386; Tesh. Maim. to *Nashim*, 28; Pr. 250-1; Am II, 81.
[83] L. 386.

tating weapon, the ban, against Jacob and his supporters.[84]
Many rabbis complied with R. Judah's wishes, wrote lengthy
discussions on the issues involved, and hurled threats at Jacob
and his supporters. Even the great Rabbi Samuel b. Salomo,
the aged teacher of R. Meir, vigorously denounced the youth
of Rothenburg and agreed that a ban be pronounced against
him and against those who upheld his cause, though he took
care to exclude R. Meir from this ban.[85]

Not all the discussions and disputations regarding this case
have been preserved, nor do we know the outcome of this heated
controversy. The few Responsa that were preserved, however,
are deeply absorbing and highly fascinating human documents,
revealing R. Meir's love for justice and his courage in face of
attack.

The complicated betrothal problems of another young
maiden again involved R. Meir in a violent quarrel. A nephew
of Rabbi Kohen Zedek permitted the betrothal of his daughter
to a young man in the presence of biblically disqualified witnesses, even though he himself as well as all those present at
the ceremony had been forewarned that the betrothal without
proper witnesses would be void. Subsequently the bride, or
her father, became displeased with the match and sought an
annulment. Rabbi Kohen Zedek, then, sent a query to R. Meir
who ruled that the betrothal was null and void, and that the
maiden was at liberty to marry anyone she pleased without
the necessity of receiving a divorce from her former bridegroom.[86]

[84] Am II, 81: כי ידעתי שהנדיב לא החריש כי קשה לו חרפתו ואלצתו שיאמרו שהכריחהו
והכריעהו לתן להם ממונו כאשר שתו עליו, ושלח הדבר לפני ישישים גדולי צרפת ושאר מקומות
וכמדומה אני שכולם הסכימו לכופו . . . וידעתי אף כי מורי גדול הדור לא יצוה לו לעבור על דברי
זקנים.

[85] Pr. 250: ואני הצעיר הסכמתי לנדות ולרדות אותו הארום עד שיכנוס או יפטור את ארוסתו
ואם ישמע תבא עליו ברכה ואם לא ישמע עונו ישא וכו' כי מחזיקי' ידי עוברי עבירה לבד ח'ו על
רב He was כבודי מהר'ר מאיר לא זכרנו אך על אחרי' לא חלקנו במקום שיש חלול השם כבוד לרב
probably mindful of *Moed Katan* 17a: תלמיד חכם שסרח אין מנדין אותו מנדין אותו בפרהסיה.

[86] See *Text*, no. 271; Am II, 42.

Rabbi Kohen Zedek wrote again to R. Meir raising doubt as to the correctness of this decision, informing him that his teacher from Spiers, though at first he agreed with this decision, finally disagreed with it; and that the young lady had meanwhile become betrothed to another man.[87] R. Meir answered that the earlier opinion of his teacher was correct, that when a woman was betrothed in the presence of disqualified witnesses no divorce was required. He, then, added: We are not at liberty to be overstringent in such cases and demand that a divorce be delivered, in order to dispel any shadow of doubt as to the girl's freedom to marry another man, since such a step would make her ineligible ever to marry a man of priestly lineage.[88]

A storm of protest arose against R. Meir's action. The Rabbis and leaders of the communities of Spiers, Worms and Mayence, became highly incensed and heaped abuse upon R. Meir for permitting a betrothed woman to marry another man.[89] They quoted several authorities in support of their view, and solemnly pronounced the ban against those involved in the action (again probably excluding R. Meir), in order to force the daughter to receive a divorce from her second bridegroom.[90]

R. Meir then wrote a sharp answer to the leaders of the three communities, in which he pointed out the clear distinction between witnesses who were rabbinically disqualified and those who were biblically disqualified. He then proved that all authorities agreed that a woman who was betrothed in the

---

[87] Am II, 41.

[88] Ibid.: ‏ואין לומר להצריך גט לחומרא דכיון דל׳צ אסור להחמיר ולפוסלה לכהונה.‏

[89] *Mordecai Hagadol* p. 212d: ‏שמעתי שהקהילות מקהו מקהייתו וקוראים אחרינו על אלה‏ ‏על אשר התרנו בלא גט קידושין שנעשו רק בפני קרובים בפני ראובן ובפני בן אחות ראובן. וקול‏ ‏התרנזם ורב בוזם עלה באזנינו ושמונו בפי כל עד שנושאות ונותנות בנו מזרות כלבנה לאמר שאנו‏ ‏מתירין אשת איש. וכהנה רבות דברים שלא נתנו ליכתב.‏

[90] Ibid.: ‏אמנם לאשר כתבו במכתבם שר׳ח בספר המקצעות והשכל טוב ואבי העזרי ורבינו‏ ‏שמחה כתבו שצריכה גט. וגם נדי את מי שאינו חייב נידוי לא יכולני להתאפק.‏

presence of biblically disqualified witnesses was free to marry
another man. The rabbis and leaders of the Rhine communities, in their eagerness to attack R. Meir, had failed fully to
comprehend the text they quoted in support of their view and
had been misled by a faulty text.[91]

With bitterness and indignation R. Meir added: 'We have
never seen revered teachers of old act in the manner of the
abovementioned community leaders. Differences of opinion
have often arisen among the great authorities, some prohibiting what others permitted, but never did anyone dare place
under the ban those who had acted contrary to his opinion.
You, the aforementioned community leaders, probably delude
yourselves with the idea that since your permission is required
before a person may divorce his wife,[91a] no scholar is permitted
to render decisions in ritual law unless he first received your
authorization. No, this is not true; for the Torah is free to
anyone who is capable of arriving at a correct decision. You
have gathered and have associated with yourselves men who
do not understand the intricacies of the laws of marriage and
divorce. I most vigorously protest against those who sought
to ruin my honor and reputation. Blessed be the Lord who
saved me from their hands'.[92]

[91] Ibid.: וכשׁ יבקש אך הש', כזו לידם, שנגה שתבא כדאי רבותי היו ולא . . . אטעינהו מוטעה וסופר
שמותו לדבריהם סעד להם נדמה כאשר מיד דברי, לסתור להוטים שהיו לפי ידעתי כי נרדף, את
ועקש. נפתל בה ואין אמת הש' תורת כי יעשה לא וכן למטה. מה למעלה מה השכילו טרם בכתובים
על וכל מכל יסמכו ולא שיורו, קודם יפה יפה דבריהם ויצהירו ויחוורו בהלכות ישכילו כן והמורים
סופר טעות מחמת האדם את מטעים לפעמים כי הפסקים דברי.

[91a] See Finkelstein, op. cit. p. 238.

[92] Ibid.: מתיר זה הגדולים בין מחלוקת היה רבות פעמים כי הכי, דעבדו קשישי רבנן חזינן ולא
שצריכין מחמת ושמא דבריו. על העובר לנדות לבו מלאו אשר מעולם מהן אחד היה ולא אוסר וזה
התורה כי לא, מיניכו. רשותא נקט לא אי להורות אדם לכל שאין אתם כמדומים גיטין להסכמת לכם
ונגד . . . וקידושין גיטין בטיב יודעים אדם בני שאין עמכם וכנפתם ולקטתם כהלכה. שיורה אך הפקר
הש"י וברוך כבודינו. לעקור שכיוון מי כל תלונת רק תלמידו, אני כי מקפיד איני משפירא ה"ר מורי
לשיניהם טרף נתנו שלא. Is it possible, then, that in spite of *Moed Katan*, 17a, the
ban was pronounced even against R. Meir?

Thus, because of his boldness and self-reliance, R. Meir occasionally found himself involved in heated controversy and passionate contention. He learned his lesson, however, and became very careful in his dealings with community leaders,[93] and quite hesitant in his decisions regarding marriage and divorce.[94]

[93] Thus in the case of the community that hired a cantor for three years, dismissed him shortly after he was hired, and appointed another in his place, R. Meir resorts to strange circumlocutions with the object of pointing out the injustice the community committed against the cantor; taking great care, however, not directly to offend the community leaders. See Am II, 234. On another occasion he shows great reluctance in deciding on matters of taxation; see Am II, 141:
דעו כי מאד מאד הקשיתם לשאול לבקשני להכריע בדבר זה, ובמרומים סהדי כי בשביל ממון גדול לא הייתי משתדל, אך אחרי שככה השבעתני והודעתני שאם אמשוך את ידי אז יבא לידי קטטה גדולה בטלתי רצוני מפני רצונכם . . . ואינכם צריכי' לשלוח לי עוד בשביל דין זה כי לא אפסוק בע"א כלל.
Cf. also Pr. 982.

[94] See Tesh. Maim. to *Nashim* 1: ואם יסכימו רבותי טוב, ואם לאו הני נמשך וננרר אחריהם לכל אשר יעשו וטוב בעיני שלא להחמיר להצריכה גט לחומרא, פן יתן המקדש כתף סוררת ואני כתבתי דעתי כאשר :ibid. 3 כדי לעננה או ירחיק נדוד ונמצאת זאת העלובה כל ימיה עגונה הראוני מן השמים ואיני חפץ כלל שתסמוך עלי להתירה בלא גט אם לא תשלח דברי לרבותי אשר סביבותיך ולרבותינו שבצרפת, ואם יסכימו לדעת תלמידם מוטב, ואם לאו דעתי מבוטלת כנגדם ואני איני כדאי שתסמכו על דברי אמנם אם יסכים מה"ר אליעזר ואתם ושאר רבותי אשר :ibid. 9 שם התירוה להנשא ואם לאו דעתי מבוטלת להם.

CHAPTER IV

R. Meir and Community Government.

R. Meir's true greatness is reflected in his relations with the communities of Germany. In his conception and analysis of the ideas of human freedom, government by consent, legal assumption of agreement, limitation of the power of the majority, and group responsibility, R. Meir is revealed as a profound thinker and theorizer on the subject of political organization. He delved into the very depths of the problem of human relation and cooperation.[1] The complexity of community organization, the multiplicity of its problems, the bitter struggle of private interests pitted against one another, and the lack of decisive means of coercion within the community, often occasioned an appeal to the great moral power wielded by the leading talmudic scholar of the age.[2] In pondering over the many queries regarding community rule sent to him, R. Meir used to advantage the fruitful political opinions of his predecessors,

[1] See subdivision 8 of this chapter. The problems of community self-rule are analyzed here in considerable detail not only because of the light it sheds on R. Meir's political thoughts, which in themselves are highly significant since R. Meir died as a political prisoner, but because the value of these Responsa as historical documents is dependent largely on the gravity with which they were composed, on the role they played as legal documents, and on the judicial and political power and standing of their author. A thorough understanding is required of the political organization of the communities of Germany and France, the position of the outstanding talmudic scholar in that political organization, and the complete control of all phases of community life by talmudic law, before one may make full use of these Responsa as historical sources.

[2] See *Maase ha-Geonim*, Berlin, 1909, p. 70; Joel Mueller, תשובות גאוני מזרח ומערב, 165; ibid. 205; Joel Mueller, תשובות חכמי צרפת ולותיר, 21–22; ibid. 24; ibid. 27; ibid. 29; ibid. 88; ibid. 97; Mord. B. K. 179; R. Eliezer b. Nathan, ספר ראב'ן, p. 139c–d; ibid. p. 137b; R. Isaac b. Moses of Vienna, *Or Zarua*, sec. *Responsa*, 751; ibid. 775; Mord. B. B. 477; ibid. 490; Mord. Kid. 561; ibid. 564.

reinterpreted a vast array of talmudic dicta on this subject, and, applying many ideas of his own, constructed a logical legal system for community government, and defined the powers, prerogatives and limitations of such government.[3]

In order to understand fully R. Meir's conception of the legal background for community government, and his theories regarding human freedom as a basis for political organization, we must review the history and development of the German communities, and epitomize the various views and opinions propounded by outstanding scholars which were instrumental in molding community government in Germany. We are not concerned here with a description of the community itself, the number of its officers and constituted agencies, and their duties and functions. We are primarily concerned with the scope of authority wielded by the community organization whatever its form, the source and legal basis of such authority, and the part played by talmudic law in shaping and controlling such authority.

1. Origin of Community Self-rule.

Jewish self-government in the Middle Ages came into being through the strong desire of the Jews to live fully in accordance with the dictates of their religion.[4] They came to Germany

---

[3] See *Text*, Nos. 527–605.

[4] The Jews found a means of organizing group life and cooperative action in their religious law. As an alien group they had to band together for mutual protection. Talmudic law provided them with the means of exercising social control, with directed leadership, and with punitive measures for the suppression of crime. See the Responsum of R. Joseph Bonfils, of the eleventh century, L. 423: אם כן יפקיע כל אחד עצמו מן המס ומכל תקנות ב'ד שאין יכולין לכוף את הרשעים בזמן הזה אלא בחרם וקנס והמבטלן מביא פריצות בישראל. The problem of finding means of social control was uppermost in their minds; see the Responsum of Rabbi Judah b. Meir ha-Kohen and Rabbi Eliezer b. Judah, of the tenth century, *Kol Bo*, 142: ועכשו יורנו רבותינו אם רשאין בני העיר למזר על קצת בני קהלם ולכופם ולהתקן עמהם בתקנתם, ושלא להפריש מן הצבור ... ויורנו רבותינו אם יוכלו בני עיר להשביע על בני עיר אחרת. That the Jews were deeply concerned with proper religious conduct we learn from a docu-

and France as an individualistic group willing to pay for the privilege of settling there, for protection of life and property, and for the right to engage in business with the local inhabitants.[5] They were not willing, however, to give up their personal freedom, their principles of justice, and their code of law; they refused to become an integral part of the feudal system, and to subject themselves to feudal law.[6]

The early privilege-documents made out to the Jews include permission to settle disputes among themselves in accordance with Jewish law.[7] These documents were drawn up at the request of the Jews, usually for a monetary consideration to the grantor; every stipulation in favor of the Jews was undoubtedly keenly sought, and specifically bargained for, by them.[8] More-

---

ment of the sixth century describing a Jew being led in chains by his brethren for refusing to abide by Jewish religious practices; see Aronius, *Regesten*, 36. In the later centuries we find community ordinances dealing with the requirement that all adults daily devote a certain period of time to the study of the *Torah*; see Finkelstein, *Jewish Self-Government in the Middle Ages*, p. 231.

[5] See the very interesting document printed by Ad. Neubauer in *R.E.J.* vol. X (1885) p. 98: אבותינו בני ישראל באו בכל ארץ מלכותו בענין שנתחייב להעמידנו בהבטחה לשמור גופנו ומאודנו ונחלתנו. ועמדנו אנחנו ואבותינו בהבטחה ההיא זמן רב מימות המלך קרל"ש עד עתה אשר הוא כבש ארצות רבות והבאים אחריהם כולם בעזר הישראלים אשר היו עמם בגופם ובממונם אשר הם בעצמם היו נכנסים בעובי המלחמה ומוסרים עצמם למיתה להצלת המלכים והשרים אשר ... עמהם כי דבר ידוע הוא וכתוב במקומות רבים בינינו. Thus the Jews paid for the protection of their life and property not only by money contributions, but through active military service. Nevertheless the relation between the king and the Jews was founded on a contractual basis, and not on a political. There was a pact between the government and the Jews to protect them for a consideration. The Jews kept their part of this pact and expected the king to keep his.

[6] Charlemagne had granted the Jews the right to settle all disputes among themselves in accordance with Jewish law. See Aronius, op. cit. 78: *Si Judeus contra Judeum aliquod negocium habuerit, per legem suam se defendat.* There is no doubt that this law was sought by the Jews and adopted at their request.

[7] See Aronius, op. cit. 78, 81, 82, 170(14), 171, 547. The discussion of Berthold Altmann, op. cit. pp. 78–96, is not entirely relevant in this connection, since we are mainly interested here with the ambitions and desires of the Jews, but not with the legal forms of the period that complied with these ambitions within the framework of existing legal institutions and concepts.

[8] The famous privilege-document of King Henry IV, granted to Judah b. Kalonymos, David b. Meshulam, and Moses b. Guthiel, of Spiers, explicitly

over, through these documented privileges they merely sought
to receive legal recognition of conditions already existing. Thus
the right to self-government was granted to them in the same
manner as the right to transact business in the King's territory,
the right to live in accordance with their religious principles, and
the right to remain undisturbed in their own property. The self-
government of the German and French Jews, therefore, came
into being because of their own ardent desire for freedom and
independence, and not at all as a result of administrative ex-
pediency on the part of the secular government.[9]

states that they approached the king with the request that he grant them his
protection and certain privileges; see Aronius, op. cit. 170. Moreover, a study of
the privileges granted reveals that they conform perfectly with talmudic law,
which in itself is sufficient proof that the privileges were, on the whole, drawn up
by the Jews themselves, and that the king affixed his signature to the document
because of substantial considerations. The well known law that a buyer of movables, which were later proven to be stolen property, was entitled to reimbursement of his original investment (170, 6), and the stipulation that a Jew should
not be condemned through the testimony of Gentile witnesses (170, 12), and that
a Jew be permitted to clear himself by his oath alone (Aronius 547, 2, 3, 7), pre-
suppose an intimate knowledge of Jewish law as well as conformity to talmudic
law of evidence. A comparison with the crude laws of evidence enacted by Charlemagne (Aronius, op. cit. 73, 76) confirms this view. As to the manner of receiving
a privilege-document, cf. Herbert Fischer, *Die verfassungsrechtliche Stellung der
Juden in den Deutschen Städten während des dreizehnten Jahrhunderts*, Breslau,
1931, p. 64.

[9] The ordinances enacted by the synods of the communities providing that
no person should bring his litigation before the courts of the land, that whoever
directly, or even indirectly, caused his litigation to come up before such court
was to be considered an informer, and that no one should seek to gain power and
authority over the Jews through the aid of the secular government (Cr. 78, cf.
Finkelstein, op. cit. pp. 151–60), speak eloquently of the fact that the Jews strongly
desired to live according to the laws and regulations of the Talmud, and that
they were greatly opposed to the secular government's interference in their internal
affairs. Cf. Pr. 247: ומה שמנום אפי' אם תפטור אמו שרוצה לקבול עליה בפני הדוכוס, תפס
חבלא בתרי רישי . . . ראוי לנדותו על הדבור ולהבדילו מעדת ישראל . . . כ"ש וכ"ש אם ילך בערכאות
של גוים. Cf. also B. p. 323, no. 978; Cr. 185b; Pr. 103; 717; 994; L. 334; ibid.
247–8; P. 311; Mord. B. K. 55; ibid. 195; Tesh. Maim. to *Nezikin*, 15; ibid. 15b.
See O. Stobbe, *Die Juden in Deutschland während des Mittelalters*, Braunschweig,
1866, pp. 140–2, 152; Schroeder, *Lehrbuch der deutschen Rechtsgeschichte*, 6th
Edition, pp. 245–6, 505 f. The Geonim permitted enlistment of the help of the
civil authorities in special cases; see *Shaare Zedek*, 7, 4; *Ginzei Schechter*, II, 127.

The Jews paid heavily to kings, archbishops, and overlords, both lay and ecclesiastical, for the permission to govern themselves; but they never considered the rights of the community over the individual based on the authority granted to the community by the secular government. Not once, in the entire Responsa-literature of Germany and France of the eleventh, twelfth, and thirteenth centuries, do we find community leaders claiming coercive powers over the members of their communities on the ground that such powers had been granted to them by the overlord.[10] On the other hand, they repeatedly asserted that their power was derived from sound talmudic law,[11] and not at all from the regulations and privileges emanating from the secular government. These privileges, granted to the Jews on various occasions, merely permitted them to continue their self-rule undisturbed, but did not institute it; and though these government regulations often circumscribed the extent of the autonomous rule of the Jews, they scarcely affected the inner life and function of the community government.[12]

[10] Moreover the use of such powers received at the hands of the secular government was strictly banned. See Cr. 78: ועוד גזרנו והחרמנו שלא יהא אדם רשאי ליטול שררה על חבירו ע"י שר ושופט ומלך כדי לענוש ולקנוס ולכוף לא בדברי הבאי ולא בדברי שמים ... . ואם יחטא איש לאיש יפללו אלקים אך אצבע נוי עע"ז לא ינע ולא יעבור בתוכם. Note the great commotion created in the community when a person became *parnes* through the promptings of the overlord, Mord. *Kiddushin*, 564: אפוטרופוס ראובן תבע עלבון הרב שנתפס הוא ובחוריו מכח שמעון שרצה לדחוק אותם שימחלו לשמעון על אשר אמר לרב שהוא בחרם, ועוד נתפס פעם שניה והושב במגדל בתחתיות שבועיים ועוד הוצרך לצאת מן העיר עבור זאת העלילה ותובע יציאותיו ונעילת דלת שיעשה שירשהו ליכנס בעיר. וגם שנטל פרנסות של הקהל מעצמו ע"י עובד כוכבים שלא ברשות הקהל. וגם קורא לבית הכנסת של הרב, 'גלו'ק, הוא בית אנקות, ושמעון משיב שהשר דחקו להיות פרנס ונתרצו הקהל, ולרב לא עשה דבר לא בדבור ולא במעשה. On the other hand, the secular arm was used as the ultimate means of enforcing community rulings. See Pr. p. 158b: וכל אשר יעבור על תקנות הללו יהיה בנדוי כל הקהילות. Cf. also Pr. 968. ואם ישהא במרדו חדש ימים יהא ממונו מותר למסור למלך או לשלטון.

[11] *Kol Bo*, 142; Mord. *Hullin*, 711; L. 108; ibid. 423; Am II, 127: והאפוטרופ' [של הקהל] השיב שמנהג הוא מימים קדמונים בורידבורג כשהיו נדולים בתורה ופרנסים דרים שם ... ; cf. also Pr. 46, 104, 106, 245, 383, 708, 716, ועתה כשנתפשנו יעצונו חכמים ובונים לתן מס 934, 940, 941, 968, 994; L. 248; Cr. 10, 165, 230.

[12] See Stobbe, op. cit. p. 140–1. The laws enacted by the secular authorities for the purpose of regulating the relationship of the Jews toward one another

How, then, did the community come into being as a unit of self-government? In order to live a strictly Jewish life, the Jews who came to Germany and France in the early Middle Ages banded together to form small communities. A Jew was in need of a synagogue, a quorum of ten for community prayer, a teacher for his children, a ritual slaughterer, and a ritual bath-house; he needed protection against his Gentile neighbors, and a person to represent him before his overlord. These a Jew could obtain only in cooperation with his brethren.[13] A community, therefore, was a cooperative body created for the purpose of providing for the common needs of the individual members and for mutual help.[14]

The early communities resembled large families. The individual members were intimately interested in one another's welfare. A wedding as well as a funeral was everybody's concern, and a betrothal usually took place in the presence of the elders of the community.[15] Orphans, widows, and the poor,

(see Aronius, op. cit. 547; Stobbe, op. cit. note 132) were devoid of any meaning, since they rarely brought their litigation before the secular courts.

[13] A Jew who separated himself from the community in taxation matters often found himself at the mercy of the overlord. Note the tragic fate of a wealthy Jew who lacked the support of his brethren, described at great length in *Text* no. 572.

[14] See the description of the duties and functions of the community, given by R. Meir: הן לברר הראשים הן לברר חזנים הן לתקון כיס של צדקה הן למנות גבאיהם לבנות או לסתור בביהכ"נ להוסיף ולגרוע לקנות בית חתנות ולקנות בית האומנים ולכונן ולסתור כל צרכי הקהל Ber. p. 320, no. 865; Tesh. Maim. to *Kinyan*, 27; *Text*, 529.

[15] Pr. 1015: על ראובן ששלח את שמעון לקדש לו לאה, וכאשר בא שמה הושיב שמעון חשובי הקהל כמו שרגילים לעשות והראה להם ההרשאה שמינהו ראובן שליח לקדש. The origin of this custom is wrapped in obscurity. Rabbenu Tam and Ri held different views on this subject. Thus we read in the *Tosaphot* to *Nedarim*, 27b. ואור"ת שלכך נהגו לאסוף כל בני העיר בשעת שידוכין היינו כי היכי דליהוי ב'ד חשוב ולא יהא ערבון אסמכתא, ואין נראה לר"י שהרי כמה פעמים אין שם אלא קרובים. In Spain a similar procedure was often required, but its motivation was clearly in order to curb mock marriages. Communities specifically declared marriages unlawful unless they were performed in the presence of a quorum of ten men. See Rashba I, 1206: שאלת עוד קהל שעשו תקנה מחמת הפריצי' שכל מי שיקדש אשה בלא מעמד עשרה שלא יהא קידושי קידושין הודיעני אם יש כח ביד הקהל לעשות כן; also ibid. 550. In Germany and France, however, there is no mention of such a motivation. See *Sefer Rabn* p. 139c–d: וכבר היה מעשה בקולוניא בבחור שהיה משדך בקרובתו נערה מן אביה ואמה ומתוך כך קפץ אחד בעל נכסים ושידכ' וי(ר)אותו לקדש' לו, והושיבוה אביה ואמה לקבל קידושי השני וקראו לקהל כמנהג המקדיש וכשעמד השני לילך

were taken care of like brothers and sisters.[16] Even in its relation to the overlord the community acted as a unit, and paid
the taxes for its members in one lump sum.[17]

The Jews of Germany, however, could not lead a strictly
Jewish life, in complete accordance with talmudic law, unless
they could establish an authoritative body to enforce that law;
for that part of the *halakah* which provided for a system of
courts, judges, and police officers, was not valid for the Jews
of medieval Europe since it depended upon a process of ordination which had been discontinued for many years.[18] Even
in a very pious and God-fearing community the Talmud was
bound to become a dead letter unless there was an authoritative body to enforce its rulings.

For this reason the Jewish communities organized themselves into corporate bodies which claimed for themselves
coercive powers over their members, that almost compared

לקדשה קדמו לפניו קרובי הראשון ברמאות וקידשוה לפני עדים שהיו להם מזומנים . . . ואבי הנערה
בא למנצא וקיבץ כל חכמי הקהילות למנצא ויועדו שם בבית הכנסת. Yet no mention is made
of any *takkanah* against such marriages. Moreover we find that at a divorce too
the community was assembled; see R. Hayyim Or Zarua, *Responsa*, 157: ועשה
שליח להולכה את שמואל ב"ר יעקב הכהן ובטל כל מודעות ואמר שמרצון נפשו צוה לכתוב הגט בלא
שום אונס, ואמר כך בפני שניהם ובפני הקהל שהיו שם שני מנינים ועוד. We must assume, therefore, that this assembling of the community, at a betrothal, marriage, and divorce,
was motivated by a feeling of kinship and family-like relationship of the members
of the community, in the early settlements, which later became crystalized into a
rigid custom. See also *Sefer Hassidim*, ed. Wistinetsky 1300: בעיר אחת עשו חרם
שלא ישיאו את בנותיהם אלא ברשות טובי העיר שיראו שירא העיר שלא יהא איש רע ביניהם. Thus the
community officers had to approve the match.

[16] See Cr. 308: וששאלתם על אחד מן האחים שמת והניח בן קטן וזה אומר ינדל בן אחי אצלי
וזה אומר ינדל בן אחי אצלי וכו' אין הדבר תלוי באחין להיות אפוטרופוס אלא בגדולי העיר אביהם
של יתומים הנראה בעיניהם יותר טוב יעשו; cf. Pr. 896; 591–3; 574; 755; ibid. 74–5; P.
512; Am II, 231; Tesh. Maim. to *Kinyan*, 28.

[17] Pr. 104; 106; 331; 708; 716; 941; L. 108; 423; Am II, 17; 127; 139; 141.
See below for a detailed discussion of the functions of the community.

[18] See Maimonides, *Mishne Torah, Hilkot Shoftim*, ch. 4. Prof. Zeitlin
(*Religious and Secular Leadership*, p. 112) disagrees with this view. The fact,
however, that in all the numerous litigations regarding the legality of community
governmental power, the authority derived from *Semiha* was never mentioned as
a factor (see especially *Mordecai Hagadol* p. 213), has confirmed us in our view.

with those vested in a *Sanhedrin*. The community claimed the
right to enact ordinanaces, impose fines, inflict corporal punishment, confiscate property, and wield the power of excommunication.[19] It used this power and authority in order to enforce
the rulings of the Talmud, as well as its own ordinances and
regulations,[20] and thus became a mighty force that gave unity,
solidity, dignity and power to the Jews of medieval Germany
and France.

2. Community's Sphere of Activity.

The Community organization had a difficult and complicated task to perform. It controlled intimately the educational,
religious, economic, social, and political life of its members. It
had diversified activities.

1. The community granted permission, or denied it, to outsiders to settle in its locality.[21] Undesirable individuals were
not permitted to settle in the midst of it,[22] and violent persons
were often expelled from town.[23]

---

[19] See *Kol Bo* 142: והמרובין רשאין להשביע ולנזור ולפדות ולהחזור ממונו ולעשות סייג
לכל דבר ... ולא טבעיא בדבר שצריך לעשות סייג וגדר לתורה אלא אפי' בדבר הרשות כגון מס
Sefer Maase ;ושאר תקנות שמתקנין הקהל לעצמן אין היחיד יכול לבטל ולהוציא עצמו מתקנתן
תשובות ,Joel Mueller שרשאין אנשי המקום ללקות ולנדות ולהסיע על קצתן :ha-Geonim, p. 70
ואם נעשה הדבר הזה בפני חשובי העיר ... וכל שלשה שנתמנו בית דין :27 ,חכמי צרפת ולותיר
הלכך מה שעשו :97 .ibid ;על ישראל הרי הן כב"ד של משה לענוש נכסים ולהיות הפקירן הפקר
הקהלות גזירתם גזירה ומעשיהם מעשה ואין לשמעון לעבור על גזירתם ... ושלום גרשם בן יהודה

[20] See Cr. 10; 49; 53; 111; 121; 156; 165; 188; 190; 209; 222; 228; 230; Pr.
359; 546; 815; 825; 968; 980; 1012; 1017; L. 48; 79; 111; 213; 215; 217; 369; 423;
Am II, 122; 127; 128; 130; 132; 140; Berl. p. 320, no. 864.

[21] Pr. 46: שבא שמעון להחזיק בישוב מכח מחילה שמחלו לו היישוב כל הקהל שהיו דרים שם
באותה שעה ;L. 78: ראיתי בתשובת הבאים מאיי הים ששאלו זקני מזקני רומא אם נמלכו הקהל
;והתירו נזירת הרם היישוב לראובן שנה הן חסר הן יתר ושוב רוצים לגרשו ואינו שומע מה דינו
ראובן הדר בישוב מרשות הקהל ומתירים לו מזמן לזמן וכבר דר בישוב כמה שנים :Am II, 244
עתה יש מקצת הקהל שאינם רוצים להתיר לו יותר ואומרים שיפנה מיד משם. Cf. Pr. 100; 101;
382; 983; 1001; L. 77; 79; 111; 120; 213-6; 476; Cr. 9.

[22] R. Tam was of the opinion that the *herem hayishub* applied only to undesirable persons, see L. 111: ורבותינו כתבו בתוס' ב"ב כי ר"ת ז"ל לא היה מודה בחרם
היישובים כי אמר קדמונינו לא הנהיגו חרם היישוב אלא בשביל אלמים ומוסרים ושאינם רוצים לפנות
לתקנת הקהל ושאינם רוצים לפרוע מס עמהם אבל על אחר אין חרם.

[23] Cr. 6; Pr. 1001: ופעמים רבות ראיתי בקהלות שלוקחים היישוב עבור דבר מועט.

2. It was responsible to the authorities for the taxes of its members.[24] It negotiated and bargained with the overlords as to the amount of taxes due them.[25] It exacted an oath from each member as to the value of his possessions,[26] determined who should pay taxes,[27] what kind of property should be taxed,[28] and the exact amount due from each member.[29] It collected the taxes and paid it to the authorities.[30]

3. It supervised and regulated the sale of real-estate. It instituted definite procedures in the transfer of real property in order to insure a clear title to the purchaser,[31] and its

[24] The overlord would levy the tax on the community and leave it to the latter to collect it from its members. See Cr. 10; 49; 53; 111; 121; 222; 228; Pr. 104; 106; 131; 134; 331; 369; 918; 932; 944; 995; L. 108; 134; Am II, 19; 122; 127; 128; 130; 139; 141; B. p. 320, no. 866.

[25] Stobbe, op. cit. p. 28, refuses to believe that the Jews negotiated with the government authorities as to the amount of the tax, bargained with them, and finally came to an agreement as to the sum due. In the Responsa, however, we find frequent references to such negotiations which were termed להתפשר על המס; see Am II, 127; Cr. 53; 222: ונכנס לעיר תחלה לדעת כן שנתפשר בפני עצמו עם השר על המס; ibid. 305; Pr. 104: ופעמים אח'כ מתפשרים בממון; ibid. 932; 944; L. 108: וטרם שבא דכיון דהקהל לא רצו לתן עם האלמנה ונתרצה עמהם שיתפשרו לבד :Am II, 19; נתפשר עם השר חוץ מן האלמנה; ibid. 128; Aptowitzer, op. cit. p. 454: כי כל עם מדינת המלך יודעים שתדיר ראשי הקהל באים לפני השר ומתפשרים כאשר יכולים, ואינם שואלים לכל איש ואיש בטרם ילכו לפני השר האלך ואתפשר גם בעבורך. See especially *Text*, 609.

[26] See Pr. 981; 1012; Am II, 17; 127; Pr. p. 158b: ואם ישבע אדם לקהלו שאין לו כי אם כך וכך לתן ממנו מס. See also *Sefer Hassidim*, no. 1292.

[27] See Pr. 331; 708b; 716; Cr. 121; 156; L. 108.

[28] Pr. 941; Am II, 141; B. p. 276, no. 58.

[29] Usually each member declared under oath the value of his taxable possessions, and the rate was adjusted according to the sum total of the assets thus declared by all the members of the community. See Am II, 127, 17. Occasionally, however, no declaration was required, but the community officials apportioned the tax according to their own estimate of each person's wealth; see L. 423. Cf. Joel Mueller, תשובות נאוני מזרח ומערב, 205.

[30] See Pr. 106; 716; 825; 995; Am II, 139.

[31] See Cr. 262; Am II, 238: וששאלת ראובן חפץ למכור ביתו שהחזיק בו כמה שנים ושמעון מוחה ואומר שיש לו עליו טענה, וראובן אומר ארד עמך לדין, ושמעון אומר איני חפץ עכשו אלא לכשארצה וכו', עבור דברים כאלו הורגלו בכל מלכותנו שכל מי שמוכר קרקע מחרימי' בבית הכנסת על כל היודע שום ערעור על קרקע זו שיניד בפני טובי הקהל קודם שיצא מבית הכנסת ואחר שמדקדקים בערעורים ורואים שאין בהם ממש כותבים כך וכך החרמנו ביום פלוני ולא יצא לא קול ולא טענה על קרקע פלוני כלל ועכשיו זיכינו פלוני באותו קרקע ואם יבא שום אדם מכאן ואילך

representatives signed the bills of sale and recorded such purchases.[32]

4. It strictly controlled the business transactions in its locality. It did not permit outsiders to invest money in its town (except to make short term loans on market days);[33] it stopped unfair competition,[34] protected the property of its members;[35] set up a maximum rate of interest on loans to Gentiles;[36] tried to eradicate evil practices in business;[37] and was ever watchful lest individuals bring a calamity upon the entire community through their business methods.[38]

See. שהיה כאן באותה שעה ויהרהר עליו לא יהא ממש בדבריו ולא יהא רשאי לזוק לדין זה
also Mord. B. M. 396 כתב רבינו מאיר וזה לשונו: מצאתי בתשובת ר' פלטוי גאון דכל היכא
דהלוקח בעיר אין להשוות המיקח עד שישלח ויודיעו למצרן שאינו בעיר אם חפץ לקנותו בכך, אלא
המוכר בא לפני הקהל ואומר פלוני חפץ לקנותו בכך וכך, אם המצרן או אחר במקומו או אחד מקרוביו
ומאוהביו חפץ לקנותו בכך מוטב ואם לאו תו לא משהינן ליה להודיעו ויזכה הלוקח במקחו, וכן
כתבתי לרבותינו שבוירצבורק והוקשה למקצתם תחלה לשנות מנהגם ואעפ"כ קבלו וכן דנין עכשיו
שמה בכל יום.

[32] See Pr. 118: אמנם מה שטוען אפוטרופא של בני החצר שכל החצר שלהם מחמת שכתוב
בשטר, [מכר] פלוני בית חתנות של הקהל, וטובי הקהל חתומים עליו; cf. Text, no. 538. See also the bills of sale published by Brisch in his Urkunden, an appendix to his Zur Geschichte der Juden in Cöln, II.

[33] Pr. 359; 983; Am II, 140; Cr. 121; 156; Text, 544; 545; 555; 558; 559.

[34] Pr. 359: בני הקהל שאתם מלוים בעירם יכולים לעכב עליכם בלא יומא דשוקא אם אותו
ראובן היה מתעסק באומנתו ובא שמעון ועסק בה אחריו, :677 .ibid; המקום אינו של שר שלכם
[וצוח] ראובן לגזור לבל יעסוק בה אחר; cf. ibid. 983; Joel Mueller, op. cit. 87; 88.

[35] Finkelstein, op. cit. p. 130, note 2; Mord. B. M. 257, and Joel Mueller, תשובות חכמי צרפת ולותיר, 97. Cf. Pr. 695; 814; 1005.

[36] Pr. 980: ועוד שתקנת הקהל שלא להוסיף על ב' פשיטין מן הליטר' לשבוע כל אשר יעלה
על הקהל. This proof is not conclusive, since the ordinance might have applied only to loans contracted by the community, as the last phrase כל אשר יעלה על הקהל seems to indicate. Were such the case, however, the ordinance would have had no relevance to the case under discussion, since no loan to the community was involved. The interpretation given in Text, 590, therefore, is probably correct. Note also that M. A. Bloch, in the Budapest edition, was very careless in copying this text.

[37] See Pr. 677; 815; Am II, 123: אלא אתה מורי וקהלך אם נראה שנעשה דבר מכוער
כזה כמו שנראה לקנסו לתן צדקה הנראה לכם הכל לפי מה שהוא אדם.

[38] See Pr. 980; L. 246: על נזקי מעות . . . ועוד שמכשיל את הרבים כשירנישו בהם כשיצאו
Pr. p. 160a: מיד ישראל אחר אז יבא לידי סכנה ואי איישר חיל השואל והנשאל ימתחו על העמוד; חרם שלא לקח גניבות כגון תועבות.

5. It enforced peace and orderliness;[39] imposed heavy fines on those who dared strike their neighbors,[40] or even threatened to do so;[41] restrained its members from bringing their cases for trial before the civil authorities;[42] and punished informers by flagellation or excommunication.[43]

6. It regulated marriage and divorce. It supervised pre-marital negotiations and arrangements as well as the betrothal ceremony,[44] fixed the amount a woman was to receive upon her divorce, or upon the death of her husband,[45] punished husbands for beating their wives,[46] did not permit anyone to divorce his wife without its permission,[47] and determined the method of disposing the property of a young couple in the event one party

[39] Pr. 994: כדרך שרגילים כל קהל וקהל לקנוס את עוברי עבירות ופורצי פרצות שמסיעין על קיצותן. See also Teshubot Geonim Kadmonim, 125: וראובן שחבל בשמעון ותלש בזקנו. See also תלישה משונה ומכוערת ועל רוב קילקולו שראו הקהל הוסיפו על קנס הקצוב ק' דינ' Sefer Hassidim, 1293.

[40] Finkelstein, op. cit. p. 177; ibid. p. 194; Pr. 994.

[41] Pr. 383: ועל שמעון שאחז בגרונו ושלף סכינו עליו ואמר ארוץ גולנלתך לא ידעתי מה אשיב, אמת הוא שנבלה גדולה עשה ואין דיני דיני קנסות וחבלות בזה"ז, ובכל קהלה וקהלה נוהגין לעשות תקנה גדולה וגדר לפי הענין . . . והמנביה ידו אעפ"י שלא הכהו, כ"ש תפס בגרונו והרים אגרופו עליו ורוצה לדוקרו בסכין, ואם היה במקומנו היינו מלקים אותו.

[42] Pr. 717; 979; 994; L. 248; 334; Cr. 78: ונמנינו וגזרנו ונידינו והחרמנו על כל איש ואשה קרובים ורחוקים אשר יביא את חבירו בדיני גוים עע"ז או יכופנו ע"י גוים עע"ז, הן שר, הן הדיוט, הן מושל, הן סרדיוט, אם לא מדעת שניהם, ובפני עדים כשרים Cf. Finkelstein, op. cit. p. 153; also Mord. B. K. 195: ונהי דר' אפרים לא טוב עשה בעמיו וראוי למתוח אותו על העמוד, כי הלך בערכאות של עכו"ם תחלה . . . ואעפ"י שהכריחו אלא לדת יהודית לא היה לו לעשות דבר זה אלא עפ"י קהלו או על פי הגדולים שבמלכות; also Berl. p. 323, no. 978.

[43] L. 248; Pr. 994; P. 220; Cr. 231: אמנם אם אמת שדבר שמעון לשר כך כמו שכתוב ועל שעשה שלא כהוגן שקבל עליו לנוי. ibid. 304: מעבר, הקהל יעניישוהו הכל לפי מה שהוא אדם איני דן דין קנסות אמנם הקהל הרשות בידם לקנוס ולענוש על דבר מכוער, הכל לפי מה שהוא אדם לפי המביייש והמתבייש.

[44] Pr. 1015; Sefer Rabn, p. 139c–d; Tosaphot to Nedarim 27b: ואותר ר"ת שלכך נהנו לאסוף כל בני העיר בשעת שידוכין היינו כי היכי דליהוי ב"ד חשוב ולא יהא ערבון אסמכתא. Cf. Cr. 90; Pr. 854; Jeol Mueller, op. cit. 27.

[45] See Irving A. Agus, שיעור הכתובה בתור קנה מדה לעושרם של היהודים בימי הבינים, Horeb, 1939; ibid. "The Development of the Money Clause in the Ashkenazic Ketubah", J.Q.R. XXX (1940), pp. 221–56.

[46] Cr. 291; Pr. 81; 927; B. p. 319, no. 780. See Text, 297–8; Finkelstein, op. cit. pp. 216 f.

[47] Pr. 87; 946; Mordecai Hagadol, p. 212d. Cf. Finkelstein, op. cit. pp. 29 f.

died shortly after marriage,[48] and the amount a *levir* was entitled to receive upon performing the ceremony of *halitzah*.[49]

7. It protected its members against the injustices of the civil authorities,[50] negotiated the release of those who were imprisoned by the latter for purposes of extortion,[51] and tried to shield its members from impending evil.[52]

8. It established courts of justice,[53] invested them with the right of summons,[54] forced its members to try their cases

[48] Pr. 483: מצאתי חרם קדמונים הנושא אשה ומתה תוך שנתה בלא ולד של קיימא מחזיר
ליורשיה כל הנדוניא והכשיטיה ובגדיה בלי ערמה ואם מתה תוך ב' שנים יחלוקו ;ibid. 934; Cr. 72;
Mord. Ket. 287; ibid. Kid. 551; Hag. Maim. to *Ishut*, 22, 1; Tesh. Maim. to
Nashim, 35; R. Asher b. Yehiel, *Responsa*, 54, 1.

[49] Pr. 563; Mord. Yeb. 22. Cf. Finkelstein, op. cit. p. 57 f.; Pr. p. 159a.

[50] Finkelstein, op. cit. p. 226: ואם המלך או ההגמון יאמר לשום יהודי תן לי כך וכך
ואם ילשין אדם את חברו למלך:.ibid ;או תלוה לי כסף או יקח לו שוה כסף ישתתפו לו כל הקהל
או להגמון או לשלטון ויזיק לשום יהודי, או בחוב או בהלואה, ישתתפו ויעזרו כל הקהל בהפסדו . Cf.
Am II, 127; Cr. 54; Pr. 992.

[51] Pr. 241; 977: ושמעון משיב כך היה הענין שנתפשת ושלחוני הקהל להשתדל בשבילך;
Am II, 19; 127; cf. Pr. 39.

[52] Pr. 980; 994; Am II, 127; *Kol Bo*, 142; Cr. 78; Pr. p. 160a: חרם שלא לקח
.גניבות כגון הועצות או גביע ובגדים צואים וספרי תפלות ומשמשיהם מפני הסכנה

[53] The leaders of the community usually constituted the court of justice. See
Sefer Rabn p. 139c–d: ואבי הנערה בא למנגצא וקיבץ כל חכמי הקהילות למנגצא ויועדו שם
and חכמי הקהילות ;thus the terms בבית הכנסת וירד בעיני כל הקהילות את המעשה אשר עשו
הקהילות, were synonymous. The Community was considered a *bet-din*; see ibid.
p. 137b; Joel Mueller, op. cit. 21; 24; 27; 29; 97; Pr. 904; 912; see also Tesh. Maim.
to *Ishut* 35: והלכה האלמנה לווירצבור"ג להוציא נדונית מיד בעלה ולא רצו לתת לה
כלום כי מתחלה אמרו בני ווירצבורק לא קבלו עליה תקנת הקהלות ואח"כ חזר ואמר לא תקנו
הקהלות אלא במקום שהאב קיים והנדוניא יצאה מכיסו, אבל בכה"נ לא, ושלחו מווירצבור"ק אלינו
קהל מנגצ"א לרבותינו שבווירמש"א ושבשפיר"א ואנו תמהנו מאד על מעשה הרע הזה, וקהל ווירמש"א
עמדו ולא ענו דבר כי קרוב להם האיש למקצתם וקהל שפיר"א חייבוהו להחזיר חצי מה שנתנה האלמנה
ואם יסרב see also Pr. p. 160a: בעצמה, והודיענו מה נראה בעיניך, ושלום ברוך ב"ר שמואל
ידינהו הקהל ע"י השליח; Pr. 591. We also find that the communities not only established courts, but compelled them to pass judgement on cases brought before
them; see Pr. 715: אבל בזמן הזה שמכריחים הדיינים לדון עפ"י חרם הקהלות; see also Pr. 249:
מה אעשה לכם בני בופרט עמיתי ר' אברהם בראש ושאר שכינים. על אודות האלמנה ובנה. דעו אם
היה תלוי בדעתי היה רצוני שלא בא שום דין לפני . . . ושלום חיים בן אמ"ו הר"י .R. Hayyim
b. Yehiel Hefez Zahav was a member of the court of Cologne; see Brisch, ibid.
For a detailed discussion of community courts see Moses Frank, *Kehilot Ashkenaz
u-Batei Dineihem*, Tel Aviv, 1933. See also Cr. 230; Pr. 950; 978; 1001; L.267.

[54] See Pr. 249; 546; 825; 904; 912. See Moses Frank, op. cit. pp. 71–90; Pr.
p. 160a: תקנת קדמונים שיעשו לאחת מן הערים בהזמנה לתובע שירד עמו לדין באחת מן נ' הערים
.הכמוכות שיש שם ב"ד . . . ואם יש אדם חשוב בקרוב יזמינו על פיו

before a court of arbitration whenever one party to the suit demanded it,[55] and enforced the rulings of such courts.[56]

9. It helped its members in their search for and recovery of lost or stolen property,[57] in collecting evidence, and in forcing witnesses to testify.[58]

10. It took care of the religious needs of its members; erected synagogues and houses of study,[59] sold honors and rights there to its members;[60] collected contributions toward their upkeep;[61]

[55] See P. 290; Berl. p. 319 no. 679; Pr. 917. Such courts were required to render a legal decision, in accordance with talmudic law, but were not permitted to compromise. If the judges were in doubt as to the proper decision, they would send an inquiry to a leading scholar; see Pr. 960: הלכך ידונו בעירם ואם הדייני' יודעים הדין יפסקו להם, ואם הוצרך הדבר לשאול הדבר תלוי בדיינים לישאל למי שירצו ואין זה הדבר תלוי בבע"ד כלל לשאול למי שהם רוצים. A great part of the Responsa of R. Meir were written in answer to such inquiries. For this reason many of the queries sent to R. Meir bear the signatures of the three individuals who constituted the court; see Am II, 33; 69; 127; 209; Cr. 11; 53; cf. also Cr. 17; Pr. 355. Litigants often hired certain persons to listen to and record their claims and counter-claims and to send such records to an outstanding scholar for a final decision. See R. Isaac of Vienna, *Or Zarua*, Responsum 775: כבר נהגו בכל המקומות ששוכרים להם בעלי טענות ושולחים במקום ששניהם חפצים . . . וכן הנהיג רבינו שמשון זצ"ל; see also Pr. 880.

[56] Cr. 280; Pr. 523; 1001: ראיתי בקהלות . . . כ"ש בי דינא דמר דאלים לאפוקא ממונא; ibid. 249: הנה כתבתי הפסק דין לענ"ד . . . ואכתוב מרורות על האשה אם תגבה מחובות בעלה עד שיופרע מה שפסק לו אביו נדן ובגדים גם אכתוב מרורות על כל מחזיקי ידיה ותומכיה נגד דין תורה.

[57] Joel Mueller, op. cit. 97; Mord. B. M. 257; *Sefer Rabn*, p. 93c; Pr. 770; ibid. 153; p. 158a: ומי שאבדה לו אבידה יש לו כח להכריח הקהל ולהושיב החזן עד שיכנסו כלם: בחרם שכל מי שיודע ממנו שום דבר שיאמר לו.

[58] *Teshubot Geonim Kadmonim*, 148; Joel Mueller, op. cit. 29; Pr. 576; 712; 978: וצוה ראובן להכריז באזהרת לא יניד כל מי שיודע משמעון שהוא חשוד יבא ויניד בפנינו ולפני בין שהוא במדה"י בין שאינו במדה"י והאשה: Pr. p. 160a; ראשי הקהל. והנה באו עדיות רבות אם הוא ירא שיש בהם מי שיכבוש עדותו יכול: P. 296; תובעת מזונות יחרימו כל היודע משלו להכריחכם ע"פ הדיינים שיחרימו על כל היודע ועד כדין שבועת העדות; Aptowitzer, op. cit. p. 456.

[59] Am II, 240.

[60] Cr. 209; Pr. 139; L. 113; Berl. p. 320, no. 865: לבנות הן לסתור בביהכ"נ להוסיף ולגרוע.

[61] Pr. 692-3; 998; L. 269; Berl. p. 293, no. 371; Synagogue expenses were often defrayed out of the income from a special fund invested for profit, see ibid. p. 321, no. 883: הנה ראיתי באשכנז . . . אשר היו מפרישים מנכסיהם לצדקה לצרכי בתי מדרשם ובתי כנסיות ונותני' הממון ליד הגזברים ומלוין אותם קרוב לשכר ורחוק להפסד, ודבר זה הרביץ תורה בישראל כי כל עניים לומדים מאותם וגם מספיקים לתלמידי' הללו אשר לומדים בישיבה לפני גדולים, וגם בתי כנסיות עומדי' על מכונם במאור יפה ובשמושיהם ובחזניהם וכל צרכי בדקיהם.

hired a Rabbi, a cantor, and a ritual slaughterer;[62] built community buildings,[63] and took care of community property and of the streets.[64]

11. It levied a special tax on its members for the purpose of defraying the expenses of its charities,[65] invested charity funds for profit,[66] took care of itinerant indigents as well as of its own poor,[67] and buried impoverished members at its expense.[68]

12. It also protected the interests of orphans, acted as their trustee,[69] and supervised the disposal of the property of many a deceased member.[70]

3. Means of Coercion.

In order to carry on efficiently these manifold governmental activities and functions, and in order to compel its members to accept its authority, the community made use of age old Jewish weapons: the *niddui* and the *herem*,— the minor and

[62] Pr. 90; 942; L. 110; 112; Am II, 234; cf. R. Isaac of Vienna, *Or Zarua I*, *Hilkot Zedakah*, 26: שמחמת כן בני העיר מפרנסים ... חבר עיר היינו חכם המתעסק בצרכי צבור אותו מחמת טובה שעושה להם שמתעסק בצרכיהם.

[63] Berl. p. 320, no. 865; Pr. 118.

[64] Pr. 118; 233-5; 236; 527.

[65] R. Isaac of Vienna, op. cit. *Hilkot Zedakah*, 4; Mord. B. B. 490; Tesh. Maim. to *Kinyan*, 27b; Pr. 74: מעות מעשר יראה אחרי שהחזיקו לתחם לעניים אין לשנותם למצוה אהרה ... ibid. 75: אבל מעות מעשר כספים כבר זכו בו עניים ע"י מנהג שכך נהגו כל הגולה 918; Cr. 10; P. 512; Am II, 231.

[66] Pr. 73; 196; 752; 755; L. 208; 234; 425; 426; 478; Cr. 101; 109.

[67] Pr. 512; Tesh. Maim. to *Kinyan*, 28. The poor were usually taken care of by the members of their synagogue: see Am II, 231.

[68] Pr. 149; 926; 964; Cr. 60.

[69] See Pr. 591: על מעשה בראובן שצוה וקובל להקהל על יתומי' קטנים בני שמעון בני שמעון שיעמידו לו אי ליכא סהדי שמינהו אבי יתומים, ב"ד אביהם ibid. 592: קהל אפוטרופוס כי יש לו עליהם דין של יתומים אפי' בשבועה לא יניחוהו לעסוק בנכסים אי לא מהימן להו לבי דינא ibid. 593; 745; Berl. p. 278, no. 85; Cr. 308: ששאלתם על אחד מן האחים שמת והניח בן קטן וזה אומר אני יגדל בן אחי אצלי וזה אומר יגדל בן אחי אצלי וכו' אין הדבר תלוי באחין להיות אפוטרופוס אלא בנדולי העיר אביהם של יתומים הנראה בעיניהם יותר טוב יברור. Young orphans were not required to pay taxes; in many important communities they did not pay taxes till they were married. See P. 520.

[70] See Pr. 896; L. 220; 235.

major excommunications.[71] Although it often imposed heavy
fines as disciplinary measures,[72] inflicted severe corporal punishment,[73] and even recruited the aid of Gentiles in forcing
recalcitrant members to obey its orders,[74] its ultimate, and
most powerful, weapon was the *herem*; for its entire administrative system and its whole complex of sanctions and means
of group control depended on the *herem*. Thus the promulgation of community ordinances and regulations was accompanied
by a pronouncement of the *herem* against anyone who would
not abide by them;[75] the assessments for taxes were based upon
declarations of possession made by the individual members
under fear of the *herem*;[76] litigants were forced to go to court,[77]

[71] For a clear definition of the terms *niddui, shamta*, and *herem*, see *Shaare
Zedek* (Responsa of the Geonim) 5, 14: ששאלתם חרם ושמתא דבר אחד. ר' פלטוי זצ"ל.
הוא או לא, איזהו חרם ואיזהו שמתא, שמתא היא נדוי שמנדין אותו וכוחבין עליו פתיחא, לאחר שמנדין
מכלל ישראל אותו ומוציאין חרם כוחבין עליו שהיה במה חוזר ואין יום ל' אותו. Cf. also
R. Isaac Alfasi, *Responsa*, 146; ibid. 281. For a detailed discussion of this subject
see R. Nissim Girundi, *Responsa*, 65. For the use of the *niddui* as a means of
coercion, see *Shaare Zedek*, 1, 14; ibid. 5, 14; ibid. 7, 38; *Hemdah Genuzah*, 22; 60;
Maaseh ha-Geonim, p. 70; L. 423: שאין לכוף את הרשעים בזמן הזה אלא בחרם וקנס והמבטלן
מביא פריצות בישראל.

[72] See *Teshubot Geonim Kadmonim*, ed. David Cassel, Berlin 1848, no. 125:
וראובן שחבל בשמעון ותלש בזקנו תלישה משונה ומכוערת ועל רוב קלקולו שראו גדולי הקהל הוסיפו
על קנס הקצוב ק' דינר; Pr. 994; Am II, 123; Cr. 304; P. 220; cf. Finkelstein, op. cit.
p. 177; ibid. p. 194.

[73] See Pr. 81: ואף לקוץ ידו אם רגיל בכך; ibid. 485; L. 246; 108; P. 294; Berl.
p. 323, no. 978; cf. *Maaseh ha-Geonim*, p. 70.

[74] See Cr. 78: ואנחנו החתומים מבקשים כל קרובים למלכות לרדות ע"י נוים כל העוברים
על אחת מנזירתינו ... יעקב ב"ר מאיר, שמואל בה"ר מאיר; see also Pr. 968; L. 423; Pr. 943:
ומה שכתבתם שמנהג הוא שהקהל מעבירים ע"י נוים כל מי שחייב מס ואינו חפץ לתן.

[75] See Pr. p. 158b: ויהא בנדוי כל הקהילות עד אשר יתקן קלקולו ... וכל אלו הדברים
כל אלו תקנות תקננו ע"פ החרם והדשנו עתה בתחק'ף לפרט מה; ibid. p. 159: גזרנו עפ"י החרם
וכל קהל שפיר"א מענ"ץ ווירמש"א :ibid.; שתקנו קדמוני' מקדם לפני כמה שנים פה במענע"ץ בחרם
הסכימו וחתמו ורבינו שמואל ב"ר מאיר ורבינו יעקב אחיו ורבנו אליעזר ב"ר נתן צפנת פענה ורבינו
אליעזר ב"ר שמעון וכל הרבנים וההכמים [שבאו] לאנייא וצרפת ובכל הארץ הסכימו וגזרו בחרם
בנידוי ובשמתא ובשם מיתא ובגזירת יהושע בן נון. See also Cr. 78; *Kol Bo*, 142; L. 423;
Mord. B. M. 257; Berl. p. 320, no. 865. See below for a discussion of the legal
basis for the efficacy of community ordinances and regulations.

[76] See note 26 above.

[77] See Joel Mueller תשובות חכמי צרפת ולוהיר, 29. The *herem Bet Din* was originally
instituted in order to force the members of the community to bring their cases

witnesses were compelled to come forward and to testify,[78] the debtors and bailees of the defendant were ordered to reveal the assests of the latter in their possession,[79] and the decision of the court was strictly enforced,[80] all through the threat of excommunication. The entire business of the community was carried on because of the fear of *niddui* and *herem* that hung over its members.

Excommunication carried a double punishment: social ostracism and the curse. In the Middle Ages a Jew needed the goodwill and cooperation of his brothers socially, politically,[81] economically, and religiously. Complete ostracism was, therefore, a terrible blow to him. To increase its effectiveness as a social force, a community would enlist public opinion on its side by obtaining the consent of famous talmudic scholars to its *herem*, as well as the sanction of the leading communities of the country.[82] A person, therefore, could not hope adroitly to evade social ostracism by moving to another community.

before the local court. Thus R. Samson b. Abraham explained: מנהג חרם של ב״ד שבעירנו אודיעך כי אחד מבני העיר מזמין את חבירו לדין ע״כ ידון כאן ואין יכול לדחותו ולומר אלך לבית הועד או לבית דין הגדול. The *Takkanah* of Rabbenu Gershom, however, was an extension of this ancient ordinance, to include those who were not members of the community but who chanced to pass through the town. See the wording of this *takkanah* in Pr. p. 158a, as well as the versions quoted by Finkelstein.

[78] See note 58 above.

[79] See Pr. 998. Although in this instance the community acted for its own benefit, there is no doubt that private plaintifs had the same privilege; see Pr. 814: ראובן נתחייב מנה לשמעון . . . ובא שמעון ובקש מן הקהל לנזור לו חרם על כל מי שיש בידו ממון; Pr. p. 160a: ראובן שיחתנו לשמעון; also Pr. 695. והאשה תובעת מזונות יהרימו כל היודע משלו

[80] See *Shaare Zedek*, 5, 14; Pr. 249; 251.

[81] Thus we find that those who separated themselves from the community by paying their taxes directly to the overlord, lacked the protection that the community offered. They sometimes paid with their lives for such separation. Note the stark tragedy unfolded in Am II, 19–23; *Text*, 572.

[82] Although the communities were independent of one another and did not admit that one community could exercise any restraint on another (see below), we nevertheless found that in extreme cases appeals were made to many distant communities as well as to outstanding scholars; see L. 108; Pr. 250-1; Am II, 81; Berl. p. 319, no. 679. The appeals, however, were for moral support and for the enlistment of public opinion; see *Shaare Zedek*, 5, 14: מהאהרמתא כך כותבין פלוני

A *herem* was also accompanied by numerous terrifying curses which were pronounced in a holy and impressive atmosphere filling the heart of every Jew with religious fear.[83] It was, therefore, an effective weapon in the hands of communities and their leaders, which gave meaning and power to the autonomous government of the Jews in the middle ages.

Nevertheless, the real source of strength of the community organization was the great prestige of talmudic law and the Jew's strong attachment to his religion. The great social control exercised over the Jews by their religion gave meaning and power to the minor and major excommunications.[84] Consequently no community organization could exercise any restraint over its members or wield control over them, unless

בן פ' לחכמים וראשי כנסיות וזקנים ולבוררין ופרנסי כנסיות שלומכם ירבה מודיעין אנו אתכם פלוני בן פ' יש עליו ממון מפ' וחתכנו עליו ולא קבל, או עבר עבירה פלונית, ונדינו אותו ל' יום ולא חזר ולא תבע להתירו מן הנידוי, צוינו והחרמנו אותו על פתח ב"ד אף אתם כשמניעין אצלכם פתחא ואחרמתא כי ידעתי שהנדיב לא ;see also Am II, 81: דא החרימו ונדו אותו כל יום תמיד והכריזו עליו החריש . . . ושלח הדבר לפני ישישים גדולי צרפת ושאר מקומות וכמדומה אני שכולם הסכימו לכופו . . . וידעתי אף כי מורי גדול הדור לא יצוה לו לעבור על דברי זקנים, ואם ישלחו גזרתם יקשה לך לעבור עליה ולבטלה פן ירבו מחלוקת בישראל.

[83] See *Nusaḥ ha-Ḥerem, Kol Bo,* 139; see also Pr. 840: וששאלת יש בני אדם החשודים על השבועה ומאחר שמשביעים אותו שבועת היסת ומקללין לפניו ואינו מודה, מהו להחרים ולקלל עוד על דבר זה עד זמן מרובה כדי שיפחד ויודה. Moreover, it was believed in the middle ages that if a person transgressed a *herem* or an oath, his children would die (based on Ket. 4b); see L. 393. The high rate of mortality among children during the Middle Ages, which hardly left a single family untouched by tragedy, must have been a powerful factor in enhancing the terror of the *herem*; see Joel Mueller, op. cit. 22: וششאלת פעמים התירו אנשי קבלון כל גזירות שעליהם מפני פורעניות הבאות. This belief also explains the traditional awe and reverential fear associated with the recitation of *Kol Nidrei* on *Yom Kippur* eve; every parent must have been consciously or unconsciously accusing himself of having been the cause of the death of his children through his having broken a vow, an oath, or a *herem*, intentionally or inadvertently.

[84] One must keep in mind that in the middle ages a Jew could easily escape all restrictions, abuses, discriminations and persecutions, he had to suffer as a Jew, by accepting Christianity. The very fact that he remained a Jew, therefore, showed his strong attachment to his religion and his willingness to suffer great hardship for his religious convictions. This feeling of piety was the source of strength and the very basis of community government. It affords an excellent example of the great power religion may wield in organizing and controlling group life.

its own powers and prerogatives were based on talmudic law, and its scope of authority defined and limited by the *halakah*. In Germany especially, where the communities enjoyed freedom from control by the secular government, where the community organization depended on no royal charter, and did not base its right to impose fines and penalties on a king's patent,[85] the community derived its authority exclusively from Jewish law.

4. Legal Basis of Community Rule.

From what source, therefore, within the framework of Jewish law, did the community as an organization claim to have received the right to weld independent individuals into a tightly knit political body, to wield coercive powers, impose fines, inflict corporal punishment, and hold the threat of excommunication over its members? What were the rights and prerogatives it claimed to possess according to the *halakah*?

[85] There was a marked difference between Germany and Spain. In the latter country the strong central government exercised strict control over its Jewish communities, while in Germany the control by the central government was very mild. See Abraham A. Neuman, *Jews in Spain*, vol. I, pp. 22–33; ibid. pp. 112–5. See the justification of the practice of capital punishment given to R. Asher, *Responsa*, 17, 8: ואמרו לי כי הורמנא דמלכא הוא. No scholar of Germany or France would ever give such a reason. R. Asher who was still steeped in the customs and manner of legal thinking of his native land, found great difficulty in accepting a king's patent as a legal basis for the competence of a Jewish court; other reasons were, therefore, given to him. He was told that capital punishment as practised by the Jews was really an emergency measure, that it saved many lives that would have been taken had such matters been left to the secular courts, and that the Gentiles would find cause to ridicule the Jews because of their religion, should they display signs of weakness. Yet R. Asher was hesitant about permitting the execution of the person involved. In cases, however, where the German and French communities also resorted to capital punishment, R. Asher was not hesitant any longer; his logic was clear, his proofs were based on sound, Jewish law and his decision was straightforward and final; see ibid. 17, 1–6 regarding informers. The emphasis Frank (קהלות אשכנז ובתי דיניהם) pp. 35–7) put on the privilege-documents as a determinative for the power and authority of the Jewish courts, was due to a misunderstanding of the real forces operating within the Jewish community.

A detailed study of these sources of authority should be of great interest to the political theorist, as well as to the student of Jewish law, since it reveals a system of government based on high ideals of justice and human rights; for talmudic law is primarily interested in and deeply concerned with justice and kindness. This government evolved under no military pressure of any kind,[86] but out of the great need of a group of people for mutual help and cooperation, and was genuinely democratic while, at the same time, it protected the individual against the tyranny of the majority. It was workable even in extremely dire circumstances, as on occasions when the community had to force each individual to part with the greater part of his worldly possessions in order to save the lives of its members. It was able to guide, protect, and cause to survive a hated, alien group, for well over eight hundred years, in a bigoted and intolerant Europe where anything foreign, or any deviation from the norm, was regarded with fear and horror. Such a system of government essentially democratic, dependent for the enforcement of its authority entirely upon public opinion, the subtle forces of social approval, the deep religious feeling of the group and its unusual reverence for a study of what constitutes humanity and justice (the Talmud), should be of great interest to every serious student of government and sociology.

Let us therefore examine the historical development of the legal status of the community and the legal foundation of its power as understood and defined by those who were concerned with the legality of the community organization and its scope

[86] For contrast see Rudolph Sohm's exposition of the origin of law and justice, in *The Institutes*, translated by James C. Ledlie, Oxford, 1901, p. 24: "Law is the formal expression of the means whereby a people organizes itself for the struggle for existence. Accordingly it is war that generates law. War, it is said, is the father of all things. Under the stress of the perils of war a people consolidates into an army, into a state. So far from being the power that destroys societies, war is the power that builds them up. Legal order has its ultimate origin in military order and in this sense the soldier is 'pater patriae'."

of authority — the talmudic scholars of the eleventh, twelfth, and thirteenth centuries.

The early communities were small, their affairs were not very complicated, and cases of criminal extortion by the over-lord were very rare.[87] The early communities, therefore, were ruled mostly by subtle, social control exercised by the local aristocracy. The rich and scholarly members of the community were naturally looked upon as the leaders. These highly respected individuals assumed leadership as a matter of course, and the humbler members of the community rarely dared oppose their decisions.[88] As self-appointed leaders the rich citizens and the scholars managed community affairs, passed regulations and decrees, and held the threat of excommunication over recalcitrant members. The poorer and less learned among the members were the weak followers who had no voice in the administration of community affairs, and who accepted the rule of the upper class by tacit agreement.[89] The leaders of the community used their power and influence for the benefit of

---

[87] A fairly good picture of the life of the communities in the eleventh century can be reconstructed from the Responsa of R. Judah ha-Kohen, the author of the *Sefer ha-Dinim*, that are incorporated in the Prague edition of R. Meir's Responsa (see Pr. 451, 874–913).

[88] See *Kol Bo*, 142: שאלה זו שאלו רבני טרויי"ש לרבי יהודה כהן ב"ר מאיר ולרבי אליעזר ב"ר יהודה ז"ל . . . ועוד יורנו כגון אנו שקהלנו מתי מספר וקטנים שבנו נשמעים לגדולים ולא מחו בעולם בכל תקנותינו ומודים לנו בכלן כשאנו גוזרים גזירה אם צריכין אנו לשאול לכל אחד ואחד אם רצונו ודעתו לדעתנו.

[89] Ibid.: ושכתבתם שבמקומכם נהגו קטנים לשמוע לשמוע לגדולים ולא מחו לעולם בידם דין הוא שהקטנים נשמעים לגדולים לכל אשר יגזרו עליהם. See Finkelstein, op. cit. p. 121 (א), where ורב מן המהוגנים מתרצים, is quoted as a מנהג קדמונים; cf. Am II, 140, where the same version is quoted by R. Meir. In the centuries before Rabbenu Gershom, therefore, the opinions of only the important members of the community, were considered; while lowly individuals were ignored. There also grew up the idea of tacit agreement as expressed in the phrase במעמד אנשי העיר. Matters were not put to a vote, but were decided upon by the aristocratic members of the community in the presence of the people, and if no outspoken opposition developed, the decisions were considered binding as if they were unanimously agreed upon by the whole community. See *Kol Bo* ibid.; R. Hayyim Or Zarua, *Responsa*, 65.

the entire community; their ordinances were, therefore, rarely contested.[90]

As the community grew in power and importance, however, social, economic and political pressure forced the community leaders to enlarge their field of activity and to assume strong coercive powers in order to force the acceptance of their rulings and decrees. Many individuals who had to bear the brunt of such measures began to question the authority of the community leaders.[91] Even in such communities where the leaders were elected by a majority or even by a unanimous vote,[92] voices of protest were often raised against the usurpation of power by the community administration.[93] They challenged the right of the community leaders to apportion taxes, punish sinners, impose fines on disturbers of the peace, or pronounce the *herem* at will.[94] Individual members of the community put

---

[90] See the description of a *parnas*, Mord. *Taanit*, 619: ומכאן נהגו לעבור לפני והאפוטרופא. See also Am II, 127: התבה בר'ה וביו'כ פרנסין המנהיגין המנינין על הדור שלהם השיב שמנהג הוא בורידבורג מימים קדמונים כשהיו גדולים בתורה ופרנסים דרים שם שאדם נותן [מס]. The community representative held that the custom of paying taxes from borrowed money, was binding upon the members of the community since it had been introduced long ago with the consent of great scholars and *parnasim* who had lived in Friedberg. A *parnas* was usually the rich member of the community. This statement, therefore, is an echo of the aristocratic leadership of earlier times.

[91] See Pr. 359; 941; 968; 980; 995; L. 108; Am II, 140-1.

[92] Frank, op. cit., p. 3, note 4, claims that election of community officers first began in the thirteenth century. See, however, the Responsum of R. Joseph Bonfils (eleventh century), L. 423, which mentions elected officers; also *Sefer Rabn*, p. 111c.

[93] See Joel Mueller תשובות גאוני מזרח ומערב, 165; ibid. 205; תשובות חכמי צרפת ולותיר, 24, ibid. 97; *Sefer Rabn*, p. 137b; ibid. p. 93c; *Or Zarua, hilkot Zedaka*, 4; Mord. B. B. 480-2; 490; 517; Mord. Kid. 561; 564; R. Hayyim Or Zarua, *Responsa* 65; 153; 206; 222; Pr. 998; Am II, 127.

[94] Although Responsa emanating from Spain are not entirely relevent to the discussion of this chapter, the following Responsum by R. Solomon b. Adret describes a very characteristic situation of the type that would arouse tempers and bring about heated discussion and litigation, in order to discover the limits of community authority; see Rashba I, 783; ibid. IV, 315: איש אחד עשיר וזהיר במצות ולא יצא עליו שם רע מימיו פסק עם בנאיו לבנות לו חצר בסך ידוע . . . ולשבת אחרת בנו בחצר והעלו אבנים בדימוס, וכשראה זה לא ידע אם זה מותר או לא. ואחר שחזר לביתו חשש לאיסור ושלח

forth the claims that their leaders assumed powers which they
did not possess according to talmudic law, that they encroached
upon the personal liberties and immunities assured to the Jew
by the *halakah*.[95] Others protested that the decrees and measures passed by the majority of community members, were not
binding upon them since they were passed against their will,
and that the community officials elected by the majority had
no coercive powers over the dissenting minority.[96] Many individuals were even loath to become part of the community; they
refused to share the community's burden of taxes, to help
shoulder its obligation to its poor, and to defray their share
of the expenses involved in procuring protection of life and
property.[97]

Such protests, claims and litigations were brought before
leading talmudic scholars who were forced to look for a sound talmudic basis for the coercive powers that the community organizations were exercising over their members. Upon the scholar
lay the burden of discovering the talmudic basis for the rights

לבנאים לעכבם ולבטל המלאכה. וכשהלך שם שלוחו מצא שם יהודים מונעים אותם ומבטלין המלאכה.
וליום הראשון קראוהו ראשי הקהל שהם י"ב ואמרו מה זאת עשית. ונשבע בנקיטת חפץ שלא ידע שעושים
מלאכה שם וקבל עליו מה שהדין נותן ועוד שיתן קנס על מה שאירע ולא רצו והסכימו ונידוהו. ועוד
הטילו קנס על נדויו. וחרה לו עד מות על נדויו וישב בנדויו חמשה ימים ולכשהתירוהו נשבע בנק"ח
שלא יאכל בשר ולא ישתה יין ולא יפרע הקנס עד בא תשובתם לדעת אם יתן הדין במה שנידוהו אם לא.
[95] See David Cassel, *Teshubot Geonim Kadmonim*, 125: וצועק ראובן עתה ואומר
שלא כדין עשו לי ראשי הקהל לפי שקנס קצוב [אינו] אלא כ' דינר והם הוסיפו עד ק', ואין לי ולאשתי
דירה אחרת אלא אותה ששמו לשמעון ועוד שהיא משועבדת לכתובת אשתי. See also Pr. 118;
195; 241; 918; 932; 941; 943; 968; 980; 995; 1012; Cr. 9; 10; 49; 53; 111; 114;
121; 156; 188; 209; 222; 292.
[96] See *Kol Bo*, 142; Am II, 127; 140; L. 423; Cr. 156; 165; Tesh. Maim. to
Kinyan, 28; Mord. B. B. 480: אין כח בבני העיר להכריח אחד מהם למה שירצו; ibid. 482:
והוצרכתי להאריך לפי שיש מרבותי שאומרים דתניא רשאין בני העיר לקיים תנאם ולהסיע על קיצותן
ה"מ אם כולם נאותו יחד והוא עמהם ושוב עבר הקציצה.
[97] See Joel Mueller, *תשובות גאוני מזרח ומערב*, 205; L. 423; Cr. 10; Pr. 918; Tesh.
Maim. to *Kinyan*, 27b; Mord. B. B. 490: שאל הרב ר' יוסף את ה"ר יצחק ב"ר אברהם
על הצדקה שפוסקין בני העיר ויש יחידים שמסרבים על דעת הרבים ולא אבו שמוע, ואני שמעתי
שכתב רבינו שמעיה בשם ר' יוסף ט"ע אין מעשין על הצדקה ... ולהסיע על קיצתן נמי אין ראיה
דהתם מדעת כולם היה כדפר"ה.

of the community over its members,[98] circumscribing the scope
and limitations of these rights,[99] establishing a procedure for
the election of community leaders, and defining the rights and
prerogatives of such leaders.[100]

Thus at the end of the tenth century, or at the beginning
of the eleventh, the following query was sent by the community of Troyes to Rabbi Judah b. Meir ha-Kohen, surnamed
Leontin,[101] and Rabbi Eliezer b. Judah,[102] the leading scholars
of that day:

> In the synagogue, in the presence of the congregation, A,
> complained that B's Gentile maidservant had come to
> his house the previous day, and had reviled and cursed
> him. He reminded the congregation that this maidservant
> was a habitual vilifier and had showered abuse upon many
> of them. Several individuals confirmed A's statement
> that she had abused them on a number of occasions.
> Whereupon A asked the congregation to decree, as a
> disciplinary measure, that for half a year the aforesaid
> maidservant should derive no benefit from any Jew. A
> volunteered to pronounce the decree himself, whereupon
> the community empowered him to pronounce the speci-
> fied decree, and A did so. B, however, protested against
> the decree and stated that he would never abide by it
> since it was enacted by an individual hostile to him.
> The community averred that the decree had been en-

[98] See L. 77; 423; Am II, 122; 130; 140; 141; Cr. 10; 165; 230.

[99] See Pr. 359; 708; 940; 941; 968; 980; 994; L. 77; 248; 423; P. 220; Am II,
123; 140–1; 240; Cr. 10; 230; Tesh. Maim. to *Kinyan*, 28.

[100] See Berl. p. 320, no. 865: אם יש קטטה בין קהלכם ואינם יכולים להשוות דעתם לברור
להם ראשים בהסכמת כלם, זה אומר ככה וזה אומר ככה, ומחמת חלוק בוטל התמיד ומדת הדין לוקה
ואין אמת ומשפט שלום בעיר ולא במלכות הנגררת אחריהם, איך יעשו, נראה בעיני שיש להושיב בעלי
בתים הנותנים מס, ויקבלו עליהם בברכה שכל א' יאמר דעתו לש"ש ולתקנת העיר וילכו בה אחרי
הרוב הן לברר הראשים הן לברר חזנים; see also R. Hayyim Or Zarua, *Responsa*, 65.

[101] He was the teacher of Rabbenu Gershom; see *Tashbetz*, 572: רבינו שלמה
ספר מעשה . . . וכתב רבינו יצחק ראיותיו לפני רבינו ליאונטי"ן רבו של רבינו גרשם מאור הגולה,
מפני שר' ליאון רבי שלמדני רוב תלמודי זצ"ל :Pr. 264; ושמו רבינו יהודה בר מאיר הכהן הזקן
חכם טופלא . . . וחתמתי נרשם ב"ר יהודה. See also Michael, *Or ha-Hayyim*, no. 1001.

[102] See Zunz, *Literaturgeschichte*, p. 612; *Monatsschrift*, XLI, p. 469.

acted by the congregation and not by an individual, that A had merely acted as its deputy, and that the decree had been enacted against the maidservant because of her abuse of several members of the community other than A. B, then, stated that he was not bound by this decree because many of those who had participated in its enactment had been friendly to A and hostile to himself. The community vigorously protested against this imputation of partiality on its part, and warned B and his followers on several occasions not to transgress the decree. A and his friends, however, remained stubborn, whereupon the community withdrew itself from them and treated them as excommunicates. Since, however, the members of the community feared that B and his friends, living so near the synagogue, would remove the Scrolls of the Law and other community articles therefrom, they transgressed the ban on several occasions, all on account of B. The question arose: Are the inhabitants of a town permitted to enact decrees which would act as a restraint upon some of their members and force them to abide by the community regulations? Is B justified in his contention? It is obvious that if B's claim is just, every dissenting minority is in a position to put forth similar claims and thus may free itself from community obligations.[103]

---

[103] *Kol Bo*, 142: שאלה זו שאלו רבינו טרוי"ש לרבי יהודה כהן ב"ר מאיר ולרבי אליעזר
ב"ר יהודה ז"ל: ראובן בא לבית הכנסת וצעק ואמר אי קהל הקדוש, גויה אחת עומדת בביתו של שמעון
ובאה אמש בביתי והרפני ונדפני ואתם יודעי' שהיא מועדת ורגילה לעשות כן לכלכם, וענו כל הקהל
כן הוא כדבריך אף לנו הרעה אותה גויה. זה אומר אותי הכה במקל. וזה אמר אשתי קראה זונה.
וזה אומר אותי קראה קרנן. וענה ראובן אחרי שהיא מועדת בבקשה מכם גזרו שלא תהנה מישראל
עד חצי שנה אולי תחזיר. ואם הצווני, אני אגזור הגזירה. וצווהו וגזר כדברי הקהל, אלא אותו שמעון
בלבד לא הסכים בדבר ואמר לעולם לא אקיים גזירתכם כי גזירתכם אינה נזירה לפי ששונאי גזר.
ואמרו כל הקהל הוא לא גזר אלא אנו דעתינו ולא על אודותיו בלבד גזרנו אלא על דבר שאר בני קהלנו.
ועוד אמר אותן שמעון אין אנו משניחין לגזירתכם יש בכם שהסכימו בגזירה אוהבי' לבעל דיננו ושונאים
אותנו. וענו כל הקהל ח"ו חלילה לנו לגזור נזירה עבור אהבת איש כי כשם שאנו אוהבי' לו כך אוהבי'
לכל ישראל, ושארית ישראל לא יעשו עולה. והתרינו בהם כמה כמה ימים וכמה ימים שלא יפקרו כל כך ולא
השגיחו. ובראו' קהלנו כך נבדלנו מהם והיו יראים כל הקהל שלא ינזלו מהם את ספרי התורה וכל
הדברים שהם של צבור מפני שביתם סמוך לבית הכנסת, ולא ימנעום מהם מלהוליכם בכל מקום
שירצו, ועברו על אותה נזירה, וכל זאת בהוראתו של שמעון. ועכשיו יורונו רבותי' אם רשאין בני
העיר לגזור' על קצת בני קהלם ולכופם ולהתקן עמהם בתקנת' ושלא להפריש מן הצבור, ואם יש ממש
בהוראתו של שמעון שא' כדבריו, כל איש ואש' שירצו לפרוק עול יבא לעשות עול ולומר כדבריו של זה.

Another question arose: are the inhabitants of one town
competent to enact decrees binding upon the inhabitants
of another town, thus exercising authority over them, or
are the latter in a position to say to the former: "We are
independent of you and are not bound by your oaths or
your bans"?[104]

Then there arose another problem: We have always been
a small community, and the humble members among us
have abided by the leadership of our outstanding members, dutifully obeyed their decrees, and never protested
against their ordinances. Now, when we are about to enact
a decree, must we ask each individual member whether
or not he is in agreement with it? In case we enacted the
decree by tacit agreement without obtaining positive consent, may a person who failed openly to protest against
the decree at the time of its enactment, claim exemption
from that decree on the ground that he did not openly
state his agreement thereto? Please explain in detail the
legal reasons for your decisions.[105]

In their response to this query Rabbi Judah b. Meir ha-
Kohen and Rabbi Eliezer b. Judah evolved two principles as
the basis for community rule:

A. The children of Israel are enjoined to compel one another
to live in accordance with "truth, justice, and the laws and
commandments of God".[106] Therefore it follows: a) If the
majority of the community members agree to pass a decree that
will serve to uphold the *Torah* and "form a fence around the

[104] Ibid.: ויורנו רבותי' אם יוכלו בני עיר להשביע על בני עיר אחרת ולכופם שם בעירם
לכל דבר אע"פ שהם רחוקים מהם כמה פרסאות ואין כפיה להם על אלו. ואם יכולין לטעון לה אנו
בשלנו ואתם בשלכם ואין אנו משניחין לנזרתכם ולא על שבועתכם.

[105] Ibid.: ועוד יורנו כגון אנו שקהלנו מתי מספר וקטני' שבנו נשמעי' לגדולים ולא מחו בעולם
בכל תקנותינו ומודים לנו בכלן כשאנו גוזרים גזירה אם צריכין אנו לשאול לכל אחד ואחד אם רצונו
ודעתו לדעתנו. ואם אין אנו שואלין וגם אם הוא שותק ואינו מוחה אם יכול אדם לומר שלא לדעת
אותו שלא נשאל ממנו נגזרה נזירה אע"פ שאינו מוחה לא בשעת הנזירה ולא לאחר זמן. הכל יורונו
טעמי השאלות באר היטב.

[106] Ibid.: כך דעתנו נוטה שחייבי' כל ישראל לכוף ולהכריח איש את חבירו כדי להעמידו על
האמת ועל המשפט ועל חקי האלקים ותורותיו ודבר זה מצינו בתורה בנביאים ובכתובים.

Law", all must accept the decree and subject themselves to their rulings.[107] b) A majority of community members may pronounce the *herem* against individuals in order to force them to comply with Jewish law, and such *herem* cannot be lifted by the dissenting minority.[108] c) The majority may even confiscate private property, if such action is necessary in order to check lawlessness and advance the cause of proper Jewish conduct.[109]

B. Decrees passed by the community by majority vote that provide for the secular needs of the community, such as decrees dealing with protection of life and property, taxation, and business competition, must also be observed by the minority even though they serve no religious purpose.[110]

The first principle, giving the community coercive powers in matters concerning religion and proper Jewish conduct, is based on the assumption that in religious matters a community constitutes a court of competent jurisdiction over its own members, one possessing legislative as well as judicial powers and endowed with those privileges and prerogatives that the entire Jewish nation, in solemn assembly, possesses over each Jew whether present or absent.[111] The devotion of Jericho was

---

[107] Ibid.: לכן כשהקהל מסכימי׳ יחד לעשו׳ סייג ונדר לתורה אין היחיד יכול להוציא עצמו מן הכלל לבטל דברי הטרובי׳ לומר לא הסכמתי בהסכמה זו, אלא בטל יחיד במיעוטו.

[108] Ibid.: והטרובין רשאין להשביע ולגזור ולפדות ולהפקיר ממונו ולעשות סייג לכל דבר. ומצינו סמך לזה בכמה מקומות בתורה: מנין שאינו יכול להוציא עצמו מן הכלל . . . ואם כדברי המשיב היה לו לעכן לומר ולטעון לא הסכמתי בהסכמת החרם, אלא לא כל הימנו . . . לנדוי מנין שאין היחיד יכול לבטל דברי הטרובין דכתיב אורו מרוז. ואמרי׳ בארבע מאה שפורי שמתיה ברק.

[109] Ibid.: להפקיר ממון מנין דכתיב כל אשר לא יבא לשלשת הימים וכו׳ וכתיב אלה ינחלו אליעזר הכהן וגו׳ וכי מה ענין ראשים אצל אבות אלא לומר לך מה אבות מנחילים לבניהם כל מה שירצו, אף ראשים מנחילים לעם כל מה שירצו (see Git. 36b). Ordinances and regulations intended to check lawlessness and advance the cause of proper Jewish conduct, are classified as תקנות למגדר מלתא, regulations for the purpose of erecting a fence around the Law.

[110] Ibid.: ולא מבעיא בדבר שצריך לעשות סייג ונדר לתורה אלא אפי׳ בדבר הרשות כגון מס ושאר תקנות שמתקנים הקהל לעצמם אין היחיד יכול לבטל ולהוציא עצמו מתקנתן.

[111] Ibid.: ואין לאיש לעזור לקרובו להחליש כח ב׳ד . . . ואם הגביה יד ב׳ד. The proofs adduced for the competence of the community are taken from cases where the

binding even upon Achan, not because it was pronounced by
Joshua, the ordained leader of his people, or by the Sanhedrin
of seventy elders, but because all the Jewish people were
present at the time. When the town of Meroz was cursed by
Barak and the town of Yabesh Gilead by the assembled tribes,
the curses and bans were legally binding because they were
pronounced by the Jewish people in solemn assembly. The
right of King Saul to condemn to death anyone who ate on the
day of battle, was not based on the extraordinary powers of the
crown, but on the fact that the ban was pronounced in the presence of the Jewish people.[112] The entire community, therefore,
in solemn assembly, possesses the same rights and privileges,
the same solemn authority, over its own members, as those possessed by the Jewish nation over every Jew; while in either case
a majority is coextensive with the whole.

A community, therefore, may elect or appoint its rabbis,
judges, and executive officers, and endow them with the powers
possessed by the ancient Sanhedrin;[113] these powers, however,

---

entire Jewish people in solemn assembly pronounced the *herem*, as in the case of
Joshua, Barak, Yabesh Gilead, and Saul. Rabbi Judah and Rabbi Eliezer, therefore, compared the community to a solemn assembly of the Jewish people.

[112] See ibid. If the devotion of Jericho was binding because of the extraordinary powers possessed by Joshua or his Sanhedrin, the incident would have had
no bearing upon our case; nor would the *herem* of king Saul be relevant in this
connection. The fact that they are cited as proof in this Responsum shows that
Rabbi Judah and Rabbi Eliezer considered the binding power of the *herem* in
these cases to issue from the fact that they were promulgated by the Jewish people,
and not because they were based upon the prerogatives of its ordained or crowned
leaders. Note also the expression: ומצינו שהסכים הקב"ה על ידו ועל יד ישראל דכתיב דכתיב חרם
בקרבך ישראל, which emphasizes the fact that the devotion of Jericho was ordered
not by Joshua alone, but by the entire people Israel. In the case of Yabesh Gilead,
the motivation is: ועוד מצינו באנשי יבש גלעד שנתחייבו כליה על שלא חשו לגזרה שגזרו עליהם
אחיהם, for they disobeyed the ordinance of their brothers; the ordinance was binding upon the people of Yabesh Gilead not because it was promulgated by the
Zekenim, or the Sanhedrin, but because it was enacted by the people, "their
brothers", even though the inhabitants of Yabesh Gilead were not present at
the time.

[113] The fact that proof of the competence of the community was adduced
from the power of the court of Ezra to confiscate property, and from the power

they hold only over the Jews of that particular community. The community may also promulgate decrees to enforce proper Jewish conduct and may pronounce the *herem* over its members with the same power and effectiveness as did the court of Joshua the son of Nun.[114]

The second principle, giving the community the powers of a secular government, to apportion taxes and control business, is based on the talmudic passage of *Baba Batra* 8b which reads as follows: "The townspeople are permitted to fix weights and measures, prices and wages, and to fix penalties for the infringement of their rules".[115] Rabbi Judah b. Meir ha-Kohen and Rabbi Eliezer b. Judah interpreted this passage to mean that a majority of the inhabitants of a town may force the dissenting minority to abide by their rules and regulations regarding secular matters that serve to improve living conditions in the town.[116]

of the Sanhedrin to excommunicate Rabbi Eliezer b. Hyrcanus, shows that the power of the community was considered equal to that of the Sanhedrin of Ezra or of Yabne.

[114] This was the accepted view among scholars and community leaders; see *Maase ha-Geonim* p. 70: וצערא דגופא לא מחיל אינש בין כך ובין כך בין בחבלה שיש בה חסרון כיס ובין בבושת שאין בו חסרון כיס כי לא מחיל לו דנין מנהג אנשי מקומו לענשו ממון בין לנדות ובין ללקות כדי לעשות נדר וסייג, שרשאין אנשי המקום ללקות ולנדות ולהסיעו על קיצתן שיש להם סמך מן המקראות הללו: ואשר לא יבא לעצת הזקנים (עזרא י, ח) וכתיב ואריב עמם ואקללם והפקר ב"ד הפקר לכן הקהל רשאין להענוש (נחמיה יג, כה). See also *Sefer Rabn*, p. 137b: לאחר בממון וגם להלקותו, ולא לעבור על דברי תורה אלא לעשות סייג לתורה. ומניין שהפקר ב"ד הפקר שנ' וכל אשר לא יבא לשלשת הימים בעצת השרים והסגנים יחרם כל רכושו. See also Cr. פרק השולח גט (גיטין דף מו.) רבי יצחק אמר עשרה דכתיב כי נשבעו להם נשיאי העדה. מכאן :165 פסק אבי' העזרי' הלכה למעשה שאם טובי העיר עשו תקנה וההרימו חרם שחייבין כל בני העיר לשומרה בין שמעו בין לא שמעו החרם והגידו להם ואמרו נואש ולא נכנסו לא בתקנתם ולא בחרמם אף על פי כן הלה עליהם החרם ועליהם לשמרה. ואפילו אם אמרו בשעה שעשו החרם לא נכנס בתקנתם ובחרמיהם ושאר טובי העיר אמרו לא תיפטרו בכך, חלה עליהם החרם וחייבין לשומרה כדאמר בשמעתא שלא נשבעו להם אלא שנים עשר מנשיאי העדה ואף על פי כן לא הכום בני ישראל משום שבועת נשיאי העדה.

[115] B. B. 8b: ורשאין בני העיר להתנות על המדות ועל השערים ועל שכר הפועלים ולהסיע על קיצותן.

[116] *Kol Bo*, 142: ולא מבעיא בדבר שצריך לעשות סייג ונדר לתורה אלא אפילו בדבר הרשות כגון מס ושאר תקנות שמתקנין הקהל לעצמם אין היחיד יכול לבטל ולהוציא עצמו מתקנתן דתניא רשאין בני העיר להתנות על המדות ועל השערים ועל שכר הפועלים ולהסיע על קיצותם. הלכך לא יעלה דבר זה על לב איש לעולם.

Thus, on these two principles did Rabbi Judah and Rabbi Eliezer base the right of the majority of the members of a community to establish an administrative organization that should regulate the secular as well as the religious activities of the community.

Regarding the question whether the inhabitants of one town are competent to enact decrees binding upon the inhabitants of another town, Rabbi Judah and Rabbi Eliezer are of the opinion that in secular matters the inhabitants of a town are completely independent of outside communities and need brook no interference. If the inhabitants of a town, however, transgressed a law of the Torah, perverted justice, or decided wrongly in ritual matters, the inhabitants of another town are both competent and duty bound to pronounce the ban against them and to coerce them in other ways until they repent.[117]

A very interesting note is added by Rabbi Judah and Rabbi Eliezer in their response to the question of the effectiveness of tacit agreement. Asserting again that the decree passed by the majority prevails even against the loudly protesting minority,

---

[117] Ibid.: ומה ששאלתם אם בני עיר אחת יכולין להשביע ולכוף בני עיר אחרת שם בעירם אף על פי שהם רחוקים, כך נראה לנו אם תקנה זו שהן מתקנין יש בה צורך ישובם כגון מס או מדות או שערים או שכר פועלים, כגון אלו ודאי אין רשאין לכוף אלא בני עירם כדאמרינן רשאין בני העיר להסיע וכו' בני העיר אין, בני עיר אחרת לא. אבל אם היו עוברים בני עיר אחת על התורה או על הדין או שהורו על אחת מכל המצות שלא כהלכה, רשאין בני עיר אחרת לכופם ולהחרימם כדי להחזירם למוטב ואינן יכולים לומר אנו בשלנו ואתם בשלכם אלא כל ישראל מצוים להכריחם שכן מצינו בזקן ממרא ובני עיר הנדחת שיושבי לשכת הגזית כופין אותם ודנין אותם. This view was also accepted by later scholars and was never disputed. Even R. Tam, the great champion of the rights of the individual (see below) threatened to excommunicate a scholar who dwelled in another community (in Melun), see *Sefer ha-Yashar*, *Responsa*, 46, 4: באלה ושמתא יהיו כל השומעים לך אם אתה התרת דברים הללו שכתבתי, ואם לא ישמעו אלינו ננזור ונחרים בכל קהלותינו על כל השומעין לך. See also the attempt to force the hand of R. Meir when he permitted the allegedly betrothed of one man to marry another, *Text*, 271. R. Meir held that his decision was correct and that he committed no sin; but he did not dispute the right of the communities to pronounce the *herem* against him, in case he did transgress the law. See also the legal basis and logical explanation of this law by R. Joseph Bonfils, Pr. 940: כללו של דבר אין לאלו כח כפייה על אלו חוץ מרדוי עבירות שבאי' מחמת טענה שנתפסי' תחתיהם דכתיב וכשלו איש באחיו, איש בעון אחיו, מלמד שכל ישראל ערבין זה בזה.

and ruling that silence signifies agreement, and that it is assumed therefore that all those who have failed to protest against an enactment have agreed to it, they further declared that the common people are required to agree with the opinion of their elders, the outstanding scholars and men of position among them, for the Lord himself respects men of learning and authority.[118] It is important to state at this point, however, that this assertion of the divine rights of the "elders" was rarely again mentioned in any decision on community rule during the subsequent centuries,[119] except in reference to the particular reverence and obedience due a teacher by his disciples.

5. Individual Versus Community.

Rabbi Judah's and Rabbi Eliezer's analysis of the rights of the community in religious matters, as outlined above, was never disputed.[120] There was no unanimous agreement, however, by outstanding scholars on the opinion that the principle "the majority rules", in secular matters, was wholly in conso-

[118] *Kol Bo*, 142: דין, ושכחתבת שבמקומכם נהגו קטנים לשמוע לנדולים ולא מחו לעולם בידם
הוא שהקטנים נשמעין לנדולים לכל אשר ינזרו עליהם . . . ואם תאמר הקטנים רבו על הנדולים וימאנו
שמוע אליהם, כיון שהם שתקו בשעת מעשה ולא מאנו ולא מחו שוב אינן יכולין ואע׳פ שהקטנים רבו
על הנדולים דין הוא לשמוע לזקניהם ולנדוליהם, שכן מצינו בכמה מקומות שהמקום חלק כבוד לזקנים
ולנדולים דכתיב ונגד זקניו כבוד.

[119] The opinion that Jewish law was wholly in consonance with an aristocratic form of government, was prevalent in the Geonic period. See *Shaare Zedek*, p. 57a:
וינזרו הזקנים גזירה וישימו את הדבר עליהם לחק ולמשפט, וכל אשר לא ישמע ולא יקבל עליו חק
הזקנים ינדוהו ויחרימוהו וינזרו אותו עד שיחזור למוטב, וכך הוא שכל מקרה שיקרה לבני המדינה
וכולם שוין בו ותקנה הוא להם וצריכים לו כופין זה את זה לאותו דבר והסכמת הזקנים נוהגת בם
וכל בני המדינה נכנסים תחתיהם כעניין שנאמר וכל אשר לא יבא לשלשת הימים בעצת השרים והזקנים
יחרם כל רכושו והוא יבדל מקהל הנולה, ואמרו רבותינו רשאין בני העיר להתנות על השערים . . .
וזה כולו במנין הזקנים, ממקראות ושמועות הללו נלמד שרשות ביד זקני העיר לתקן תקנות לבני עירם
ולכוף לבני עירם למה שתקנו.

[120] See *Maase ha-Geonim*, p. 70; Joel Mueller, op. cit. 21; 24; *Sefer Rabn*, p. 137b; R. Tam, *Responsa*, 34, 6; Cr. 10; 165; Pr. 940; Am II, 140; Berl. p. 320, no. 865. One must keep in mind, however, that the term "religious matters" was used here in a very broad sense; thus it included the talmudic penal code, and every ordinance that might be construed as having been instituted למנדר מלתא, "to form a fence around the law".

nance with talmudic law. The very fact that the community of
Troyes was in doubt whether unanimous tacit agreement
was sufficient, was eloquent proof of the fact that many scholars
required expressed unanimous agreement before a community
decree became law.[121] These scholars probably felt that Jewish
law protected the rights and immunities of the individual,
especially in money matters, against any tyranny, even that
of the majority.

Rabbenu Gershom b. Judah, the "light of the exile", who
was the student of Rabbi Judah b. Meir ha-Kohen,[122] based the
secular powers of the community leaders on the principle that
those elected by the community have the status of a *Bet-din*, a
court of law, and that even if they are not learned they may
wield the same authority as Shamai and Hillel.[123] Community
leaders possessed, therefore, the right of confiscation of property
which was based on the famous talmudic principle הפקר בית
דין הפקר (confiscation of private property by the court is valid).
Community leaders also possessed all the other rights and prerogatives implied in this all-inclusive principle. There is no
proof, however, that Rabbenu Gershom agreed with his teacher's
view that "the majority rules" is a basic talmudic principle; his
takkanot, as pointed out below, seem to show that he disagreed
with it completely.

---

[121] In the later centuries we find this opinion clearly expressed; see R. Hayyim
Or Zarua, *Responsa*, 222: והארכתי לפרש לפי שיש מרבותי שהיו אומרים דהא דתניא רשאין
בני העיר לקיים תנאם ולהסיע על קיצתם ה"מ אם כולם נאותו יחד והוא עמהם ושוב עבר על תנאם,
דומיא דהנהו תרי טבחי אבל בלא דעתו לא אלימי לעשות, והפקר ב"ד הפקר לא שייך הכא, כך היה
אומר מורי הזקן ממיין זצוק"ל ואני את אשר עם לבבי כתבתי, ואם שניתי הורני רבותי . . . אליעזר
ב"ר יואל הלוי, ורבנו ברוך מצא בסוף הישר של ר"ת זצ"ל שפירש כן בבבא בתרא פ"ק דאין רשאין
בני העיר להסיע על קיצתן אא"כ נאותו כלם.

[122] See note 101 above.

[123] Joel Mueller, op. cit. 97; Mord. B. M. 257: גם מפני תקנות הקהלות צריך שמעון
להחזיר האבדה לראובן אפילו אם נתייאש ראובן דהפקר ב"ד הפקר שנאמר וכל אשר לא יבא . . .
וליכא למימר דוקא בדורו של שמאי והלל או של ר"ג שהרי אמרו חכמים למה לא נתפרשו שמותן של
זקנים שלא יאמר אדם פלוני כאלדד ומידד, פלוני כנדב ואביהו ואומר וישלח ד' את ירובעל ואת
בדן ואת יפתה ואת שמואל, לומר לך יפתה בדורו כשמואל בדורו ומי שנתמנה פרנס על הצבור כאביר
שבאבירים.

The principle of "the majority rules" was probably challenged quite often in the Jewish communities of France and Germany, so that Rabbenu Gershom found it necessary to convoke a
synod of the communities in order to establish this principle,
so necessary for organized government, upon a firm foundation.
That the question of majority versus minority was a grave
problem in community life, the cause of many disputes and
quarrels, is indicated by the very wording of the *takkanah*
adopted by this synod: כי אין ב"ד לישב על זה כי הכל הולך
לפי ראות טובי העיר, כי כן מנהג קדמונים, אי נמי צורך שעה[124]
"For no court may sit in such a case, since everything depends
on the opinion of the elders of the town, for such is the custom
of the ancients, or the need of the hour". No court should
concern itself with such complaints! These must have been

---

[124] See the various versions cited by Finkelstein, op. cit. p. 121. It is important to note that an ordinance for the benefit of the poor was explicitly mentioned in this *takkanah*. Finkelstein, op. cit. p. 132, note 4, wondered why the
helping of the poor was clearly specified and singled out as an instance. The
reason was, however, that obligatory payment of charity was a moot problem in
community life. Many individuals had poor relatives, or such relatives residing
out of town, whom they preferred to help rather than the other poor. The community, on the other hand, demanded that all charity funds be handed over to
the community charity chest and that distribution be equitably administered. In
such instances the individual clashed sharply with the community, and the principle "majority rules" was put to a severe test. Thus R. Joseph Bonfils is reported
to have favored the individual as against the majority in disputes regarding the
collection of charity funds. See Mord. B. B. 490: בשם רבינו יוסף ט"ע אין מעשין על
הצדקה אפילו למצוה שנאמר כי בגלל הדבר הזה יברכך ושנינו כל מצוה שמתן שכרה בצדה אין ב"ד
של מטה מוזהרין עליה ואין הדבר תלוי אלא בנדיבות [הלב] ומדברי הרצאה... והשיב ר"י ב"ר
אברהם. See *Tosaphot* to B. B. 8b, s. v. ושמחתי בדברים כי עכשו מצאתי גאון כדברי
עליה... ואר"ת דהאי כפייה בדברים... ועוד תירץ דהכא קבלו עליהם שיכופו אותן הגבאי; ואת והוא בפרק כל הבשר אמר כל מ"ע שמתן שכרה בצדה אין ב"ד של מטה מוזהרים: אכפיה לר' נתן
ועוד היה מפרש רבינו תם זצ"ל דודאי אין בני העיר יכולים *Or Zarua, Hilkot Zedakah*, 4:
לכוף אחד לצדקה ולא לכל דבר שאינו תקנת העיר, והא דכפיי' רבא לרב נתן בר אמי היינו שהיה
כבר קצבה ותנאי ביניהם ונתרצו בה מעיקרא ועתה לא רצה לקיים הקצבה... ורבי יצחק בר אברהם
זצ"ל השיב הלכה למעשה שאם אדם אינו רוצה ליתן בקופה של צדקה שיכולין בני העיר לכוף אותו...
וגם ר' שמשון אחיו זצ"ל פי' כדבריו. The reference is probably to Tesh. Maim. to *kinyan*,
27b. Note also the special *takkanot* regarding charity funds; Pr. p. 159b: תקנה שלא
ורנמ"ה תקן לחדשה בכל שנה ;note also: לסרב לכנוס בחרם להרים מעשר. See also Cr. 10;
Pr. 75; 343; 755; P. 13; 512; L. 506.

numerous and troublesome; they must have cropped up on the slightest provocation!

Thus the synod did not claim that "the majority rules" was a talmudic law. It merely stated that the rules and regulations enacted by a majority vote ought to be binding upon the minority since such was the accepted custom of the early settlers.[125] According to the Talmud an accepted custom had the status of law.[126] As the later synods always reiterated the earlier *takkanot* in order to validate them for their own generation,[127] even so did the synod of Rabbenu Gershom endeavor to reestablish this custom of the ancients as a general *takkanah* in order to emphasize its validity. Lest anyone dispute the fact that "the majority rules" was "the custom of the ancients", the words אי נמי צורך שעה were added; meaning that if no such custom existed, it should hereby be established as a *takkanah* enacted as an energency measure.[128] A *takkanah* of a synod was probably unanimously agreed upon by the assembled representatives of all influential communities and by the leading scholars of the country present at the gathering. It was felt that no individual would dare protest the enactment of the greatest scholars and leaders of the country and that everyone would tacitly agree to the *takkanah*, thus making it a law unanimously agreed upon by all the Jewish inhabitants of the country.[129]

[125] Note that no other *Takkanah* of this early recension gives a reason for its validity. There is no doubt that the question of "majority rules" was the subject of many disputes, as well as learned arguments.

[126] B. K. 116b: שלא ישנו ממנהג החמרים . . . ובלבד שלא ישנו ממנהג הספנים.

[127] See Pr. p. 159a: כל אלו התקנות תקננו עפ"י החרם וחדשנו עתה בתתקף לפרט מה שתקנו קדמונים מקדם . . . ואח"כ חדשנו תקנות אלו עפ"י החרם אעפ"י שהיתה כבר תקנה ישנה.

[128] The words אי נמי צורך שעה appear in almost all the versions and there is no doubt that they were included in the original *takkanah*. The fact that these words are very awkward and appear strange in their context, bears out our contention that the views of R. Judah b. Meir ha-Kohen and R. Eliezer b. Judah were not accepted by many scholars and community leaders.

[129] See the discussion of *herem d'Rabbenu Gershom*, R. Nissim Girundi, *Responsa*, 48: ואותן מנהגות הן נקבעין על זה הדרך שאדם חשוב שבעיר מנהיג איסור בדבר אחד לעשות סייג לתורה ובני עירו נשמעין אליו ונוהגין איסור בדבר ובניהם אחריהם מפני שראו אבותיהם שהיו נוהגין

That the principle "the majority rules" had many weak-
nesses, that it often wrought grave injustices and therefore
needed limitation and control, became obvious to the scholar
in many disputes between individuals and their communities.
The following query, sent by the community of Troyes to
Rabbi Joseph Bonfils (the elder),[130] a younger contemporary
of Rabbenu Gershom, may serve as an example:

In order to collect the king's tax the townspeople enacted
a solemn decree that every person contribute to the tax
a fixed amount per pound of value of his money, merchandise, and other saleable possessions. The fixed amount
paid from every pound of value, depended on the exigencies
of the moment. Leah possessed several vineyards. She
was requested by the townspeople, therefore, to pay the

איסור בדבר אף הן נוהגין כמותן דור אחר דור וכל מי שבא לאותה העיר ג״כ חייב לנהוג המנהג שלהם
מתקנת חכמים . . . אבל בית דין הגדול שהחרים דבר אחד על כל אנשי גלילותיו עליהם ועל זרעם
וק ב ל ו ה ו ע ל י ה ם . . . שחרם זה אין המקום גורם אלא אקרקפתא דגברא רמי. Moreover
there was one source of authority which transcended personal liberty: that of the
teacher to whom a student owed respect and obedience. A teacher had the right
to excommunicate his pupil long after the latter left his school. Consequently
the student had to accept all ordinances and regulations passed by his teacher or
incur his wrath and censure; see L. 77. The great scholars who assembled at a
synod of the communities were the teachers of all the lesser scholars in the country,
who in turn were the teachers of the community leaders and every man of importance (המהוגנים) in the community. Whatever was decreed by the teachers was
automatically approved by the students, whatever was decreed by a synod was
automatically approved by all the communities that participated in the synod.
This source of authority is sometimes pointed out in the text of the *takkanot*.
See Cr. 78; Pr. p. 159b: והיו כל ישראל מובדלים . . . והעובר על נזירתינו יהא באלה ובנידוי ;
ממנו חתומים ואינם חתומים ותלמידיהם ותלמידי תלמידיהם וחבריהם גדולים וקטנים ; see also the
Responsum of Rashi, Joel Mueller, op. cit. 21: שכשנינו מנודה לעיר אחרת אינו מנודה
לעירו, לא שאנו אלא במנדין לכבודם אבל במנדין לכבוד שמים אף המנודה לתלמיד מנודה לרב
וכ״ש לעיר אחרת . . . וכ״ש רבי׳ גרשם זכר צדיק וקדוש לברכה שהאיר עיני גולה וכולנו מפיו חיין
וכל בני גולת אשכנז וכיתים תלמידי תלמידיו הן. Consequently, it was assumed that a
takkanah was accepted unanimously. Thus R. Tam when he referred to the
takkanah of Rashi regarding the payment of taxes on borrowed money said (Mord.
B. K. 179): ואפילו מן החצי שהוא מלוה לא נהנו אלא מפני שקבלו עליהם מתחלה מדעת כולם.

[130] See Introduction to *Teshubot ha-Geonim Kadmonim*; R. Tam, *Responsa*,
46, 4; *Tosaphot* to *Pesahim*, 30a, s. v. אמר; ibid. 115a, s. v. והדר; to *Nazir* 59a,
s. v. אמר; to *Gittin* 85b, s. v. ולא; to A. Z. 74b, s. v. והקורא. See also V. Aptowitzer,
op. cit. p. 352 f.

fixed amount upon every pound of value of her vineyards, her harvested grapes, and her other possessions. They claimed that vineyards were in the same category as the capital of a loan, while the harvested crop was equivalent to the interest. Since they themselves paid taxes from both the capital and the interest of their money investments, from their merchandise as well as from its profit, they held that Leah should do likewise. Leah, on the other hand, pointed out that a vineyard could not be compared to the capital of a loan, or even to merchandise; for a vineyard required a yearly investment in money and effort, a great deal of expensive labor in upkeep and in harvesting its crop. In a vineyard a person invests a great deal of labor, and money, but is rarely sure of his profit. Then the lords of the land come every year and carry away their fat portions; sometimes there is too much rain, sometimes too little; sometimes the weather is too hot, and sometimes too cold; and sometimes there is no crop at all. The profit, therefore, is very uncertain and meager [and can be counted merely as the profit on the invested labor and effort, not on the value of the vineyard itself.] Money investments, on the other hand, require no labor and no additional expense. The creditor is always in a position carefully to guard his pledges and is secure in his initial investment, while his capital automatically increases with the passing of time. The merchant too is sure of his profit with but little effort and small risk. The value of the vineyard itself, therefore, cannot be considered capital for the purpose of taxation.[131]

Rabbi Joseph Bonfils saw the justice of Leah's argument; he cited the custom of the communities not to tax land, as a decisive argument; and appealed to the community of Troyes to deal prudently and justly with Leah, and not make her lose her vineyards through an unwise taxation policy.[132]

[131] Pr. 941.

[132] Ibid.: .... נמצאו מכלין קרן ופירות ונשמט בעל הקרקע ויצא ריקם ח״ו לא תהא כזאת בישראל
ומנהג הקהלות נותני׳ עיניהם על הפקחין כענין שנאמר ואתה תחזה מכל העם וגו׳ ויושבי׳ ומדקדקי׳
ומטילי׳ על כל או״א בצדק איש לפי עמלו ולפי טיפולו.

Merchants and money lenders, who sometimes constituted a majority in the community, often attempted to shift the burden of taxation to property owners. The talmudic scholars, however, fortified by a widely accepted custom of long standing, rarely permitted such encroachment upon the rights of the minority.[133] At an earlier period, when farmers and landowners were predominant in the community, or in particular localities where farming was common among the Jews, real property was taxed as a matter of course, and such taxation received the sanction of the talmudic scholar.[134] It was only when farmers constituted a small minority in the community, and the enormous profits of the merchant and the money lender caused taxes to rise in conformity with such high rate of profit, that the few landowners needed protection as a minority group.

The sense of justice of the talmudic scholar revolted against any form of arbitrary compulsion, and the idea of the special prerogatives of the community as a solemn body possessing divine rights of rulerships over its members, began to suffer an eclipse as soon as profound talmudic scholarship became firmly established in France and Germany. A different source of power for the community organization was beginning to come

---

[133] See ibid.: ושאלת על ראשי הקהל הבאים לשנות ולהטיל מס כל כך על שוה ליטרא קרקע [כשוה] ליטרא מעות, בכל מלכותינו אין נותני' כלום מס מן הקרקעות ופעמים רצו בעלי כיסין דכמה פעמים צוחו קמאי דקמאי לתח מס Am II, 127:. לשנות ובא המעשה לפנינו ולא הנחנום מקרקעות ומספרים במסים גדולים כאלה יותר מס' שלא נשאר חלק עשירי בידם ובאו לדין על כך כך ונפטרו בעלי הקרקעות והספרים כמנהג קדמונים שתקנו כך.

[134] See Joel Mueller, 165:, תשובות גאוני מזרח ומערב כולה: כיון שקבלו עליהם בני הקהל ונכללו בעלי הכפרים להכליל הפריעה שעל הכפרים כולם ולהטיל על כל כפר וכפר לפי מדת קרקעותיו וכן להשתוות בהשחדה שמשחידין לסלק האונס מעליהם וכתבו מקבלה זו כתב וחתמו בו, אין למקצתם רשות לבטל אותה קבלה . . . עד שיסכימו כולן על בטולן Moreover, it seems that at this early period real property was the chief object of taxation, while the merchants tried to evade being taxed. See ibid. 205: א'כ הוא כמו שכתוב בה שיש ביניהם בני אדם שאין להם כרמים ולוקחים פירות מן הגוים וממלאים אוצרות מפירות כרמים שלוקחים מן הגוים והם מבני מס שלכם ואף יש אצלכם אחרים מקצאו'ת רוטה ואינם מבני מס שלכם אבל הם קבועים ונשאו נשים אצלכם ונפלו להם נכסים מחמת נשותיהם ומחמת לקוחות ואינם רוצים לא אלו ולא אלו לסייע אתכם . . . כך נראה בעיני שיש מן הדין להעמיד שלשה בני אדם הבקיאים במס ויטילו על כל אחד ואחד לפי ממון, מי שיש לו קרקע יעלו אותו בחשבון ומי שאין לו כרמים וקרקעות ויש עטו זהובים במה שיסחר ובמה שלוקח פירות מן הגוים ויטילו על הכל.

to the fore: voluntary agreement. A community had the right to apportion taxes and enforce payments to the charity chest, because these rights were given to it by voluntary agreement on the part of the members.[135] Voluntary agreement, however, precluded the principle "the majority rules" as a basic legal force in community government. Unanimous agreement alone can be called voluntary on the part of each member of the community. It is true that tacit unanimous agreement on a decree beneficial to a particular individual was often assumed by the court (on the ground that each member must have agreed to a decree that would also be beneficial to him should he find himself in circumstances similar to those of the present beneficiary),[136] but the basic principle of the inalienable rights of the individual that could be encroached upon only with his personal consent, was not abrogated through such assumption of unanimous consent, for the ultimate basis of the legality of such decree was still voluntary agreement. This new attitude to the source of community prerogatives showed a tendency toward a deeper democratic feeling, and toward a greater sensitivity to the rights of the individual as against those of the majority.

This change of attitude may be seen in the basic difference between the response of Rabbenu Gershom and that of Rabbi Eliezer b. Nathan, in connection with a similar situation. Let us, therefore, examine the answer given by Rabbenu Gershom to the following query:

---

[135] Even the secular government, according to R. Samuel b. Meir derived its prerogatives from the voluntary agreement on the part of its constituents. See his commentary to B. B. 54b: והאמר שמואל דינא דמלכותא דינא. כל מסים וארנוניות ומנהגות של משפטי מלכים שרגילים להנהיג במלכותם דינא הוא, שכל בני המלכות מקבלין עליהם מרצונם חוקי המלך ומשפטיו, והלכך דין גמור הוא ואין למחזיק בממון חבירו ע״פ חוק המלך הנהוג בעיר משום גזל.

[136] See *Sefer Rabn*, p. 93c: אבל אם בקש ראובן מן הקהל וגזרו הקהל על כל בר ישראל שיבוא אבידתו לידו שיחזירנה לו, חייב להחזיר מפני תקנת הקהל, שתקנה זו תקנה היא לו וניחה ליה בה שאם יוארע לו כמו זה יעשו כמו כן תקנה.

Some Jews were traveling by ship. Part of their cargo consisted of gold packed in boxes. The ship was wrecked, but the people were rescued. One Jew hired a Gentile to help him save some of A's gold. The Gentile dragged one of A's boxes out of the water, but because the box was too unwieldy, he broke it open and transferred the gold to another ship. Meanwhile many Gentiles were attracted by the loot, and some of them seized part of A's gold. Next day the Jews bribed the lords and judges of the locality, so that they issued an order that anyone who had salvaged or looted any valuables from the wrecked ship, must restore them to the original owners. Many Gentiles returned the looted property, but some of them had to go through the ordeal by fire and the trial by combat in order to prove their innocence. In order to help the travelers recover their loss, the communities that were assembled there also enacted a decree requiring that every Jew who obtained any valuables from the wrecked ship to restore them to the original owners. Within thirty days after the wreck, a Gentile sold some of A's gold to B. A demanded his gold from B, but B refused to part with it, citing in his defense the talmudic law that goods washed ashore were considered ownerless property (B. M. 22a).[137]

Rabbenu Gershom ruled that the decree of the communities was binding and consequently B had to restore the gold to A upon the receipt of the same amount of money he had paid the Gentile for it. Rabbenu Gershom based his decision on the principle הפקר ב"ד הפקר, the confiscation of property by a court was valid.[138] Thus he assumed that a community possessed the rights and prerogatives of an ordained court, and could deprive an individual of his legally acquired possessions. About a century and a half later, however, in an exactly similar case, Rabbi Eliezer b. Nathan, a contemporary of Rabbenu

[137] Joel Mueller, תשובות חכמי צרפת ולותיר, 97; Mord. B. M. 257.
[138] Ibid.: ואפילו נתייאש ראובן אפי' הכי כיון שגזרו הקהל שהיו שם על כל מי שיבא לידו כלום מכל מה שנאבד באותה שיחזיר לבעלים, צריך לשמעון זה להחזיר אותו היותר לראובן אע"פ שהתורה זכתה לו שהפקר ב"ד הפקר.

Tam, though ruling that the ordinance of the community was valid, based his decision not on the principle of ד"ב הפקר הפקר, but on the assumption that when the ordinance had been enacted B was satisfied with it and voluntarily agreed to it, because of the consideration that a similar ordinance would be enacted for his benefit whenever he should be in A's position.[139] This shift of emphasis from the all-powerful community to the voluntary agreement on the part of the individual, indicates a radical departure from the original opinion regarding the legal basis of community rule.

This greater consideration for the rights of the individual as against those of the group was clearly expressed by Rabbi Jacob Tam, who denied the community the right to pass ordinances and regulations, in secular matters, when a minority openly protested against them.[140] The talmudic statement רשאין בני העיר להסיע על קיצותן (Baba Batra 8b) used by Rabbi Judah b. Meir ha-Kohen and Rabbi Eliezer b. Judah to prove that even in secular matters the principle "the majority rules" prevailed, was interpreted by Rabbi Jacob Tam to mean that after the townspeople had unanimously enacted a certain decree, they were permitted to force any individual among them to abide by its ruling.[141] The word קיצותן (their decree), ac-

---

[139] *Sefer Rabn* p. 93c; R. Eliezer b. Joel ha-Levi also ruled that the *herem hayishub* was binding only on the members of the community where the *herem* had been pronounced to the effect that they ought to avoid having any business or social relations with a person who came to settle in their midst without their permission, but he held that the community had no power to place a curse or a *herem* on the prospective settlers; see Mord. B. B. 517: כתב אביאסף וזה לשונו ... ורשאין בני העיר להסיע על קיצתן ולעשות תקנה, נ'ל על עצמם רשאין לגזור שכל מי שיבא בעיר שלא מרצונם שלא ישאו ויתנו עמו; cf. L. 77.

[140] *Or Zarua, Hilkot Zedakah,* 4; Mord. B. K. 179; ibid. B. B. 490; Cr. 230; R. Hayyim Or Zarua, op. cit. 222.

[141] See Tesh. Maim. to *Shoftim* 10; Mord. B. K. 179: ומה שטוען ראובן שרוצה לתקן לתת משל אחרים מעתה והלאה ושמעון מעכב, הדין עם שטעון אם הוא מישובו, דהא דאמרינן ורשאין בני העיר להסיע על קיצתן הכי פירוש ורשאין בני העיר להסיע ולהפסיד ממון את העובר על הקצבה שקצבו והתנו ביניהם לדעת כלם, שנתרצה בתחלת התקנה ועתה עובר עליה, והוא שעשאוה בחבר עיר, כי הני דתרי טבחי שנתרצו וחזר בו האחד והואיל דליכא קנין וכמו דבר שלא בא לעולם

cording to Rabbenu Tam, meant a decree already enacted; and
the phrase להסיע על קיצותן meant to give townspeople the
right to enforce a decree that had previously been enacted;
the legal method of enacting a decree was not at all treated
in this talmudic passage.[142] The enactment of a decree, as a
legal act, must conform to the general talmudic principles of
justice and human rights, which principles do not permit any
group to encroach upon the rights and liberties of an individual,
guaranteed to him by the *halakah*, unless he himself consents
thereto. Talmudic law does not grant a majority the right to
tyrannize over its minority. The community, according to
Rabbenu Tam, may not even force an individual to contribute
to the charity chest, since that too would constitute the curb-
ing of a person's freedom of action, a thwarting of his will, and
an unlawful coercion. It is true that the Talmud cites the case
of Raba who forced R. Nathan b. Ami to give charity, but the
reason for this use of force by Raba was that the community
of R. Nathan b. Ami had previously unanimously enacted a
decree granting its charity officers the right to force every member to pay his share of the charity requirements.[143] Raba merely
enforced a legally enacted decree.

הוא צריך חבר עיר וכן מפורש בתוספתא על מי שיראה לשלטון או להגמון יתן כך וכך, אבל להפקיע
ממון שלא מדעת בעלים אסור אם לא ע״י הפקר צבור או ב״ד וקודם מעשה זה אני מורה כן לכל שואל,
ומה שנוהגים במלכות זה לתת משל אחרים לא נהגו אלא מן החצי שהוא מלוה לו ולא מן החצי שהוא
פקדון, ואפילו מן החצי שהוא מלוה לא נהגו אלא מפני שקבלו עליהם מתחלה מדעת כולם, ומשל
עובדי כוכבים אין נותנים כלום דכולי פקדון, וכן תיקן רבינו שלמה זקיני במלכותינו ושלום יעקב
ב״ר מאיר.

[142] R. Solomon b. Adret held a similar view; see *Responsa*, IV, 185: שאלת אם
רשאין הצבור לעשות תקנות והסכמות וגדרים ביניהם ולקנוס ולענוש על הסכמותיהם שלא מדין התורה
אם לאו... דבר ברור הוא שהצבור רשאין לגדור ולתקן תקנות ולעשות הסכמות כפי מה שיראה
בעיניהם והרי הוא קיים כדין התורה ויכולים לקנוס ולענוש כל העובר בכל אשר יסכימו ביניהם ובלבד
שיכימו בכך כל הצבור באין מעכב... וכן נהגו בכל קהלות הקדש.

[143] See *Or Zarua*, ibid.: ועוד היה מפרש רבי׳ תם זצ״ל דודאי אין בני העיר יכולין לכוף
אחד לצדקה ולא לכל דבר שאינו תקנת העיר והא דכפיי׳ רבא לר׳ נתן בר אמי, היינו שהי׳ כבר
קצבה ותנאי ביניהם ונתרצו בה מעיקרא ועתה לא רצו לקיים הקצבה לפיכך אכפייה ופעמים היה
רבי׳ תם זצ״ל מפרש שקיבלו עליהם בני עירו של ר׳ נתן בר אמי שיהא רשות לגבאים לכוף אותם
אכפיה לר׳ נתן. לפיכך כפה אותו רבא. Cf. Mord. B. B. 490; *Tosaphot* to B. B. 8b, s. v.

It is obvious, however, that even according to Rabbenu
Tam, if a community had once adopted a resolution that in all
its transactions and regulations the opinion of the majority
should prevail, that in such a community the principle "the
majority rules" would be binding in all phases of its activity.
Thus the ruling of Rabbenu Tam was not meant to weaken the
community organization, but to emphasize the rights of the
individual according to talmudic law,[144] and, in a number of
instances, to protect the minority against the rapaciousness of
the majority.

We may discern, therefore, a continous development of the
democratic idea underlying community government in France
and Germany, in the direction of laying greater emphasis upon
the rights and immunities of the individual, and of the minority
group: a) Rabbi Judah b. Meir ha-Kohen and Rabbi Eliezer
b. Judah (about 970 C. E.) still echoed the opinion held by several of the Geonim that the majority of the members of the community, if humble and non-scholarly, were enjoined to honor
and obey the aristocratic few among them, since God Himself
honored the leaders of Israel.[145] They assumed that the few

The idea of voluntary consent as the only legal basis of group organization and
government authority, was very popular in R. Tam's period. Thus Rabbi Samuel
b. Meir bases the king's very right of taxation on the voluntary acceptance of
his policy by his constituents; see note 135 above.

[144] Rabbi Eliezer b. Joel ha-Levi, on the other hand, clung to the older view
that an ordinance enacted by majority vote was binding upon the minority. See
R. Hayyim Or Zarua, op. cit. 222: ונ׳ל שאם אחד מבני העיר מוחה בדבר שרוצים ראשי
הקהל לעשות או לגזור חרם אם רוב הקהל מסכימים חלה החרם . . . אבל אם הרוב הסכימו והמיעוט
מיחו, חלה הגזרה עליהם בעל כרחם.

[145] See Shaare Zedek, p. 57a: וינזרו הזקנים נזירה וישימו את הדבר עליהם לחק ולמשפט
וכל אשר לא ישמע ויקבל עליו חק הזקנים ינדוהו ויחרימוהו וינזרו אותו עד שיחזור למוטב . . . והסכמת
הזקנים נוהגת בם וכל בני המדינה נכנסים תחתיהם. Thus the geonic view was that the elders
had unlimited authority to enact decrees and ordinances binding upon the inhabitants of their locality, provided, of course, that such decrees were calculated
for the benefit of the community. In the geonic period courts of justice were
established from above, and the members of the community had nothing to say
in the matter. See Alexander Harkavy, *Zikron Larishonim*, IV, 180; מסעות ר׳
בנימין מטודילה, ed. Asher, p. 60 f.

rich and scholarly members of the community possessed divine rights of leadership and that the majority of the members of the community should be subjected to this minority group.[146] b) Rabbenu Gershom (about 1000 C. E.) ruled that the majority group was omnipotent even in money matters; that the community, meaning this majority group, constituted a court of all-embracing competence and even possessed the right of confiscation of property. c) Rabbenu Tam (about 1150 C. E.), however, was of the opinion that in money matters the rights of the individual were inviolable, and that a community could not curb his rights except by his voluntary consent.

Let us reiterate, that in religious matters the power and authority of the community were undisputed even in the later period, which meant that the enforcement of the entire body of talmudic law, both civil and religious law, was completely and

---

[146] Even in the later period a distinction was made between the aristocratic members of the community and the commoners. Thus the *takkanah* of Rabbenu Gershom, which established the rule of the majority in all community matters, carefully stipulated ורוב המהוגנים מתרצים, or rather והרוב מתרצין והן מן המהוגנים (see various versions, Finkelstein, op. cit. p. 121). Even R. Meir writes לא כל הימנו בעודו שם למחות תקנות במגדר מלתא אחר שרוב המהוגנים שבעיר הסכימו לכך. This deference paid the "worthy ones", however, was not caused by the fact that the rights and immunities of the humble member of the community were disregarded or even slighted. It was rather the result of the talmudic law requiring that every measure adopted by a group must have the sanction of the resident scholar before it becomes law. (B. B. 9a: ה"מ היכא דליכא אדם חשוב אבל היכא דאיכא ... ולהסיע על קיצתן דאיכא אדם חשוב לא כל כמינייהו דמתנו.) When a number of the residents of a community were scholars to a greater or lesser degree, a *takkanah* of such a community had to have the sanction of its scholars, the מהוגנים, before it became law. A decree passed by the majority was not binding, according to talmudic law, unless it was so passed with the consent of the scholars of the community. Cf. R. Isaac Alfasi, *Responsa*, 13: עקר המנהג שעושין על פי והוא שרוב הקהל יתייעצו עם זקני הקהל ויתקנו תקנה כמה שיתקנו ויקיימו אותה זהו המנהג. According to R. Meir all taxpayers have a voice in the community government; nonpayers of taxes, however, have no voice (Berl. p. 320). This ruling was motivated by the fact that community regulations, on the whole, involved the expenditure of money, and it was felt that only those who were to pay for such expenditures should have a voice in authorizing them.

indisputably in the hands of the community organization.[147]
It was only in matters of taxation or extraordinary fines and
penalties that a minority group fought for its rights, and often
gained the support of outstanding scholars.[148]

6. Community Independent of Outside Interference.

The conception of the community as the Jewish people in
miniature, as a completely sovereign, august, and solemn body,
able to generate from within itself a new and vital source of all-
embracing authority, both secular and religious, made the
community completely independent of all traditional sources
of authority, such as Palestinian ordination, appointment by
the exilarch, or nomination by the heads of Babylonian *Yeshibot*;
it also made the community independent of other communities
or any other extraneous authority. The community elected or
appointed its *parnasim*, its judges, and its tax assessors, and
clothed them with complete religious and secular authority over
its members; but this authority did not stem from any outside
force, did not claim to be based on traditional rulership, such

---

[147] Thus Rabbenu Tam threatened the followers of Rabbi Meshullam of
Melun with excommunication because the latter erred in several of his decisions
in ritual law. Rabbenu Tam threatened to invite a number of neighboring communities to pronounce the *Herem*. See his *Responsa*, 46, 4: נגזור ונחרים בכל קהלותינו
על כל השומעים לך. Rabbenu Tam also instructed the judges of a certain community
to pronounce the *herem* against a litigant should he refuse to abide by their decision. See ibid. 34, 6: ומעתה אם לא יציית לכם להשיב ליד ראובן תחרימו עליו בהסכמותינו.
These matters, of course, involved religious law, and no mention is made of the
immunity of the individual. Moreover, in religious law, the community arrogated
all rights to itself, and thus even curbed the particular rights of certain individuals guaranteed to them by the Talmud. Thus the Talmud ruled: תלמיד חכם
שנדה לכבודו נידויי נידוי (Moed Katan, 16a), which gave the scholar the right to
pronounce the ban against anyone who slighted him. The communities, however,
objected to the exercise of such power by an individual and passed the famous
ordinance that no scholar should pronounce the *herem* without the consent of the
community (Pr. p. 158b).

[148] See Pr. 941; Am II, 127; R. Hayyim Or Zarua, *Responsa*, 222; Mord.
B. K. 179.

as that of the family of David, or the students of Moses, but emanated from the community itself.[149] An outsider, therefore, could not interefere with the community's government, dictate to its leaders, nor enforce any order within its jurisdiction, without its consent. The community treasured its independence and guarded it from encroachments by outsiders.

The following query sent to Rabbi Joseph Bonfils is a case in point:

> The inhabitants of T had to pay the King's tax. In apportioning this tax they accused one another of having shifted the burden from oneself to someone else. Consequently they elected trustworthy men, most expert in taxation matters, to levy the tax on each individual in accordance with their estimate of the value of his assets. The members of the community had all agreed to abide by the decision of these honest assessors, and solemnly decreed that everyone should pay to the treasurers the amount he was assessed for, and that anyone who refused to do so, should be under the ban throughout the term of his refusal, and should have to pay a fine of one pound. The whole community, because of fear of God, and the solemn decree, promptly paid the tax. Two persons A and B, however,

---

[149] In all rabbinic discussions of the sources of authority in Jewish life in Germany and France, the scope and limitation of such authority, whether exercised by the community, the court, or the scholar, no mention is made of any delegation of authority by the exilarch, the Geonim, the *Nasi* of Palestine, or of even a direct chain of tradition from teacher to pupil. This fact is brought out very clearly in R. Meir's defense against the Rhine communities (see *Text*, no. 271) at the time he was accused of having permitted the betrothed of one man to marry another. A question of ritual law was involved, and the special prerogatives of the Rhine communities as a supreme religious authority, were debated. R. Meir denied the existence of such special authority in religious matters; he wrote: ושמא מחמת שצריכין לכם להסכמת ניטין כמדומים אתם שאין לכל אדם להורות אי לא נקט רשותא טינייכו, לא, כי התורה הפקר אך שיורה כהלכה. The Torah is free, anyone who is able to arrive at a correct opinion is permitted to give a decision in ritual law. R. Meir does not claim to have received ordination from his teachers, who in turn received it from their teachers, etc. He clearly states that no ordination is required, or is of any value, the knowledge of the Law being the only requirement (see *Mordecai Hagadol*, p. 212d).

refused to obey the community ordinance, and did not
heed the solemn decree. They, then, went to the town of
Z and related there the whole incident. The people of Z
invited A and B to their homes, entertained and dined them,
and lifted from them the ban of the community of T, even
giving them a written release. The people of Z based
their right to lift the ban of the community of T, on the
talmudic interpretation (Beza 5b) of the verse "when
the trumpet soundeth long, they shall come up to the
mount (Ex. 19,13)", from which the Talmud derived the
law that whatever one *Bet-din* prohibited remained forbidden until another *Bet-din* permitted it; but which in
the opinion of the people of Z meant that whatever one
Bet-din forbade, another might permit.

When A and B returned to T they triumphantly boasted
of the whole affair. The people of T were greatly angered
for they realized that a community's means of coercion
were of no avail, if another community might nullify its
decrees. They resolved to ask the king to order his con-
stables to collect this tax directly from A and B. Upon
deliberation, however, they changed their minds and decided first to inquire whether their decree was valid, and
whether the cancellation thereof by the community of Z
was of any consequence.[150]

Rabbi Joseph Bonfils responded that since the community
elected trustworthy officials, enacted the decree at the advice
of experts [on community law], and pronounced the ban with
their consent, it was undoubtedly valid and that no community had the right to annul or lift it. Neither the fact that the
other community was greater in numbers, nor that it excelled
in scholarship, was of any consequence, since the dispute involved money matters, and in a litigation regarding money,
even the same court might not reverse itself.[151] Our sages, he

---

[150] L. 423.

[151] Ibid.: נ'ל דכיון שביררו להם הקהל נאמנים ועשו להם תקנה על פי בקיאים וגזרו גזירה
בהסכמתם אין כח לשום קהל להפר ו[ל]בטל לא משום רבוי חכמה ולא משום רבוי מתירין שדבר

wrote, have given every community the right to enact decrees
for its benefit, and no outside community can revoke or annul
such decrees (based on the above-cited statement of B. B. 8b).
A community has the right to establish a *Bet-din* competent
to confiscate property, and to impose fines and penalties even
when not prescribed by the Torah, provided such *Bet-din* uses
its prerogatives to strengthen Jewish law, and not to transgress
it.[152] In our case, he continued, the community of T acted well
within its rights, since no one was permitted to evade the payment of taxes. The people of Z, he said, have badly misinterpreted the talmudic passage cited above, and have therefore
drawn the wrong conclusions; for in civil matters no court can
invalidate a decree enacted by a community.[153] The *herem* and
the penalties are the only means of punishing transgressors
left to us, he concluded; anyone who weakens these means of
coercion is guilty of bringing about anarchy in Israel.

Thus the independence of the community was inviolable.
Even great scholars were very careful in their dealings with the
communities.[154] They made a clear distinction between the
all-embracing power vested in the community organization,
and their own lack of any authority outside their own commu-

זה דין ממון הוא, וכ"מ שהוא דין ממון בין ב' אנשים וגזרו ב"ד על החייב לפרוע, אפי' אותו מין ואותו
ב"ד עצמו אין יכולים להתיר.

[152] Ibid.: הא למדת שרשאין ב"ד שבכל קהלה וקהלה לגזור על קהלתם כפי ראייתם לצורך
השעה ואין אחרים יכולין לבטל תקנתם ובלבד שלא תהא עבריינות של תורה.

[153] Ibid.: וזה מה שהצבור עושין תקנה ביניהם וגוזרין האיך יכולים שום ב"ד לנתקה ולהתירה.
In this connection compare R. Nissim Girundi, *Responsa*, 11.

[154] Even R. Meir was very careful in his dealings with the communities; see
Am II, 234: ואינו בא לפסוק הדין בינו ובין הקהל כי לא על ככה נשאלתי ואם יצא דבר מפי אגב
אורחא אשר ממנו יודע זכות לראובן נגד הקהל סמיכנא בשמא קדישא שאל יודע לראובן,
דלא לימרו הקהל קא מנמרו טעגתא לאינשי ומפסדו להו. Talmudic scholars were very reluctant to answer questions regarding community law, and were unwilling to
venture an opinion unless assured that it would be accepted. See Am II, 141:
דעו כי מאד מאד הקשיתם לשאול לבקשני להכריע בדבר זה ובמרומים סהדי כי בשביל ממון גדול
לא הייתי משתדל . . . ואינכם צריכים לשלוח לי עוד בשביל דין זה כי לא אפסוק בע"א כלל או כמ"ש
או כמנהג העיר, ואם אין מנהג העיר הכל כמנהג המדינה. See also Tesh. Maim. to *Kinyan*, 32:
ועליך אין לפקפק ולהרהר כי כל מה שתפסוק פסוק וחתום ותו לא מידי.

nity.[155] In his own community, it is true, the scholar possessed great power and influence for the following reasons: a) He was entitled to a vote like any other member of the community;[156] b) he had personal prestige that swayed others to his point of view; c) the leading members of the community were his students who, therefore, owed him honor and obedience;[157] d) there was a prevailing opinion that no community ordinance could be passed without the consent of the resident outstanding scholar.[158] Outside of his own community, however, his authority, prerogatives and powers were almost nil. Thus even Rashi when asked to release a certain person from the ban, wrote: "Far be it from me to assume the authority of a *bet-din hashub*. Were I residing among you, my vote would have been counted together with yours to release the individual. Who am I, however, that I should assume authority in other localities [than my own]"?[159] This statement of Rashi was not prompted by

---

[155] See Am II, 123: ולהחליטו ביד ראובן, האי לאו דינא הוא אלא קנסא, והני קנסות אנן לא דייני׳ אלא אתה מורי וקהלך אם נראה שנעשה דבר מכוער כזה כמו שנראה לקנסו לתן לצדקה לא ידעתי מה אשיב אמת הוא שנבלה גדולה עשה ואין דנין דיני קנסות וחבלות Pr. 383; הנראה לכם בזה׳ז ובכל קהלה וקהלה נוהגים לעשות תקנה גדולה ונדר לפי העניין . . . ואם היה במקומנו היינו Cr. 304; איני דן דין קנסות אמנם הקהל, איני דן דין קנסות אמנם הקהל; מלקים אותו ועל שעשה שלא כהוגן שקבל עליו לנוי, הרשות בידם לקנוס ולענש על דבר מכוער.

[156] Joel Mueller, op. cit. 22: אם הייתי ביניכם הייתי נמנה עמכם בהתר.

[157] L. 77: ואם יש רב בעיר יכול [לגזור] גם על הבא לדור וחלה עליו נזירתו אם הוא רבו; see also note 129 above.

[158] This is based on B. B. 9a: ולהסיע על קיצתן . . . ה׳מ היכא דליכא אדם חשוב, אבל דכיון שביררו להם הקהל :Pr. 968; L. 423: היכא דאיכא אדם חשוב לאו כל כמיניהו דמתנו; נאמנים ועשו להם תקנה על פי בקיאים, וגזרו נזירה בהסכמתם :Tur Hoshen Mishpat, 231, 30: אבל אם יש חכם ומנהיג אפילו כל בני העיר אין רשאין לתקן כלום זולתו ואם תקנו והתנו דבר בלתי ידיעתו אינו כלום; Hagahot Maimuniot to Hilk. Mekirah, 14, 3; Mord. B. B. 483-4; Sefer Agudah, B. B. 19.

[159] Joel Mueller, op. cit. 22; cf. also R. Jacob Tam, *Responsa*, 46 end: דע כי נקהיל עליך קהלות. Rabbenu Tam had no power of coercion over Rabbi Meshullam of Melun, excepting his personal prestige which enabled him to summon communities to a synod, or have them individually protest against Rabbi Meshullam, and by aroused public opinion force him to repent. The statement of Zeitlin, *J.Q.R.* XXXI (1940) p. 31-2, that Rabbenu Tam enacted ordinances "independently of the community", is entirely unwarranted. The ordinances of Rabbenu Tam, as well as those of Rabbenu Gershom, were enacted at synods where the representatives of many communities were present, and were considered, תקנות

humility, but by a clear understanding of the limitations of the authority of a scholar in a community outside his own.

The חרם בית דין, the ban on an individual who refused to answer a summons to the local court, was also an effective measure for strengthening the authority of the community. The right to prefer a superior court, guaranteed by the Talmud to certain litigants,[160] often caused embarrassment to the community organization inasmuch as many would not subordinate themselves to the court established by the community, claiming that they would submit their case before a court of greater learning. Often such a claim was put forth merely to delay legal proceedings. The חרם בית דין did not permit such evasion of justice; it strengthened the autonomy of the community and gave its court complete judiciary authority over its members.[161]

הקהלות, community ordinances. They derived their legality from the fact that they were accepted by the people. See Cr. 72; 79; Finkelstein, op. cit. pp. 153, 159, 163. Cf. R. Hayyim Or Zarua, *Responsa*, 69.

[160] Sanh. 31b. According to Ri, only the defendant may insist on a superior court, while according to Rabbenu Tam the plaintiff has a similar right; see Mord. Sanh. 709.

[161] See Mord. Sanh. 709; Tesh. Maim. to *Shoftim*, 2: מנהג חרם של ב׳ד שבעירנו אודיעך כי אחד מבני העיר מזמין את חבירו לדין ע׳כ ידון כאן ואין יכול לדחותו ולומר אלך לבית ;הווער או לבית דין הגדול . . . וזהו מנהג העיר וכאר מפני הרמאים ושלום שמשון ב׳ר אברהם see also Berl. p. 319, no. 678: ומנהג קדמונים הוא כי התובע חבירו לדין בעיר אין לו לקרב לקח דיינים או מקבלי טענות בעירו מכל תביעות ואם הוצרכו לשאול שואלים ושולחים למורה ומי שמסרב מזה הוא סרבן בין שהוא מן הקלים ובין שהוא מן החשובים. This was an ancient custom that was extended by the *takkanah* of Rabbenu Gershom to include transients and members of other communities who ordinarily would not have been bound by the local custom of the community they happened to visit. The *takkanah* of Rabbenu Gershom made it the law of all German and French communities, and therefore binding on everyone. R. Isaac of Vienna, however, believed that the above law was instituted by Rabbi Samson. See *Or Zarua, Responsa*, 775: ועל דבר הדין שהזמינך למיידבורק לפני ה׳ר אין בדבריו כלום כי יש בעירך ה׳ר יעקב כהן שהוא מומחה לרבים ואפילו אם לא היה בעירך כבר נהגו בכל המקומות ששוכרין להם בעלי טענות ושולחים במקום ששניהם חפצים. הלכך ידונו לפני ה׳ר יעקב כי כן הדין או תבחרו מקבלי טענות ותשלחו במקום ששניכם חפצים וכן הנהיג רבינו שמשון זצ׳ל מפני הרמאים. Cf. also Finkelstein, op. cit. p. 178, 13. The jealousy of each community of its judicial autonomy was so intense that it was later assumed that every community where an outstanding scholar had once resided had judicial autonomy. This description probably applied to every community of importance. See Finkelstein, op. cit. p. 206: ואמ׳ גדולי

7. Community's Authority Beyond its Borders.

The jealous guarding by the community of its independence and autonomy, did not prevent it from attempting to
extend its authority beyond the confines of the town wall. A
well organized community had a feeling of responsibility toward
neighboring settlements and communities. During the Middle
Ages, when the life and fortune of every individual Jew depended
completely upon the opinion his Gentile neighbors held of the
whole Jewish people, the dictum כל ישראל ערבין זה בזה
(Shebu. 39a), all Israel were responsible for one another, was
felt keenly by individuals and groups.[162] A single Jew could
bring a calamity upon the whole community, a single group or
settlement could endanger the safety of all its neighbors.[163]

Four distinct reasons, aside from the natural lust for power,
prompted the community to extend its authority beyond the
town walls: a) The community was concerned that no flagrant breach of Jewish law should occur in its neighborhood.[164]
The Biblical law regarding the condemned city, the rebellious
elder, and the example of the civil war with the tribe of Benjamin
(Judges 19-20), heightened the concern of the community for
the religious mores of its neighbors, and provided it with a legal
basis for interference.[165] Thus we read in a Responsum of Rashi

צרפת שבדרוייש שנ' ה' אלפים ול'ב מקום שנזכר שהיה שם מקדם ת'ח באותה עיר ומסתמא קרוב
לודאי שהיה שם חרם ב'ד.

[162] See Pr. 940: לא מצינו בכל מקום ... כתב לבני טרויי'ש. תשובת רבינו יוסף טוב עלם,
[שבני] עיר אחת יכולי' להטיל ממון על עיר אחרת . . . כללו של דבר אין לאלו כח כפייה על אלו
חוץ מרידוי עבירות שבאין מחמת טענה שנתפסין תחתיהן דכתיב וכשלו איש באחיו איש בעון אחיו.
מלמד שכל ישראל ערבין זה בזה.

[163] See Pr. 980: וראוי היה לקונסו ביותר כי הכעיס את הכומר מקציני המלך ולא תחתיו
וכמה דמים נשפכו על ידי אלה, וכאלה פוסלי Cf. L. 233; Text, 175; L. 246: בלבד היה קודר
מטבעות היינו דאחרבינהו לאחינו יושבי צרפת והאי.

[164] See Pr. 940, and the great storm of protests against R. Meir described in
Text, 271.

[165] See Kol Bo, 142: אבל אם היו עוברין בני עיר אחת על התורה או על הדין או שהורו על
אחת מכל המצות שלא כהלכה, רשאין בני עיר אחרת לכופם ולהחרימם כדי להחזירם למוטב ואינן
יכולים לומר אנו בשלנו ואתם בשלכם, אלא כל ישראל מצוין להכריחן שכן מצינו בזקן ממרא ובני עיר
הנדחת שיושבי לשכת הגזית כופין אותם ודנים אותם.

that when two families were engaged in a severe quarrel and
were vilifying and reviling each other, a neighboring community
solemnly ordered them to desist. Rashi ruled that the decree of
the community was binding upon both families, even though the
members of one family had previously taken a solemn oath, not
to accept the order of this community. The reason the solemn
decree was binding upon individuals who were not members
thereof and who did not live within its sphere of authority, was,
according to Rashi, that the enactment of the decree was
prompted by religious reasons.[166] Rabbi Jacob Tam, the champion of the inalienable rights of the individual, threatened to
invite many communities to pronounce the ban against Rabbi
Meshullam b. Nathan of Melun, unless he admitted that he was
mistaken in several of his rulings on ritual law.[167] The threats of
excommunication hurled against R. Meir by various communities for permitting an allegedly betrothed maiden to marry
another man, were also prompted by religious reasons. R. Meir
did not dispute the right of these communities to take disciplinary measures against him; he merely defended his point of view
and proved that he was guilty of no breach of Jewish law.[168]

b) The right of a litigant to appeal to a higher court was
inviolable, and the right of the individual to sue his commu-

---

[166] See Joel Mueller, op. cit. 21: משפחות המתגרות זו בזו בחירופי' ונגאים. ונשמע לקהל
קבלון וגזרו עליהם שלא ירגילו בכך וקפצה האחת ונשבעה קודם גזירה שלא יקבלו עליהם גזירת
הקהל ... ונשבעו לשוא את שבועתם מפיהם יצתה לשקר שנשבעו לעבור על המצוה שלא
לשמור חוקי דת עברית לשמוע בקול זקניהם גודרי גדר ומחזיקי סייג, הם צריכים מלקות משבועה
ראשונה, וגמי מגזירת קהל שעברו שעל כרחם חלה עליהם, ואע"פ שהם בני עיר אחרת, שהם לשם
שמים נדו. For the same reason Rabbi Eliezer b. Nathan was justified in pronouncing the *herem* against anyone who would act in accordance with his theoretical
definition of a particular ritual law. Since a religious question was involved, he was
entitled to pronounce the ban against anyone, even members of distant communities, who would dare transgress the Law. See *Sefer Rabn*, p. 12c: ואני לא
להורות לעשות כן באתי אלא לפרש ההלכה על מכונה ואשר יקל ויפרוץ גדר הראשונים ויסמוך על
דברי מה שפרשתי יהא באלה ובנידוי ובשמתא דרבנן ואני נקי וכל ישראל.

[167] See Rabbenu Tam, *Responsa*, p. 88; H. Gross, *Gallia Judaica*, p. 352.
[168] See *Text*, 271.

nity was also upheld.[169] Many disputes within the community,
therefore, were brought before outstanding scholars who resided
in other communities, or before the courts of leading communities. It is important to note, however, that whenever a case
was appealed to a higher authority, the latter usually served
in an advisory capacity, but had no power to enforce his rulings.
The outstanding scholar or the court of a leading community
merely appealed to the conscience of the litigant community,
pointed out the correct decision according to Jewish law, and
expected the local court, or the community itself, to enforce
compliance with such ruling.[170] It is obvious, however, that
though the court of appeal had no authority inherent within
itself to force a community to accept its rulings, its decisions
carried great weight since any legal act contrary to such decision might in itself be construed as a breach of Jewish law and
might provoke a number of communities to take disciplinary
actions against the community or the individual involved.[171]
Thus did the courts of leading communities exert great influence, in the judicial sphere, over neighboring communities.[172]

[169] See Mord. Sanh. 709; Cr. 49; 111; 121; 156; 165; 167; 209; 222; 292; Pr.
104; 106; 118; 195; 241; 716; 825; 941; 968; 995; 1012; Am II, 127; 130; 140.

[170] See Pr. 968; 983; L. 109–11; 246; Am II, 141; 234; Mord. B. K. 81–2.
Thus R. Meir explains, Am II, 46: צריך אני לדקדק ולחלק על כל אנפי הדין צדדי' וצדי
צדדים שלא לתן פתחון פה לבעל הדין לחלוק.

[171] See the Responsa regarding the young man of Rothenburg who had betrothed the daughter of R. Judah of Düren and later refused to come to Düren
to marry her, Text 280; note the veiled and open threats of excommunication in
case of continued disobedience; note the gathering clouds of wrath nearing an
eventual explosion. See Am II, 81: נא מורי הכר מעליך תלונות והשיא לאותם האנשים עצה
ההוגנת להם, כי ידעתי שהנדיב לא החריש . . . ושלח הדבר לפני ישישים גדולי צרפת ושאר מקומות
וכמדומה אני שכולם הסכימו לכופו שלא לענן את הנערה שיבא לכונסה או לפטרה בגט, ודעתי אף
כי מורי גדול הדור לא יצוה לו לעבור על דברי זקנים, ואם ישלחו גזרתם יקשה לך לעבור עליה
ולבטלה פן ירבו מחלוקת בישראל.

[172] This strong religious control exerted by the large communities became
obvious whenever a general ordinance was adopted that was to be binding on all
the communities. In such instances the important communities became the prime
movers in the enactment of the takkanah; their names were explicitly mentioned
in the ordinance itself, while the lesser communities were often not even con-

In analyzing a community dispute brought before an outstanding scholar or a court of another, leading community, therefore, we must reckon with three distinct factors: the jealousy of the litigant community for its autonomy; the strong desire on the part of the community to conform to Jewish law; and the fear of censure and of sanctions invoked by neighboring communities.

c) The Jews of neighboring settlements were dependent upon the community in religious matters. They would move to town for the holidays in order to attend congregational services,[173] and they would bury their dead in the community cemetery.[174] The service in religious matters that the mother community rendered to its surrounding settlements served as a basis for the expectation of reciprocal obligations on the part of the inhabitants of these settlements. The members of the community were taxed heavily in order to defray the cost of building and maintaining their synagogue, their cemetery, and other public institutions, and of supporting the poor. They therefore expected the villagers who made use of these institutions to share the burden of their maintenance. Thus an ancient *herem* made it obligatory upon all passing through a town during the two weeks preceding the feast of Esther, to give their *Purim* contributions to the local poor, when so requested.[175] Another *herem* required villagers who participated in congre-

---

sulted. See Cr. 78: לכן נועצנו לב יחד זקני טרוויי״ש וחכמיה ואשר בגבוליה סביב כל יושבי
צרפת, יש אשר כבר הסכימו ויש אשר לא שמענו דבריהם כי היה הדבר נחוץ, וסמכנו על אשר ידענום
גדולים נשמעים לקטנים. See also Cr. 72, where the community of Narbonne is prominently mentioned; Pr. p. 159a, where the consent of the famous communities of Spiers, Worms and Mayence is specifically recorded. The consent of the lesser communities was often taken for granted; or, at least, mention of their names carried no weight, and was therefore dispensed with.

[173] See Cr. 44; Pr. 1016; Pr. p. 158b; Berl. P. 320, no. 865b: ושאלנו ע״ד קהלינו
יושבי נועטט יש מהן רוצי׳ ללכת חוץ למקומם לימים נוראי׳ ומניחי׳ חבריהם בלא מנין.

[174] Am II, 33; Pr. 249; Pr. p. 159b.

[175] Pr. p. 158b: משנכנס אדר עד הפורים כל העוברי׳ דרך עיירות אם יש מנין קבוע יש חרם
קדמונים לפרוע מעות פורים לחלק לעניי אותה העיר אם יתבעום א׳ מאנשי העיר, ואם לא יתבעם
פטורי׳ מחרם.

gational services in town on *Yom Kippur,* to leave in the synagogue the remaining portions of the large candles they had lit
there for the holy day.[176] An ordinance of the communities of
much wider scope and greater significance, established the rule
that villagers who buried their dead in the cemetery of a particular community subject themselves to the jurisdiction of the
court of that community.[177] Thus we find that Rabbi Hayyim
b. Yehiel Hefetz Zahav, a member of the court of Cologne,
forced the inhabitants of neighboring Boppard to accept his
legal decision in their local dispute, because they had been
bringing their dead to Cologne for burial.[178]

d) The community and its surrounding settlements were
often under the jurisdiction of the same overlord.[179] Although
in paying regular taxes they were at times completely independent of one another, the safety of the Jews of the whole territory
often depended on a bribe or a gift to the overlord or his friends.
In such cases complete cooperation between the community
and its neighboring settlements was required in order to safeguard life and property. When such cooperation was voluntarily

---

[176] Ibid.: ואם אנשי כפרים אשר אין להם מנין בעירם ובאים למקום הקהילות למנין ביום
הכפורים ומביאים נרותיהם בבית הכנסת שקורי' ציר'א אם לא עשה כ'א אחת יניחם שם בביהכ'נ
שהדליקו ויכולי' בני העיר להכריחו בחרם להניחו ואם עשה שנים האחד יניחו והשני יכול לשא עמו
וכל נדרים שאדם נודר בביהכ'נ שיתפלל ;cf. also ibid. p. 159a: להדליקו במקום שמתפלל קבוע
שם ישלם באותה ביהכ'נ כמנהג אנשי המקום ותקנתם אם יש קהל קבוע באותה ביהכ'נ.
[177] Ibid. p. 158b; p. 159a–b: עיר שיש בה בית הקברות כופי' בני הכפרים המוליכי'
מתיהם לשם לדון שם. Aside from these instances of compulsory dependence upon
another community, there were many of voluntary dependence, or even a voluntary acceptance of all the customs and mores of a neighboring community. See
Pr. 106: אם יש מנהג בקהלה או בעיר שננדרים אחריה ילכו אחר המנהג.
[178] Pr. 249: על אודות האלמנה ובנה דעו אם היה תלוי בדעתי היה רצוני שלא היה בא שום
דין לפני, אך כי זה העלם אמר שמעבירי' עליו הדרך, יען כי זה ב'ד קרוב גם עתה נגררי' אחר בית
עלמין שלנו; Finkelstein op. cit. p. 198, note 2, gives R. Hayyim Paltiel as the author
of this Responsum. The signature חיים בן אמ'ו הר'י, however, proves that the
author was Hayyim b. Yehiel Hefez Zahav, the famous member of the court of
Cologne. See signatures to Pr. 189; 241; 296–7; 339–41.
[179] See Cr. 121.

given, there was no problem; but often a legal basis for the right of coercion was necessary in order to enforce cooperative action, and the problem became a complicated one.[180]

To summarize, then, although the theoretical basis of community self-rule made the community completely independent of any authority outside its own border, religious, economic, and political forces drew the individual communities together and made them dependent upon one another. A flagrant breach of Jewish law in one community roused the other communities to summary action;[181] a great teacher commanded the respect and obedience of his students long after they left his school and became leaders of various communities; unfair competition between members of different communities, was checked on an intercommunity basis; and an acute political crisis of national proportions found the communities well organized for effective cooperative action.[182] In analyzing any occurrence, dispute, or litigation, of a community, one must take into consideration the interplay of the various forces tending toward both isolationism and interdependence that molded and shaped the life of the medieval community.

[180] See Joel Mueller, תשובות גאוני מזרח ומערב, 165: עייני עליהם שקבלו כיון זו בשאלה עייתי
בני הקהל כולה וכללו בעלי הכפרים להכליל הפריעה שעל הכפרים כולם ולהטיל על כל כפר
וכפר לפי מדת קרקעותיו וכן להשתוות בהשתדה שמשחידין לסלק האונס מעליהם. The Jews of
Lorrain were confronted with a serious problem of a similar nature; see Mord.
Kidd. 561: על דבר הדוכוס מלותיר אשר דרש מאת היהודים שיתעסקו באותם יהודים הדרים
בכפרים שלו תחת שרים קטנים וישובו תחתיו ואם לא כלה גרש ינרש אותם. דומה בעיני שביד הדוכוס
לנרש כולם, ואף כי אלו אומרים תמות נפשי עם פלשתים לא מהני אלא כופין אותם על מדת סדום
לחזור תחתיו ... ואם יש תביעה לאותם יהודים עבור שיש להם פסידא לעקור ממקומם, זה יטענו
לאחר כך; see also Pr. 241.

[181] See *Sefer Rabn*, p. 139c–d: ואבי הנערה בא למגנצא וקיבץ כל חכמי הקהילות למגנצא
ויועדו שם בבית הכנסת וירע בעיני כל הקהילות את המעשה הרע אשר עשו קרובי הראשון ... וכל
חכמי הדור רבי' יעקב הלוי מוורמשא וישיבתו ור' יצחק הלוי מאשפירא ובני ישיבתו היו רוצין להפקיע
קידושי הראשון. The reason for this great disturbance becomes apparent when we
read: ואשר עשו המעשה היו קרובים למלכות ולא היו בני הכרחה.

[182] See note 179 above; see Pr. 241; R. Hayyim Or Zarua, *Responsa* 110:
כשיצאו מצרפת ונתוועדו כל הקהלות למגנצא ומורי הרב רבי מנחם מוירצבורק ומורי הרב ר' היילמון
ומורי הר'ר אשר וכל הגדולים שהיו ברינוס וראשי הקהלות כי הוצרכו ליתן מס גדול למלך ל' אלף

8. R. Meir's Ideas on Community Government.

R. Meir dealt extensively with community problems and wrote many Responsa dealing with litigations in which a community was engaged.[183] The German communities turned to him for guidance in their most pressing problems. When the relationship of communities toward one another was the subject of litigation,[184] when exhorbitant taxes were levied upon a community,[185] when its entire membership was imprisoned for purposes of extortion,[186] when the strife caused by such critical conditions threatened the very existence of the community, the opinion of R. Meir was relied upon to command the respect of all factions and to check the outbreak of great hostilities and serious quarrels.[187] In studying these various problems R. Meir developed a logically consistent theory of community government which determined the course of development of community life.

R. Meir's opinions regarding the legal basis of community rule, the scope as well as the limitation of its power, and its manifold rights and duties toward the individual, were based upon a highly developed idea of human freedom. R. Meir believed that a person not only possessed inalienable rights, but that he was completely free of any obligation toward God or man. No one, not even the Almighty Himself, had a right to impose his will upon an individual. No one had a right to coerce a person to do aught against his will.[188]

---

[183] Thus more Responsa of R. Meir dealing with community law, have survived than of all his predecessors (in France and Germany) combined.

[184] See Pr. 131; 983.

[185] Cr. 53; Pr. 941; Am II, 127; 141.   [186] Am II, 127; 130.

[187] Am II, 141: דעו כי מאד מאד הקשיתם לשאול לבקשני להכריע בדבר זה ובמרומים סהדי כי בשביל ממון גדול לא הייתי משתדל, אך שככה השבעתני והודעתני שאם אמשוך את ידי אז יבא לידי קטטה גדולה בטלתי רצוני מפני רצונכם.

[188] For this reason the Torah was not binding upon the Jews until they voluntarily accepted it at the time of Mordecai and Esther. R. Meir does not treat the talmudic discussion on this subject as mere sermonic utterance. He derives

A person, however, may forego his unlimited freedom by voluntary consent. He may agree to bind himself by a certain contract and thereby become obligated to abide by its terms or suffer the penalties agreed upon. He may voluntarily accept such a vastly complicated contract as the Jewish religion (referred to in the Pentateuch on numerous occasions as a ברית, a covenant, a reciprocal treaty, a contract),[189] and then be obligated to fulfill all its commandments, be bound by all its legal provisions, and be subject to its penal code. Sanctity of contract is the very cornerstone of equitable human cooperation, the only justifiable foundation of legal or religious duties.[190]

Thus, the only reason that the Jewish people are obligated to observe the laws of the Torah, is that they voluntarily accepted it in the time of Mordecai and Esther. The acceptance of the Torah at Mount Sinai was not voluntary, and therefore not binding; the second acceptance towards the end of their long journey in the desert, also took place under strained circumstances and was, therefore, of no legal consequence. In the days of Mordecai and Esther, however, the Jews voluntarily

---

therefrom the law that the captives who were forced to obligate themselves, by a *herem*, to pay money to their captors, were free from obligation, because the *herem* was pronounced under pressure; see Pr. 938. R. Meir also decides that a community may not pronounce the *herem* against an individual, if the individual protests against it. He writes: אבל חרם אין נראה לומר אלא מדעתם לאפוקי בעל כרחם. ואם עוברים על אותו חרם אין להם עונש לאותם שלא קבלוהו כדאמר בפ' אמר ר' עקיבא, אמר רבה מודעה רבה לאורייתא אע"ג דקבלום כיון דאנוסים היו ובעל כרחם קבלוהו, אלא לאו דהדר קבלוהו בימי אחשורוש מדעתן (*Semak*, 79 end). Thus R. Meir treated seriously this talmudic statement that God could not force his will upon the Jewish people; he derived important laws therefrom, and therefore must have fully subscribed to it.

[189] See Genesis, 17, 1–2; 17, 7–14; Exodus 19, 5–6; ibid. 34, 10 f.; see contractual idea behind Leviticus ch. 26; also Dt. 31, 16–21.

[190] Thus R. Meir explains why in certain instances a community does legally possess the right to coerce recalcitrant members (Pr. 968): ורשאין בני העיר להסיע על קיצותן היינו מדעת כולם וקמ"ל לדבדבור בעלמא בלא קנין הן הדברי' הנקני' באמירה ורשאי' לקנוס את מי שקבל עליו [תחלה] ועבר על [תקנתן] רשאי' לגבות הקנס כאשר קימו וקבלו עליהם בכך וכך העובר. או ז' טובי העיר שהוברדו מתחלה מדעת כל אנשי [העיר] לעיוני במילי דמתא לקנוס ולענוש גם הם רשאי' [להסיע] על קיצותן.

accepted the Torah, and ever since they have been legally obligated to fulfill every detail of the Law, and the Almighty was
justified in punishing them for the minutest breach of that Law.[191]
Consequently, the Jews are obligated to observe all the laws of
the Torah as discussed, analyzed, and interpreted in that vast
study of the details of the Law, both written and oral, the
Talmud.

Thus when R. Meir was asked regarding certain Jews who
were thrown by some of their fellow coreligionists into prison
and, under threat of being killed, were made to bind themselves
by a *herem* to pay a certain amount as ransom, he ruled that the
captives were not bound by the *herem*, since they had accepted
it under pressure. R. Meir then discussed at length the obligation of the Jews towards the Torah and their contractual relationship with God, in order to prove that even a solemn agreement, if entered into under pressure, was not binding.[192]

R. Meir emphasized the idea of the freedom of the individual
to such an extent that he could find no legal method whereby
a community might force an individual to subject himself to
its *herem*. Thus R. Meir was asked:[193]

> In a case where some members of the community seek to
> pronounce a *herem*, a community ban, for a certain purpose,
> while others openly protest against it, are the former per-
> mitted to pronounce the ban, and when pronounced, will
> it be binding on the latter group?

[191] See Pr. 938: כשהשביע משה ע"ה את ישראל בערבות מואב [אמר] לא על דעתכם אני
משביעכם אלא ע"ד המקום ועל דעתי, שנאמר לא אתכם לבדכם וגו' ואפ"ה אמרי' בפ' ר' עקיבא
(שבת פ"ח ע"א) ויתיצבו בתחתית ההר מלמד שכפה עליהם ההר כגיגית, ואמר ר' אחא בר יעקב כאן
מודעא רבה לאורייתא, פי' משום שאם יתבע הקב"ה ממנו למה קבלתם את התורה יש לנו להשיבו
אנוסים היינו לקבלה. אמר רבא הדר קבלוה בימי אחשורוש כו' והקשה ר"י אמאי לא אמר כבר קבלוה
בערבות מואב, ותירץ דהתם נמי יראים היו מהקב"ה שמא לא יביאם לארץ.
[192] Pr. 938.
[193] *Semak*, ed. Constantinople, 79: וששאלתם אם מקצת הקהל יכולין לתת חרם בעל
כרחם של האחרים ואפילו עומדים וצווחים.

R. Meir answered:[194]

> If the decree for which the pronouncement of the ban is
> sought, is designed for the public benefit or to fill a great
> need in the community, while without such a decree the
> existence of the community will be jeopardized, the mem-
> bers of the community are permitted to coerce one another
> to adopt the required resolution and to abide by its
> provisions. A *herem*, however, can not be effectively in-
> voked upon those who protest against its being pronounced,
> since a *herem* [being in the nature of an oath or a vow]
> must first be accepted voluntarily by a person before it
> becomes binding on him.

This reduction of the solemn and terrifying power of the *herem*
to a mere verbal expression of agreement, a mere vow, was
indeed a very bold step, one that went contrary to the rulings
of outstanding scholars of previous generations[195] and was even
in opposition to Biblical precedent,[196] but one that expressed
clearly and emphatically R. Meir's strong conviction regarding
the unbounded freedom of the individual.[197]

---

[194] Ibid.: אם הוא דבר דהוי מינדר מלתא וצורך הקהל שבלא זה אי אפשר להם להיות, כופין
בני העיר זה את זה לקיים, כדאמרינן בפ'ק דבבא בתרא ובתוספתא דבבא מציעא במילי טובא, אבל
חרם אין נראה לומר אלא מדעתם לאפוקי בעל כרחם. ואם עוברים על אותו חרם אין להם עונש
לאותם שלא קבלוהו כדאמר בפ' אמר ר' עקיבא, אמר רבה מודעה רבה לאורייתא . . . וממה ששתפו
הקב"ה במכירת יוסף אין ראיה, דרצונו היה, דבלאו הכי לא היה מגלה דלא דלטור הוה, כדאשכחן
במעשה דעכן.

[195] מכאן פסק אב"י העזר'י הלכה למעשה See Elfenbein, 246-7; Cr. 165: תשובות רש"י
שאם טובי העיר עשו תקנה והחרימו חרם שחייבין כל בני העיר לשום' בין שמעו בין לא שמעו החרם
והגידו להם ואמרו נואש, ולא נכנסו לא בתקנתם ולא בחרמם אף על פי כן חלה עליהם החרם ועליהם
לשמרה. ואפילו אם אמרו בשעה שעשו החרם לא נכנס בתקנתם ובחרמיהם ושאר טובי העיר אמרו לא
תיפטרו בכך חלה עליהם החרם וחייבין לשומרה.

[196] R. Eliezer b. Joel ha-Levi bases his decision (see previous note) on the
oath of Joshua and the elders to the Gibeonites, which was binding on all Israel.
Barak excommunicated the inhabitants of the city of Meroz, certainly against
their will (see Shebu. 36a); Saul anathematized those who would eat on the day
of battle, and it included Jonathan who was not there at the time (Samuel I, 14).

[197] The *herem* contained (at least) two elements: solemn agreement and a
curse. For this reason the word ארור included the idea of excommunication (see
Shebu. 36a). The נוסח החרם (*Kol Bo* 139) consists mainly of terrifying curses.
The great dread medieval Jews had of the *herem* was caused mainly by its power
as a curse. According to R. Meir's idea of the freedom of the individual, however,

Such freedom of the individual, however, did not lead to anarchy in Jewish life, since the Jews had voluntarily accepted the Torah as their way of life and were, therefore, bound by all its rules and regulations. Regarding group responsibility and group organization the Talmud makes various provisions:

a) The inhabitants of a town may force one another cooperatively to build a synagogue, to buy Scrolls of the Law, the books of the Prophets, and the Hagiographa,[198] to provide for the transient poor as well as for the local,[199] and to pay their taxes collectively.[200]

b) A person who settles in a certain community may be coerced into sharing the burden of its taxation and into contributing to its charity chest.[201]

c) The inhabitants of a town may force one another cooperatively to build a wall around it, construct a gate in that wall. and provide all other safety devices.[202]

---

no one is permitted to curse another against his will; and the very idea of the curse is meaningless. Thus a curse can only be construed as the invocation of the anger of God and His punishment on the perpetrator of a particular forbidden act. If the person, however, did not voluntarily consent to the enactment of the particular rule, he was not bound by this rule, and committed no sin in breaking it. Consequently the Almighty had no right to punish him, and the curse was of no avail. R. Meir, therefore, was forced to adopt the principle that a *herem* must be voluntarily accepted before it becomes binding on the individual.

[198] *Tosephta*, B. M. 11, 23: כופין בני העיר זה את זה לבנות להם בית הכנסת ולקנות להם ספר תורה ונביאים [וכתובים], quoted by R. Meir in Cr. 10; Berl. p. 320 no. 865.

[199] This law was not as obvious as the others. Consequently some authorities believed that no one could be forced to contribute to the charity chest; see *Tosaphot* B. B. 8b, s. v. אכפיה לר' נתן; *Or Zarua, Hilkot Zedakah*, 4. R. Meir derived this law from B. B. 8a: כמה יהא בעיר ויהא כאנשי העיר, שלשים יום לתמחוי ג' חדשים לקופה וכו'; see Cr. 10; Pr. 918.

[200] Pr. 918: פרדכס (נה.) חזקת הבתים וכ'ש שכופין אותו כדי להשתתף במס מהא דאמר בפ' טסייע מתא וכו' . . . וכן משמע בר רב חסדא רמא כרנא ארבנן (ב'ב ח.) . . . וכן משמע בתר הכי דההוא כובס דכל בני העיר חייב' והוי כמו לפסי העיר ולשורא לפרשאה ולאינלי נפא (ב'ב ח.) דכולן חייבין.

[201] B. B. 8a: וכמה יהא בעיר ויהא כאנשי העיר, ל' . . . י'ב חדש לתמחוי . . . ל' יום לפסי העיר, quoted by R. Meir in Cr. 10; L. 108.

[202] B. B. 7b: בני העיר כופין זה את זה לבנות לעיר חומה ודלתים ובריח, quoted by R. Meir in Pr. 104; Berl. p. 276 no. 57; also *Tosephta* B. M. 11, 18: כופין בני חצר זה

d) Members of a community must contribute to the charity chest, community expenses, and the overlord's tax, in proportion to their wealth;[203] while in certain instances payments must be apportioned one-half on a per capita basis, and the other half according to the value of each member's assets.[204]

e) In all other matters, if the inhabitants of a town have unanimously agreed to enact a certain ordinance, and such agreement was reached with the knowledge and consent of the resident scholar, they are then permitted to enforce such an ordinance.[205]

f) A community organization may exercise the power of a Sanhedrin over the inhabitants of the town, enacting ordinances and regulations required for religious purposes (למגדר מלתא), for the enforcement of talmudic law, or for the safety of the group, and may force a recalcitrant minority to abide by such regulations.[206]

g) The inhabitants of one city may restrain the inhabitants of other cities from competing with them within their city limits.[207]

את זה לעשות לחי וקורה למבוי, כופין בני בקעה לעשות ביניהם חריץ ובן חריץ, quoted by R. Meir in Berl. p. 320, no. 865; cf. L. 108.

[203] B. K. 116b: שיירא שהיתה מהלכת במדבר ועמד עליה גייס לטורפה, מחשבין לפי ממון; B. B. 7b: א״ל לפי ממון נובין ואליעזר בני קבע בה מסתרות; ואין מחשבין לפי נפשות, applied by R. Meir in Berl. p. 276, no. 57. Cf. Pr. 104; 568; 1016; Cr. 10.

[204] B. K. 116b: ואם שכרו תייר ההולך לפניהם מחשבין אף לפי נפשות. Cf. Cr. 228; Berl. p. 276, no. 57. Most taxes were in proportion to one's wealth; in but rare cases were they allocated on a per capita basis; see Text 527–9; 530; 550–3; 555–9; 560; 563–8; 570–2; 576–9; 580–4.

[205] R. Meir followed the interpretation of Rabbenu Tam (cited above, see note 141) of the talmudic statement, B. B. 8b, and derived therefrom the law that in certain instances (described below) a unanimous vote was required for the enactment of an ordinance. See Pr. 968: לא אדונים הם בדבר זה כי אינם רשאים לחדש דבר בלא דעת כולם דהא דאמר (ב״ב ח:) ורשאין בני העיר להסיע על קיצותן, היינו מדעת כולם וקמ״ל דבדבור בעלמא בלא קנין הן הדברים הנקנים באמירה, ורשאי׳ לקנוס את מי שקבל עליו [תחלה] ועבר על [תקנתם] רשאי׳ לגבות הקנס כאשר קימו וקבלו עליהם [לקנוס] בכך או בכך העובר, או ז׳ טובי העיר שהוברדו מתחלה מדעת כל אנשי [העיר] לעיוני במילי דמתא לקנוס ולענוש גם הם רשאי׳ [להסיע] על קיצותן . . . אבל היכי דאיכא [אדם] חשוב לאו כל כמיניהו דמתנו. Cf. Cr. 10; 222; L. 108; Am II, 127; 141; 240.

[206] See notes 113, 114, 123, above.

[207] This is based on B. B. 21b: אמר ר׳ הונא בריה דרב יהושע פשיטא לי בר מתא אבר; and especially on B. B. 22a: הנהו עמוראי דאייתי עצרא לפום נהרא; מתא אחריתי מצי מעכב.

Thus, R. Meir states that Jewish law gives the inhabitants of a town the right to organize themselves into a political body, elect officers, enact decrees and regulations (in matters classified as למגדר מלתא),[208] establish a court of law and invest it with the powers and prerogatives over its own members of an authoritative court, or with such as may be wielded by the outstanding scholar of the generation.[209] This political body, the community, has the right to rule upon and decide all such matters by majority vote.[210] Thus R. Meir rules:[211]

Whether regarding the election of officers, appointment of cantors, or the creation of a charity chest and appointment of its officers; whether to build or destroy anything in the

see ;אתו בני מתא קא מעכבי עלוייהו אתו לקמיה דרב כהנא אמר להו דינא הוא דמעכבי עלייכו Pr. 359; 983.

[208] See Berl. p. 320, no. 865. Note that assessment of taxes is not included among the powers of the community organization elected by majority vote. As will be pointed out later, R. Meir was of the opinion that any innovation or change in the manner of allocation or payment of taxes was to be made by unanimous agreement only.

[209] See Cr. 230: וטעמא נראה לי דטובי העיר הוו בעירם כחבר עיר למה שהוזכרו כמה נדולי הדור בכל מקום. כמו שנדולי הדור הפקירן הפקר בכל מקום במגדר מלתא ותקנתא, הכי נמי דבר פשוט הוא Pr. 980: ;טובי העיר בעירם, דעלייהו סמכו כל בני העיר וכל הנסמכים עליהם ;רשאין בני העיר להסיע על קיצותן כ"ש במגדר מלתא הפקר ב"ד הפקר לקנוס ולענוש בגופו ושבחא L. 108: ואי ציית ציית, ואי לא ציית הרשות בידכם להכריחו במילי ובשוטי ובחרמות ובנידויים עד שיחזור בו.

[210] See Am II, 140: אם אותו האחד שעבר על התקנה הי' מיושב בשעת התקנה בעיר ונמנה עמהם בתקנה, או אפי' לא נמנה עמהם אלא ששתק וקבל, ואפי' מיחה, לא כל הימנו בעורו שם למחות תקנות במגדר מלתא אחרי שרוב המהוגנים שבעיר הסכימו לכך.

[211] Berl. p. 320, no. 865; Tesh. Maim. *Kinyan*, 27. R. Meir does not give the talmudic source for the principle "majority rules". Since, however, he does not base it on a *minhag*, while in Berl. p. 320, no. 865 he explicitly bases his decision on the Tosephta, B. M. 11, he must have considered it required by talmudic law. In Am II, 140, he quotes the *takkanah* of Rabbenu Gershom, but in a manner which does not at all indicate that the *takkanah* is the main basis of this rule. He seems to quote the *takkanah* merely as an explanation of the details of the principle, but not as the basis for the principle itself. R. Meir, therefore, must have derived the law "majority rules" from the talmudic expression כופין בני העיר זה את זה (as given in Berl. p. 320, no. 865) which implied the idea of coercion and thus gave the inhabitants of the town the right to coerce some of their neighbors to accept their resolutions; while the rule: אין נוזרין גזירה על הצבור אלא אם כן רוב צבור יכולין לעמוד בה (B. K. 79b), gave this power of coercion to the majority.

synagogue, or to buy a community wedding-hall or bakery, or to provide all other community needs — all such matters shall be decided by a vote of the majority. Should the minority refuse to heed the decision of the majority, this majority, or its appointed officers, shall use coercive force, whether through Jewish law or the law of the land, to compel the minority to abide by its rulings. Should an expense of money be involved therein, the minority shall have to defray its part of the expenses.

We must keep in mind, however, that all the regulations enumerated above are binding upon the individual member because they are required by talmudic law; and that talmudic law, in turn, is binding upon the individual because it was once voluntarily accepted by the entire Jewish people as its way of life. The question arises, therefore, why should an individual, born free of any duty or obligation toward God or man, be bound by a code of conduct accepted years ago by his ancestors? R. Meir never explicitly discussed this problem, but indications are that his reason would be as follows: When a person is born in a certain community it is reasonable to assume, and we do so assume, that at one time or another, after he had reached his majority, he had favored, agreed to, and voluntarily accepted the way of life of his community, and thus became bound by all its customs, regulations, and religious obligations. Therefore, a Jew is bound by and must observe all the laws of the Talmud because he himself has, at one time, voluntarily accepted the Jewish religion as practiced and observed in his community.[212]

---

[212] The idea of the freedom of the individual, and his immunity from pressure or coercion of any kind, is so clearly implied by R. Meir in all his decisions regarding the *herem*, community regulations, and tax assessments, that we must assume that he did not subscribe to the idea that a father could bind his children and their children to a vow, a *takkanah*, or a *minhag*. Thus R. Meir protested against the assumption that a son, a minor, tacitly consented to the arrangements made by his father (L. 386). How, then, can a father make a vow that would be binding upon the son? We must also keep in mind that the idea that all the genera-

R. Meir would probably give the same reason for the law that a new settler was bound by all the customs and ordinances of the community he settled in (aside from the fact that this rule was grounded in talmudic law). Thus he would argue that it is reasonable to assume that when a person decided to move into a certain community, intending to become part of it, he voluntarily accepted, and agreed to abide by, all its rules and regulations, customs and ordinances.[213] The new settler must

tions were present at Mount Sinai and thus personally accepted the Torah, would not be a satisfactory explanation for R. Meir, since he himself pointed out that the acceptance at Mount Sinai was of no legal consequence. On the other hand the fact that a Jew is bound to observe the laws of the Torah, that a new settler is bound by all the regulations of the town he moves to, and that a student is subservient to his teacher and must accept all his decrees and orders — all point to the idea that it is assumed that when a person lives within a particular environmenl, he at one time or another was pleased with and accepted the "way of life" of his environment. Cf. R. Nissim Girundi, *Responsa* 48, quoted in note 129 above.

[213] Although in some instances R. Meir bases his ruling, that a new settler is bound by the customs of the city, on talmudic law, see Cr. 10: וכן משמע בפ׳ק דבבא בתרא (ח:) כמה יהא בעיר ויהא כאנשי העיר . . . אלמא דכופין הבא לגור ליתן עמהם למילי דצדקה אע׳פ שלא נשתתף עמהם מעולם . . . וה׳ה שכופין אותו להשתתף עמהם במס מהא דאמרינן פרק חזקת הבתים (נה.) פרדכס מסייע מחא, he fails to give any basis for such ruling in those instances where no talmudic proof can be adduced. Thus in Am II, 140 R. Meir writes: ואם בזה תקנו בני העיר עליהם לתת מס יראה לי דלאו כל כמיניהו, דרשאין בני העיר להסיע על קיצוצתן על בני עירם שהיו שם בשעת התקנה או שלבסוף באו לגור שם אבל זה שלא היה מהימנו בשעת התקנה ונם עכשו אינו גר שם לאו כל הימנו. The community ordinance thus referred to by R. Meir in his argument, would have been in opposition to talmudic law and to the custom of all other communities. A community may change talmudic law, in secular matters, as well as a prevailing custom, but such change can be adopted only through the unanimous approval of all the members of the community (as below). The opinion of the new settler, however, was not included in such unanimous agreement, and he could not be bound by it. The two talmudic laws cited in Cr. 10 as proof that a new settler is bound by the custom of the town, deal only with customs that are required by talmudic law (community charity chest, paying taxes cooperatively) regarding which, according to R. Meir, the principle "the majority rules" prevails. Just as the majority may force the minority to contribute to the community charity chest, and to pay their taxes cooperatively, so it may force the new settler to do so (see L. 108). Those ordinances, however, that require unanimous approval for their enactment (see below), form a class by themselves and no ruling regarding them may be deduced from the two talmudic laws cited in Cr. 10. Consequently the line of reasoning adduced in the text is relevant to the discussion and offers a possible explanation.

have accepted the entire pattern of life of the community, and therefore could not have excepted a particular rule. Even if he expressed his disapproval of a certain custom, and stated that he intended to disregard this particular *minhag* (custom),[214] his protestations were of no avail since the pattern of life of a community was so intricately woven that upon accepting part thereof one automatically accepted the whole.

It is obvious, however, that in accordance with this line of reasoning all talmudic laws and regulations no longer operative in a person's community, are of no consequence to him and he is not bound by them. This idea has far-reaching consequences and is the basis of the ruling that custom takes precedence over talmudic law.[215] Thus a person accepts the customs prevalent in his locality as part of its way of life, but does not accept the talmudic law supplanted by that custom. A person, therefore, is only bound by that part of talmudic law that has not been changed by the customs of his community, but he is definitely subjected to the *minhag* of his locality.[216]

Moreover, that part of human activity which was regulated by custom was completely outside the jurisdiction of talmudic law; in relation to such activity the authoritative bodies which had been set up by talmudic law, such as the "community" (meaning the majority) and the *Bet-din*, were devoid of any power of coercion. Thus, neither the majority of the members of

[214] See Cr. 222: ונכנס לעיר לדעת כן שנתפשר בפני עצמו עם השר בכך וכך שלא להשתתף עם הקהל. אם מדעת הקהל נחלק מהם הרשות בידו, אבל בלא דעת הקהל אינו רשאי להפרד מהם שלא לישא בעול עמהם, אחרי שמנהג העיר כך הוא להיות כל היהודים שותפים במס, רשאים בני העיר להסיע על קיצתם. Cf. L. 108; Pr. 995.

[215] See Cr. 10: על אודות ראובן הפורש מן הצבור שלא לתת לכיס של צדקה ושלא לתת עמהם מס, אם כך נהגו בעיר מימי קדם שלא לתת ביחד אלא כל אחד נותן לבד, אינם יכולים לכופו ולשנות מנהגם אם לא מדעתו. Such custom would be in opposition to talmudic law. See also Am II, 141; Berl. p. 276, no. 57; Pr. 106; 995; L. 213–4.

[216] Thus R. Meir treats even a private custom as a vow; see Pr. 95: שאלת על מי שרגיל להתענות בכל שנה תעניות שלפני ר"ה ושבין ר"ה ליוה"כ, או מי שרגיל שלא לאכול בשר ולא לשתות יין מי"ז בתמוז עד ט' באב ורוצה לחזור בו מחמת שאינו בריא, א"ל קרובי מורי ה"ר יודא כהן ז"ל שצריך ג' הדיוטות שיתירו לו . . . דהוי כמו נדר ונשאל לחכם ומתיר לו.

a community, nor the *Bet-din* established by the community, could change a *minhag* in a purely secular matter, if such change was opposed by the minority. Such a *minhag* became operative solely because of the voluntary consent on the part of each member of the community; it could, therefore, be abrogated only through such voluntary consent.[217]

The sphere of community life that was dominated by *minhag*, and consequently was outside the jurisdiction of talmudic law, was quite extensive and included the most important phase of community government, i. e. taxation. The laws governing taxation were rooted in local custom; the method of electing tax collectors, the powers of such collectors, the manner of assessment for taxes, the nature of property assessed, and the type of individuals exempted from taxation — all were subject to local custom.[218] If no custom existed in the community, that of the country was followed;[219] some communities were accustomed to follow the *minhagim* of a leading, neighboring community, and thus became obligated to abide by all its *minhagim*, even those they never yet had occasion to practice.[220] The rules

---

[217] [אינם רשאים] לחדש Pr. 968: ;אינם יכולים לכופו ולשנות מנהגם אם לא מדעתו
אין ב״ד Am II, 127: ;ואפילו אחד מבני [העיר] יכול לעכב עליו L. 108: ;דבר בלא דעת כולם
יכול לבטל דברי ב״ד חבירו אלא מדעת כל בני העיר, כי רשאין בני העיר להסיע על קיצותן ולשנות
שירצו כמו כולם מדעת; ibid. 141: הכל כמנהג שנהגתם עד עכשיו אין לכם לשנות אלא מכח כולכם.
If, however, the new ordinance was intended למנדר מלתא, a majority vote was sufficient for its enactment even though it thus abrogated a *minhag*; see Am II, 140.

[218] See Pr. 106: ;עניני מס אינם תלוים לא בסברא ולא בגמרא אך כפי מנהג המדינה ibid.
995: למה אתם שואלים דיני מסים שמהלכות מדינה הם נהרא נהרא ופשטיה. Cf. also previous note.

[219] Am II, 141: ואם עד הנה לא הייתם רגילים לתת אלא מס קצוב ולא שינה השר ולא הכביד
עליכם כי אם מס שלו הקצוב הוא לוקח, ועתה בא לשנות יש לכם לילך אחר מנהג קהלות אשכנז ויש
לדרוש ולתור אם בכל המקומות נוהגים . . . ואם אין מנהג העיר הכל כמנהג המדינה.

[220] See Pr. 106: ואם יש מנהג בקהילה או בעיר שנונדרים אחריה ילכו אחרי
;המנהג Berl. p. 320, no. 865: ומחמת חלוק לבם בוטל התמיד ומדת הדין לוקה ואין אמת ומשפט
ואתם אם אין cf. L. 182: ;ושלום בעיר ולא בכל המלכות הנונדרת אחריהם
במקומנו אין לנו מנהג ברור ibid. 214: ;לכם מנהג יש לכם לנהג . . . כמנהג הקהילה הסמוכה לכם
בזה כי לא בא דין זה מעולם לכאן . . . ואם בא דין זה לפנינו היינו שואלים מן הקהילות מה משפט.

and regulations governing taxation, therefore, could not be changed except by unanimous consent.

Thus R. Meir recognized two distinct spheres of community activity, which were mutually exclusive, and which were governed by divergent sets of law. One sphere of community activity dealt with the regulation and enforcement of religious practice, dispensation of justice, and the strengthening of the social, economic, and political position of the community. Any regulation or ordinance enacted for such purpose, designated למגדר מלתא,[221] was governed by talmudic law and was subject to the authority of the community organization. Within this sphere of community government were included regulation of business competition,[222] business practices,[223] family

[221] In some cases R. Meir decides that the principle "the majority rules" prevails in community law, and in others, that unanimous approval by all the members of the community is required for the enactment of a regulation or decree. Prof. Louis Finkelstein was quite puzzled by this seeming irregularity, see op. cit. pp. 53–4. However, R. Meir's principle was quite clear, and he followed it with unfailing logic: All community ordinances that could be included in the group classified as למגדר מלתא, were to be enacted by majority vote; all others required unanimous approval. See *Mordecai Hagadol* p. 182b: ובלאו הכי נראה דיש כח ביד ראשי הקהל להכריחם לפשרה ולעשות מה שיאמרו הפשרנים, דקיימא לן הפקר ב"ד הפקר. ירובעל ואפי' מיחה לא כל ...בדורו; Am II, 140: דהא מ ג ד ר מ ל ת א לעשות כן... מב"ב; הימנו בעודו שם למחות תקנות ב מ ג ד ר מ ל ת א אחר שרוב המהוגנים שבעיר הסכימו לכך; וטעמא נראה לי דטובי העיר הוו בעירם כחבר עיר למה שהוזכרו כמה גדולי הדור בכל Cr. 230: מקום. כמו שגדולי הדור הפקירן הפקר בכל מקום ב מ ג ד ר מ ל ת א ו ת ק נ ת א, הכי נמי טובי העיר בעירם. The טובי העיר were usually elected by majority vote (see Berl. p. 320, no. 865), their competence was, therefore, limited to matters classified as דבר פשוט הוא רשאין בני העיר להסיע על ל מ ג ד ר מ ל ת א ו ת ק נ ת א; cf. Pr. 980: קיצתן, כ"ש ב מ ג ד ר מ ל ת א הפקר ב"ד הפקר לקנוס ולענוש בגופו ושבחא. When the officers were elected by unanimous consent, however, their power was unlimited; ומה שטען שמחלו [טובי העיר] זה לזה בלא דעתו, לאו כל הימנו למחול חלקו see Am II, 127: בלא דעתו אא"כ נבררו טובי העיר מעיקרא מדעת כולם למחול ולעשות בכל צרכי צבור כפי רצונם; או ז' טובי העיר שהובררו מתחלה מדעת כל אנשי [העיר] לעיוני במלתא דמתא also Pr. 968: לקנוס ולענוש, גם הם רשאי' להסיע על קיצותן.

[222] See Am II, 123; Mord. B. M. 395; Pr. 677; 359: בני הקהל שאתם מלוים בעירם יכולים לעכב עליכם בלא יומא דשוקא. Cf. Pr. 983; Am II, 140, where an ordinance designed to stop competition from those who left town, was classified by R. Meir as למגדר מלתא; also Cr. 121; 156.

[223] See Pr. 980: כ"ש במגדר מלתא הפקר ב"ד הפקר לקנוס ולענוש בגופו ושבחא וראוי היה לקנסו ביותר.

law,[224] police duties,[225] protection of life and property,[226] administration of the civil code,[227] management of public buildings and institutions,[228] enforcement of religious practices,[229] and care of the poor and the helpless.[230] In all such matters the will of the majority prevailed; a *minhag* could be modified or completely abrogated by majority vote, and officers elected by majority vote formed the community organization that wielded undisputed authority.[231] The legal basis of the authority thus wielded by the majority was threefold: 1) Talmudic law;[232] 2) competence of authoritative court;[233] 3) the custom of the "ancients" as formulated in the *takkanah* of Rabbenu Gershom.[234]

The second sphere of community activity dealt with those regulations that served no religious purpose, and were not even

[224] See Cr. 72; 291; Pr. 81; 87; 483; 927; 934; 946; Am II, 48; Berl. p. 319, no. 780; *Mordecai Hagadol*, p. 212d; Mord. Ket. 287; ibid. Kid. 551; Hag. Maim. to *Ishut*, 22, 1; Tesh. Maim. to *Nashim* 35.

[225] See Pr. 383: ובכל קהלה וקהלה נוהגים לעשות תקנה גדולה ונדר לפי העניין; ibid. 994.

[226] Pr. 980; L. 246: ואי איישר חיל השואל והנשאל ימתחו על . . . ועוד שמכשיל את הרבים; Pr. 717; 979; 994; L. 248; 334; Am II, 127; P. 158a. העמוד

[227] See Pr. 715: אבל בזמן הזה שמכריחים הדיינים לדון עפ"י חרם הקהלות; Cr. 230; Pr. 825; 960; 978; 1001; L. 267; Am II, 123.

[228] See Berl. p. 320, no. 865.

[229] Pr. 994: כדרך שרגילים כל קהל וקהל לקנוס את עוברי עבירות ופורצי פרצות שמסיעין ואטו משום דעבר על שבועתו קנסי' ליה להוציא הקרקע מידו ולהחליטו; Am II, 123: על קיצותן ביד ראובן, האי לאו דינא הוא אלא אלא קנסא, והני קנסות אנן לא דייני' אלא אתה מורי' וקהלך אם נראה שנעשה דבר מכוער כזה כמו שנראה לקנוס לתן לצדקה.

[230] See Berl. p. 320, no. 865. Cf. Pr. 74–5; 918; Cr. 10; P. 512; Am II, 231; L. 208; 234; 425; 478; Tesh. Maim. to *Kinyan*, 28.

[231] See notes 222–30 above. These matters are included in the phrase: דבר דהוי מינדר מלתא וצורך הקהל שבלא זה אי אפשר להם להיות (see *Semak*, ed. Constantinople, 79), regarding which the principle "the majority rules" prevails.

[232] See notes 198–207 above; see especially Berl. p. 320, no. 865: יש כח ביד הרוב או ביד מי שמינו הרוב ראשים עליהם לכופם ולהכריחם בין בד'י בין בדא'ה עד שיאמרו רוצים אנו . . . כי ההיא דתניא בתוספתא דב'מ כופין בני העיר זה את זה לקנות להם ביהכ'נ . . . וכופין בני מבוי . . . כ'ש שאר דברים שיש צורך

[233] See Pr. 980: וטעמא נראה לי דטובי; Cr. 230: כ"ש במנדר מלתא הפקר ב'ד הפקר. העיר הוו בעירם כחבר עיר למה שהוזכרו כמה גדולי הדור בכל מקום, כמו שנדולי הדור הפקירן בעירם. The power of the court הפקר בכל מקום במנדר מלתא ותקנתא, הכי נמי טובי העיר to confiscate property was also limited to matters classified as למנדר מלתא, see Am II, 99: דלא אמרינן הפקר ב'ד הפקר אלא בשביל התקנה ומנדר מלתא.

[234] See Am II, 140.

calculated to improve the social, economic, or political status of
the community, but were primarily concerned with purely
secular matters that tended to give an advantage to one member of the community at the expense of another member.[235] The
laws and regulations governing taxation came prominently
within this sphere of community activity. In these matters
the laws governing *minhagim* prevailed, and an ordinance required unanimous approval by all the members of the community before it became law.[236] Any deviation from an accepted
custom or from talmudic law, that would give a financial advantage to some members of the community at the expense of
others, required the unanimous approval of all the members of
the community.

Thus R. Meir writes:[237]

> If there is an established custom in the community of which
> A is a member, that every member pays his taxes directly
> to the authorities, and distributes his charity-funds as he
> sees fit, the community cannot force A to abandon this
> practice unless A agrees to the change. But, if the custom
> was that all the members were to pay their taxes and dis-
> tribute their charities collectively, A must abide by this
> custom. Where the community is new and no custom exists,

---

[235] The laws of taxation regulate the distribution of the burden of taxes on
the individual members. Any change in these laws and regulations tends to shift
the burden from one member to another. Consequently, R. Meir did not permit
any change in these laws except if passed by unanimous vote. In this matter he
followed Rabbenu Tam who ruled: ואם ע״י פשרה וטובי העיר הוו כחבר עיר וכל כמנייהו.
(Cr. 230). נגזרה הגזירה לאו כל כמיניהו דכל פשרה לא פקועי ממונא לא הוו כחבר עיר

[236] See Cr. 10; 222; Pr. 968; L. 108: ואפי' אחד מבני [העיר] יכול לעכב עליו; Am II,
127: הכל כמנהג שנהגתם ibid. 141: אין ב״ד יכול לבטל דברי ב״ד חבירו אלא מדעת כל בני העיר
עד עכשיו, אין לכם לשנות אלא מכח כולכם. For the same reason a *pardekat* (an idle or
retired person) had the right to evict from town a person who had no settling
rights there; for the *herem hayishub* was a *minhag* of the town, and it could not be
abrogated or waived in anybody's favor, if a single individual (even a *pardekat*)
objected thereto: see L. 215.

[237] Cr. 10.

talmudic law prevails which provides that the inhabitants of a town may force one another to pay their taxes collectively and to establish a community charity fund to which every member must contribute.

In another Responsum R. Meir writes:[238]

If you have been accustomed to be partners in the payment of all kinds of taxes to the overlord, viz.: normal taxes, exorbitant taxes, poll taxes, tallages, penalties, and whatever other levies came to his mind, you must assess each member, for the present extortion, in the same manner and according to the same procedure as heretofore. If you have been accustomed either to tax real property, or not to tax it, you may not deviate from whatever was the custom except by unanimous consent. If, however, up to the present you never paid any but normal taxes, if heretofore your overlord never demanded any extraordinary taxes, but was satisfied with collecting the regular, yearly, tax, you must search out and follow the custom of German communities. If the custom throughout Germany, when a community is arrested for the purpose of extortion, is to exempt real property from taxation, you may not tax such property; and if the custom is to assess such property at one-half, one-third, or one-quarter, of its actual value, you must follow this custom. This is required by strict law; but I would prefer that you voluntarily adjust your differences and reach some/compromise, if possible. You need not further inquire of me regarding this case, for my answer will invariably be the same: either you reach a compromise [i. e. unanimous agreement], follow your local custom, or, in case no local custom exists, follow the custom of your country.

Even when talmudic law specifically authorized the inhabitants of a town to force one another to establish a certain rule of community cooperation, R. Meir did not permit the

238 Am II, 141.

establishment of such rule if it ran contrary to the custom of the community, unless it was so established by unanimous consent.

Thus R. Meir wrote:[239]

> The Jews of T who have banded together, electing leaders and giving them authority to levy taxes and manage all communal affairs, had no right to do so even though they represented a majority of the Jewish inhabitants of T, as long as the minority took no part in the reorganization; for no new custom or institution can be established in a community without the knowledge and consent of all its inhabitants.

Although talmudic law explicitly states that the inhabitants of a town may force one another (which according to R. Meir's interpretation, in several instances, means that the majority may compel the minority)[240] to organize themselves into a cooperative group for the purpose of levying the tax and managing community affairs, R. Meir rules that they may not do so unless they have the "consent" of every inhabitant of the town, since it constitutes the establishment of "a new custom or institution". Similarly any regulation that would go beyond the limits set by talmudic law to the coercive authority of the community organization, would require unanimous approval for its enactment since it would mean the establishment of a new custom. Thus R. Meir writes:[241]

> We find no law in the Talmud that would permit members of a community to coerce one another into giving charity to the non-resident poor beyond providing a loaf of bread and a night's lodging for the itinerant pauper. If the residents of a town voluntarily agree to give more ample support to the non-resident poor, in order to silence the complaints and evil talk of passersby, they may do so. But,

---

[239] *Text*, no. 530.   [240] See Berl. p. 320, no. 865.
[241] Tesh. Maim. to *Kinyan*, 28.

should one resident dissent, and insist on giving his "tithe" (charity money) to his indigent relatives instead of to the non-resident poor, the other members of the community would have no right to interfere with him.

To summarize R. Meir's view on the legal basis of community government: The innate, unbounded freedom of the individual may justly be curbed only by his voluntary consent. A Jew has voluntarily agreed to be bound by talmudic law, and by the *minhagim* of his community and his country. A *minhag* should take precedence over talmudic law, since that part of talmudic law that was displaced by the *minhag* was never accepted by the Jew. Talmudic law permitted the inhabitants of a town to organize themselves into a political body, the community, and invested that body with certain rights in a specific sphere of community activity within which the principle "the majority rules" was to prevail. Custom and the *takkanot* have also invested certain rights in the community organization. Thus regulations and ordinances enacted for religious purposes or for the benefit of the public (both included in the term למגדר מלתא) by majority vote, were valid because of talmudic law and the *takkanot*. A regulation or ordinance that served no religious purpose, nor was calculated to be of any benefit to the public, could also be enacted by majority vote in such communities where the local custom gave the majority the right to decide on all matters, religious or secular. Where no such custom existed, however, any deviation from talmudic law or from the *minhagim*, in purely secular matters, required unanimous approval before such deviation became law. Thus by combining the ideas of the basic freedom of the individual and the sanctity of contract, R. Meir constructed an excellent theory of the legal basis of community government that served him as a guide in all his attempts to settle community disputes and litigations.

CHAPTER V

R. Meir's Later Life.

R. Meir's peaceful life as a scholar and teacher was rudely interrupted by the turbulent political events that followed the termination of the interregnum, the election of Rudolph I, of Hapsburg, as Emperor of Germany, and his firm taking over the reins of the empire. For some reason life in Germany became impossible for R. Meir. Leaving behind his large house in Rothenburg and giving up his exalted position and his beloved school, he set out for countries beyond the sea, taking with him his whole family, his daughters, and his sons-in-law.

Nor was R. Meir alone in this self-imposed exodus. Hundreds of Jewish families from Mayence, Speyer, Worms, Oppenheim, and the towns of the Wetterau, abandoned their goods, left their homes, synagogues and communities, and fled from Germany, while many others prepared to do likewise. While he was in Lombardy, however, he was recognized by an apostate who reported him to the authorities. He was then apprehended and delivered to Emperor Rudolph. Thus began the tragedy of his later years, for he was kept in prison for the rest of his life.

Jewish sources tell the story of his emigration and arrest briefly, as follows:[1]

[1] See Azulai, *Shem ha-Gedolim*, ed. Ben Jacob (Vienna, 1864), Addenda, 47:
ר"מ מרוטנבורג בר ברוך שם פעמיו לדרך לעבור הים הוא וביתו ובנותיו וחתניו וכל אשר לו, ויבוא עד עיר אחת יושבת בין ההרים הרמים שקורין לומברדש גיבורג'א בל'א ורצה לישב שמה עד אשר יאספו אצלו כל העוברים עמו. והנה פתאום ההגמון מבזילא רכב מרומא דרך אותה העיר ועמו איש אחד ושמו קינפפא והכיר מורנו והגיד להגמון וגרם שהפחה מיינהארט מנערץ שר של אותה העיר
125

R. Meir of Rothenburg, son of Baruch, set out to go across
the sea together with his family, his daughters, and his
sons-in-law. He came to a town situated in the moun-
tainous region called Lombardische Gebirge (ש"למברדי
גיבורג"א) where he intended to wait for his fellow travelers
who were to join him on this journey. The bishop of Basel,
however, on his way from Rome, rode through that town
in the company of an apostate named Knippe (or Kinpe)
who recognized R. Meir and informed the bishop. The
bishop brought about the arrest of R. Meir through the
ruler of that town, Count Meinhardt of Goerz, on the 4th
of Tammuz 5046 (June, 28th 1286). Count Meinhardt
delivered R. Meir to King Rudolph who kept him in prison
till the day of his death, on the 19th of Iyyar 5053 (April,
27th 1293).

This account of R. Meir's emigration, arrest, detention and
death, is given in two different sources: 1) The *Minhag-buch*
of Worms, written in 1625 and copied by Ahron Fuld and L.
Lewysohn;[2] 2) a written note on a *Mishne Torah* printed by
Caromly in Jost's *Annalen*.[3] These two sources, however, are
very similar in content and style, and were probably both copied
from an earlier source.[4]

The *Annales Colmarienses*, edited by Böhmer in his *Fontes
Rerum Germanicarum*, give the following report for the year
1287:[5] *Rex Rudolphus cepit de Rotwilre Judeum, qui a Judeis
magnus in multis scientiis dicebatur et apud eos magnus habe-*

תפסהו ד' תמח שנת מ'ו לאלף הששי ומסרוהו למלך רודאלף ונפטר בתפיסה בעוה"ר י"ט אייר שנת
נ'ג וקבורה לא היתה לו עד שנת ס'נ ד' אייר, ואז ערה רוח נדיבה בלב נדיב בק'ק ורנקבורט ופיזר
הון עתק עד שהביאו לקבורה בקבר אבותיו בק'ק וירמיישא, ואותו נדיב נפטר אחריו וקנה שביתתו אצלו.

[2] See L. Lewysohn נפשות צדיקים, p. 36; Ahron Fuld in *Shem ha-Gedolim*, ed.
Pollak (Frankfurt A.M.), p. 154. See also S. E. Blogg כפר החיים, ed. Hannover,
1848, pp. 304-5 who claims to have read the same account on R. Meir's tombstone. For the wording of the inscription, however, see Lewysohn, op. cit. p. 35
(quoted in note 8 below).
[3] Isaac Marcus Jost, *Israelitische Annalen*, no. 44 (1839), p. 349.
[4] See Lewysohn, op. cit. p. 35.
[5] P. 23. Cf. Wiener, *Regesten* I, p. 13, note.

batur in scienta et honore. There is no doubt that this note refers to the arrest of R. Meir, and that Rotwilre is identical with Rothenburg.[6] The Dominican monk of Colmar, however, probably heard of R. Meir's arrest half a year after it actually took place, and therefore recorded it in the year 1287. There is also the possibility that it was more than six months before R. Meir was delivered to Rudolph and conveyed to prison, and hence the final incarceration is thus recorded by the monk from Colmar as having taken place in 1287.[7] There is, therefore, no discrepancy in the date of R. Meir's arrest between the Jewish sources and the *Annales Colmarienses.* Moreover, the epitaph on R. Meir's tombstone, found in the city of Worms, gives the fourth of Tammuz, 5046, as the date of his arrest.[8]

The dramatic surprise of this strange event is greatly heightened by the fact that R. Meir's emigration was but part of a mass movement to leave Germany, a sudden exodus of the Jews on a large scale that must have been caused by deep desperation. That many Jews emigrated from Germany in the year 1286, we learn from an official letter sent by Rudolph I to the authorities and burghers of Mayence, Speyer, Worms, Oppenheim, and the towns of the Wetterau.[9] In this letter Rudolph

[6] See Graetz, *Geschichte d. Jud. Volkes*, vol. VII, note 9; Wiener, op. cit. p. XIV; Back, op. cit. p. 69.

[7] See Back, l. c.

[8] Lewysohn, op. cit. p. 35: ציון הלז לראש מרנא ורבנא מאיר בן הרב ר' ברוך אשר תפשו מלך רומי בארבעה ימים לר"ח תמוז שנת ארבעים ושש לאלף הששי, ונפטר בתפיסה י"ט באייר; cf. Yehiel שנת המשים ושלש ולא נתן לקבורה עד ארבעה ימים לירח אדר שנת ששים לאלף הששי Halpern, סדר הדורות, for year 1286: הפס ה' לאלף מ"ו שנת :ישן בקובץ מצאתי הכותב ואני מלך רומי שהיה נקרא אדולף את ר' מאיר ונפטר תוך התפיסה י"ט אייר נ"נ לפ"ק ולא נתן לקבורה עד אדר ס"ז.

[9] Schunk, *Codex Diplomaticus Mogunt.* 1797, p. 122, nos. 51–3; cf. Oswald Redlich, *Rudolph von Habsburg*, pp. 498–9; Wiener, op. cit. p. 12, no. 74; Karl Zeumer, *Die Deutschen Städtesteuern im 12. und 13. Jahrhundert*, (1878) vol. I. p. 139; Herbert Fischer, *Die verfassungsrechtliche Stellung der Juden in den deutschen Städten während des dreizenten Jahrhunderts*, Bresslau 1931, p. 15; Guido Kisch, "The Jewry-Law of the Medieval German Law Books", *Proceedings of the American Academy for Jewish Research*, Vol. X. (1940), p. 131.

asserted that since both the person and the property of the Jews as a group, and of every Jew as an individual, belonged to the king, and since a number of the Jewish residents of the above-mentioned towns had fled beyond the sea without previously obtaining the king's permission, it was fitting and proper that he should appropriate the real and personal property they had left behind; the archbishop of Mayence and Count Eberhard of Katzenellenbogen were appointed to take over and manage this property.

The exact number of Jews who participated in this mass exodus, is unknown; but it must have been considerable to occasion such extraordinary measures on Rudolph's part. In Mayence alone, we learn, the burghers appropriated fifty-four houses that belonged to Jews who had left Germany that year.[10]

What was that compelling reason that forced R. Meir, at an advanced age, to leave his exalted position and his comfortable home and to seek refuge in a strange land? What was the great catastrophe and deep desperation that caused this widespread emigration of hundreds of Jewish families to lands unknown?

Graetz, Back, and other scholars,[11] believe that the Jews left Germany because of the frequent blood accusations and massacres that took place in Germany between 1283 and 1286. Graetz cites the following cases: 1) The blood accusation and the massacre of ten Jews in the city of Mayence on the nineteenth of April, 1283; 2) the murder of twenty-six Jews in Bachrach on the same day; 3) the killing of sixteen Jews in Brückerhausen, a few days later; 4) the burning of a section of the Jewish community of Mulrichstadt in the latter part of March of that year; and 5) the blood-accusation and result-

---

[10] K. A. Schaab, *Diplomatische Geschichte der Juden in Mainz*, 1855, p. 60.

[11] See Grätz, *Geschichte der Juden*, vol. VII (fourth edition), p. 173 f.; ibid. p. 423; Back, op. cit. p. 65; Zimmels, op. cit. pp. 4 f.

ing massacre in Munich, two and a half years later, in which one
hundred and eighty Jews were burned in the synagogue.

The first four calamities happened three years before the
emigration movement started; and after these but a single,
though serious, violent action occured before 1287. Massacres
were not new to the Jews and did not surprise them. Blood
accusations and mob actions continued throughout the thirteenth century[12] and nothing new happened during the years
1280–1286 to cause the Jews to lose heart and flee from Germany
en masse. It is hard to believe that a few bloody riots com-
paratively light in number of casualties, should occasion a widely
spread exodus of the Jews of entirely unaffected localities.
There must have been a deeper reason and an all embracing
circumstance which forced the Jews to leave their well established communities and to seek new fortunes in foreign lands.[13]

Moreover, the detention of R. Meir in prison presents another perplexing problem: Why was he not released from custody? Both Jewish and non-Jewish sources tell us that the Jews
made strenuous efforts to ransom their Rabbi. The *Chronicon
Colmariense*, for the year 1288,[14] records the fact that the Jews
promised the emperor Rudolph twenty thousand *marks* to bring
to justice the murderers of the Jews of Boppard and Oberwessel,
and release their learned and highly honored Rabbi. This Rabbi,
whom the *Chronicon* describes as the head of the Jewish school
and as being divinely honored by his fellow Jews, could be none
other then R. Meir. At the same time, Rabbi Hayyim b. Yehiel

---

[12] For massacres of Jews during the thirteenth century, see Aronius, op. cit.
nos. 413, 469, 472, 473, 474, 529, 539, 540, 542, 543, 546, 666, 669, 695, 704, 705,
728, 740, 748.

[13] Cf. Karl Brisch, *Geschichte der Juden in Cöln und Umgebung aus ältester
Zeit bis zur Gegenwart*, 1879, p. 163. *Die Ursache, welche die Auswanderung vieler
rheinischer Judengemeinden in letzten Viertel des dreizenten Jahrhunderts ver-
anlaste, zu ermitteln, hat noch nicht recht gelingen wollen; den Verfolgungen haben
vor — und nachher stattgefunden, ohne dass die Betroffenen den Wanderstab ergriffen
hatten. Es scheint somit tiefer liegende Beweggründe demals mitgewirkt zu haben* . . .

[14] Böhmer, op. cit. p. 72; cf. Grätz, op. cit. note 9.

of Cologne[15] tells us in one of his Responsa[16] that in 1287 twelve communities promised to give to King Rudolph twenty-three thousand pounds, if he would grant their request. The two sources speaking of promises made to the emperor of twenty thousand *marks* and twenty-three thousand pounds respectively, probably refer to the same request made to him, viz: justice and protection for the Jews of Boppard and Oberwessel, and the release of R. Meir.[17] Thus we see that the Jews were prepared to expend an enormous sum of money in order to ransom their beloved teacher; why, then, was he not released?

Graetz and Back believe that R. Meir did not allow the communities to ransom him at such a high price, so that the Gentiles should not resort to the capture of great rabbis as a means of extorting large sums of money from the Jews.[18] This assumption is based on the statement of R. Solomon Luria in his שמעתי על מהר"ם מרוטנבורק which reads: יים של שלמה[19]

ז"ל שהיה תפוס במגדל איינשהיים כמה שנים והשר תבע מן הקהילות סך גדול והקהלות היו רוצים לפדותו ולא הניח כי אמר אין פודין את השבויים יותר מכדי דמיהם.

This report heard by R. Solomon,[20] however, cannot be entirely true. R. Asher, commenting on the talmudic statement

---

[15] See Michael, *Or ha-Hayyim*, no. 876; R. Hoeniger, and M. Stern, *Das Judenschreinsbuch der Laurenzpfarre zu Köln*, Berlin, 1888.

[16] Pr. 241; cf. Excursus II.

[17] Cf. Graetz, l. c.; Back, op. cit. p. 74. R. Hayyim b. Isaac Or Zarua also reports a similar payment that was to be made to the king while R. Meir was in prison. See *Responsa* 110: ועוד כי אני הייתי ברצונם כשיצאו מצרפת ונתוועדו כל הקהלות למגנצא ומורי הרב רבי מנחם מוירצבורק ומורי הרב ר' היילמון ומורי הר'ר אשר וכל הגדולים שהיו ברינוס וראשי הקהלות כי הוצרכו ליתן מס גדול למלך ל' אלף ותבעו בעלי מטלטלין ליתומים מן הקרקעות כי ברצונם נהגו שאפילו יש לאדם כמה בתים שוים כמה אלפים אינו נותן מס מהם ושמעתי באותה שעה שמורינו ורבינו מאיר זצ"ל אמר אפילו אם היו חייבים ליתן מס מן הקרקעות לא היו חייבים ליתן כי אם רביע שווים מההיא דפיאה, ומפי מורי לא שמעתי כי היה תפוס אבל מפי מורי הרב ר' שלמה זצ"ל שמעתי כן בהיותי בפרונא. R. Hayyim b. Isaac must refer here to the same payment made to Rudolph, while the ל' אלף is probably a corruption of כ. אלף.

[18] Grätz, l. c.; Back, op. cit. p. 78.   [19] *Gittin*, IV, 66.

[20] We must draw a clear distinction between R. Solomon's Responsum 29, where he inserts a copy of an historical document that was written by a contemporary of R. Meir, and his statement in the יס של שלמה, which was based on

אין פודין את השבויים יותר מכדי דמיהם, explicitly decides that talmudic scholars should be ransomed at any price, and makes no mention of the heroic gesture ascribed to R. Meir.[21] Further in a Responsum written in prison R. Meir says:[22] ופי' זרעים וטהרות שלי לכשאצא בשלום אטרח ברצון שיהיו מועתקים לך. ובתפיסתי את בוראי לא שכחתי ובתורתו ובירְאתו דבקתי. והמתנדבים יחזו את ה' בנועם. וכתם זהב לא יועם. This shows he expected to be released soon. On other occasions he also wrote that a Jew cannot expect to be released from the clutches of his captors unless he pays a heavy ransom.[23] He must have expected to be released through the payment of a ransom. Furthermore, the clause והמתנדבים יחזו את ה' בנועם must be interpreted as an expression of thanks to those princes in Israel, the leaders of the various communities, who volunteered to raise the ransom money;[24] while the words וכתם זהב לא יועם[25] express a prayer and a wish that the payment of such money be effective in obtaining his release. Again, in the Responsum of R. Hayyim b. Yehiel cited above, the author asserts that at first Rudolph promised to grant the request of the communities, but subsequently refused to live up to his promise; that nevertheless he enforced collection of the sum promised by the communities.[26] Thus we learn from this source that the ransom money was paid, but that Rudolph still refused to release R. Meir.

R. Meir, therefore, remained in custody not because he forbade the communities to ransom him, but because of the

---

an oral report, notoriously subject to error. An oral statement made almost three hundred years after the event is usually devoid of historical truth.

[21] Asheri to Gittin, IV, 44: אין פודין את השבוין יותר על כדי דמיהם . . . וכן תלמיד חכם שנשבה בהא לא תקון כדאמרינן . . . כל שכן מי שהוא כבר אדם גדול [שצריך לפדותו אפילו יותר מכדי דמיו].

[22] L. 151.

[23] See Cr. 33; L. 345; Pr. 39.

[24] The expression יחזו את ה' is probably based on Exodus 24, 11: ואל אצילי בני ישראל לא שלח ידו, ויחזו את הא' ויאכלו וישתו.

[25] A reference to Lamentations 4, 1.

[26] Pr. 241: ועל כל זה הלכו וקבצו מס על הקהלה שלנו.

treachery and double dealing of the emperor. The perplexing problem remains, therefore: Why did Rudolph refuse to release R. Meir, and what did he expect to gain from R. Meir's continued confinement?

We believe that the reason for both, the sudden exodus of hundreds of Jewish families from Germany and the continued retention of R. Meir in custody, is to be sought in the political situation of the time; more specifically, in the severe struggle on the part of each of the three powerful political bodies, the emperor, the lay and ecclesiastical nobility, and the burghers, to increase its power at the expense of the other two. The prosperous, Jewish communities constituted a lucrative source of income highly coveted by the emperor, the overlords, and the burghers, and were jealously guarded by those who acquired it (mostly during the interregnum) by fair means or foul. The right to tax the Jews thus became the bone of contention over which the three powers fiercely fought for decades; while, in the process, they mercilessly crushed under foot the security, the freedom, and the dignity of the German Jews.

Let us, therefore, in order to find the solution to our problem consider the relationship of the Jews to the civil authorities during this period, their political status from the point of view of the civil authorities as well as from their own point of view, and the changes in such relationship and status wrought by the interregnum. As the great majority of R. Meir's Responsa were written after 1250, they should serve as reliable sources for the period under consideration.

In R. Meir's Responsa we find that the Jews paid taxes to the lay or ecclesiastical lord of the town,[27] or to the burghers.[28]

---

[27] See Pr. 134; 226; 331; 359; 595; 677; 708; 938; 944; 1001; L. 108; 217; 381; Am II, 19; 122; 127; 128; 139; 141; 157; Cr. 9; 32; 33; 49; 53; 305; 307; Mord. B. K. 190. Cf. Aronius, op. cit. nos. 319; 325; 385; 430; 434; 455; 552; 564; 569; 574; 575; 581; 591; 615; 636; 637; 644; 664; 676; 710; 751.

[28] See Pr. 104; 995; Mord. B. B. 475; Berl. p. 276, no. 58; cf. Aronius, op. cit.

In the more than sixty of these Responsa dealing with taxation, however, we do not find a single case where the Jews of Germany paid taxes to the king.[29] The local chief of the town or settlement, taxed his Jews according to their volume of business;[30] he allowed rich Jews apart from the community to pay their taxes directly to him;[31] he made arrangements with new settlers as to the amount of taxes they would have to pay;[32] he attracted new settlers by granting them release from taxation for a certain period of time.[33] Further he helped the Jews in their business transactions and in enforcing collection of their debts;[34] but sometimes he levied extraordinary taxes on the Jews[35] and even imprisoned them in order to extort large sums of money from them.[36] Yet no mention is made of any taxes paid to the king. We must conclude, therefore, that during the years 1250 and 1286 the great majority of the Jews of Germany paid no taxes to the king.[37]

---

nos. 604; 622; 645; 662; 672–3. For taxes paid to the king see Isert Roesel, *Die Reichssteuern der deutschen Judengemeinden von ihren Anfängen bis zur Mitte des 14. Jahrhunderts*, Reprint.

[29] Three of R. Meir's Responsa deal with paying taxes to the king. Let us examine them, however: a) Pr. 131: ואשר שאלה מעניני מס שהורגלו היהודים בכל מלכות המלך לתת בשותפות. This Responsum, however, was sent to Bohemia and dealt with taxes paid to the king of Bohemia. See Excursus I. b) Pr. 943: אם המלך העביט הקהל והעליל עליהם בשביל ראובן שלא בא ליום מועד ולקח מהם ממון. According to R. Meir, however, the king extorted money from the community; we cannot, therefore, classify it as taxation; c) Tesh. Maim. to *Kinyan*, 2, is also a case of extortion.

R. Meir does speak about taxes paid to the king in L. 381: ה'מ במס הקצוב שנובה המלך בכל שנה קצבה וסכום יחד מכל בני העיר. This statement, however, probably refers to talmudic times. Thus in this very Responsum R. Meir asserts that each overlord is completely independent of any central authority: אבל עכשיו כל שר ושר הוא במלכותו כמו מלך ומי יאמר לו מה תעשה.

[30] See Pr. 331; 983; L. 217.

[31] See Pr. 134; 331; 708; 944; L. 108; Am II, 122; Cr. 10.

[32] See Pr. 1001; L. 108; Am II, 122; Cr. 9.   [33] See L. 108.

[34] See Pr. 105; 677.   [35] See Pr. 995; L. 381; Am II, 141; Cr. 53.

[36] See Pr. 226; 595; 938; Cr. 32–3; 305; 307; Am II, 19–22; 127–8; 157; Mord. B. K. 190.

[37] For non-Jewish sources regarding the payment of taxes to the local rulers, see Aronius, op. cit. nos. 319; 325; 385; 430; 434; 455; 552; 564; 569; 574–5; 581;

The emperors of Germany throughout the thirteenth century bestowed their income from various Jewish communities as gifts upon the local rulers;[38] while during the interregnum this alienation of the income of the crown grew apace.[39] Moreover, during the interregnum the local rulers appropriated to themselves the right to tax the Jews in their territory regardless of whether or not they ever received such rights from the king. Thus, in a Responsum regarding a Jew who moved out of a certain town and refused to pay his taxes together with the community, R. Meir wrote:

> I have seen many instances where men who had left their town and had moved to places scarcely half a mile away, no longer paid their taxes to the community. Formerly, when the country had a king, the Jews of the surrounding territory — even those who lived eight miles away from town, in fact those who lived in the entire bishopric — would pay their taxes to the king collectively. [But this is no longer done].[40]

The Jews, on the other hand, were not averse to this change since it heightened their feeling of independence and personal freedom. Upon settling in a particular place the Jews negotiated with the local ruler as to the amount of taxes they were to pay him.[41] If the overlord proved himself too oppressive, the Jews

591; 604; 615; 622; 636-7; 644-5; 662; 664; 672-3; 676-7; 681; 703; 710; 714; 733; 751-2.

[38] See Aronius, op. cit. nos. 379 and 548 (bishopric of Mayence); 384 (the Jews of Mayence, Erfurt and other places); 459 (the Jews of Regensburg); 385 (to the bishop of Worms); 434 (to the church of Worms); 563-4 (to the bishop of Würzburg, cf. nos. 593; 675); 569 (the Jews of Helmstedt are under the jurisdiction of the abbe).

[39] See Aronius, op. cit. nos. 583; 591; 591a; 615; 664; 672-3; 676; 687; 701; 710; 751; 763.

[40] Cr. 121: וכהנה וכהנה ראיתי שהרבה הלכו ממקומם לגור במקום אחר שהוא בטורח חצי פרסה מן העיר ולא נתנו מס עם הקהל. כי אם כשהיה מלך בעולם אז היו נותנים למלך עמהם אפילו עד ח' פרסאות כל מה שהיה שייך להגמוניא.

[41] See Am II, 122; L. 108: ועתה חשקה נפש ראובן לצאת ולדור עם שמעון וחביריו תחת שרם בעירם, וטרם שבא נתפשר עם שר של שמעון בכך וכך לשנה.

left him and moved to the territory of a more liberal overlord.[42]
They jealously guarded their right of freedom of motion, their
right as free and independent individuals who could leave a
settlement at will, without first obtaining the overlord's permission.[43] According to R. Meir the Jews paid taxes to the lord
of the town because he permitted them to live and to earn
profit in his city. The tax paid to the overlord, therefore,
resulted from his ownership of the town, and not from any
servile relationship on the part of the Jews.[44]

From the Responsa we also learn that the burghers coveted
the right to tax the Jews. During the interregnum the burghers
became a strong power in the town and the Jews were afraid
to arouse their enmity.[45] The thirteenth century witnessed the
growth and development of the German town, and the long,
continuous struggle of the burghers for the control of it.[46] They
were anxious to weaken the power and authority of the overlord of the town within its limits, and during the interregnum
they took full advantage of the general chaos. Accordingly
they were interested in decreasing the overlord's income from
the Jews, and therefore, strove to prevent him from levying extraordinary and extortionate taxes upon the Jews of the town.[47]

[42] See Berl. p. 286, no. 348: וכשראה שמעון שהפקיד העליל עליו בקש מן השרים ומן
שתי עיירות לבקש הפקיד ליתן לו רשות לדור בעיר אחרת שהיא תחת ממשלתו כמו כן ונתן לו השר
רשות. Mord. B. K. 190; Cr. 305; Pr. 1001.

[43] See L. 114; Aronius, op. cit. no. 588; ibid. no. 676.

[44] See Pr. 941: וע״ז סמכו הקדמונים שלא להטיל מס על הקרקעות כי כל המס אינו אלא
מן המשא ומתן; ibid. 1001: ומי [להתישב בעיר] אבל הכא העיר של השר ולמי שחפץ נותן רשות
שאינו טוב לפניו יכול לעכב עליו אפילו דריסת הרגל... אבל בכסף גולגולת ומסים אינו חייב
אבל שאר מסים קצבתם שנותנים בכל שנה ושנה למס: Berl. p. 276 no. 58: כשאינו גר תחת השר
כגון מסים: Mord. B. B. 475b; L. 108: לשר או לעירונים זכו מחמת רוחים שמרויחים בעיר
להעלות לשר העיר שכל שמירת העיר מוטלת עליו להצילם מן הנייסות.

[45] See Pr. 995: ונם העירונים נרמו לנפשותינו לעשות כמו שעשו ברינוס; R. Hayyim Or
Zarua, Responsa 110: אבל כאן אם יאמרו לעירונים לא ניתן לא יקחו אשר להם לא ממון ולא
בתים, אלא מחמת שכפופים להם בעוונותינו שרבו, הם יריאים שישנאו אותם וירע להם בכמה דברים
מהמת כן צריכים לקיים צוום וליתן מה שאומרים. Cf. Herbert Fischer, op. cit. pp. 108–19.

[46] Herbert Fischer, op. cit. pp. 54–98.

[47] See Aronius, op. cit. nos. 593; 621; 636; 644; 672; 673; 674; 675; 676; 681;
687; 701; 709; 710; 715; 716; 717; 751; 760.

At the same time the burghers were eager to establish their own right to tax the Jews of their town. In many places where the Jews were accustomed to guard personally part of the walls of the town, the burghers substituted a tax in lieu of such duties.[48] The amount demanded from them was often much higher than was necessary to hire guards for the walls, but ostensibly the tax was payment for such guard service.[49] Often the burghers used no other excuse for taxing the Jews than that of force. Thus we read in a Responsum of the claims of a woman who refused to pay her share of the taxes which had been paid to the burghers before she came to town.[50] The community's reply was, in part: "The burghers threatened to do what they did on the Rhine". The woman averred: "The tax was not paid in order to save your lives; you always paid taxes to the burghers, whenever they demanded them from you". Thus in order to compel the Jews to pay taxes to them, the burghers often resorted to exaggerated threats of violence.

The Jews, therefore, were often compelled to pay taxes to two masters: to the lay or ecclesiastical head of the town, and to the burghers. These two tax recipients carefully watched over the Jews, not permitting anyone to molest them and thus diminish their ability to pay taxes. In a Responsum regarding a Jew who was imprisoned by his powerful debtor and forced to cancel the latter's debt, R. Meir asserts that the lord imprisoned the Jew in order to extort additional money from him, and not in order to force him to cancel his debts.[51] He argued thus:

> Moreover, we must assume that A's captors would not commit such an outrage against the bishop and the burghers

[48] See Pr. 104; cf. Aronius, op. cit. no. 582.

[49] Herbert Fischer, op. cit. pp. 99–106. Sometimes the strengthening of the town walls furnished the excuse for taxation; see Hayyim Or Zarua, *Responsa* 110.

[50] Pr. 995; *Text*, 557.

[51] Cr. 305: יעוד אנן כהדי שלא היו עושין פריצות גדול נגד העירונים וההגמון רק כדי לפטור מחוב מקולקל שכבר נעשו עליו מחוסרי אמנה שקורין טרוולי'ש (treulos).

merely to cancel a debt of a faithless debtor who had already lost his credit. Your contention that A's captors were intent on cancelling the above debt in order that the over-lord should not be called a defaulter, is indeed untenable. The duke did not object to becoming known as a thief, a robber, a highwayman, and an extortionist; why should he object to the appellation defaulter? It is incredible.

Thus the imprisonment of a Jew was considered an outrage committed against the burghers and the bishop of the town. The overlord and the burghers vigorously opposed any one who tried to extort money from the Jews living in their territory. We, therefore, find continuous wrangling between the burghers and the overlords regarding their respective right of taxation over the Jews, each party restraining the other from oppressing them, since mistreatment often meant extortion of money under false pretexts.[52]

Already in 1244, archbishop Siegfried II of Mainz found it necessary to assure the burghers that he would deal justly with the Jews of that town.[53] In 1252, the Jews of Cologne demanded the burghers' guaranty that the privileges granted to them by the archbishop would not be infringed upon by him;[54] and six years afterwards the burghers of Cologne became aroused because the archbishop mistreated the Jews.[55] Throughout the interregnum and even towards the end of the century, we find the burghers endeavoring to diminish the control of the lay or ecclesiastical lord of the town over its Jewish inhabitants, and striving to gain the right to tax them. We find evidence of this encroachment of the burghers upon the rights of the over-lords in Luzern,[56] in Worms,[57] in Constance,[58] in Halle,[59] in

---

[52] See following notes; also Herbert Fischer, op. cit. note 3; also pp. 106-22.
[53] See Aronius, op. cit. 548.
[54] Ibid. nos. 588; 644.   [55] Ibid. 636.
[56] In the year 1252, see ibid. 290.
[57] In the year 1258, see ibid. 637; also in the year 1263, see ibid. 687.
[58] In the year 1255, ibid. 621.   [59] In the year 1261, ibid. 674.

Strassburg,[60] in Würzburg,[61] in Hagenau,[62] in Augsburg,[63] in Quedlinburg,[64] and in Regensburg;[65] we note the efforts on the part of the burghers to restrain anyone from extorting money from the Jews and in turn to levy their own taxes upon them.

Consequently, when Rudolph I, of Hapsburg, was elected emperor in 1273, he found very few Jewish communities under the direct control of the crown. Two of R. Meir's Responsa deal with Rudolph's taking money from Jews; in both cases the king resorted to false pretexts for such action, and R. Meir labeled them illegal extortion.[66] The local rulers held fast to their Jews, and neither they nor the burghers were willing to relinquish their rights of taxation over them.

Moreover, during the interregnum the Jews scattered all over Germany and formed new settlements under the protection of the local rulers. Such settlements were very small, often consisting of not more than two or three Jewish families; but they were probably numerous.[67] Thus many Jews lived in new towns and villages, the local rulers of which Rudolph could not accuse of having alienated the income that had formerly belonged to the crown, since no Jews had lived there before 1250.[68]

Rudolph was therefore confronted with various difficulties in his endeavor to exact taxes from the Jews. The local rulers

---

[60] In the year 1261–2, ibid. 673, 681, respectively.

[61] In the year 1261, ibid. 675.

[62] In the year 1262, ibid. 682.

[63] In the year 1266, ibid. 716; in the year 1271, ibid. 751.

[64] In the year 1278, ibid. 763.

[65] In the year 1231, ibid. 582; also in 1297, see Fischer l. c.

[66] Pr. 943; Tesh. Maim. to *Kinyan*, 2. The latter bears the signature מאיר ב"ר ברוך זלה"ה. It was therefore, written after 1275, and thus refers to Rudolph.

[67] See Pr. 1001; 1006; L. 310; Am II, 41; Cr. 121.

[68] For a similar situation, though on a smaller scale, see Mord. *Kiddushin*, 561: על דבר הדוכס מלוחיר אשר דרש מאת היהודים שיתעסקו באותם יהודים הדרים בכפרים שלו, תחת שרים קטנים, וישובו תחתיו, ואם לא כלה גרש ינרש אותם. דומה בעיני שביד הדוכוס לגרש כולם. ואף כי אילו אומרים תמות נפשי עם פלשתים, לא מהני אלא כופין אותם על מדת סדום לחזור תחתיו. ועוד שקצת נוטה כדבר הדוכוס דדינא דמלכותא דינא. ואם יש תביעה לאותם היהודים עבור שיש להם פסידא לעקור ממקומם, זה יטענו אחר כך . . . ושלום עזריאל בן יוסף.

protected the lives, property, and investments of the Jews in their territory and would not permit the king to molest them, imprison them, or extort money from them. Moreover the local rulers who profited by taxing the Jews, were numerous and powerful. Any move to regain the lost or alienated taxation rights of the crown would meet with powerful and widespread opposition. Again small groups of Jews were widely scattered throughout Germany, and the king could not reach them by direct taxation, especially against the opposition of local rulers.

Rudolph, therefore, had to find a legitimate excuse for exacting an additional tax from the Jews over and above the taxes they had paid to the local rulers. In order to establish his right to impose taxes on the Jews of the empire, in addition to their local tax obligations, he made the claim that the person as well as the property of the Jews belonged to the crown.[69] This claim he based on the *servi camerae* relationship of the Jews to the king, which, according to his interpretation, meant that they were actually servile to the king and that he might therefore dispose of their persons as well as of their property in any manner he saw fit.

The term *servi camerae* was already used before Rudolph to denote the Jew-king relationship; but previously the term did not possess the actual connotation of servility, and did not imply that the property of the Jews belonged to the king.[70] We

[69] Schunk, ibid. *cum universi et singuli Judei utpote camere nostre servi cum personis et rebus suis omnibus specieliter nobis attineant* ... Rudolph must have first made the claim that the property of the Jews belonged to him, in the year 1283, when he confiscated the property of the Jews killed in Mayence. For Rudolph's decision in the Mayence massacre, see Oswald Redlich, op. cit. p. 498.

[70] For the various opinions on the history and development of the *servi-camerae* idea, see Otto Stobbe, *Die Juden in Deutschland während des Mittelalters*, 1866, pp. 8-10; George Caro, *Social und Wirtschaftsgeschichte der Juden im Mittelalter*, 1908, vol. 1, pp. 396-404; ibid. pp. 412-5; Eugen Täubler, *Mitteilungen des Gesamtarchives der deutschen Juden*, vol. III (1914), pp. 44-58; J. E. Scherer, *Die Rechtsverhältnisse der Juden in den deutschösterreichischen Ländern*, Leipzig, 1901, pp. 70-8; Aronius, op. cit. no. 314a; Ernst Kantorowicz, *Kaiser Friedrich der Zweite*,

are not concerned here with the origin and development of the *servi-camerae* idea, but rather with its final phase; i. e. with the new formulation of the idea which implied that the property of the Jews and all their earnings belonged directly to the king. This, most important and most far-reaching phase, was invented by Rudolph. We are further concerned with the reaction of the Jews to Rudolph's formulation of their status, with the ideas and opinions the Jews themselves held regarding their status, and with their fierce opposition to any change of such status that would contain an imputation of servility.[71]

Whatever the processes whereby Rudolph arrived at his interpretation of the status of the Jews, whether historical, theological, or juridical, whether completely motivated by economic forces or by opportunism,[72] the reaction of the Jews to such formulation of their status was violent and bitter.[73] The Jews had always considered themselves free men possessing the status of free owners of property.[74] They were even con-

Berlin, 1927, pp. 244 f.; Solomon Grayzel, *The Church and the Jews in the Thirteenth Century*, Philadelphia, 1933, pp. 51 f., 348 f.; James Parkes, *The Jew in the Medieval Community*, London, 1938, pp. 106 ff.; Rapheal Strauss in *Zeitschrift für die Geschichte der Juden in Deutschland*, vol. VII (1938), pp. 234–9; Herbert Fischer, article "Kammerknechtschaft" in *Encyclopaedia Judaica*, vol. IX, pp. 860–2; Berthold Altmann, op. cit. pp. 73 ff.; Guido Kisch, "Jewry-Law in Medieval German Law Books", in *Proceedings of the American Academy for Jewish Research*, vol. X (1940), pp. 130–184.

[71] The change in the status of the Jews brought about by the rigorous policy of Frederick II (see Ernst Kantorowicz, l. c.), did not shock the Jews, since it came about as part of a gradual process and had no immediate practical applications. Moreover, during the interregnum the policy of Frederick II and his strong emphasis on the *servi-camerae* idea, were completely relaxed, and the Jews reverted to the status they held in the eleventh and twelfth centuries. In their dealings with the local rulers political theories carried no weight and were of no significance, since financial considerations were uppermost in the minds of the protectors and the protected. The policy of Rudolph with its serious practical implications, therefore, was a severe shock to the Jews precipitating a powerful reaction.

[72] See Guido Kisch, op. cit. pp. 152–163.   [73] See below.

[74] See Pr. 1001: וגם היהודים אינם מכורדנים להתחייב בכל מקום שהם כמו שהגוים מכורדנים, אלא רואין אותן כמו שהן בני חורי' שירדו מנכסיהם ולא נמכרו ממכרת עבד.

vinced that the government officially recognized their free
status and treated them accordingly. Thus R. Meir wrote:[75]

> For Jews are not subjugated to their overlords as the Gen-
> tiles are, in the sense that they have to pay taxes to a par-
> ticular overlord even when they do not live in his domain.
> The status of the Jew in this land, is that of a free land-
> owner who lost his land but did not lose his personal liberty.
> This definition of the status of the Jews is followed by the
> government in its customary relations with the Jews.

The famous Tossaphist Ri wrote:[76]

> The law prevalent throughout these countries, provided
> that when a Jew had moved away from his settlement, the
> overlord of that settlement did not possess the right to
> appropriate the real property the Jew had left behind; for
> every Jew had the right, according to the law of the land,
> to leave his home town at will, and freely to move from
> place to place.

On another occasion Ri wrote:[77]

> For we saw throughout the country that the Jews had the
> legal right, similar to the right of the knights, to live (liter-
> ally: to stay) wherever they wanted to; and the law of the
> kingdom provided that the overlord should not appropriate
> the Jew's property after he had moved away from his
> town. This was the custom throughout Burgundy.

In the time of Rabbenu Tam an attempt was made, in a
particular terrritory, completely to subjugate the Jews to their
local rulers and to rob them of the right to freedom of domicile,

---

[75] Pr. 1001; *Text no. 591.*

[76] See Pr. 661: ואם ברח יהודי מעירו והניח קרקעותיו והחזיק בם השר . . . נראה לר' שאין
לישראל אחר לקנותם שקרקע אינה נגזלת . . . כי הדין הוא בכל המלכויות האלה שכשהיה יהודי יוצא
מן העיר שבדין מלכות לא היו המושלים מחזיקין בביתו לפי שמשפט היהודים ללכת אנה ואנה בכל
מלכות שירצו, ואם שעוותו את הדין, אין זה דין מלכות אלא גזל מלכות
מקום שירצו.

[77] *Tosaphot* to B. K. 58a, s. v. אי נמי: ואומר ר"י שאם בא ישראל וקנאם מיד השר מחזירה
לבעלים ונוטל מה שהנהו, דאין זה דינא דמלכותא, כי ראינו במדינה שבסביבותינו שמשפט היהודים
לעמוד כמו פרשים בכל מקום שירצו. ובדין מלכותא היו תופסים שלא יחזיק המושל בנחלת היהודים
כשיצאו מעירו, וכן היו נוהגים בכל ארץ בורגוניא.

by forcing them to go surety for one another and thus guaranty
that no one would leave his residence without the consent of his
overlord. Rabbenu Tam took stern measures to combat this attempt to enslave the Jews. He brought about the promulgation
of a *Takkanah* to the effect that no Jew, man or woman, should
go surety for another to guarantee that the latter would not
move away from town.[78]

Similarly we find that in 1252 the Archbishop of Cologne,
in his enumeration of the privileges granted to the Jews, expressly recognized their right to leave his territory.[79] In 1261
the burghers of Halberstadt, at the request of the bishop, con-
ceded this right to the Jews.[80] Most documents containing
privileges granted to the Jews, were drawn up at their own request.[81] We must, therefore, recognize in these two documents
the struggle of the Jews to maintain the right to change their
domicile at will.

Thus the Jews considered themselves free men possessing
full rights to their real and personal property, and endowed
with the right to move freely from place to place. No personal
tie bound them to their overlord, they swore no oath of fealty
to him; for their relation to him was based on an agreement
between two free and independent parties.[82] The Jews jealously

---

[78] See Hayyim Or Zarua, *Responsa*, 179; L. 114: ועוד מזקנים נתבונן דר"ת עשה
תקנה אחת המתחלת מי משלנו למלך ישראל וז"ל. ועל כן בן ברית איש ואשה גזרנו באלה אשר יתערב
נגד השרים היושבים תחת השלטון הצרי משיקוע כל אדם ואם ח"ו יעבור על גזירתינו, גזרנו על המתערב
על כך שלא יפצנו, ועל כל בני ברית נזרנו שלא להושיב ב"ד על כך. This שלטון הצרי was undoubtedly
a local ruler of a certain territory. The *takkanah* was meant for that territory
only, since R. Moses b. Hisdai (Taku) derives from this *takkanah* the law that
ordinarily when a Jew goes surety for a friend that he will not leave the overlord's
territory, the surety is entitled to reimbursement for all damages he suffers as a
consequence thereof.

[79] See Aronius, op. cit. no. 588.

[80] Ibid. no. 676.

[81] Cf. Herbert Fischer, op. cit. p. 64 f.

[82] See the attitude of R. Meir in Am II, 122: ואשר שאלת על יהודי שיש לו עול
גדול מן השר ומהלואות ומסים ונכנס לעיר תחלה לדעת כן שנתפשר בפני עצמו עם השר בכך וכך
ושלא להשתתף עם הקהל . . . אינו רשאי להפרד מהם . . . ומה שאומר שאינו שוה לו למתפס חבלא

guarded their freedom and would not permit any encroachment upon their rights. The formulation of their new status by Rudolph, therefore, was a severe shock to them, and they were ready to resort to extreme measures, even leaving Germany altogether, in order vigorously to combat this imputation of servility.

Let us, therefore, follow the steps that led to this grave decision of the Jews: In 1284 Rudolph levied an extraordinary tax on the towns, which amounted to three and one-third per-cent of the working capital of the town dwellers. This levy aroused great opposition throughout Germany, an opposition which almost amounted to a rebellion.[83] Those opposed to Rudolph's tax, gave lavish support to the pseudo-Frederick II, who appeared in that year in Neuss and later moved to Wetzlar.[84] It is hard to believe that when Rudolph levied this tax on the towns, he did not put a similar tax on the Jews. Thus we find that the Jews were ardent supporters of the pseudo-Frederick.[85] It is therefore fair to assume that in the same year, 1284, Rudolph put a heavy tax on the Jews. The opposition of the towns to Rudolph's tax policy, and the affair of the pseudo-Frederick, lasted for almost a year. The impostor was finally delivered to Rudolph by the town of Wetzlar in the summer of 1285.[86] Rudolph having been successful in his special levy on the towns, and desiring to gain control over the Jews as well as to punish them for their support of the pseudo-Frederick, became more oppressive in his demand of taxes from them.[87] It was at this

בתרי ראשי לתת בפ"ע ולחזור ולתת עם הקהל, הלא יכול לילך אל השר ולומר לו אדוני אין זה דיננו להפרד זה מזה במסים ושלא לשא בעול כי אם יחדיו, וכל היהודים שבמלכות מריבים אתי בזה, אין רצוני עוד לתת בפ"ע אלא עם שאר חבירי.

[83] For a discussion of this extraordinary tax and of the opposition it aroused throughout the Empire, see Oswald Redlich, op. cit. pp. 491 ff.

[84] Ibid. pp. 533 ff.

[85] See Brisch, op. cit. p. 164.

[86] See Oswald Redlich, l. c.

[87] Cf. Brisch. l. c. "Jetzt zog Rudolph alle Anhänger seines falschen Gegners zur Rechenschaft, in erste Reihe natürlich seine Kammerknechte."

time probably that he promulgated his new formulation of the *servi camerae* relationship of the Jews to the king in order to reestablish his right to tax them regularly.[88] He was not satisfied with a fine; he wanted a regular income, and he pressed the idea that both the person and the property of the Jews belonged to the crown, and that, consequently, the king had a right to take part of that property at any time he chose to do so.

The Jews, on the other hand, refused to accept this degraded status. We must keep in mind that at this time the Jews of Germany were still bold, proud, and liberty loving. They were not yet broken in spirit and body by the persecutions and massacres of Rindfleisch and by the Armleder brothers, and those following the black plague, the confinements within Ghetto walls, the terrible extortions, oppressions, and inhuman restrictions of the fourteenth, fifteenth and sixteenth centuries. Throughout the Responsa of R. Meir we find that the Jews of that period were self-reliant, resourceful and courageous.[89] The outrageous demand of the king and his effort to rob them of their liberty, humiliate, and even enslave them, aroused them to a high pitch of indignation, and many of them decided to leave Germany forthwith. R. Meir was probably the leader of this opposition. His ideas regarding the basic freedom of the individual, his passion for justice and righteousness,[90] led him to revolt against Rudolph's attempt to reduce the Jews to servility. Consequently he was among the leaders of this mass exodus.

We find other instances where heavy and extortionate taxation drove the Jews to migrate to other countries or ter-

[88] Cf. note 69 above.

[89] The courage of the Jew of that period can be seen especially in his dealings with his overlord. Cf. Pr. 134; 137; 226; 241; 595; 677; 708; 938; 944; 980; 1001; 1005; L. 108; 114; Am II, 19; 122; 180; Cr. 9; 32–3; 49; 53; 305; 307; Berl. p. 286 no. 348. Note also the attitude of R. Meir toward the law of the land and the legal rights of the overlord.

[90] See previous chapter.

ritories. Thus, in the same century, the Jews of England, when a heavy tax was imposed on them, asked the king to permit them to leave the country.[91] In a Responsum regarding Jews who were imprisoned by the local ruler, R. Meir stated that although the ruler imprisoned the Jews, his intention was to tax them but not to kill them; that since he desired to impose on them an exceptionally heavy tax, he feared that they might flee from his territory, and therefore ordered their arrest. He added further that had the overlord been sure that the Jews would pay the desired tax and not flee from the country, he would not have taken the trouble to imprison them.[92] Cases of mass imprisonment of entire communities were quite frequent in the thirteenth century,[93] and must have all been motivated by the same anxiety on the part of the overlord that the Jews would flee from his territory. We may safely assume, therefore, that the reason many Jews left Germany in the year 1286, was the effort of Rudolph to enforce his claim of being the direct master of the Jews, the actual owner of their persons and possessions, and his consequent right to tax them whenever, and in whatever form, he chose.

Even those who remained in Germany did not acquiesce in Rudolph's demands, but fought bravely for their independence. Relying on the strength of their local rulers they stubbornly defied Rudolph, disregarded his demand for taxes, and thus nullified the practical application of his claim regarding their new status.[94] Rudolph, therefore, resolved to use the

[91] See A. M. Hyamson, *History of the Jews in England*, pp. 55, 58, 77-8.

[92] Mord. B. K. 190: אע"ג דפתח המושל בתפיסה הדבר ידוע שלא בא אלא על עסקי ממון, אלא לפי שרוצה להכביד עליהם ולשאול יותר מדי וירא פן יברחו, צוה לתפשם, ואילו מובטח היה שלא יברחו לא היה תופסם כמו בפעם אחרת, והדבר ידוע וברור שאין זה אלא כשאר מסים. See especially *Text*, 772: "Many Jews resort to this practice whenever they are forced by their overlord to take an oath that they will not move out of the overlord's town."

[93] See Pr. 22 6; 339; 595; 938; L. 114; 381; Am II, 19–22; 127–8; 141; 157 Cr. 32–3; 305; 307; Mord. B. K. 190; Berl. p. 286, no. 342; ibid. no. 348.

[94] See Pr. 241.

arrest of R. Meir as a means of forcing the Jews to accept their new status.

A clear description of the sly maneuvering, double dealing, and treachery, employed by Rudolph in his effort to force the Jews to pay him taxes, is given in the Responsum of Rabbi Hayyim b. Yehiel Hefetz Zahav,[95] a participant in the battle of wits with the emperor. Rabbi Hayyim tells us of the negotiations carried on between the Jews and King Rudolph whereby they agreed to pay him twenty-three thousand pounds on condition that he grant their request. What the nature of the request was we learn from the *Chronicon Colmariense* for the year 1288, which reports that the Jews promised King Rudolph twenty thousand *marks* to save the Jews of Boppard and Oberwessel from the peril of death, and to release from prison the Rabbi of the Jews, their highly venerated teacher on whom their school depended,[96] meaning none other than R. Meir. As pointed out above, the negotiations with the king described in Rabbi Hayyim's Responsum and those in the *Chronicon*, must be identical since in one case the Jews promised the king the enormous sum of twenty-three thousand pounds and in the other twenty thousand *marks* (the value of the pound was not constant, the two sums must, therefore, have been equal in value), and since both sources date the negotiations at about 1287-8.[97] Thus the condition upon which the Jews promised money to the king, referred to by Rabbi Hayyim, was relief for the Jews of Boppard and Obverwessel and the release of R. Meir.

[95] Ibid.

[96] Böhmer, *Fontes Rerum Germanicarum*, II, p. 72: *Judei regi Rudolfo ut eis de illis de Wesela atque Porpardia justiciam faceret, et eos a periculo libraret mortis, et ipsorum Rabbi i. e. supremum magistrum, cui schola Judeorum et honores divinos impendere videbantur, quem rex captiverat, a captivitate carceris libraret viginti sibi millia marcarum promiserunt.*

[97] As to the date of R. Hayyim's Responsum, see Excursus II.

Regarding these negotiations, therefore, Rabbi Hayyim
wrote:

> Last year only twelve communities promised to pay twenty-
> three thousand pounds to the king with the understanding
> that should he fail to carry out his promise, we, the twelve
> communities, should not owe him anything. Subsequently
> the king willfully retracted and refused to do what he had
> promised. Were we, then, under obligation to pay him
> anything? Of course not! .... Moreover, I participated
> in the negotiations as an individual and not as a delegate
> of our community. I was even expressly ordered by the
> community not to participate in these negotiations. I re-
> peated the terms to the king saying three times: 'We are
> under no obligation to you. If you fulfill your solemn
> promise to us, you shall be paid, and even I shall endeavor
> [to persuade the community of Cologne to pay its share],
> otherwise you will not receive even a penny.' The king's
> answer was that he was satisfied with these terms. He
> said: 'If I keep my part of the bargain, all will be well;
> otherwise you shall not pay me anything.' Consequently,
> when the king failed to keep his promise, I said to the com-
> munities that they should not levy any tax on our commu-
> nity. All the talmudic scholars who were present at the
> time, ruled that our community was free from obligation,
> and even gave us a written court order to that effect.
> Nevertheless, a share of the tax was imposed upon us; and
> the king and count Eberhard were directed to collect it
> from us. Had not the members of our community realized
> that they (the community members) would not be able to
> enforce collection of their debts, they would still refuse to
> pay anything. As a matter of fact they [the king's tax
> collectors] are still searching for insidious ways of collecting
> their full quota.[98]

---

[98] Pr. 241: ואשתקד לא היינו אלא י״ב שנדרו למלך כ״ג אלפים ליטר' ע״ת אם לא יקיים לא
היינו חייבי' לו כלום, ונסוג אחור ולא קיים תנאו ובמזיד, וכי על אותן י״ב לתן הממון, חלילה, כ״ש
בנדון זה שכבר התחיל בנקמה לולי נאנס. ואף אני לא הלכתי שם בשליחות הקהל ומיחו בי שלא
לילך והתניתי עם המלך ג' פעמים שאין לנו דין ודברים עמך, אך אם תעשה מה שנדרת יתנו לך, וזה
אעסוק, ואם לאו לא יתנו לך פרוטה. ואמר המלך איני רוצה יותר, אם אעשה מה שנדרתי מוטב ואם

The fact that the communities promised to pay money to
Rudolph on condition only that he fulfill his promise, that Rabbi
Hayyim had to emphasize that condition three times, that the
community of Cologne was very suspicious of the king and
openly warned its representative not to take part in the negotiations, speaks eloquently of the severe struggle of the Jews
against Rudolph's attempt to lay claim to their persons and
property and thus to infringe upon their status as free men.
The Jews of the particular communities involved[99] tried to
emphasize again and again that the king had no right to tax
them, and that they were under no obligation to him.

We can now understand why R. Meir was not released from
prison. The Jews were willing to pay money for R. Meir's release, but they refused to concede that the king had a right to
tax them.[100] In 1284, when the king imposed a tax on them,
they refused to pay it. When they now offered him money, they
clearly stipulated that they were willing to pay ransom for R.
Meir, but they still maintained that the king had no right
to tax them. This is the meaning of Rabbi Hayyim's words to
the king: שאין לנו דין ודברים עמך אך אם תעשה מה שנדרת לנו
יתנו לך וזה אעסוק ואם לאו לא יתנו לך פרוטה. The most adamant
in their stand were the communities, like Cologne, the income
of which had long ago been alienated by the crown, and which
would have been obligated to the king only if they accepted
the new formulation of the status of the Jews.

לאו אל תתנו, וכשנסוג המלך אחור אמרתי אל הקהלות אל תטילו על הקהלה שלנו מאומה וכל תופשי
התורה שהיו שם פסקו שהקהלה שלנו פטורה וכתבו לנו פטור והפסק בידי, ועל כל זה הלכו וקבצו מס
על הקהלה שלנו והראה המלך והפחה עפרהרט, ולולי שראו הקהל [כי] לא יכלו להוציא מחובותיהם,
כלום היו צריכי' לתן, ועדיין אורבים ומצפים אם ימצאו מקום לגבות קצבתם.

[99] It is important to note that R. Hayyim represented the community of
Cologne which was under the protection of the archbishop of Cologne, and which
did not pay any taxes to the king already during the rule of Frederick II (1215–50);
see Aronius, op. cit. nos. 299; 325; 382; 588; 591; 614; 636; 644.

[100] Even those communities that were immediately under the king's protection and paid their taxes directly to him, were afraid to offer ransom money for
R. Meir lest the king discover their ability to pay heavier taxes.

Rudolph, on the other hand, wanted to emphasize his right to tax the Jews and to force them into accepting their new status as real *Kammerknechte*. He, therefore, demanded the promised amount as a tax, and not as a payment for a royal favor. Were Rudolph to release R. Meir after receiving the money from the Jews, such money would appear to be received in payment for R. Meir's release, and not as the payment of a direct levy. Rudolph therefore refused to release R. Meir and to help the Jews of Boppard and Oberwessel, in order to emphasize the fact that the money he had collected was in payment of a direct tax upon the Jews.

Rudolph made a strenuous effort to collect this money from the Jews; he even went so far as to threaten to release their debtors and thus cause them to lose their investments (a procedure that was quite common in the fourteenth century).[101] These, however, were mostly protected by the local rulers.[102] The Jews paid as little as they could in order to save many an unprotected investment, but they did not pay the entire amount promised.[103] To bring justice to bear on the murderers of the Jews of Boppard and Oberwessel, the Jews resorted to their local rulers and bribed the Archbishop Siegfried of Cologne who executed two of the murderers before he was himself captured by Johann von Brabant.[104] In 1288 the Jews, hoping to force Rudolph to release R. Meir, appealed to Pope Nicolas IV and he urged Rudolph to free his captive.[105] The intervention of the

---

[101] This is implied in the words (Pr. 241): ולולי שראו הקהל [כי] לא יכלו להוציא מחובותיהם.

[102] See Cr. 305; Pr. 105.

[103] Implied in the words (Pr. 241): ועדיין אורבים ומצפים אם ימצאו מקום לנבות קצבתם.

[104] On June 5, 1288; see Oswald Redlich, op. cit. pp. 657-8. For the effort on behalf of the Jews of Boppard and Oberwessel, see Excursus II.

[105] Langlois, *Registres de Nicolas IV*, no. 313; Böhmer and Redlich, *Registii Imperii Rudolphi*, no. 2185: *Papst Nicolaus IV an König Rudolph: es sei ihm von seite einiger Juden die Klage vorgebracht worden dass er den jüdischen Magister*

Pope, however, was of no avail, and R. Meir remained in prison.

When the Jews found that Rudolph collected the money promised to him without granting their request, they no longer offered him any more money as ransom for R. Meir. They feared that the king would repeat the process and again demand the newly promised sum as a tax, without granting their request. Rudolph, on the other hand, after collecting the greater part of the twenty-three thousand pounds as a direct levy upon the Jewish communities, expected to receive additional funds for R. Meir's release. He would not release a prisoner of such importance without receiving a large sum of money as ransom. R. Meir was, therefore, kept in prison until his death, and his body was retained for fourteen years after his death. Even then the Jews were afraid to offer any ransom money for the release of his body.[106] An individual Jew, however, could make an offer of paying ransom without any fear that his payment would be construed as a tax, or that it would become a precedent for further exaction. It was an individual Jew, therefore, R. Alexander b. Salomo Wimpfen, who finally succeeded in ransoming the body of this great teacher by paying to King Albert a large sum of money out of his own pocket.[107]

It is possible that the communities were willing to compromise with Rudolph in order to gain the release of their beloved Rabbi, but that R. Meir urged them not to forego their freedom under any circumstances; he refused to allow the communities to give up their independence on his account. He was willing to die the death of a martyr rather than become the

Mehir von Rotenburg gefangen halte, obwohl der selbe nichts gegen die christliche Religion oder den König noch sonst etwas verbrochen habe, und ermahnt ihn, wenn sich dies so verhalte, den Mehir freizulassen.

[106] This struggle between the Jews and the German emperors who sought to gain and enforce the right of direct taxation over them, continued for over fifty years. Cf. G. Caro, op. cit. vol. II, pp. 127–42.

[107] See R. Meir's epitaph in Lewysohn, op. cit. p. 35; quoted in note 8, above.

means whereby the Jews would be coerced into accepting a status of servility. This was probably the circumstance that occasioned the traditional account of the reason for his continued retention, later recorded by R. Solomon Luria.

The sources mention two places where R. Meir was held prisoner: Wasserburg,[108] and Ensisheim,[109] each of which is described as a *migdal*, tower. We have only a few references to R. Meir's stay in Wasserburg, and quite a number about talmudic discussions held with his students in Ensisheim; we even possess a few Responsa that were written here.[110] We may, therefore, infer that R. Meir was in Wasserburg for a short time only, while he spent the greater part of his seven years of imprisonment in Ensisheim.

There remains now the question: which was the first place of R. Meir's confinement? Although in his text Back assumes that Wasserburg was the first place, he makes an effort, in a lengthy note,[111] to prove that R. Meir was first taken to Ensisheim, but that after the communities promised Rudolph a large sum of money, he was transferred to Wasserburg which was more comfortable than Ensisheim. Back bases his opinion on the quotation in the שלשלת הקבלה of the statement of R. Judah b. Asher, which reads: ואז הרחיבו את בית הר"ם בבית הסהר;[112] and on the *Yozer* that R. Meir composed while in Wasserburg,[113] in which he wrote: שכמי מסבל דוחקו וממוסרות עבות נתקו, which seems to refer to a change for the better. This view of Back, however, is untenable. We possess a Responsum written by R. Meir in the tower of Ensisheim in which he complains that his imprisonment has lasted already

---

[108] See Back, op. cit. p. 72, note 1.
[109] Ibid. p. 73, note 1.
[110] All quoted by Back, op. cit. pp. 72–3, in the notes. Cf. *Ohalot*, chaps. 5, 9, 15.
[111] Ibid. p. 80, note 1.
[112] Gedaliah b. Joseph Ibn Yahia, ספר שלשלת הקבלה, Zalkow, 1802, p. 40
[113] Leopold Zunz, *Literaturgeschichte*, p. 361, note 4.

for three and one half years.[114] Thus R. Meir was in Ensisheim
at the beginning of the year 1290, while the transfer referred
to by R. Judah b. Asher took place in 1287. The tower of
Ensisheim was, therefore, the place to which R. Meir was transferred after Rudolph's negotiations with the communities failed
to bring about his release.

Ensisheim is identified with the small town of that name in
Oberelsas;[115] while there is no town or place in Germany called
Wasserburg. Back believed that it was the name of a house in
Mayence,[116] and Wallescz was of the opinion that it was a castle
surrounded by a moat filled with water.[117] He is inclined to
believe that R. Meir was held in the castle of Mayence. Thus
the location of the tower to which R. Meir was confined could
not be identified with any degree of certainty. We do know,
however, that the tower was situated in a town where more
than ten Jewish adults lived.[118]

R. Meir was given some privileges while in prison. His
students were permitted to visit him; and they continued
to discuss ritual and legal problems with him, and recorded
his practices and opinions.[119] Within the walls of his prison

---

[114] Tesh. Maim. to *Ishut*, 30: כי . . . תשובה מורי רבינו למה״ר אשר ממגדל אינזינשהיים
מה לעני יודע שיושב חושך וצלמות ולא סדרים זה ג׳ שנים ומחצה.

[115] Back, op. cit. p. 73.

[116] Ibid. p. 80, note 1; cf. Wallescz, *R.E.J.* LXI, p. 54, note 4. Wasserburg,
however, is referred to as a *migdal*, a tower, and could hardly have been a house
in Mayence.

[117] Ibid.

[118] See *Tashbetz*, 207: אמנם הר״ם ז״ל אמר שבספר מיימון יש במקום שיש מנין אם יש יחידים
שאין יכולים לבא, או שלא היו בבית הכנסת בשעת קריאת ההלל, אפילו הם שלשה אין להם לברך
על קריאת ההלל, וכן עשה כשהיה באישפרוקה. That אישפרוקה is to be identified as Wasserburg, can be learned from the fact that Rabbi Perez, a friend of R. Meir, in his
glosses to the *Sefer Mitzvot Katan* (146b), records the same practice of R. Meir,
but gives the version: וכן עשה הר״ם כשהיה בבית הסהר

[119] See Hag. Maim. to *Hilkot Tefillah*, 14: במגדל אינזינשהיים הודה מורי לדברי ואמר
וזכורני כשהייתי אצל מורי במגדל ושבורג ;to *Hilkot Shabbat*, 6: לי שחזר בו מן המנהג ההוא ;to
Hilkot Teshubah, 5: ובמגדל אינזינשהיים תירץ לי מורי רבי׳ ;to *Hilkot Keriat Shema*, 1:
וכן הסכים מורי לכל דברים אלה במגדל אינזינשהיים.

R. Meir began to compile his novellae to the various tractates of the Talmud.[120] These novellae contained many of his Responsa[121] and probably resembled the *Mordecai* in structure and form. Excepting the *Tosaphot* to *Yoma* and to *Ohalot*, however, we do not possess R. Meir's novellae in his own redaction. Most of them were probably incorporated in the works of his students: R. Mordecai b. Hillel, R. Meir ha-Kohen, R. Samson b. Zadok, and the anonymous collectors of his Responsa.[122]

R. Meir's literary compositions may be divided into three distinct classes:[123]

I. Tosaphot, Novellae and Commentaries.

He wrote Tosaphot and novellae to the following tractates: *Berakot, Yoma, Shabbat, Erubin, Ketubot, Yebamot, Gittin,*

---

[120] See Hag. Maim. to *Hilkot Shabbat*, 19: ושוב קבע תשובה זו במגדל אינזינשהיים; Tesh. Maim. to *Ishut*, 30: וקבעה מורי רבינו בחדושיו; to *Kinyan*, 31: כתב בחדושיו; to *Mishpatim* 60: במגדל אינזינשהיים; עכ"ל אשר כתב בחדושיו בפרק האומנים תשובת ... מורי רבינו מגדל אינזינשהיים וקבעה בחדושיו. See also *Ohalot*, ch. 5, end.

[121] See previous note.

[122] It is indeed a dubious question why R. Meir's novellae, so often referred to by the author of the *Hagahot Maimuniot* (*Hilkot Zizit*, 1; *Maakalot Asurot*, 9; *Hilkot Shabbat*, 6; ibid. 16; ibid. 17; *Hilkot Shebuot*, 11; *Hilkot Sekirut*, 2; ibid. 5; *Hilkot Malveh ve-Loveh*, 4; ibid. 5; ibid. 27; *Hilkot Ebel*, 6; Tesh. Maim. to *Ishut*, 30; ibid. 29; to *Mishpatim*, 60; ibid. 61) and by the *Mordecai* (Yeb. 19; *Shebuot*, 759; *Shabbat*, 456; B. K. 215; *Mordecai Hagadol* p. 236d; ibid. p. 237b), did not reach us in their original form, and why even the Rabbis of the next century were not acquainted with them. R. Meir's Responsa were quoted very often in the later centuries (see the numerous references in the *Sources* to the *Text*), but his novellae were rarely mentioned (see Joseph Kolon, *Responsa*, 36). There is a possibility, however, that the *Mordecai* is simply an enlargement of R. Meir's Novellae, that R. Meir gave his works to his students for revision and amplification. We find that he suffered in prison from a lack of books. Thus he did not possess the *Tosaphot* to the Talmud, nor any of the codes current in his day (see Am II, 108: תוספי גטין אין בידי ולא ספרי פסקים בארץ הנגב ... ואם ימצאו שהתוס' וספרי (הפסקים חולקי' עלי בשום דבר דעתי מבוטלת, כי מה לעני יודע ...). He was probably not permitted (or was afraid) to keep many books in prison. He was, therefore, forced to give them to his students (cf. Tesh. Maim. to *Kinyan*, 35: ועיין בפירשתי בנדרים והם ביד חברינו ה"ר יצחק מנוטינגן ז"ל) who incorporated them in their own works.

[123] For the sources, see Wellescz, *R.E.J.* LXI. pp. 45-7.

Kiddushin, Nedarim, Sota,[124] *Baba Kama, Baba Mezia, Baba Batra, Shebuot, Sanhedrin, Menahot, Bekorot, and Hullin.* He wrote commentaries to the two orders of the Mishnah: *Zeraim and Taharot.*[125]

II. Compendia of laws for special purposes.

a) *Piske, or Hilkot Erubin.*

b) *Halakot Pesukot.*

c) *Hilkot Berakot.*

d) *Hilkot Semahot.*

e) *Hilkot Shehitah.*

f) *Hilkot Hatmanah.*[126]

g) A collection of the customs connected with the marriage ceremony, and the wording of the *ketubah.*

h) A collection of customs called מנהגי הר"ם רוטנבורק probably compiled by one of his students.

III. Responsa.

We possess four different editions of his Responsa:

a) Cremona, 1557; b) Prague, 1608 (reprinted in Sdilkow, 1835, and in Budapest, 1895); c) Lemberg, 1860; and d) Berlin, 1891–2; aside from those incorporated in the works of his students.

To these must be added R. Meir's *piyyutim,* especially his elegy שאלי שרופה באש; and a collection of masoretic explanations in manuscript in the Vatican Library.

[124] Not mentioned by Wellescz, but see Mord. *Yebamot,* 19: כתב מור"ם ז"ל בסוטה פרק ארוסה.

[125] See L. 151: ופי' זרעים וטהרות שלי לכשאצא בשלום אטרח ברצון שיהיו מועתקים לך. R. Yom Tob Lippman Heller used R. Meir's novellae to the order *Tohorot,* in his commentary תוספות יום טוב to that order.

[126] See Mord. *Shabbat,* 456: לשון מור"ם ז"ל בהלכות הטמנה.

R. Meir died in 1293, but his body was not delivered to the Jews for internment until the year 1307.[127] As stated above, R. Alexander b. Salomo Wimpfen, a resident of Frankfort a. M. ransomed his body for a large sum of money from king Albert.[128] He was, then, buried in Worms, on the fourth of *Adar*, 5067 A. M. Soon afterwards (on the eleventh of *Tishri*, 5068) R. Alexander b. Salomo himself died and was buried alongside R. Meir.[129]

[127] See his epitaph in Lewysohn, op. cit. p. 35; quoted in note 8 above.
[128] See his epitaph, Lewysohn, op. cit. pp. 39–40.
[129] See ibid. pp. 35–40.

Excursus I

The Addressee of Responsum Prague 131.

"For many years, the Jews of the entire kingdom paid their taxes to the king collectively. Then the king gave part of his kingdom to his son, and stated that henceforth the taxes of the Jews in that territory should be paid to his son. But the communities of the rest of the kingdom still demand the regular taxes from the Jews of the territory presented to the king's son (Pr. 131)."

Back (op. cit. p. 47f.) identifies the king in this Responsum with Rudolph I, who in 1282 gave his son Albrecht the rulership over Austria, Styria and Carinthia. Since R. Meir in his answer displayed ignorance of the details connected with the feudal grant made by the king to his son, Wellescz (R. E. J. XL, p. 64) rightly pointed out that the king could not be identified with Rudolf, for if he were Rudolf, R. Meir would have been better informed. There is no doubt that Wellescz's objection is a serious one. Had the German communities been involved in a tax suit with the communities of Austria, Styria and Carinthia, R. Meir's community would also have been a party to the suit, and R. Meir would have known the details of the king's grant to his son. Moreover, the German communities never paid their taxes to the king collectively. The record of the taxes of the German cities to the emperor, for the year 1241 (see Rösel op. cit. pp. 10–19), lists the receipts of every community separately. Throughout the 13th century, the kings of Germany pledged or gave away as gifts the income derived from individual communities. Rudolf himself in 1286 pledged the income from the Frankfurt community for 200

156

marks (Rösel op. cit. p. 70). The German communities, therefore, did not pay their taxes to the king collectively; consequently, the above cited Responsum could not refer to Rudolf's
grant to his son. It must have been written for a foreign country.

I believe that this Responsum was written in the year 1249
to the communities of Bohemia and Moravia, and that it was
occasioned by the treaty entered into between King Wenceslas I
of Bohemia and his son Premysl Ottakar, on August 16, 1249,
by the terms of which treaty the latter was endowed with the
margravate of Moravia and the entire income of that territory
(see A. Bachmann *Geschichte Böhmens* I, p. 543; Franz Palacky
Geschichte von Böhmen II, p. 133; B. Dudik, *Mährens allgemeine
Geschichte* V, p. 373).

That the Jews of Bohemia paid their taxes to the king collectively we learn from a Responsum sent to the community
of Pribram by R. Abigdor b. Elijah ha-Kohen (of Vienna, see
Michael *Or-ha-Hayim*, no. 10). The Responsum is quoted in
Mordecai B. K. 180 (cf. *Germania Judaica* pp. 281, 282) and
reads as follows: אם מתחילה הטיל המלך מס על בני פיברם ס'
זקוקים בפני עצמם ובקשו שאר הישובים מן המלך או משלוחיו לחברם
עמהם במס כדי להקל עליהם בחבור זה והתנו בהם בני פיברם שלא
לעשות החבור, אם נתברר הדבר שעברו על התראה זו ועל דבר חשובי
פרא"ג שאמרו להם שלא לעשות . . . ואף אם מתחלה היה מנהג להטיל
מס עפ"י המלך בחבור, ועכשיו מעצמו שנה להטיל מס בפירוד.
The last clause proves conclusively that the communities of
Bohemia had paid their taxes collectively.

Moreover, B. Bretholtz, in his book *Geschichte der Juden in
Mähren im M. A.* pp. 99–102, satisfactorily proves that during
the middle of the 13th century many Jews lived in the cities
of Moravia. We are convinced, therefore, that Responsum Pr.
131 was sent by R. Meir to the communities of Bohemia and
Moravia, and that it was written in the year 1249.

Excursus II

Responsum Prague 241.

Responsum Pr. 241 is of great historical value not only because it was written by one of the leaders of the community of
Cologne but because it discusses important negotiations between
Jews and an archbishop, and between twelve Jewish communities and the king. A detailed discussion of its meaning and
implications is relevant to our subject, and we shall, therefore,
quote it in full: אשיבכם כפי ע"ד. נ"ל אחרי.שראובן ובנו לא מעלו
בשליחות ועשו כל היכולת, אך שאירע אונס הידוע שנתפס ההגמון אחרי
שהתחיל בנקמה להרוג שניהם מהם, והשאר צוה לכותבם להתחייב
הריגה, שאף יחיד שעשה חבירו שליח בעוד שלא מעל ופשע ושינה
בשליחות דיכול לאמר לתקוני שדרתיך ולא לעותתי שחייב לקיים כל
מה שנדר כמו הנותן מעות לקנות חטי' ופחתו פחתו למשלח (וב"ק ק"ב
ע"א), וכ"ש בנדון זה, דזהו מנהג פשוט בכל המקומות תפוצות גולה שאם
מצווים לפרנס אחד לילך בשליחותם ועשה שליחתו לשם שמים ולא שינה
שהקהל מצוים לסלקו, ואם א' או שנים צעקו נגד הדבר אף מראש ועד
סוף, בשביל זה לא יפטרו דבטל יחיד במעוטו. ובדידי הוה עובדא כמה
פעמי' כשהייתי שליח קהל קולוניא ור' זלקמן כהן צעק כמה פעמים
אל תדור עלי כלום, בשביל זה לא נפטר להכשיל את הרבים בפעם
אחר. וכ"ש בנדון זה שעת הסכנה היה הדבר מגופים והדבר נחוץ ושנו ושלשו
במכתבם להזהירו לזרז הדבר ועשה כל יכלתו דאין להרהר אחריו,
דמסתמא לא שדי איניש זוזי בכדי, ועליהם ליתן את החובן כדי שלא
תנעול דלת בפני הטורחים עבור רבים, אין לדקדק ולמצוא דקדוק
עניות והעושה כך אין לבו לשמים. גם במכתבם אין כתוב שום תנאי אלא
רק לזרזו, ואם יאמרו הקהל בעל פה על תנאי כזה וכזה נדרנו, לא אתי
בע"פ ומרע לשטרא, דאי לא תימא הכי אין לדבר סוף ווכין כל פעם
ופעם יאמר על תנאי זה נדרתי כך וכך. ואשתקד לא היינו אלא י"ב שנדרו
למלך כ"ג אלפים ליטר' על תנאי אם לא יקיים לא היינו חייבי' לו כלום.

158

נסוג אחור ולא קיים תנאו ובמזיד. וכי על אותן י"ב ליתן הממון, חלילה,
כ"ש בנדון זה שכבר התחיל בנקמה לולי נאנס. ואף אני לא הלכתי שם
בשליחות הקהל, ומיחו בי שלא לילך, והתניתי עם המלך ג' פעמים שאין
לנו דין ודברים עמך אך אם תעשה מה שנדרת לנו יתנו לך, וזה אעסוק,
ואם לאו לא יתנו לך פרוטה. וענה המלך איני רוצה יותר, אם אעשה מה
שנדרתי מוטב, ואם לאו אל תתנו. וכשנסוג המלך אחור אמרתי אל
הקהילות אל תטילו על הקהילה שלנו מאומה. וכל תופשי התורה שהיו
שם פסקו שהקהלה שלנו פטורה וכתבו לנו פטור והפסק בידי. ועל כל
זה הלכו וקבצו מס על הקהלה שלנו, והראה המלך והפחה עפרהרט.
ולולא שראו הקהל וכין לא יכלו להוציא מחובותיהם[,] כלום היו
צריכים לתן, ועדיין אורבים ומצפים אם ימצאו מקום לגבות קצבתם.
וחרה אפי במטילי המס והראיתי הפסקים של תופשי התורה, ואמרו אין
אנו משגיחים בפטפוטים כך דין קהלות מקדמונים. ראו איך מי שעורר
מדנים אלו אין לבו לשמים. אך הקהל ישבו ועיינו בדבר מראש ועד סוף
וישלמו כפי חלקם המגיע, שלא לנעול דלת בפני כל אדם. ושלום חיים
בן אמ"ו הר' יחיאל חפץ זהב.

Graetz (*op. cit.* note 9) and Back (*op. cit.* p. 74) believe
that this Responsum discusses the negotiations between the
Jews and emperor Rudolf for the release of R. Meir, and that
the 23,000 pounds mentioned therein constitute the ransom
money promised for such release. Back identifies the *Hegemon*
with the Archbishop of Cologne, who was captured in the battle
of Worringen on June 5, 1288, by Johann of Brabant (O. Redlich
op. cit. pp. 657f.). The Responsum, therefore, was written in
the year 1288. Wellescz (R. E. J. LXI, p. 53) takes issue with
Back and concludes that the *Hegemon* referred to was the Archbishop of Mayence, Werner d'Eppenstein, who (according to
Graetz, VII, note 9, but see Herbert Fischer *op. cit.*, note 5)
protected the Jews of Mayence in 1283. This would place the
writing of the Responsum in 1283; the negotiations described
therein, therefore, would have nothing to do with the ransoming of R. Meir. Wellescz's objection to Back's view, however,
is based on an error (which Zimmels *op. cit.* note 53 p. 78f,
failed to notice). Back translated שאירע האונס הידוע "*da trat*

das bekannte unglückliche ereignis ein", and Wellescz objected
that R. Hayyim b. Yehiel would not have called the capture
of the archbishop a misfortune (*un malheureux événement*).
But the term אונס does not always mean a misfortune; its usual
meaning in Rabbinic literature is "an unavoidable accident,"
and this is its meaning in the present context. A and his son
were successful in their mission to the *Hegemon* and the latter
began his vengeful work by killing two of the murderers and sen-
tencing others to death; but he was prevented from completing
this work by the unavoidable accident of his being taken prisoner. We may, therefore, safely assume that the *Hegemon*
referred to was Siegfried, the archbishop of Cologne, that the
Responsum of R. Hayyim was written in 1288, and that the
23,000 pounds referred to were promised to Rudolf of Habsburg
in 1287.

Why did R. Hayyim refer to the case of the twelve communities who had promised money to the king? What relation did
it bear to the case on hand, and what did R. Hayyim expect to
prove by citing it?

It seems to me that the question submitted to R. Hayyim
was as follows: A certain community delegated A and his son
to negotiate with the Archbishop of Cologne to induce him
to bring to justice the murderers of the Jews of Boppard and
Oberwessel. It was within the power of the archbishop to do
so, since these two towns belonged to his archbishopric. A and
his son faithfully fulfilled their mission and paid a sum of money
to the archbishop (דמסתמא לא שדי איניש זוזי בכדי), upon the
latter's promise to fulfill their wish. The archbishop executed
two of the murderers and sentenced the others to death. Meanwhile, however, the archbishop himself was captured by Johann
of Brabant, and therefore the rest of the murderers went unpunished. A and his son demanded of the community repayment of the amount they had paid to the archbishop. The community, however, recalling the facts connected with the attempt

to ransom R. Meir, no doubt warned A not to give any money
to the archbishop until he carried out his promise. Consequently, the community refused to compensate A and his son
for their trouble and expense.

We can now understand R. Hayyim's Responsum. He
argued that A and his son had faithfully fulfilled their mission;
that the custom throughout the country required that after a
representative had faithfully carried out a task delegated to
him by the community, it was to refund him all the expenses
he had incurred in connection therewith; and that even though
one or two members of the community were opposed to entrust-
ing the mission to such representative, they were nevertheless
obligated to pay their part of the expenses. R. Hayyim, then,
related his personal experiences as community representative.
He had often been sent by the community of Cologne to negotiate with the authorities, and R. Zalkman Kohen had warned
him on a number of occasions not to promise any money to the
authorities on his behalf. Nevertheless, R. Zalkman was
obligated to pay his share of the amount promised. Moreover, during the previous year twelve communities had promised
to pay 23,000 pounds to the king for certain considerations.
He, R. Hayyim, was not sent as a delegate by his community
and was even warned not to take part in the negotiations with
the king. Subsequently the king refused to keep his promise,
but demanded the pledged sum nevertheless. R. Hayyim's
community, though it took no part officially in the negotiations
with the king and was therefore not responsible for the loss
incurred, nevertheless had to pay its share. R. Hayyim concluded, therefore, that a community which tried, on a mere
technicality, to evade refunding the expenses of its representatives was not acting honorably.

A and his son were sent by a community. The phrase ש"כו
מגופים היה הסכנה שעת זה בנדון, coincides with the statement
of the Colmar chronicler regarding Boppard and Oberwessel:

et eos a periculo liberaret mortis. The Jews of these two towns were still in danger of death when A and his son were sent to Siegfried of Cologne. It seems, therefore, that after the twelve communities were forced to pay the amount they had offered for the king's favor, even though their request was not granted, they no longer dared enter into further negotiations with the king and left the Jews of Boppard and Oberwessel, as well as R. Meir, to their fate. A and his son, therefore, were probably sent by the community of Boppard and Oberwessel, who, fearing a repetition of the negotiations with Rudolf, advised A and his son not to give the archbishop any money until he granted their request and carried it out to a successful conclusion.

Excursus III

A misinterpreted Responsum.

In order to illustrate how the cryptic style, complicated discussions, and use of special terms in the Responsa literature, may mislead even trained rabbinic scholars, we offer here the following example. R. Meir writes: וששאלתני על קהלך שכבר עשו תקנה ביניהם ובהסכמתך קרובי כהן צדק שכל מי שיצא מן העיר לגור במקום אחר שלא יכנס לעיר לזקוף חובותיו בלא דעת הקהל לראות אם יוכל להפרע שאז לא יזקוף חובותיו, אם אחד מן הקהל חפץ ליתן דמי החוב ולסלקו יש לו להסתלק ואם זקף בלי דעת הקהל קנסוהו לתת מכל אשר ימצא לו ו' קולני"א מן הזקוק ועתה עבר אחד על ככה.

Moses Hoffman (*Der Geldhandel der deutchen Juden*, "Anhang", 189) translated the term לזקוף *aufzustellen*, and therefore, interpreted it to mean *Schuldkonten abzuschlissen und einzuziehen*. Accordingly the *takkanah* of the community provided that upon leaving town, a person should not collect all his debts at once, without the knowledge of the community, as this might lead to a panic (ibid. p. 80). Thus, according to Hoffman, the rapid withdrawal of capital from a town in the Middle Ages, would cause a money crisis. If this interpretation of the Responsum is correct, our entire outlook on the money economy of the Middle Ages and their system of credit would have to undergo a radical change. Zimmels (op. cit. p. 44), though not referring to Hoffman, gives this same interpretation of the above mentioned Responsum. Thus he writes: *Die Gemeinde eines Verwandten R. Meirs verordnete, dass jeder, der die Stadt verlässt und sich in einer anderen Siedlung niederlässt, nicht in der Stadt die Schulden ohne wissen der Gemeinde einkassieren dürfe, sonst wurde er bestraft werden*... This interpretation of

163

the above quoted Responsum, however, is entirely unacceptable; for the term לזקוף never meant to collect debts.

The talmudic term זקפו עליו במלוה (B. M. 72a), meaning:
"he settled the interest on the debtor as a loan", received a
special meaning in the Middle Ages. In order to collect their
debts, the Jews were often forced to lend additional sums
to their debtors and combine the old debt with the money
newly lent as a single debt, for which the Jews received
better-pledges as security, or more reliable sureties. This process
of lending additional funds in order to insure the collection of the
money already due, was called זקיפה. Thus we read in Cremona
וכן עשה שיצא הוא וביתו לעיר אחרת ושהה שם ימים רבים ...121:
ומה שהלוה לשרים כדי שיזקפו לו הכל ביחד ויפרעו לו הכל, גם מזה
הקהל 156: also ibid ;פטור כיון שלא יכול להוציא חובו בענין אחר
יש להם לשבע שהוא כדבריהם שהלוה אותם בעירם או זקפם, כי בענין
אחר לא היה חיב על הזקיפה אם לא היו רוצים לפורעו אלא לזוקפו
מה הוה לו למעבד.

We can now understand the community ordinance referred
to in Am. II, 140. The community leaders were unwilling to
allow persons, who were not residents of their town, to invest
their money there for profit (see Pr. 359). They knew the custom of the German communities not to collect any taxes from
those who moved out of a town, but who were forced to lend
additional funds to their debtors in order to insure the collection of their old debts (see quotation of Cr. 121, 156 above,
also R. Meir's answer to Am. II, 140). In order that no one
should use his perfectly secure old debt as a mere pretext for
lending additional funds to his debtors, the community leaders
passed a decree to the effect that a person who moved out of
their town should lend additional funds to his debtors, only
with the knowledge and consent of the community, who first
had to determine whether or not those debts could be collected
without lending additional funds to the debtors. Furthermore,
if a member of the community desired to take over a debt from

one who had moved out of town, the latter member was forced
to assign that debt to the former.

R. Meir's answer was that if the individual left the community after the above-mentioned decree was passed, he was
bound by its terms even though he had originally protested
against it; but if he had left the city before the ordinance was
passed, he was not bound by its terms since a community can
not force a non-member to accept its decrees: דרשאין בני העיר
להסיע על קיצותן, על בני עירם שהיו שם בשעת התקנה או שלבסוף
באו לגור שם אבל זה שלא היה בשעת התקנה וגם עכשיו אינו גר שם לאו
כל הימנו.

L. Finkelstein (op. cit. p. 53) interpreted R. Meir's answer
as follows: "In this Responsum R. Meir ... adds the novel
principle that, provided the community is not unjust, it may
even protect its citizens by calling on non-members doing business within its jurisdiction to obey its decrees". This interpretation, however, is in direct contradiction of R. Meir's view
that a non-member is not bound by the special decrees of individual communities, but is subject to the custom of the country
only: ואם לא יכלו להוציא קודם, מנהג הוא בכל הקהלות שאין
לקח מהם מס (ibid.).

DEMOCRACY IN THE COMMUNITIES OF THE EARLY MIDDLE AGES

By Irving A. Agus, Yeshiva University

A.

One of the most popular subjects for historical research during the past century, a subject that occupied the best European historians for a hundred years and was discussed in innumerable articles and books, was the origin and development of the European towns, and the social, political and economic institutions evolved therein during the Middle Ages.[1] Modern life in most of its phases is a direct outgrowth of the institutions, practices and ideas developed in the medieval towns. Our present civilization is urban and cannot be fully comprehended without a clear grasp of the elements creating the multifarious life of the early towns.

Vast research has therefore been devoted to this subject, and a number of theories have been set forth to explain the sudden emergence of free corporations in a medieval world, and the growth of democratic institutions in an overwhelmingly autocratic environment; theories have been advanced about the freedom of the individual, in spite of the

[1] For a bibliography of the subject see Dahlman-Waitz, *Quellenkunde der Deutschen Geschichte*, 9th edition, Leipzig 1931, pp. 156–7 and 453–6; *Cambridge Medieval History*, vol. 5, pp. 904–8: J. W. Thompson, *An Economic and Social History of the Middle Ages*, New York, 1928, pp. 848–50; J. C. Gemperle, *Belgische und Schweizerische Städteverfassungsgeschichte im Mittelalter*, Wetteren, 1943, pp. 349–66.

א

all pervading idea of servility and dependence.[2] The problem of the origin of the European town and of its characteristic institutions, has, as yet received no adequate solution, and none of the theories so far propounded by various schools of historians since W. Arnold[3] and G. L. Maurer,[4] have satisfactorily explained all the matters involved.[5] To cite a single example, George von Below, after a lifetime of laborious and fruitful research, was forced to conclude: "Unter diesen Umständen bleibt uns nur übrig zu konstatieren dass es im grossen und ganzen gar keinen Anknüpfungspunkt für den entstehenden stadtrat gegeben hat."[6] The paucity of studies on town origins by scholars of the present generation is not due to the fact that the problem has been considered solved either by Keutgen,[7] Rietschel,[8]

---

[2] An excellent summary of the various theories propounded during the active period of the controversy, will be found in G. Seeliger, "Stadtverfassung", *Reallexikon der Germanischen Altertumskunde*, ed. by J. Hoops, vol. IV, Strassburg, 1918, pp. 244 ff. Cf. *Cambridge Medieval History*, vol. 5, pp. 631–7; J. W. Thompson, *op. cit.*, pp. 766–73; C. Stephenson, *Borough and town*, Cambridge, Mass., 1933, ch. 1.

[3] *Verfassungsgeschichte der deutschen Freistädte*, 2 vols., Hamburg and Gotha, 1854.

[4] *Geschichte der Städteverfassung in Deutschland*, Erlangen, 1869–71, 4 vols. For a criticism of Maurer, see A. Heusler, *Der Ursprung der deutschen Stadtverfassung*, Weimar, 1872, pp. 157 ff., 236 ff.

[5] Even the mercantile theory of Pirenne and Rietschel, which is the most favored theory at present (C. Stephenson, *ibid.*), is based mostly on conjecture, takes many things for granted, and does not explain the origin of many characteristic town institutions. It merely states, without evidence from earlier sources, that such institutions were usually set up by merchants. Cf. K. Frölich, *Zeitschrift der Savigny-Stiftung für Rechtsgeschichte*, Germanische Abteilung, LI (1931), pp. 628 ff.; A. Coville, "Les Villes du Moyen Age," *Journal de Savants*, 1928.

[6] *Die Entstehung der Stadtgemeinde*, Düsseldorf, 1889, p. 97.

[7] *Untersuchungen über den Ursprung der deutschen Stadtverfassung*, Leipzig, 1895. Cf. F. W. Maitland, "The origin of the Borough," *English Historical Review* XI (1896), pp. 13 ff.; *ibid.*, *Doomsday Book and Beyond*, Cambridge, 1897.

[8] *Die Civitas auf deutschen Boden*, Leipzig, 1894; *Markt und Stadt in ihrem rechtlichen Verhältniss*, Leipzig, 1897.

Dopsch,[9] or Pirenne,[10] but is rather due to a conviction that the problems involved are unsolvable.[11]

It is therefore important to examine a parallel political corporation that developed side by side with the town commune, that has been in daily contact with it socially, economically, and even culturally, and that has often antedated it by centuries in the development of characteristic town institutions. Such a political corporation was the Jewish community, which in many localities had already been established by the time the town commune began its characteristic development immediately adjacent to this community. A study of the Jewish community, therefore, may shed new light on the subject, and may even lead to a satisfactory solution of some of its most intricate problems. Moreover, there is a great paucity of source material for the growth of the European town, during the tenth and eleventh centuries, although we do possess very valuable material for the study of the community during this period.[12]

Thus in the Responsa literature of the end of the tenth and the beginning of the eleventh centuries, the Jewish community already appears as a unit of self-government with fully developed institutions, with firmly rooted

[9] *The Economic and Social Foundations of European Civilization,* tr. from the German, London, 1937, esp. chs. X and XI.

[10] "L'Origine des Constitutions Urbaines au Moyen Age," *Revue Historique,* LIII (1893), pp. 52 ff., LVII (1895), pp. 57 ff.; *Belgian Democracy,* Manchester, 1951; *Medieval Cities,* Princeton, 1925; *Les Villes et les Institutions Urbaines,* Brussels, 1939, 2 vols.

[11] Since the turn of the century most studies of the town life deal with separate towns and depend on localized sources, but are not concerned with general theories of origin. See Stephenson, *op. cit.,* first two chapters, and the detailed bibliography in J. C. Gemperle, *ibid.*

[12] A detailed discussion of the constitutional history of the Jewish community in the middle ages, is given by the present author in his book *Rabbi Meir of Rothenburg,* Philadelphia, 1947, pp. 54–124.

customs, and with an established method of cooperation with neighboring communities.[13] From a Responsum of Rabbenu Gershom we learn that several communities were assembled in one place, and that they pronounced the ban to help restore the stolen goods of a Jew, and that the pronouncement of a ban for such a purpose was a well established custom "in most Jewish communities."[14] R. Gershom affirms in his answer that the community is a legal entity having the judicial and legislative authority of the Sanhedrin, the High Court of Jerusalem.[15] The European towns, on the other hand, did not generally exercise such authority till the end of the twelfth and the beginning of the thirteenth centuries.

The community at this early period already paid its taxes to the king, or overlord, in a lump sum, assessed each member for his share of the tax, and used several well-established and ingenious methods of assessment,[16] — in which respects, again the community antedated the town commune by more than a century. In the second half of the tenth century the community maintained peace between its members, and fixed specific money-fines for particular breaches of the peace — a characteristic function of the town commune two centuries later.[17]

[13] See the Responsa of Rabbenu Gershom in תשובות חכמי צרפת ולותיר, nos. 85, 87, 88 and 97; and the Responsa of R. Joseph Tob-Elem found among the Responsa of R. Meir of Rothenburg, Prague ed. nos. 940–1; Lemberg ed. no. 423, cf. תשובות גאוני מזרח ומערב, nos. 165, 205.

[14] Joel Mueller, תשובות חכמי צרפת ולותיר, no. 97; Mordecai, B. M. 257: והקהילות שהיו נקבצים שם נתעצמו על אבידת (אביהם) [אחיהם] וגזרו גזירה באלה ובשבועה על מי שיגיע לידו מכל מה שנאבד באותה ספינה שיחזיר לבעל אבידה כמנהג הנוהג ברוב קהילות ישראל שכל מי שיפסיד כלום או בגניבה או בשום ענין, שעושין לו תקנה וגוזרים על כל מי שיבא לידו אבדה פלונית שאבד פלוני שיחזיר לבעלים.

[15] Ibid., loc. cit.

[16] See Responsa of R. Joseph Tob-Elem cited in note 13 above.

[17] Teshubot Geonim Kadmonim, 125; ibid., 135; L. Ginzberg, גנזי שכטר, II, p. 274; For a survey of the dates of the establishment of similar institutions in the European towns, see Cambridge Medieval History, vol. V, chapter XIX,

The most important phase of community activity, however, was its system of government. We encounter in the communities of the thirteenth century a government, democratic in form, based on ideals of justice, freedom and equality. The principle that "the majority rules" is generally accepted in the matter of election of officers and in legislation designed for the public welfare and for strengthening of religious observance, while unanimous agreement is required for the introduction of arbitrarily new practices.[18] The question therefore arises: what were the steps in the development of this elaborate and mature system? and principally, what were the factors that determined the direction of such growth?

Two alternatives present themselves: A. The communities of the tenth century had an aristocratic form of government, similar to the one described in geonic Responsa,[19] but later changed through the adoption of the democratic principle "the majority rules," while in the final stage of their constitutional development, during the twelfth and thirteenth centuries, the communities came to recognize the rights of the minority and instituted safeguards for its protection, so that in certain instances unanimous agreement was required. B. The constitutional development within the community was mainly conditioned by the ideas of its environment. Therefore, in accordance with Germanic lines of development, unanimous agreement was required for all community activities during the tenth century; while in the twelfth and thirteenth centuries, because of the renewed interest in Roman law in the European towns, the principle "the majority rules" was introduced in the Jewish communities.[20]

[18] See Irving A. Agus, *op. cit.*, pp. 108–24.

[19] See *Shaare Zedek*, p. 57a.

[20] See Prof. Yitzchak (Fritz) Baer, היסודות וההתחלות של ארגון הקהלה היהודית בימי הבינים, *Zion*, 1951, pp. 37–40. It is very doubtful, however,

The present writer in his book on R. Meir of Rothenburg accepted the first alternative,[21] and came to the conclusion that the democratic system of government in the communities was an outgrowth of Jewish law in its constant adjustment to the problems of life. A continuous growth was shown in the sensitivity of community government to the interests of each individual member.[22]

Prof. Yitzchak (Fritz) Baer in a recent article has accepted the second alternative.[23] He gives an excellent description of the history of the community system of government, marshalling an abundance of source material in order to prove that this system had already been in existence in the Judean towns in the days of the second Temple. He has shown that although it developed side by side with the Hellenistic cities, it was an immanently Jewish creation, and that in spite of the opposition of official Judaism (embodied in the Mishna, Talmud, and geonic literature) it flourished throughout the first millenium of our era, until it became firmly established in the West. Although Prof. Baer brilliantly points out that as a political unit possessing autonomy, judicial power, a penal code, and powerful social institutions, the Jewish community antedated the town commune by several generations,[24] he nevertheless insists that the Jews became familiar with the democratic system of government through the contemporary learned jurists and canonists, who in

whether the old Germanic idea of unanimous consent was still known in Germany and France during the tenth and eleventh centuries. Long before this time the autocratic idea became paramount in western Europe, thus wiping out any trace, or even a memory, of the custom of free association of equals. See O. v. Gierke, *Genossenschaftsrecht*, vol. I, pp. 98, 103, 121, 153.

[21] *Op. cit.*, pp. 94 f.

[22] See *ibid.*, pp. 108–24. [23] See note 20 above.

[24] *Ibid.*, pp. 32–6; see also his article on Rashi in ספר היובל לכבוד יעקב נחום אפשטיין, Jerusalem, 1950, p. 320.

turn arrived at the principle "the majority rules" during
the revival of the study of Roman law in the twelfth
century.

Thus Baer writes: "Accordingly we conclude therefrom
that the tosaphists and the German rabbinical scholars,
because of their long, traditional training in talmudic
dialectics, antedated the Christian scholars in the exact
formulation of political conceptions then vaguely current
in the air, [and used them] before their neighbors were
able to arrive at distinctly clear definitions. Basically,
however, in this matter the Jewish scholars learned and
received their ideas from their friends, the Christian jurists
and canonists, and not from their own, talmudic tradition.
The principle "follow the majority" was not applied by
the Talmud to town corporations nor to communities —
for, as pointed out before, such institutions were not within
the scope of interest of the talmudic scholars — nor do we
find that such a problem could practically have been discussed in the geonic period. In European society, however,
toward the end of the twelfth century they began seriously
to discuss such matters."[25]

[25] *Ibid.*, p. 38: כדרכנו נסיק מכאן, כי רבותינו בעלי התוספות וחכמי אשכנז,
בזכות לימודם התלמודי המסור בידיהם מדורות, קדמו לחכמי הנוצרים ופירשו לעצמם
מושגים פוליטיים שהיו רווחים באוויר, אלא ששכניהם הנוצרים לא הספיקו עדיין
להגדיר אותם בכל הבהירות הדרושה. אך בעיקר העניין למדו כאן חכמי ישראל את
תורתם מפי חבריהם היוריסטים והקנוניסטים הנוצרים, ולא מן המסורת התלמודית.
הכלל של „אחרי הרבים להטות" לא נלמד בהלכה התלמודית על הקורפורציות
העירוניות והקהילתיות — כי מוסדות אלה לא נכנסו בתחום התעניינותם של חכמי
התלמוד, כפי שראינו — ובתקופת הגאונים לא מצאנו, כי בעיה כזאת יכלה לעמוד
לדיון להלכה ולמעשה, אבל בחברה האירופית התחילו מסוף המאה הי"ב ואילך
לדון בשאלות כאלה בכובד-ראש.

[The principle of "the majority rules" was in vogue in the Second
Commonwealth and was adopted in the synagogues (assemblies) and
conclaves. Decisions were made according to the majority after taking
a vote. These decisions affected not only the religious, but Jewish
life as a whole. This may be deduced from the expression נמנו ורבו found
in tannaitic literature (compare also the expression נמנו וגמרו). The principle of "the majority rules" was also observed in the Jewish communities

The problem of the origin of democratic ideas in the
communities, however, could easily be resolved if we were
able to discover the approximate date of a Responsum sent
by R. Judah b. Meir ha-Cohen and R. Eliezer b. Judah to
the community of Troyes.[26] The matter here involved was
as follows: The people of Troyes had enacted a resolution
by majority vote, and had strengthened it by a *herem*,
enjoining the members of the community from employing
a particularly obnoxious servant for a period of six months.
The employer of the servant, however, refused to abide by
this resolution holding that it was carried through by a
personal enemy. The community, therefore, inquired of
R. Judah and R. Eliezer whether an enactment passed by
the majority of the members of the community was binding
upon the minority in spite of the latter's protest. In their
answer these scholars gave a detailed explanation of the
principle "the majority rules" as applied to community
government, and gave elaborate proof of its validity in
Jewish law.

The present writer has subscribed to the opinion of S. D.
Luzzatto[27] and H. Gross[28] in identifying R. Judah b. Meir

of France. Professor Baer states that the principle of "majority
rules" was not mentioned in the geonic literature. This silence is
understandable since the Babylonian communities were not as
democratic as the Judaean-Palestinian. On the other hand, the
Franco-German Jewish communities were a continuation of the
Palestinian communities and followed the principles that were in
vogue among the Jews in Judaea-Palestine. S. Z.]

[26] *Kol-Bo*, no. 142: שאלה זו שאלו רביני טרוייׄׄש לרבי יהודה כהן ב״ר מאיר
ולרבי אליעזר ב״ר יהודה ז״ל; printed also by S. D. Luzzatto in מנד ירחים,
pp. 8–10, from a manuscript of the *Orhot-Hayyim*, II, p. 235.

[27] *Ibid.*, p. 10: העתקתי כל זה מפני שנראה לי כי זה ר' יהודה הכהן הוא רבו
של רבנו גרשם מאור הגולה, ור' אלעזר ב״ר יצחק הוא הנקרא ר' אליעזר הגדול.
כי הנה בשבולי הלקט כ״י אשר ביד ידידי החכם יוסף אלמנצי מצאתי: רבנו שלמה
זצ״ל שמע מרבו על יהודה הכהן ב״ר מאיר שהיה אומר דריחא מלתא, ור' אלעזר
בן גילו חולק ומורה דלאו מלתא היא ..." The second signature in the
Orhot-Hayyim mss. quoted by Luzzatto and that in the Seminary is
אלעזר ב״ר יצחק, though the heading clearly states אליעזר ב״ר יהודה.

[28] *Monatsschrift*, XVIII (1869), pp. 537–8; *Galia Judaica*, Paris,

as R. Leontin, the teacher of Rabbenu Gershom, who had been active toward the end of the tenth and the beginning of the eleventh centuries. He thus had decisive proof of the fact that the principle "the majority rules" was operative within the Jewish community almost two centuries before "European society began seriously to discuss it."[29]

Baer, however, refuses to accept this identification and suggests that R. Judah and R. Eliezer were students of R. Perez (of the thirteenth century). He insists that, unless decisive proof be found to the contrary, this Responsum be considered as belonging to the end of the thirteenth century since its contents are in consonance with the stage in constitutional development reached by the European towns at that time.[30] As proof, Baer cites: a) the fact that the above-mentioned Responsum appears at the end of a chapter entitled "the decisions of R. Perez"; b) the comparative length of the Responsum; c) the peculiarity of finding a Responsum of R. Leontin only in the *Kol-Bo*; and d) that the nature of the charges brought against the unruly servant (that she struck a man with a stick, called the wife of another "a prostitute," and called the third "a cuckold") is not in consonance with manners at the turn of the eleventh century, but rather fits in well with the the thirteenth.[31]

1897, p. 224: "Cette consultation fut adressée à cette communauté par Juda ben Méir Haccohen (identique très certainement avec Sire Léontin, qui vécut vers l'an 1000 et fut le maitre de Rabbenu Guerschom) et Eliezer b. Juda . . ."

[29] *Op. cit.*, p. 76 f.

[30] *Op. cit.*, p. 38, note 31.

[31] *Ibid.*: — ליאון 'ויהיה זה חידוש מעניין למצוא בס' כל בו תשובה גדולה של ר' ליאון
רק ככה נקרא שמו, עד כמה שידוע לי בדברי תלמידו המפורסם עצמו! אלא שהתשובה
הנ"ל נמצאה בס' כל בו בתוך .דינים מה"ר פרץ', תלמידו של ר' יחיאל ב'ר יוסף
מפריש, וכל עוד שאין ראיה ממשית נגדית צריך להניח, כי התשובה שייכת לסוף המאה
הי"ג. וכן מוכיחה האריכות של דברי המשיב בעניין זכות הצבור, המרובין, לגבי היחיד,
ואין דרכו של רנמ"ה בתשובותיו האמתיות להאריך בצורה כזאת. וגם המעשה הנשאל

The objections of Baer to the antiquity of the Responsum under discussion, however, are not very serious. This Responsum is found in manuscripts of the *Orchot Chayyim II*,[32] and of other collections of rabbinic lore.[33] Although it usually follows the decisions of R. Perez, it did not necessarily emanate from his school. Students in the thirteenth century usually included much older material in the collections of their teachers' decisions. Thus we find geonic Responsa in practically all collections of rabbinic lore of this period.[34] A student of R. Perez did indeed copy the above-mentioned Responsum and placed it among the decisions of his teacher, but this act should never be used as a criterion of its age. It may serve as a *terminus ad quem*, but not a *terminus a quo*.

Nor is it strange to find a Responsum of R. Leontin exclusively in the *Kol Bo*. We find geonic Responsa in the *Mordecai* that are not found elsewhere. This is also true of Responsa in the *Shibbolei ha-Leket*, in the *Shaare Dura*, in the *Teshuvot Maimuniot*, in the *Orchot Hayyim*. The *Shibbolei ha-Leket*, vol. II, still in manuscript, contains Responsa of R. Gershom not found elsewhere; why then should it be so strange to find a Responsum of R. Leontin in the *Kol Bo*?[35]

עליו יוכיח, בנייה שעומדת לחרף ולנדף את היהודים, .זה אומר אותי הכה במקל
וזה אומר אשתי קראה קראה זונה וזה אומר אותי קראה קרנן' .קרנן' הוא כנראה לשון גנאי,
ולא כדאי להרבות בדברים כדי להוכיח כי התשובה הנ'ל היא מאוחרת. Incidentally, the word קרנן probably means the same as today in German *Hörner aufsetzen*, i. e., to cuckold; using the noun, however, instead of the verb.

[32] See מגד ירחים, II, pp. 8 f.; also the Seminary ms. *Orhot Hayyim*, II, p. 338.

[33] See Halberstamm catalogue, קהלת שלמה, no. 170; also described in "Descriptive Catalogue of Hebrew Mss. of the Montefiore Library," *JQR.*, o. s. XIV (1902), p. 180.

[34] See especially the Prague edition of the Responsa of R. Meir of Rothenburg which contains, among many others, eleven Responsa of R. Gershom, forty-one of R. Juda haCohen, two of R. Joseph Tob-Elem, eight of Rashi, twenty-eight of R. Tam, some of which are not found elsewhere.

[35] Moreover, though the *Kol-Bo* consists mainly of a systematic

The length of the Responsum is certainly no criterion, as anyone acquainted with Responsa literature will admit. It is not unduly long, especially when one takes into consideration the fact that it answers three questions. We possess Responsa of Rabbenu Gershom of equal length.[36] The Responsa of R. Meir of Rothenburg range from a few lines to several hundred, the length depending on the problem involved and the prestige of those who propounded the question.[37] Nor do the charges brought against the servant predicate a particular age or century.

Serious study of the text of the Responsum of R. Judah and R. Eliezer will convince the student of rabbinic Responsa that it was composed at the turn of the eleventh century, for the following reasons: a) The authors cite many proofs for their view that the principle "the majority rules" is sound Jewish law, but they never mention authorities, such as Rashi, R. Tam, Rabiah, R. Meir, or any of the celebrated tosaphists — an unusual omission in discussions of the thirteenth century. Nor are the widely accepted customs of the French and German communities (during the thirteenth century) ever referred to as proof.[38] b) The authors derive legal principles directly from the Bible.

---

arrangement of many branches of Jewish law, the last part of the *Kol-Bo* contains a haphazard collection, without any discernible order, of rabbinic lore, halakic decisions and Responsa of talmudic scholars who lived within a period of four centuries before the compilation had been made.

[36] Cf. Joel Mueller, תשובות חכמי צרפת ולותיר, nos. 85, 98, 99; אוצר החיים III (1927), pp. 97–102.

[37] See especially Cremona edition, no. 111, versus Berlin edition, pp. 146–53. Moreover, one can not compare one authority with another, even if they are of the same period. Thus R. Meir usually wrote brief answers while those of R. Eliezer b. Joel are unusually long sometimes constituting elaborate treatises. The famous *Iggeret* of R. Sherira Gaon is also not a model of brevity.

[38] R. Meir of Rothenburg constantly refers to the customs of the communities as the deciding factors in community law; see Cremona ed. nos. 49, 111, 121, 156, 230; Berlin ed., pp. 205, 209, and many others too numerous to list.

This is indeed a decisive proof. The very beginning of their answer: דבר זה מצינו בתורה ושנוי בנביאים ומשולש בכתובים is such as is rarely, if ever, found in rabbinic writing after the middle of the eleventh century. The rabbis of the middle ages relied exclusively on the Talmud, and on talmudic interpretation of biblical verses. One can hardly find an author of Responsa from Rashi on who derives law directly from the Bible.

Talmudic scholars never re-inforced their views thus, as is well known. Nevertheless, R. Judah and R. Eliezer indulge in a long, midrashic, interpretation of biblical sources,[39] comparing the community to the congregation of Israel in solemn assembly, its decision to that of the Sanhedrin under Joshua the son of Nun, and its authority to that of king Saul, without citing any proof from the Talmud that such comparisons are admissible.[40] Some parts of the Responsum read exactly like a *Midrash*, but a diligent search has failed to reveal any other source for most of these interpretations.

Traces of such a practice are found in the Responsa of

[39] *Kol Bo* 142: וכתוב, כתוב בתורה ובאת אל הכהנים הלוים ואל השופט
שופטים ושוטרים תתן מלמד שהשוטרים מקבלים שכר כשופטים ושכר אלו ואלו שקולים.
בנביאים דכתיב והיה ה' עם השופט. בכתובים דכתיב ואריב עמם ואקללם. ואין
לאיש לעזור לקרובו להחליש כח ב"ד ואם עשה כן מה כתיב שם ואם העלם יעלימו
ונומר. וכתוב ושמתי אני את פני. ואם הגביה יד ב"ד והחליש כח קרוביו מה שכרו
יורו משפטיך ליעקב וגו' ברך ה' חילו, מה טעם, משום האומר לאביו ולאמו וגו' . . .
ומצינו סמך לזה בכמה מקומות בתורה מניין שאינו יכול להוציא עצמו מן הכלל
דכתיב לא אתכם לבדכם וכתיב את אשר ישנו פה וגו'. וכתיב פן יש בכם איש או
אשה וגו'. וכתיב והיה כשמעו את דברי האלה הזאת וגו'. בנביאים דכתיב והית'
העיר חרם ואע"פ שהחרימה יהושע שלא על פי הדיבור . . .

[40] *Ibid.*: ומצינו שהסכים הקב"ה על ידו ועל יד ישראל דכתיב חרם בקרבך ישראל.
וכתיב לא אוסיף להיות עוד עמכם אם לא תשמיד החרם מקרבך. ואם כדברי המשיב
היה לו לעכן לומר ולטעון לא הסכמתי בהסכמת החרם, אלא לא על כל הימנו. ועוד
מצינו בשאול . . . ועוד מצינו באנשי יבש גלעד שנתחייבו כלייה על שלא חשו לגזירה
שגזרו עליהם אחיהם דכתיב . . . לנדרו מניין שאין היחיד יכול לבטל דברי המרובין
דכתיב אורו מרוז. ואמרי' בארבע מאה שפורי שמתיה ברק.

Rabbenu Gershom[41] and R. Joseph Tob-Elem.[42] They, too, occasionally derive legal principles directly from biblical verses. This extraordinary use of biblical verses by the two leading scholars of the end of the tenth and the beginning of the eleventh centuries confirms the view of the present author that the above-mentioned Responsum was composed in this period.

More decisive proof of the antiquity of the Responsum under discussion, however, can now be advanced. One of the three questions asked, by the community of Troyes, of R. Judah and R. Eliezer was whether one community might presume to exercise authority over another and effectively pronounce the *herem* against its members.[43] This question is set forth in general terms with no description of the circumstances involved. The present author, however, fortunately discovered an unpublished Responsum of R. Joseph Tob-Elem, apparently addressed to the other community involved, in which are given all the details that occasioned the incidental query included by the community of Troyes in their questions to R. Judah and R. Eliezer.

This Responsum of R. Joseph Tob-Elem, the text of

---

[41] *Orhot Hayyim*, II, p. 574; Responsa R. Meir, Prague ed. 928; *Mahzor Vitri*, p. 96 f.; *Mordecai* B. B. 600: ואע"ג דלאו בפירוש כתיב האי דינא איכא למימר מדוקיא דקראי ומדוקיא דמתני'. דוקיא דקראי דכתיב איש כי ימות ובן אין לו והעברתם את נחלתו, משעת מיתה האב עוברת הנחלה.

[42] Responsa R. Meir, Prague ed. 941; Cf. Responsum at end of this article: והלא אין גוזרין גזירה על הציבור אא"כ רוב הציבור יכולין לעמוד בה שנאמר (איוב ל"ז, כ"ג) ושדי לא מצאנוהו שגיא כח. Our Talmud, however, derives this law from another verse, see B. K. 79a, B. B. 60b, A. Z. 36a, Horayot 3b. See also *Mahzor Vitry*, p. 357: ומקרא מעיד וצוח הרימו מכשול מדרך עמי.

[43] *Kol-Bo, loc. cit.*: ויורנו רבותינו אם יוכלו בני עיר להשביע על בני עיר אחרת ולכופם שם בעירם לכל דבר אע"פ שהם רחוקים מהם כמה פרסאות ואין כפיה להם על אלו. ואם יכולין לטעון לה אנו בשלנו ואתם בשלכם ואין אנו משגיחים לגזירתכם ולא על שבועתכם.

which is appended to this article, is found in the *Mordecai Hagadol*, the Goldsmith manuscript, in the Jewish Theological Seminary library.[44] This Responsum undoubtedly belongs to R. Joseph Tob-Elem the elder, who was active at the turn of the eleventh century, since it bears the full signature יוסף בר שמואל טוב עלם,[44a] and parts of it are quoted by the famous tosaphist R. Isaac b. Abraham (end of twelfth century) who refers to the author as "gaon."[45] This title was given to the scholars of France, Germany, and Spain, who lived at the time when talmudic learning first appeared in the West.[45a] Following is a digest of the question put to R. Joseph Tob-Elem:

Some Jews of Rheims, while on their way to the fair of Troyes, were attacked and taken captive. The charitable members of the latter community interceded on their behalf, negotiated with their captors, and agreed to pay a ransom of thirty pounds. The greater part of the ransom money was paid by the captives themselves, while, in order

[44] P. 298a.

[44a] See Rappaport, Introduction to *Teshubot Geonim Kadmonim*; *Sefer Hayashar*, no. 46d; *Mahzor Vitry*, pp. 352–3; *ibid.*, p. 357; *Tossaphot to Pesahim*, 30a, s. v. אמר; *ibid.*, 115a, s. v. והדר; *Nazir* 59a, s. v. אמר; *Gittin* 85b, s. v. ולא.

[45] *Mordecai*, B. B. 490: שאל ה"ר יוסף את ה"ר יצחק בר אברהם על הצדקה שפוסקים בני העיר ויש יחידים שמסרבין על דעת הרבים ולא אבו שמוע. ואני שמעתי שכתב רבינו שמעיה בשם רבינו יוסף טוב עלם אין מעשין על הצדקה אפילו למצוה שנאמר כי בגלל הדבר הזה יברכך ושנינו כל מצוה שמתן שכרה בצדה אין ב"ד של מטה מוזהרין עליה ואין הדבר תלוי אלא בנדיבות הלב ומדברי הרצאה עכ"ל. ותלמידך חוכך להחמיר . . . והשיב ר"י ב"ר אברהם וז"ל . . . וכתב רבינו יוסף דאין מעשין עליה משום דמתן שכרה בצדה. יפה כתב אני לא ידעתי ושמחתי בדברים כי עכשיו קמצאתי גאון כדברי. Cf. *Tossaphot* to B. B. 8b, s. v. ואכפיה; *Teshubot Maimuniot* to *Kinyan* 28; *Or Zarua, Hilkot Zedakah*, 4. Part of this Responsum is found in Responsa of R. Meir, Prague ed. 940 with the superscription: תשובת רבינו יוסף טוב עלם. כתב לבני טרויי"ש בסוף התשובה.

[45a] See Samuel Poznanski, *Babylonische Geonim im nachgaonaischen zeitalter*, Berlin, 1914, pp. 105–111; Joel Mueller, Introduction to תשובות גאוני מזרח ומערב, and to תשובות חכמי צרפת ולותיר; *Tashbetz*, 575; *Or Zarua*, II, p. 117, middle of first column; *ibid.*, no. 275 end; *Mordecai Pesahim*, 594; *Tarbitz*, VIII (1937), p. 169.

to raise the remainder, the community of Troyes ordained that their own members and those of the neighboring communities, Sens, Auxerre, and Chalon-sur-Saône, should contribute one shilling per pound. They further ordained that anyone who would refuse to contribute his share should together with his children be placed under the ban; that partaking of his bread and wine should be forbidden; and that he should pay a fine of thirty shillings. They added that no one should release a community or individual from this ban.

The community of Sens, however, formally released its members from the ban on the ground that they had become impoverished, because of recent harassment and serious trouble; and, furthermore, they maintained that they were completely independent of the community of Troyes and were under no obligation to share in its burdens. The representative of Troyes was aware that the people of Sens were in serious difficulty because some one had destroyed a church (or a cross) in their locality. They, nevertheless, sent their voluntary contribution to the people of Troyes. The question was, therefore, whether the community of Troyes had a right to pronounce the ban, and whether it was binding upon the people of Sens. Thus there can be no reasonable doubt that the part of the Responsum of R. Judah and R. Eliezer referred to above, and the Responsum of R. Joseph Tub-Elem, deal with the same incident; and that both were, therefore, written about the same time. There is no other case, where one community tried to dictate to another community, reported in the entire literature of Germany and France of the eleventh twelfth, or thirteenth centuries. To assume that the two Responsa dealing with such a case, and both involving Troyes, refer to two separate incidents, would indeed tax our credulity. Moreover, in his book the present author discussed at length the legal relationship of the communities to one another, the jealousy of each community for its independence,[46] and the widespread acceptance of political and constitutional theories by the twelfth and thirteenth centuries, theories that would make it impossible, during that period, for one community to attempt to coerce the members of another.[47]

In view of the internal and external evidence cited above, we must conclude that the Responsum of R. Judah and R. Eliezer, which gives a clear and detailed description of the principle "the majority rules" as applied to community government, was written at the turn of the eleventh century, at a time when "European society" was not at all confronted with such problems (especially in Germany and France), and a century and a half before jurists and canonists discussed them. Hence, the rabbis could not have learned this principle from their Christian neighbors, but must have relied solely on their interpretation of the Talmud and on their own efforts in applying Jewish law to new circumstances.

We must now try to identify R. Judah b. Meir ha-Cohen and his colleague R. Eliezer b. Judah. As stated above, S. D. Luzzatto and H. Gross believe that the former was R. Leontin the teacher of Rabbenu Gershom.[48] L. Zunz is not certain of his identity,[49] while Abraham Epstein[50] suggests that he was R. Judah ha-Cohen, the author of the *Sefer Hadinim*,[51] a student of Rabbenu Gershom, and that his colleague was R. Eleazer b. Isaak, known as the Great.[52]

---

[46] *Op. cit.*, pp. 96–107.   [47] *Ibid.*, pp. 79–96.

[48] See notes 27–8 above.

[49] *Literaturgeschichte der Synagogalen Poesie*, p. 612.

[50] "Glossen zu Gross' Gallia Judaica," *Monatsschrift* 41 (1897), p. 469.

[51] For the *Sefer Hadinim*, see Zunz, *op. cit.*, p. 611.

[52] Lived in the first half of the eleventh century. Luzzatto, *op. cit.*, accepted the reading at the end of the Responsum in the *Orhot Hayyim*,

The fact that a certain incident occasioned the putting of queries before these scholars and before R. Joseph Tob-Elem, who is considered a younger contemporary of Rabbenu Gershom, would incline many scholars to agree with the opinion of A. Epstein.

The present writer, however, is still convinced that R. Judah b. Meir of our Responsum is to be identified with R. Leontin, the teacher of Rabbenu Gershom, for the following reasons: a) It is very doubtful whether the father of the author of the *Sefer Hadinim* was named R. Meir; none of the authentic sources tells us his name.[53] R. Leontin, on the other hand is clearly known as R. Judah b. Meir.[54] b) We find R. Leontin closely associated with a R. Eliezer.[55] c) We have a number of Responsa from the

ms. אלעזר ב״ר יצחק as the correct reading, and identified him with R. Eleazar the Great. In this identification A. Epstein agrees with Luzzatto.

[53] Whenever R. Judah the author of the *Sefer Hadinim* is quoted, the name of his father is not mentioned. See *Maase ha-Geonim*, p. 50; *Sefer ha-Pardes*, nos. 24, 290; *Rabiah* II, p. 533; *ibid.*, no. 994; *ibid.*, no. 1011; *Or Zarua* I, nos. 440, 694; *ibid.*, II, 275; Responsa R. Meir, Prague edition, nos. 451, 861, 887, 891; ed. Lemberg no. 63; ed. Berlin, p. 26; *Mordecai*, B. M. 222; *Piske Rikanti* 287. Although Zunz, *ibid.*, is of the opinion that the name of the father of the author of the *Sefer Hadinim*, was Meir, the source material does not support such an opinion.

[54] See *Tashbetz*, 575: רבינו שלמה סיפר . . . וכתב רבינו יצחק ראיותיו לפני הגאון רבינו ליאונטי״ן רבו של רבינו גרשם מאור הגולה ושמו רבינו יהודה בר מאיר וכן פסק ריב״ם כ״ץ רבו של רבנו גרשם שהיה הכהן הזקן; *Shaare Dura*, no. 35: ורבנו יהודה ב״ר cf. האנור ספר, Sidilkow, 1834, p. 108b: מכונה שי״ר ליאו״ן מאיר הזקן רבו של רבנו גרשם.

[55] See *Shibbolei Haleket*, II, mimeograph edition by Hassida, p. 58: רבנו שלמה זצ״ל שמע מרבו על ר׳ יהודה כהן ב״ר מאיר שהיה אומר דריחא מלתא. ור׳ אליעזר בן גילו חולק ומורה דלאו מלתא, והתיר הפת. That this R. Judah is the teacher of Rabbenu Gershom we learn from *Shaare Dura*, loc. cit., where the law is clearly reported in the name of R. Leontin; cf. also *Shibbolei Haleket* II, p. 59: וכן אומר הרב ר׳ מנחם הלוי נ״ע משם רבינו יהודה כהן הזקן. The fact that R. Eliezer is called by Rashi's teacher בן גילו of R. Judah, shows that the two were closely associated.

Sefer-Hadinim[56] and we never find in them the extraordinary practice of deriving law from biblical verses, a
practice so liberally resorted to in the Responsum of the
Kol Bo. As stated above, this practice is occasionally
found in the Responsa of Rabbenu Gershom and R. Joseph
Tob-Elem.[57] It seems reasonable to assume, therefore,
that the teacher of Rabbenu Gershom engaged in this
archaic practice rather than his pupil.

The fact that the Responsum of the *Kol Bo* was written
at a time when R. Joseph Tob-Elem was already an outstanding scholar, does not exclude R. Leontin from being
its author. R. Joseph Tob-Elem was probably active
toward the end of the tenth and the beginning of the
eleventh centuries. There is little evidence that would
force one to assign a later date for the activities of R.
Joseph.[58] The convenient arrangement of the scholars of
the early centuries into teachers, students, and students of
students, is very misleading; for a scholar was often active
for more than half a century. He could therefore be
contemporaneous with the teacher of another scholar, with
the scholar himself, and with his students. Thus R. Meir
of Rothenburg wrote important Responsa for over forty-
four years,[59] although it was never mentioned that he was
very old when he died; while R. Leontin is known as
hazaken.[60] Moreover, one of the younger students of
Rabbenu Gershom, while acting as judge in a particular

[56] See Responsa R. Meir, ed. Prague, nos. 451, 874–913; cf. Zunz,
op. cit., p. 611.

[57] See notes 41–2 above.

[58] See Rapoport, Introduction to *Teshubot Geonim Kadmonim*, p. 5a;
Gallia Judaica, pp. 308 f.; Zunz, *Zur Geschichte und Literatur*, p. 192.

[59] See Agus, *op. cit.*, pp. 156–7, where it is proven that R. Meir
wrote an important Responsum to the communities of Bohemia and
Moravia in 1249. R. Meir died in 1293, a span of activity of at least
44 years.

[60] See sources quoted in notes 54–5 above.

case, sent a query to R. Leontin.[61] It was, therefore, possible for R. Leontin and R. Joseph Tob-Elem to write Responsa about the same case.

In any event, whether R. Leontin or the student of Rabbenu Gershom was its author, the Responsum of R. Judah and R. Eliezer was written in the first half of the eleventh century at the latest, and is now, therefore, of paramount importance in the study of democracy in the communities of the early Middle Ages.

THE RIGHTS AND IMMUNITIES
OF THE MINORITY

By IRVING A. AGUS, Yeshiva University

JEWISH public law is a subject very important for Jewish
history. Historians must take cognizance of this fact. Since
the destruction of the Jewish state nearly two thousand
years ago, the Jews have been subjected to various masters
and overlords. In the political field they were passive and
never had an occasion to carry out their ideas on public
law — so runs the usual argument.[1]

In reality, however, Jewish public law has played a very
active, and even controlling, role in the life of our people
for the past two millenia. Since the "dispersion" the Jews
have lived in semi-autonomous groups, regulating their
lives in accordance with Jewish law, and organizing their
social, economic, political and religious affairs through
institutions exercising the full power of government.[2] Although their self-government was often limited in scope by
the state, it was nevertheless a highly potent and vigorous
form of self-rule affecting the inner life of the individual.
The Jewish community, for the past two thousand years,

[1] For this reason our modern books on Jewish ethics and philosophy,
rarely deal with Jewish ideas on government, in spite of the fact that,
as demonstrated below, it was in the development of modern democracy
that the influence of Jewish ideas was most powerful and most significant.

[2] See Louis Finkelstein, *Jewish Self-Government in the Middle Ages*,
New York, 1924; Abraham A. Neuman, *The Jews in Spain*, Philadel-
phia, 1942, pp. 34–147; Irving A. Agus, *Rabbi Meir of Rothenburg*,
Philadelphia, 1947, pp. 54–124; Salo W. Baron, *The Jewish Community*,
Philadelphia, 1942, vol. 1; Moses Frank, קהלות אשכנז ובתי דיניהם, Tel
Aviv, 1938; and recently Yitzchak (Fritz) Baer, היסודות וההתחלות של
ארגון הקהלה היהודית בימי הבינים, *Zion*, 1951.

כ

though small and weak and lacking in full sovereignty, nevertheless exercised fully all the functions of the modern state. Since during this long period, thousands of such communities were organized on the basis of Jewish public law, and have lived a full and vigorous life as miniature states, the full scope and development of such law is of compelling interest to the scholar.

It is not our intention to discuss here Jewish public law in all its ramifications, but we shall limit ourselves to a single phase of the vast subject, namely: the form of the political organization of the community as a unit of local government. More specifically, we are mostly concerned here with the problem, whether the intricate form of the political organization of the German and French Communities of the 12th and 13th centuries,— a form revealed in the sources of this period,— was developed in Europe under the influence of Germanic law and contemporary institutions, or was a purely Jewish form handed down by tradition from the days of the Second Temple.

Elsewhere the present writer has pointed out that in the 11th, 12th and 13th centuries, the Jewish scholars of Germany and France showed a remarkable interest in the moral and legal foundations of government, that they dealt seriously with the ethical problems involved in social and political organization, and that they came to the conclusion that Judaism postulates, as a fundamental principle, the absolute freedom of the individual.[3] A human being was free, and no one could coerce him to do aught against his will; nor could any one exact money from him, or confiscate his property without committing a serious breach of Jewish law. Hence the establishment of a ruling body, whether autocratic, oligarchic or democratic, inasmuch as it would

---

[3] See I. Agus, *op. cit.* pp. 108–11; *ibid.* תשובות בעלי התוספות, pp. 16–18; *ibid. JQR* XLIII (1952) pp. 153–71.

occasionally have to impose its will upon an individual, or exact taxes from him, would constitute a serious crime in Jewish law. Use of the mere title of king, prince, government, or state, would not render the criminal act of coercion or robbery, any the more legitimate.[4]

On the other hand such absolute freedom, though just and ethical, would necessarily lead to complete anarchy. No group cooperation or group organization would be possible unless some coercion was used in order to arrive at decisions quickly and efficiently. Perfect harmony and unanimous agreement on the part of all members of a group are rarely encountered in practical situations. In order to survive in the fierce struggle for existence, a group must adopt some method of compulsion, some means of constraint. The more serious the dangers besetting the group, the harsher the restrictive measures required. The ideals of exalted freedom, absolute justice and pure ethics, were thus pitted against the harsh and cruel demands of practical life.

The rabbis of the Middle Ages resolved this dilemma by postulating the principle that a person may forego his unlimited freedom by voluntary consent. He may agree to bind himself by a certain contract and thus become obligated to abide by its terms. Since the Jewish people have voluntarily accepted rabbinic law,[4a] they were legally bound by the provisions of this law. Consequently, rabbinic law may serve the Jews as the foundation of their social and political organization, without infringing upon, or compromising with, high ideals of ethics and freedom.[5]

---

[4] For an exposition of the view of the Tosefists on the rights and powers of a king, see the *Responsum* of R. Tam in תשובות בעלי התוספות, ed. I. Agus, no. 12; also *ibid*. pp. 16–18. The view of the Spanish school is expressed in *Hilkot melakim*, of Maimonides.

[4a] Comp. *Sifre*, 238; Shab. 88a.

[5] See Agus, *R. Meir of Rothenburg*, pp. 108–13.

The principles of government in rabbinic law, as reflected in tannaitic literature, seem to have been founded upon the recognition of the strong obligations of the individual toward his group. For man does not live alone; nor can he provide for his needs by his own efforts. In seeking the cooperation of his neighbors, he must necessarily bend his will to theirs, and must recognize his obligations as a neighbor, as a member of the group. Thus the absolute freedom of the individual should be curbed by his obligations to his neighbors, to the community, and to the nation, as well as by the obligations he himself might have incurred through voluntary agreement or by contract.

It is, therefore, very significant that in tannaitic literature the laws governing a town, a community, or a merchant-association, are conceived as part of "the Laws of Neighbors."[6] Government, in Jewish law, apparently is an outgrowth of the responsibilities and the obligations of the individual as a neighbor, as a part of a community. Government is not sanctioned by any divine rights, is not endowed with special or extraordinary privileges, it is merely a means of providing cooperatively for the security and the needs of the group.[7]

The question, however, of placing the exact limits to the rights and powers of the ruling body still remained. When was coercion criminal, and when was it legitimate? How should a community organize itself so that it be fully and efficiently provided for, without, however, encroaching upon the rights and immunities of the individual?

Accordingly, the legal authorities of the above mentioned communities believed that Jewish law made a very clear distinction between community matters that could be

[6] See Tosefta, B. M. ch. 11; Mishnah, B. B. ch. 1; note how the laws of a community, a town, or a group, are integrated with, and form part of, the laws of neighbors.

[7] Cf. especially the view of the Tosefists, I. Agus, *op. cit.* p. 140 f.

determined through enactions by majority vote, and matters that required determination by unanimous agreement
as to enactment into law. They, therefore, divided community legislation into two distinct categories: a) The
category technically designated למגדר מלתא ולתקנת הקהל,
which included all community enactments designed for the
purpose of strenghtening religion and religious observance,
and also those measures that tended to increase the power
and promote the health of the community, and to assist it
vitally in its struggle for existence. In all matters included
in this category, the principle "majority rules" was fully
accepted. b) The second category, occasionally designated
רווחא להאי ופסידא להאי, included those measures that did not
appreciably strengthen the community, but rather tended
to shift the burden of taxation from one group to another,
to change the customary legal interrelationship of individuals so that one would benefit at the expense of the
other, or arbitrarily to introduce any constitutional changes.
In all such matters unanimous agreement was required for
enactment into law.[8]

Thus the communities of Germany and France arrived
at a system of organization which provided for efficiency in
government, while, at the same time, it gave protection to
every individual against the encroachment upon his private
interests and rights by a tyrannical majority. It was indeed
this remarkable system of organization that was the basic
reason for the great success of the community form of self-
rule in Europe for over a millenium, made it possible for the
community to weather many critical storms, and rarely
gave occasion for inner strife;[9] for it provided adequate

[8] *Ibid.* pp. 114–24.
[9] Considering the fact that in Germany and France there were hundreds of Jewish communities, with a continous history of several centuries, the number of the inner disputes and strifes, as recorded in the
Responsa of the period, is indeed extremely small.

protection for the minority, as well as an effective check to the assertiveness and oppressions of the majority.

It is, therefore, very important to note that several centuries later the town communes of Germany, and the various Gilds, also adopted this division of legislation into two distinct categories. A distinction was made between a) general legislation intended for the benefit of the community, in the sphere of which the principle "majority rules" was adopted; and b) particular legislation encroaching upon the rights and immunities of the individual, in which sphere unanimous agreement was required.[10] This division of legislation into two categories, as adapted by the town commune, parallels in practically every detail the division practised centuries earlier by the Jewish communities. Such parallelism could not be accidental; it rather points to direct borrowing of principles and ideas, by one political body from the other.[11]

The problem we are mainly concerned with, therefore, is whether this remarkable division of legislation into two categories was a fresh creation of the European communities, a natural development in a new environment and under changed conditions; or whether it was the continuation, or the revival, of an old practice. Was the democratic system of government adopted by the medieval Jewish communities of Germany and France the result of a con-

[10] See Otto v. Gierke, *Das deutsche Genossenschaftsrecht*, vol. II, Berlin, 1873, pp. 230–2; and pp. 478–9.

[11] For a history of the majority principle, see T. Baty, "The History of Majority Rule," *Quarterly Review*, vol. CCXVI (1912), pp. 1–28; Wolodymyr Starosolskyj, "Das Majoritaetsprincip," *Wiener staatswissenschaftliche Studien*, vol. XIII, Vienna 1916; Joseph Stavski, *Le Principe de la Majorité*, Danzig, 1920; J. G. Heinberg, "History of the Majority Principle," *American Political Science Review*, vol. XX (1926), pp. 52–68; H. Pirenne, "Les Origines du Vote à la Majorité dans les Assemblées Politiques," *Société d'Histoire Moderne et Contemporaine, Bulletin*, ser. IV, no. 24 (1924), pp. 456–61; Arthur M. Wolfson, "The Ballot etc." *American Historical Review*, vol. V.

tinuous process of growth and adaptation containing, therefore, new, and even foreign, elements;[12] or was it merely the
continuation of an old and well developed system of town
government, a system rarely referred to by the Talmudim
but kept alive, nevertheless, by actual usage? The pre-
ponderant evidence of the sources seems to support the
latter view.

Thus the Tosefta makes a clear distinction in group
legislation between measures that are of vital concern to
the group, providing for the mutual needs, requirements,
and safety of its members; and those measures that
are intended to regulate the relation of the individuals of the group toward one another.[13] In the former
group of measures, the Tosefta uses the formula כופין
בני העיר (בני חצר, בני בקעה, בני מבוי) זה את זה; while in the
latter group the formula is

רשאין בני העיר (הצמרין, והצבעין, הנחתומין, החמרין, הספנים)
להתנות (לומר).

Although the expression כופין בני העיר זה את זה, is not
very explicit, there can be no doubt that it implies the
principle "majority rules." The term כופין, they may coerce, implies the forcing of individuals to do something
against their own will. Hence there are dissenters, and
there are those who have the power to coerce them. To
assume that the Tosefta gives the power to the minority to
coerce the dissenting majority would be very unreasonable,
especially in the case where those who possess fields in a
particular valley would seek to force all those who also have
fields there to construct a canal bringing in irrigation.[13a]
Moreover, such a law would go against the principle, often

[12] This is the opinion expressed by Y. Baer, *op. cit.* p. 38 f.

[13] Tosefta, B. M. ch. 11.

[13a] *Ibid.* ed. Zuckermandel, ch. 11, no. 18: כופין בני בקעה זה את זה לעשות
ביניהם חריץ ובן הריץ.

repeated in talmudic law, that no ordinance may be enacted unless it meets with the approval of the majority.[14]

The meaning of the Tosefta, therefore, is: the majority of the residents of a town may force the dissenting minority to contribute its share to the cost of building a synagogue, buying a Torah-scroll or a scroll of the Prophets; the majority of the residents of a courtyard may force the minority to contribute its share to the cost of placing a stake and a beam at the entrance of their alley, or of erecting a roof over the courtyard; the majority of the farmers whose fields are located in a particular valley, may force the minority to help in the construction of a main canal and a contributary canal for the purpose of irrigating the fields in the valley.[15]

The Mishna states the same law more emphatically: "A resident of a courtyard may be compelled, by the other residents, to contribute to the building of a porter's lodge and a door for the courtyard."[16] Here, indeed, is a clear statement to the effect that the individual may be coerced by the group, the minority by the majority, and not vice versa.

The measures enumerated by the Tosefta and the Mishna deal with the vital needs of a group, with needs that the individual cannot provide for himself without the cooperation of his neighbors, and in cases where the obligation of each neighbor toward the other members of his group is quite clear. Hence when the farmers of a particular valley need an irrigation canal, every farmer of that valley would benefit from the construction of such a canal. Here we have a cooperative undertaking that would benefit every member

[14] See Mishnah, Shek. 5,2; Tosefta, Sanh. 2,13; A. Z. 36a; Yer. Shab. 1,4; Yer. A. Z. 2,8.

[15] B. M. ch. 11, nos. 16, 18, 22, 23.

[16] B. B. 1,5: כופין אותו לבנות בית שער לחצר . . . כופין אותו לבנות לעיר חומה דלתים ובריח.

of the group, but which could be obstructed by the supineness or obstinacy of a few. The law, therefore, recognizes the obligation of the individual to the group, and permits it to force its collective will upon him.

On the other hand the expression רשאין בני העיר להתנות (לומר), does not imply any dissension or coercion. The terms להתנות and לומר designate, throughout tannaitic literature, the voluntary and uncoerced expressions of a person's will. The Tosefta, therefore, deals with a case where the residents of a town have unanimously agreed to pass certain enactments regulating weights or measures, prices or wages. This Tosefta merely provides that a measure unanimously agreed to, shall become binding upon the residents, and that the town administration shall then have the power to impose the fines originally agreed to by all.[17]

The Tosefta specifies the following measures, the enactment of which would require unanimous agreement: to regulate prices, weights, measures and wages; to impose specific fines for informing, and for the reckless grazing of one's livestock; to form monopolistic pacts, to impose business or manufacturing controls, or to agree to certain cooperative or insurance arrangements.[18] A careful scrutiny of these measures will reveal that they do not affect cohesiveness of the community or enhance the growth of the strength of the group as a whole. It is apparent that some members of the group might indeed have doubted whether they would personally benefit from such mea-

---

[17] Notice the careful choice of terms in Tosefta, B. B. ch. 11, no. 23: כופין בני העיר, which implies coercion; ורשאין להתנות which implies no coercion at all; and ורשאין לעשות, for the imposition of the agreed fines.

[18] *Loc. cit.*, nos. 23–6: ורשאין הן בני העיר להתנות על השערים ועל המידות ועל שכר פועלים . . . רשאין בני העיר לומר כל מי שיראה אצל פלוני יהא נותן כך וכך, וכל מי שיראה אצל מלכות יהא נותן כך וכך. וכל מי שתרעה פרתו בין הזרעים יהא נותן כך וכך . . . רשאין הצמרין והצבעין לומר כל מקח שיבוא נהיה כולנו שותפין בו. ורשאין הנחתומין לעשות רגיעה ביניהם. רשאין החמרין לומר כל מי שאבדה לו את ספינתו נעמיד לו חמור אחר . . . רשאין הספנים לומר כל מי שאבדה לו את ספינתו נעמיד לו ספינה אהרת.

sures;[19] and that rugged individualists might even have insisted, in some cases at least, that it would be more salutary for the community or the group to do without such controls. For the enactment of such measures the Tosefta required unanimous agreement.

Thus we find in tannaitic literature the same division of legislative measures into two categories, that we encounter in the European communities of the twelfth and thirteenth centuries. The political theories of the medieval communities, therefore, were not based on a new development, and were not an outgrowth of changed conditions and a new environment, but were rather an adaptation of old, traditional ideas and customs,— community practices that were kept alive, not through the academic studies at the *Yeshiboth*, but through a living tradition of generations of community leaders, officials and *parnasim*. This oral tradition, rich in content, and highly significant for a study of Jewish public law, thus played a very important role in the administration of Jewish self-government in the Middle Ages.

The characteristic division of legislation into two categories (guaranteeing as it does the rights and immunities of the minority) of these medieval communities, apparently has vitally affected the form of organization of the European democratic towns, and through them the democracies of today, the most important characteristic of which is the protection of the basic rights and vital interests of the minority through constitutional guarantees. This protection of the rights of the minority, is a phase of modern democracy significantly lacking in the Greek and Roman democracies of the ancient world, and has apparently been derived by direct borrowing and imitation from Jewish public law.

[19] See especially nos. 24 and 25.

I
ORAH HAYYIM

1 (D)

Q. Is it proper to wear *zizith* (fringes) made of flax?

A. No, flaxen *zizith* are permitted to be worn only with a flaxen *talith*. But since it is not proper to wear a flaxen *talith* (cloak), one must never wear flaxen *zizith*.

SOURCES: Pr. 444; cf. L. 230.

2

Q. If a person has a burn on his arm, how can he put on the phylactery of the arm?

A. There is enough room on the arm for two phylacteries; he can therefore, put it either above or below his burn.

SOURCES: Cr. 40; Pr. 425.

3

Q. Must a person who puts on only the phylactery of the head say both blessings [*Lehaniah Tefilin*, and *Al Mitsvat Tefilin*]?

A. Authorities differ on this law, Rashi requiring one blessing and R. Amram and R. Tam requiring two blessings. I am inclined to agree with the last two that he must say both blessings.

SOURCES: Cr. 41; Pr. 424; Rashba I, 874.

4

Q. Is a person who has had a nocturnal pollution permitted to put on the phylacteries?

A. The custom is widely accepted to permit such a person to study the Torah, to recite his prayers, and to put on his phylacteries.

SOURCES: Cr. 37; cf. L. 223–4.

5

Phylacteries which lost their square shape through age and use must be reshaped before they can be used. But *zizith* (fringes) are fit for use at any time if, when they were made, they were of the required shape and size.

SOURCES: Pr. 68.

6

R. Tam decided that a minor may not be counted among the ten men required to make up a *minyan*, and we can not go against his decision. Therefore, when you find yourself in a position where the other congregants are about to count a minor among the required ten, the best thing for you to do is to leave the synagogue, and thus avoid being the cause of a transgression.

This Responsum bears the superscription: "to my teacher, R. Eleazar."

SOURCES: L. 268; P. 298.

7

Q. Ten Jews are present in the synagogue; one of them is praying privately and can not join in the responding of *Amen.* May the remaining nine persons conduct congregation services and recite *Kaddish* and *Barku?*

A. Yes, although it is better to wait and give the tenth person an opportunity to join in the response of *Amen.*

SOURCES: Pr. 529; L. 202. Cf. Maharil, *Responsa* 150.

8 (D)

Q. May a person, who, while sitting in his house, hears the congregation recite *Kedushah*, *Barku*, and *Kaddish*, join in the proper responses as if present in the synagogue?

A. Yes, he may.

SOURCES: Pr. 530; Wertheimer 10.

9

Q. Must a person, reciting the prayer *Yaale Veyabo* on the day the new moon falls on a Sabbath, mention the term Sabbath in that prayer?

A. No.

SOURCES: Pr. 635.

10 (D)

Q. Is a person who has suffered severe divine punishment permitted to serve as cantor?

A. Yes. The Lord prefers the prayers of a person broken in spirit.

SOURCES: Cr. 249.

11

Q. Should the *Hazan* (Reader) call out "Kohanim" (Priests), the usual invocation to the priests to bless the congregation, when only one priest is present to perform the ceremony of blessing the congregation?

A. If there is only one priest to officiate, the *Hazan* refrains from saying "Kohanim".

SOURCES: Cr. 21; L. 363; Pr. 323; Wertheimer 17.

12

Q. In a town where there are only two or three Israelites and many *Kohanim*, or where there are only *Kohanim* and no Israelites, who should be called up to read the Torah?

A. Where there are only two or three Israelites, they should be called up several times, after one *Kohen* has read the first two portions, until the seven portions are read. If there are no Israelites, women and children are called up in their place. But, if there are only *Kohanim* and no women or children, the Torah may not be read, as no *Kohen* may be called up to the third, fourth, fifth, sixth or seventh portions of the readings, lest the onlookers get the impression that he is not of pure lineage.

This Responsum is addressed to Rabbi Asher b. Moses.

SOURCES: Cr. 8; Pr. 108; Mord. Git. 402–3; Hag. Maim., *Tefilah* 12, 200. Cf. Weil, *Responsa* 3.

13

Q. Is a *Kohen* permitted to forego his prerogative and allow one not of priestly lineage to lead in saying grace after a meal?

A. Yes, he is permitted to do so.

This Responsum is addressed to "My teacher, R. Asher," i. e. R. Asher b. Moses.

SOURCES: Cr. 7; 8; Pr. 107; Mord. Git. 401.

14

Q. Is a *Kohen* permitted to board a boat wherein a dead body is lying?

A. If the boat is small so that it shakes whenever a person walks thereon, a *Kohen* may not board it since he is bound to shake the body. If the boat is large, he may board it, but he is not permitted to come within four cubits of the body.

SOURCES: Cr. 141; Mord. M.K. 865; Hag. Maim., *Abel* 3,1.

15

Q. How many persons should be called (in the Synagogue) to the reading of the weekly portion on *Rosh-hodesh* (day of the new-moon) or *Hanukkah* when they fall on Sabbath?

A. Many of our ritual customs are based on the *Siddur* of Rav Amram, the *Halakot Gedolot,* and the tractate *Soferim.* From these sources we have derived our custom that the first seven persons read the portion of the week, and the *maftir* (one who concludes the reading of the Torah) reads the por-. tion pertaining to the special occasion.

SOURCES: Pr. 110.

16

Q. What *Haftarah* (portion of the Prophets) is read on the Sabbath between *Rosh-Hashanah* and *Yom-Kippur?*

A. In our synagogue we read *Shuvah Israel* (Hosea 14: 2ff.).

SOURCES: Cr. 41; Pr. 426.

17

Q. Is the Reader (of the Torah) permitted to recite the *piyyutim* called *dibra* (דברא) while reading the ten commandments to the congregation?*

A. No, on reading the scroll of the Law the reader is not permitted to add any extraneous material lest it be confused with the Text in the minds of the listeners.

SOURCES: Pr. 59.

18

Q. A donated a plot of ground to the community for the purpose of erecting a synagogue thereon. However, when the members of the community made ready to build the synagogue

---

* See L. Zunz, *Literatur Geschichte der Synagogalen Poesie,* 76. *Dibra* is a *piyyut* recited on Pentecost after each of the ten commandments.

they were restrained by the "students of Jesus" (probably theological students). The community, therefore, decided to build a Talmudical school instead; whereupon A objected that he did not donate the ground for such purpose.

A. Since A did not originally stipulate the condition that in case a synagogue is not built on said ground, it shall revert to him, he may no longer withdraw his gift, and the ground belongs to the community who can use it for any purpose it sees fit. The mere designation of an object for a sacred purpose does not sanctify the object, and it may still be used for a secular purpose. Therefore, were A not a resident of that town, the community would be free to use said ground for building the school. But if A is a resident of that town, since a community can not use for one purpose, community property originally designated for another purpose, unless such change be unanimously approved by the members of the community, or approved by a resident, outstanding scholar of the caliber of R. Ashi, the community can not build a school on the ground, since the protest of A does not permit a unanimous approval of the plan. Therefore, the community can do nothing with the ground till either the Christian priests permit them to build a synagogue, or A withdraws his objection.

This Responsum is addressed to "My teacher Rabbi Asher."

SOURCES: Am II, 240; Mord. Meg. 821. Cf. *Agudah* B.B. 21.

19

Q. The oil-lamp of our synagogue emits a dense smoke which causes damage to the congregants and occasionally compels them to leave the synagogue altogether. Some persons have donated money for the purpose of buying oil for the synagogue. Must we continue to bear the smoke of the oil-lamp, or may we divert the donated money to another purpose?

A. The money may be used for buying waxen candles. The purpose for which the money was given may be changed by the members of the synagogue (though it can not be so changed by the donor) for the following reasons: a) Preparing an object for sacred use does not sanctify the object until it is actually used for such purpose; b) candles and oil used in a synagogue are not intrinsically sacred; nor are they even considered *tashmishe kedushah* (objects used for a sacred function) since they are not indispensable to the function of the synagogue.

SOURCES: L. 269; P. 299–300.

20

Q. Are we permitted to make use of the garret of the synagogue building? I see no reason why its use should be prohibited, since even the garrets of the *Azarah* (Temple court) were not invested with holiness.

A. I know of no actual prohibition against making use of the synagogue building, but we should be very careful not to perform there any profane, degrading, or indecent acts, since the prohibition against such acts is implied in the talmudic statement (Shab. 11a): "a city, the houses of which tower above the synagogue, will eventually be destroyed."

SOURCES: Sinai VI (1943) 13, no. 475; Mord. Shab. 228; ibid. 451.

21

Q. A customarily bought the honors connected with the second scroll of the Law of the synagogue. This time, however, the community sold these honors to B for half a pound. Now A seeks to exercise his priority rights in the acquisition of such honors.

A. If, when the community sold the honors to B, A was in a position to pay half a pound for them but failed to do so, he forfeited his rights to them when he consented to their being sold to B. Therefore, if witnesses testify that A had originally consented to such sale together with the rest of the community, A has no claim to these honors. Or, in the absence of such testimony, if witnesses testify to B's undisturbed possession — since B claims that A had consented to the sale — the honors belong to B. However, if, when the honors were sold to B, A could not afford to buy them, but now that he has the means he wants to recoup his rights and privileges, A is entitled to his rights of priority.

SOURCES: Cr. 209; Mord. B.B. 533; Tesh. Maim. to *Shoftim*, 7; *Mordecai Hagadol* p. 109c.

22

Q. A and B inherited from their father the sole right to make alterations or additions to the synagogue building. A desires to sell his privilege to a wealthy man.

A. The privilege given to A's father, was personal to him and his children, and, therefore, cannot be sold without the consent of the community. Every right, privilege, and authority over the Jewish public, such as the priesthood, kingship, service of the Levites, or even the post of *parnas*, is given to be enjoyed by a person and his children, but must not be sold to another.

SOURCES: Pr. 139; Mord. B.K. 108. Cf. Moses Minz, *Responsa* 6.

23

Q. The father of R. Zadok, R. Zadok himself, and his sons, have successively had for eighty years the honor of providing the synagogue with wine for *kiddush* and *habdalah*. Another member of the community now offers to give one *mark* per year, if he is permitted to provide the wine.

A. Since the sons of R. Zadok have had the honor of providing the wine for more than three years, and since there are witnesses that their father had that honor before them, we put forth the claim on their behalf that their father or grandfather bought from the community the exclusive right to this honor for himself and for his descendants. Even if the honor was not sold to the grandfather, but the community agreed to grant it to him or his son, it cannot be taken away from R. Zadok's children, for the law requires that children should inherit their father's position and authority in the community, if they are worthy of doing so.

This Responsum is addressed to Rabbi Samuel.

SOURCES: Sinai VI (1943) 13, no. 420.

24 (D)

Q. A claims: (1) that he pledged a Scroll of the Law with the synagogue, as security for money he owed to a holy cause; (2) that without his knowledge or permission the trustees sold the Scroll to B; (3) that when he learned about the sale, he protested to B who said to him: "If the Scroll is still in the city, it is yours;" and (4) that the Scroll was in the city at the time. A, therefore, demands that B return the Scroll to him. B, however, claims: (1) that he bought the Scroll for five pounds from the leaders of the community in the presence of the Rabbi; (2) that the beadle delivered possession of the Scroll to him; (3) that while buying the Scroll, he specified that he was donating it to his community and thus received it for half a pound less than the price asked for; and (4) that he had already donated it to his community and it was thus out of his hands.

A. Since B bought the Scroll from reliable people, the sale is valid. B, however, would do a praiseworthy deed were he to return the Scroll to A and take his money back, since this method of acquiring a *Mitzvah*, by depriving one of the opportunity to redeem his property, is not commendable.

SOURCES: Pr. 925.

25

Q. I placed a carpet on the stone floor in front of the ark of our synagogue, for, whenever the cantor would fall on his face in prayer, it would appear as if he were bowing (in adoration) to the stones. Was my act justified?

A. You have done a meritorious act. For bowing on a stone floor even without extending the arms and legs, is forbidden by Rabbinic enactment. Although many venerable men are very careful and turn sideways instead of prostrating themselves (cf. Ber. 34b), yet many ignorant cantors actually fall on their faces in prayer. If it will be within my power, I shall abolish this practice. I shall proceed cautiously, however, in order not to create undue disturbance.

SOURCES: Am I, 94; cf. Mord. Meg. 807.

26

Q. The tablets of the covenant used to lie flat in the holy ark of the Temple. Why are not the Scrolls of the Law, in our day, placed in the ark in a horizontal position?

A. It is preferable to make the ark wide and place therein the Scrolls in a horizontal position.

SOURCES: Cr. 66; Pr. 352; Hag. Maim., *Sefer Torah* 10, 8.

27

If a critically ill person eats on the Day of Atonement, he should mention the holiday when he says grace after his meal. Since he is permitted to eat, the Day of Atonement is to him like any other holiday.

SOURCES: Pr. 71; *Tashbetz* 568; Hag. Maim., *Hilkot Berakot*, 2, 2.

28

Q. Three persons vowed to refuse to accept any favor or benefit from one another during a particular day. May they be counted together for common grace on that day if they ate in the same room, the objection being that neither one can eat the other's food without breaking his vow?

A. No, they may not.

Sources: Pr. 330.

29 (D)

Q. Does a minor complete the quorum necessary for the purpose of mentioning the name of God in the invocation to grace after the meal?

A. There are many conflicting opinions on this subject. R. Tam held that such a minor could complete the necessary quorum, but he himself did not permit such a practice. I have seen many great authorities doing so. But when I was in Provence I said grace several times at the table of my great teacher in the presence of nine men and one minor in his thirteenth year, and he did not allow me to mention the name of God in the invocation. Subsequently I inquired of my teacher R. Judah whether my great teacher was correct in forbidding me to mention God's name; and he replied that he was, thus confirming his opinion.

Sources: L. 488.

30

Q. When are we supposed to recite the blessing "over the washing of hands?"

A. The blessing "over the washing of hands" is recited when one washes his hands upon rising from bed. It is also proper to recite this blessing when one comes out of a privy, and washes one's hands in order to recite the *Minha* services.

Sources: Pr. 40–41; L. 346; Rashba I, 1124. Cf. Wertheimer 4.

31

Q. Must one who comes out of a privy and wants to eat [bread] wash one's hands twice, first in order to recite the blessing "who has created Man", and second, for one's meal?

A. There exists a difference of opinion among the Geonim, but I believe that he should wash his hands once, and recite two blessings: the first "on the washing of hands" and the second "who has created Man", and then eat.

Sources: Pr. 42; L. 347; Hag. Maim., *Berakot* 6, 50.

32

Q. When does one recite the blessing over the study of the Torah?

A. I recite this blessing only once during the day; if I study before the morning services I recite this blessing before I commence to study, otherwise, I recite it (during the Services) in the synagogue.

Sources: Pr. 43; Rashba I, 851; Wertheimer 3.

33 (D)

Q. Must we recite the blessing *al hagefen* after drinking the wine of *kiddush* and *habdalah* [before beginning the meal]?

A. Since reciting the blessing over the wine of *kiddush* and *habdalah* obviates the necessity of reciting another blessing over the wine drunk during and after the meal, the drinking of the wine of *kiddush* and *habdalah* forms part of the meal, and the reciting of the *al hagefen* after such wine and before the meal is unnecessary.

Sources: L. 398; Cf. *Tashbetz* 294.

34

If a person has eaten fruit and has recited the blessing "who creates the fruit of trees", and another species of fruit is brought before him, which also requires the same blessing, he must repeat the blessing before eating the second fruit since the latter fruit was not before him, and he did not intend to eat it when he pronounced the blessing over the former fruit.

SOURCES: Pr. 67; cf. *Tashbetz*, 310.

35

Upon reciting *al hamihya, al hagefen,* or *al haetz,* on Hanukkah or Purim, one need not make mention of the festival.

SOURCES: Pr. 70.

36 (D)

Q. Is there a custom of abstaining from work on Saturday night and the day of the new moon?

A. There is such a custom for women for the day of the new moon.

SOURCES: Pr. 13; L. 420.

37

Q. Are women permitted to wear shawls in the streets on the Sabbath?

A. They are permitted to wear shawls the ends of which are tied together, making it impossible for the wind to blow them off.

SOURCES: L. 186; *Tashbetz* 48.

38

Q. Are the Jews who travel on the roads permitted to wear their belts in which their money is sewed, on the Sabbath?

A. No, such act is prohibited.

SOURCES: Cr. 112; Pr. 94; *Tashbetz* 569.

39

Q. May a person attach a metal buckle to his girdle as an ornament, and then file the buckle into the shape of a key with which he can unlock the door of his house, and then wear this buckle on the Sabbath?

A. People do not usually wear metal keys on their girdles as ornaments. Therefore, this key is not considered an ornament and he is not permitted to wear it on the Sabbath.

SOURCES: Pr. 532; Mord. Shabb. 350; Hag. Maim. to *Shabbat*, 19, 4. Cf. Maharil, *Responsa* 84.

40

Q. Is a person permitted to wear, on the Sabbath, a ring which encloses a loose stone or a piece of lead in a hollow cavity, thus emitting a tinkling sound when moved?

A. A person is not permitted to produce musical sounds on the Sabbath, and some authorities believe (Ulla, in Erub. 104 a) that one is not permitted to produce on the Sabbath any sound that will serve a specific purpose. Since the ring in question produces neither a musical sound nor serves a useful purpose, a person is permitted to wear it on the Sabbath.

SOURCES: L. 139; Hag. Maim., *Shabbat* 23, 2; *Tashbetz* 61.

41 (D)

Q. Is a person permitted to carry objects on the Sabbath from a planted garden to the house and from the house to the garden, when the garden is adjoining the house?

A. If the major portion of the area of the garden is planted, it is considered a separate enclosure and a person is not permitted to carry objects on the Sabbath from the house to the garden or vice versa. But, if only a small part of the area of the garden is planted, the garden is considered part of the courtyard.

SOURCES: L. 144; cf. Mord. Erub. 485.

42

On the Sabbath, a Jew is not permitted to pour sewage into a stone-trough, which is situated partly in his yard and partly in the public domain (used to carry off sewage into the street), unless the trough is covered for four cubits length in the public domain.

SOURCES: Cr. 69; Pr. 31; L. 341; Rashba I, 850; Mord. Shabb. 375.

43

Q. On the Sabbath, may a Jew use latrines which are built in the city wall and open into a ditch surrounding the wall, so that the feces falling into the ditch are moved (by his force) from one Sabbath domain into another?

A. He should fasten a board beneath the seat (within not more than three *tefahim* below the latrine walls) so that the feces first fall on the board and then into the ditch. Should the board break on the Sabbath, he would still be permitted to use the latrine on that day.

SOURCES: Cr. 178, 179; Pr. 96; L. 349; Mord. Shabb. 376; Hag. Mord. Shabb. 461; *Tashbetz* 38; Hag. Maim., *Shabbat* 15, 4; *Kol Bo* 31 (p. 34a). Cf. *Terumat Hadeshen* 66.

44

Q. Is it permissible to manipulate the rectum with a spigot, on the Sabbath, in order to stimulate defecation?

A. This is permissible when the spigot is held in a different manner than it is usually held, e. g., when it is held with two fingers.

SOURCES: L. 147; *Tashbetz* 62; *Tur Orach Hayim* 312.

45

Q. Is a Jew permitted to attach a belt to his trousers (without pinning or sewing) on the Sabbath?

A. Yes, even if the belt is new.

SOURCES: Pr. 65.

46

Q. Is a Jew permitted to milk a cow on the Sabbath?

A. No, but because of the danger to the cow in not being milked, one is permitted to tell a Gentile to milk it and keep the milk for himself.

SOURCES: Cr. 182; Pr. 49, 638; Hag. Mord. Shabb. 466; cf. *Shaare Teshubah* (Geonic Responsa), 221; Asheri Shabb. 18, 3; ibid. B.M. 2, 29.

47

Q. Is it proper to permit a Gentile servant to warm the winter house on the Sabbath, when he does it of his own accord?

A. Although in France such practice was not objected to, and Rabbi Jacob of Orleans even permitted one to tell a Gentile explicitly to fix the fire, it is not to be permitted in our country where many are accustomed to consider it a desecration of the Sabbath.*

SOURCES: Cr. 5; Pr. 92; Rashba I, 857; Hag. Maim., *Shabbat* 6, 6; *Kol Bo* 31 (p. 30c); Maharil, *Responsa* 166.

48

Q. A teacher rendered a decision permitting Jews to instruct a Gentile on the Sabbath to go outside of the city limits in order to be ready to assist relatives of a deceased in their burial operations.

A. The decision of the teacher is incorrect, for ordinarily whatever a Jew is not allowed to do on the Sabbath, he is not permitted to tell a Gentile to do.

This Responsum is addressed to R. Nathan, an uncle of

---

* R. Meir adds that in his own home he constructed an enclosure for his stove, which he would keep locked on the Sabbath to prevent his servant from making a fire in the stove.

R. Meir. But according to Cr. 20, it was sent to R. Hezekiah of Merseburg.

SOURCES: Cr. 20; Pr. 637; Wertheimer 15; Mord. Shabb. 314; Hag. Maim., *Shabbat* 6, 9.

49

Q. Before leaving his place in order to participate in congregational services, A gave money to a Gentile and told him to hire workers immediately and build A's house. Is such an act permissible?

A. A Jew is not permitted to tell a Gentile before the Sabbath to work for him on the Sabbath.

SOURCES: Cr. 44; Rashba I, 875.

50

1) *Q.* Is a Jew, who lives alone among Gentiles, permitted to ask his Gentile friend to hire laborers to do his work on the Sabbath?

A. He is not permitted to do so lest the members of his family or occasional Jewish guests, think that he hired the laborers himself.

SOURCES: Cr. 42; Pr. 427; cf. Rashba I, 875.

2) You were justified in forbidding the practice of the Jews who used to enter a Gentile's store on the Sabbath, choose hats for themselves, put them on their heads, and walk out with them, even though they bargained for them on the following day; for the hats might have been finished on that very Sabbath.

SOURCES: Wertheimer 13.

51

Q. Slaughtering of an animal on the Sabbath is punishable by stoning, while eating forbidden meat involves only the trespassing of a negative commandment. Why, then, are we permitted to slaughter an animal on the Sabbath for the benefit of the critically ill, when feeding them forbidden meat would involve a lesser deviation from the Law?

A. Work done on the Sabbath for the benefit of the critically ill is considered as if done on a week-day, thus involving no infringement of the law.

SOURCES: Cr. 200; Am I, 41; Asher, *Responsa* 26, 5; Asheri *Yuma* 8, 14.

52

Q. Is a woman who has had an ulcer on her body for the past four years permitted to treat it with calcined ashes on the Sabbath?

A. It is permissible to dust calcined ashes on an ulcer during the week, but not on the Sabbath unless thereby to save an endangered life.

SOURCES: Mord. Shabb. 381.

53

Q. Is it permissible to cure a person's headache or eye-sore by a charm, on the Sabbath?

A. It is permissible.

SOURCES: Mord. Shabb. 385.

54

Q. Since according to the Talmud (Shabb. 25b) a person is required to light the Sabbath candles, one should eat the evening meal in the light of these candles. Why, then, do we often leave the candles in the house and eat the evening meal in the courtyard?

A. The Sabbath candles are intended to enhance the pleasures of the Sabbath, and not to detract from it. Since we derive greater pleasure from eating in the open air and away from the flies [that infest the house], we are permitted to do so.

SOURCES: Hag. Maim. Shabb. 5, 20; cf. *Tashbetz* 3.

55

Q. When, on occasion, the stocks of wine in our locality
are completely exhausted, are we justified in assuming that
our beer is "the wine of the country" and thus may be used
as wine for all religious purposes?

A. The term "wine of the country" is applied to a drink
when no real wine is available throughout an entire country.
Thus no wine is available in Westphalia. But, there is an
abundance of wine throughout your country. Moreover, even
in your locality wine is available in large quantities most of
the year. If toward the end of the year a shortage develops,
you have no right to call your beer "the wine of the country".
Knowing how superior wine is, and how much it is preferred
to other drinks for *kiddush* and other religious uses, you should
provide yourself with enough wine to last throughout the year.
A bottle,* of wine, which costs twelve pennies, should last you
a long time.

SOURCES: L. 146; *Tashbetz* 301.

56

A person who has neither wine nor any other liquor should
nevertheless recite the *habdalah*, for the *habdalah* is similar to
grace, and although grace should be said over wine, we must
say it even when we have no wine. This law applies only if
wine is not procurable in that place, otherwise he must make
a strenuous effort to procure it.

SOURCES: Cr. 100.

57

Q. Do the stakes and cross-beam, set up at the entrance
of a courtyard to form a *zurat hapesah* (the semblance of a
gate to comply with the laws of *Erub*), require also an "indication of hinges"?

* *Tashbetz* reads: "two full *lugin.*"

A. According to my interpretation of the talmudic source (Erub, 11a) an "indication of hinges" is also required in a *zurat hapesah.*

SOURCES: P. 295.

58

Q. Is a gatelike structure consisting of two stakes and a beam, one end of which rests on one of the stakes and the other end rests more than a *tefah* away from the other stake, to be considered a gate in reference to the laws of *Erubim?* Some scholars believe that such a structure is considered a gate since one end of the beam rests on one of the stakes.

A. This structure is not considered a gate. In the laws of *Erubim* the minimum requirement of a structure to be called a gate, is a beam resting on a stake at one end, and on another stake at the other end.

SOURCES: Cr. 51; L. 336; Mord. Erub. 478; Hag. Maim., *Shabbat* 16, 60.

59

Q. The occupants of an alley performed the ceremony of *shittuf-mabo* [association of courtyards which open into a common alley by placing a cross-beam over the alley-entrance, and placing food belonging to the occupants of the alley in one court-yard, thus transforming the different court-yards and the alley into one single domain, held jointly by the occupants, in the limits of which it is permitted to carry objects on the Sabbath]. If the cross-beam over the alley-entrance broke down, are the occupants permitted to carry objects on the Sabbath within the limits of their respective court-yards, and from one court-yard to the next one?

A. All the court-yards from which one can enter, directly or through other courtyards, into the one where the common-food has been deposited, without having to cross the alley, form a single domain within the limits of which, objects may be carried on the Sabbath. In the remaining court-yards, one is not permitted to do so.

SOURCES: Cr. 39; Pr. 422; Mord. Erub. 518; Hag. Maim. to *Erubin* 3, 6.

60

If the occupants of court-yards which open into a common alley-way, have associated their court-yards through the ceremony of *shittuf* (cf. M. Erub. 7, 6) ,the courtyards, together with the alley-way, become a single domain within which objects may be carried on the Sabbath. Such a ceremony renders unnecessary any further association of the different premises within each court-yard through the ceremony of *Erub*.

SOURCES: Pr. 89; cf. Hag. Maim., *Erubin* 1, 9.

61

Q. A's courtyard abuts on that of a Gentile. The two courtyards are separated by a wall which has a window more than ten *tefahim* above ground. If A did not rent the Gentile's yard for the Sabbath, is he permitted to carry objects through the window on the Sabbath?

A. If A's yard, the Gentile's yard, and the yard of another Jew, open into a common alley, and this alley has not been made available for Sabbath movements by means of an *Erub*, nothing may be carried through the window on the Sabbath unless A rented the Gentile's yard. If the Gentile's yard, however, does not open into a common alley, nor into A's yard, A may use the above window on the Sabbath.

SOURCES: Mord. Erub. 519.

62

Q. Wheat containing cracked grains (cracked by moisture) which constituted less than one-sixtieth of the whole was ground up before Passover. Is it permissible to eat such flour on Passover?

A. No, such flour is not fit for consumption on Passover.

This Responsum is addressed to R. Hayyim.

SOURCES: L. 332; Rashba I, 831.

63

If a grain of wheat is found in a chicken after boiling water was poured over it, the chicken may be eaten on Passover, since boiling water, once poured into a second vessel, does not cook; and, consequently, the chicken was not cooked with leaven.

SOURCES: Pr. 438.

64

Ears of corn parched in a hot stove may be eaten on Passover.

This Responsum is addressed to: "My teacher Rabbi Eliezer".

SOURCES: P. 291; Am. I, 61; Hag. Maim., *Hamets uMatsah*, 5, 4; *Mordecai Hagadol*, p. 73b.

65

Q. Is not the liturgical poet, who first writes that clay vessels in which leaven was cooked must be broken before Passover, and then states that they may be stored away in wooden sheds, guilty of a contradiction?

A. It is poetic license to state together two conflicting talmudic opinions.

SOURCES: Pr. 441.

66

Vinegar that has been mixed with the yeast of beer must be sold to a Gentile before Passover (in order not to violate the commandment of Ex. 12,19 and 13,7, which prohibits a Jew from possessing leaven during the Passover week). The Gentile may be told that if he holds the vinegar until after Passover, a Jew will buy it from him.

SOURCES: Cr. 68; Pr. 31; L. 340; Rashba I, 850.

67 (D)

Q. Is a Jew enjoined to remove (before Passover) the leaven of a Gentile deposited with him, for which he has accepted responsibility as a gratuitous watchman?

A. Since the Jew would be held responsible for the leaven, were it lost or stolen because of willful neglect, he must remove it before Passover.

SOURCES: Am I, 62.

68

One is not permitted to carry books back from the synagogue to the house on a holiday, unless he intends to study them.

SOURCES: Mord. *Beza*, 658.

69

Q. Many candles are usually lit in the synagogue on the morning of a holiday. Some persons want to forbid such a practice on the ground that the light of a candle is useless in the daytime, and one is not permitted on a holiday to light a candle the light of which serves no use.

A. The light of many candles in the synagogue, whether in daytime or at night, enhances the spirit of festivity and rejoicing. Were it not for this reason, the practice of lighting many candles in the synagogue for Friday evening services, when a holiday falls on Friday, would be forbidden, since services are usually over before dark and the candles are not needed for their light; and the lighting of many candles on a holiday night would be forbidden, since a single candle dispels darkness. The practice referred to is, therefore, perfectly in order.

R. Meir added: Please forgive me for not having answered your questions. I was very busy and forgot to answer. I even lost your letter. I could find no one who travelled regularly to your parts, and I did not often inquire from travelers about persons who might travel to your locality.

SOURCES: L. 125; P. 125; Am. I, 47; Berl. p. 295 no. 387; *Mordecai Hagadol*, p. 94a. Cf. Maharil, *Responsa* 53.

70

Q. On the eve of a holiday, why do women light their candles long before evening, extinguish them immediately afterwards, and then rekindle them at the proper time?

A. This is done on the eve of *Rosh-ha-Shana*, of a Sabbath that immediately precedes a holiday, or of a holiday that immediately precedes the Sabbath, for the purpose of having the wicks of the candles prepared on a week-day for their being lighted both on the first and on the second holy days.*

SOURCES: Mord. *Beza*, 644; *Mordecai Hagadol* p. 93d.

71

Q. Why do we permit children to eat on holidays cakes whereon letters and words are inscribed, since they erase words on a holiday when they eat the cake?

A. Erasure on a Sabbath or a holiday is Biblically prohibited only because such erasure produces space for further writing (Shabb. 75b), while eating the cakes has no such effect. Rabbinically, however, even the form of erasure brought about by eating is prohibited; but we pay no attention to children who eat such cake, since the Court is not enjoined to restrain children from eating forbidden food.

SOURCES: Mord. Shabb. 369; *Mordecai Hagadol* p. 51d.

---

* It is much easier to relight a candle that has burned previously, than to light a fresh one. Thus the first lighting of a candle prepares it for subsequent relighting. Therefore, a candle that was burning on the Sabbath may not be rekindled for the holiday immediately following, otherwise the candle would thus have been prepared on the Sabbath for its being kindled on the holiday. The above procedure prepares the candle, on a week-day, for its being lighted on both holy days.

72

Regarding the taking of *Hallah* on a holiday, I usually take *Hallah* and recite the required blessing whenever one of the following dwells in our town: a young "priest" who has not yet experienced pollution, a "priest" who immersed himself in a ritual bath after pollution, or a "priest" who could neutralize said *Hallah* through mixing it with a greater volume of ordinary bread.

SOURCES: Cr. 45; Rashba I, 876.

73

Rabbi Shlomiel is commended on his decision that one is not permitted to eat on a holiday the food prepared with an egg laid on the same holiday, since this food may be eaten after the holiday without hesitation.

SOURCES: Cr. 46; Pr. 100; L. 368.

74

Q. Is a Jew permitted to refine silver on *Hol-haMoed* for his Gentile customer, who would otherwise transfer his business to a Gentile refiner?

A. No, he is not permitted to do so, for refining silver is considered real labor.

SOURCES: Pr. 60.

75 (D)

Q. A hired workers to erect a building for him, and contracted with them for the whole structure. Before finishing the building, however, their work was interrupted because of the holiday. The workers refused to waste time and threatened to leave the building unfinished unless they be permitted to continue their work. May A allow them to finish the building on the intermediate days of the holiday, since otherwise he may suffer an irreparable loss?

A. A may not permit the workers to finish the building on the intermediate days of the holiday, for Jewish passersby will think that A has specifically hired these workers to do the work on the semi-holiday.

SOURCES: Cr. 142.

76

A person who fasts on a Friday, has to fast only till after the Sabbath-eve-service, the time of such service beginning in the middle of the afternoon.

SOURCES: Mord. Erub. 494.

77

Q. A was accustomed to observe the arbitrary fast-days preceding *Rosh-hashanah* and *Yom-Kippur*. B abstained from eating meat or drinking wine between the 17th of Tammuz and the 9th day of Ab. Because of illness, they seek to discontinue these practices.

A. Their customs and practices were tantamount to vows and can be discontinued only if A and B are released by a court consisting of three laymen.

SOURCES: Pr. 95; L. 179; Mord. Pes. 602, Hag. Maim. to *Shebuot* 12, 3.

78 (D)

Q. A woman obligated herself to fast on Monday and Thursday of every week until *Rosh Hashanah.* After the holiday of Passover she asked when she ought to begin her fasting.

A. It is customary to consider the whole month of *Nissan* as a period of semi-festivity. Thus we do not recite the *Tahnun* throughout this month. Therefore, since her fasting was to begin after Passover, she should begin her fast after the expiration of the month of *Nissan*.

SOURCES: L. 442.

79 (D)

Q.   *Rosh-Hashanah* fell on Thursday and Friday. On Wednesday A forgot to perform the ceremony of *Erub-Tabshilim* [which would have enabled him to prepare food on the holiday for the Sabbath]. May he perform the ceremony on Thursday with the condition that if Thursday is *Rosh-Hashanah*, and Friday is a week-day, the ceremony is void, but if Friday is *Rosh-Hashanah*, and Thursday is a week-day, his ceremony of *Erub-Tabshilin* will be valid. [This is based on the assumption that *Rosh-Hashanah*, like all other holidays, really consists of one day, but that we observe two days not knowing exactly which day it is.]

A.   No, but he is permitted to cook on *Rosh-Hashanah*, for the Sabbath, just enough for his bare needs. Moreover, he may cook and bake on the holiday more than he needs for the holiday, and eat the remainder on the Sabbath.

SOURCES: Pr. 317.

80

Q.   A set aside two days as *Yom-Kippur*. [He would fast on the 10th and 11th of Tishri]. If *Yom-Kippur* should fall on a Thursday [for A, therefore, Thursday and Friday], may he ask his neighbors to prepare meals for him on Friday for the Sabbath?

A.   No, but he may partake of anything his neighbors and friends have prepared for themselves.

SOURCES: Pr. 76.

81

Q. If upon seeing a Hanukkah candle one recited the blessing of *sheheheyanu* must he repeat the blessing when he lights his own Hanukkah candles?

A. No, to recite the *sheheheyanu* once is sufficient.

Sources: Pr. 57.

82

Q. Where should one put the Hanukkah candle in the synagogue?

A. Wherever there is no *mezuzah* on the right side of the entrance (to necessitate the putting of the candle on the left side) one should put the candle on the right side, and in the synagogue, near the opening of the ark.

Sources: Pr. 66.

83 (D)

Q. A person vowed to fast a certain period of time which included Hanukkah or Purim. Must he fast on these days of rejoicing?

A. Vows are interpreted according to the meaning of words and phrases in common parlance. Since people do not, generally, fast on Hanukkah or Purim, he, also, is exempt.

Sources: Pr. 295.

84

Q. The Mishna (Meg. 6b.) states: "The only difference between the first (month of) *Adar* and the second *Adar* consists in reading the scroll of Esther and giving presents to the poor." Does this statement mean that we ought to celebrate *Purim* on the fourteenth of the first *Adar* (in a leap-year) and fast on the thirteenth of this month?

A. No, the above cited statement means that the reading of the scroll of Esther on the fourteenth of the first *Adar*, even though it was so read before the leap-year was decided on, does not free one from the obligation of reading the scroll on the second *Adar*. The statement does not mean that all other laws connected with *Purim* apply to the first *Adar*.

SOURCES: L. 195; *Tashbetz* 178.

85

In a new town it is forbidden to introduce the custom of giving presents to Gentile servants on *Purim*. R. Ephraim applied to this custom the verse: "and I multiplied unto her silver and gold, which they used for Baal (Hos. 2, 10)." However, in places where the custom has already been well rooted, it should not be discontinued lest it disturb peaceful relations with the Gentile neighbors.

SOURCES: L. 184; Hag. Maim. to *Megillah* 2, 5; *Orchot Hayyim* II, p. 236, misconstrued by editor.

II

YOREH DEAH

86 (D)

A ritual examiner (of slaughtered cows) who passed as *kosher* (ritually fit for eating) two or three cows that were ritually unfit, must be removed from his post until he completely repents of his act. He should be punished by flagellation or by a fine, for what he has done, according to his circumstances; such punishment to be further determined by the seriousness of the crime, whether it was committed through negligence or ignorance, or with vicious intent.

Sources: P. 294.

87 (D)

Q. Is a calf whose brain is decayed and soft, watery in texture, fit to eat?

A. If only a small part of the brain is thus softened and that part is completely surrounded with healthy brain, the calf is fit to eat; otherwise, it is not.

Sources: L. 322.

88 (D)

Q. A worm was found in the opening of the cranium of a cow at the very base where the brain joins the spinal cord. Is the cow fit to eat?

A. Above the medulla oblongata a puncture of the membrane of the brain, but not the presence of a worm, renders the cow unfit for eating purposes. But, below that region of the brain only a severance of the major part of the cord renders the cow unfit.

Sources: L. 323.

89

A blister on the thin extremity of the lung, which penetrates the thickness of the lung and extends from one side to the other, does not render the animal *trefah*, unless the subdivision of the bronchia is visible in the blister.

This interpretation of the obscure Pr. 66 is based on the clearer statement in *Tashbetz*, 325.

SOURCES: Pr. 66; *Tashbetz*, 325.

90

Q. A butcher removed the lungs from several ritually slaughtered sheep. Later, adhesions were found on one of the lungs. Are we to suspect that the ritual examiner had been at fault and had overlooked these adhesions, or are we to presume that a Gentile had mixed a lung from a *trefah* sheep with the other lungs?

A. Whenever a presumption is possible we resort to it, since a ritually slaughtered animal is considered *kosher* until it is proven to be *trefah*.

SOURCES: B. p. 291, no. 363.

91

A cow with one kidney is fit for eating purposes.

SOURCES: P. 292; Am. I, 76.

92

Q. Meat is sometimes salted on pieces of wood in a bath-tub, and the brine flows into the bathtub. Does this process render the bathtub unfit for use?

A. Boiling-hot food may not be placed in such a bathtub, nor may any food be pickled there, for pickling is tantamount to cooking.

SOURCES: *Tashbetz*, 337; *Mordecai Hagadol* p. 130b.

93

You have rendered unfit for eating purposes meat that was not rinsed before it was salted and cooked. Your decision in this case, however, is not correct since the talmudic law requiring that meat be rinsed before salting is a requirement previous to the act (לכתחלה) which law does not render unfit for eating purposes meat that was already salted without a previous rinsing (בדיעבד).

SOURCES: Cr. 55; Pr. 992; L. 337; Rashba I, 870. Cf. Wertheimer 8; *Sefer Haparnes* 30.

94

Q. What should be done with a chicken that was salted before its liver was removed?

A. The chicken may be eaten if it be peeled at the place of juncture with the liver.

SOURCES: Pr. 59; *Sefer Haparnes* 41.

95

Q. A sheep's stomach was salted together with other pieces of meat before its *heleb* (forbidden fat) was cleaned off. Are the pieces of meat and the stomach fit for eating purposes?

A. If the volume of the stomach is sixty times the volume of the *heleb*, the stomach may be eaten after its *heleb* is cleaned off. Each piece of meat whose volume is sixty times the volume of the *heleb* is fit for eating purposes, but the smaller pieces are not fit for eating purposes if they touched the *heleb*.

SOURCES: Pr. 617; Mord. *Hulin*, 683. Cf. *Sefer Haparnes* 25.

96

Q. A large intestine was salted before its suet was removed, together with a quantity of meat more than sixty times its volume. Does the salting of the meat together with the suet of the intestine render the meat unfit to eat?

A. The intestine is unfit, but the meat is fit to eat.

SOURCES: Tesh. Maim. to *Maakalot Asurot* 16.

97

Q. Are we permitted to eat a species of bird, about the cleanliness (fitness for food) of which we have no tradition, but which possesses the following tokens of cleanliness: an extra talon and a gizzard whose inner skin is easily peeled off?

A. Scholars have expressed conflicting opinions on this subject.

SOURCES: Pr. 614; Mord., *Hulin*, 646.

98

Q. Do you compare vegetables having a sharp taste, to asafoetida to the effect that you forbid the use of such vegetables if they are cut with a knife that is *trefah* (unfit for use) even though no *trefah* food was cut with such knife within the day. (cf. A. Z. 39a)?

A. Sefer haTerumah compares leek, onion, radish, and garlic to asafoetida, and we follow this ruling. But since many authorities disagree with this view, I do not protest against those who do not compare the other vegetables to asafoetida.

SOURCES: *Tashbetz*, 359; *Mordecai Hagadol* p. 130 c; Asheri A.Z. 2, 38.

99

Q. A pot which had been used for cooking meat was thoroughly washed and a vegetable soup was made in it. Is a person permitted to eat cheese immediately after eating this soup without previously wiping his mouth and washing his hands?

A. Even if meat had been cooked in the pot on the same day that the vegetable soup was made in it, a person is permitted to eat cheese immediately after eating the soup without first wiping his mouth or washing his hands.

SOURCES: Wertheimer 11; *Mordecai Hagadol*, p. 129c.

100

Q. If one wants to eat meat after cheese, may he first wipe his mouth (by eating a piece of hard bread) and then rinse it, or must he first rinse it and then wipe it?

A. The order makes no difference.

SOURCES: Pr. 531; Wertheimer 12; Hag. Maim. to *Maakolot Asurot*, 9, 2.

101

Q. We have heard that you refrain from eating meat after cheese for the same interval as cheese after meat, and that you do eat poultry-meat after cheese. Is this report true?

A. Yes, one may conduct oneself more strictly than required by the Law in order to make sure that one be not exposed to sin, without being guilty of the sin of adding anything to the Law.

R. Meir adds that in his youth he used to scoff at those persons who were so meticulous. He even considered their practice heretical, until he once found small particles of cheese between his teeth hours after he ate it. He, therefore, decided to be more careful.

SOURCES: Pr. 615; L. 500; Mord., *Hulin*, 68; cf. *Tashbetz*, 355.

102

Q. Brine from ritually salted meat flowed into a vessel which contained water. Was the brine neutralized in the water?

A. Brine and water are not identical liquids. Therefore brine is neutralized when mixed with a quantity of water sixty times its volume.

SOURCES: Mord. *Hulin*, 671.

103

Q. A drop of milk fell upon the outside of a boiling pot of meat. The volume of the pot and its contents was more than sixty times that of the milk. Are the contents of the pot as well as the pot itself fit for use?

A. In France I witnessed a great controversy over this matter. But, at the time, I failed to inquire into the reasons of both those who permitted and those who forbade the use of the pot and its contents. I also discovered that Ri forbade the use of the pot and its contents, probably for the reason that the drop of milk first rendered the pot unfit for use, and the pot, in turn, rendered its contents unfit for use.

SOURCES: L. 121. Cf. Mord., *Hulin*, 679; P. 515; Hag. Maim., *Maakalot Asurot* 9, 3; Asher, *Responsa* 20, 26; *Sefer Haparnes* 19.

104

Q. A drop of milk fell on the outside of a (meat) pot covering the greater part of it. Are the pot and its contents fit for use?

A. Rabbenu Samson permits its use while Ri forbids it. Ri bases his opinion on the fact that a drop of milk does not spread over the whole pot, and since the part of the pot affected is not sixty times the volume of the milk, the milk is not neutralized. Therefore, even according to Ri if one could gage the volume of the milk and find a ratio of one to sixty to the volume of the part of the pot affected, the milk would be neutralized. In any event, if the loss be an appreciable one, or the enjoyment of the Sabbath or a holiday be involved, one may be lenient, in view of R. Samson's opinion.

SOURCES: P. 515; Mord., *Hulin*, 679; cf. L. 121; Asher, *Responsa* 20, 26; *Sefer Haparnes* 19.

105

Q. A fly was found in a bowl of soup from which some of the soup was poured into plates. Did the fly contaminate the soup, the bowl and the plates?

A. The fly contaminated neither the soup, nor the bowl nor the plates. For the fly probably fell into the bowl when the soup was no longer boiling. Moreover, the law stating that a creature is never neutralized in a mixture, is applicable only to cases where the creature is not removed from the mixture. In this case, however, after the fly is removed from the soup, its taste is neutralized and the soup is fit to be eaten.

SOURCES: L. 143; *Tashbetz*, 350; *Orhot Hayyim* II, p. 309.

106

Rabbi Samuel of Eisenach, a relative of R. Meir, permitted the eating of ritually slaughtered chickens with which a *trefah* chicken was mixed up. He based his decision on an opinion he said he had received from R. Jacob, that the law stated in Mishna Ab. Z. 5, 9, and interpreted in the Talmud Ab. Z. 74a, is the accepted law governing mixtures. This talmudic interpretation implies, that only objects possessing both characteristics: a) items usually sold by the piece, and b) forbidden objects, the profitable use of which is prohibited (*issurei hanaah*), are never neutralized in a mixture. However, objects lacking one of these characteristics do become neutralized in the proper mixture.

R. Meir took issue with R. Samuel, pointing out, that the accepted authorities never mention the foregoing view as the final law. On the contrary, these authorities decide that items usually sold by the piece, even though they be not forbidden objects the profitable use of which is prohibited, are never neutralized. Moreover, R. Samuel contradicted himself and ruled that a "piece fit to be offered a guest", even though it be not *issurei hanaah*, is not neutralized; but a whole chicken is also considered "a piece fit to be offered a guest". R. Meir, therefore, pleads with R. Samuel to acknowledge his mistake, and change his decision, lest it become a misleading precedent which may be followed by future generations.

SOURCES: Cr. 14; Am I, 75.

107

Since vinegar is used in flavoring food, it does not lose its identity even when mixed with a substance more than 60 times its volume.

SOURCES: Pr. 100; Cr. 46 end; L. 368 end. Cf. *Sefer Haparnes* 22.

108 (D)

Q. An oven was greased with fat-tail, and before it was reheated, bread was baked therein. Is it permissible to eat this bread?

A. This bread may not be eaten, lest perchance one eat it with milk. However, it may be sold to a Gentile, since in a Rabbinical prohibition we do not take into consideration the remote possibility that the Gentile will resell the bread to a Jew.

This Responsum is addressed to R. Tobiah.

SOURCES: Am I, 77.

109

Q. Is it permissible to eat with meat, bread which was baked in an oven at the same time with cheese pie?

A. This question involves the controversial subject of *reha milta hi* (whether the odor of an object is considered to have substance). In practice, we do not permit the baking of bread together with cheese or meat-pies; but if it had been done so, we do not prohibit the eating of such bread with meat or cheese. Onion baked in the same oven with forbidden meat, may not be eaten, since the odor of onion definitely has substance and absorbs from the forbidden meat. We, however, are permitted to eat (on Passover) unleavened bread that was baked in the same oven with leavened bread, since we find no mention (in the Talmud) of a problem regarding the odor of two types of bread.

SOURCES: Am I, 68; Pr. 25, 26, 27; Hag. Maim., *Makalot Asurot* 15, 70; Rashba I, 849; cf. *Tashbetz*, 332; Mord. *Hulin*, 665.

110

Q. A court is not enjoined to restrain a child from eating forbidden food (Yeb. 114a; Git. 55a; Shabb. 121a). Is a father obliged to restrain his child?

A. A father is enjoined to train his son in the performance of the *Mitzvoth*. Lack of disapproval on the part of the father means approval. Therefore, a father must restrain his child from eating forbidden food, if eaten in his presence. This law, however, applies to the father, but not to the mother.

SOURCES: Cr. 200; Am I, 88.

111 (D)

Children are permitted to wear around their necks a medicinal collar designed by a recognized (medical) expert to ward off an evil eye. But, if such collar was not designed by an expert, they may not wear it. For, we are not permitted to urge young children to do things forbidden to us (Yeb. 114a).

SOURCES: L. 140.

112

Q. Is a Jew permitted to eat fish smoked by a Gentile?

A. Smoking and salting are methods of preserving fish (and not of cooking them). Therefore, a Jew is permitted to eat fish smoked or salted by a Gentile, although he is not permitted to eat fish cooked by a Gentile.

SOURCES: Pr. 58.

113

Q. Is a Jew permitted to eat bread from flour belonging to a Jew, baked solely by a Gentile, without the Jew's having even stirred the embers of the fire?

A. In France such bread is not eaten by Jews; even the sale of such bread to a Gentile is prohibited, lest the latter resell it to a Jew. The reason for this is that a Jew is permitted to eat bread baked by Gentiles from flour belonging to Gentiles, but he is not permitted to eat bread baked by a Gentile from flour belonging to a Jew.

SOURCES: Pr. 33; L. 342. Cf. Mord. A. Z. 830; Hag. Maim., *Maakalot Asurot* 17, 90; *Agudah* A. Z. 29; *Sefer Haparnes* 93.

114 (D)

Q. Are we permitted to eat butter bought from Gentiles?

A. R. Tam, Ri, and some of the Geonim (in their Responsa), permit the use of such butter. However, R. Nathan of Africa writes in a Responsum, (found among my Geonic Responsa), that until now the use of such butter was permitted, but since the Gentiles began to mix forbidden fat with their butter, we anathematize all persons who eat it. Moreover, throughout Germany, excepting the towns bordering on France, the custom is well established not to eat such butter. But, since the former great authorities have permitted its use, we do not declare unfit the vessels wherein the butter of Gentiles was fried, even if it was so used by persons who usually do not eat it.

SOURCES: L. 193.

115

Q. Is it permissible to scald in the same tub vessels needed for Passover use and vessels bought from a Gentile, when such vessels were not used for some time (more than one day) and, therefore, would impart an unpleasant taste to each other?

A. Yes, for during the scalding process vessels actively exude all the substances they have absorbed before, and do not absorb any new substances. After the period of exuding is over the vessels may begin to absorb again, but whatever they will absorb will impart an unpleasant taste to them, and therefore, will not render them unusable.

SOURCES: Pr. 429.

116

Q. One repaired a pan which contained a hole. Must he immerse the pan in a ritual bath before he is permitted to use it?

A. Whether the hole was formed on the bottom or on the side of the pan, the pan needs immersion, since, when repaired, it is considered as a new vessel.

SOURCES: Pr. 620; Mord. A. Z. 859.

117

Q. Has a wooden pail which is fastened with iron hoops, the status of an iron vessel in regard to the laws of immersion in a ritual bath?

A. A vessel has the status of its supports (in this case, the iron hoops) in the laws of immersion as well as in the laws of *Tumah* (uncleanliness).

SOURCES: Pr. 621; Mord. A. Z. 859; *Agudah* A. Z. 73.

118

Q. Is it permissible to scald large kneading-basins, which cannot be submerged in boiling water because of their size, by pouring boiling water over them [thus preparing them for use on Passover]?

A. No, but they may be filled with water and the water heated to the boiling point to render them fit for Passover use.

SOURCES: Pr. 439.

119

Q. Is it permissible to scald the handle of a frying pan by pouring boiling water over it?

A. Yes, since the leaven the handle absorbed was poured over it, it will exude in the same manner as it absorbed.

SOURCES: Pr. 440.

120

Q. Is the wooden handle of a leather bag* considered an interposition when the bag is to be immersed in a ritual bath?

A. Handles, that are permanently attached to vessels, are not considered interpositions.

SOURCES: L. 194; *Tashbetz* 363.

121

Q. What is the meaning of the term "wine touches wine" as distinguished from the term *nitzok* (uninterrupted flow)?

A. When a Gentile pours wine from a vessel, that part of

---

* *Tashbetz* reads: "frying pan."

the wine which is already outside of the vessel is considered "forbidden wine" because the Gentile exerted energy in pouring it from the vessel. When the Gentile stops pouring the wine, the last drop dribbling from the vessel is still considered "forbidden wine" because of the energy exerted, while the drop with which it was in contact and which separated from it and remained in the vessel not only itself should become "forbidden wine", because of its actual contact with the last drop that dribbled from the vessel, but should render the rest of the wine in the vessel "forbidden". This actual contact of the wine remaining in the vessel with that poured out of it, is termed "wine touches wine". When a Gentile, however, had actually touched the wine contained in a certain vessel, thus rendering it *yayin nesek* (forbidden wine), and subsequently a Jew poured wine from a cask into the vessel containing the *yayin nesek*, a contact was thus made by the uninterrupted flow of the wine from the cask into the vessel. This contact is termed *nitzok*. Some authorities rule that this contact renders the wine in the cask *yayin nesek*, while other authorities hold that it does not. However, even according to the former authorities, when a Gentile pours wine from a vessel he does not render the wine remaining in it "forbidden wine", for the reason that the wine he did pour out of the vessel, though "forbidden wine", is not considered *yayin nesek* in the full sense of the term. The mere exerting of energy by a Gentile in connection with the wine, without his actually touching it, renders it "forbidden" in a limited sense.

SOURCES: Sinai V (1941) pp. 298–300; *Mordecai Hagadol* p. 119a; cf. Tesh. Maim. to *Maakalot Asurot* 12.

122

Q. A Gentile maid went down to the cellar to bring up beer. She made a mistake, however, and instead of drawing the liquor from the beer-cask, she drew it from the cask containing wine-vinegar. She did not learn of her mistake, however, till she had replaced the bung.

A. Since the maid must have touched the flowing liquid, even though she was ignorant of its true nature, the wine-vinegar in the cask became forbidden liquor. However, if the oxidation of the wine in the cask was so far advanced that when poured on the floor it bubbled, it was no longer in the category of wine, and was not rendered forbidden liquor by the touch of the Gentile.

SOURCES: Cr. 233; Mord. Ab. Z. 847; Hag. Maim. *Maakalot Asurot* 11, 8.

123

Q. A Gentile woman poured wine without touching it into a bottle or glass, thinking it was whiskey.

A. Since she did not touch the wine and did not know that it was wine, we assume that she did not discover its true nature by its odor. For our wines are clear and weak in comparison with the wines of the talmudic period. Therefore, the use of the wine, even the wine she poured into the bottle, is permitted.

SOURCES: B. p. 296 no. 390; *Mordecai Hagadol* p. 118b.

124

Q. After a Gentile drank wine from a cup, a Jew forcefully emptied the cup and then drew wine from a cask into the cup. It is not known, however, whether or not the cup was still "moist enough to moisten other objects" (A. Z. 60a) when the Jew drew the wine from the cask. Was the wine in the cask rendered "forbidden wine"?

A. Since there are many reasons for being lenient in this matter, we may try again forcefully to empty the cup to see whether or not the cup remains "moist enough to moisten other objects". Moreover, the wine in the cask ought to be declared fit for use, even if the cup does remain "moist enough to moisten other objects", in accordance with the view of R. Simeon (A. Z. 60b), because otherwise the result would be a great financial loss.

SOURCES: *Mordecai Hagadol*, p. 126b; cf. *Tur Yoreh Deah*, 126; *Terumat Hadeshen* 204.

125

Q. Thieves broke into A's cellar and inserted a tap into a cask of wine. Subsequently it was discovered that a great deal of wine was missing from the cask. Rabbi Jedidyah, however, permitted the use of the wine that was left in the cask.

A. Though the majority of thieves are Gentiles, and the talmudic dictum regarding Pumbeditha (A.Z. 70a) does not apply to other places, the use of this wine is permitted nevertheless, for there is no evidence that thieves broke into the cellar. Thus the cellar was found locked, while thieves do not trouble themselves to lock a door after their work is done. Therefore we assume that a member of the household inserted the tap, a common enough occurrence. Each member of the household, though he knows that he himself did not tamper with the cask, is nevertheless permitted to drink the wine, for he may assume that one of the other members of the household inserted the tap.

SOURCES: B. p. 295, no. 389. Cf. Asher, *Responsa* 19, 1.

126

Q. Thieves entered a place where many casks of wine were stored. Some of the casks were provided with faucets, while others were entirely sealed. The thieves inserted a faucet in one of the sealed casks and drew part of its wine. I believe

that the wine in the casks which have faucets should be considered "forbidden wine" since we suspect that the thieves drew
wine from these casks also.

A. We must not be too strict in our ruling when it is uncertain whether wine has been dedicated to an idol. Since there
is no indication that the casks which had faucets were tampered
with by the thieves, we do not assume that the thieves drew
wine from them. Faucets are usually inserted in casks which
contain ordinary wine, while sealed casks are used for wine
of superior quality. The thieves preferred to insert a faucet in
a sealed cask probably in order to draw the superior wine
rather than obtain inferior wine from the open casks. Moreover,
they did not draw out all the wine even from the sealed cask.
There is no reason to suspect, therefore, that they also drew
wine from the open casks.

SOURCES: *Mordecai Hagadol,* p. 119b; cf. B. p. 295, no. 389.

127 (D)

A Jew is not permitted to offer a Gentile forbidden wine
(*yayin nesek* — wine touched by a Gentile). I often wondered
how this custom, to offer forbidden wine to Gentiles, became
so widely accepted. If the perpetrators had been duly warned
against this practice and did not heed the warning, they need
no longer be disturbed; for it is better that they transgress
innocently than rebelliously. Our own wine, of course, we are
permitted to offer to a Gentile (although this wine becomes
yayin nesek as soon as the Gentile touches it).

SOURCES: L. 145.

128

Q. May a Jew rent his cellar to a Gentile for the purpose
of having the Gentile store his *yayin nesek* (forbidden wine)
therein?

A. No, he may not, for a person may derive no such benefit from forbidden wine. The only difference between the *yayin nesek* of the talmudic period and that of our own day is that the *yayin nesek* of today may be taken from a Gentile in payment of his debt, as we thus recover our money from him.

SOURCES: *Tashbetz,* 376; *Orhot Hayyim* II, p. 264; cf. ibid. p. 244; *Kol Bo* 96.

129

Q. Does the touch of a Jew "who has his prepuce drawn forward" render wine *yayin nesek* (forbidden wine)?

A. No, it does not.

SOURCES: *Tashbetz,* 380; *Mordecai Hagadol* p. 121 d; *Orhot Hayyim* II, p. 245; *Kol Bo* 96.

130 (D)

The wine of a (Jewish) infidel or of a Karaite, who does not trust the teachings of the Rabbis, is *yayin nesek* (forbidden wine), for, although they are not idolators themselves, they do not guard their wine from being handled by Gentiles.

SOURCES: L. 231.

131

Q. A claims that he lent two pounds to B for investment purposes for one year, on condition that B pay him one pound if B's profit from this investment should exceed one pound, or the whole profit in case B's profit be less than one pound. B, however, claims that he was to pay A a uniform interest at the rate of one pound a year, and that it was a usurious transaction, and, therefore, not binding.

A. A's claim is sustained. Since A could have received a pound a year legally, had he lent the money to B through a Gentile, we must believe the truth of his (A's) present claim.

SOURCES: Cr. 57; Pr. 146; Rashba I, 871.

132

Q. A gave a pledge to B telling him that it was a Gentile's pledge, and that he would allow B to collect the interest on the loan he had extended to the Gentile if B would refund him the principal of that loan. B gave him the money and took the pledge as security. Subsequently, A told B that he was not entitled to any interest since the pledge belonged to a Jew and that he had previously lied to him concerning the original owner of the pledge.

A. B may insist that he believes A's first statement only, even if A is ready to take an oath as to the truth of his second statement. Therefore, if A gave the pledge to B at the time B gave him the money, B may keep the pledge until A pays him the promised interest.

Sources: Pr. 142; Rashba I, 858; Mord. B.M. 338, Cf. L. 448.

133

Q. A claims that B lent him money on a pledge, and that when he came to redeem the pledge B exacted interest from him. Since he had contracted the loan directly from B, the latter was not allowed to take any interest on this loan. A, therefore, demands that B pay him back the interest. B, on the other hand, claims that the loan was originally contracted through a Gentile intermediary and that he was entitled, therefore, to the interest.

A. It is assumed that a person who might have gained an advantage by following a certain legal procedure, did not fail to follow such procedure. Since B could legally have been entitled to interest on his money had he granted the loan through a Gentile intermediary, we assume that he did grant the loan through such intermediary. Therefore, B is entitled to his interest and is not required to take an oath.

Sources: L. 197.

134

Q. A borrowed ten pounds of charity-money on the following conditions: a) that he pay three pounds per year out of his profits; b) that should his profit be less than three pounds, he would have to pay only half of that profit; and c) in case there be a loss, A would suffer the entire loss himself. For ten years A paid the three pounds per year regularly and thus has paid thirty pounds to the charity-chest. Now, however, being somewhat depleted in finances he is in no position to return the ten pounds. Since it is forbidden to lend charity-money on condition that the lender share in the profits but not in the losses, the thirty pounds paid by A is considered *abak ribbit* (shade of usury). Although A can not collect, by judicial process, the *abak ribbit* he has paid, he ought to be able to retain the ten pounds in exchange for the unlawful interest he has paid. Signed: Hayyim b. Machir.

A. If one lends money on condition that he share in the profits but not in the losses, the terms of this transaction, being unlawful, are void. We must, therefore, substitute other terms in their place. We must choose one of the following alternatives: a) the transaction is a pure loan bearing no profit; b) the lender is liable for his share of the losses and is entitled to his share of the profits. Since a person lends money with the intention of earning a profit, and such profit constitutes the main purpose of the transaction, we prefer the second alternative. Therefore, we must calculate what percentage of the entire profit (earned by A through the use of the ten pounds) the three pounds per year was expected to form, and, then, charge the charity-chest with the responsibility for the same percentage of the losses. If, during the ten year period, the thirty pounds paid by A exceeded the percentage of the total profit, A is entitled to deduct such excess from the principal; otherwise, he must repay the entire principal.

R. Hayyim b. Machir raised objections to R. Meir's decision. He brought proof to the effect that the transaction ought
to be changed into a pure loan bearing no profit, and that A
be entitled to retain the ten pounds of the principal against
the illegal profit he has paid. He even cited (by number) another
Responsum of R. Meir wherein the latter decided that a transaction such as the above be considered a pure loan bearing no
profit. (Cf. Cr. 62, Pr. 151; Am. II, 169.) He assured Rabbi
Meir, however, that he would follow his decision.

R. Meir replied: I was always of the opinion that the aforesaid transaction ought to be considered a pure loan bearing no
profit. But, when your query reached me I had just received
the book (Code) of Maimomides, and I decided to "ask the
Oracle" (see what Maimonides says on the subject). When I
discovered that Maimonides requires the lender to share in the
losses as well as in the profits, I adopted his view. For all his
words are based on tradition. Even if this decision be based on
reason, I have to bow to his opinion since my inferior reasoning
ability could never compare with that of Maimonides who is
a profound master in that art. Moreover, I see the wisdom of
his view. For a person who lends money to another does so
because he hopes to profit thereby. Were he mainly interested
in the safety of the principal (as you seem to infer) he would
keep the money in a safe place and never lend it to anybody.
Were we to ask a lender who had stipulated that he do not share
in the losses, whether he would prefer to change his voided
agreement into a pure loan transaction bearing no profit, or
choose to share in the profits and the losses, he would certainly
prefer the latter. Furthermore, when the active partner lends
the money against adequate security, the chances of earning
a profit are much greater than the chances of losing part of the
principal.

SOURCES: L. 426; P. 477.

135

Q. A borrowed money against pledges from the charity-trustees, at a stipulated rate of interest. After A had held the money for over half a year, B asked A to lend it to him. B undertook to release A from his obligations to the charity-trustees as to both principal and interest, and was ready to substitute his pledges for those of A. A agreed to this arrangement and gave the money to B.

A. If B cannot extricate himself from the charity-trustees without paying interest on A's loan, as in case the trustees claim to have lent the money to A through a Gentile, A must pay the required interest to B, since his loan to B constituted a usurious transaction and the court enforces the reimbursement of money collected as usury. On the other hand, if B could extricate himself from the charity-trustees without paying interest on the loan, but in order to do so, he would have to sue the charity-trustees, A should pay B for his efforts on his behalf; otherwise these efforts would constitute *abak ribbit* (a shade of usury). However, a court does not enforce the reimbursement of *abak ribbit*.

Sources: Mord. B.M. 327.

136 (D)

Q. A claims that B owed him three and three-eighths *marks*, that B gave him valuables to pledge with the charity treasurers for a loan of the same amount (the money of which A was to take in payment of the above debt), that B asked him to pledge with the charity treasurers additional valuables of his own, which he (A) was to lend to B, should B's valuables prove insufficient security for the loan, and that B promised to redeem these valuables. A, therefore, demands that B redeem his pledges. B, while conceding the above, claims that originally A lent him only three *marks*; that the additional three-eighths of a *mark* A is demanding, constitutes the interest on this loan; and that such interest is unlawful usury from Jew to Jew since the loan was made by A directly to him [without a Gentile intermediary].

A. B must take an oath that the three-eighths of a *mark* constitutes interest on a loan made directly to him, and thus be free from obligation for this sum. Although by taking this oath B will incriminate himself [since borrowing money on interest is also a sin] such oath will have full legal effect when applied against A. For the testimony of a witness that incriminates the witness himself, is nevertheless acceptable as valid testimony against, or in support of, the litigants (Sanh. 25 a).

Sources: L. 208.

137

Q. A trustee loaned money belonging to orphans to A on interest, at the rate of one quarter per *mark*. A refused to pay the interest. Moreover, A claimed to have repaid part of the loan, which claim the trustee denied. The inquiring judges decided that even money belonging to orphans can not be loaned to a Jew at a definite rate of interest.

A. Your decision was correct and the trustee's stipulation of a definite interest was illegal and, therefore, void. However, under the circumstances, the loan is as if made by the Jewish court — the natural trustee and protector of all orphans — on the usual terms [made when orphans' money is loaned]: "to share in the profits but not in the losses." Therefore, if A earned profits with the money, he must pay to the trustee, the stipulated quarter per *mark*. If A admits that the money he borrowed belonged to the orphans, but claims to have repaid part of it, the trustee is believed as to the amount he received from A, (in repayment of the loan), and is not required to take an oath since the trustee is a disinterested third party. But if A states his belief that the trustee loaned him his own money, and not the orphans' money, the trustee must take an oath as to the amount he received from A in repayment of the loan, though he is not required to take an oath to the effect that the money he loaned belonged to the orphans.

SOURCES: Pr. 969; Mord. B.M. 332; *Agudah* B.M. 98.

138

Q. How are we to invest money belonging to orphans; are we permitted to lend such money on interest?

A. The Talmud provides that such money be invested with a rich and trustworthy person, one who obeys the laws of the Torah and is careful not to bring upon himself a ban of the Rabbis. It should be invested on condition that the orphans share in the profits but not in the losses (B. M. 70 a). To invest such money in mortgages on houses, fields, or vineyards, is preferable, since money may be lost but land lasts forever. The written contract attesting the transaction, should be deposited with a trustworthy person or with the trustee of the orphans. But, we are not permitted to lend such money on a definite rate of interest.

SOURCES: L. 235.

139

Q. A young man lent money to A stipulating that the latter be responsible for the loss of it through theft, but not through unavoidable accident. The former also tutored A's son. In return for both services A paid the young man's living expenses. Is the lending of the aforesaid money considered a legitimate transaction?

A. If while the arrangement was made with the young man to rehearse the lessons with A's son in return for receiving his sustenance, the stipulation was made that the young man lend money to A, the transaction is considered usurious, even though A would have been content to pay the young man's living expenses in return for his tutoring alone. The fact that the money was not given as an actual loan, since A was not to be responsible for its loss through unavoidable accident, does not materially change the situation, since the Talmud considers the renting of money a usurious transaction (B. M. 69b). But, if it is true, what you write at the end of your letter, that the young man gave A his money as an outright gift so that he is at liberty, should he so desire, never to return the money to the young man, the transaction is a legitimate one.

SOURCES: Cr. 257; Am II, 151; Mord. B.M. 316; Tesh. Maim. to *Mishpatim*, 45; *Agudah* B.M. 88. Cf. Maharil, *Responsa* 37; Moses Minz, *Responsa* 72; *Terumat Hadeshen* 302.

140

Q. When a person sells to another a debt due him from a Gentile, how does the buyer gain title to the debt, since the principle that a debt may be assigned "in the presence of the three parties involved (B. B. 148a)" does not apply when one of the parties is a Gentile?

A. A person's admission against his own interests is equivalent to the testimony of a hundred witnesses (Git. 40b). Since the seller admits that the money due from the Gentile really belongs, and has always belonged, to the buyer assignee, the latter is entitled to collect the debt from the Gentile. This procedure, however, does not remove the prohibition against usury, since the interest accruing after the sale still belongs to the seller.

SOURCES: Sinai VI (1943) 13, no. 461. Cf. Israel Bruno, *Responsa* 160; ibid. 209.

141

Q. B claims that he deposited a Gentile's pledge with A as security for a loan, that subsequently thereto he repaid both the principal and the interest to A, but that the Gentile failed to pay him, B, the interest. A avers that when B came to redeem the Gentile's pledge, he asked B whether the Gentile paid him the interest, and that B replied that he had. Is A entitled to any interest on his loan to B?

A. A is not entitled to any interest on his loan to B, even if the Gentile paid interest to B, unless B transferred the Gentile's debt to A, at the time A extended B the loan, and B completely withdrew from the transaction with the Gentile.

SOURCES: *Mordecai Hagadol*, p. 277a.

142

Q. To redeem his pledges C, a trustee, assigned to A and B a debt due him from a Gentile, on condition that A and B collect the interest as well as the principal. May A and B collect the interest from the Gentile?

A. They may not; a debt due from a Gentile can not be assigned in any manner, even if accompanied by a *kinyan* or made in the presence of the three parties involved in the transaction; hence the accrued interest belongs to the original creditor.

SOURCES: Pr. 354; 989; L. 404; Mord. B.B. 614. Cf. *Agudah* B.B. 197; Israel Bruno, *Responsa* 160; ibid. 209.

143

Q. A claimed: a) that B owed him ten *marks;* b) that when he demanded that money from B, the latter transferred to him an investment of ten *marks* in the hands of the bishop, and told him to collect both the principal and the interest from that day on; and c) that B thus owed him the principal and the interest of such investment. B, however, refused to pay the interest to A. Thereupon the judges by arbitration decided that B pay A the greater part of such interest, and transfer the debt to him.

A. The arbitrators and the witnesses have transgressed the commandment: "thou shalt not lay upon him interest (Ex. 22, 24)", while the creditor has violated several negative commandments. A debt in the hands of a Gentile can not be transferred to another by a simple agreement of the three parties concerned. Such a debt may legally be transferred to a third party in the following manner only: The creditor must say to the Gentile debtor and to the sureties: "Obligate yourselves to pay to A the debt which you owe me; if you will do so, I shall release you from your obligations toward me." Should the debtor and the sureties agree to the arrangement, only then will the debt be transferred to A.

SOURCES: Tesh. Maim. to *Mishpatim*, 68. Cf. *Agudah* B.B. 197; Weil, *Responsa* 33.

144 (D)

Q. A lent money to a Gentile on a monthly rate of interest and received as security a pledge worth double the amount of the loan. A, needing money, asked B to take over the Gentile's loan and collect the interest. B paid A the amount due the latter from the Gentile and A said: "From now on it is yours." Subsequently, the Gentile failed to redeem the pledge. Is A permitted to recover the pledge and pay B the principal plus the interest accumulated during the time the pledge was in B's possession, or would such payment of interest constitute usury? Moreover, since a Jew does not gain title to a Gentile's pledge (Pesach. 31b), may B refuse to return the pledge to A on the ground that A sold his rights in that pledge to B?

A. Since A did not gain title to the pledge, it is assumed that he surrendered all his rights to the pledge upon handing it to B. Therefore, B became the creditor of the gentile (and not A's creditor) and was entitled to the interest on his loan. Thus B, upon surrendering the pledge to A, has a right to receive from A the principal plus the interest due B from the Gentile; and B has the further right to keep the pledge for himself.

SOURCES: Pr. 795; cf. Mord. B.M. 338.

145

Q. A and B lent money on interest in partnership. Subsequently, A withdrew from the partnership and gave his part of the loan to B. Is this transaction valid?

A. A healthy person can assign his loans to another only in the presence of all three interested parties, viz: the assignor, the assignee, and the debtor. This mode of assignment is valid only if the interested parties are Jews. Since in this case the debtor was a Gentile, the assignment of the loan was not valid and the accrued interest belongs to A.

SOURCES: Cr. 61; Pr. 150; L. 376.

146 (D)

Q. R. Eliezer (a relative of R. Meir?) and B jointly lent money to a Gentile. When half of the debt was repaid, R. Eliezer permitted B to take the entire half, as his full payment of his part of the loan. Would this constitute a termination of the partnership entitling R. Eliezer to the entire interest that will accrue on the remaining one-half of the debt?

A. Yes. A partnership may be dissolved by the mere verbal consent of all the members thereof.

SOURCES: Pr. 1008.

147

Q. A's father, before his death, deposited his books with B (a trustee) as security for a dowry of twenty-four *marks*, which he promised his son C. He subsequently paid B eighteen *marks*, leaving a balance of six *marks*. C's brother, A, representing his mother, Bruna, now demands that B permit him to redeem his father's books for six *marks*. B, however, claims that when C demanded the six *marks* from his mother, she, in payment of that amount, assigned to C a debt of twenty-three pounds D owed her, and pledged the books for that amount. B, therefore, demands twenty-three pounds to be paid to C before he returns the books. A, however, claims that anything paid to C above six *marks* will constitute usury.

A. B's testimony is accepted without reservation since B is a trustee. According to that testimony, the payment of twenty-three pounds to C would constitute usury. B must, therefore, return the books to A and his mother upon the receipt of six *marks*. Moreover, the loan of the value of twenty-three pounds never really belonged to C, since a loan can not be legally assigned to a third party.

R. Meir sent substantially the same answer to Rabbi Yedidyah which answer begins as follows: "According to the (record of) claims sent to me by the judges, the widow, Bruna, did not admit that the loan originally belonged to them (to B and C). She claims only to have given them the loan in exchange for the pledges . . . ."

SOURCES: Pr. 985–6; L. 503.

148

1) *Q.* A and B planned to lend money to a Gentile in partnership at the rate of four *Heller* denarii per pound [per week]. However, A had more money to put in the partnership than B had. They agreed, therefore, that when in the future

they would divide the profit, A should first take out of such profit four denarii [per week] per every pound he had invested more than B, and that the remainder should be equally divided between them. When they came to negotiate the loan with the Gentile, however, he asked them that in addition to lending him the money they undertake to feed his horses for a certain period of time. He offered to pay only three *Heller* denarii per pound [per week] interest, but the liberal compensation he offered for feeding his horses induced them to accept his terms. They agreed, therefore, that at the expiration of the designated period the Gentile pay A and B a certain sum of money, which sum represented payment of the principal and the interest, plus remuneration for feeding the horses. Now B claims that out of his share of the profit from feeding the horses he is paying A four denarii per every pound the latter had invested more than he himself had; and that such payment constituted usury.

A. The above agreement between A and B is valid. No question of usury is involved. A Jew is permitted to pay interest to another Jew for a loan extended to a third party, as long as the first Jew is not responsible for the repayment of the principal.

2) *Q.* A claims that he gave more feed to the horses than B gave.

A. A should take an oath as to the amount and value of the feed he has given in excess of that of B, and be entitled to collect this difference. If A gave the extra feed at a time the price of feed was lower than it is at present, A must state under oath whether he had intended to lend feed or the price of feed to B, and be entitled to collect accordingly.

3) *Q.* A claims that he bought four measures of feed from B and paid him for it; that when he came to take it, B told him that he had none and advised him to buy some from an-

other person and charge it to him; and that consequently he bought two measures of feed from another person for thirteen schillings. He now demands two measures of feed plus thirteen schillings from B. B avers that since the original transaction was not binding, because mere payment of money does not legally conclude a sale of movables, he now refuses to enter into such a sale, and owes A only the money received from him.

A. B must give thirteen schillings and two measures of feed to A, or he would incur severe punishment from Heaven. Although the mere payment of money does not conclude a sale, a person who retracts his word incurs severe punishment from Heaven.

SOURCES: Cr. 253–4–5; cf. Hag. Maim., *Malveh* 5, 40.

149

Q. A was deputy in lending B's money to a Gentile upon interest. Thus A took the money from B and gave it to the Gentile in B's name; the Gentile's friends went surety to B. Subsequently, the Gentile, a violent man, concocted false charges against A and ordered him to repay both the principal and the interest to B out of his own pocket. The Gentile also told B that A would pay his debt for him. A, therefore, brought the principal and the interest to B. The latter, however, being a religious man, refused to accept the interest lest it be considered usury from Jew to Jew.

A. B is permitted to accept the interest, for A merely acted as B's deputy. He was never responsible to B for the money. The fact that the Gentile forces A to repay his debt for him, is no concern of B.

SOURCES: Cr. 309; *Mordecai Hagadol*, p. 368a.

150

Those who throw keys or money into the hands of their wives during their menstruation period, should be sharply rebuked. Throughout this period until her immersion in a ritual bath, the wife should put down such articles for the husband to pick up, and the husband should put them down for the wife to pick up, but, throwing articles to each other at this period is prohibited.

SOURCES: Cr. 124.

151

Q. A woman believed herself pregnant for eight weeks, showing all the symptoms of pregnancy. At the end of this period, however, during coitus, she felt that she was beginning to menstruate. She told her husband about it, and he withdrew hastily.

A. The husband has committed a sin punishable with *kareth* (extermination), for he should have waited till his penis relax, before withdrawing. However, since he has committed the above sin inadvertently, fasting will atone for it. Let him fast for one day each week from now, the tenth of *Iyyar*, till *Rosh Hashanah*. If he cannot fast, however, let him give twelve denarii to charity [for each fast-day].

SOURCES: Mord. Sheb. 754; *Mordecai Hagadol*, p. 338 b. Cf. *Agudah* Sheb. 7; Moses Minz, *Responsa* 26; Isserlein, *Pesakim* 60.

152

Q. A woman cohabited with her husband out of her "fixed period" (period of menstrual flow), and found blood on her sheet next morning. What penance should be inflicted upon her?

A. Since she did not expect a flow of blood at the time,

such flow is considered an unavoidable accident; therefore, she did not sin, and needs no penance.

SOURCES: Pr. 622; Mord. Sheb.; *Hilkot Niddah*, 731. Cf. Hayyim Or Zarua, *Responsa* 112; Asher, *Responsa* 29, 2.

153

Q. While urinating Leah sees on the urine particles of blood of a pale color. May she cohabit with her husband?

A. If she examines herself after urinating and finds blood on the examining rag, she is not permitted to cohabit with her husband. But if examining herself after urination she finds no blood for three consecutive times, she no longer has to examine herself and is permitted to cohabit with her husband.

SOURCES: Pr. 630; L. 403; Mord. Sheb. 735. Cf. Israel Bruno, *Responsa* 248; ibid. 250.

154

Q. After urinating Leah usually finds blood on her "examining rag" (*ed*); the Rabbis of Cologne are of the opinion that she is permitted to cohabit with her husband, since the ruling of R. Jose is accepted that a woman who finds blood in her urine is ritually clean (Niddah 59 b).

A. Even R. Jose would admit that upon finding blood on her "examining rag", after urination, the woman would be ritually unclean. (For R. Jose's opinion is based on the belief that blood found in urine does not come from the interior of the womb, but from a wound or sore; cf. Pr. 630; Mord. *Niddah* 735. That blood on the "examining rag" after urination however usually comes from the interior of the womb, is universally accepted.) I have often wondered at the compilers of some codes who decide in accordance with the view of R. Jose, yet fail to make the above distinction.

SOURCES: Am II, 51; cf. Pr. 630; L. 403; Hag. Maim. to *Issurei Biah*, 5, 2; Maharil, *Responsa* 173.

155

We have carefully investigated and found that this woman has a wound in her womb; for every time she urinates she suffers severe pain. Occasionally, but not always, she finds blood in her urine; but no blood is found immediately after urination, neither upon wiping herself nor on the "examining rag". I, therefore, agree with you that this woman is permitted to co-habit with her husband, for, when a woman says she has a wound in her womb from which the blood exudes, she is to be believed.

This responsum is addressed to Rabbi Yekutiel; the *Mordecai Hagadol*, however, ascribes the question to Rabbi Asher.

SOURCES: Am II, 52; *Mordecai Hagadol*, p. 339a.

156

L has a wart in her vagina which bleeds during copulation and even when touched by the "examining rag". I am inclined to believe that L is ritually clean since we assume that her blood comes from the wart and not from the interior of the womb. During her regular period (of menstruation), if she definitely feels that the blood comes from the wart, she is ritually clean; otherwise she is unclean. At other times she is ritually clean even when she does not definitely feel that the blood comes from the wart. She can recognize the menses by a greater flow of blood than that which usually comes from the wart. At her menstruation period she must count the same number of days as hitherto. Moreover, knowing exactly where the wart is situated, she should be able to manipulate the "examining rag" in such a way as to discover whether there be present any menstrual blood.

SOURCES: Am II, 53; cf. Pr. 626; Mord. *Niddah*, 735. Cf. Maharil, *Responsa* 173.

157

The blood stains on the shirt and sheets of a leprous woman do not render her impure. For these stains came from her leprous skin rather than from her womb. A stain on her shirt does not render her impure even during her "period", if she examined herself.

SOURCES: L. 185; *Tashbetz* 481; *Orhot Hayyim* II, p. 126.

158

Q. A woman who is presumed to be (levitically) clean discovered a (blood) stain on her person or on her clothes. May she continue to consider herself clean by assuming that the stain was caused by other factors, than a flow of blood from her womb?

A. If there were present other factors that could have produced the stain, she might assume that the stain was produced by these factors.

SOURCES: *Tashbetz*, 476.

159

Q. A lived normally with his wife L for some time. Later, however, L detected discharges of blood during copulation on three occasions. Should L "examine herself" (Niddah 66a, with a lead tube, in order to discover whether the blood flows from the interior of the womb or from the walls of the vagina) or must A divorce her immediately? In case of divorce, is L entitled to her *ketubah*?

A. Rashi and Ri hold opposite views on this subject. We are not at liberty to disregard Rashi's view and, therefore, can not permit A to live with L even if an "examination" will produce favorable results. However, we must make the following distinction: If the three acts of copulation during which blood was detected were consecutive, A must divorce L forthwith; but, if they were not consecutive and between each act there were other acts during which no trace of blood was detected, A is permitted to live with L. If the copulations during which blood was detected, occurred on specific dates, or at regular intervals, A must refrain from copulation on such dates. Moreover, if A is not anxious to remarry, and is willing to allow L to live away from him in another district and to deal with her through an intermediary or only in the presence of a third party, he does not have to divorce her. In case of divorce, however, L is entitled to the *Ikkar-ketubah* and to her dowry, but she cannot collect the additional jointure, since some authorities are of the opinion that under the circumstances she is not entitled to the additional jointure.

This Resp. is addressed to "my relative Rabbi Baruch ha-Kohen."

SOURCES: Am II, 49; Rashba I, 839, 40; Pr. 625; Mord. *Niddah*, 735; Hag. Maim., *Isurei Biah* 8, 3. Cf. *Sefer ha Terumah* 106–7; Maharil, *Responsa* 173.

160 (D)

Q. B betrothed his daughter C to his nephew D, the son of B's brother, A, while C and D were still minors. D married C while she was still a minor, and entrusted his dowry, into the hands of his father-in-law, B, as a loan. After the first night, blood was found on the bridal sheet in spite of the fact that D did not yet cohabit with his wife, C. The fact was then discovered that C dripped with blood whenever she micturated or defecated. D, who kept away from his wife for a half year, was advised to cohabit with her on the ground that he thus might cure her. D did so and C's blood flowed profusely. D, therefore, sent C back to her father. D's mother claimed that C had this illness before she was betrothed to D; that long before C's marriage she once found C soaked in blood; that D's marriage to her was, therefore, contracted in error; and that C was therefore not entitled to her *ketubah*. B, however, claimed that it was D's misfortune that he could not cohabit with C, and, therefore, B demanded C's *ketubah*.

A. As soon as a person marries a woman, even if he does not cohabit with her, she is entitled to her *ketubah*. Therefore, D must pay C her *ketubah* unless he can conclusively prove that C was dripping blood before her bethrothal.

SOURCES: Pr. 868.

161

Q. Are the "days of purity" [the days between the seventh and the fortieth day after the birth of a son, and between the fourteenth and the eightieth day after the birth of a daughter during which a flow of blood does not render the woman unfit to cohabit with her husband] still in effect? Alfasi rules that the "days of purity" are not in effect at present.

A. I have not at hand Alfasi on the laws of *Niddah*, but I once examined carefully the statement of Alfasi, referred to, and found that he did not mean to convey your meaning at all; for there is no doubt that the "days of purity" are still in effect.

R. Meir adds: When I studied under my teachers in France, my father asked my teacher whether the "days of purity" were still in effect. My teacher was surprised that this should be doubted at all, since no opinion to the contrary is quoted in the Talmud. He asked me so to inform my father. But, when I subsequently returned to this kingdom I was told that Alfasi had decided that the days of purity were no longer in effect. A closer examination of the text of Alfasi, however, did not bear this out. Therefore, if one wants to be stringent, he may be stringent; but the one who chooses to be lenient, may do so without compunction.

SOURCES: Am II, 54. Cf. Mord., *Hilkot Niddah*, 738.

162 (D)

A woman is permitted to cohabit with her husband immediately after her immersion in the ritual bath, even if such immersion took place in the daytime [of the eighth day]. However, R. Tam holds that a woman is not permitted to immerse herself in a ritual bath during the daylight time of Sabbath even if it be her eighth day.

SOURCES: L. 507; P. 288.

163

Q. I have heard that you permit a woman to attend the bath-house for further lavation, after her required immersion in a ritual bath.

A. I can find no reason for prohibiting such practice. For the original prohibition against washing in ordinary water after immersion in a ritual bath, was directed only against persons preparing themselves for sacred duties; while a woman prepares herself for a secular purpose. My teacher R. Isaak of Vienna, was wont to prohibit such practice; nevertheless, when I once presented my point of view discussing the matter at length in his presence, he did not contradict me. I also heard from young men from Mantua, that when he (?) inquired about the matter from Rabbi Isaiah of Burgundy [of Trani], the latter also permitted the practice.

SOURCES: P. 289; Am. II, 55; cf. Mord. Sheb. 750.

164

1) *Q.* Water was drawn with a leaking vessel from a ritual bath until less than forty *seah* remained in it. The vessel had a hole, the size of a finger, in its side, immediately adjacent to the bottom. There is no doubt, therefore, that at least three *lugin* of water leaked back from the vessel into the bath, thus rendering the bath unfit for ritual purposes. Therefore, no inflow of fresh water could ever purify it for ritual purposes. The obvious solution would be completely to drain the bath until less than three *lugin* of water remain therein. But the natural inflow of fresh water is so intense that the bath can not be so drained.

A. I should prefer to have the bath completely drained and thus be spared the trouble of discovering legal grounds to declare the bath fit for ritual purposes. Since, however, that is impossible, I declare that the bath is ritually pure for two reasons: a) since the hole in the vessel is immediately adjacent to the bottom so that the vessel can not retain any water, it is legally not considered a vessel. Therefore, the water dripping therefrom is not considered *maim sheubim* (drawn water) and does not render the bath unfit for ritual purposes. b) This ritual bath, being a natural spring, does not become unfit by the admixture of *maim sheubim*.

2) *Q.* Does water scooped up in a winnowing shovel, (that has a rim on three sides but is open on the fourth side) and poured back into the ritual bath render the bath unfit for ritual purposes?

A. Since such shovel can not retain water, it is not considered a vessel and the water scooped up therein is not considered *maim sheubim*.

This Responsum is addressed to Rabbi Jonathan.

SOURCES: Am I, 95; Mord. Shebu. 746. Cf. Asher, *Responsa* 30, 4; *Terumat Hadeshen* 258.

165

Q. A solemnly vowed not to play cards. He broke his vow, however, and now plays cards frequently. Should we release A from his vow so that he should no longer commit a sin every time he plays cards?

A. No court should release A from his vow, for regarding such cases it is said: "Let the wicked gorge himself with his sin till he die (B.K. 69a)".

SOURCES: Cr. 124.

166

Q. A vowed to quit gambling and promised to give one *mark* for a holy cause should he break his vow. He subsequently gave money to a friend to gamble for him. Must he pay the promised *mark?*

A. Vows are interpreted according to common parlance. If the phrase "I will not gamble again" includes, in common parlance, gambling by proxy, he must pay the fine. If, however, the implications of the phrase in common speech can not be determined, we must follow Biblical use of terms. In Biblical law a person is responsible for the acts of his agent unless the agent himself commits a sin by carrying out his mission. Although A's vow was made in the form of *Asmakta,* it is binding since all promises to a holy cause, even when made in the form of *Asmakta,* are binding.

SOURCES: Cr. 299, 300; Pr. 493, 494; L. 211, 212; *Mordecai Hagadol* p. 337b.
Cf. Asher, *Responsa* 13, 2; *Agudah* B.K. 51.

167

Q. A vowed to quit gambling and promised five *marks* to charity should he break his vow. He did break his vow, but refuses to give the promised five *marks* to the charity trustees of his town, stating that he will give it to the poor of another town.

A. A must pay the five *marks* to the charity chest of his own town.

Sources: Pr. 500; Mord. Meg. 825; *Mordecai Hagadol* p. 107a. Cf. Moses Minz, *Responsa* 73.

168

Our friend, R. Samson, informed me that he vowed that he would not take an oath nor make any promise to his father-in-law or to his wife by which he would bind himself not to deal treacherously with them, and that he made this vow on condition that it could not be dissolved except with the unanimous consent of Rabbi Perez, Rabbi Hayyim, and myself. I have inquired and have become convinced that no peace was possible between R. Samson and his wife unless this vow is dissolved. I for my part, therefore, fully consent to its dissolution and agree that the others do likewise. Moreover, since the dissolution of R. Samson's vow is a meritorious act that would re-establish domestic tranquility, his vow may be dissolved without our consent. The correct procedure would be first to annul the condition that a unanimous consent of the three Rabbis be required — for this condition in itself constitutes a vow and lends itself to the same manner of dissolution as other vows — and finally to dissolve the vow itself.

Sources: *Semak* ed. Constantinople, no. 79 end, ed. Cremona, 82 end; *Mordecai Hagadol*, p. 218d; Tesh. Maim. to *Haflaah* 4.

169

Q. A vowed to abstain from having intercourse with his wife. He stipulated, however, that such vow be void if it involve a violation of the law.

A. If A did not procure his wife's consent to his abstention, prior to making the vow, it is void. If he did procure his wife's consent thereto, the vow is binding unless A be released from it by three laymen.

R. Meir adds that he can not release A from his vow unless A personally appear before him, for one can not release a person from a vow through a messenger.

This Responsum is addressed to Rabbi Moses.

SOURCES: Mord. Kid. 550; Tesh. Maim. to *Ishut.* 2; Hag. Maim. *Ishut* 14, 3. Cf. Weil, *Responsa* 2.

170

Q. A swore by the Ten Commandments that he would never live with his wife again and that he would divorce her, if she would not take a ritual bath on that particular night. Can such an oath be dissolved by a scholar?

A. During the period of the Geonim the strict law was adopted that no oath could be dissolved by a scholar if such oath was taken by the pronouncing of the name of God, by the Torah, or by the Ten Commandments.

SOURCES: Cr. 18; Pr. 120, 121, 122; Mord. Sheb. 758; Rashba I, 854. Cf. R. Haim b. Isaac Or Zarua, *Responsa*, 12; Maharil, *Responsa* 129; Moses Minz, *Responsa* 47.

171

Q. A and L bound themselves, by a ban of the communities, to get married to each other. Subsequently, A apostatized. He repented, however, and returned to the fold. Now L refuses to marry him; must she seek release from the ban?

A. During the time that A was an apostate, the ban was voidable. Therefore, if L appeared in court at the time A was an apostate, and was advised that the ban was void, even though she did not marry another before A repented, she no longer

needs seek release from the ban. If she did not receive a ruling
from the court, however, she must now seek release from the
ban by a scholar. The release may be effected only in A's
presence or, if he is not present, with his consent.

SOURCES: Mord. Sheb. 781.

172 (D)

Q. A and B entered into an agreement and bound themselves by a severe oath, to help each other against murderers
and informers. A failed to carry out the terms of the agreement.
Does A's breaking of the agreement absolve B from his oath
and release him from his obligations to A?

A. Three laymen may absolve B from his oath on the
ground that it was his expectation, at the time he bound himself to the terms of the agreement, that A would carry out his
part of the obligation.

SOURCES: Pr. 841.

173

Q. Certain Jews received permission from their overlord to
imprison and torture their fellow Jews in order to extort money
from them. They threw a few Jews into prison and, by threatening to kill them, made them bind themselves by a *herem* to pay
a certain amount of money to their captors. Must the captives
fulfil their promise after they are released?

A. No, the *herem* is not binding upon them since they
accepted it under pressure, and since they probably thought that
the threats of murder would not be carried out, that the overlord
would probably not agree to murder, and that the captors
themselves would be afraid to commit murder, a sin punishable
by God and man. However, in order to be doubly certain, and
for the sake of appearances, the captors should be asked to
free the others from the *herem;* and knowing that the *herem* is

not binding anyway, the captors should not hesitate to do so. But, if the captors refuse to free the captives of the *herem*, the latter are free from obligation anyway, and need not even seek absolution by a scholar.

SOURCES: Pr. 595, 938; Mord. Gitt. 395; Tesh. Maim. to *Haflaah*, 7; *Agudah* Sheb. 14. Cf. Weil, *Responsa* 53; Isserlein, *Pesakim* 73; ibid. 252.

174

Q. The burghers forced some Jews to take an oath on the Scroll of the Law that they would not clip the coins. While taking the oath the Jews made mental reservations, to their verbal statements, which they believed invalidated the oath. They proceeded, therefore, to clip the coins.

A. Whether or not one has taken an oath not to clip coins, the doing so is a serious crime, the perpetrators of which deserve severe punishment. Clipping coins is tantamount to stealing and robbing, and robbing Gentiles is a crime. Furthermore, such an act creates a public nuisance as it may result in causing great injury to other Jews innocently passing on these coins. It may even cause widespread disaster, and has already led to a great deal of bloodshed. Thus, clipping coins brought about the destruction of our brethren in France and Britain. In addition to committing a basic crime, these Jews broke their solemn oath to the burghers. Mental reservations do not invalidate an oath occasioned by legal circumstances. The talmudic ruling (Ned. 28a) that a person may invalidate his oath to extortionists and murderers by mental reservations, does not apply in this case; for, while extortionists and murderers, by administering an oath, strive to bolster their criminal purposes, it is legal and proper for a king or civil authority to forbid the clipping of coins. Therefore, their oath to the burghers was valid despite their mental reservations. Moreover, when the Gentiles will learn that the Jews clipped coins despite their oath — and they are bound to discover it sooner or later — they will suspect the Jews of wilfully breaking their oath. Should the latter inform the Gentiles that they disregarded their oath because of mental reservations, the consequences might be still more serious; for Gentiles will never again believe a Jew under oath. Therefore, if your authority and my authority carry enough weight, these Jews should be properly flogged.

This Responsum is addressed to: "My teacher Rabbi Judah."

Sources: L. 246; *Mordecai Hagadol*, p. 337c.

175

Q. A Jew stole a horse from a Gentile. The court decided that he should take an oath, in the presence of other Jews, denying the charge of stealing. The Jews are aware that he intends to take a false oath. What should they do?

A. The Jews should state that they do not want to listen to this oath. Moreover, they would do a very meritorious deed if they would settle with the Gentile for a definite sum of money. Then they would be entitled to collect that sum from the thief. The Jews were required to force the thief to such a settlement, in order that he should not cause the name of God to be profaned.

Sources: L. 233; Hag. Asheri *Shebuot* 4, 1.

176

"They that swear by the sin of Samaria" and mainly rely on Christian oaths in the conduct of their business are guilty of a misconduct. I have often protested most vigorously against it, but they would not heed me. I have often repeated that on account of such practices family fortunes have been ruined and investments lost, but I have been unable to abate these practices; for those who indulge in them state that they rely

on great authority, on R. Tam, who permitted such practices
on the ground that the Gentiles of today were not idolators.
Nowadays the Gentiles swear by their sacred objects but do
not consider the objects themselves to be deities. Though they
appeal to Heaven and mean Jesus, they do not expressly mention his name. [Regarding the prohibition involved, see Sanh.
43b]. Moreover, since these Jews do not heed outright prohi-
bitions, how can one expect them to abstain from practices
that some authorities permit? However, the person who reported to you that I sanction such practices, did not speak the
truth; for whenever a difference of opinion exists between our
great authorities I follow the strict opinion, except when the
lenient ruling has been widely accepted as an ancient custom.

SOURCES: B. p. 294 no. 386; *Mordecai Hagadol* p. 113a. Cf. Israel Bruno,
Respona 271.

177

I have not found the Responsum dealing with a solemn
hand-clasp. But, Rabbi Isaak b. Rabbi Menahem wrote that
Rabbi Joseph b. Simon* used to enforce the collection of money
promised to the plaintiff by a solemn hand-clasp.

SOURCES: Cr. 62; Am II, 169; cf. Hag. Maim., *Shebuoth* 11, 3.

178

Q. A swore by the sacred table (of the Temple), or by
other sacred vessels. Is such an oath valid?

A. The oath is invalid. However, if A is an ignorant person,
he should be punished therefor, in order that he refrain from
making a habit of uttering such oaths.

SOURCES: Mord. Sheb. 788.

---

* In Cr. 187 R. Meir states that he possesses a Responsum of Rabbi Isaac b. Abraham
who reports that Rabbi Joseph b. Isaac used to enforce etc.

179 (D)

Q. A seeks from a scholar absolution of a vow. May he make a request of absolution in writing, or must he appear personally before the scholar?

A. He can not be absolved of a vow, unless he appears in person before his absolver.

Sources: Pr. 204.

180

1) *Q.* Does a father have the authority to restrain his son from emigrating to the Holy Land?

A. Since it is a *mitzvah* to settle in the Holy Land, a father has no authority to restrain his son from fulfilling this *mitzvah;* for one must honor the Almighty above one's father.

2) *Q.* Will a person whose wife refuses to accompany him on his emigration to the Holy Land, be liable to punishment for divorcing her?

A. Were any punishment connected with divorcing one's wife under such circumstances, the Rabbis would not have permitted such a divorce, and would not have released the husband from paying the wife's *ketubah.*

3) *Q.* Have you heard what were the reasons that prompted the prominent men to order their sons to return from the Holy Land?

A. It seems to me that the following were the reasons: a) No mercy was shown there; b) they were constantly troubled by the necessity of earning their bread, so that they could not devote their time to study; c) consequently they were lacking in knowledge of the *Torah,* and they were uncertain regarding the details of ritual law. I believe that I heard the above reasons from their children.

SOURCES: Am II, 28; ibid. 79.

181

Q. Why do we, nowadays, partake of secular festivity-meals and secular wedding-feast meals (such as at the wedding of a priest to a daughter of an Israelite, or of a daughter of a scholar to a commoner) in view of the fact that the Talmud explicitly states (B. Pesah. 49a): "A scholar may not partake of any but religious festivity-meals?"

A. We recite, at such meals, hymns of praise and thanksgiving to the Lord and thus convert them into religious feasts.

SOURCES: Pr. 605; Mord. Pesah. 605; *Mordecai Hagadol* p. 77b.

182 (D)

Q. B swore to leave all his disputes with A, to C and D for arbitration. Subsequently, B vilified A's father calling him shameful names, to which A retorted: "not my father, but your father". B became enraged at the insult to his father who had been a scholar and a sage. Both fathers were dead at the time. Now B demands that A be duly punished for vilifying a scholar after his death.

A. We have no right to adjudicate fines, but a court is permitted to take emergency measures whenever necessary. However, if A will take an oath to the effect that he did not fully understand the charge B had made against his father but automatically replied, "your father", he will be free from obligation. Moreover, B must leave this dispute also to C and D for arbitration. He can not press this charge separately without transgressing his oath. On the other hand, since people customarily and automatically reply "your father" whenever someone vilifies their father, B deserves greater punishment than A since he was the first to use vile language. In any event, both A and B should appear before a scholar seeking atonement for their sin of having vilified the dead.

SOURCES: Cr. 298.

183

Q. A rich man called the son of a worthy and scholarly family "bastard, son of bastards". What should be his punishment?

A. The Talmud prescribes thirty-nine lashes, and the judges may punish him more severely, if he makes a practice of offending people. The punishment should also depend on the high qualifications of the man and the family insulted. But for his own salvation, he should fast, chastise himself, give charity to the poor, and ask the Lord for mercy and forgiveness; for he has offended scholars in their graves which is, indeed, a serious sin.

SOURCES: Cr. 285; Pr. 132; Rashba I, 855; Mord. B.K. 105. Cf. Weil, *Responsa* 28.

184

Q. L contends that A reviled her, and that he said to her husband: "Why do you live with a wife who is a prostitute!" A denies her charge, but on the other hand, contends that L vilified the dead. She denies this charge.

A. If L's contention were supported by witnesses, the community would have to punish A by flagellation or imposition of a fine, in accordance with the status of the individuals involved. But, since there are no witnesses, and A denies her charge, no oath is to be imposed on A. Similarly, if A's contention were supported by witnesses, or if L admitted his charge, she would have to visit the grave of the dead person she had vilified, and in the presence of ten Jews, ask forgiveness from the dead. But, since there are no witnesses, and each one denies the other's charge, they are free from obligation. In order to pacify L and A, however, the community may pronounce a solemn curse in the synagogue, such curse to fall on A or L if they are not telling the truth. This procedure should force them to admit the truth.

SOURCES: Mord. B.K. 81–2. Cf. Menahem of Merseburg, *Nimmukim* (78).

185

Q. A promised to give two *marks* for a holy cause should he cohabit with his wife, within the year. He did cohabit with her within that time. If such promise of a gift were made by an individual, even had such money been actually delivered to the donee, it would be considered an *asmakhta* and would be void. Therefore, this conditional promise for a holy cause should also be void, for, although a mere verbal promise for a holy cause is as valid as an actual delivery (of money and valuables) to a private person, it has no greater validity than such delivery; and any transaction classified as an *asmakhta* is invalid even if the money and valuables are actually delivered. Although a conditional promise classified as *asmakhta*, if accompanied by a *kinyan* and made before an authoritative court, is valid, its validity stems from the powers of confiscation inherent in the authoritative court, but not from an act of the promisor.

A. A must pay two *marks* to the holy cause. A mere verbal promise to a holy cause is as binding as a similar promise to an individual accompanied by any manner of conveyance that serves to validate such promise. Since a conditional promise classified as *asmakhta* is valid if accompanied by a *kinyan* and made before an authoritative court, a mere promise of this kind made to charity or to a holy cause is binding, even though the promise was not made before an authoritative court. The validity of a conditional promise made before an authoritative court does not stem from the court's power of confiscation, otherwise no *kinyan* would have been required. Moreover, the power of confiscation by a Jewish court is invoked only for the furtherance of proper conduct in accordance with Jewish principles (למגדר מלתא) but not for the sake of validating private transactions.

This responsum was addressed to Rabbi Solomon "a prominent scholar from France".

SOURCES: Am II, 99; Mord. B.K. 44; cf. Cr. 299–300; Pr. 493; *Agudah* B.K. 51; Asher, *Responsa* 13, 2; Isserlein, *Pesakim* 53.

186 (D)

Q. A promised to give a certain sum of money to charity, but did not specify the particular purpose for which he intended to give the money. Which is more important, candles for the synagogue, or the care of the sick?

A. A should preferably give the money for the care of the sick.

SOURCES: Pr. 692.

187

1. *Q.* A promised ten *denarii* to the charity fund of Merseburg to commemorate the soul of his departed mother. Subsequently he learned that his mother had already contributed to the same fund for the same purpose. Can he retract his promise?

A. No, since he made the promise without any verbal reservation, he must keep his promise.

2. *Q.* May A give ten *denarii* to a charity fund of another place?

A. No, A's promise to give money to the poor of Merseburg is in the nature of a vow and must be fulfilled.

SOURCES: Pr. 342; 343.

188

Q. The community demanded from L, a widow, the one pound she had vowed to give to charity. L denied having vowed to give anything to charity. A single witness, however, supported the claim of the community.

A. Although L is not required to take a Biblical oath in order to counteract the testimony of the single witness, since no such oath is imposed on a litigant in a dispute over charity funds, she is required to take a Rabbinical oath (B. M. 58a). Should one of the members of the community, however, give a fixed sum of money to the charity-chest in full payment of his share of the charity burden, he would thus become a disinterested witness in this case, and his testimony together with that of the other witness would impose upon L the obligation of paying one pound to the charity-chest.

This Responsum is addressed to "my teacher Rabbi Israel."

SOURCES: *Mordecai Hagadol*, p. 175c.

189

Q. After A's death, his widow and her mother revealed that A had left a Scroll of the Law and his large, good prayer-book to charity. They suggested that the community should choose one of them on the following terms: if they choose the Scroll they must undertake to memorialize A's soul together with the souls of the other departed; but if they choose the prayer-book they must undertake to use it constantly for ten years [that the *Hazzan* use it in conducting the prayers of the congregation]. The community chose the prayer-book. But, the widow and her mother, then, asserted that they had agreed to deliver the prayer-book on condition that it be used for ten years to the exclusion of all other prayer-books. At court the representative of the community stated that the community would be ready to accept the prayer-book on the original terms, while the widow's representative denied ever having offered the prayer-book to the community. The community representative retorted that such offer was made in the presence of many witnesses. Accordingly a solemn ban was pronounced against anyone who had heard the widow make the offer and would not appear at court to offer testimony. Some members of the community, then, testified that the widow offered the prayer-book to the community on condition that it be used for ten years. Others testified that they heard the widow's mother make such offer but did not hear it from the widow herself. Some testified that they heard the widow's mother stipulate the term "exclusively", while others heard no exclusive stipulation.

A. Since the prayer-book has allegedly been offered to the community, the members of the community, as interested parties, are considered disqualified witnesses. Therefore, in the absence of qualified witnesses, if the widow will take an oath to the effect that she had never offered the prayer-book, to the community, she will be free from obligation.

SOURCES: B. p. 293 no. 371.

190

Q. We, the undersigned, were chosen as examiners and recorders of the claims of A and the widow L. Consequently, witnesses have testified before us: a) that when A was ill he asked his wife, R, to agree to an arrangement that would bring solace to their souls; b) that A and R, therefore, made a legally binding arrangement in their presence, to the effect that if A died first R would give three *marks* and A's clothes to a charity stipulated by him; and if R died first A would give six *marks* and R's clothes to a charity stipulated by her; and c) that subsequently A recovered from his illness, but R became critically ill and died of her illness. R's mother, L, came before us and claimed that, before her death, R appointed her (L) trustee of the six *marks* and the clothes, and that she asked her to distribute the same to any charity she saw fit. L, therefore, demanded the six *marks* and R's clothes from A. A on the other hand, claimed that he asked his wife before her death why she had not stipulated the recipients of this charity, and in reply she authorized him to spend two *marks* on the cemetery, either for the purpose of constructing a wall or for obtaining sand; to give half a *mark* for the sick, and to give the rest to R's needy relatives. Neither L nor A have any witnesses to support their assertions. Regarding the garments demanded by L, A claimed that L had already taken away all of R's clothes with the exception of one cloak. A demanded that L return to him his wife's seven gold rings, the two pieces of silver jewelry, the two Cologne gulden, and the money that was in R's pocket, which L had taken. L averred that she had returned to A everything that belonged to him. L further demanded that A pay her the expenses she incurred in transporting her daughter's body to another place for burial. A averred that he had paid for the casket and the shrouds; that L had transported R's body without his knowledge and consent; that he had intended to bury her in our town since there was a cemetery in our town; and that L had incurred unnecessary expenses in having R's relatives accompany the body to the place of burial. L, on the other hand, claimed that A had known of her intentions to transport her daughter to another town for burial, that A had consented to it, and that she could prove the truth of these contentions through the testimony of A's tutor, should the latter be forced to testify by a *herem*. A's tutor was summoned before us and testified to the following facts: A told him that he, A, would have accompanied his wife's body to the place of burial were he able to leave the house; he asked the tutor whether he was willing to take his place;

the tutor agreed and accompanied the hearse as instructed.
Three days after the claims in question were placed before us,
L further claimed that A had been at odds with her daughter
and, therefore, the latter did not entrust to him the charity
money, and preferred that L distribute it. A denied this claim
asserting that there was never any enmity between him and
his wife, and that, on the contrary, she became very affectionate
toward him during her illness and tried to show this affection
in many ways. L also claimed that she had already distributed
R's clothes in accordance with the latter's instructions; while
A claimed to have warned L not to give anything away without
his consent. A discovered some of the garments distributed
by L in the hands of the recipients. Please explain in detail
who is to be entrusted with the distribution of the charity
money, and please write your answer on the reverse side of
this parchment. Signed: Samuel b. Eliezer haKohen; Kalonymus
b. Asher; Nahman b. Nathan.

A. If L claims that A was present when her daughter
appointed her the distributor of the money and the clothes,
A must take cognizance of her claims and must take an oath
denying such claims. After taking such an oath, A will have
to give to charity in the presence of witnesses the six *marks* and
the clothes still in his possession. But, if L admits that A was
not present at the time she was thus appointed distributor of
the money and the clothes, A is under no obligation to L and
must proceed to give them to charity in the presence of witnesses. L., on the other hand, must take an oath to the effect
that she did not take anything belonging to A, that she has
distributed R's clothes in accordance with the latter's instructions, and be free from obligation. As to the expenses of R's
funeral, if some of R's relatives, or some of A's relatives, had
been transported and buried in the cemetery to which R's
body was transported, A was under obligation to bury R in
that cemetery, since a husband is obliged to bury his wife with

all the honor and dignity customary in her family, or in his
family, whichever be the greater. Therefore, A must pay L
the expenses she incurred in the burial of her daughter, and
must also repay all loans extended to L for that purpose. Moreover, even if no relatives of A or R were ever buried in this
cemetery, since A sent his tutor to participate in the funeral,
he thus gave his consent to the proceedings and must pay the
expenses thereof. The amount of such expenses are to be attested to by L under oath. However, A is responsible only for
the expenses strictly necessary for the funeral, but not for any
unnecessary extravagances.

Sources: Am II, 33.

191

Q. A and B transgressed a community ordinance and a
fine was imposed on them to pay a certain amount to charity.
There are two synagogues in town, however, one having a
large membership and the other a small membership. A frequents one synagogue, while B frequents the other. Must the
fine-money be equally divided between the two synagogues,
or must it be distributed in proportion to their respective
memberships?

A. The distribution of charity and fine-money is governed
either by custom or by agreement on the part of the community
(members). However, if no custom exists in your town and the
community can come to no agreement, the money should be
distributed in proportion to the number of charity recipients
belonging to each synagogue; for A and B were ordered by
the community to pay to charity, and all the poor of the town
have an equal claim to the charity of that town. A distinction
is drawn in Jewish law between the poor related to the donor
and the poor of the town, between the poor of the donor's town
and those of another town. But we find no distinction drawn

between the poor of the donor's synagogue and those of another synagogue in the same town.

SOURCES: Am II, 231; *Mordecai Hagadol*, p. 300d.

192

We find no law in the Talmud that would permit members of a community to coerce one another into giving charity to the non-resident poor beyond providing a loaf of bread and a night's odging for the itinerant pauper. If the residents of a town voluntarily agree to give more ample support to the non-resident poor, in order to silence the complaints and evil talk of passersby, they may do so. But, should one resident dissent, and insist on giving his "tithe" (charity money) to his indigent relatives instead of to the non-resident poor, the other members of the community would have no right to interfere with him.

SOURCES: Tesh. Maim. to *Kinyan*, 28.

193

Since the custom has been established throughout the diaspora of giving the "tithe"* to the poor, one can not give it away for any other purpose. The use of such money for other purposes would be tantamount to robbing the poor of what is due them.

SOURCES: Pr. 74.

194

In a community where no rule exists to the effect that all tithe-money must go to the community charity-chest, one is permitted to feed his grown-up, independent children with his tithe-money.

SOURCES: Pr. 75, cf. *Tashbetz*, 405.

---

* The Jews of Germany in the Middle Ages used to give a certain percentage of their income to the poor and called it מעשר "tithe-money." Cf. Finkelstein, *Jewish Self-Government in the M. A.*, pp. 18 and 185.

195

Q. According to the custom prevalent in A's town, a person is not required to give to the Community Charity-Chest one half of his tithe-money; but may distribute that half to the poor of his own choosing. Is A permitted to give that half of his tithe-money to the sons and daughters of his relative B, who are supported by B, when B himself is not eligible to receive charity?

A. As long as B's children are being supported by him, even though they have reached majority, their acquisitions belong to him. Since he is not entitled to receive charity, none may be given to his dependents.

SOURCES: P. 13; Mord. B.M. 241; Tesh. Maim. to *Nezikin*, 5; Wertheimer, 7; *Agudah* B.M. 22.

196

Q. The wife of a supposedly poor man was buried at the expense of the Charity Fund. It was subsequently discovered that the woman's husband had money. The community wishes to collect the funeral expenses from the husband.

A. Conflicting opinions are recorded in the *Yerushalmi* regarding the case of a private individual, who paid the expenses for the burial of another man's wife, and no definite decision was reached there. However, since in this case the money came from the charity fund, the community may collect the funeral expenses from the husband. For a man who possesses more than 200 *zuzim* is not permitted to accept charity money for the burial of his wife.

SOURCES: Cr. 60; Pr. 149.

197

Q. A mother demanded support from her three sons. One son has no money except his salary as teacher. The second son possesses fourteen *marks*. The third son is rich but does not live in the same town. Who must support the mother?

A. It is the accepted law that children are obligated to support their widowed mother only out of the possessions they inherited from their father, but not out of their own possessions. However, children of means may be forced to support their mother as an act of charity [since a Jew may be forced to give charity to the poor]. Therefore, any son who would himself be thrown upon charity were he forced to support his mother, can not be forced to do so. But those sons who have means should support their mother in proportion to their wealth. These sons, however, cannot be forced to support their mother out of their own money, but can do so out of the money they are usually obliged to give to charity, although they would thus incur the curse of the Rabbis who say: "Cursed be he who feeds his father out of the poor man's tithe" Kid. 32a.

SOURCES: Cr. 198; Pr. 541; Tesh. Maim. to *Shoftim*, 15; *Mordecai Hagadol*, p. 197d.

198

Q. Leah entrusted twelve *marks*, which she promised to donate for charitable purposes, to A for investment, of which half the profits was to go to impoverished scholars engaged in the study of the Torah, and the other half was to belong to A. A applied some of the profit earned as instructed and added to the principal four pounds from the remaining profit. A died and Leah does not wish to leave the money with his widow.

A. If Leah entrusted the money to A as a loan for no definite period of time, she may demand it at any time after the lapse of thirty days from the time the loan was made. But, if she gave the money to A for a definite period of time, which time is not yet up, she can not demand it before the expiration of the agreed period.

SOURCES: Cr. 58; Pr. 147; Rashba I, 1100; Mord. B.K. 146; *Agudah* B.M. 166.

199

Q. B gave A two *marks* to invest and, from the profits, to pay every year a certain amount to charity to commemorate the soul of his departed wife. Now B demands that A pay him back the principal plus the accrued interest. A, however, claims that he received the two *marks* from B in order to give it, together with the interest, to any charity he pleases. He, therefore, refuses to return the money to B.

A. If B admits that the principal was also meant for charity, but claims that he wants to distribute it himself, A is free from any obligation to B, and is not even required to take an oath, since no actual money loss to B is involved.

SOURCES: Cr. 87; Pr. 286; Mord. Shebu. 767.

200 (D)

Q. A promised ten *marks* to charity. He gave the money to B for investment purposes on condition that B pay to the poor of a certain community ten quarter-*marks* per year.

A. B should not give the ten quarter-*marks* to the poor of that community, since it would constitute unlawful usury. If, however, B earned profit with the ten *marks*, he must give part of the profit to the poor of another city, since one is not permitted to profit from charity money.

SOURCES: Pr. 999.

201

Q. Is it permissible to lend charity-funds at a definite rate of interest?

A. This is undoubtedly prohibited. But since the lending of charity-funds at a definite rate of interest became such a widespread custom throughout the Kingdom that the prohibition of the practice would not be heeded even if the law became known we refrain from publicising this prohibition. This opinion is expressed, however, in order to urge the compliance with this prohibition in the future (but R. Meir would express no opinion as to the necessity of repaying the interest already collected).

SOURCES: Pr. 73; L. 478. Cf. L 234; Cr. 101, 109; Tesh. Maim. *Mishpatim*, 14; R. Asher, *Responsa* 13, 8; *Agudah* B.M. 73.

202

Q. I heard that you permit the lending of charity-funds on condition that the lender share in the profits, but not in the losses, resulting from its investment by the borrower. Such a transaction is forbidden by Rabbinical decree; why, then, should it be permitted in connection with charity-funds? Signed: Hayyim b. Machir.

A. Lending charity-funds on condition that the lender share in the profits but not in the losses, is forbidden. The Rabbis who said (B. M. 70a) that a person lending money on such a condition is called "wicked" made no distinction between rich and poor. Since a poor person is not permitted to lend his money on condition that he share in the profits but not in the losses, we are not permitted to do so for him.

Note: The following introduction precedes the answer: Please excuse me for the brief response. For the last two weeks I have been confined to bed and have lost the taste for food. I wrote to you a lengthy response regarding the lending of charity-funds, and sent it to you through a messenger named Marvel. I forgot the lengthy argument and discussion. I remember, however, to have agreed with your reasons and arguments, and to have added the following ....

SOURCES: L. 425; P. 476. Cf. *Agudah* B.M. 73.

203

Q. What is the legal basis for permitting the lending of charity-funds upon a definite rate of interest?

A. Perhaps some persons have mistakenly ruled that charity-funds are in the same category as Temple-funds. However, this is incorrect, for the Talmud considers charity-funds as money belonging to "thy brother" and, therefore, must be included in the commandment: "unto thy brother thou shalt not lend upon interest (Deut. 23,21)". You know, however, how readily people will heed those who permit the forbidden.

SOURCES: Cr. 101. Cf. *Agudah* B.M. 73.

204

Those who lend charity-funds upon a definite rate of interest are doing an improper thing, for charity-funds are included in the commandment: "unto thy brother thou shalt not lend upon interest (Deut. 23,21)." However, such funds may be lent on condition that the profits but not the losses be shared.

SOURCES: Cr. 109; *Mordecai Hagadol*, p. 276b. Cf. *Agudah* B.M. 73.

205

A person is not permitted to lend charity-funds on interest, and it makes no difference whether or not the recipients of the funds are designated by name or the amounts they are to receive, determined (cf. B. K. 93a end). The poor are included in the term "thy brother" used in the law which prohibits the charging of interest. I lend out the charity funds in my possession for investment purposes only, to share equally in the profits and the losses; but I do not lend these funds on interest.

R. Meir adds: What you claim to have heard in my name that when a person gives a certain sum to charity he may consecrate it and be permitted to lend it on interest, then redeem it against a penny and throw the penny into the river, is untrue. I never said it, and I do not even understand the meaning of this babble.

SOURCES: L. 234; cf. Asher *Responsa* 13, 8.

206

Q. A boy was born Friday evening after the congregational evening services were over, but before stars appeared in the sky. When should his circumcision take place?

A. The boy was born while it was still Friday, and should be circumcised eight days later, on Friday. Even if the boy was born Saturday evening before the stars appeared in the sky, he would have to be circumcised the following Saturday, for there is no doubt that legally a day extends till the time stars appear.

SOURCES: Sinai VI (1942) 1–3 no. 359; Hag. Maim. *Hilkot Milah* 1, 8; cf. *Sefer Haparnes* 288.

207

Q. If a child is to be circumcised after the prescribed date, may the circumcision take place at night?

A. No, a child must be circumcised in the daytime.

SOURCES: Cr. 22; Pr. 324; L. 364; Wertheimer 18; Rashba I, 877.

208

You were right, of course, in postponing the circumcision of the boy whose blood was not yet absorbed by his tissues, even though his brothers had not died from circumcision. We were surprised, however, when the report reached us that your postponement was made not in order to permit the child's tissues to absorb his blood, but in order to establish his viability.

SOURCES: Sinai VII (1944) 8–9 no. 57; Hag. Maim., *Milah* 1, 30.

209

Q. A's son was an eight-month's baby and was very weak when it was born. A appointed B as his *Mohel* (circumciser) and informed him that the circumcision was to take place a month after birth, at which time the child would be proven to be viable. Subsequently A informed B that the date of circumcision would be postponed until such time as the child would be strong enough to undergo the operation. B left the city on community business and returned one day before the end of the month. Meanwhile, however, A had decided to circumcise his son immediately after he would be a month old, and, fearing that B might not return on time, he engaged an out-of-town *Mohel* promising him that the *Mitzvah* will be his even though B would return before the ceremony. B now demands that he be permitted to perform the rite. In general, may a father who has already appointed someone as a *Mohel* or *Baal Berith* (the one who holds the child during the rite), change his mind and give the honor to someone else? Please let us know the laws governing these situations since disputes often arise regarding them.

A. If the child was not circumcised yet, B should perform the rite of circumcision since he was promised the *Mitzvah* originally. If the circumcision, however, had already taken place, B would have no claim, since no question of money is involved.

This Responsum was addressed to R. David b. Kalonymus.

SOURCES: Pr. 949; cf. Mord. Shabb. 472; *Mordecai Hagadol*, p. 385 margin. Cf. Moses Minz, *Responsa* 101.

210

It is not necessary to write the Scroll of the Law in such a manner that each column begin with the letter *Vaw*. Often this practice, introduced by a scribe of his own accord and

blindly followed by others, spoils a column by the necessity
of cramming or spreading out the letters of the last lines in
order to start the next column with the letter *Vaw*. Therefore,
in writing the scroll of Esther, this practice need not be followed.

SOURCES: L. 142; Hag. Maim., *Sefer Torah* 7, 7; *Tashbetz*, 181.

211

Q.   A Scroll of the Law was torn, the tear traversing three
written lines. The torn parts were glued together. Is this
sufficient?

A.   Gluing torn parts of a Scroll of the law, is not sufficient,
for in handling the Scroll the glued parts may come apart
again. Therefore, the entire sheet must be replaced.

This Responsum was addressed to Rabbi Asher b. Yehiel.

SOURCES: Am I, 96; Asheri, *Sefer Torah* 14.

212

Q.   To which row of stitches should a Scroll of the Law be
rolled (after reading), to the one before or to the one after the
last portion read?

A.   It is preferable to roll a Scroll of the Law as little as
possible; therefore, it should be rolled to the nearest row of
stitches.

SOURCES: Pr. 69.

213

You write that I should exhort the people to fasten *mezuzot*
to their doors in order that I thus turn many away from iniquity.
A human court is not enjoined to enforce compliance with a
commandment the reward for which is explicitly stated in the
Torah. However, those who say that a tenant is not enjoined
to fasten a *mezuzah* to his door, are undoubtedly in error, for,

to fasten a *mezuzah* to the door is the tenant's duty (Pes. 4a), whether he pays rent or not. Moreover, if people knew the advantages of having a *mezuzah* on the door, they would not transgress this commandment; for I am convinced that no demon can harm a house properly provided with *mezuzot*. Thus, in our house we have close to twenty-four *mezuzot:* I fastened a *mezuzah* to the house of study, the winter house, the door of the house proper, the gate of the courtyard that opens into the street, the door of the house that opens into the courtyard, the cool upper chamber where I eat in the summer, and the room of every student.

Sources: Cr. 108; cf. Asheri *Hilk. Mezuzah* 10; Maharil, *Responsa* 94.

214

Q. What rules govern the writing of the Scroll of Esther?

A. All the rules and laws that govern the writing of the Scroll of the Law, apply also to the writing of the Scroll of Esther.

This Responsum is addressed to R. Shneor.

Sources: Cr. 66; Pr. 351; cf. L. 183; Isserlein, *Pesakim* 23.

215

Q. Does the law requiring a blank space the width of a column at the end of the Scroll of the Law, apply to the Scroll of Esther?

A. The Scroll of Esther is called a book and, also, a letter. Therefore, all the laws governing the writing of books apply also to the Scroll of Esther. However, since it is also called a letter, only three (*Tashbetz:* ten) of its seams are required to be sewed with dried tendons, the others may be sewed with threads of flax.

Sources: L. 183; *Tashbetz* 180; cf. Pr. 351; *Kol Bo* 45.

216

Q. *Mahzorim* (holiday prayer books) are often illuminated with figures of animals and birds. Why do you not protest against such a practice? Is not the painting of any figure or form forbidden to us?

A. This practice ought to be condemned for the reason that the drawings distract attention at the solemn hour of one's praying to one's heavenly father. But the drawing of the figures is not forbidden. Even though the forming of three dimensional figures is forbidden, a Jew is permitted to paint figures, since paintings have no thickness. Moreover, the Talmud (Ab. Z. 43 a-b) seems to imply that a Jew is permitted even to make three dimensional figures of animals and birds, since only the fashioning of figures of the human body or the quadruple figure of man, lion, ox and eagle is forbidden.

This Responsum is addressed to R. Asher.

SOURCES: Cr. 24; Am I, 97; Tos. *Yuma* 54a; Mord. Ab. Z. 840. Cf. *Agudah* B.B. 95.

217

Q. A person tanned a piece of leather specifically for the purpose of making it into a cover for a holy book. Before using it for this purpose, may he change his mind and use it for repairing shoes?

A. Preparing something for use as a holy object does not make it holy; therefore, the leather may still be used for repairing shoes.

SOURCES: L. 138; *Tashbetz*, 423; *Mordecai Hagadol*, p. 106d.

218

Q. A is the owner of a vineyard. Is he permitted to plant in it branches of a vine that has not yet borne fruit?

A. Whether the branches are taken from a vine that has already borne fruit, or from one that has not yet borne fruit makes no difference. For the life of the new vine begins with the time the branch is planted in the ground. Even if the branch bore fruit before it was replanted, nevertheless, its fruit after replanting will be *Orlah* for three years. The fruit of the fourth year may be eaten after redeeming it for a penny, grinding the penny and throwing it into the river. However, the fruit from a branch of an old vine, planted in the ground without severing it from the old vine, may be eaten even during the first year.

SOURCES: L. 196; *Tashbetz* 365.

219 (D)

Q. When do the three years of *Orlah* begin for a tree?

A. The three years begin immediately upon planting the tree.

SOURCES: Cr. 118.

220

1) *Q.* A rented his vineyard to a Gentile for one year. The Gentile planted vines therein during that year. Is A permitted to eat the fruit of such vines that will grow during the second, third and fourth years?

A. No, he may not eat the fruit, for the law of *Orlah* applies also to trees planted by a Gentile.

2) *Q.* May A rent out the aforesaid vineyard to a Gentile for three years so that the Gentile may eat the fruit of the young vines during the period that the fruit is considered *Orlah?*

A. A is not permitted to rent this vineyard to a Gentile for the first three years, since a Jew is not permitted to derive any benefit from *Orlah.*

3) *Q.* What should a person do with fruit of *Orlah?*

A. The fruit that can be burned should be burned; whatever can not be burned, should be buried in the ground.

SOURCES: *Tashbetz*, 366–8.

221

Q. Are we permitted to give the redemption money of a first-born son to a daughter of a priest?

A. No, for it is recorded in the Pentateuch (Num. 3, 51) that Moses gave the redemption money to Aaron and his sons. The term "sons" excludes the daughters.

SOURCES: L. 329; Rashba I, 836.

222

Q. A bought from a Gentile a cow that already was yielding milk. Should the cow bear a male calf in A's house, would such calf be unfit for eating purposes for fear lest it be a firstling?

A. The fact that a cow yields milk is no proof that she has already given birth to a calf, for it sometimes happens, though very rarely, that a cow yields milk even though she has not as yet given birth.

SOURCES: Cr. 312; L. 187; *Orhot Hayyim* p. 21. Cf. Moses, Minz, *Responsa* 34; ibid. 35; *Terumat Hadeshen* 271; Isserlein, *Pesakim* 129; ibid. 167.

223 (D)

1) *Q.* Do we believe the casual remark of a Gentile that a certain cow has already given birth to a calf?

A. The casual remark of a Gentile is believed only when it refers to the death of a Jew, and is so believed in order to prevent the latter's wife from remaining an *agunah* (deserted wife).

2) *Q.* Do ridges on the cow's horns, which indicate that the cow is old, prove that the cow has already given birth before?

A. Even if we know definitely that the cow is old, as long as we do not know for certain that she has already given birth before, her newly born calf is considered a firstling.

3) *Q.* What is the difference between a calf that is definitely a firstling, and one whose status is doubtful?

A. Upon contracting a blemish, the firstling must be given to a priest; the calf whose status is doubtful may be consumed by the owner.

Sources: Cr. 313.

224

Q. A duke's servants who occasionally engaged in plundering the countryside, sold a pregnant heifer to A. At the time the sale took place, the vendors told A to allow the original owner of the heifer, a Gentile woman, to redeem it, when she was ready. Subsequently the woman appeared and offered to redeem the heifer. A agreed to the transaction, but, before the woman had the opportunity of producing the money, the heifer gave birth to a firstling. Is the calf a consecrated firstling (which can not be sold to a Gentile)?

A. When the robbers took the cow away from its owner, he abandoned all hope of recovery. Therefore, when A bought it he acquired clear title thereto because of this abandonment of hope and of the change of domain. The subsequent consent by A to allow the original owner to redeem the cow, did not transfer the title to the owner. Thus the firstling was born to a cow belonging to a Jew and was, therefore, consecrated.

Sources: L. 312.

225

Q. Is it permissible to avoid the consecration of a firstling by granting or selling to a Gentile the ear of its mother?

A. It is permitted to avoid the consecration of a firstling by granting or selling to a Gentile the ear of its mother before the firstling is born.

SOURCES: Pr. 18. Cf. *Sefer Haparnes* 300.

226

Q. A Jew made a fictitious sale of his cow, that eventually gave birth to a firstling, to a Gentile. The sale was concluded through the taking of money from the Gentile, but it was not accompanied by the delivery of the cow to the Gentile. According to Rashi such a sale is valid, but according to Rabbenu Tam it is not. How are we to deal with this firstling? Are we permitted to overstuff him with food till he die?

A. Since a firstling loses its sacred character when it receives a blemish and may be consumed by a priest, we are not permitted to bring about its death.

This Responsum is addressed to Rabbi Baruch.

SOURCES: Cr. 216. Cf. Moses Minz, *Responsa* 5; ibid. 34; ibid. 35; *Terumat Hadeshen* 270; Isserlein, *Pesakim* 169.

227

Q. A firstling was born to a priest who is a poor man; is he permitted to give it to a rich priest?

A. If the rich priest is willing to accept the firstling, the owner is permitted to give it to him. The rich priest, however, may refuse to accept the firstling from a brother priest since, in this case, the giving constitutes a secular donation, which may be refused.

SOURCES: L. 188; *Tashbetz* 385. Cf. Weil, *Responsa* 127.

228

Q. 1. A is a *Kohen* (of priestly lineage). His enemies, in order to put him to great expense and inconvenience, permitted their cattle to give birth to firstlings while in their possession, and gave the firstlings to A. Such firstlings are holy, must be fed and taken care of, but cannot be put to any use. Are Jews permitted to do so purposely, and can A collect damages from them for the loss he has suffered through them?

2. A Jew, an ignorant person, intentionally inflicted an injury on one of A's firstlings. Is A permitted to slaughter this firstling?

3. A's firstling caused damage in a Gentile's garden and was detained by the Gentile without A's knowledge or consent. Must A redeem the firstling? How much ransom must he pay?

A. 1.   All these people were guilty of various sins: a) They permitted the birth of a public nuisance. b) They perverted the will of the Lord who intended His 24 gifts to the priesthood to be a boon to them and not a nuisance. c) They have been guilty of despising consecrated objects. d) They derived satisfaction from giving a priests' gift to a particular *Kohen*. However, A can do nothing about it.

2.   A cannot slaughter the blemished firstling since the person who caused the blemish, though an ignorant person, was nevertheless a Jew.

3.   A must ransom the firstling, but is not obliged to pay more than its market value.

SOURCES: Pr. 78. Cf. Weil, *Responsa* 127; Isserlein, *Pesakim* 166.

229 (D)

Q. May one derive benefit from the manure formed by the dung of a consecrated firstling?

A. If the manure has been deposited by many firstlings and thus has a money value, it (or its value) must be given to a priest. But if its value is negligible and it has been mixed up with the dung of other cows, an Israelite may use it without compunction.

SOURCES: Pr. 604.

230

Q. I was wondering at your method of taking *Hallah* from unleavened cakes; for, after they were baked you put all the cakes into a basket and took one cake as *Hallah* for the rest. It is true that in the Mishnah (*Hallah* 2, 4.) R. Eliezer decides that cakes taken from different pieces of dough may be joined for the purpose of taking *Hallah* by putting them in one basket. But this law of R. Eliezer is only a restrictive measure in order to require the taking of *Hallah* from small pieces of dough (by putting them together in a basket), which are, by themselves, too small to necessitate the taking of *Hallah* from them. But R. Eliezer never meant his law to be a palliative measure. I, therefore, take a small piece from each quantity of dough that is separately mixed, and then join the small pieces into one piece as *Hallah*.

Signed: R. Isaac b. Simeon.

A. Throughout France *Hallah* is being taken from un-leavened cakes by uniting them in a basket. This method is approved by the author of *Sefer ha-Terumah*, and the author of *Eben ha-Ezer*. But your method is not to be followed, for while the small pieces are being accumulated they become leaven.

SOURCES: Cr. 21; Pr. 322; L. 366; Rashba I, 834; Wertheimer 16; cf. Am. 57; Pr. 279.

231

Q. Is it obligatory to take *Hallah* from coarse bread baked especially for (fattening of) geese, but which is also fit for human beings?

A. The talmudic sources are at variance with one another, making it impossible to arrive at any definite law. To free oneself from doubt, one should not only have the intention, while kneading, of eating the bread himself, but actually eat some of it, in order to necessitate definitely the taking of *Hallah* from it.

SOURCES: Pr. 61.

232

Q. Dough of a Gentile [which is exempt from the law of *Hallah*] was mixed with a piece of dough belonging to a Jew which by itself, was sufficient to become subject to the law of *Hallah*. How can the Jew take *Hallah* for, or from, the mixture?

A. In order to make sure that he takes *Hallah* from dough that is subject to that law, the Jew must take as *Hallah* a piece that is larger than the Gentile's dough.

SOURCES: Cr. 40; Pr. 423; P. 225; cf. Am I, 59.

233 (D)

Q. A person baked a pie which consisted of meat and dough, and forgot to take *Hallah*. May he do so from the remaining dough?

A. Yes, he may.

SOURCES: Pr. 309.

234

Q. Why do certain women, when they prepare a special dough for making dumplings, first bake a small part thereof as a wafer, and then take *Hallah* from the wafer?

A. I have instructed many women to follow this procedure; it is a meritorious practice, for the following reason: Our authorities hold conflicting views on the problem whether dough specially prepared for making dumplings is subject to the law of *Hallah*. Therefore, one should first bake a wafer on coal, out of such dough, the wafer would thus undoubtedly be subject to the law of *Hallah*, then one should place the wafer next to the rest of the dough, and take *Hallah* from both, the cake and the dough. Thus one would obviate the doubt as to whether he was required to take *Hallah* from such dough (and whether he had legitimately recited the blessing: "to take *Hallah* from the dough").

SOURCES: Mord. *Pesahim*, 592; cf. Asheri, *Pesahim* 2, 16; ibid. *Hilkot Hallah* 2.

235

Children under the age of twelve are exempt from the law of mourning, but their garments must be rent.

SOURCES: Pr. 437.

236

A. A *baal-berith* (the person who holds the child during circumcision) is permitted to change his clothes and to bathe on the day the child is circumcised, even if such day be within his "period of mourning" (thirty days). The prohibition against changing one's clothes and bathing within the "period of-mourning" is based on custom and does not apply to persons performing a *Mitzvah* (religious duty). Within the thirty days of mourning, however, a person is not permitted to take part in a religious banquet, though one is permitted to return a visit to a secular feast. Therefore, the *baal-berith* is not permitted to take part in the banquet following circumcision.

SOURCES: L. 227, 8, 9; cf. Mord., *Moed katan*, 891.

237

Q. A close relative of A died four days before Passover. The eve of Passover fell on a Saturday. Some Rabbis permitted A to bathe Friday afternoon, others forbade it.

A. A should not bathe Friday afternoon. He may bathe in cold water on Saturday, or he may take a regular bath during the intermediate days of the holiday.

SOURCES: Cr. 314; Pr. 430.

238

If a man heard about the death of his parent on the thirtieth day after such death, he must observe the seven days of strict mourning and the thirty days of mourning. But if he heard on the thirtieth day which was a Sabbath day or a holiday, he must observe only one day.

SOURCES: Pr. 436; Mord. M.K. 883; Hag. Maim. to *Abel*, 7, 1, 2.

239 (D)

Q. Is a mourner permitted to grind wheat during the first week of mourning, if otherwise he would have no bread?

A. Even when the mourner has bread, but prefers it fresh, he is permitted to grind wheat.

SOURCES: Pr. 20; cf. Rashba I, 845; Mord. M.K. 929.

III

EBEN HAEZER

240

Q. L had been married to A, a person of blemished descent. After A died, no one wanted to marry L. [She maintained, however, that she had originally been granted permission to marry A, and demanded that the stigma attached to her because of her marriage to him be removed from her. May this be done?]

A. It is true that I have known a woman who was reported to have received permission to enter upon marital relations with a Gentile. I have also heard in France that some women were permitted to have marital relations with Gentiles. I failed, however, to inquire for the reasons that prompted the granting of such permission. I, for my part, can find no justification for granting permission to a woman who wants to live with a Gentile merely in order to gratify her carnal desires.

Sources: *Mordecai Hagadol,* p. 358d.

241

Q. Are the women among the group of forced converts from Rockenhausen who escaped from their captors, permitted to resume their marital relations with their husbands?

A. Nowadays that the Gentiles are all powerful, a Jewish woman who was held captive by them, even though only for the purpose of extortion, is not permitted to live with her husband (Ket. 27b). But, since in this case many Jews were held captive together, they are now able to testify which women were not violated by their captors; such women who can furnish this testimony, even by a single witness and even by a woman witness, are permitted to resume their marital relations with their husbands. The fact that the captives did not give their lives for their religion does not disqualify them as witnesses. Although a Jew is enjoined to choose death rather than be forced to worship idols, should he violate this law he would not become disqualified as a witness though he would be guilty of having committed a sin. Moreover, according to the account given by the captives, they never actually embraced Christianity, but merely listened without comment to the priest's recitation of his senseless ritual in the presence of the Gentiles. Thus, the captives never committed a sin; for a Jew is not enjoined to choose death rather than allow the Christians to deceive themselves into believing that they have converted him.

SOURCES: Am II, 80; cf. Hag. Maim., *Isurei Biah* 18, 6.

242

Q. A, of priestly lineage, saw his wife L go to a secluded place with a certain young man. They stayed there only for a short time, for L's mother walked toward them with a lighted candle. On another occasion, while lying in bed late at night, A heard, on the other side of the wall, the heavy breathing of his wife and the young man as they were arduously embracing each other, which to him was clearly indicative of consummated sexual intercourse. The same incident was repeated on another night. On these occasions L was late coming to bed. Next morning, however, when A rebuked L for her lewd conduct, she protested vigorously. Nevertheless A was convinced that his wife commited adultery and was, therefore, forbidden to him. A had always loved and catered to L, but she had never returned that love, and had never submitted to him willingly.

Rabbi Hezekiah b. Jacob, to whom the question was first submitted, ruled that L be forbidden to A.

A. One judge is not at liberty to permit what another has prohibited. Were I present at the time when Rabbi Hezekiah received the query, I would have argued the case with him. A woman is not forbidden to her husband unless either: a) the husband is jealous of a certain man, and warns her against private meetings with this man, and the wife disregards this warning in the presence of witnesses; or b) they actually be found in a position indicative of fornication. But, heavy breathing itself is no indication that illicit sexual intercourse took place. Therefore, I shall wait till Rabbi Hezekiah recuperates from his illness, whereupon I shall discuss this matter with him.

SOURCES: Pr. 98; Am II, 63; Rashba I 832–3; Tesh. Maim. to Ishut, 8; Hag. Mord. Kidd. 549. Cf. Asher, *Responsa* 32, 11; Weil, *Responsa* 8; ibid. 88; Israel Bruno, *Responsa* 5; ibid. 7; Isserlein, *Pesakim* 222.

243

Q. A reported that his wife secluded herself with a certain Gentile, and thus rendered herself forbidden to him. Since, however, A had no witnesses to corroborate him, nor did he witness any actual intimate relations between the Gentile and his wife, are we nevertheless to give credence to his words to the extent that we should no longer require him to support her?

A. Your question regarding the wife's sustenance indicates that you are convinced that she is forbidden to her husband. This is not so, however, for a woman is not forbidden to her husband unless either: a) he is jealous of a particular man, warns her against private meetings with him, and witnesses testify that subsequent to the warning she secluded herself with that man; or b) the husband finds his wife with another man in a compromising position. In any event, even if the husband maintains that he saw her with the Gentile in a compromising position, as long as his statement is not supported by witnesses, she is not to be deprived of her right to sustenance and to her *ketubah*.

SOURCES: Wertheimer 14; *Mordecai Hagadol*, p. 214d.

244

Q. L, a married woman, admitted that she willingly had sexual intercourse with another man.

A. L's husband may refuse to lend credence to L's admission, and thereupon, be permitted to have marital relations with her. If the husband, however, lends credence to L's statement, he is not permitted to have marital relations with her. Moreover, if L made the above statement in the presence of witnesses, her husband may divorce her without paying her the *ketubah*. However, if L can give a plausible excuse for having made the self-accusing statement, even though it was false, she may still claim that the statement was false. Similarly, if a husband says he had seen his wife have sexual relations with another man, and there are no witnesses to corroborate his statement, his personal statement does not deprive her of her right to the *ketubah*. It has the effect, however, of forbidding him to cohabit with her, unless he gives a plausible explanation for having made a false statement.

SOURCES: Mord. Kid. 547.

245

Q. Rabbi Eliezer B. Joseph betrothed L through a deputy. Subsequently it was discovered that at the time of the betrothal L was pregnant through harlotry.

A. If L refuses to accept a divorce, Rabbi Eliezer is permitted to marry another woman. Rabbenu Gershom had intended that his prohibition against bigamy should apply only

when the first marriage was legitimately contracted; but he
had not intended to protect by his *takkanah* the marriage of a
loose and immoral woman. Those who impute such intentions
to Rabbenu Gershom will receive severe punishment from
Heaven for defaming this saint's character and malignantly
ascribing to him silly ordinances in order to make him appear
ridiculous and thus discredit his other *takkanot*. Thus, the
Rabbis are intent upon breaking up the marriage of a man to a
woman pregnant by another. Would, then, Rabbenu Gershom
protect such a marriage by his *takkanah*! I am even inclined
to the opinion that the betrothal itself was invalid since the
bridegroom was ignorant of facts, the knowledge of which would
have prevented him from marrying L. There is no doubt, however, that Rabbi Eliezer is permitted to marry another woman
in case L refuses to accept a divorce.

SOURCES: Cr. 161.

246

R. Isaac left his wife Sarah in the month of *Adar* of the year
5031 (1271), and travelled to a distant place in search of sustenance for his family. Next year he learned that his wife had
played the harlot and had thus become pregnant. He returned
home, and in the month of *Ab* of the year 5032 (1272) he appeared before us and asked us to investigate his wife's conduct
during his absence, since she bore a child in the month of Adar
of the same year (1272), twelve months after he had left her.
Sarah asserted, however, that she was pregnant when her
husband left her. Therefore we, the undersigned, wrote to R.
Shealtiel and his two sons, who lived in the same village with
Sarah, and they testified in writing that Sarah bore a child
twelve months after R. Isaac left her. The signatures and seals
of the deponents have been attested to by reliable witnesses.
Then, a person appeared before us because of the ban (proclaimed against all those who knew anything relating to this case

and did not appear as witnesses) and testified that on the evening
of *Shabuot* of the previous year (1271) he went to Sarah's home
in order to recite the *kiddush* in her presence, and found Gentiles,
loafers, who caroused with her, caressed and embraced her. We
concluded, therefore, that she must have become pregnant at
that time. Other persons testified to have seen her on *Purim*
of this year (1272) in the last stages of pregnancy. On previous
occasions, however, in the month of *Elul*, she violently protested that she was not pregnant, and cursed and abused those
who had said to her that she was pregnant. Moreover, before
the evil report reached the town, Sarah's father appeared before
us and asked us to allow him to put his daughter to death by
drowning her. When asked for his reasons, he stated that a
daughter of his (meaning Sarah) was an incorrigible harlot, who
bore a bastard daughter by a Gentile and then killed her child.
When asked whether he tried other means of controlling her,
he answered that whenever he reproved her she threatened to
apostatize altogether and pleaded that she was not the first
woman who ever sinned. She had left the house on a number of
occasions but was persuaded to return by the entreaties of her
mother. The father feared lest she turn to evil and, therefore,
asked for permission to kill her. However, we did not permit
him to carry out his design. We sent the testimony to Rothenburg to the great luminary, Rabbi Meir. Since the Rabbis of
Erfurt who are near us, and those of Würzburg, who are far
from us, as well as Rabbi Meir of Rothenburg, all agree to allow
R. Isaac to divorce Sarah even against her will, the divorce
has been given in our presence. Signed: Moses Azriel b.
Eleazar hadarshan, Eleazar b. Yehiel, Ephraim b. Joel.

R. Meir's opinion was as follows:

The testimony of R. Shealtiel and his sons is of no consequence for two reasons. a) They are related to each other;
their testimony is that of a single witness, and, therefore,

insufficient. b) The foetus could have lingered in the mother's womb for twelve months (cf. Yeb. 80b). Sarah's giving birth to a child twelve months after her husband left her, is, therefore, no proof of her depravity. The testimony of the other witness regarding Sarah's indecent behavior on the evening of *Shabuot*, being the testimony of a single witness, does not deprive Sarah of her right to her *ketubah*. If R. Isaac believes the afore-mentioned witness or if he takes the word of his wife's own father, he must divorce Sarah even against her will. If she renders it impossible for him to divorce her, he may marry another woman without divorcing Sarah as a warning to all indecent and depraved women. But he must pay Sarah her *ketubah*. However, if Sarah admits her guilt, or acknowledges the truth of the testimony regarding her indecent conduct on the evening of *Shabuot*, or if she cannot satisfactorily explain why she denied her being pregnant in the month of *Elul* of the previous year, or answer all other questions regarding her conduct, she loses her right to her *ketubah* and is entitled only to whatever is left of the valuables she had brought with her upon her marriage.

SOURCES: L. 310; Tesh. Maim. to *Nashim* 25; Hag. Mord. to Yeb. 121; cf. Sinai vol. V (1941) p. 296; Asher *Responsa* 32, 11; Weil, *Responsa* 8; ibid. 88; Isserlein, *Pesakim* 22.

247

Q. A, of priestly lineage, married a woman within three months [of the death of her husband]. The authorities would have forced A to divorce her — even though he was of priestly lineage and would not be able to remarry her once he divorced her — had he not postponed asking them about the matter till long after the three months had expired and after it had become definitely certain that she had not been pregnant by her former husband. What is your opinion on this subject?

A. The ban that is pronounced against a person who marries a widow within three months of her husband's death, is not a punitive measure, but is a means of forcing such a person to divorce her in order that he should not live with her within the three months of her former husband's death [so that the child born seven, eight, or nine, months later would not be of doubtful parentage]. After the three months have passed, therefore, there is no longer any reason for pronouncing the ban, and persons already married prior to the expiration of that period may be permitted to continue their married life undisturbed. The same rule applies to a person who married a nursing widow before her child was twenty-four months old. If no action was taken against him before the expiration of the twenty-four months, none should be taken against him after the expiration of that period. At the same time we make no distinction between a person who married a nursing widow because he was ignorant of the transgression involved, and the person who did so fully aware that he was doing wrong, since forcing a person to divorce his wife whom he married in a forbidden period, as referred to above, is not a punitive measure.

SOURCES: *Mordecai Hagadol*, p. 157c.

248

Q. How long should a nursing widow wait until she can remarry?

A. The accepted law is that she must wait 24 moon-months (from the day the child is born), i. e. months of alternating length of 29 and 30 days. If one of the years is a leap year, she must wait 25 such months. However, were I not afraid to differ with the decisions of my teachers, I would require her to wait 24 full months of 30 days each, or 720 days, and in a leap year 25 moon-months of alternating length, in order to be sure to comply with all possible interpretations of the opinions of the authorities of the Talmud.

This Responsum is addressed to R. Yekutiel.

SOURCES: Pr. 79. Cf. Mord. Yeb. 19; Israel Bruno, *Responsa* 192; ibid. 193; ibid. 194; *Terumat Hadeshen* 216; Isserlein, *Pesakim* 82; ibid. 178.

249

Q. A, of priestly lineage, married a nursing widow, Leah. Before the marriage took place, Leah, following the advice of Rabbi Jacob (of Cracow), gave her infant to a wet-nurse who made a vow *Al Daat Rabbim* (the interpretation of said vow to lodge with an undetermined number of people, and, therefore, incapable of annulment) not to resign her position till the infant be of age to be weaned (two years). Many have disputed the efficacy of this procedure, and gave their opinions that A must divorce Leah. Rabbi Jacob pleaded that A be not required to divorce Leah since A, being of priestly lineage, would not be able to remarry her after the two year period of nursing be over.

A. A person who married a nursing widow must divorce her, even though he was of priestly lineage and consequently could not remarry her, once he divorced her. The wet-nurse's vow is of no avail since her husband could annul it even though it was made *Al Daat Rabbim*.

SOURCES: Pr. 864; Tesh. Maim. to *Nashim*, 24; cf. R. Asher, *Responsa*, 53, 2; *Tur Eben Haezer* 13.

250 (D)

Q. A went to a village and expected to return the same day. He did not return, and on that day a murdered man was found in the nearby forest. Although the body was unrecognizable as it had been mutilated by dogs, it was identified as A's body for the following reasons: (a) People said that a Jew was

murdered; (b) the garments on the dead body were recognized
as belonging to A; (c) A's wife identified a mole on the dead
body as the one her husband had. May A's wife remarry?

A. Neither a general rumor, nor the finding of one's garments on a dead body, are sufficient to establish the death of an
individual. But a woman is believed when she identifies her
husband's body through a mole. A's wife may, therefore,
remarry.

SOURCES: Pr. 371.

251

Q. L's husband disappeared. Her relatives sent inquiries
to the surrounding towns in an effort to locate him. Meanwhile
a Gentile came to the Jews of a neighboring town, and asked
them why they did not fetch the body of the murdered Jew
from T (the town where L's husband had lived) that was lying
in place X. The Gentile added that for one pound he would
himself convey the body in his wagon to T. Since the Gentile
mentioned money, we were doubtful whether his statement
should be admitted in evidence.

A. I have considered the above case from all angles, and
find no reason why L should not be permitted to remarry. The
fact that the Gentile mentioned money did not weaken his
testimony, but rather strengthened it; for, not only did he make
a report in his innocence, he even offered to prove the truth of
it. Therefore, if no other Jew is missing from T, L should be
permitted to remarry. Moreover, I have seen the letter of R.
Jacob b. Mordecai, bearing the signature of Rabbi Eliezer,
which stated that a certain Gentile told a Jew that he killed
L's husband. This statement by the murderer is to be admitted
in evidence; and should, in itself, serve as a basis for permitting
L to remarry.

Rabbi Meir adds: I am not worthy to be relied upon, unless

my teacher Rabbi Eliezer, you yourselves, and the other teachers agree with me. Otherwise, my opinion is void.

This Responsum is addressed to Rabbi Abraham and Rabbi Mordecai.

SOURCES: Tesh. Maim. to *Ishut*, 9; Sinai VII (1943) 5–6 no. 33. Cf. *Terumat Hadeshen* 239; Isserlein, *Pesakim* 161; ibid. 223.

252

Q. A Jewish young man and three Gentiles were together in a boat on a rough sea, full of rocks, reefs and floating ice. Another Jew and many Gentiles heard them crying: "Help! oh Lord, we are drowning." Their boat was subsequently found overturned and empty; but the young man's body was not found. One Jew is willing to testify that the young man is dead since he searched for his body together with experienced fishermen who assured him that no one could come out alive under the circumstances. May we permit the young man's wife to remarry?

A. The Rabbis did not permit remarrying by the wife of a man, lost in a body of water of which not all the boundaries are visible, and no distinction was made as to the nature of the water, or the shore. We would be very happy were we able to find a legal basis for allowing the woman to remarry; but many before us have tried to find such a basis and were not successful. We must, therefore, accept the decision of the Rabbis.

SOURCES: Pr. 971.

253

Q. A and B were married to two sisters. Since A frequented B's house, B suspected him of adulterous relations with his wife, and threatened to kill him. One day A went out of town leaving his books and his valuables with his wife, his manner indicating that he intended to return shortly. He never came back, however, and a search for him proved futile. Subsequently, three Gentile thieves came to the house of a Jew of a neighboring town to sell a stolen article; and casually remarked that A, from the nearby town, was murdered through the instigation of his brother-in-law, and was buried in his clothes in an upright but inverted position. The Jew asked the thieves to show him where A was buried, and they answered that they would show him the place if he gave them one *mark*. On the same day, however, before they had a chance to point out A's grave, the thieves were apprehended for stealing and were hanged. Subsequently, a Jew arrived in town who told the relatives of A's wife that he had seen A alive in France. This Jew, however, had been an apostate and later returned to Judaism, but not wholeheartedly. He was one of those despicable creatures who wander from town to town and alternately appear as Jews or as fanatical Christians. Nevertheless, the relatives of A's wife sent a man with the apostate to France, and the man investigated thoroughly but could find no trace of A. Meanwhile a long time has passed, and the grass widow, lonely, miserable, and distressed, has not heard a word about the whereabouts of her husband.

A. Whenever a Gentile makes an informal statement to the effect that he witnessed the death of a Jew, we accept such statement as reliable evidence and permit the Jew's wife to remarry. Thus, the unsolicited remarks of the three thieves are to be considered as the testimony of three witnesses. Although the statement of the apostate contradicted the words of the thieves, we do not admit into evidence the testimony of a single witness in the face of the testimony of three witnesses. It is true that, although in a case involving the release of a grass widow we admit into evidence the testimony of ordinarily unqualified witnesses (such as women and Gentiles), the testimony of a single qualified witness is nevertheless considered equal to that of a hundred unqualified witnesses. In our case, the three Gentile witnesses were not contradicted by a qualified witness, for the apostate cannot be considered a qualified witness, since his return to the fold was not sincere. He and the others of his kind call themselves Jews in order that people should give them food, and that they should have a chance to steal and to indulge their base appetites. Therefore, if the communities of Rita and Kublin should agree, I would permit the woman to remarry.

SOURCES: Mord. Ket. 306; Yeb. 81; Tesh. Maim. to *Ishut*, 10. Cf. Weil *Responsa* 164; Israel Bruno, *Responsa* 28; ibid. 29; ibid. 32; Isserlein, *Pesakim* 138; ibid. 220; ibid. 221.

254

Most scholars hold the opinion that a woman whose husband fell into a body of water whose final boundaries are not discernible, and who, though not permitted to remarry, defiantly transgressed against the prohibition of the Rabbis and did remarry, need not be divorced from her second husband. This opinion they base on the talmudic ruling that the law prohibiting the remarriage of a woman whose husband fell into a "boundless" body of water, applies only before, but not after, she has remarried. I once saw a prominent personage of our kingdom remarry under such circumstances without any one admonishing her. All our prominent scholars decided that she need not be divorced, once she has remarried. A great French scholar was then staying in our kingdom, and he, too, permitted her to stay married claiming that he had witnessed a similar case in France and that all the great scholars of France ruled that she need not be divorced. I also gave my consent to his decision though I was hesitant. However, I have finally come to the conclusion that such an opinion is untenable. For, were this opinion correct the prohibition of the Rabbis would be rendered senseless, useless, and ridiculous, since no woman would heed such prohibition and would transgress against it rather than stay single all her life. Why, then, would the Rabbis prohibit such remarriage to begin with! Therefore, we must say that the talmudic ruling which does not require the remarried woman to be divorced, refers only to that woman who remarried because she innocently believed that a scholar had permitted her to do so, as in the case of Hassa (Yeb. 121b) and that of R. Shila (Yeb. 121a); but that it does not refer to the woman who defiantly transgressed the prohibition of the Rabbis. This latter interpretation of the pertinent talmudic sources clarifies the words of the Rabbis and renders them logical and tenable. Therefore, a woman who remarried without receiving permission from a scholar must be divorced, or the husband be put under the ban till he divorce her. We must not be concerned lest a relative of the woman permit her to remarry (thus flouting the prohibition of the Rabbis), for the following reasons: a) only a scholar holding the position among scholars that R. Nahman (the scholar who inadvertently caused the wife of Hassa to remarry) and R. Shila held in their day, is empow‑ ered to permit such a woman to remarry; b) a scholar permitting such a woman to remarry would bring upon himself the ban.

SOURCES: Cr. 194; Am II, 97; Mord. Yeb. 128; Tesh. Maim. to *Nashim*, 11, Pr. 612; *Tashbetz*, 468. Cf. Weil, *Responsa* 128.

255

꩜. B claims that he gave A fifteen pounds to lend it on interest for two years and then give the principal and the interest to B's son if he should consent to marry A's daughter. B's son, however, refused to marry A's daughter and B wants his money back. A claims that he had originally accepted B's money as a dowry for his daughter, that he had taken possession of the gift for her, and that the money, therefore, belongs to her.

A. A dowry gift becomes the property of the donee only if the marriage takes place. Therefore, neither A nor his daughter has ever gained title to B's money, and A must return the principal plus the interest to B. Even if B expressly stipulated that he will forfeit the 15 pounds if the marriage does not take place, such a stipulation is considered an *Asmakhta* and is not valid. B, however, must pay A for his trouble in managing B's investments.

SOURCES: Cr. 86; Pr. 285; Mord. B.B. 615; *Agudah* B.B. 198.

256

Q. A negotiated a marriage between his daughter and B who was from out of town and whom A did not know very well. A deposited a pledge of twenty-five *marks* on condition that should his daughter refuse to marry B, the pledge would belong to B. A had stipulated, however, that the agreement be void in case he be prevented by unavoidable accident from carrying out his part of the agreement. Subsequently it became known that B was an epileptic. A's daughter, therefore, refused to marry him.

A. Even according to Rabbi Joel, who was doubtful whether or not an epileptic might be forced to divorce his wife, the pledge must be returned to A, since in cases of doubt we do not give a verdict in favor of one seeking to collect money from the other party to the suit. Moreover A had stipulated that his agreement with B should be void in case of unavoidable accident; the discovery that B was an epileptic and the rightful refusal, hence, of A's daughter to marry B because of the danger involved, constituted an unavoidable accident and thus voided the agreement. We must also take into consideration the possibility that B's children will be epileptic. Although the admonition of the Talmud (Yeb. 64b) not to marry into a family of epileptics applies to a family of which at least three members are epileptic, this admonition applies to the marrying of a person who is himself an epileptic even though no other member of his family is so afflicted. Moreover had B already married A's daughter, and were she to demand a divorce on the ground that she can not live with an epileptic, she would have been entitled to the return of her dowry; since no marriage has taken place, B is not entitled to receive any money from A. Even if the pledge was already delivered to B, there is not the slightest doubt that he must return it to A.

SOURCES: *Mordecai Hagadol*, p. 165a.

257

Q. A promised his daughter, a minor, in marriage to B, and stipulated the condition that should his daughter, upon reaching her majority, refuse to accept *kiddushin* from B or from his deputy, A would pay B one *mark* of gold. Subsequently, but while A's daughter was still a minor, he betrothed her to another man. A maintains that he owes nothing to B since his daughter is prevented from accepting *kiddushin* from B by circumstances beyond her control.

A. If A's daughter would herself have made the above-mentioned agreement with B, and her father would subsequently betroth her to another, she would have had a plausible excuse for her not complying with the agreement. Since A himself, however, entered into an agreement with B, he not only guaranteed thereby that his daughter would accept *kiddushin* from B, but also that he himself would not prove a hindrance to the betrothal. B, therefore, is entitled to collect one *mark* of gold from A. B, however, must wait till A's daughter grows up before he will be entitled to collect the penalty, since in the meantime it may happen that A will not be prevented from fulfilling his original agreement with B.

SOURCES: *Mordecai Hagadol*, p. 200c.

258

Q. B promised his young daughter in marriage to A's minor son. He gave A a written document obligating himself, from the time of the promise, to be A's debtor for 20* *marks* should his daughter refuse to accept *kiddushin* from B's son when he will have arrived at his majority, or in case A himself should refuse to accept the *kiddushin* for his daughter. B died before A's son reached the age of 13, and his daughter married someone else. Now A demands the 20* *marks* from B's heirs.

A. Since B has been prevented, by death, from fulfilling his promise, he never became obligated to pay the 20* *marks* to A. Consequently his heirs owe nothing to A.

This question was also sent to R. Meir by his father, R. Baruch, who was one of the judges in this case.

SOURCES: Cr. 31; Pr. 50; Pr. 939; L. 355; Mord. B.M. 247; cf. Jacob Weil, *Responsa* 105; ibid. 142.

259 (D)

Q. A and B arranged a match between their children. At the time the amounts of dowry and parents' gifts were agreed upon, A and B stipulated that the bride and groom, if they subsequently quarrel, should divide their combined possessions

---

* In some sources (Pr. 50, L. 355) the reading is "2 *marks*." The discrepancy arose because of the similarity of the two Hebrew letters of *Khaf* and *Beth*, which stand for 20 and 2 respectively. The Cremona source and the Mord., however, used the word *Esrim*, 20, specifically.

equally between themselves. Now the groom refuses to abide by such stipulation claiming that he is not bound by his father's agreements.

A. Since the possessions of the young couple originally came from their parents, the former are bound by the stipulations of the latter regarding the disposal of such possessions. For the dowry and the presents were originally given on condition that the agreement between the parents be carried out.

SOURCES: Am II, 129.

260 (D)

Q. A went to a distant country, leaving behind a wife and a daughter. His wife betrothed her daughter to C and promised him a dowry. C demanded that A's brother, B, become surety for the dowry. B did so, and A's wife deposited valuables with B to be used in the discharge of B's suretyship. A's wife died. When A returned, he demanded that B restore to him the valuables his late wife had entrusted to B.

A. A's wife had no right to promise a dowry or give anything to B or C without A's permission. Her promises and gifts were, therefore, void and B must return to A the valuables A's wife had deposited with him.

SOURCES: Pr. 858.

261

Q. A (verbally) promised to give a definite amount of money to his sister upon her marriage. After her marriage A refused to keep his promise. Can A's sister enforce his promise?

A. Only a father's verbal promise to his child on his first marriage is binding. All other promises of marriage gifts are not binding unless accompanied by a *kinyan* (a formal binding act). If, however, A's sister was poor, he is bound to pay her the promised sum, because a promise to give charity is binding.

The Responsum is addressed to R. Eleazer Kohen.

SOURCES: Pr. 97; cf. Cr. 151 where the opposite opinion is given.

262 (D)

Q. A had promised to give a dowry to his sister, an orphan, but after her marriage refused to keep his promise.

A. Any person who promises a marriage-gift before the wedding of a couple, must keep his promise. The ruling of the Palestinian Talmud that such a promise by a brother of the bride or the bridegroom is not binding, must be construed to apply only to the case where the brother promised his father's money, for this interpretation eliminates a contradiction between the Palestinian and Babylonian Talmuds (Yer. Ket. 5,1; Bab. Ket. 102a).

SOURCES: Cr. 151. Cf. Hag. Maim. to *Ishut.* 23, 9.

263

Q. Since the written betrothal agreement makes no mention of a *kinyan*, it should not have the force of a legal document. Obviously, greater trust was place in him (the intended father-in-law) than in a legal document. Moreover, the witnesses do not recall the contents of the written agreement that bears their signature.

A. There are a number of documents that contain no *kinyan* clause and yet have the force of legal documents. Although the witnesses do not recall the contents of the document that bears their signature, the document is legally binding nevertheless.

SOURCES: Cr. 210; Mord. Ket. 284; Tesh. Maim. to *Mishpatim* 39. Cf. Weil, *Responsa* 94.

264

Q. A had a sickly, epileptic daughter. He promised B a large dowry, and for this reason B married her. A's daughter died within the first year of her marriage, after having given birth to a child who, in turn, died before he was thirty days old. Since A's daughter left a child when she died, we decided that B was entitled to collect the dowry from A.

A. Since the child died before he was thirty days old, his viability has not been established. Therefore, his existence was of no consequence. Thus, I am greatly surprised that you considered the existence of the child a determining factor in the case. Moreover, Rashi and R. Tam hold conflicting opinions regarding the question whether a widower is entitled to collect the dowry his father-in-law had promised him (*Tosaphot* Ket. 47a, s. v. כתב). I am greatly surprised, therefore, that you dare decide between the two conflicting opinions; for whenever there exists a difference of opinion between authorities, we do not enforce the collection of money by either party. Your contention that since A's daughter was a sickly person B had a stronger claim on her dowry, is also baseless, for the law draws no distinction between a healthy and a sickly wife. Indeed, the *takkanah* of R. Tam to the effect that when a wife dies within the first year of her marriage the husband must return her dowry to the original donors, is only valid in those communities where this *takkanah* was accepted. My decision in this case, however, is not based on this *takkanah*, but on Rabbinic law which is valid everywhere.

Sources: Cr. 159.

265

Q. L's father gave five pounds to L's fiance, C. Her father deposited with B the rest of L's dowry, with the provision that B deliver it to C one year after he marries L. C married

L, but she died within the first year of her marriage. C, now, demands L's dowry from B.

A. When a woman dies within the first year of her marriage, the ordinance of Rabbenu Tam undisputably prevails that her dowry must be returned to the donors. The communities have further ordained that when a woman dies within the second year of her marriage, half of her dowry must be returned to the donor. We are not certain, however, whether or not this latter ordinance was accepted. Moreover, even according to talmudic law the dowry mentioned above is not collectible, since according to R. Tam's interpretation of the pertinent talmudic ruling (ket. 47a) a person may not collect the dowry that had been promised to his wife, who subsequently died, unless he collected it before she died. There is no doubt, therefore, that C is not entitled to collect L's dowry from B (talmudic law), and that he must even return the five pounds he had already received (because of the ordinance of R. Tam). Should C deny having received the five pounds, he would have to take an oath in support of his denial. Since C, however, does not inherit L's dowry, he is under no obligation to pay for L's funeral. Therefore, he is not to be charged with the funeral expenses spent by L's father. Similarly, C is under no obligation to discharge L's pledges to charity, unless C had instructed L to make such pledges at his expense.

SOURCES: Tesh. Maim. to *Ishut*, 35. Cf. Maharil, *Responsa* 61; ibid. 76; ibid. 80; Weil, *Responsa* 40.

266

I have observed that persons misunderstand and misinterpret the words of Rabbenu Tam who derived from the Talmud the law that a father, whose daughter died within the first year of her marriage,* was under no obligation to pay the dowry he

---

* This phrase was probably inserted by mistake. The law of R. Tam is not limited to the first year of marriage. Consequently, this Responsum did not contradict the

had promised. This ruling, however, applies only to the father
who had merely promised a dowry but failed to give it to his
son-in-law before his daughter died. In our case, however, the
son-in-law gained title to the dowry, for it was secured through
pledges the father had deposited with trustees, or because sureties have guaranteed its delivery. The dowry was merely
entrusted to the father-in-law that he do business therewith,
and earn profit for the benefit of the young couple until they
grow up. Therefore, the son-in-law is entitled to collect the
dowry.

SOURCES: Hag. Mord. Ket. 287; cf. Maharil, *Responsa* 61.

267

Addressed to R. Mordecai haKohen: You committed no
sin in marrying a deaf maiden, especially since you married her
in the presence of her father and with his consent. You should
be careful, however, not to permit her to eat *hallah*, as this is
forbidden to her even in these days when we have no Biblically
consecrated *Terumah* (Yeb. 113a).

SOURCES: Sinai V (1941) 4, no. 114.

268

Q. In the presence of witnesses Leah asked A to betroth
her. While she was in a yard not owned by her, A threw a ring
into her lap for the purpose of betrothal. The witnesses, although they saw Leah shake her dresses in order to brush the
ring away, did not see whether or not the ring actually fell into
her lap. Does Leah need a divorce from A?

A. Had the witnesses seen the ring fall into Leah's lap,
she would need a divorce in spite of her claim that she never

community ordinance regulating the return of dowry which was limited to the first
year of marriage. Cf. *Hiddushei Anshei Shem*, ad loc., who was misled by the above
phrase.

intended to become A's wife and that she was joking when she asked him to betroth her. For we would, then, be concerned only with facts and not with her thoughts and unexpressed intentions. But, since the witnesses did not see the ring fall into Leah's lap, and the yard where the incident took place did not belong to Leah, she needs no divorce, for no betrothal took place. R. Meir adds: If my teachers agree with my decision, all will be well. But if they do not agree I shall subscribe to whatever they decide to do. However, I should prefer not to be strict in this matter and not to require Leah to obtain a divorce, lest A become rebellious and refuse to divorce her, and lest he travel to a distant land and thus render it impossible for the unfortunate woman ever to marry again.

This Responsum is addressed to: "My teacher Rabbi Haim and his court."

Sources: Pr. 993: Mord. Git. 451; ibid. Kid. 548: Tesh. Maim. to *Nashim*, 1.

269

Q. Without any previous courting A gave money or presents to Leah saying they were tokens of love. The witnesses testify that A did not speak to Leah about marriage while he gave her the money, and that she did not express her consent.

A. If there are witnesses that A proposed to Leah on a previous occasion and that she accepted his proposal, she is betrothed to A, even though A did not expressly say he was betrothing her. When there are no such witnesses, but both, A and Leah, admit that they had a previous understanding between them, or that at the time A gave the money to Leah they both intended the money to bind them in betrothal, Leah is betrothed to A. Moreover, the mere statement of A to Leah that he gave her the money as a token of love may constitute a betrothal, and therefore, Leah needs a divorce from A before she can marry another.

SOURCES: Cr. 19; Pr. 519–520; Mord. Kid. 521; Tesh. Maim. to *Ishut*, 4.

270

The betrothal of a woman in the presence of a single witness, is void. We do not require that she receive a divorce, for the mere sake of strictness, since such an act would bar her from marrying a person of priestly lineage. Nor are we apprehensive of a spreading report to the effect that the woman was betrothed, since such report would also include the information that the betrothal took place in the presence of a single witness, thus automatically nullifying the effect of the report. If it was originally reported, however, that a bona fide betrothal took place, and later it became known that the betrothal took place in the presence of a single witness, a divorce would be required, if we did not deliberately cancel false reports. Rabiah, however, ruled that we should cancel false reports.

SOURCES: Pr. 133; Mord. Kid. 537; ibid. 548; Tesh. Maim. to *Nashim* 2; Rashba I, 856.

271

Q. A, a nephew of Rabbi Kohen Zedek, asked the latter for advice regarding the planned betrothal of his daughter. A informed him that in his (A's) locality there were no qualified witnesses (unrelated to the bride) but that he intended to invite two strangers from another locality to act as witnesses to the betrothal. These two strangers, however, were brothers-in-law and one was the nephew of the other. Rabbi Kohen Zedek, then, told A that since these two were related to each other they were disqualified witnesses and consequently the betrothal would be void. A, however, answered that no great harm would be done even if the betrothal were void since the bridegroom would ultimately betroth the bride again, at the time of the marriage. A repeated this answer to the widowed sister of Rabbi Kohen Zedek who later witnessed the betrothal and protested that the witnesses were disqualified. Must A's daughter receive a divorce in order to free herself from the bridegroom?

A. Since the two witnesses were related to each other, they were disqualified and the betrothal was not binding. Therefore, A's daughter needs no divorce. As to the spreading rumor that a betrothal took place, the opinion of Rav is accepted that when the court discovers that a certain rumor [of betrothal] had no foundation in fact, the court silences such rumor. Moreover, a rumor is of no consequence unless the probability of its truthful origin has been upheld in court (cf. Git. 89a f.), while in our case the rumor is known to be baseless.

Rabbi Kohen Zedek wrote again to Rabbi Meir raising doubt as to the correctness of R. Meir's decision, and informing him that his (R. Meir's) teacher from Spiers at first agreed with this decision but later disagreed with it; and that meanwhile A's daughter became betrothed to another man.

Rabbi Meir answered that the first decision of his teacher was correct; that in the case of a woman who was betrothed in the presence of two witnesses, one of whom was later discovered to be related to the bridegroom, Rabbi Joel haLevi decided in a Responsum that the woman did not need a divorce, and permitted her to remarry; and that he enclosed a copy of Rabbi Joel's Responsum in order to prove that his own decision was based on a solid foundation. He added: A rumor is of no consequence unless it be current in the town where the alleged betrothal took place. In this case, however, A and his sons were the only Jewish residents of the settlement, and they were told beforehand that such a betrothal would be void. Moreover, even the authorities who hold that we cannot dispel a rumor, agree that when a rumor is self-contradictory, or the statements made therein are not untrue but harmless, such rumor is of no consequence. We are not at liberty to be overstringent in such cases and demand that a divorce be delivered in order to dispel any shadow of doubt as to the girl's freedom to remarry, since such a step would make her ineligible to marry a man of priestly lineage.

The leaders of the communities [Spiers, Worms, and Mayence] upon learning that R. Meir permitted A's daughter to become betrothed to another man without first receiving a divorce from her first bridegroom, became highly incensed and heaped abuse upon R. Meir for having permitted a married woman to remarry. Rabbi Mordecai [of Worms, cf. Mord. Ket. 290] and his associates wrote that Rabbi Hananel in his *Sefer Hamikzoot*, the author of *Sekel Tob*, Rabiah, and Rabbi Simha [of Spiers], all ruled that a woman who was betrothed in the presence of unqualified witnesses, must receive her divorce before she is permitted to remarry. They placed A and his daughter [but probably not R. Meir] under the ban in order to force A's daughter to receive a divorce from her second bridegroom.

R. Meir became highly indignant. He pointed out the clear distinction between witnesses who were rabbinically disqualified and those who were Biblically disqualified. He proved that the above-mentioned authorities as well as Alfasi, Rabbi Kalonymus, and the author of *Ittur* [Rabbi Isaac b. Abba Mari of Marseilles] all agreed that a woman who was betrothed in the presence of Biblically disqualified witnesses required no divorce and was free to marry another. He showed that not a single authority contravened this view, and that the Rabbis of Spiers were misled in their haste and zeal by a faulty reading of the *Sekel Tob*.

R. Meir added: if the Rabbis of the communities subsequently discover an authority who ruled that such a woman must receive a divorce, they should realize that such a divorce was not required by Biblical law nor by rabbinic law, but that the authority of his own accord ruled that a divorce take place merely to dissipate evil gossip. Since the first betrothal of A's daughter took place in the presence of two witnesses who were beyond a doubt Biblically disqualified witnesses, as one of them was the nephew of the other, the betrothal was void; especially so since even at that time it was known to all bystanders that the betrothal possessed no validity whatsoever. Since she was subsequently betrothed to another, having first received permission from an authoritative court, no authority in the world would require that the Biblically valid second betrothal should be dissolved merely in order to dissipate unfounded doubts. Moreover, we are expressly enjoined by the Talmud from requiring that she receive a divorce from her second bridegroom, since such divorce would disqualify her from ever marrying her first bridegroom (Yeb. 11b). If the leaders of the communities are highly sensitive and are bent on dissipating any doubt in the matter, they should force the first bridegroom to grant a divorce to A's daughter and I, on my part, shall compel her to accept the divorce. Although such a divorce is unnecessary, and hence should not be granted, as it would bar the woman from ever marrying a man of priestly lineage, I should overlook this point in honor of the Rabbis of the communities. Accordingly A's daughter will wait for a divorce till the feast of *Purim*. If the communities will be unable to effect the divorce within that time, because of the stubbornness of the bridegroom and his refusal to comply with their request, we shall go against the wishes of the community leaders and allow A's daughter to marry her second bridegroom; as we shall not permit that she be put in a position where she can never remarry.

We have never seen revered teachers of old act in the manner of the above-mentioned community leaders. Differences of opinions have often arisen among the great authorities, some prohibiting what others permitted, but never did any one dare place under the ban those who acted contrary to his opinion.

You, the aforementioned community leaders, probably delude yourselves with the idea that since your permission is required before a person may divorce his wife (see Finkelstein op. cit. p. 230), no scholar is permitted to render decisions in ritual law unless he receives your authorization. No, this is not true, for the *Torah* is free to anyone who is capable of arriving at a correct decision. You have gathered, and have associated with yourselves, men who do not understand the intricacies of the laws of marriage and divorce. I am not in a position to protest against my teacher of Spiers since I am his student [and owe him the respect and subservience of a student], but I protest against those who sought to ruin my reputation and honor. "Blessed be the Lord who hath not given us as a prey to their teeth". (Ps. 124, 6). "For they hid snares to take me". (Jer. 18, 22). "The snare is broken and we are escaped". (Ps. 124, 7).

SOURCES: Am II, 41–2; *Mordecai Hagadol*, p. 212d f.; R. Judah Mintz, *Responsa* 11.

272

Q. B admits that when A first appointed him his deputy for the purpose of betrothing L for A's wife, he stipulated that B betroth her on condition that she has no physical defects. When A formally appointed B his deputy in the presence of witnesses, however, he failed to mention such a conditional arrangement; nor did B make any reference to such an arrangement when he betrothed L for A. L has protruding glandules on her neck and legs, and A refuses to marry her. Was the betrothal void?

A. If the glandules are situated in a place where sometimes they may be seen while at other times they are hidden from view, the betrothal was concluded under error and was, therefore, void. The betrothal would have been void under such circumstances even if no condition had been stipulated by A. If the glandules, however, were situated in a place where they were always exposed to view, A must have seen them and must therefore have determined to overlook them, and certainly such was the case with reference to the glandules on her legs; the betrothal was therefore valid. The condition he had stipulated was of no avail since it must have referred to other defects besides the glandules. Moreover, we know that a condition was stipulated only through B's admission, which is not sufficient evidence. If A did not know L and had never seen her, however, the betrothal was void even if no condition had been stipulated. We should not permit A, however, to marry another woman since we have no record that the great Rabbis, our predecessors, ever permitted such a marriage in practice. You are at liberty, though, to act as you see fit.

This Responsum is addressed to "my teacher Rabbi Israel b. Urshrago".

SOURCES: *Mordecai Hagadol*, p. 168b.

273

Q. B sent A to betroth Leah as his wife on his (B's) behalf. A came to Leah's town, invited the important persons of the community, showed them proof that he acted as B's agent, and appointed witnesses, but when he came to betroth Leah as B's wife, he said: "You are hereby betrothed to me", instead of "You are hereby betrothed to B." When the witnesses objected, A said that it was a slip of the tongue, that he did not intend to betroth Leah as his wife, especially since he was married already and that he would not violate the prohibition of polygamy by Rabbenu Gershom. He, therefore, repeated the ceremony and betrothed Leah to B. Must A divorce Leah before she may marry B?

A. No, A is to be believed that he did not intend to betroth Leah as his wife, and his unintentional act is not valid.

R. Meir adds: I wrote you my opinion but I do not want you to rely on it to free Leah without a divorce until you have inquired of the Rabbis of the surrounding territory and of the Rabbis of France. If they agree with me you may accept the above decision; but if they do not agree with me, their opinion is to take precedence over mine.

SOURCES: Pr. 586, 1015; Mord. Kidd. 522, 548; Tesh. Maim. to *Nashim*, 3.

274

The reason, for the custom to betroth again a wife whom one has betrothed through a messenger, is that a personal betrothal is the greater *Mitzvah*. However, the majority of the Jews do not follow this practice.

SOURCES: Pr. 432.

275

Q. A betrothed L with a copper ring.

A. Since A said: "I betroth thee with this ring", and not "with this ring of gold", the betrothal was valid.

SOURCES: Cr. 107; *Orhot Hayyim* II, p. 56.

276

Q. A betrothed L with a ring which the witnesses to the betrothal, and a goldsmith, declared that it was made of gold. Half a year later, however, it was discovered that the ring was made of copper.

A. Since L relied on the opinion of the witnesses as to the quality of the ring, and since this opinion was erroneous, the betrothal was void, for a false statement made by the witnesses to a betrothal should have the same force as such a statement made by the groom (cf. Kid. 48b). In practice, however, I should not dare release L without a divorce.

This Responsum is addressed to: "my teacher Rabbi Jonathan".

SOURCES: Tesh. Maim. to *Ishut*, 20; Hag. Maim. *Ishut* 8, 2; *Mordecai Hagadol*, p. 211b.

277 (D)

If a minor betroths a woman, his act is of no consequence, even rabbinically.

SOURCES: Cr. 106.

278

The talmudic statement, that a man may direct his young daughter (a minor) to accept *kiddushin* (Kid. 19a), implies that having once directed her to receive *kiddushin*, he may no longer withhold his consent from her doing so. Although the Talmud prohibits the betrothal of a minor (Kid. 41a), this prohibition only means that a father should not himself take the betrothal-money of his young daughter (a minor), but he may permit her to accept the money herself. Thus have I acted in the case of my own young daughter; I told her to receive her *kiddushin*, if she wanted to do so.

SOURCES: P. 293; cf. Rashba I, 867; *Terumat Hadeshen* 213. Cf. Isserlein, *Pesakim* 33.

279

Q. Are a bride and a bridegroom permitted to live in the same house after betrothal?

A. They are not permitted to live in the same house because there may be occasions when no chaperons are about, and a person is not permitted to cohabit with his betrothed before they are actually married. Moreover, there is danger lest familiarity may breed contempt.

SOURCES: L. 141; *Tashbetz*, 450; *Mordecai Hagadol.* p. 145c; *Orhot Hayyim* II, p. 60; *Kol Bo* 75.

280

We were obliged to try the case of a betrothed, L, who demanded that her bridegroom, A (Jacob), come to her father's house and marry her there. A's father, B (Moses), representing his son, brought forth the following claims: a) When he (B) had arranged the match with L's father, C (Judah), he had promised C to send his son to live in C's house; b) he kept his promise, and, after A betrothed L through a messenger, he sent A to C; c) at the time the match was arranged C promised to clothe A suitably, to support him, and to hire a capable teacher for him; d) after A stayed in C's house for one year, he was sent back to his father and C took no further notice of him; A was forced to interrupt his studies and he, B, with very limited means, had to support him for five difficult years; and, f) he asked many persons to urge C to keep his promise of support to A, but C refused. The undersigned (R. Meir) also, sent many letters to C, asking him to have pity on his son-in-law who suffered poverty and privation — all to no avail. Moreover, we have learned (from a letter) that C does not at all desire the consummation of the marriage, but has set his heart on a divorce since A displeased him. Thus, B claims that he has fulfilled his promise and sent his son to C; but, that the latter put A to shame and now he, B, can no longer force A to return to C's house; that A is afraid to return to C's place of residence since many persons have warned him that C's servants were threatening to do him injury unless he agree to divorce L; that though A cannot, and will not, return to C, he is nevertheless ready to marry L whenever she will come to his place of residence.

Taking the above into consideration, we have decided that
A cannot be compelled to settle in C's town, marry L, and live
with her there; nor can he be forced to divorce L. Our decision
is based on irrefutable proof: Thus, the majority of our leading
authorities agree that a man living in one country who betrothed
a woman living in another country, may force the woman to
come and live with him in his country. Although the Tosephta
(Ket. 13, 2) and the Palestinian Talmud, (Ket. 13, 10) seem to
disagree on this score, we believe that our interpretation of the
statements in these two sources removes the discrepancy and
shows that both agree regarding this law. Moreover, when the
man betrothed the woman through a messenger, there is not
a shadow of a doubt that according to both sources given
above, the woman ought to be forced to move to her husband's
place of residence. This opinion is shared by Rashi, Maimonides
and other leading authorities. R. Tam, however, believes that
these sources deal with cases in which we force the husband to
change his place of residence to that of his wife. Therefore, in
view of this difference of opinion (although I do not agree with
the view of R. Tam) we must accept the strictures of each
opinion. Thus, we are forced to decide that neither the husband
nor the wife can force a change in the other's place of residence.
We cannot compel the husband to change his place of residence
because of the opinion of Rashi, Maimonides, and the other
leading authorities; but neither can we compel the wife to
change her place of residence, because of the opinion of R.
Tam. Although B had agreed at the time of the betrothal that
A would settle in C's town, B had no right to bind A to such
terms and we can find no evidence that A had voluntarily
agreed to change his place of residence. The fact that A went
to visit C is no evidence of such voluntary agreement. Moreover,
he went on this visit after the betrothal, while we are concerned
with his intentions at the time of the betrothal. Therefore,
this agreement between B and C is void. Furthermore, had A

himself voluntarily agreed at the time of the betrothal to move to C's place of residence, we should not be able to force A to keep his part of the agreement since C, on his part, had made many promises at that time which he later failed to keep.

Some Rabbis wrote their opinion that A should be compelled to move to L's place of residence since it was not dignified for a woman to move from place to place, as expressed by the verse: "All glorious is the king's daughter within the palace" (Ps. 45, 11; cf. Git. 12a). Moreover, it is humiliating for a woman to pursue her husband into a distant place. However, I regard this manner of reasoning as very strange indeed; for in the talmudic period women were more honorable and discreet than today, and yet talmudic law required them to move to their husband's place of residence. The aforementioned Rabbis also wrote that since, according to the Talmud, a woman's station may be elevated through marriage but not lowered, L should not be forced to move to A's town. For L was brought up in great luxury and abundance, and were she to move to A's house she would have to share his poverty and privation. However, L would not have to suffer privation. C had promised A a large sum of money as a dowry; with that money A should be able to support L in a manner befitting her station, and on a standard equal to that of the other women of her family. Although she would miss some of the extravagances of her father's house, she would have to bear with such minor inconvenience. In conclusion, since A is ready to marry L whenever she will come to live in his town, we cannot compel A to move to L's town or to divorce her. This decision is required by talmudic law and the Rabbis made no distinction between a poor woman and a rich woman. Signed: R. Meir b. Baruch.

SOURCES: L. 386; Tesh. Maim. to *Nashim*, 28; Hayyim Or Zarua, *Responsa* 147. Cf. *Hagahot Asheri* Ket. 12, 3; Asheri Ket. 13, 17; *Tur Eben Haezer* 75.

The following Responsa by R. Samuel b. Salomo, R. Jacob
B. Joseph, R. Yehiel b. Jacob ha Levi, and R. Eliezer B. Ephraim, refer to the same case:

This letter is written regarding the youth of Rothenburg
who betrothed, through a messenger, the daughter of R. Judah
of Düren. At the time the match was concluded the youth's
father had agreed that his son would take up his permanent
abode with his father-in-law. After the betrothal the bridegroom came to stay with R. Judah who hired a teacher for him
and treated him honorably for a long time. A year later the
youth became sick and R. Judah, thinking that this was a
result of the change of climate, sent him home accompanied
by his teacher, and expended large sums of money on him.
Subsequently, R. Judah sent for the youth to come to his house
and marry his daughter. The youth, however, changed his
mind on the matter of residence, and refused to come to Düren,
stating however that he was ready to marry his bride if and
when she came to live in Rothenburg. Thus it is apparent that
the youth was intending to exact money from R. Judah. Therefore, it is my opinion that the youth be forced either to marry
his bride on her terms, or divorce her. First, it is obvious
that at the time of her betrothal the bridegroom had intended
to settle in Düren. Secondly, his father had explicitly agreed
with R. Judah to the youth's change of abode. Therefore,
we assume that the youth also had agreed to it, since a young
son does not dare to oppose his father and usually subscribes
to the father's arrangement of his affairs. Again in agreements arising between the various parties interested in a
marriage, the conditions apparently implied, though not expressly stated, are presumed to form part of such agreements
(see Git. 65b; Ket. 54b; 79a; B. B. 132a). Thus, in our case,
it is apparent that R. Judah did not intend to have his daughter
leave him and her mother and remove from the country of her
birth, and suffer privation in Rothenburg with her poverty

stricken husband; that he did not intend to spend the large
sum of money required to finance the safe conduct of one who
was the daughter of a magnate whose name was known throughout the countries. Thus, the overlord of Rothenburg acting
on the mere rumor [that R. Judah's daughter was coming to
settle in Rothenburg] already sought ways of subjugating R.
Judah to his will [using his daughter as a hostage]. Finally, according to the Talmud (Ket. 110b) a husband cannot force his
wife to move from a humble to a more sumptuous dwelling
since she can hold that such change of abode, even though it was
for the better, would cause her many inconveniences. Any
woman who gives plausible reasons against the change of abode
demanded by her husband, therefore, cannot be forced to undertake such a change. In our case the bride's reasons against a
change of abode are numerous and reasonable. Therefore, the
youth ought to be forced by flagellation or the use of the ban
either to marry his bride or to divorce her. This case was
already brought before us last year, and we decided in the bride's
favor. Because of these reasons, I have agreed to ban and
chastise the bridegroom until he either marry his bride on her
terms or divorce her. If he refuses to comply with our order
he shall bear his sin and those who support him shall likewise
suffer. None is excluded from our ban, excepting, of course,
our honored teacher Rabbi Meir. Rabbenu Gershom requires
that a husband be coerced into divorcing his rebellious wife
lest the latter turn to mischief. Although many authorities
disagree with Rabbenu Gershom and we do not follow his
decision, in cases similar to the one at hand, however, we must
protect the daughters of Israel lest unscrupulous youths use
the inability and unwillingness of daughters of rich men to
change their place of residence, as a means of extorting money
from their fathers. Signed: Samuel b. Salomo (Pr. 250).

Wailing and complaint that cannot be silenced, arose because of Jacob b. Moses who betrothed the daughter of R.

Judah . . . . The bridegroom may be coerced either to marry
the bride on her terms or divorce her. R. Tam decided that
a court must compel a levir to marry, or give *halitzah* to his
brother's childless widow, even by the use of force; and that it
is even permissible to have Gentiles use force on the levir until
he comply with the decision of the Jewish court. Although
according to the Jerusalem Talmud whenever the Mishna fails
expressly to allow the use of coercion we can use no physical
compulsion (Ket. 11, 7), and although the ban is a strong
form of coercion, nevertheless, since R. Tam allowed the use
of physical compulsion (in a case where the Mishna does not
expressly allow the use of such measures, cf. B. Yeb. 39a) we
ought to ban the bridegroom until he comply with our decision.
Moreover, custom changes law; whenever we are uncertain
regarding a certain law, we observe and follow the accepted
practice. Thus, the custom is universally accepted of performing the marriage ceremony in the house of the bride's father.
Therefore, we invoked against the youth all the curses great
and small, until he comply with our decision. Signed Jacob b·
Rabbi Joseph (Pr. 251).

To our Rabbis of Germany, your love has obliged me to
express my opinion regarding the above. Since witnesses testify
to the fact that there was a stipulated condition at the time of
the betrothal, such condition is binding and the bridegroom
must live up to its terms. Even if there are no such witnesses,
the fact that his father-in-law kept him in his house together
with his teacher, even though he returned home because of
illness, proves that the father-in-law intended that the wedding
take place in his house. It is difficult to imagine that the latter
intended to brave the grave danger of sending his daughter
and his money to Germany, which is very unsafe country. Furthermore, a man may not force his wife to leave her country
and to come to live in his country. Therefore, we may force
the bridegroom to do one of two things: either marry his bride

and come to live in her place of residence, or divorce her. The Rabbis ought to coerce him by the use of chastisement and the ban, for fear lest his bride remain a deserted wife. We find many instances where the Rabbis decreed special laws and took extraordinary measures in order to prevent the possibility of a woman remaining a deserted wife. Signed: Yehiel b. Jacob ha Levi (Pr. 251).

To my teacher Rabbi Meir. I saw the decision of the judges in the case of the honorable R. Judah of Düren who betrothed his daughter to Jacob b. Moses of Rothenburg. At the time of the betrothal Moses agreed to send his son Jacob to Düren in order that he marry his bride there. Moses kept his agreement and sent his son to R. Judah. But, when the latter saw that Jacob was small in stature, homely, and despicable, he had pity on his daughter. Fearing lest she begin to despise her bridegroom, he sent Jacob back to his father to stay there till he grow up. When the bride grew up and R. Judah was told that Jacob also gained in strength, he sent for the latter to come and marry his bride. However, Moses refused to send Jacob to Düren. As time dragged on and R. Judah's daughter saw that her bridegroom refused to come to her, she sent a messenger to Rothenburg to demand that Jacob either marry her on the conditions previously agreed upon, or divorce her. But Jacob answered that he did not personally agree to move to Düren, that he did not join in his father's agreement on that score, that he would not come to her father's house, and that he would marry her only if she come to Rothenburg. Thereupon it was decided [by R. Meir] that she could not compel Jacob to move to Düren nor force him to divorce her. This decision, however, is very strange, and, in my opinion, is a perversion of justice for a number of reasons. a) Some of our great authorities quote the opinion of R. Tam to the effect that both the Mishna (Ket. 13, 10) and the Tosephta (Ket. 13, 2) which treat of the conditions under which a party to a marriage may be forced to remove to the place of residence of the other party, deal with forcing the husband to move to the place of residence of the wife. Therefore, the conclusion of both sources is that the husband who married a wife living in another country must move to that country. Again, whenever the talmudic sources state that the husband be so forced to move, the implication is that upon refusing to do so he must divorce his wife and pay her the *ketubah*. Next, it is well known that the bride's home is luxurious and comfortable [for which reason she ought not to be forced to remove to her husband's humble abode], that her traveling to Rothenburg would entail great difficulties and serious hazards since the entire road is infested with lurking dangers, and that her very stay in Rothenburg would be perilous because of her father's great reputation for wealth. Therefore, Jacob cannot force her to take such a step. Besides, even if she wanted to go to Rothenburg, her father's repeated objections would not allow her to do so, and she could do nothing about it. Therefore, this case is similar to the one quoted in the Mishna (Ket. 13, 5), in which case Admon decided that the bride might demand from her bridegroom that he either marry, or divorce her. Finally, Jacob is bound by his father's agreement, since it is customary for the parents of a couple to enter into all agreements governing the marriage, and for such agreements to be considered binding on the couple. Although the principle is accepted that "the consent of the father does not imply the consent of the son (Kid. 45b)", this principle applies only to the actual betrothal but not to the other arrangements appertaining thereto. Moreover, the fact that he came to live in Düren proves that he had agreed to his father's arrangement; while his having been sent home temporarily, because of illness, did not invalidate the original agreement.

Therefore, it seems to me that the decision cited above was a perversion of justice, or, at least, against common sense, and not in the interest of the public welfare. For were we to accept the principle implied in your decision, the interests of the wealthy would suffer greatly. Thus many unscrupulous persons, knowing that the daughters of the rich cannot move away from their home towns, would betroth such women and then extort money from their fathers by refusing to marry them until either the women move away from their homeland, or their fathers pay exorbitant sums of money. And you, my teacher, R. Meir, how did you come to subscribe to such a decision? Everybody is wondering at this. For R. Judah is ready to fulfill all his previous promises and more; he wants Jacob and the bride also wants him. They are ready to give guarantees that they will not act treacherously against him; and, in case he does not want her, she is ready to accept her divorce and forego her *ketubah*. In the face of such facts, how can any Rabbi, student, or judge, give heed to those who insidiously demand that R. Judah's daughter come to live in Rothenburg, knowing full well that she can not do so! It is obvious that these persons are only interested in extorting money from R. Judah, and it is not becoming your dignity to uphold the cause of these extortionists. Should we allow an Israelite daughter to become a deserted wife because her father is averse to becoming a victim of extortion? I know that R. Judah did not acquiesce; that he could not bear the idea of being coerced and forced to part with his money; and that he sent inquiries to the elders, the greatest authorities of France, and to other places. It appears that those authorities have all agreed that Jacob ought to be forced to marry his bride on her own terms or to divorce her. Although you are the greatest authority of our generation, you will not find it easy to oppose the decision of our great authorities, lest dissensions multiply in Israel. "Therefore, leave off contention, before the quarrel break out" (Proverbs 17,14). Signed: Eliezer b. Ephraim. (Am. II, 81).

281

Q. What is the meaning of the following statement in Yer. Yuma, 1, 1: "Those who wed widows must marry them long before sunset in order that they perform no act of possession on the Sabbath day."?

A. The *Huppah* ceremony is the marriage proper for a maiden, while the essential marital act for the widow who remarries is cohabitation. Therefore, a person marrying a widow must consummate the marriage before sunset (on Friday) lest he first cohabit with her on the Sabbath and thus perform an act of possession on the Sabbath.

SOURCES: L. 151.

282

Q. A demands that his wife leave her home town and live with him in another place. She, however, refuses to do so.

A. A husband may force his wife to move from one town to another of approximately the same size; and from one home to another, similar to it within the same country. He cannot, however, force her to move from a town to a city or from a city to a town, from a poor home to a rich home or vice versa. The *Tosephta* rules that a woman who has married a man must move to his home wherever it be, but you should not follow this ruling in practice, since the Palestinian Talmud apparently opposes this view.

SOURCES: Cr. 36.

283 (D)

Q. Regarding the three countries into which Palestine is divided in reference to the laws of marriage, to the effect that a husband may not force his wife to move from one country to another, what is considered a country nowadays?

A. France, England, Germany, and Bohemia, are to be considered separate countries in reference to the laws of marriage, since a different language is spoken in each of these lands.

It is indeed reasonable to assume that only territories within which a different language is spoken are to be considered as different countries in the above sense. Were we to consider Saxony, Franconia, Alsace, the Rhine province, and Bavaria, separate countries, then Palestine, a land of four hundred miles by four hundred miles, would have had to be considered a land containing more than three countries.

SOURCES: Cr. 117; *Beth Joseph* to *Tur Eben Haezer* 75.

284

Q. L, while not quite twelve years of age, was married by her brother(s) and mother to A, a resident of another town. The match was originally concluded on condition that the couple settle in L's town; and after the marriage they lived there for nearly half a year. Subsequently, however, A went back to his father and then demanded that L follow him. L, who was in possession of the valuables of the household, refused to do so. Without L's knowledge or consent, her mother appeared before prominent persons and reached an agreement with A that L live out of town. She also bound herself by a valid *kinyan* to deliver the valuables mentioned above to A. L, however, protested vigorously against this agreement claiming that she refused to deliver the valuables to A lest he run away from her leaving her penniless.

A. L's mother had no right to enter into agreements to L's disadvantage without the latter's consent. Therefore, the agreement between L's mother and A is void.

SOURCES: Cr. 217; Am II, 82; *Mordecai Hagadol*, p. 192d; ibid. p. 374c.

285

Q. A married his daughter to B, a resident of another kingdom. The marriage took place in A's town and the couple lived there for about three months. Now, B wants to force his wife to move to his country. A and his wife claim that at the time of the betrothal they stipulated the condition that B reside in their town. B denies that such condition was ever stipulated. Since A's daughter is in possession of the couple's property, may we rely on A's oath.

A. A, as a relative, can take no oath in a litigation between his daughter and his son-in-law. Nevertheless, B may not force his wife to move to another country. For R. Tam is of the opinion that the Talmud enjoins a husband, who married his wife under such circumstances, from forcing her to remove to another town.

SOURCES: Cr. 218; Am II, 83; *Mordecai Hagadol*, p. 192d; ibid. p. 376a.

286

Q. Does the clause of the *Ketubah*: "and I will labor, honor, nourish and sustain thee" provide that a husband may be coerced into hiring himself out as a laborer in order to support his wife?

A. A number of legal proofs have been marshalled to the effect that a husband may be forced to work in order to support his wife; but none is conclusive. However, I have observed that great teachers in France forced husbands to hire themselves out in order to support their wives, and I am content to follow my teachers.

SOURCES: Cr. 126.

287

Q. May a husband, who says he has no money with which to pay for his wife's sustenance, compel her to give her consent to his sale of his real property, as such sale would provide the funds for her sustenance?

A. The husband may not compel his wife to permit him to sell his real property. If he says he has no money, the court will sell his real property, and will use the money exclusively for the wife's sustenance in the manner prescribed by the Talmud (Ket. 107a). When this money is spent, the husband will be forced to work in order to support his wife, in accordance with the clause of the *ketubah*: "and I shall work, honor, and sustain thee. . ." Although some authorities are opposed to a literal interpretation of this clause of the *ketubah*, I have noticed that our Rabbis of France follow this literal interpretation in practice. It must be understood, however, that after the court sells the real property for the wife's sustenance, she will no longer be able to seize such property in payment of her *ketubah*.

This Responsum was addressed to Rabbi Menahem b. Natronai.

Sources: Tesh. Maim. to *Ishut.* 31; *Mordecai Hagadol*, p. 159a. Cf. Weil, *Responsa* 78.

288

Q. While A was absent in a foreign country, his wife borrowed money for her sustenance. Upon his return, A refused to pay his wife's debts claiming that she could have supported herself by her work.

A. Biblical law requires that a husband must provide his wife's sustenance; therefore, A must pay whatever his wife borrowed for her sustenance.

Sources: Pr. 232; L. 383. Cf. P. 11; Mord. Ket. 273.

289 (D)

Q. [While her husband was away] L borrowed money for her sustenance.

A. If L borrowed the money without specifying any terms of repayment, her husband must repay her debts; but, if the creditor gave the money to L saying that he expected her husband to repay him, the husband is free from obligation.

SOURCES: Cr. 248.

290

The court may dispose of a man's property for his wife's sustenance, not only after a lapse of three months after the husband has left for lands beyond the seas when the wife demands her sustenance (Ket. 104b), but also whenever the husband moves to another place and the wife is unable to borrow money for her sustenance. However, if the husband is not too far away and the wife can borrow money to last her for a short period, the husband should be informed of the situation before the court sells any of his property.

SOURCES: Am II, 35.

291

Q. Leah, a married woman, borrowed money from her father to buy herself clothes. Leah's father demands the money from A, Leah's husband. The latter, however, refuses to pay his wife's debt.

A. If Leah bought herself clothes in accordance with the rank of his, or her, family and borrowed the money from her father as a personal loan, A must pay that debt. But, if Leah's father gave her money and hoped that A would repay him, A is free from the obligation of repayment. Even in the former case, if A claims that his father-in-law owed him an equal sum of money, he (A) is under no obligation to pay, but must take an oath to support his claim. If Leah bought excessive clothes, A is under no obligation to pay for them.

SOURCES: Pr. 82. Cf. P. 11; Mord. Ket. 273, *Terumat Hadeshen* 317.

292

Q. A was arrested for purposes of extortion. At the same time, but quite independently of him, A's wife was also arrested, and was tortured in prison. Her relatives carried on negotiations with her captors, and finally succeeded in ransoming her. These relatives now seek to recover their expenses from the valuables of A that he had deposited with B for safe keeping. However, A is still being held by his captors. No one knows how much money will be required in order to effect his release. He may need the valuables mentioned above for his own ransom. Must B deliver A's valuables to the relatives of A's wife?

A. The release from captivity of a wife takes priority over that of her husband, since a wife is in danger of being outraged. Therefore, the relatives of A's wife are entitled to collect their expenses from A's valuables, and B must deliver these valuables to the relatives.

SOURCES: Hag. Mord. Ket. 288; *Mordecai Hagadol,* p. 359c. Cf. Weil, *Responsa* 148.

293

Q. A has two sons and several daughters, some under six years of age, and some older. These children possess property of their own which they received as gifts. Must A nevertheless provide them with food and sustenance? Your pupil is inclined to think that A is under no obligation to do so, since feeding one's children is considered by the Talmud to be a charitable act (Ket. 50a), and A's children need no charity.

A. Your reasoning is correct as far as the older children are concerned, but does not apply to those under six years of age, for as the Rabbis decreed that a husband must provide his wife with food and sustenance even if she has property of her own, they also decreed that a father feed his children until they reach the age of six, even though they have property of their own.

The query was sent by Rabbi Asher.

SOURCES: Am II, 242, 244; cf. Asheri Ket. 14; *Tur Eben Haezer,* 71.

294 (D)

Q. We are to be guided by the disposition of the deceased
father as to the amount for which the heirs are to be assessed
for a daughter's outfit (Ket. 68a). If upon considering the
father's disposition we are convinced that he would have given
his daughter more than one tenth of his estate, are we to assess
the heirs for more than one tenth of the estate?

A. We cannot assess the heirs for an amount greater
than one-tenth of the estate, unless we have irrefutable proof
that the father would have given more to his daughter.

SOURCES: Am II, 75.

295 (D)

Q. An orphaned daughter is entitled to a dowry equal to
one-tenth the estate left by her father. Is she entitled to one-
tenth of the movables forming part of her father's estate?

A. She is entitled to one-tenth of the immovables only.
Although nowadays, because of the ordinance of the Saburaim,
a woman collects her *ketubah,* and all other obligations stipulated
therein, from movables, the dowry of a daughter is not an
obligation included in the *ketubah,* and, therefore, is not included
in the abovementioned ordinance.

SOURCES: L. 237; cf. Hag. Maim. *Ishut* 20, 2.

296

One-tenth of the property, to which a minor daughter is
entitled out of her father's estate according to talmudic law,
means real property only. Thus a minor daughter is entitled
to one-tenth of the real property left by her father, but is not
entitled to any part of the movable property left by him.

SOURCES: L. 182; *Tashbetz,* 458.

297

Q. A often strikes his wife. A's aunt, who lives at his home, is usually the cause of their arguments, and adds to the vexation and annoyance of his wife.

A. A Jew must honor his wife more than he honors himself. If one strikes one's wife, one should be punished more severely than for striking another person. For one is enjoined to honor one's wife but is not enjoined to honor the other person. Therefore, A must force his aunt to leave his house, and must promise to treat his wife honorably. If he persists in striking her, he should be excommunicated, lashed, and suffer the severest punishments, even to the extent of amputating his arm. If his wife is willing to accept a divorce, he must divorce her and pay her the *ketubah.*

Sources: Pr. 81; cf. Cr. 291.

298

Q. A often beats his wife. She begged him to promise not to beat her any more, but he refused to make any such promise. Even when she appeared in the Synagogue to demand that A pay the debts she had contracted in order to pay for her sustenance [probably during a period of separation], A stubbornly refused to promise that in the future he would refrain from beating her.

A. A must pay for his wife's sustenance since by his action he has shown that he had not decided to desist from his shameful practice. One deserves greater punishment for striking his wife than for striking another person, for he is enjoined to respect her. Far be it from a Jew to do such a thing. Had a similar case come before us we should hasten to excommunicate him. Thus, R. Paltoi Gaon rules that a husband who constantly quarrels with his wife must remove the causes of such quarrels, if possible, or divorce her and pay her the *ketubah*;

how much more must a husband be punished, who not only quarrels but actually beats his wife.

SOURCES: Cr. 291; B. p. 319 no. 780; *Mordecai Hagadol,* p. 182a.

299

Q. L claims that her husband is impotent.

A. The law considers such a claim by a wife to be valid, on the assumption that a woman would not dare present against her husband claims he knows to be false. Nowadays, however, there are many impudent and brazen women, and the above assumption is no longer true. Moreover, in this case there is reason to believe that L is lying since her husband has had children with a former wife. Even though he might have weakened since, we can put no trust in L's words. Therefore, we must not force the husband to grant L a divorce, but we ought to persuade him to do so.

SOURCES: Cr. 271; Pr. 947; Mord. Kid. 542; Tesh. Maim. to *Nashim,* 7; cf. Asher, *Responsa* 43, 2; ibid. 43, 5; Weil, *Responsa* 22; Israel Bruno, *Responsa* 266.

300 (D)

Q. A is impotent. His wife demands that he divorce her.

A. We may force A to divorce his wife, especially if she has no children.

SOURCES: Cr. 150; cf. Cr. 271; Pr. 947.

301

Q. L says that her husband is impotent and has had no sexual intercourse with her for the two years since their wedding day. She demands, therefore, that he divorce her and pay her the *ketubah.* L's husband admits that he is impotent but attributes this to his being bewitched.

A. Since L's husband admits that he is impotent, there is not the slightest doubt that he must divorce her and pay her the *ketubah*. If L pleads that she wants to be free to remarry and to have children who will comfort and support her in her old age, we are permitted to force her husband, even by flagellation, to divorce her. If she enters no such plea, however, we can not force him by flagellation but we can by threats of dishonoring him. When he does divorce her he must pay her the *Ikkar ketubah* and her dowry, but is under no obligation to pay her the additional jointure. If she admits having brought in as dowry a sum less than the fifty pounds written in her *ketubah* — in your town these fifty pounds are interpreted to mean one hundred *marks* — she is entitled to such a sum only. If witnesses testify to the exact amount she brought in as her dowry, she is entitled to receive that amount only. If there are no witnesses, however, she is entitled to receive the full fifty pounds as her dowry. In case, however, her husband gave away his personal property as gifts to others to make it impossible for L to collect her *ketubah*, the following distinction must be made: If while granting the gifts he mentioned the contingency of his death, she is still entitled to collect her dowry from such gifts; if he gave his personal property away as outright gifts, however, she may not collect from these gifts. Should her husband brave the disapproval of the Rabbis and refuse to divorce her, we must add to her *ketubah* three denars per week for the entire period of his refusal.

SOURCES: *Mordecai Hagodol*, p. 378 d. Cf. Cr. 271; Tesh. Maim to *Nashim*, 7.

302

Q. A has been dripping blood for the past four years. During that period he refrained from sexual intercourse with his wife on the ground that his doctors forbade him to have intercourse as it endangered his life. Is A to be considered a rebellious husband and hence should three denars per week be added to his wife's *ketubah* for the period of his abstention?

A.   Since A was forced by illness to refrain from intercourse with his wife, he is not to be considered a rebellious husband. A rebellious husband is one who refuses to live with his wife because he is angry with her or because he hates her. A person who is physically unable to live with his wife, however, is not considered a rebellious husband. A, however, must divorce his wife and must pay her the *ketubah*, since he is in the same category as a leper for whom coitus is harmful (Ket. 77b). Although A's sickness does not disable him permanently and is curable, we do not compel his wife to wait indefinitely in the hope that he might be cured. Thus Maimonides (M. T. Ishut 14, 7) rules that under such circumstances a woman must wait only six months. Although we have compared A to a leper for whom coitus is harmful, nevertheless we should not force A by flagellation to divorce his wife, but should only resort to persuasion. We should merely tell him the law requires him to divorce his wife and pay her the *ketubah*; should he refuse to do so, he would be called "transgressor". Whether A divorces her or not, however, we force him to pay his wife the *Ikkar ketubah* and her dowry, but we do not force him to pay her the additional jointure since some authorities hold the opinion that under the circumstances she is not entitled to the additional jointure. Should A's wife aver that she does not believe that A's doctors told him to refrain from sexual intercourse, and insist that he is a rebellious husband, he would have to take an oath in support of his assertions. Should A refuse to take the oath, we would have to add to his wife's *ketubah* three Tyrian denars per week for the entire period of his abstention. I have sufficient proof to support my view that the three denars prescribed by the Mishnah (Ket. 5, 7) mean Tyrian denars. Should A admit that he had refrained from sexual intercourse with his wife because he was angry with her and that he had lied about both his sickness and the advice of his doctors, and should he declare that he now desires to resume marital relations with her, the aforementioned amount would be added to her *ketubah* and she would be required to resume her marital duties. Regardless of what happened in the past, A may now claim that he is well and that he is able to live normally with his wife, since the truth of his claim is bound eventually to be proven or disproven.

This Responsum is addressed to: "Rabbi Isaac, my relatives Rabbi Joel and Rabbi Ephraim".

SOURCES: Sinai V (1941) pp. 203-6; ibid. pp. 294-5; *Mordecai Hagadol*, p. 159c; Pr. 574.

303

Q. A wife refused to have conjugal relations with her husband for a long time, with the result that she lost her *ketubah* according to Mishnaic law (M. Ket. 5, 7). She repented and wanted to resume marital relations with her husband, but the latter refused. Must he pay for her sustenance?

A. When the woman lost her rights to the money she was entitled to under the *ketubah* she also lost her other rights enumerated therein, and her husband is under no obligation to support her any longer.

SOURCES: Pr. 228, 946; Rashba I, 861; Hag. Maim, *Ishut*, 14, 8; Mord. Ket. 290; P. 242.

304

Q. L rebelled against her husband. She refused, however, to accept her divorce from him, stating that she disliked him and wanted to cause him pain and annoyance. Nevertheless, heretofore they had lived in harmony.

A. L should be persuaded to forego her *ketubah* and accept her divorce. Should she refuse to forego her *ketubah*, her husband should be permitted to marry another woman. L should remain a deserted wife tied to her husband until she consents to forego her *ketubah* and accept her divorce. We can not permit a situation wherein L's husband would be prevented from fulfilling his duty of propagation. Were we to allow L's conduct to go unpunished, great misfortune would ensue, for the daughters of Israel would turn to mischief.

SOURCES: *Mordecai Hagadol*, p. 162c.

305

Q. L rebelled against her husband and left him. She took with her some of his valuables which he now demands. L, however, claims that he gave her these valuables as an outright gift. Are we to give credence to L's assertion? Moreover, is a widow permitted to keep valuables she claims to have received from her husband as an outright gift?

A. If the valuables were not seen in the woman's possession, we must give credence to her assertion, since she could have denied having taken them or could have claimed to have returned them (principle of *Miggo*). But, since in this case the fact of their being in L's possession is established, L must return the valuables unless she produces witnesses to substantiate her claim.

SOURCES: Cr. 268; Am II, 32; *Mordecai Hagadol*, p. 313d.

306

Q. A married off his son to B's daughter, giving a dowry of twenty *marks* which A deposited with B. Subsequently, A's son quarrelled with his wife and returned to his father's house. He appointed his father his trustee and the latter demanded that B return the dowry deposited with him since it was given to him for safe-keeping only. B claimed that he gave the money to his daughter while the young couple still lived happily together; that his daughter used the money in business since she was active in business and earned the income for the family, while her husband devoted all his time to studies; that A's son never asked him for the money, and that A never told him not to give the money to his daughter. B also mentioned his daughter's complaints that A's son did unmentionable things to her, conducting himself in a disgusting manner, and thus became hateful to her. She now demanded that he divorce her and pay her the *ketubah*, as she said that she despised her husband, would never live with him again, and would rather go begging from door to door than remain with him.

A. B must take an oath to the effect that he gave the money to his daughter while she was still living in peace and harmony with her husband, and thus be free from obligation. Since B's daughter was a rebellious wife she ought to be dealt with as such. I already wrote to you, while I was in Konstanze, my opinion regarding the law governing a rebellious wife. We follow the ordinance of the Geonim and permit her to keep all she brought to her husband as dowry (*Nikse Zon Barzel*), and whatever he brought is returned to him, nor is she entitled to the *Ikkar ketubah*; she is then to wait until either he consents to divorce her, or she decides to go back to him. If we suspect, however, that she does not dislike her husband but revolts against him because of financial considerations, or because her father, her mother, or her relatives induce her to quarrel with him, we take away from her even her dowry. In such a case we must follow the law in all its strictness and give all the possessions of the couple to the husband, for the ordinance of the Geonim mentioned above does not apply to the woman who rebels against her husband because she is persuaded to do so by others.

Sources: Cr. 93, 94; L. 327, 328; Mord. Ket. 186–7; cf. *Mordecai Hagadol*, p. 160d; *Terumat Hadeshen* 220; Isserlein, *Pesakim* 264.

307

Q. Leah loathes her husband and demands a divorce. Her father who did not, as yet, give the dowry to her husband, handed the dowry over to Leah. Is the father's act justified?

A. Leah's father was justified in his act for a number of reasons: a) A woman who loathes her husband and demands a divorce is entitled to collect from her husband everything that is left of her dowry. There is no doubt, therefore, that she may retain such dowry. b) R. Jacob Tam took into consideration the fact that a father promises a dowry to his daughter in the expectation that she will live with her husband. He, therefore, ruled that a husband whose wife died before he collected her dowry, can no longer collect it. The same principle applies to our case. c) If a man seizes the property of a debtor for the benefit of a single creditor while the debtor owes money to other creditors, such seizure is of no avail, and the other creditors may take away said property. But, if the man who seized the property hands it over to the creditor for whose benefit he seized it, the act is valid and the other creditors can do nothing about it. In our case, too, Leah already received the money from her father.

SOURCES: Pr. 230; Mord. Ket. 290; cf. Hag. Maim., *Ishut* 14, 20.

308

Q. Within the first year of her marriage to A, L claimed that she detested him and could not live with him. Before their marriage, money had been given to L by her father, as a present, on condition that A never have a right to it. L, therefore, demanded this money and the accrued income thereof. On the other hand, L's father had promised a dowry to A but had postponed the date of delivery of such dowry, having expressed the fear that L might rebel against her husband within the first year of her marriage. A, therefore, demands the dowry from L's father.

A. Although no present can be given to a married woman on condition that her husband have no right thereto, such a present may be given to her during the period of betrothal and thereupon the husband will have no right to such present or the income thereof. Therefore, the present and the accrued income must be returned to L. This decision is effective only if L's dislike of A is deep and genuine and is not induced by anyone. The community must pronounce the ban (*herem*) against anyone holding information relative to this matter; and if it be discovered that someone has induced L to rebel against A, then the money may be withheld from her as a punishment until she repents. The court always has a right to punish one even unduly, if such punishment will help to check lawlessness and indecency. In this case the punishment of L will serve as a warning to other women. Moreover, should A desire to marry another woman, I believe that he should be permitted to throw a bill of divorcement to L even against her will, since she is the rebellious party. A, however, is not entitled to the dowry promised to him by L's father, since the latter had expressed his intention of giving such dowry only in the event that L and A lived happily together.

SOURCES: Am II, 48.

309

Q. A promised under a ban that he would never deal treacherously with his wife, L, and that should he break his promise, he would give her half of his money. Subsequently he broke his promise, whereupon L left him and he paid her half of his money in accordance with his agreement. They later became reconciled to each other, however, and lived together again in harmony and love until her mother persuaded her to leave him. Now A demands the return of his wife and the restoration of his money.

A. If A's promise was not accompanied by a *Kinyan* made before an authoritative court, it was merely an *Asmakhta* and was void. L, then, must restore the money to A. He should atone in a manner that the Rabbi might prescribe for him for having transgressed the ban. Although a rebellious wife is entitled to receive the money she brought with her as her dowry, L is not entitled to such money since she did not rebel against A of her own accord, but was persuaded to do so by her mother. Thus the communities, [at their synod held] in Würzburg, passed an ordinance to the effect that whenever a woman shall be led to rebel against her husband through the persuasions of her relatives, and shall refuse to heed all warnings, all the possessions of the couple shall become the sole property of her husband, and he shall be permitted to divorce her, even against her will, without giving her a penny. I believe that all Israel should abide by this ordinance which was instituted for the public benefit, especially since the money of the couple belongs to the husband according to talmudic law, and we need not resort to an ordinance. Since the law prescribes that whatever a woman acquires belongs to her husband (Gitt. 77b), why should we seek to infringe upon his rights, and especially in a case where the woman loves her husband, but was merely persuaded by her relatives to rebel against him, and where, therefore, there is no fear lest she resort to mischief? In such a case we must follow the law in all its strictness and give all the possessions of the couple to the husband, for the ordinance of the Geonim to the effect that the dowry be returned to the rebellious wife does not apply to the wife who rebelled against her husband not for personal reasons, but because she was persuaded to do so by others.

SOURCES: *Mordecai Hagadol*, p. 160d; Hag. Maim. to *Ishut* 14, 30. Cf. Hayyim Or Zarua, *Responsa* 126; ibid. 155; ibid. 69; Asher, *Responsa* 43, 8; Asheri Ket. 5, 35; Hag. Asheri Kidd. 3, 16; *Kol Bo* 75; *Tur Eben Haezer* 77; Weil, *Responsa* 22; Israel Bruno, *Responsa* 208.

310

A claims that his father-in-law, B, alienated his wife's affections and also withheld his money. B claims: a) when he gave his daughter to A he stipulated the condition that A deposit sixty pounds with him; b) A agreed to this condition and gave the money to B and to his daughter stipulating that should A overindulge in food and drink or generally squander his money, he and his daughter would withhold the money until A bettered his habits; c) this agreement was accompanied by a *kinyan*; d) that A drew up a bond to that effect which bond is still in B's possession; e) A abstracted the sixty pounds from his wife, and therefore she refuses to live with him, or to give him money that was originally designated for buying her ornaments. A disclaims signing such bond, and denies having squandered any money or being guilty of any improper behavior. He denies having abstracted the money from B's daughter for the purpose of squandering it, but says that he had taken it only because he was afraid lest B rob him of his money and deprive him of his wife, as B had done with his other sons-in-law.

A further claims that B turned him over to a wicked Gentile who almost murdered him. A, therefore, demands that B be punished. B, on the other hand, gives a different account of the affair. He says that a Gentile, a violent man, placed a *mark* (8 ounces) of gold in pledge with him; and he, in turn, deposited it with A. When A wanted to leave town, B fearing lest the Gentile bring false accusations against him upon failing to produce the pledge, demanded that A return the gold *mark* to him. A invited B to go to the Gentile, and promised to free B from obligation to the Gentile. The Gentile, however, refused to listen to A and warned B that he (the Gentile) would collect double its value should his gold *mark* be lost. B, therefore, grabbed A by the clothes and said to the Gentile that his gold *mark* was in A's possession. The Gentile, then, angered by A's words made extreme threats against A. Nevertheless, A suffered no bodily injury nor any loss of money on account of this incident.

A. If the agreement was made at the time of the betrothal, it is binding on A. At a betrothal, verbal agreements are binding, and whenever verbal promises are binding — as in charity-gifts, Temple-gifts, or vows — they are binding even when made in the form of conditional promises which are usually classified as *asmakhta.* If the money in question was part of the dowry given by B to his daughter, the agreement is certainly binding on A. Moreover, even if the agreement was entered into after the betrothal, it would also be binding if it was accompanied by a *kinyan* made before the notables of the community, who normally constitute an authoritative court.

Regarding A's complaint that B informed against him, A is not entitled to compensation since he suffered no damages. As to punishing B for complaining to a Gentile against A, I have no authority to impose fines. The community, however, has the right to impose fines, and also to punish a member for improper acts committed by him. Such fines are to be imposed in accordance with the status of the individuals involved.

SOURCES: Cr. 304; P. 219, 220; *Mordecai Hagadol,* p. 181a.

311

This is in answer to your query regarding A who demands that his father-in-law permit his wife to join him. Even if she is sick, she must immerse herself in a ritual bath. If she refuses to do so, she is considered a rebellious wife.

SOURCES: Mord. Ket. 185.

312

Q. A says that he was on good terms with his wife when she went to her mother's home for her baby to be delivered, and that as now she refuses to return to him, somebody must have persuaded her to rebel against him. He, therefore, demands that his wife resume her marital duties. The trustee of A's wife states that A used to beat his wife even during her menstruation period and that he caused her so much pain and humiliation that he became repulsive to her.

A. A's wife can not be compelled to live with A, even though she had children with him, ("for we cannot force anyone to live with a snake"), nor can A be forced to divorce her. They are to remain apart until either A's wife consents to resume her marital duties, or A consents to divorce her. Meanwhile, A must return to his wife whatever is left of her dowry.

SOURCES: Pr. 946.

313

Q. A rebellious wife who refuses to live with her husband admits that she has never allowed her husband to come near her. What should be done to her?

A. Since the women of our generation are loose in their manner of life, we do not permit the husband to remarry while she is forced to remain single till old age, which procedure was recommended by R. Eleazar b. Nathan, and we do not require a waiting period of twelve months till the divorce be granted. Therefore, the elders of the community should endeavor to persuade both parties to a speedy divorce without resorting to coercion of either party. Upon the granting of the divorce the woman should receive only what she actually brought in as dowry, but not the full fifty pounds of dowry written in her *ketubah*; for when the husband received her dowry and evaluated it at fifty pounds, though actually it was worth less, he did so because he wanted to marry her and live with her. Now that she refuses to live with him she loses the extra value placed on her dowry, the additional jointure promised her by the husband, as well as the 200 *zuzin* prescribed by the Talmud. Though in this country the same amount of dowry is written in the *ketubah* of a rich as in that of a poor bride, irrespective of the amount she actually brings in, in order not to shame the brides who bring in a small dowry, this rebellious wife is not entitled to collect the full amount of dowry written in her *ketubah*, since she never lived with her husband.

SOURCES: Pr. 442–443.

314

Q. How are we to treat a rebellious wife, who asserts that she despises her husband?

A. She is to receive whatever she has brought in to her husband as dowry (*Nikse Zon barzel*), and whatever is left of her own property to which her husband has had the right of usufruct (*nikse melug*). She is, then, to wait until her husband consents to divorce her.

Your objection to this procedure on the ground that any woman upon seeing her husband losing his property and sinking into poverty would become a rebellious wife, seize his remaining property and enjoy its use, is not very serious as she would not enjoy it very much, for, her husband may refuse to divorce her. According to R. Eleazar b. Nathan he may even remarry while refusing to grant her a divorce.

This Responsum is addressed to R. Jacob and R. Joseph.

SOURCES: Pr. 946; P. 241; Rashba I, 859, 860; Hag. Maim., *Ishut* 14, 30.

315

Q. Must a woman who rebelled against her husband, before she receives her divorce, return the presents her husband had given her before their betrothal, which, at the time, were not intended for immediate consumption or wear?

A. If the woman rebelled against her husband, she must return even those presents which were intended for immediate consumption or wear.

SOURCES: Pr. 946.

316 (D)

Nowadays the talmudic law regarding a rebellious wife no longer applies. The ordinance of the Saboraim prevails instead, that when a woman refuses to live with her husband, he is immediately to be coerced into granting her a divorce. This ordinance was instituted in order that Jewish women should not turn to mischief. The woman is to receive whatever she has brought in as her dowry (*Nikse Zon Barzel*), and whatever is left of her own property to which her husband had the right of usufruct (*Nikse Melug*). The Geonim ruled that she was also entitled to the *Ikkar ketubah*. The husband is to be coerced, by threat of excommunication, into granting the divorce, for who will dare contradict the decisions of the great luminary Rabbenu Gershom, the Geonim, Alfasi, Maimonides, and R. Isaac di Trani? One may not object that such favorable treatment would encourage many women to rebel against their husbands; Heaven forfend, Jewish daughters are not suspected of such malefaction. They prefer to stay married even in adverse circumstances, and would not seek a divorce unless actually driven thereto.

SOURCES: B. p. 285, nos. 337–9; P. 494. Cf. Weil, *Responsa* 78.

317

Q. Leah rebelled against her husband A, the son of Mendel Kern. When warned that she might lose her *ketubah* and the dowry (which she brought in upon her marriage) and that she might be forced to wait for many years for her divorce she

threatened, among other things, to go and live among the
Gentiles. Since the women of Regensburg were always arrogant
in their relations to their husbands and now are even more
supercilious than ever, Leah should be dealt with in a manner
that would serve as a warning to her haughty sisters. A should
be permitted to remarry immediately in accordance with the
view of R. Eliezer b. Nathan, while Leah should be forced to
wait for her divorce for many years. However, Leah should
not be left entirely to the mercy of her husband who, after
marrying another woman, might demand an exorbitant sum
for Leah's divorce, or might refuse to divorce her altogether.
We, therefore, leave it to you to decide upon a proper punishment for Leah.

A. In order to curtail the possibility of Jewish women
turning to mischief, and in order that people might not say:
"This one is A's wife and this one his paramour", we should not
permit the husband to remarry before he divorces his rebellious
wife. Therefore, A should receive a limited amount of money
and give Leah her divorce, or, he should give Leah a divorce
on condition that the divorce become valid (from now and)
twelve months, or two years, after date. After the delivery of
such a conditional divorce, A may be permitted to remarry immediately. If, however, Leah had good reason to detest her
husband, she should be dealt with more leniently. Therefore,
you should use your judgment in determining the severity with
which Leah is to be punished.

SOURCES: Pr. 946; *Mordecai Hagadol,* p. 161b.

318

1) *Q.* L's representative claims that her husband has
seized her garments and refuses to return them. L's husband
avers that the garments were deposited with him as security
against a debt.

A. If the garments are not now in the husband's possession, or if they were identified in his possession as L's garments, he must return them to L, for a wife's garments are in the category of objects that are usually lent or rented out, regarding which one may not claim that he has bought them (Sheb. 46b). If no one, however, saw the garments in the husband's possession, we uphold his claim; since if he wanted to lie he could have denied having taken them.

2) *Q.* L's representative claims that her husband has seized her jewelry of gold and silver, and refuses to return it. L's husband avers that this jewelry was given to him as part of his wife's dowry.

A. The wife has the right to the use of the vessels of gold and silver she has brought with her as her dowry, for, had she intended to give them to her husband for his exclusive use, she would have given him money instead.

SOURCES: Cr. 252; *Mordecai Hagadol,* p. 160b.

319

Q. A's wife bound herself by a ban in the presence of the people of the town, not to do a certain thing. The terms of the ban were written down, and all the townfolk signed the document. Subsequently she transgressed the ban several times, as attested to by witnesses. A transgressing woman, if properly forewarned, loses the right to her *ketubah.* We are doubtful, however, whether A's wife had to be properly forewarned before losing her right to the *ketubah.* We are inclined to believe that no such forewarning was necessary since she was warned at the time the ban was pronounced that she would lose the right to her *ketubah* should she transgress the ban, and she agreed thereto without inserting any qualifying conditions. Does A's wife lose the right to her *ketubah?* Furthermore, is A permitted to divorce her against her will?

A. Even if proper forewarning were required before a transgressing woman loses her right to the *ketubah*, one such warning would be sufficient. Otherwise a woman would be able, without any restraint, continually to cause her husband to sin. For, when forewarned by witnesses, she would temporarily abstain from sin, and, later, return to her mischief. Moreover, any situation that would require the administration of testing-water to a *Sotah* (a woman suspected of faithlessness), would cause her to lose the right to her *ketubah*; and the forewarning of a jealous husband, even though preceding by many days the seclusion of his wife with another man, would require the administration of testing-water, as evidenced by the statement of the Baraita (Yeb. 58b): the jealous forewarning of a betrothed would require the administration of testing-water after she married [if she secluded herself with that other man after the marriage took place]. Therefore, a forewarning does not necessarily have to precede a transgression immediately.

The question was again sent to R. Meir: A's wife brought witnesses who testified before us that A also had transgressed the ban. We decided, therefore, that she did not lose the right to her *ketubah*, since she did not intend to commit a sin. Moreover, a woman must be forewarned immediately before committing a sin in order to be classified as a transgressing woman. The Baraita cited above offers no proof to the contrary since it deals with a case where the sinful seclusion immediately followed the jealous forewarning (i. e. the seclusion took place before the marriage).

A. I still believe that a forewarning does not necessarily have to precede the transgression immediately. Thus Rashi offers two interpretations of the aforementioned Baraita. The first, and most important, interpretation assumes that the seclusion took place after the marriage, and, thus, long after the jealous forewarning. Moreover, the Talmud (Sotah 26a) clearly states that a woman who was jealously forewarned before her marriage and secluded herself with another man after the marriage, must either drink the testing-water or lose the right to her *ketubah*. However, since A too has transgressed the ban, we must make two distinctions. a) If the wife's sin consisted of merely disregarding the ban, while her act was not sinful in itself, A is not permitted to divorce her; for transgressing a ban causes the death of the transgressor's children, and is, therefore, ground for divorce; but, since A himself transgressed the ban, he can have no objection to a similar act on the part of his wife. b) If A's wife, however, transgressed Mosaic law and Jewish custom, A is permitted to divorce her even against her will; he need not seek the consent of the communities, and he is not required to pay her the *ketubah*.

SOURCES: Cr. 185; L. 393; Tesh. Maim. to *Nashim* 16; Rashba I, 864–6; Hag. Asheri Ket. 7, 9. Cf. Isserlein, *Pesakim* 68.

320

𝒬. Up to the present the custom was prevalent in our country to enforce the collection of *ketuboth* written many years previously to their being presented for collection even when such *ketuboth* bore witnesses' signatures that were not known to the court. Recently, however, some defendants disputed the authenticity of a certain *ketubah* and demanded legal identification of the signatures on the document. Since no such identification was possible, the case was protracted by the defendants and the woman was forced to reach a compromise and accept a less amount than that written in her *ketubah*. From now on this procedure will probably be followed by all other defendants in similar cases [which will cause great hardship to widows and divorcees]. I have before me a Responsum of Rabbi Menahem who rules that a woman who lost her *ketubah*-document did not thereby lose her right even to the additional jointure. Although the consensus of opinion is that the additional jointure is also considered a *maase beth-din* (an obligation imposed by the Rabbis on all husbands, the existence of which obligation, therefore, need not be proved), it is considered a *maase beth-din* only in those countries where a standard *ketubah* is written for all women, containing a fixed amount of dowry and additional jointure. In our country, however, there is no general standard and each family has its own custom in this matter. Those families who follow a definite custom and write the same *ketubah* for all the women of the particular family, would encounter no difficulty on this score, as each woman would be entitled to collect as her *ketubah* the amount fixed in her family. Sometimes, however, the custom of the family is not clear and is not known even to the members of the family. In such cases the Geonim rule that when a woman has lost her *ketubah*-document, the *ketuboth* of three members of her family are to be examined and the woman should be entitled to receive the smallest of the three amounts written in these *ketuboth*. In our case, however, the *ketubah*-document was not lost and its money clause is written plainly; why should the woman be forced to take a lesser amount? Sometimes a woman has no family, or we do not know to what family she belongs, or all her relatives are dead. We should not permit that an identification of the signatures by a court be required before a woman can collect her *ketubah*, since in many cases indeed no such identification of signatures is possible even in *ketuboth* that are brought to court a short time after the wedding. Indeed, legal endorsement of *ketuboth* at the time of the wedding should have been required, but we never heard that our fore-fathers or teachers insisted upon such endorsement. Moreover, we should restrain a husband from living with his wife unless her *ketubah* bears a legal endorsement, since without such endorsement her *ketubah* is useless. Why is no attention paid to this matter? Perhaps the reason is that, unlike bonds and notes of indebtedness, the identification of the signatures on *ketuboth* is not required and not necessary. Perhaps also we do not suspect that women would forge *ketuboth*, for the reason that not one woman in a thousand knows how to write, nor are women familiar with the required legal phraseology. Nor do we suspect that persons who know how to write would be so degraded as to write forged *ketuboth* for the benefit of others.

A. I have considered your problem in all its aspects and could find no solution for it, unless each family should write an equal amount of additional jointure for all its members. If a family has no established custom of writing a uniform *ketubah* for all its members, the procedure prescribed by the Geonim and mentioned above, must be followed, unless the signatures on the *ketubah* can be identified. We do indeed suspect that the woman had a scribe write a forged *ketubah* for her, or even that a scribe wrote several *ketuboth* for her which she expects to present for collection at different courts.

Sources: Sinai VI (1943) 7–8 no. 408. Cf. Isserlein, *Pesakim* 232.

321

Q. L's husband was killed on a day of rioting and massacre. L lost her *ketubah*-document; is she entitled to collect her *ketubah*?

A. L is entitled to collect the *Ikkar ketubah*, since no document is required to prove the existence of an obligation classified as *maase-beth-din*, an obligation imposed by the Rabbis on all husbands alike, as a mere verbal claim of having discharged such obligation is of no avail unless one can produce documentary evidence (B. M. 17b). Therefore, if L can prove through witnesses that her husband married her as a maiden, she will be entitled to collect two hundred *zuzim* as her *Ikkar ketubah*; otherwise she will be entitled to collect only one hundred *zuzim.* As to the fifty pounds of dowry and fifty pounds of additional jointure that we generally include in the *ketubah* of our wives, I am doubtful whether these sums may be considered as *maase-beth-din.* It seems to me, however, that since we have a firmly established custom throughout our kingdom to write the aforementioned amounts in the *ketubah* of all maidens, the same law should apply to these amounts as to a *maase-beth-din.* We should, therefore, not put forth the claim, for the benefit of the heirs, that the widow has already received payment of the dowry and the additional jointure. Moreover, since witnesses testify that L and her husband lived a normal married life when he was killed, we can not put forth the claim that she has already received payment of the aforementioned amounts, for we have no reason for supposing that the husband deposited valuables with L to be used in payment of her *ketubah.* Thus Rabbi Simon of Jointville ruled that when a man suddenly dies we need not suppose that he deposited valuables with his wife to be used by her in payment of her *ketubah,* for while he is alive the *ketubah* is not an obligation requiring payment, and as long as he is well, he does not think of the possibility of his death.

SOURCES: *Mordecai Hagadol,* p. 179 margin. Cf. Asher, *Responsa* 85, 1; ibid. 86, 1; *Terumat Hadeshen* 330.

322

Q. How much money is a woman entitled to collect as her *ketubah,* upon divorce or the death of her husband?

A. The amount of money to which a woman is entitled as her *ketubah,* is dependent on local custom. In Würzburg and its vicinity, the dowry and the additional jointure are valued at one hundred pounds of two *marks* per pound; in the Rhine communities, it seems to me, they are valued at one hundred *marks.* These sums do not include the *Ikkar ketubah*

of two hundred *zuzim*, or five hundred pennyweights of silver,
each *zuz* equalling two and one half pennyweights of silver.
If no custom, as to the value of the *ketubah*, exists in your town,
you should follow the custom of the town where the wedding
took place. If no such custom exists there, you ought to follow
the custom of the community nearest to you to which you usually look for guidance. But, if no such custom exists in the
latter, the women of your locality are entitled to collect one
hundred pounds of the coins current there, plus five hundred
pennyweights of silver. Before a woman may collect her *ketubah*
she must take an oath that she did not give away or waste
(while her husband was alive or after his death) anything belonging to her husband, and that she did not retain anything
for herself. Everything she takes from the husband's house,
such as her bedding or her clothes even, is to be appraised
and deducted from her *ketubah*. The orphans are to pay the
balance due her either in real property or in moveable property,
whichever they prefer.

SOURCES: L. 182; *Tashbetz*, 457.

323

Q. What is the value of the one hundred pounds that a
person obligates himself, in the *ketubah* document, to pay to
his wife in case of death or divorce?

A. In Würzburg a well established local custom is followed
to permit a woman to collect two hundred *marks*. This custom,
however, is not logical, for the term "pound" is thus interpreted
to mean a pound by weight (16 ounces) which is equivalent
to two *marks*. But if this interpretation is correct why do we
not explicitly write in the *ketubah*: "one hundred pounds by
weight"? Thus, I once saw my teacher and relative Rabbi Judah
haKohen order the insertion of such phrase in the *ketubah* of

one of his relatives. Since, however, we unqualifiedly write "one hundred pounds", we probably mean the coin "pound" and refer to the largest money unit current in the particular town. Rabbi Simha established the custom of paying the widow or divorcee one hundred *marks* as her *ketubah*, thus interpreting the above mentioned phrase to mean one hundred pounds of heavy coins (ליברייﬡ"ש), one pound of which is equivalent to a *mark*. Indeed, I have heard that in Worms only one hundred pounds *Heller* are paid; this custom of paying pounds current in the particular town seems to me preferable to all other customs. However, one must follow the custom of his locality. In the absence of a local custom, the custom of the town where the wedding took place should be followed. If no custom exists in this town either, one should pay one hundred pounds of the coins current in his present place of abode or in the town where the wedding took place — whichever is of lower value*.

SOURCES: Cr. 95.

324

a) *Q*. A married L in Mayence, or in another locality, where the *ketubah* is valued at two hundred *marks*. They then removed to a different locality where the *ketubah* is valued at much less. They lived in the latter place until A's death. How much money is L entitled to as her *ketubah*?

A. The opinion of R. Simon b. Gamaliel (Ket. 110b) is accepted that a woman is entitled to the *ketubah* current in the locality where her marriage took place.

b) *Q*. After A died L took over, and managed, his estate. Why, then, did you write that the estate was considered, nevertheless, to be in the possession of the orphans?

A. R. Hananel decided that the estate managed by the widow is considered to be in the possession of the orphans.

---

* The last statement is quite obscure since the talmudic source quoted in its support is in complete disagreement therewith.

The widow is merely a managing trustee. Therefore, all the profit accruing because of her management, belongs to the orphans and she can not collect her *ketubah* therefrom. When the widow demands her *ketubah* she loses her right to receive her sustenance from the estate. She must, then, take an oath while holding the Scroll of the Law; and whatever she thus states under oath to have given away, or to have retained for herself, to have given to her daughter, or to have given to charity, is deducted from her *ketubah*.

c) ℺. L lent some of the money to lords and "men of violence", and it is doubtful whether the latter will pay their debts.

A. L is responsible for these bad investments. Ordinarily when heirs pay the *ketubah* to a widow, they may give her in payment any kind of property, or any object even bran; but they cannot pay her by transferring to her money due them from others, since the collection of debts often involves litigations to which a woman is not accustomed. However, in our case, the orphans may transfer to L the money she has invested with the lords and the "men of violence", in payment of her *ketubah*, since she had no right to make such unsafe investments.

d) ℺. While L managed the estate she gave presents to certain persons thinking she had the right to do so. Are the orphans entitled to take back the presents?

A. The recipients are entitled to retain these presents since they may claim that L gave them out of her own property, and since it appears that the market ordinance (*takkanat hashuk*) was to apply to property given away as presents.

e) ℺. Do we put forth the claim for the benefit of the orphans that L may have been a widow when she married A, or that A may have paid her one *Mina*.?

A. We surely put forth the above claims for the benefit of the orphans. However, if a report circulates that L was a virgin when she married A, she is entitled to the *ketubah* of a virgin, since the majority of women are married while virgins. [The principle of "a majority of cases" presumes that what is true in most instances, is also true in our case.] Although in litigation over money matters the principle of "a majority of cases" is not a factor, it is so when the claimant is in actual possession of the litigated money. In our case, L is in actual possession of the money; therefore, the combination of a "majority" and a "report" in her favor, is conclusive.

SOURCES: Cr. 127–8–9–30–31; L. 480–1–2–3.

325

Q. A woman produced for collection a *ketubah* in which the sum of two hundred pounds was stipulated. But the *ketubah* did not specify whether the coin "pound" [the value of which differed in each locality] was meant, or the weight "pound" [which equalled two *marks*, or sixteen ounces of silver] was meant. How much is the woman entitled to collect?

A. It all depends upon the custom of the place where the woman married. In Würzburg and its surrounding country, the one hundred pounds of the *ketubah* are interpreted to mean two hundred *marks*. On the Rhine, there are places where the one hundred pounds of the *ketubah* are interpreted to mean one hundred pounds *Heller*. If the woman comes from a place where there is no established custom, she receives two hundred pounds of the coin current in her locality.

SOURCES: Pr. 284; Mord. Ket. 281; Tesh. Maim. to *Nashim*, 13.

326 (D)

Q. The *ketubah* of a widow contained the following clause: "you shall collect whatever you have brought in, as your dowry, over and above the amount you are entitled to as your *ketubah*",

without description of what the dowry consisted. The widow
seized some articles stating that her late husband had given
them to her as a present. Are we to believe her statement (in
accordance with the rule of *Miggo*), since if she had wanted to lie
she might have claimed that said articles were part of her dowry?

A. A mere claim to the effect that the articles had formed
part of her *ketubah* would have been insufficient. Since her
ketubah did not enumerate the articles and valuables that made
up her dowry, she would have to prove what the dowry consisted
of before she would be entitled to collect any part thereof.
Therefore, we do not have to believe her statement.

SOURCES: L. 243.

327

Q. A sold his immovable property. Do the protests of A's
wife invalidate such sale [since his wife's *ketubah* is a lien upon
his real estate]?

A. If the property was set aside by A to be used in payment of his wife's *ketubah* in case of divorce or his death, or,
if it originally formed part of the wife's dowry, the sale is
invalid. Otherwise the sale is valid until A's death, or until
A divorces his wife, at which time the latter will be permitted
to seize such property in payment of her *ketubah*.

SOURCES: Cr. 250; L. 124; Mord. B.B. 545. Cf. *Agudah* B.B. 90.

328

Q. A wants to buy a house. He is afraid to do so, however,
lest his wife later legally restrain him from reselling it [since a
wife's *ketubah* constitutes a lien on the husband's immovables].
Should A stipulate that he buys the house on condition that
his wife be unable to restrain him from selling it, and if she
formally agrees thereto, would such an agreement be binding on the wife; or would it be null and void since she would
thus have agreed to a thing that as yet had no existence?

A. The above agreement would be binding on A's wife, for a person may relinquish his claim to rights and privileges before they are created.

Sources: Cr. 263; Mord. Ket. 212; Hag. Maim. *Ishut* 23, 2. Cf. Moses
Minz, *Responsa* 39.

329

Q. A quarrelled with his wife. Subsequently it was discovered that A bought real estate but had the deeds made out in the name of his relative, B, intending by means of these transactions to evade paying his wife's *ketubah.*

A. A's wife is entitled to collect her *ketubah* from this real estate, for, transactions that are intended to nullify a rabbinical ordinance are void.

Sources: Mord. B.B. 649; *Mordecai Hagadol,* p. 336a; Asher, *Responsa* 78, 1;
ibid. 78, 3; *Tur Hoshen Mishpat* 99.

330

Q. What should be done to a man who revolted against his wife and gave away his money to others to avoid paying her the *ketubah?* Please explain in detail the laws concerning rebellious husbands and rebellious wives.

A. If the husband refuses to support his wife he can be forced to support her. If he does support his wife, but refuses to cohabit with her, he should be told that according to the Rabbis he is required to divorce her or be called *abaryana* (renegade), but he cannot be forced to divorce her. If, however, he refuses to do either, he can be forced to grant her a divorce.

Sources: Pr. 946.

331

When Rabbi Zamlan was ill he sent for Rabbi Asher in order that the latter help him dispose of his property in a manner that would make it impossible for his wife, L, to appropriate his possessions in payment of her *ketubah* or for her sustenance. Rabbi Asher refused to come, but Rabbi Zamlan implored him and pleaded with him saying: "What can I do for my only son who, after my death, will have to go begging from door to door?" Rabbi Asher then agreed to act as a witness, and Rabbi Zamlan gave away to his son and to other persons, all of his property as an outright gift effective immediately. After his death, L's relatives summoned Rabbi Zamlan's son to the court of Rabbi Perez. The latter recorded the claims of the two parties and sent the claims to Rabbi Meir without giving the names of the litigants and without expressing any opinion on the subject. Rabbi Meir ruled that L was entitled to collect her *ketubah*, or to draw her sustenance, from the possessions of Rabbi Zamlan which he had given to his son; his reason being that even an outright gift to an heir is considered an inheritance and that the widow's *ketubah* is a lien upon it.

Rabbi Perez took issue with Rabbi Meir quoting Alfasi's decision that the ordinance of Usha — which ruled that a person who divided all of his property among his children may derive his sustenance as well as that of his wife's from such property — was not accepted.

Rabbi Meir reproved Rabbi Perez for resorting to Alfasi when the Talmud specifically decided that the ordinance of Usha was not accepted. R. Meir contended, however, that only that part of the ordinance was not accepted which gave the right to the donor, and to his wife while he was alive, to derive their sustenance from the property he had given away; while the rule that the widow may collect her sustenance or her *ketubah* from such property after the donor's death, was accepted before the ordinance of Usha was promulgated, and has remained in force independently of such ordinance.

Meanwhile L's relatives have written to Rabbi Meir asking for his decsion in this matter. R. Meir answered that he usually

refrained from sending legal opinions to litigants, or to their
relatives, and confined his responses to judges. But, when
Rabbi Perez, in his second letter, gave the names of the litigants,
R. Meir realized that the letters from L's relatives dealt with the
same case. R. Meir recalled that among these letters was found
a letter from Rabbi Asher which explained the circumstances
of the gift mentioned above. Therefore, R. Meir added (in
his second letter to Rabbi Perez) that since according to Rabbi
Asher's letter, the donor mentioned the contingency of death
when he summoned Rabbi Asher, he therefore made the gift
to his son *causa mortis* (cf. B. B. 151a), and a widow is undoubtedly entitled to collect her *ketubah* from *causa mortis*
gifts.

SOURCES: Cr. 192; Am II, 46–7; cf. Hag. Maim. to *Ishut* 16, 4; Mord. Ket.
161. Cf. *Agudah* B.M. 29; Moses Minz, *Responsa* 66.

332

Q. A's widow, Leah, and his children put forth their claims,
through representatives, regarding real property left to A by
his mother on condition that after A's death the property be
transferred to A's children and not be used to pay Leah's *ketubah*.
Leah claimed that the said property never belonged to A's
mother since the latter received it in payment of her *ketubah*,
but failed to take the required oath before collecting such
ketubah. Leah, therefore, demanded her *ketubah* from this
property. A's sons, then, produced a document to the effect
that A, foregoing the required oath, permitted his mother to
take the property of his deceased father in payment of her
ketubah, and bestowed upon her as a gift whatever amount the
property was worth in excess of her *ketubah*. Leah, however,
claimed that as soon as her father-in-law died, his property,
automatically falling to her husband, was subject to the lien of
her *ketubah*, and that A, therefore, had no right to waive the oath

his mother was required to take and to bestow gifts upon her without her (Leah's) permission.

A. The property belongs to the grandchildren who were already born at the time the gift was made by A's mother, and Leah cannot collect her *ketubah* therefrom. We have no proof that A's mother received more than the amount specified in the *ketubah*. A's document bestowing on his mother as a gift whatever she received over and above her *ketubah* does not prove that she actually received more than was due her. Leah's claim that A had no right to bestow gifts without her permission is valid only in regard to real property, but a husband may sell or give away personal property without his wife's permission. Therefore, A's mother had a right to give her property to A and to his children. Moreover, since Leah is not certain that A's mother collected more than her *ketubah*, and can take no oath to that effect, the property goes to A's children.

This Responsum is addressed to "my teachers and relatives, Rabbi Menahem and Rabbi Hillel."

Sources: Cr. 205; Pr. 987–8; *Mordecai Hagadol*, p. 153c; Tesh. Maim. to *Mishpatim*, 7; cf. ibid. 43; Maharil, *Responsa* 75.

333

Q. In order to be entitled to her *ketubah*, a widow must take an oath that she did not steal, retain, or use any of her husband's property in any manner not specifically permitted by her husband. It is, however, only natural for a wife, during her marital status, to donate small sums of her husband's money (to relatives or to charity) without the husband's knowledge. Of such money, she usually keeps no account, and is not in a position to remember each donation. How, then, can a widow take this oath without violating her conscience?

A. If the widow can not approximate the exact sum she spent without her husband's knowledge or permission, let her forego a great part of her *ketubah* rather than hazard the taking of a false oath.

SOURCES: Pr. 117.

334

Q. A set apart the land upon which he dwelt for the payment of his wife's *ketubah*. After his death, the trustee of the orphans demanded that A's widow take an oath to the effect that she did not appropriate anything that belonged to her husband, before she be permitted to collect her *ketubah* from this real estate. Is the trustee justified in his demand?

A. Since the property was mortgaged to A's widow, she is now considered to be in possession of her *ketubah*. And as long as she does not demand her *ketubah*, she is not required to take an oath (Ket. 87b) unless the orphans claim positive knowledge of her having appropriated anything that belonged to their father. Therefore, A's widow is not required to take an oath.

SOURCES: Cr. 266; Am II, 6; Mord. Ket. 224. Cf. Moses Minz, *Responsa* 96.

335 (D)

Q. A died and left a widow, a son and a daughter. The widow, without taking the usual oath regarding her *ketubah*, came to an agreement with the orphans regarding A's estate, and undertook to support them until they reach a certain age. The daughter died while she was still young. Now, the son demands from his mother the amount not expended for the support of the daughter.

A. The widow owes nothing to her son.

SOURCES: Pr. 860.

336 (D)

Q. A formally released his mother, L, from the obligation of taking the required oath regarding her *ketubah*, and gave her the right to will the property to whomever she might please, to sons and to daughters, to give more to some and less to others, on condition that she transfer to A a particular piece of real property forthwith. Immediately after the formal release, however, A said to his mother that since this real property was mortgaged, her release was not to become effective till she redeem it for him. L promised to redeem it. Now, however, she refuses to do so.

A. Unless L redeem the above property, her agreement with A is void, for A's last stipulation proves that he had originally agreed to release L on condition only that she transfer the property to him unencumbered by mortgages. Moreover, a stipulation made immediately after an agreement is concluded, but while the matter is still being discussed, becomes part of the agreement (B. B. 114a).

SOURCES: Cr. 96.

337

Q. L, a widow, summons to court her father's half-brother, A, who with L's father were children of the same father, B, but not of the same mother, and claims that the movables, immovables, and books which A inherited from his mother did not belong to his mother since she did not take the required oath regarding her *ketubah*. A avers that his mother told him: a) that his father, B, left no money beyond what was necessary to repay his debts; b) that he left a house, vineyards, and books; and c) that he gave her the house and the vineyards as an outright gift. A further claims: a) that his father gave him the books as a gift; b) that his father freed his mother from the necessity of taking an oath and forewent the return of any money she might have taken from him; c) that the above transactions were properly recorded by B in a written instrument; and d) that A's brothers and even L and her husband, forwent their claims against his mother and gave her written instruments to that effect.

A. If A was in undisturbed possesssion of the litigated immovables for three years, or if his mother had dug pits and trenches in the immovables or had sold parts thereof three years prior to her death, we uphold A's claim if supported by an oath, since he had recourse to a *miggo* (he could have claimed that he had purchased the immovables from his brothers, or that his mother had purchased them); otherwise, A must return the immovables to his father's estate. Regarding the books, however, if witnesses did not see B's books in A's possession, A would be entitled to retain them upon taking an oath in support of his claim. If witnesses saw B's books in A's possession A would have to return them to the estate. L, on the other hand, will not be entitled to any part of the property thus returned to the estate, unless she takes an oath to the effect that she had never relinquished her rights to such property.

Sources: Mord. B.B. 527; *Agudah* B.B. 72. Cf. Moses Minz, *Responsa* 96; *Terumat Hadeshen* 330.

338

Q. When A died he was survived by his wife, L, his son, C, and his daughter. Subsequently L married B and brought him as her dowry that which she had taken from A's estate, namely: fifty *marks* and a half interest in A's books. The other half interest in the books she gave to her son C. The money and books, however, did not cover the amount L was entitled to according to her *ketubah*. Furthermore, when L gave her money to B she stipulated that he clothe and sustain her son and daughter, that he hire teachers for her son, and that he provide a dowry for her daughter. When C grew up, B decided to dissolve his partnership with C in the books. He invited the worthies of the community and in their presence the books were equally divided by lot between B and C. Subsequently L died. Whereupon C demanded that B return to him all he had received from L, since the latter had not taken the required oath regarding her *ketubah* and consequently had nothing of her own to give to B.

A. Unless C can prove that L had taken from A's estate more than the amount that was due her according to her *ketubah*, B owes nothing to C. If L were alive she would have been required to take an oath regarding her *ketubah*, but no oath is required of her heirs. However, if L gave immovables to B, as part of her dowry, the burden of proof regarding L's title to these immovables would lie with B, for the legal advantage enjoyed by the litigant who is in possession of the litigated money, is entirely absent when immovables are the subjects of the litigation.

SOURCES: Mord. B.B. 547. Cf. Moses Minz, *Responsa* 96; *Terumat Hadeshen* 330.

339

Q. L, A's widow who has had no children with A, gave away his books to religious (or charitable) institutions of two or three communities, before she took the required oath regarding her *ketubah*. A's heirs summoned her to court claiming that she had taken from A more than was due her according to her *ketubah*. L appeared in court and was ready to take the required oath regarding her *ketubah*, but died before she could do so. L's trustee asked the judges how to dispose of the books that were entrusted to him, and the judges instructed him to deliver them to the donee institutions. Now A's heirs demand the return of these books.

A. This is a highly controversial subject. The court of Würzburg — and I believe also of Speyer, following a decision by R. Simha — usually follow the decision of R. Eliezer (Shebu. 48a) which in our case would be in favor of the donees. However, we follow the ruling of Rav and Samuel (ibid.) that the entire estate belongs to the heirs. According to our opinion, therefore, even if the donee has already taken possession of the widow's gift, it should be returned to the heirs; but, if the donee has originally taken possession of the gift at the instruction of a court, we usually uphold the court's decision on the assumption that the court has followed the opinion of R. Eliezer (ibid. 48b). However, you state that the court has also decided that L's heirs have no claim on A's estate; they followed, therefore, the opinion of Rav and Samuel. Thus their decision in favor of the donees can no longer be construed as following the opinion of R. Eliezer, and must be considered a mere error.

SOURCES: Cr. 88.

340

Q. Leah, A's widow who was now the wife of C, had taken the proper oath regarding her *ketubah* before a court, whereupon the court had transferred to her A's house in payment of her *ketubah*. This house had been originally given to A by his father, B, who had distributed the rest of his property among his (B's) sons-in-law as gifts *causa mortis*. B's sons-in-law now claim to possess a deed to the effect that B gave the house to A with the stipulation that, in case A died childless, the house should belong to B's daughters. [Since A died childless] B's sons-in-law demand the house.

A. Since A was the legal heir to the house, B had no power to terminate A's normal right of conveying his inheritance to his heirs (cf. B. B. 133a). Therefore, B's stipulation limiting A's normal right of inheritance was void; the house unreservedly belonged to A, and Leah, his widow, had the right to collect her *ketubah* therefrom.

SOURCES: Cr. 260; P. 287; Mord. B.B. 595; Hag. Maim., *Zekiah* 12, 3; Asher *Responsa* 84, 2; *Tur Hoshen Mishpat* 248; *Agudah* B.B. 180.

341

1) *Q.* A married a widow, B, and lived with her for eight years till her death. B had not taken the customary widow's oath regarding her *ketubah* due her from her former husband. When she married A she was not considered very rich and no one suspected that she owned more than the value of her *ketubah*. But, after her death, when A declared, under oath, to the community (leaders, probably for purposes of taxation) the value of his assets, it was discovered that he had inherited from B more than the value of her *ketubah* from her former husband. The heirs of the latter, therefore, demand that A return the excess to them.

A. If the valuables B brought to A were undistinguishable and no one recognized them as having belonged to B's former husband, A is free from obligation for five reasons. a) Even if the valuables B brought to A were worth more than the value of her *ketubah*, such valuables may not all necessarily have come from the estate of her former husband, for she might have received some gifts or found a treasure. b) Were B still alive she would have been obliged to take an oath [to the effect that she did not take from her former husband more than the value of her *ketubah*], but now that she is dead, A is free from the obligation of taking an oath, since he is not supposed to know his wife's affairs. c) A is not even required to take the oath of an heir — that B never told him, and that he did not know that she had received from the estate of her former husband more than the value of her *ketubah* — since the heirs of

B's former husband are not positive in their claim. The heirs, however, may pronounce the ban (*herem*) in the synagogue against anyone who does possess such knowledge and does not reveal it. Such ban would include A. d) Whatever a person would have retained, had he taken an oath, his heirs may retain without the necessity of taking an oath. e) Some authorities require A to take the oath of an heir; but since many great authorities absolve him from such oath, and since A is in possession of the aforesaid valuables, the burden of proof is upon the plaintiff. For similar reasons A would be free from the obligation of taking an oath, even if some of the valuables brought to him by B were distinguishable and were recognized as having belonged to B's former husband, if the valuables thus recognized were in themselves not worth more than the value of B's *ketubah*. But, if the distinguishable valuables are in themselves worth more than the value of B's *ketubah*, A must return the difference to the heirs of B's first husband.

2) *Q*. Witnesses have testified to the effect that B and her former husband, C, had made a binding agreement that in the event of the death of one party, the surviving party would share the property with the heirs. After C's death, B settled with all of C's heirs, except the youngest, D, who was born after the drawing up of the agreement. D, therefore, is now pressing his claim.

A. D was entitled to his share even though he was born after the agreement was made, for in it B did not bestow benefits on anybody; she merely relinquished her rights to C's property up to a certain extent, and D later became heir to the relinquished property. However, A may claim that B brought him nothing from C's estate, or he may contend that B had already settled with D, and be free from obligation for the reasons enumerated above.

Sources: Am II, 17; cf. Hayyim Or Zarua, *Responsa* 86; ibid. 165; ibid. 191.

342

Q. A drew up a legal document in which he used the following words: "Effective as of today, but to be executed after our (meaning himself and his wife, L) deaths, our daughter R shall inherit an equal share with her brothers, those already born and those that might be born, in whatever will remain of my estate." After A's death, his children and his widow, L, interpreted the document to mean that A had appointed L trustee over his estate. When L proved a very inefficient, careless, and wasteful trustee, A's sons reached an agreement with L, whereby she was to receive forty *marks* for turning over the estate to A's sons immediately. Before relinquishing her trusteeship, L and her youngest son B (who was eighteen years of age) agreed to allow R's husband to take his wife's share of the estate immediately, without having to wait for L's death. A's two other sons object to this latter agreement.

A. A's heirs were entitled to take over his estate at any time they wished to do so. The giving of forty *marks* to L in order that she relinquish her trusteeship, was entirely unnecessary, for A's document, while making the collection of R's share in A's estate dependant on L's death, did not appoint L trustee of said estate. Moreover, had A explicitly appointed L trustee of his estate, the court would have removed her at no expense to the heirs, since she had proven to be inefficient, careless, and wasteful. The second agreement is not binding on A's two sons since L, not being a trustee of the estate, had no legal power to dispose of part of the estate. B, however, was able to forego his own part of R's share, and his act is binding upon such part if R (or her husband) was in possession of her share at the time of the latter agreement. Thus R would be entitled to receive one third of her share (B's part of her share) immediately, while B's two brothers would manage the other two-thirds for their own profit and gain until L's death.

Although the brothers are entitled to manage R's share for
their own profit, they are not permitted to sell or otherwise
alienate any part of it; and their responsibility thereto would
be that of a gratuitous watchman. Thus any increase that
will accrue until L's death will belong to the brothers, while,
any decrease of value caused by theft, loss or unavoidable
accident will be suffered by R. Should the brothers be called
upon to pay L her *ketubah*, one quarter of such payment should
come out of R's share. R may not claim that her father has
made her an outright gift, free of any lien or obligation, since
A did not intend to give R a greater share than that of his sons.
After L's death, R may exact an oath from her brothers to the
effect that they did not retain for themselves anything belonging to her.

2) *Q.* L's trustee claimed that L's property which she had
given to her husband, had been given only to gratify him, but
had not been intended as an outright gift. Therefore, this
property had belonged to L; and she gave it to her mother
by right.

A. This property was not listed in L's *ketubah*, and was
thus considered *niksei melug* regarding which a woman may
not claim that her gift thereof to her husband was not actually
meant to be binding but was given in order to gratify him
(B. B. 50a). Therefore, the gift was binding, and she no longer
had any claim to said property. She had no right to give it
to her mother.

This Resp. is addressed to: "My teacher Rabbi Eliezer
b. Ephraim."

SOURCES: Cr. 30; Pr. 243–4; Am II, 18.

343

Q. A claims that his father before his death declared in
his will that a certain amount be given to A's mother. A wants

to pay that amount to his mother, but she insists on collecting her *ketubah*.

A. Since A's father did not declare his last will in the presence of his wife, she was not bound by such will. She is therefore entitled to collect her *ketubah* in full.

SOURCES: Mord. B.B. 587.

344

Q. A rented a house to B for five years and received the rent for the entire period in advance. He promised to repay B the expenses for any structures he might erect in the house, and gave him a written guaranty to this effect. B spent six pounds on such structures. Subsequently, A died and his widow, L, took over the house in payment of her *ketubah*.

A. B must vacate the house; for L's *ketubah* was a lien upon it, before it was rented to B. L may remove anyone from the house, whether buyer, renter, or creditor; provided, of course, that her marriage to A took place, and A was owner of the house, before he sold it, rented it, or borrowed money. Therefore, if A left no movables and his estate does not exceed L's *ketubah*, B can not reclaim his money. If, however, A left movables with a third person, these movables ought to be turned over to B in payment of the obligation due him, and any excess should go to L. Whenever a creditor and a widow press their claims to an estate consisting of movables — unless the movables had previously been set aside by the husband for the payment of his wife's *ketubah* — the creditor has priority over the widow. The creditor's priority, however, as against the widow extends only to the payment of the *Ikkar ketubah*, the additional jointure, and that part of the dowry which the husband wrote in the *ketubah* in excess of what she actually gave him as dowry — thus in our *ketubah* we uniformly write that the wife brought in a dowry worth fifty pounds, regardless of the actual value of her dowry, and in our country a woman collects one hundred *marks* as her dowry, since we interpret the term "pound" to be a pound of weight, consisting of two *marks*. In regard to whatever the widow actually brought in as dowry she is considered a creditor sharing equally with other creditors in collecting from movables. Although a woman is entitled to collect the entire amount her husband wrote in the dowry clause of her *ketubah* in excess of what she actually brought in, she does not have equal right with a creditor in collecting that excess. Therefore, since in collecting her actual dowry from movables, L is on an equal footing with B, the movables mentioned above must be equally divided between L and B (and not in proportion to the respective obligations). When an estate consists of movables and immovables, and the latter do not suffice to cover the *ketubah*, the widow collects the *Ikkar ketubah*, the additional jointure, and the excess dowry, from the immovables, while she takes her part of the movables in payment of her actual dowry. The creditor may not claim that the immovables taken by the widow are in payment of her actual dowry, while she may not collect the rest of the *ketubah* from the movables until he, the creditor, collects his full debt therefrom, for the *Ikkar ketubah* and the additional jointure are liens upon the immovables, while in regard to the actual dowry she is considered a creditor entitled to share with the other creditors in collecting from movables (cf. Ket. 86a).

Sources: Am II, 67.

345

Q. After L, a widow, remarried, she presented for collection the *ketubah* she had received from her first husband. In the absence of unencumbered property, L sought to collect her *ketubah* from a piece of the real estate which her former husband had sold to A. A, in turn, had sold the real estate to B; and after the latter's death, it fell to his orphans some of whom were minors. L contended that her husband had sold the real estate without her consent, and without obtaining her signature to the deed.

A. If L will take an oath to the effect that she did not as yet collect any part of her *ketubah*, and that she did not consent to the sale of the above property, she will be entitled to evict B's heirs from it. The talmudic statement you quote in the query: "after a widow remarries, the burden of proof lies on her shoulders (ket. 96b)", does not apply to a case where the widow seeks to collect her *ketubah*. Moreover, the *ketubah*-document in itself constitutes adequate and sufficient proof of the fact that the widow did not collect her *ketubah*. The fact that B's heirs are able to prove three years of undisturbed possession, also has no bearing on the case. A widow is not required to protest the occupancy by another of real property which does not belong to her, but which she may eventually come to seize in payment of her *ketubah*.

This responsum is addressed to: "my teacher Rabbi Joseph".

SOURCES: Tesh. Maim. to *Ishut 5*; *Mordecai Hagadol*, p. 310c.

346 (D)

Q. A widow, who seized the property left by her husband but did not take the required oath regarding her *ketubah*, donated part of such property to a sacred cause. Has the donation become sacred?

A. Since the property did not belong to the widow, she could not render it sacred, and the orphans are entitled to take it back.

SOURCES: Am II, 16.

347 (D)

Q. A widow seized the property of her late husband. She kept it for years; some of it she squandered, and some of it she gave away as presents. Now the orphans demand that she take an oath regarding her management of the aforesaid property.

A. The orphans are justified in their demand that the widow take an oath regarding the property she has squandered or given away. Although the Yerushalmi rules that a widow who seized the property of her late husband is not required to render an accounting, Ritzba (R. Isaak b. Abraham) is of the opinion that this ruling of the Yerushalmi applies only when the widow is expected eventually to take an oath regarding her *ketubah*.

SOURCES: Am II, 14.

348

Q. L, B's widow, seized all of his movables in payment of her *ketubah*. Subsequently, A, B's creditor, produced B's note of indebtedness and by the use of force took away the movables from L.

A. A acted within his rights. The ruling of the Talmud (Ket. 86a), which gives the debtor precedence over the widow in the settlement of an estate, is to be enforced even if the widow has already seized her husband's property.

SOURCES: Cr. 195; Hag. Maim., *Ishut* 17, 2. Cf. Asher, *Responsa* 79, 1; Weil, *Responsa* 30.

349

Q. A widow demands her *ketubah* and a creditor demands his money from an estate. Who has priority in collecting from the estate?

A. The creditor has priority over the widow. Moreover, even when the estate consists of assets only to satisfy one of the claimants, the creditor is paid in preference to the widow. In our times, since the creditor as well as the widow collects from unencumbered movables, the creditor has priority over the widow in collecting from such movables.

SOURCES: Cr. 140; P. 283. Cf. Asher, *Responsa* 79, 1; Weil, *Responsa* 30.

350

Q. A creditor demanded his money from a critically ill person. The latter admitted the indebtedness and ordered his heirs to repay the debt. Do you follow the decision of R. Tam that a widow has priority over a creditor in collecting (her *ketubah*) from movables, or the decision of Alfasi and the Geonim that the creditor has priority over the widow?

A. No difference of opinion exists between R. Tam and the Geonim in regard to this law. Even the former admits that nowadays, when the ordinance of the Saburaim gives the creditor the right to collect his debt from movables even after the debtor's death, the creditor has priority over the widow in collecting from movables.

SOURCES: Pr. 334; Am II, 68; Tesh. Maim. to *Ishut*, 23.

351

Q. The trustee of the charity-chest claims that he lent money from the charity-chest to A, L's late husband, and that the money is now in L's possession. L avers that she does not know who gave this money to her late husband, but that she took whatever she could find belonging to him in payment of her *ketubah*.

A. If the trustee cannot produce A's note of indebtedness, he has no claim against L, since she may deny the indebtedness altogether, or may maintain that her husband repaid his debt to the charity-chest. If the trustee, however, produces A's note of indebtedness, the signatures of which were identified in court, he takes precedence over L in collecting from A's estate. Even if L has already taken possession of A's valuables in payment of her *ketubah*, these must be taken away from her and given to the trustee in payment of A's debt. We rendered a similar decision in Frankfort some time ago.

SOURCES: *Mordecai Hagadol*, p. 171c.

352

1) *Q.* A owed one *minah* to B. He promised that he would repay the money on a specified date, or that his sureties, C and D, would either repay it themselves or would eat two meals a day to be charged to A. A made a binding promise to C and D, accompanied by a solemn hand-clasp, to compensate them for any losses they might suffer on account of their suretyship; and he gave them a written document to that effect. Before the debt fell due, however, A died leaving orphans and a widow, but not enough property to cover the latter's *ketubah*. B demands that the sureties either eat at the expense of A's estate, or pay him one *minah*. Who has priority in collecting from the estate, the creditor or the widow? Is this case similar to the case when interest is accumulating on the obligations of young orphans [in which case the court must attend immediately to the affairs of the estate in order to save the money of the orphans], or is it not similar to this case for the reason that in our case the orphans can receive no part of the estate in any event?

A. Nowadays that a creditor may collect his debt from the movables of an estate, he has priority over the widow in collecting from movables. The orphans are not considered at all in this case, since they can receive no part of the estate in any event.

2) *Q.* When A married L she had small children. She said to A that she would give him a dowry of thirty *marks*, and

would keep her remaining twenty *marks* for her children. The twenty *marks*, however, were not kept separately and they (A and L) did business with the entire sum. Subsequently A died, and L claimed that the greater part of the money he left belonged to her young children. Do we assume that since A did business with the money it belonged to him?

A. If the money is in L's possession and we have no evidence (but her admission) that she possesses it, L must take an oath in support of her claim. We must be satisfied with this oath since she could have successfully denied possessing the money. But, if the money is not in her possession, or we have evidence that she possesses it, she must produce witnesses in support of her claim.

3) *Q.* Does a widow who is not admitted to oaths, lose her *ketubah* since she cannot take the required oath?

There is no answer to this query. The three questions bear the signatures of: Joseph b. Moses, Nathan b. Jacob, and Isaac b. Solomon.

SOURCES: Am II, 69–70.

353

Q. A widow seized notes of indebtedness and bonds of Gentiles, that were made out both in her name and in the name of her husband. Does this act constitute seizure of the debts?

A. The widow has to produce evidence to the effect that the money represented by the notes and the bonds was actually her money. Furthermore, possession of notes and bonds, does not imply the right to the money and property described therein. Thus seizure of the notes and the bonds does not constitute seizure of the debts.

SOURCES: P. 282; Mord. B.B. 562; *Agudah* B.B. 123. Cf. Maharil, *Responsa* 75.

354

Q. A left four daughters and no sons. His widow claims that B owed money to her deceased husband, and seeks to recover it in payment of her *ketubah.*

A. In talmudic times a widow could collect her *ketubah* from real property only; therefore, it is stated in the Talmud that when a person dies, his debtors or depositaries shall repay their obligations to the person's heirs and not to his widow. But, the Geonim enacted a law that a woman may collect her *ketubah* from movable property and even from property her husband has given away to his heirs before his death. Nowadays, then, a woman may collect her *ketubah* from her husband's property in the hands of debtors and depositaries. Therefore, if the widow will swear that A did not leave her enough property to cover her *ketubah,* B must pay her the money he owed A. If B denies that he owes anything to A, he must take an oath to that effect and be free from obligation.

Sources: Cr. 85; Pr. 211; Am II, 8.

355 (D)

Q. Does a woman collect her *ketubah* from a loan that has been secured by a pledge at the time the loan was contracted? Does a first-born son receive a double share from such a loan?

A. A woman may collect her *ketubah* from all loans, even from loans that are not secured by pledges. Nowadays especially, since a woman may collect her *ketubah* from movables — and even after the loan is repaid to the orphans she may demand the money thus repaid in payment of her *ketubah* — she is entitled to collect directly from the debtor. Moreover, the custom of collecting the *ketubah* from movables and from loans, is well established in our time. Such a custom may be justified by the fact that the major part of our business consists of loans and investments. Similarly a first-born is entitled to a double share from a loan that had been secured by a pledge, since such a loan is not considered *raui* (a potential asset) but constitutes a real asset of the estate.

SOURCES: Am II, 66.

356

Q. A Gentile stole a book from A, who never gave up hope of recovering it. After A's death the book was recovered from the thief. Did this book, at the time of A's death, constitute an actual asset of A's estate, in which case A's widow would be entitled to collect her *ketubah* therefrom; or did it constitute merely a potential asset?

A. A's widow is entitled to take the book in payment of her *ketubah*; for, wherever the book was at the time of A's death, it belonged to A.

SOURCES: Mord. B.B. 574.

357 (D)

Q. A's estate was not sufficient for the purpose of paying his wife's *ketubah*. The widow, however, improved the estate. Is she entitled to collect her *ketubah*, from the increase in value that resulted from her efforts? I believe that such increase belongs to the orphans.

A. Your decision is correct. Since the widow derived her sustenance from the property of the orphans*, the fruit of her labor belonged to them.

SOURCES: Am II, 15.

358

Q. The property A left when he died was sufficient to cover but part of his wife's *ketubah*. The widow claimed A's

---

* As long as the widow did not take the required oath regarding her *ketubah*, the estate belonged to the orphans.

entire property in payment of her *ketubah*, and refused to allow the use of any part of it to pay for A's burial expenses. Is the widow entitled to her claim?

A. The widow is under no obligation to pay for her husband's burial. She is entitled to collect her *ketubah* from all of A's property; and if nothing is left to pay for A's funeral expenses, such expenses must be covered by charity funds.

Sources: Cr. 243; Pr. 176, 964. Mord .Ket. 157; Rashba I, 1103; *Tashbetz,* 491; *Mordecai Hagadol,* p. 177a; Hag. Maim. *Ishut* 17, 4. Cf. Cr. 184; Weil, *Responsa* 78; ibid. 156; Moses Minz, *Responsa* 22; ibid. 53.

359

Q. A's mother defrayed the expenses of A's funeral but did so only in the nature of a loan to his estate. His widow, however, refused to repay the money to A's mother and insisted in taking his entire estate in payment of her *ketubah*.

A. A's funeral expenses must be defrayed with money taken from his estate, before his widow can collect her *ketubah* from it. Thus a person may not give away all his possessions to his heirs in the expectation that his funeral expenses would be paid from public funds (Ket. 48a); the same principle should apply when one gives away all his possessions to his wife. The claims of a creditor, however, should have priority over the decedent's funeral expenses, since the appropriation of a creditor's own money to pay another person's funeral expenses would constitute downright thievery. On the other hand, just as an exemption of bedding, food for thirty days, and clothing to last twelve months, is allowed to a bankrupt debtor (B. M. 113b), so an exemption of the bare funeral expenses should be allowed in the case of a decedent's insolvent estate as against both the creditor and the widow.

This Responsum is addressed to Rabbi Israel, and the decision is in direct contradiction of that recorded in Cr. 184;

ibid, 243; Pr. 176; ibid. 964; Mord. Ket. 157; Rashba I, 1103; and Tashbetz, 491.

SOURCES: Pr. 926; *Mordecai Hagadol*, p. 176c.

360

Q. R. Eliezer bound himself by a *herem* to give his daughter Gutlin, a minor, in marriage to Miriam's son, Isaac Levi, also a minor; and Miriam also obligated herself by a *herem*. Both parents put up a trust fund of three pounds for the couple, on condition that in case one of the parties dies before marriage the parents should divide between themselves the principal and the accrued interest. R. Eliezer died, and subsequently, but before her marriage, his daughter also died. A young son by a former marriage, who is also motherless, and a widow survived him. The trustee of the orphan, appointed by the community, and the widow, both made claims to one half of the trust-fund money. To whom should it be given?

It seems to me that the orphan is entitled to this money since it was not an actual asset at the time R. Eliezer died, and a widow collects her *ketubah* only from actual assets. The fact that the widow is in possession of the money, as the court gave it to her temporarily, does not make this asset any more actual as is evident from the case, quoted in the Talmud, of the woman with whom notes of indebtedness were deposited (Ket. 85a). Neither does the principle of *Miggo* apply to her since the money was given to her by the court and since the previous year she was obliged to make out a detailed statement of her assets, for the purpose of taxation and assessment for charity, in which statement the trust-money was listed. Signed: Moses Azriel.

A. Since half of the fund which belonged to R. Eliezer was to be given to the couple on their wedding day and was to be returned to R. Eliezer in case of death, it did not leave R. Eliezer's possession, and was, therefore, at the time of his death, an actual asset of his estate from which his widow is entitled to collect her *ketubah*. The widow is further entitled to collect her *ketubah* from the interest that accrued on the investment up to R. Eliezer's death, but not from the interest that accrued after his death.

SOURCES: Pr. 981; *Mordecai Hagadol*, p. 172b.

361

Q. While still in good health, A deposited a sum of money with B and instructed him to give it to his (A's) son C upon the latter's marriage. A died. Subsequently, but before his marriage, C also died. Can A's widow collect her *ketubah* from the money deposited with B, or must B return the money to C's heirs?

A. Since C did not marry before A's death, and since the money never came into C's possession, it never belonged to C, and A's widow is, therefore, entitled to collect her *ketubah* from that money. A widow is entitled to collect her *ketubah* from all bequests made *causa mortis*, and from all gifts that are not legally to be delivered to the donee (as in cases where the donor died before the stipulated date of delivery of the gift) but which must be so delivered for the reason that "it is a meritorious act to fulfill the expressed wishes of a dying person" (Gittin, 15a).

SOURCES: Pr. 966; Mord. B.B. 629.

362

Q. A entrusted valuables to B to be given to A's daughter upon A's death. A and his daughter died at the same time. A's widow claims that the daughter died first and demands the valuables in payment of her *ketubah*. B claims that A died first, and therefore wishes to give the valuables to the daughter's heirs.

A. Even if A died first, his widow is entitled to the valuables in payment of her *ketubah*. A widow is entitled to the payment of her *ketubah* out of all gifts made by the husband which were to become effective after his death, even though he was in good health at the time that he made the gift.

SOURCES: Pr. 99.

363

Q. Rachel's husband became an apostate. She gave him one-half *mark* as the price of his granting her a divorce. After the divorce was delivered, the witnesses to the instrument went to R's father, and with his permission tore up R's *ketubah*. A had in his possession a deposit belonging to R's husband. R demanded that A give her the deposit in payment of her *ketubah*. The apostate, on the other hand, threatened A with great injury unless he returned the deposit to him.

A. Although the tearing of R's *ketubah* by her father does not cancel the apostate's obligation to R, A may not be forced to risk his life or property by handing over the deposit to R. A, therefore, should try to settle with the apostate for as little as possible, and give the remainder to R.

This Resp. is addressed to "my teachers and relatives, R. Joseph Kohen and R. Jacob."

SOURCES: Cr. 288; Pr. 974; Tesh. Maim. to *Nezikim*, 7; *Mordecai Hagadol*, p. 194b; ibid. p. 379c.

364

Q. A widow seized for her sustenance all the money left by her late husband. The orphans claim that she thus seized more than the value of her *ketubah*. May she be compelled to return the money?

A. Although R. Isaac b. Abraham believes that the talmudic ruling, "a widow who seized (her husband's) valuables for her sustenance may retain such valuables (Ket. 96a)," applies to cases where it is known that the widow seized less than the value of her *ketubah;* his brother, R. Samson b. Abraham, and Maimonides, believe that the ruling applies to any amount seized by the widow, for the amount a widow may need for her sustenance is indeterminate. Therefore, the widow may retain the money she has seized for her sustenance. She need take no oath as to the amount seized, since such oath would serve no purpose. However, should she subsequently demand additional funds for her sustenance, she would have to take an oath as to the amount she seized and to the manner she used it. She may restrain the orphans from selling immovables they inherited from her late husband since her sustenance is a lien upon such property, but she can not invalidate a sale already concluded.

Sources: L. 394; Am II, 3; Mord. Ket. 251; Tesh. Maim. to *Nashim,* 27; Asheri Ket. 11, 3. Cf. Cr. 129b.

365

Q. A's heirs refuse to support, out of their inheritance, all the members of the household of A's widow.

A. If the widow had a servant while A was alive, she is entitled to have one now that A is dead; and this servant must be supported out of A's estate.

Sources: Cr. 275; L. 244; *Mordecai Hagadol,* p. 371a.

366

Q. A died leaving several bad debts (investments). Since these debts are worth very little, may A's widow and daughter use the money exclusively for their own sustenance, while A's sons may be forced to go begging from door to door?

A. The law, which provides that daughters be entitled to derive their sustenance from movables left by their father, was instituted by the Geonim. Male and female orphans were placed by them on an equal footing in regard to such movables.

Sources: Cr. 267; *Mordecai Hagadol*, p. 183a; ibid. p. 322d.

367

Q. Does the custom of the Galileans prevail, which provides that the widow is entitled to receive her sustenance out of her husband's estate all the days of her widowhood until she demand her *ketubah*; or is the custom of the Judeans to be followed, which provides that the heirs may discontinue providing her sustenance as soon as they are ready to pay her the *ketubah* (Ket. 52b, 54a)?

A. Opinions differ on this subject and I should not dare to decide between the authorities. However, we always follow the decisions of Alfasi whenever they are not contradicted by the Tosaphists. In this case the Tosaphists specifically agree with Alfasi that the custom of the Galileans was to be followed. The fact that two or three members of your community found it necessary to insert, in the *ketubot* they gave to their wives, the clause: "after my death, should you desire to remain a widow the rest of your life you may take possession of all my property" does not prove that your community has adopted the Judean custom. These individuals may have merely re-iterated the accepted custom for the sake of emphasis. More-over, this clause is not entirely superflous even in a community where the Galilean custom prevails; for it strengthens the widow's position inasmuch as it makes her master of the estate, while according to the Galilean custom she is only to receive thirty-day allowances at a time. Neither does the fact that some widows in your community have been ousted from their husbands' estates by being paid their *ketubah*, prove that you

have adopted the Judean custom. Mere ignorance of their
rights may have been the only reason these widows did not
protest against such an ouster.

SOURCES: P. 281; Am. II, 4; Mord. Ket. 170. Cf. Moses Minz, *Responsa* 5;
ibid. 17; *Terumat Hadeshen* 335, Isserlein, *Pesakim* 223.

368

Q. A left two daughters, one of whom is married. May
his widow collect money for her sustenance from the possessions
of A's married daughter?

A. A's married daughter must support his widow, or pay
her the *ketubah* only from the valuables she inherited from A,
but not from any gifts she received from him during his life,
unless such gifts were made *causa mortis*.

This Responsum is addressed to R. Moses.

SOURCES: Cr. 287; Pr. 224; *Mordecai Hagadol*, p. 178c.

369

Q. L, a widow, demands her father-in-law's possessions
from her levir. Is she entitled to collect them?

A. You did not state your question clearly. If L received
halitzah and now demands her *ketubah*, she is entitled to collect
it from her husband's share of his father's estate, provided
her husband died after her father-in-law. If L married the
levir, she thereby transferred to him all of her husband's possessions, both actual and potential.

SOURCES: Cr. 264. Cf. Mord. Ket. 170; Israel Bruno, *Responsa* 21.

370

Q. A died a short time after his marriage. According to
Rabbi (Alexander) Susskin ha-Kohen, an ordinance had been
adopted by the communities to the effect that where either

husband or wife died within two years of marriage, the heirs of the deceased person were entitled to half the dowry (i. e. half the presents given to the deceased person by his, or her, relatives at the time of the marriage). Is A's widow entitled to the full amount of her *ketubah*, or does the rule of the communities prevail?

A. R. Meir answered that he never heard of such an ordinance before he was told of it by R. Susskin; that he still doubted its existence; and that he found it hard to believe that the communities would adopt an ordinance the effect of which would be to rob a woman of her *ketubah*. He, therefore, referred the author of the inquiry to the Rabbis of Würzburg, whose decision, in regard to community ordinances, he accepted as final.

SOURCES: Pr. 934. Cf. Maharil *Responsa* 76.

371

Q. Mice nibbled at a *ketubah*-document tearing out pieces thereof.

A. The husband must write a new document. Although a legal writ is still valid even when torn, except when rent by a court cancellation (B. B. 168b), when words are missing it is invalid.

SOURCES: Tesh. Maim. to *Mishpatim*, 62.

372

Q. May we coerce an epileptic by flagellation to divorce his wife?

A. Although the proof adduced by Rabbi Simha from the Yerushalmi (Ket. 7, 8) that an epileptic may be coerced, is convincing, while the objections raised by Rabiah may easily be removed, we never heard that the great Rabbis, our predecessors, have here used means of coercion. How, then, can we, orphaned and humbled as we are, resort to such strong measures.

This Responsum is addressed to Rabbi Menahem.

SOURCES: B. p. 281, no. 154; cf. Mord. Ket. 201.

373

Q. A wants to emigrate to Palestine, but his wife, L, refuses to accompany him. Is he permitted to divorce her?

A. The Talmud (Ket. 110b) rules that under the circumstances, the husband is permitted to divorce his wife and is not required to pay her the *ketubah*. Although some scholars believe that this talmudic ruling applied only during the period of the Temple, while Israel dwelt on his land, and that it does not apply at present, we must make no such distinction, for the contradiction between the statement of the Babylonian Talmud (ibid.) and that of the Palestinian Talmud (Ket. end), may be reconciled if we assume that the latter refers to the present. Regarding the payment of the *ketubah*, however, A is not required to pay L the *Ikkar ketubah* and the additional jointure, but he is required to pay her whatever she has brought in as her dowry (*niksei tson barzel*) and whatever is left of her *niksei melug* (private property of the wife). Moreover, should A subsequently return from Palestine, he would be required to pay L or her heirs the *Ikkar ketubah* and the additional jointure.

This Responsum is addressed to Rabbi Isaac and Rabbi Yekutiel haLevi.

SOURCES: Cr. 199; Am II, 78; Mord. Ket. 280. Cf. Moses Minz, *Responsa* 96.

374

Q. Witnesses testified that A's wife had committed an act forbidden to her by ban and oath. Moreover she brought forward a scoundrel who was in love with her and who threatened to kill A should he mistreat her. Is A permitted to divorce his wife against her will? Is she entitled to her *ketubah*?

A. A is enjoined to divorce his wife since she disregarded a ban and an oath and thus transgressed against Mosaic law. The ban of Rabbenu Gershon against divorcing one's wife without her consent, was not directed against those husbands who perform meritorious deeds by divorcing their wives. However, since A's wife claims that she was not forewarned of the consequences of her deed, and A can produce no witnesses to prove that she was so forewarned, she will be entitled to collect her *ketubah* after receiving her divorce.

Sources: L. 245; Hag. Maim. to *Ishut*, 24, 4; Mord. Ket. 196. Cf. *Hagahot Asheri* Ket. 7, 9.

375

1) *Q.* A promised to give his wife two *marks*, of the money current at the time, before *Hanukkah* on condition that she receive her divorce. Subsequently, the burghers decreed that the use of the current coin be stopped on the first day of *Hanukkah*, and that the Friedberg Coin (וריברג״ש) be substituted as money-current.

A. Since A's promise was to pay her before *Hanukkah*, he should give her the old coin, if he pays her before the first day of *Hanukkah*.

2) *Q.* A's wife expressed the wish that her father should inherit the two *marks* in case she dies before *Hanukkah*. Since the expression "inherit" does not imply an outright gift, her father should not receive the two *marks* unless he is her rightful heir. Would not A be her rightful heir if she died before she received her divorce?

A. No; since A made known his design to divorce his wife, he is no longer her heir.

SOURCES: Pr. 1000; Mord. B.K. 113.

376

Q. Leah promised her husband, by solemn hand-clasp, to accept her divorce or pay a fine. While in the city of Worms, she expressed regret for having made such a promise. The Rabbis of Speier, having heard of her change of mind, refuse to permit the delivery of the divorce. Should Leah be fined for breaking her promise?

A. Leah only expressed her feelings. The Rabbis of Speier do not carry out her orders; she is, therefore, not responsible for their actions.

SOURCES: Pr. 87.

377 (D)

Q. A, who fell sick, gave a bill of divorce to his wife on the condition that it be valid from the time of its delivery if he should die as a result of that sickness. A died as a result of that sickness and the people did not allow his wife to touch him, weep over him, or even walk after his hearse, claiming that such action on her part would invalidate her divorce.

A. The people were wrong. It is not within the province of a wife to invalidate her divorce.

SOURCES: Pr. 857; *Mordecai Hagadol,* p. 230c.

378

Q. While critically ill, A gave a bill of divorcement to his wife on condition that should he die from this illness, she should be divorced therewith from the day she receives the divorce. After the bill of divorcement was thus delivered to A's wife,

it was torn up. Subsequently A's condition improved; he
got up from bed, walked to the synagogue and to the market
p!ace without a cane, and even arranged his mother's funeral
out of town. Twenty-eight days thereafter, however, he fell
ill again and died. During these twenty-eight days he was at
times lying in bed, and at other times he was upon his feet.
Was the bill of divorcement effective?

A. The bill of divorcement was ineffective. First, according to R. Tam and Ri the stipulated condition mentioned
above, is to be interpreted to mean that A intended the divorce to become effective an hour before his death. Since
on the day of A's death the bill of divorcement was already
torn up, no divorce took place. A similar query was sent
to me from Acco (Aachen?) and I ruled that no divorce took
place. I always advise women who receive such conditional
divorces to guard their bills of divorcement carefully till their
husbands die. Secondly, even according to Rashi, who believes that the divorce becomes effective immediately upon
the delivery of the bill of divorcement, if the husband subsequently dies from his illness, the fact that A was walking thereafter without the support of a cane nullified the bill of divorcement. In any event the advice of a medical authority would
be required in order to decide whether or not A died from his
first illness; and nowadays we have no medical authorities on
whose expert opinion we can definitely rely in such a vital
matter.

R. Meir adds: I do not possess the *Tosaphot* to tractate
Gittin, nor the code books from the south (Alfasi and Maimonides). I composed the above with the help of heavenly guide;
if you find that the *Tosaphot* and the codes hold another opinion, my opinion is nullified by theirs; for what does a poor
man know, one who dwells in darkness and gloom for three
and one half years.

This responsum was sent to Rabbi Asher from the tower of Ensisheim and was placed in his (R. Meir's) novellae in his own handwriting.

Sources: Am II, 108; Tesh. Maim. to *Nashim*, 30; *Mordecai Hagadol*, p. 229b.

379

Q. Rabbenu Tam interprets the talmudic statement: "this is thy letter of divorce, effective as of today; if I shall die ... the divorce is valid" (Git. 72a), to mean that such divorce becomes effective one hour before the man's death. According to Rabbenu Tam, therefore, what would be the status of the woman who received a letter of divorce from her husband with the provision: "this is thy letter of divorce effective as of today, if I shall not return within the next twelve months", if this letter of divorce was lost or burned within the twelve months, and her husband did not return?

A. You have done well to distinguish between the above two cases. Although in the former case, when the divorce is given by a critically ill person in order that his wife be not forced to accept *halitzah*, the phrase "effective as of today" is taken to mean one hour before the man's death, in the latter case the phrase "effective as of today" is to be taken literally.

This Responsum is addressed to "My teacher Rabbenu Perez".

Sources: Mord. Git. 430.

380

Q. A minor orphan girl was betrothed to A. She wants to exercise the right of "Refusal" (סירוב). May the testimony of female witnesses be accepted that the girl is only eleven years old and, therefore, may still exercise the right of "Refusal"?

A. The mere ceremony of betrothal, without cohabitation, is binding only because of Rabbinic enactment, but is not binding according to Biblical law. The testimony of women is acceptable in the annulment of a marriage that is valid only according to Rabbinic enactment. Therefore, since A did not cohabit with the orphan, the testimony of the female witnesses is to be admitted in evidence.

SOURCES: Cr. 286; Pr. 569; L. 389; Mord. Yeb. 60, 61; Tesh. Maim. to *Nashim*, 14.

381

Q. L, an orphan, was betrothed by her mother to A. Subsequently A was killed on a day of rioting and massacre leaving a year-old brother. L is eleven years old according to the testimony of women, and has no symptoms of pubescence. May L sever her dependence upon A's brother by "Refusal"?

A. We follow Alfasi (Yeb. 107b) who rules that a minor may sever her dependency upon her levir by "Refusal". In this case we accept the testimony of the aforesaid women regarding her age and condition.

This Responsum is addressed to Rabbi Yakar haLevi.

SOURCES: Cr. 81.

382

Q. Before his death, A bequeathed sixty pounds *Heller* (denarii of Halle) to his brothers and sisters. His childless widow, however, retains all of A's property and refuses either to marry, or to take *halitzah* from her levir.

After protracted litigation, the widow (of Speyer) and her levirs finally came to court and chose their judges. These judges asked the opinion of R. Meir who put them off and advised them to ask the great (Jewish) leaders of the

Kingdom (Germany) regarding the ordinances passed by the communities affecting the relations of a widow and her levirs. The leaders all agreed that after the rite of *halitzah* is performed, one half of the husband's estate belongs to the widow and one half to the levirs. R. Meir states that he knows no further details regarding these laws of the communities, and renders the following decision in accordance with talmudic law:

A. If A's widow, three months after his death refuses to undergo the rite of *halitzah* or marry her levir, she is to be considered as a rebellious wife and all of A's property is to be taken away from her, except that which she has brought in as a dowry, upon her marriage to A. If, however, she consents to undergo the rite of *halitzah*, she receives half of A's property, as is the *Takkanah* of the communities. From this amount is deducted the sum she admits, under oath, to have wasted, lost, and given away as presents, while A was alive and after his death.

SOURCES: Pr. 563; Mord. Yeb. 23. Cf. *Terumat Hadeshen* 220; Isserlein, *Pesakim* 262; ibid. 263; ibid. 264.

383

Q. A refuses to marry or give *halitzah* to his brother's childless widow claiming that, because a year has not yet passed since his brother's death, his deep sorrow prevents him from either marrying her or giving her *halitzah*.

A. A's temporizing is baseless and useless. Our sages have decreed that three months, and not a year or two, after a person died leaving no children, his brother must either marry the widow or give her *halitzah*. Therefore, no temporizing is permitted. A should be coerced, either by persuasion or by flagellation, into giving *halitzah* to the woman immediately. Let Gentiles belabor him till he agrees to do what he is told to do. I should prefer, however, that A be misled or deceived by offers of money till he voluntarily gives her *halitzah*. Thus the widow may officially forego her claim to her husband's money that is in A's possession, and even bind herself thereto by a *kinyan*. After the ceremony the widow would still be entitled to collect this money from A, for the court that has a right to inflict corporal punishment on A, has a right to confiscate his property if it be required by considerations of public welfare. I should prefer to practice deception on A rather than inflict flagellation, since the latter might involve great hardship, have very serious consequences, and even cause A to abscond.

SOURCES: Cr. 244; Pr. 492; P. 10; Moses Minz, *Responsa* 10.

384

Q. A believed that his brother's (childless) widow had retained from her husband's estate more than the amount due her for her *ketubah*, and he refused to go through with the ceremony of *halitzah*, unless she paid him some money. They finally agreed on the sum of 20* *marks*. Before the ceremony of *halitzah* she gave the money to a trustee in A's presence. A said to the trustee: "After the ceremony, you must give me the 20* *marks*". To this, the trustee replied, "I shall." After the ceremony, the widow produced her *ketubah*, swore that she had not received enough to cover same, and demanded the 20* *marks* back. The court decided that the 20* *marks* belong to the widow. Is the decision of the court correct?

A. The question is not sufficiently clear for us to express an opinion. If the widow told the trustee, in A's presence, to give the money to A after the ceremony, the money belongs to A; since this money is simply a gift which the trustee received for A's benefit. But, if the widow said nothing while she gave the money to the trustee, A's words are of no avail, and she can reclaim her money in payment of her *ketubah*.

SOURCES: Cr. 65: Pr. 30; L. 339; Mord. Yeb. 24.

* In Mord. ibid. L. ibid. the reading is — 2 *marks*.

385

Q. Must a levir pay for the sustenance of his brother's widow in case he is sick and is thus unable either to marry her or give her *halitzah?*

A. The levir must pay for the widow's sustenance since he is the cause of the delay in giving her *halitzah.*

SOURCES: Pr. 855.

386

Q. A levir performed the rite of *halitzah* with a shoe sewed with flaxen thread, but which did not belong to him. The levir refuses to repeat the rite with another shoe. The law provides that *halitzah* performed with a shoe not belonging to the levir is valid *bediabad* (after the act has been performed). What does *bediabad* mean in this case; does it mean after the rite was performed, or only after the woman remarried?

A. Bediabad, in this case, means after the rite was performed. Nevertheless, the aforementioned performance of the rite is invalid, for a different reason: the shoe used was sewed with flaxen thread and, therefore, was never fit for this purpose. Since, however, the levir performed an invalid rite of *halitzah,* neither he nor his brothers are now permitted to marry the widow. *Halitzah* by the same levir being the only manner of releasing her, he may be forced, by persuasion or by flagellation, to repeat the rite with the proper shoe. For now the *Mitzvah* revolved on him alone, and we are permitted to scourge a Jew until he perform the required *Mitzvot.*

This Responsum is addressed to Rabbi Menahem of Würzburg.

SOURCES: Am I, 93, 94.

387

Q. A died childless and left two brothers. One brother is an apostate, the other lives in a distant country. May A's widow accept *halitzah* (cf. Deut. 25; 7–9; Mishnah, Yeb. 12) from the apostate?

A. Since the other levir is a Jew, the widow should not accept *halitzah* from the apostate.

SOURCES: Pr. 491; Mord. Yeb. 30; B. p. 280, no. 130. Cf. Maharil, *Responsa* 100; *Terumat Hadeshen* 223; Judah Minz, *Responsa* 12.

388

Q. When a levir is required to grant his brother's widow both a divorce and *halitzah* (Yeb. 50a), which is granted first?

A. *Halitzah* is the complete and final severance of the tie that binds the widow to her levir; therefore, it must be granted last.

Regarding your request for a form of such letter of divorce, I have no such form. But, it seems to me that you ought merely to insert the words "my *yebama* (sister-in-law) and betrothed" in place of the words "my wife" in the ordinary letter of divorce

SOURCES: Cr. 278–9; *Mordecai Hagadol*, p. 138a.

RABBI MEIR OF ROTHENBURG

HIS LIFE AND HIS WORKS AS SOURCES FOR THE RELIGIOUS,
LEGAL, AND SOCIAL HISTORY OF THE JEWS OF GERMANY
IN THE THIRTEENTH CENTURY

The publication of this book has been made
possible through the generosity of the renowned
Maecenas of Talmudic-Rabbinic Culture

MR. HARRY FISCHEL

whose unique patronage of true Hebrew learning
and passionate devotion to numerous philanthro-
pic endeavors have gained for him the love and
admiration of Jewry throughout the world.

RABBI MEIR
OF ROTHENBURG

HIS LIFE AND HIS WORKS AS SOURCES FOR
THE RELIGIOUS, LEGAL, AND SOCIAL HISTORY
OF THE JEWS OF GERMANY IN THE
THIRTEENTH CENTURY

By

IRVING A. AGUS, Ph.D.

VOLUME TWO

TABLE OF CONTENTS

Volume II

IV

HOSHEN MISHPAT

Q. Two litigants agreed to abide by A's decision in their dispute. They asked him not to arbitrate but to render the decision according to strict law (דין תורה). A listened to their arguments, returned to his home town, and sent his decision through a messenger who read it before the litigants. Is A's decision valid?

A. If A's decision is a correct one, it is binding although A did not conform to the usual procedure of reading the decision personally, while seated, before the standing litigants. The procedure used in reading a court decision does not affect the legality of the decision. Moreover, since the litigants chose A as their judge and completely relied on his decision, such decision is binding regardless of the manner of its rendition.

SOURCES: Cr. 282; Pr. 526.

390

Q. A and B placed their dispute in the hands of two mediators subject to a final decision between the two, of C, the third mediator. They agreed before an authoritative court, that should one party refuse to abide by the decision of the mediators, that party was to pay five *marks* to the cemetery fund or to the synagogue. They deposited valuable pledges with C to enforce their agreement. The mediators reached a decision on the second day. A, however, refused to abide thereby claiming that, at the time of the making of the agreement, it was understood by both parties that the decision of the mediators was not to be postponed till the second day. A brought two witnesses, one of whom testified that such was the understanding; the other witness was not sure whether the condition was made at the time of the agreement or subsequent thereto. C and the subscribing two witnesses denied A's allegation that such a condition was made at the time of the agreement. The Rabbis, therefore, decided that A must pay the five *marks* fine. A, then, changed his mind and expressed his desire to be bound by the decision of the mediators. Must he still pay the fine?

A. As soon as A refused to accept the decision of the mediators, he became obliged to pay five *marks* to the sacred cause. Therefore, A must pay the five *marks* fine.

SOURCES: Pr. 975; Cr. 289; *Agudah* Sanh. 5.

391 (D)

Q. Two litigants appeared in court. They agreed to settle their dispute by arbitration, and bound themselves to that agreement by a *kinyan* in the presence of the worthies of the community. May one of the litigants still refuse to abide by the ruling of the court?

A. An agreement accompanied by a *kinyan*, especially if made in the presence of the worthies of the community, is binding. Moreover, arbitration by three judges requires no *kinyan*.

SOURCES: Cr. 215.

392

If litigants request that the judges adjudicate their case at night, and they solemnly agree to abide by such adjudication, the judges are permitted to hold court at night, and their decision, in such case, is binding. Therefore, a *kinyan* of an *Asmakta* transaction, made at night before an authoritative

court, is binding since it is made with the consent of both
parties.

SOURCES: Cr. 29.

393

Q. B, the defendant, in litigation with A, is willing to be
bound by the decision of local judges. A, the claimant, insists
upon having the local judges only hear the case, but demands
that copies of the arguments be forwarded to a court of a different city for the decision. Must B comply with A's demands?

A. No; only creditors can compel their debtors to appear
before a higher court. In all other claims, claimants as well
as defendants must rely on their local court, if either party
insists upon it. The judges of the local court can either rely
on their own judgment, or, in case of doubt, send an inquiry
to any Rabbinical authority they (the judges) desire, disregarding the wishes of either party to the litigation.

SOURCES: Pr. 960.

394

Q. One of two opposing litigants wants his case to be
tried by the local court of Rothenburg, while the other litigant
insists on bringing it before the *Beth Havaad* (superior court)
at Marienburg.

A. The Talmud differentiates between litigants, giving
a creditor the right to choose the court for the trial of his case
(Sanh. 31b). At present, however, an ordinance of the communities prevails to the effect that, in a place where an authoritative court exists, no litigant may insist on taking his case
before the *Beth Havaad.* Therefore, the litigants (of Rothenburg)
must choose a court that will hear their claims; and the court,
in turn, will refer their claims to a superior court of its own
choosing.

SOURCES: P. 290. Cf. Weil, *Responsa* 155.

395 (D)

Q. When a widow seeks to collect her *ketubah* from the heirs, who has the right, she or the heirs, to compel the other to rely on a local court or to compel that other to appear before an authoritative court outside of the community?

A. If both parties agree to rely on the local court, the matter is left to the court either to rely on their own judgment, or to inquire of an authoritative court of their own choosing. But, if the parties to the suit come to no agreement, and one of the litigants demands that the case be brought before an authoritative court, the claimant has the right to determine before which court the case shall be tried. In this case the widow is the claimant.

SOURCES: Cr. 98.

396 (D)

Q. A was involved in a litigation with B and C who were powerful leaders of the community. They summoned A to the local court. A, however, claimed that he could expect no justice in that court since B and C were in a position to overawe the judges, and A himself would be mentally intimidated and thus be unable to put forth his claims in the proper fashion.

A. A may force B and C to try the case in a court of a neighboring town.

The author adds: In a similar case my grandfather R. Isaac permitted R. Eliezer to refuse to appear before the court of Troyes in his litigation with R. Abraham because the latter was the leader of that town. For the same reason R. Samson b. Abraham permitted the bridegroom, R. Samson, a resident of Troyes, to refuse to appear before that court. R. Judah of Paris dealt similarly with R. Yom Tov b. Eliezer. I decided, therefore, to follow my elders.

SOURCES: Pr. 546; Berl. pp. 318–319 no. 677.

397

Q. An insane person fell heir to an estate. In his locality, however, no Jewish court exists to declare him insane and thus to permit the appointment of a trustee to manage the estate for his benefit. May a court declare him insane upon the testimony of two witnesses who have observed him in his locality?

A. If the testimony of two witnesses is sufficient to deprive a person of his life, it should be sufficient to declare him insane and incapable of managing his affairs. The trustee thus appointed would have complete charge of his affairs, and, if need be, would be permitted even to provide him with a wife.

This Responsum is addressed to: "My teacher and relative Rabbi Yakar haLevi".

SOURCES: Cr. 160.

398

Q. When we are confronted with a case regarding which authorities differ in their decisions, are we permitted to exercise our discretion in adjudicating such a case?

A. Only the outstanding scholar of the age and an authorized judge are permitted to exercise judicial discretion (שודא דדייני) in a few cases prescribed by the Talmud. Otherwise the rule prevails that the burden of proof is upon the person seeking to collect money from his friend.

SOURCES: Cr. 274; L. 241; Mord. Ket. 243.

399

(1) *Q.* If A claims that the judges rendered an erroneous decision against him, can he summon the judges before a court?

A. Yes, for we have heard of no ban or ordinance passed by the communities against the summoning of judges before a court. Moreover, it is a daily occurrence that litigants complain against their judges and summon them to court. Therefore, if the court of appeal shall decide that the judges erred, the latter will have to reverse their decision; should they refuse to reverse their decision, they will have to compensate A out of their own pockets.

R. M. adds: In our days, since the judges do not exercise the power of summons, but are compelled by a ban of the communities to sit in court and render judgment to those who appear before them voluntarily, the talmudic law — that the decision of the judges remains valid and the judges must compensate the injured party out of their own pockets — cannot be applied.

(2) *Q.* The judges allowed A a definite period of time within which to appeal his case before another court and A agreed to it. Now the specified term has expired; can A still appeal his case?

A. Since A's agreement to the term for appeal set by the judges was not accompanied by a *kinyan*, it is not binding and A can still appeal his case.

SOURCES: Pr. 715; Mord. Sanh. 676–7.

400

You asked me regarding the judges. I usually refrain from expressing my opinion before a litigant, lest I suggest advice to him as against his opponent.

SOURCES: *Tashbetz,* 518.

401

Q. A and C were negotiating a marriage. They deposited pledges with B. When a dispute arose between them, they brought their case before the worthies of the community who ordered B to deliver the pledges to C. This decision was later proven to be erroneous. Now A demands that B compensate him for the loss of his pledges.

A. Since B claims that A and C had undertaken to abide by the decision of the community leaders, and that he merely obeyed such decision, he is free from obligation. Although these leaders were ignorant in the law, their decision was nevertheless binding since A and C had accepted them as judges. The leaders and worthies of a community, because they are generally accepted by the members of their community and are in the same category as the Syrian courts (Git. 23a), form an authoritative court. Should A deny B's claim (that he obeyed the order of the community leaders), B would be free from obligation since a witness supports his claim. Moreover, no oath is exacted from a trustee who claims to have carried out his commission. Even if the mistake of the court became known before B delivered the pledges to C, and B nevertheless obeyed the order of the court, he is free from obligation, for A and C originally agreed to abide by the decision of the community leaders; and the custom is widely accepted throughout our kingdom that whatever obligations a person assumes in the presence of the community leaders become binding and unretractable. The leaders of a community wield the same authority over the members of their community regarding matters for which they were elected, as the great scholars of each generation wield over all of Israel.

SOURCES: Cr. 230; Tesh. Maim. to *Shoftim*, 10; *Mordecai Hagadol*, p. 298d; ibid. p. 349c. Cf. Moses Minz, *Responsa* 39.

402

Q. A, wishing to appeal to a higher court, demands that the local court give him a written statement as to the reasons underlying the court's decision in his case versus B. Can B be enjoined from issuing execution on the rendered judgment until such time as the appeal has been disposed of?

A. No, B may collect his money immediately.

SOURCES: Cr. 280; Pr. 523; L. 128; Hag. Maim. to *Sanhedrin*, 6, 8.

403

Q. How long after a decision of a court has been rendered, is a party to the suit entitled to a statement as to the reasons underlying such decision? Within what period, after a decision has been rendered, can a person appeal to a higher court? Must one declare before the local court that he will seek an appeal?

A. If a party to a suit originally wanted to bring his case to a higher court but was forced to try it at the local court, he is entitled to a written statement of the reasons for the decision, and he may appeal his case at any time. But if both parties agreed to have their case tried by the local court, the court is under no obligation to give any written opinion.

SOURCES: Cr. 281; Pr. 524; Mord. Sanh. 708; Hag. Maim. *Sanhedrin*, 6, 7.

404

Q. How much time is a defendant allowed to comply with the court's decision and pay the claimant, before further action is taken against him?

A. A defendant is allowed thirty days to comply with the decision of the court, if he is ordered to pay money to the claimant. If, however, the court's order is that he take an oath, he must do so at the next court session. Moreover, action is immediately taken against a defendant who admits that he has money, but refuses to comply with the court's decision.

SOURCES: Pr. 945; Cr. 103; Mord. B. M. 414.

405

Q. Does the plaintiff or the defendant pay the expenses of the messenger [hired to procure the Responsum from a talmudic authority]?

A. Both the plaintiff and the defendant share equally in such expenses.

SOURCES: Pr. 46; L. 352; *Mordecai Hagadol,* p. 308a. Cf. end of Cr. 70; Pr. 32.

406

Q. Several partners sue A for money. A demands that the partners choose a representative to present their arguments, for he may be at a disadvantage in having to answer the arguments of several people. May each partner claim that he wants to present his arguments personally for his own interests?

A. Each partner has a right to present his claims personally. Furthermore, any testimony of one partner disadvantageous to the other partners is treated as the testimony of a single witness; and the testimony of two partners disadvantageous to the other partners is treated as the testimony of two witnesses.

SOURCES: Pr. 332; Mord. Ket. 299; Rashba I, 1107.

407

Q. A claims that he will not be able to argue his case properly because the partners, his opponents, being many, will confuse him. He demands that his friends be near him while he presents his arguments. May the partners object on the grounds that they do not want A's friends to listen to their private affairs, and that A's friends may direct A's presentation of his arguments by sly hints and facial expressions?

A. A cannot have his friends present at the trial, neither can the partners be present while one of them presents his claims, so that A may not be confronted with all the partners at the same time. Each partner shall present his claims separately and the verdict shall be passed on the accumulated evidence. If the court finds difficulty in remembering all the facts and claims, let the partners present their claims before two or three courts, or in two or three days to the same court, or let the court keep a written record of all claims.

SOURCES: Pr. 333; Mord. Shebu. 761; Rashba I. 1107.

408

When a person sues, or is being sued by, a partnership, he may not demand, on the ground that the multiple claims of the various partners will overburden and confuse him, that one partner represent the partnership. Each partner may insist on personally presenting his claims for his share. On the other hand, at the trial a statement made by a partner, supporting one of the claims or counterclaims of the opponent, has the force of testimony by a single witness, either to obligate the partners to take a Biblical oath, or to free the opponent from the obligation of taking such an oath.

SOURCES: Hag. Mord. Ket. 299.

409

Q. In the dispute between A and B the court found that B owed A money. A demanded either immediate payment, or that B put up a bond to insure such payment. B, however, asked for the usual thirty days' interval in which to carry out the decision of the court. Are A's demands justified?

A. B is entitled to the thirty days' interval. The system of justice current in Israel is guaranty enough for A that after the thirty days will have passed the court will enforce its ruling. The reason for allowing a person only thirty days within which to comply with a court's decision, while, according to the

Talmud, an *adrakta* is written after a ninety day interval, is this: An *adrakta* is written when the court finds no property from which to collect; but, if the property of the debtor is within reach, a judgment is enforced after the thirty days' interval has passed.

Sources: L. 267; P. 297.

410

a) *Q.* Is a person who reached his majority, permitted to appoint a legal representative to argue his case in court? The Palestinian Talmud (Sanh. 2, 1) definitely implies that a high priest is permitted to appoint such a representative.

A. The statement in the Palestinian Talmud does not necessarily imply that an ordinary person is permitted to appoint a legal representative. It is possible that only a high priest is permitted to appoint such a representative, in order to save him the humiliation of appearing before a court having less authority than himself; but an ordinary person may not be permitted to make the appointment. In any case, all are agreed that a levir is not permitted to appoint a legal representative when his brother's widow demands that he fulfill the positive command (of God) to perform the ceremony of *halitzah* or to marry her. Moreover, a person commits a wrong when he consents to become a legal representative to a levir, thus helping to postpone the fulfillment of this positive command, and injuring the interests of the widow.

b) *Q.* Is a legal representative permitted to present before the court claims and arguments that will improve his client's case but which he knows to be false?

A. The plaintiff, or defendant, himself is not permitted to lie in order to improve his case in court; a legal representative, therefore, is surely not permitted to lie.

Sources: Cr. 246; L. 126, 127; Mord. B. M. 276; cf. P. 519; *Mordecai Hagadol*, p. 270a.

411

Q. A claims that his representative caused him to lose his case against B by willful neglect, for the representative pleaded in court those arguments which A asked him not to plead, and neglected to plead those arguments which he specifically asked him to. A, therefore, demands that his representative compensate him for the loss caused him.

A. If A lost money through his representative's willful neglect, the latter must make good A's loss. But, if the case is such that had the representative pleaded A's arguments, A would have had to swear and be able to recover, or swear and be free from obligation, and now the case is that the oath has either been transferred to B, or that now B may collect without taking an oath, the representative is free from obligation, since the damage to A's interests is not clear and remains problematical, as no one can be sure that A would have taken the required oath. However, if the case is such that had the representative pleaded A's arguments, A would be free from obligation and would not be required to take an oath, and now B collects from A without being required to take an oath, the representative is guilty of willful neglect.

SOURCES: Cr. 157; Pr. 242; Mord. B. M. 290; Rashba I, 1106.

412

Q. A promised B that he would not summon him to court at all if he did not do so before a certain date. The specified date passed and A did not summon B to court. May A summon B to court hereafter?

A. A verbal release does not require a *kinyan*, but a conditional promise of release is not binding unless accompanied by a *kinyan*.

SOURCES: Pr. 718; cf. Mord. *Sanhedrin*, 677.

413

A owed money to B and refused to pay his debt. The Rabbis of Spiers, basing their decision on the statement of R. Nahman (B. K. 27b) that a man is permitted to take the law into his own hands, gave B permission to break into A's house and forcefully take possession of A's valuables in payment of the debt.

R. Meir wrote to the Rabbis of Spiers not to ascribe legal absurdities to R. Nahman; for such interpretation of the words of R. Nahman was not only in opposition to an explicit statement of the *Mishna* (B. M. 9, 13) but was even against the very words of the Pentateuch (Deut. 24,10). A person is permitted according to R. Nahman, to enter into another person's house and take away an object definitely known to be his own, but he is not permitted to touch an object belonging to the other person, unless accompanied by a law-court official.

SOURCES: Cr. 102; Pr. 950; L. 148; cf. Tesh. Maim. to *Nezikin*, 14; *Beth Joseph* to *Hoshen Mishpat* 388.

414

Q. A court decree reads: A must pay to the other party to the suit, a certain sum of money, but said decree does not indicate who the other party is.

A. A must pay the specified sum to the bearer of the above document.

SOURCES: Pr. 521; Mord. B. B. 647.

415(D)

Q. Do the judges or the witnesses (who heard the court's decision) sign the court's decree?

A. If the judges sign the writ, it must be phrased as a decree; if the witnesses sign it, it must read as testimony.

SOURCES: Pr. 522.

416

Q. Must a court decree be dated, since, otherwise, a creditor who obtains a later decree would be able to enforce his rights thereunder, prior to the creditor who received the former decree.

A. It is advisable to include the date in a court decree, but not for the reason cited. A creditor, whose bond is dated before the bond of his fellow creditor, should receive a prior lien if execution is to be issued upon real property; but if execution is to be issued upon personal property, the creditor who seizes the property first has a prior lien without regard to the date of his bond. In any case, the date of the court decree is immaterial. Moreover, no undated document is invalid except a divorce.

Sources: Cr. 281; Pr. 525.

417 (D)

You have written correctly: R. Alexandri may not compel the witnesses to reveal their testimony, until they appear in court to have it recorded by order of the judges. Furthermore, he may not cause the ban to be pronounced against the witnesses, if they are willing to testify without recourse to the ban. However, if R. Alexandri fears that other witnesses may withhold their testimony, he may, by the authority of the judges, compel you (the community?) to pronounce the ban against any and all witnesses who refuse to testify.

Sources: P. 296.

418 (D)

Witnesses may be examined and their testimony admitted as evidence, only if the examination took place in the presence of the litigant against whom they testify.

Sources: Cr. 207; Pr. 166; Tesh. Maim. to *Shoftim*, 6.

419

Q. Some persons maintain that A and B are disqualified to serve as witnesses. I believe, however, that they are so qualified.

A. A person who committed a sin that disqualified him Biblically from serving as a witness, became so disqualified at the very time he committed the sin, even though a court did not proclaim him a sinner. A person, however, who committed a sin that disqualified him as a witness only according to Rabbinic enactment, must first be proclaimed as a sinner by a court before he becomes disqualified, and his disqualification dates from the time of the court's proclamation.

SOURCES: Sinai V (1941) 5–6, no. 197.

420

Q. In a litigation in which he was a defendant, A agreed to admit in evidence the testimony of two interested witnesses. After the witnesses testified before the court, A asked the court to reject their testimony on the ground that they were interested witnesses.

A. A's request should not be granted in view of the fact that he did not object before the testimony of the interested witnesses was presented. After witnesses present their testimony the case is closed and neither the defendant nor even the witnesses themselves can reopen it.

SOURCES: Cr. 48; Pr. 708, 915; L. 370; Rashba I, 868. Cf. Judah Minz, *Responsa* 6.

421

Q. A advanced many claims against B. Having no Jewish witnesses to testify on his behalf, he produced Gentiles as witnesses. B consented to admit in evidence the testimony of a certain Gentile; this consent was accompanied by a *kinyan*. When, however, B felt that the Gentile was perverting the truth — probably having received a bribe — he protested the admission into evidence of the Gentile's testimony.

A. Since B had accepted the Gentile as a trustworthy witness and had accompanied the acceptance by a *kinyan*, the testimony of the Gentile was equivalent to that of Jewish witnesses. Therefore B's protest was of no avail.

SOURCES: Cr. 245; P. 284; *Agudah* San. 15; cf. *Or Zarua* I, 752b.

422

Q. One of the witnesses to a document subsequently became related to the beneficiary named in the document.

A. The document has no value unless witnesses testify that they saw the document, and recognized the signatures of the witnesses, in the hands of its present possessor before the witness in question became a relative of the beneficiary.

SOURCES: Pr. 115, 919, Am. II, 101; Mord. Sanh. 696. This Responsum relates to Pr. 50. In Cr. 31, L. 355, the two parts are printed together.

423

Q. R. Tam is of the opinion that a person whose claim is supported by the testimony of a single witness is entitled to collect his claim without being required to take an oath. However, the Talmud, B. M. 28a, states: Where two persons lay claim to an object found by a third, each of the two giving the proper identifying marks and one of them supporting his claim by the testimony of a single witness, the testimony of that witness is of no avail. Does not this talmudic law contradict the statement of R. Tam?

A. There is no contradiction. R. Tam means to say that whenever a person would be entitled to collect his claim were he to take an oath to support it, such an oath would not be required if he obtain the testimony of a single witness supporting the claim. Thus, the testimony of a single witness directed against a litigant has the effect of requiring an oath (denying the truth of such testimony) when otherwise no oath would have been required; and such testimony in favor of a litigant has the effect of rendering unnecessary an oath that otherwise would have been required. However, when two persons lay claim to an object found by a third and both give the proper identifying marks, no oath is accepted from either of the claimants and the object is not delivered to either of them. Therefore, the additional testimony of a single witness does not change the situation.

This Responsum is addressed to: "My teacher, and relative, Rabbi Menahem", of Würzburg.

SOURCES: L. 343; Mord. B. M. 417; Tesh. Maim. to *Mishpatim*, 6; Asheri B. M. 1, 3. Cf. *Terumat Hadeshen* 334.

424 (D)

Q. B lent money to A. The latter promised to give to the former half of the profits he would derive from all his business transactions, including those transactions in which money borrowed from a third party would be employed. Is this promise binding on A?

A. If the promise was accompanied by a *kinyan* in the presence of witnesses, it is binding; otherwise it is a mere *asmakhta* (exaggerated promise) and is not binding.

SOURCES: Pr. 676.

425 (D)

Q. A advanced forty ounces (of silver) to B for purposes of investment to share equally in the profits. After the lapse of some time, B gave A ten ounces, telling him that it was his share of the profits. Subsequently, B gave A a pound and told him that the first ten ounces he gave him were part of the principal; that his transactions brought in no profits, and that, for fear lest A would immediately demand his money, he had originally lied to him by telling him that the ten ounces were profit.

A. Since B still owes money to A, and since B could have denied owing anything to him, B is to be believed upon the taking of an oath that his transactions with A's money brought no profit. Therefore, if B takes such an oath, the ten ounces B has given A as profit, are to be considered as part of the principal.

SOURCES: Pr. 827.

426 (D)

Q. A advanced one Mina to B for investment purposes, to share equally in the profits. B died; A presented B's note of indebtedness and demanded his money from B's heirs.

A. A is entitled to half the amount he advanced to B, if he takes an oath that he received no money from B in payment of that claim (cf. B. B. 70b–71a).

SOURCES: Pr. 846.

427

Q. A and B appeared in court. A claimed that two years previously he had lent money belonging to orphans to B for investment purposes on condition that the orphans share equally in the profits as well as in the losses. He demanded that B return this money since B was not financially as well off as he had been two years previously and might lose the orphans' money. B, on the other hand, claimed that the money was given to him by the grandfather and mother of the orphans with the condition that he do not return it under any circumstances, not even to themselves, until the orphans grow up and get married; that he now intended to abide by this agree-

ment even though the grandfather died meanwhile and his
heirs have demanded the return of this money; and that he
was richer at this time than two years previously, since at that
time he owned no real estate while now he did, and also had
property of his own.

A. If the grandfather and the mother of the orphans were
not trustees — never having been duly appointed by the court,
the father of the orphans, or the orphans themselves — they
had no right to administer the latter's money. Therefore, the
agreements they had entered into regarding this money, were
void. If they were duly appointed as trustees for the orphans,
they ought to be discharged for lending money belonging to
orphans without adequate security, and without receiving
notes of indebtedness, and on terms injurious to the orphans'
interests; since according to the agreement the orphans were
to share in the losses, as well as in the profits, resulting from
B's transactions. Such money must be lent to a rich and trustworthy man, on adequate security, and on condition that the
orphans share only in the profits but not in the losses. Any
trustee not heeding this rule could be discharged without notice
for damaging the orphans' interests, and the agreements he had
entered into would become void at the time he was discharged.
Since B admitted that the money lent to him belonged to
orphans, and that it was lent to him on conditions injurious to
the latter, the agreement he entered into with the trustees of
said orphans, was void, and he had to return the money.

SOURCES: Cr. 211; L. 220; Tesh. Maim. to *Mishpatim*, 40. Cf. Moses Minz,
Responsa 72.

428

Q. A claims that: a) B personally lent him money for
investment purposes to share equally in the profits, b) he
secured this loan by delivering his pledges to B, c) subsequently

he gave ten *marks* to B, which amount constituted B's part of the profits, d) he then repaid the principal to B but the latter failed to return the pledges, e) meanwhile B's house burned down, the pledges were damaged by the fire, and the magistrate took them together with other valuables that belonged to B. Now, A demands that B pay him back the ten *marks*, since his investments earned no profits. He further demands that B pay him for the pledges since they were lost through B's failure to return them (after having received his money), which failure constituted a wilful neglect on B's part. B, on the other hand, claims that: a) the money he lent to A belonged to orphans, b) the money was lent to A by a third party, c) he took the pledges because he was the trustee of the orphans, d) he is not responsible for the loss of the pledges since he did not hinder A from taking them away after the debt was paid.

A. B is free from obligation, and is not required to take an oath to support his claims, for the following reasons: a) The money-lending transaction was legitimate even if it was carried out in accordance with A's version thereof; b) a creditor is not responsible for a loss of pledges through unavoidable accident, if he received such pledges at the time the loan was contracted; c) after A gave ten *marks* to B as B's share of the profits, A may no longer claim that he had made a mistake, and that ultimately his investments earned no profits.

SOURCES: Cr. 224; L. 326.

429

Q. A lent money to B on condition that they share equally in the profits. After a Sabbatical year passed, B refused to pay his debt to A, claiming that the Sabbatical year released him from the obligation. A is ignorant of the fact that were he to claim that he had a *prosbol*, which was lost, he could collect his debt in full. May the judge inform A of his rights?

A. No, he may not. In talmudic times, people often wrote *prosbols*; therefore, a judge was allowed to inform a creditor of his right to claim that he had had a *prosbol* but lost it. Nowadays, however, people rarely write *prosbols* and a judge is not permitted to suggest to a creditor to put forth an unusual claim.

Sources: Pr. 972; L. 198; Rashba I, 1075; Tesh. Maim. to *Mishpatim*, 10; *Mordecai Hagadol*, p. 219d; ibid. 369a.

430

Q. A claims that L(eah) delivered him into the hands of Gentiles and caused him a loss of one hundred and five pounds. L denies A's charge. A further claims that he lent L twelve pounds for investment purposes to share equally in the profits. L avers that A lent her ten pounds upon interest [the interest was to be two pounds], that she has repaid five pounds and still owes him five pounds of old coins.

A. Regarding the first charge, if L will take an oath in support of her claim, she will be free from obligation. Regarding the latter claim, although I have heard in the name of R. Tam that the principle "a person will not let stand what is permitted and eat what is forbidden", as applied to the case where the creditor claims to have lost his *prosbol* (Git. 37b), is also applicable to a case such as the one mentioned above, some great scholars draw a clear distinction between the case of *prosbol*, where the debtor does not know whether or not the creditor has had a *prosbol*, and a claim such as the one mentioned above where the debtor knows the terms of the agreement, and his denial, therefore, of the creditor's claim, ought to carry weight. Moreover, R. Tam's decision probably applies only when the creditor had received a pledge and, thus, was in possession of his money. But, in our case, A seeks to collect. Therefore, L may take an oath to the effect that she owes A only five pounds of old coins, and, after repaying that sum, be free from further obligation.

SOURCES: Cr. 167; Am II, 143.

431

Q. Leah lent A one pound for investment, and was to receive half of the profits. She claims: a) that she gave the money to A partly on trust, and partly because she received clothes as security from him; b) that she made a condition with A that he lend the money only if adequately secured; c) that later A asked her to return to him his wife's coat (which was part of the security), and promised to give it back to her after the holiday; d) that he never returned the coat, and e) that he paid her only 60 pennies of the principal. A claims: a) that Leah lent him the money without any security; b) that he was supposed to lend it as he saw fit; c) that the clothes he deposited with Leah were deposited for safe-keeping only, because he was angry with his mother-in-law, and not as security for the loan; d) that he lent the money to others without security, and e) that his debtors failed to repay the loans.

A. Leah shoud swear that she made a condition with A to lend the money only if adequately secured. A must swear that his investments brought no profit (but if he did make some profit, he must give Leah her share of it) and Leah is entitled to keep A's clothes unless he redeems them.

SOURCES: Pr. 86.

432

Q. R(achel) lent L(eah) twenty *marks*, secured by pledges, for the purpose of investment and was to share equally in the profits. Part of the money, according to R, belonged to orphans and the other part was deposited with her for the purpose of educating the orphans and contributing to other religious causes with the profit derived therefrom. Subsequently, L paid back to R sixteen *marks*, gave her a pledge worth ten *solidi* which a Gentile had deposited with L as security for a loan of one *mark*, told R that the investments had brought in a profit of fourteen *marks*, and said that she took for herself seven *marks* which constituted her part of the profits. Two days later, however, L claimed she had searched her assets and investments carefully and could find no trace of the seven *marks* profit coming to R, and that she did not know what had become of that money. She demanded that R return her pledges in exchange for the three *marks* she still owed R on the principal. R said that when L paid her the sixteen *marks*, the pledges were left in her (R's) possession as security for the four *marks* of the principal and the seven *marks* of profit coming to her; that she would not return the pledges until the eleven *marks* were paid to her; that L had probably spent the seven *marks* on her sustenance, since she had no money and no source of income; and that she (R) ought not to suffer any loss on the one *mark* loan made to the Gentile against a pledge worth ten *solidi*, since she had expressly instructed L to lend the money against adequate security only. L rejoined that R had given her no such instructions; that she knew the Gentile very well, had always trusted him and at one time had lent him ten pounds without security which he had repaid in full; and that when she extended the loan to the Gentile she acted in good faith and was, therefore, not responsible for the loss resulting therefrom. L denied having spent the seven *marks* on her sustenance, and further denied that her pledges were left in R's possession as security for the seven *marks* profit, claiming that these pledges were deposited as security for the principal only. The court set up to register the claims [for the purpose of sending it to an authoritative court for decision] thoroughly questioned L regarding the disappearance of half of the fourteen *marks* she had originally

admitted she had earned, but could receive no clear explanation
from her. She claimed that whenever she earned a profit of
ten or twenty *solidi* she spent half of it for her daily needs and
added the other half to the principal, since such was her understanding with R; that she had thus spent seven *marks* out of
the profit, and that when she finally counted up her assets she
could find no trace of the seven *marks* profit coming to R.
She believes that the money was either lost or stolen, or disappeared in some other manner unknown to her.

A. A person with whom money is deposited for investment
purposes and who is to share equally in the profits, assumes the
responsibility of a debtor for one half of the money [the profit
of which half belongs to him], and the responsibility of a bailee
for the other half [the profit of which belongs to the depositor].
If, in addition to the money, the depositor pays a small token
fee to the bailee as compensation for his trouble in managing
the investments, the latter has the responsibility of a paid bailee
for the second half of the deposit; but when no such fee is paid,
the responsibility of the bailee thereto is that of a gratuitous
bailee. Since L claims to have added the seven *marks* profit
to the principal, her responsibility to this profit became the
same as to the principal. Therefore, if R paid L a token fee for
her trouble in managing the investments, L was responsible for
the loss or theft of the seven *marks*. Although some authorities
would disagree with this decision, we follow the authorities
favoring R's interests, since she is in possession of the pledges.
But, if R paid L no such fee, the latter will be responsible for
only half that amount, upon the taking of an oath to the effect
that the seven *marks* were lost through no negligence on her
part, and that she did not misappropriate them. However,
should R claim that according to her agreement with L the
profit was not to be joined to the principal and that it was to be
given to her immediately, or that it was left with L as a loan
and not for reinvestment, R will be entitled to collect the entire

seven *marks* upon the taking of an oath to the truth of such claim. We must be satisfied with such oath, since she is in possession of the pledges. Regarding the loan to the Gentile against inadequate security, R may take an oath to the effect that she had specifically instructed L not to lend the money unless adequately secured, and be entitled to collect the one *mark*; or she may demand that L take an oath as to the truth of her (L's) claim.

This Responsum is addressed to R. Jacob, R. Solomon, and R. Shemaiah ha-Kohen, the court that registered the claims.

SOURCES: L. 380.

433

Q. A summoned B, the brother of his wife L, to court. A claimed that his wife, L, who took part in managing his business, had transferred to her brother, B, a debt of four pounds of coins due her from C; that in B's presence L told C to pay his debt to B, and that the latter would be under obligation to repay to her that money as well as half of the profit he (B) would earn therewith; that L released C from obligation to her because B had undertaken to be responsible for the money; that C promised by solemn hand-clasp to repay his debt to B, and that the latter consequently promised L by solemn hand-clasp to repay her the money and half of his profit therefrom; and that L permitted B to retain for himself the chickens he might receive from his Gentile debtors as presents.*

B averred that L had stealthily taken the four pounds from A and had lent them to C; that she acted stealthily because she was afraid of her husband; that subsequently she

---

* Cf. *Hagahot Maimuniot*, Constantinople edition, to *Hilkot Malveh*, chap. 9: אם המקבל לוקח עצמו הדורונות שמביאין הגוים כעבאים לפדות את משכנותיהן בהא נראה דסני בשכר עמלו. Thus Gentile debtors used to bring presents to their creditors, when they came to redeem their pledges.

encountered difficulty in collecting the money from C who
had no money with which to repay her; that consequently she
asked B to collect the money for her; that he, B, obligated himself to pay L the principal plus half the profit he might earn
therewith, should he succeed in collecting the money from C;
that his obligation to L was not to begin till C repaid his debt;
and that C never paid him the money. B further claimed that
he had not in C's presence provided L with sureties for the
debt nor came to an agreement with her regarding the conditions of the transaction; but that L merely told C to repay his
debt to B, without any further qualification; that when he
subsequently came to demand the money from C, the latter
asked him for an extension of the loan for four weeks; that L
advised him to grant C that extension; that in all his dealings
with C he consulted L and followed her instructions; that he
reminded L repeatedly that his obligation toward her would
not begin till C repay his debt, and that she invariably agreed
with him.

The trustee appointed by L confirmed (in her name) A's
claims and denied those of B. The trustee further claimed
that L had stipulated in her agreement with B that he invest
her money only against pledges, and that B violated this agreement by granting C an extension. Does the granting of permission to the active partner to receive gifts from the prospective
Gentile debtors legitimize the aforesaid seemingly usurious
transaction (for the plaintiff thinks that such stipulation does
legitimatize the transaction) according to which B was to be
responsible for the entire principal and was also expected to
share the profits with L?

A. If L released C because B took over C's obligation and
told L to release C, B's responsibility was that of a surety who
guaranteed a loan at the time it was consumated, and was,
therefore, responsible even if his act was not accompanied by
a *kinyan*. But, if L merely told C to pay his debt to B, the

latter is not responsible for the debt, even if he did not expressly stipulate the condition that his responsibility begin only after C had repaid his debt. Although L claims that B promised by solemn hand-clasp to go surety for C, since B denies this claim he is free from obligation and is not required to take an oath. Had B made such promise by solemn hand-clasp, we would compel him to carry out his promise. However, we impose no oath on a person who denies having promised by solemn hand-clasp, when such a person would be under no obligation to the alleged promisee if he truly made no promise by solemn hand-clasp. Therefore, if B take an oath to the effect that L did not release C because of B's promise, or that he, B, had expressly stipulated the condition that he was not to become obligated till C has repaid his debt, he would be free from obligation. B's alleged solemn hand-clasp, however, does not take the place of such oath. Since aside from that hand-clasp, B would have been under obligation to L if her other claims were true, such a hand-clasp does not take the place of a judicial oath administered while holding the Scroll of the Law.

SOURCES: Am II, 165; Sinai VII (1943), 5–6, 53; *Mordecai Hagadol*, p. 361a.

434

Q. B gave one *mina* to A's wife, for investment purposes. Since a husband is reluctant to have his wife degraded by appearing in court, is B permitted to summon her to court? Furthermore, since any profit earned by a wife belongs to her husband, may A demand the profit his wife earned with this *mina*?

A. A's wife may send her representative to court in her stead. A is entitled to the profit earned by his wife.

SOURCES: Cr. 175–6; Am II, 30.
The former source bears the signature of R. Isaac b. Abraham, while the latter source bears the signature of R. Meir b. Baruch.

435

Q. We are in doubt concerning the implications of the following ruling of the scholars of Nehardea: When one person gives goods to another in order that the latter trade therewith and the former share in the profits, half of the value of such goods is considered a loan (at the risk of the active partner) and the other half, a trust (at the risk of the investor). Does this statement imply that the part which is considered a loan is subject to all the laws governing loans, even to the extent of being cancelled by a Sabbatical year? Would it not work to the disadvantage of the investor?

A. That part which is considered a loan is subject to all the laws governing loans and is subject to cancellation by a Sabbatical year. However, the investor can safeguard his interests by writing a *Prosbol.*

This Responsum is addressed to R. Shemariah.

SOURCES: L. 490; Mord. B. M. 390.

436

Rabbi Dan's report in my name is correct, that when one person gives goods to another in order that the latter trade therewith and the former share in the profits, half of the value of such goods is considered a loan (the other half is considered a deposit), even to the extent that a Sabbatical year effects its cancellation. I always consider it a loan in every respect. The law that such half be considered a loan is stated in the Talmud without qualification (B. M. 104b). The stipulations of Raba are specific; they do not go beyond those mentioned by Raba.

R. Meir adds: Your requests, Rabbi Samuel and Rabbi Dan, that I forgive Rabbi Hananiah for his insults to me are granted. I fully absolve him of guilt.

SOURCES: P. 304; Pr. 973; Tesh. Maim. to *Mishpatim*, 12; Mord. B. M. 390.

437

Q. D claims that A, B, and C, had asked him to pay thirty pounds of old (invalidated) coins to a certain Gentile on the promise that they would repay him with new coins; that at first he had refused to do so thinking the transaction a usurious one, but that when they assured him that the difference in value between the new coins and the old would be charged directly to the duke, he accepted their proposition and paid the old coins to the Gentile. At first A admitted to the court the truth of D's claims, but a considerable time later he retracted his admission.

A. A can not retract his admission. Therefore, if the duke repaid new coins to A, B, and C, they in turn must pay D new coins; but if the duke repaid them with old coins they must pay D the value of the coins he paid to the Gentile at the time he made the payment.

SOURCES: *Mordecai Hagadol*, p. 276c.

438

1) *Q.* R(achel), a widow, entered into the following agreement with B and his wife L(eah): 1) B and his wife undertook to provide food for R and her servant-girl until her death; 2) R, on the other hand, was to give to B and L her late husband's chain valued at fifteen *marks*; 3) B and his wife were to come to live in R's house (R owned a half interest in a house) and were to pay the interest to the mortgagee of R's house who was a Gentile; 4) in case B or his wife survived R the fifteen *marks* would be forfeited; and 5) in case both, B and his wife, died before R, she was to receive from their estate fifteen *marks* minus one-quarter *mark* for every year from the time of signing the contract. R delivered the chain to B and L. Subsequently B died and L moved to a place where there was no

minyan. R demands from L her board and the interest due on the mortgaged house. L claims that she cannot afford to live in one place and provide food for R and her servant in another place. R refuses to leave her city, her daughter, her relatives, and the place where she can pray with a *minyan*. Can R compel L to provide food for her in R's city; and is not the contract void since in case L died before R and the latter reclaimed her money, the food L provided her with would constitute illegal interest?

A. L cannot force R to come to live with her, and R can not force L to support her while L is away, for neither of them would have entered into the original agreement had they forseen such eventualities. Moreover, the contract is void since there is a possibility that the food R receives from L would constitute illegal interest on R's money. L, therefore, should deduct from the fifteen *marks*, the amount she expended on R's food, and return the rest to R.

2) *Q.* R drew an instrument in which she stated that from then on and after her death, her (real) estate should belong to her brother, to certain people and to charity, on condition that she retain the right to sell any part of it if hard pressed for funds with which to feed and clothe herself. R, now, desires to sell part of her property claiming that she needs the money for her sustenance. The charity-trustee refuses to grant her permission to do so, claiming that R is not hard pressed for funds since she receives her food from L and since she has sufficient clothes.

A. If it is known that R is not in dire need of money for her sustenance, she may not sell any part of her property. But if this is not a known fact, R may promise under oath that she will not sell any part of her property unless she will need the money for her sustenance. She will be permitted, then, to sell such part of her property the proceeds of which will suffice for her sustenace for a period of six months. That money should be deposited with a trustee who would pay her a monthly allowance.

SOURCES: Pr. 1006.

439 (D)

Q. L borrowed money from B, with a verbal promise to repay. Subsequently she married A and gave him money as her dowry. Is A obligated to pay L's debt, out of that dowry? Are we permitted to exact an oath from L in case she denies B's claim?

A. Authorities differ regarding the rights of a husband over his wife's dowry. Some authorities decide that a husband has the rights of a buyer [who is not responsible for the seller's debts] while others hold that his rights are those of an heir [who is liable for the debts of his benefactor]. Since we can not choose between these conflicting opinions, we allow the money to remain in the hands of the present possessor. And since L has no money and will have no money till she be widowed or divorced, there is no sense in exacting an oath from her. We give B a written verdict, however, to the effect that in case L be widowed or divorced she then must take an oath denying B's claim or pay that debt.

SOURCES: Am II, 25, 27, 29. Cf. *Agudah* B. B. 185.

440

Q. B admits that he borrowed a pound from A, but refuses to repay it because, he claims, A is indebted to his wife.

A. If B's wife is dead, or if she is alive and she instructs A to repay his debt to B, then B is justified in retaining A's money.

This Responsum was sent to R. Yekutiel.

SOURCES: Cr. 56; Pr. 145.

441

Q. When A demanded of B the return of the money he had given him, B repaid part of it and provided A with a surety for the rest. The fact that B provided A with a surety is attested to by witnesses. Now, however, B claims that this money was originally given to him by A not as a loan but as an outright gift, that consequently he owes nothing to A, and that when he provided A with a surety he acted "inside the line of justice."

A. The testimony of the witnesses to the effect that B provided A with a surety, is convincing proof that A had given the money to B as a loan. Although a person will sometimes buy what by law belongs to him in order to avoid litigation, this principle applies only when the rightful owner is not in possession of the disputed property, while in our case B was in possession of the money. Moreover, even if there were no such witnesses, we would have put no credence in B's assertion that he provided A with a surety only because he acted "inside the line of justice." For the principle of *Miggo* — that we ought to believe B's present statement since, were he inclined to lie, he could have denied altogether having provided A with a surety — does not apply to this case, since we are thoroughly convinced that had B not owed the money to A, he would not have repaid part of it.

Sources: Cr. 166; Am II, 164.

442

Q. Can A's creditors collect their claims against A from garments and jewels that A's wife brought with her upon her marriage?

A. No, for the garments and jewels a woman brings with her upon her marriage belong to her exclusively.

This Responsum is addressed to R. Haim.

Sources: Cr. 84; Pr. 210; L. 359; Tesh. Maim. to *Mishpatim*, 8. Cf. Moses Minz, *Responsa* 96.

443 (D)

Q. A lent money, on trust, to B who subsequently left for a distant country where he was robbed of all his possessions. Upon his return he settled with A for three halves (half-pounds, *marks*), and gave A a note of indebtedness in which no specific date of month or day, but the calendar year since the creation of the world appeared, and which contained a clause to the effect that A is to be believed without an oath should any litigation arise concerning this debt. After B's death his widow seized his property in payment of her *ketubah*, which property barely covered ten percent of her claim, without taking the usual oath required of a widow upon the collection of her *ketubah*. Ten years after the death of B's widow, A presented his note for collection and demanded the full amount from B's sons. The latter claimed that their father left them nothing, that they inherited valuables from their mother only, and that B had paid A part of the debt contained in the note. A single witness testified, and A himself finally admitted, that B had repaid one-sixth of the debt.

A. A controversy exists regarding the status of the property seized by a widow in payment of her *ketubah*, if the widow died before taking the required oath. Some are of the opinion that the entire property reverts to the husband's estate; while others hold that the part of such property which is valued at no more than half of the amount of the widow's *ketubah* remains part of the widow's estate, while anything above that amount reverts to the husband's estate. The latter opinion is accepted. Therefore, if B's sons take an oath that they inherited nothing from their father, they are free from any obligation to A. If, however, they are willing to repay their father's debt, they may demand that A take an oath as to the amount actually due him, since he has been proven to be untrustworthy.

SOURCES: Pr. 859.

444

Q. A sent his messenger to take wine from his Gentile debtor in payment of his debt. The messenger carried out his order and pulled the wagon of wine for the purpose of taking possession thereof by this act. However when the Gentile brought the wine to town he gave it to his other creditor, B. Now A sues B for that wine.

A. The law of agency does not apply to a Gentile, nor can he confer a benefit, for the law of conferring a benefit is deduced from the law of agency. Therefore when the Gentile gave the wine to the messenger for A's benefit, his act was not valid. Furthermore, since the messenger strove to take possession of the goods of a debtor for the benefit of one creditor though the debtor owed money to other creditors, his act was invalid (Ket. 84b). Moreover, perhaps Rashi's opinion is accepted that one cannot acquire ownership of a Gentile's property by a *kinyan* of pulling. Finally, B may not be called "wicked", for interfering with another man's business, since the Gentile owed him money.

Sources: Am II, 245.

445

Q. Ten Jews individually loaned various sums of money to a feudal lord, each one receiving pledges as security, independently of the others. One day, the feudal lord called them together and told them that he preferred to deal with them collectively instead of individually. He also wanted an extension of the loans. Furthermore, he stipulated that whenever he would pay them a sum of money as interest they should divide it among themselves in proportion to their oans, and whatever he would repay on the principal should also be so divided. The creditors agreed to this arrangement. Subsequently, however, one creditor succeeded in collecting his debt independently of the others. Must he share with the others the amount he has collected?

A. Since the creditors did not actually pool their money, their efforts, or their pledges, and did not form a partnership by any binding act, no partnership existed. Each creditor had a right to act in pursuance of his own interests. However, if the loan of the creditor who collected his debt independently was well secured by pledges or sureties, or if the security was sufficient to warrant a new loan by him, he may be called "wicked" for having damaged the interests of the other creditors. This is in accordance with the talmudic law (Kidd. 59a): If a poor man "turneth a cake" and another takes it away from him, the latter is called "wicked".

SOURCES: P. 286.

446 (D)

Q. A claims that he advanced money to L, a widow, who assured him that the exact amount would be returned to him in Erfurt; that L promised to repay all expenses he might incur in collecting the money, should he find it difficult to collect it in Erfurt; that when he came there he was put off time and again and was obliged to send three messengers in order to collect the money, thus spending three pounds. He, therefore, demands these three pounds. L denies any knowledge of A's expenses, but is ready to pay the amount that, A will state under oath, is due him.

A. L's promise to A was a mere *Asmakhta.* Since this promise was not made before an authoritative court, even if it was accompanied by a *kinyan*, it was not binding.

SOURCES: B. p. 276, no. 53.

447 (D)

Q. A lent money to B. Before repayment was due, the coins were discontinued and new coins were issued in their stead weighing more than the old coins. The increase in weight, however, was less than twenty-five percent (cf. B. K. 98a). How is B to repay his debt to A?

A. If A specified at the time the loan was made that he was to be repaid a certain number of coins, B must repay him the same number of new coins, though he will thus repay more precious metal than what he borrowed, since an increase in the metal of less than twenty-five percent does not affect prices. But, if A did not specify the manner of repayment, he is to receive the same amount of precious metal as he lent to B, in new coins.

SOURCES: L. 209.

448

Q. A claims he has no cash and wants to repay his debt to B with goods. B demands that A swear that he has no cash. Is it not true that the court can not require an oath from A since no actual loss of money to B is involved?

A. The fact that there is no actual loss of money to B does not, of itself, absolve A from taking an oath. A is not required to take the oath for another reason. B can not claim to be certain that A has cash, and no one is required to take an oath when his opponent is not certain of his claim.

This Responsum is addressed to Rabbi Asher b. Moses.

SOURCES: Cr. 7, 8; Pr. 109; L. 360. Cf. Am II, 224.

449

Q. A owed money to several persons. When B demanded his money from A, the latter admitted the debt but claimed that since he did not possess enough money or valuables to cover all his obligations, he preferred to divide his possessions equitably among his creditors. Since A admits, in court, his debt to B, may the latter force A to repay that debt in full, before he divides his property?

A. Since A owes money to several persons, and since he owes more than the total value of his possessions, each creditor is entitled to receive an equal share of such possessions irrespective of the amount due him. The debtor, however, may distribute his assets among his creditors in proportion to the amount due to each, before they come to court; such distribution would be irrevocable, and would even constitute a praiseworthy act. Since A is willing so to divide his possessions, no judge can force him to favor one creditor at the expense of the other creditors. However, before receiving his share of A's possessions, movables or immovables, each creditor will have to take a creditor's oath — the same oath that a creditor takes upon collecting his debt from encumbered property.

SOURCES: Cr. 219; Am II, 45; Tesh. Maim. to *Mishpatim*, 41.

450

Q. A verbally contracted a loan from B. Subsequently A conveyed all of his property to C in order to withhold it from B.

A. We suspect A and C of conspiracy to defraud. Therefore, the court should force A to renounce all benefit from this property.

SOURCES: Mord. B. B. 648; *Mordecai Hagadol*, p. 335b.

451 (D)

Q. C gave the thirty *marks* A owed him to B as an outright gift. Thereupon, A transferred to B full ownership of the money by means of a valid *kinyan*. The whole transaction, however, was merely intended as a means of putting this money beyond the reach of C's creditors.

A. If B was present when C told A to give the money to B, the latter became legal owner of the money. Should C's Gentile creditors now institute garnishee proceedings against B, B may take an oath, to the effect that he has none of C's money, with a clear conscience. However, if B was not present when C told A to give the money to B, the mere statement of C, unaccompanied by a *kinyan*, did not transfer the money to B. Therefore, it still belongs to C.

SOURCES: Cr. 120.

452

Q. A owes money to B and B owes the same amount to a Gentile. B told A, in the presence of the Gentile, to pay his debt directly to the Gentile. The Gentile released B and depended upon A for payment. A successfully avoids payment to the Gentile because of an old debt due him from the latter. Since, according to Jewish law, the transaction was not valid and A's indebtedness to B was not legally transferred to the Gentile, A must pay his debt to B. But why should B be permitted to rob the Gentile? Is not robbing a Gentile prohibited? Moreover, the Gentile presses A for payment and eventually may force A to pay him his money; must A pay his debt to B?

A. Robbing a Gentile is prohibited, but one is permitted to annul a Gentile's debt (if he can do so by using plausible excuses and without causing the name of the Lord to be profaned). But, if A will be forced to pay the debt to the Gentile, he will not have to pay anything to B.

SOURCES: Cr. 227; Pr. 327; L. 385; Am II, 119.

453

Q. A claimed that he gave B a coat of mail and thigh plates as security for a loan. He repaid that loan, and therefore demands back his security. B answered that he received from

A only a coat of mail which he was ready to return upon the latter's payment of money still due B. Upon hearing B's reply, A said to the judges that he knew that the law required them to charge B with an oath, but that B was not qualified to take an oath since he was a notorious thief and was suspected of swearing falsely. A made a public announcement that whoever knew anything that might disqualify B from taking an oath, should appear and testify before the court and the community leaders, in accordance with the Biblical injunction (Leviticus, 5, 1). Many witnesses appeared, but the testimony of only three persons was valid. One of these testified that B had stolen one pound from him; the second said that B had testified against him in a Gentile court and thus had caused him to suffer damages; and the third testified that B had bound himself by a *herem* to redeem his pledged horse, and had failed to do so. Since these misdemeanors had happened long ago and B might have repented since then, was the testimony of these witnesses sufficient to disqualify B from taking an oath?

A. B should be disqualified from taking an oath because of the testimony of the first and third witnesses. The Talmud (B. K. 62a) came to no conclusion regarding the trustworthiness of an informer; therefore, the testimony of the second witness is of no consequence.

SOURCES: Pr. 978.

454

Q. A claims he deposited a pledge with B to secure a loan, and now wishes to redeem it. B claims that the pledge had to be redeemed before a certain date or become forfeited. When the time of payment arrived, A asked for an extension of time and said: "Take formal possession so that the pledge henceforth be yours if I do not repay you before that date". A made no payment on the date due after the extension; B, therefore, claims that the pledge became forfeited. A denies having said, "Take formal possession . . . . henceforth".

A. Usually a statement, such as A is alleged to have made, is classified as *Asmakhta* and is not binding. But since B is in possession of the pledged articles, and since B has done a favor to A in lending him money, this satement is no longer classified as *Asmakhta* and is binding. Therefore, if B takes an oath that A made the statement: "Take formal possession. . . . . henceforth", the pledge belongs to B.

SOURCES: Cr. 1; Pr. 91; L. 333; Rashba I, 1103; *Tashbetz*, 490; cf. Mord. B. M. 321.

455 (D)

Q. A sent a pledge to B through a Gentile as security for a loan to be contracted through the Gentile. Upon A's seeking to redeem the pledge, B refused to accept the money, claiming that the Gentile had sold him the pledge.

A. The Gentile had no right to sell A's pledge; consequently, A has a right to redeem it.

SOURCES: Pr. 728.

456 (D)

Q. A claims to have pawned with B, for thirty schillings, objects worth ten pounds. He is now willing to repay the thirty schillings and demands that B return the pawned objects. B, on the other hand, claims to have followed A's instructions and to have pawned the objects with the *Cahorsin*. To A's charge that the objects are still in B's possession, B retorts that he subsequently bought them from the *Cahorsin*. A also claims that B gave false testimony against him and caused him a loss of eleven pounds. B denies this charge. A further claims that he has provided B's Pentateuch with punctuation marks, that he was not paid for his labor, and that he can prove through witnesses that B owes him three pounds. B, however, claims to have already paid his obligations to A.

A. Regarding B's claim that he had paid his obligations to A, if he will take an oath to this effect, he will be free from obligation to A. Regarding A's first claim, however, the following distinction must be made: If B admits that A had originally pawned the objects with him for thirty schillings, even though subsequently thereto A told him to pawn them with the Gentile, he must return the objects to A upon the receipt of thirty schillings; but, if both A and B admit that originally A merely sent B to pawn the objects with the Gentile, B must state under oath the amount he paid to the Gentile for the return of the objects, and must return them to A upon the receipt of such amount.

SOURCES: B. p. 292, no. 370.

457

Q. It is the law that the responsibility of a creditor toward a pledge he received as security for a loan is that of a paid bailee. Does this responsibility also extend to the amount by which the pledge exceeds the loan?

A. Since Ri ruled that the opinion of Rabba prevails, that the responsibility of a keeper of a lost object is that of a gratuitous bailee (B. M. 82a), the responsibility of the creditor toward the excess value of the pledge is also that of a gratuitous bailee. Although some authorities are of the opposite opinion, the very fact that a difference of opinion exists creates a doubt as to the law; and in case of doubt we do not render a verdict to collect.

SOURCES: Am II, 161; Mord. Sheb. 774; Tesh. Maim. to *Mishpatim*, 56; *Agudah* Sheb. 36; cf. Pr. 185; ibid. 699b.

458

Q. A lent money to B receiving a pledge as security thereof. He stipulated at the time that he be not held responsible for the pledge in case of loss. Is A responsible if the pledge was lost through his wilful neglect?

A. A is not responsible. Although a creditor is in the category of a paid watchman regarding the pledges he receives as security, he is not even in the category of an unpaid watchman, if he renounces his responsibility thereto; and he is not responsible even though the security be lost through his wilful neglect.

Sources: Pr. 229; Mord. B. M. 361; Tesh. Maim. to *Mishpatim*, 11; *Agudah* B. M. 127.

459 (D)

Q. A loaned money to a Gentile and received a pledge as security. Being in need of money he rehypothecated the Gentile's pledge with B. B lost the pledge. When the Gentile repaid his debt he demanded for his lost pledge double its actual value. A demanded that B indemnify him for the loss he suffered because of his obligation to the Gentile, since the pledge was lost while in B's possession.

A. B is responsible for the actual value of the pledge only. Whatever the Gentile demanded in excess of that amount is illegal extortion and must be suffered by A.

Sources: Pr. 694.

460

Q. A had paid off the greater part of the loan he had contracted from Gentile money-lenders against a pledge. B wanted to borrow money from these money-lenders. He asked A to permit him to borrow money against this pledge of A that was still in the hands of the Gentiles, and A assented. Subsequently, the Gentile's house burned down and A's pledge was lost [in the flames]. Must B compensate A for this loss?

A. Since B did not take possession of A's pledge, he never became responsible for its safety. Therefore, B owes nothing to A. Although the burning of A's pledge cancelled B's debt to the Gentiles (by the law of the land), and thus directly benefited B, Heaven bestowed a blessing upon him; why should he therefore share it with A?

This Responsum was addressed to Rabbi Asher.

SOURCES: Am II, 159; Mord. B. M. 371; Tesh. Maim. to *Mishpatim*, 60; *Mordecai Hagadol*, p. 289b.

461

Q. A's heirs demand from B A's *Humash* (one book of the Pentateuch) which witnesses saw in B's possession. B claims that A deposited the book with him as security for the two *marks* A owed him. Some of A's heirs admit having heard A say before his death that the book was deposited with B as a pledge. Is a *Humash* classified as an object which is usually borrowed or hired and regarding which a person is, therefore, not believed when he claims to have received it as a pledge?

A. Throughout the kingdom, Rashi's view is accepted that a *Humash* is not an object that is usually borrowed or hired. B therefore may take an oath that the book was pledged with him for two *marks*. However, B should be careful in taking his oath; for, if A did not actually owe him two *marks*, but promised to give B two *marks* if the latter effect a reconciliation between A and his son, A became indebted to B only for the latter's wages for the time and effort expended, but not for full two *marks*.

SOURCES: Pr. 1007.

462

Q. A demands that B return his book. B avers that the book was pledged with him for ten pounds. He refuses to explain, however, under what circumstances the book was pledged with him.

A. If B claims to have forgotten under what circumstances the book had been pledged with him, he is free from obligation. However, if B merely refuses to explain how the book came into his possession, there is evidence of fraud, and a thorough investigation is required. Therefore, if B should fail to explain under what circumstances the book was pledged with him, he would have to return the book without compensation.

SOURCES: Mord. B. M. 223. Cf. *Terumat Hadeshen* 343.

463

a) *Q.* B demands from A the books he deposited with him. He maintains that all the members of the community are ready to testify that he deposited his books with A only as security against money he owed to the holy cause, while A was the trustee of that cause, and that he subsequently repaid this obligation. A claims that the books have been pledged with him as security for nine *marks* still due him from B, and pleads that the members of the community are hostile to him and should therefore be disqualified as witnesses.

A. Jews are not suspected of bearing false witness against a person even though hostile to him. The members of the community are, therefore, qualified to serve as witnesses in this case. If witnesses had seen B's books in A's possession, and if witnesses will testify that the books had been deposited with A as security against B's obligation to the holy cause, A will have to return the books to B. But if B's books had not been

seen in A's possession, A is entitled to claim that these books
were pledged with him for a personal loan.

b) *Q.* A claims that B made a complaint against him to
the Gentiles and thus caused him a loss of five *marks*.

A. B should take an oath that either he did not inform
against A, or was unaware to what extent he had damaged
A's interests, and then he would be free from obligation. Should
B take the latter oath, he would be free from obligation only
if A could not prove through witnesses the extent of the damage
B caused him.

SOURCES: *Mordecai Hagadol,* p. 369b.

464 (D)

Q. A sold a cloak to B for twelve halves (half-pounds, or
marks). B postponed payment for it from day to day; and when
finally A brought him to court, he claimed that he had already
paid A. The court ordered A to take an oath, but B kept on
postponing the taking of such oath until he died. A now demands payment from B's son.

A. B's son must take the ordinary oath of an heir that his
father told him nothing regarding the debt to A.

SOURCES: Pr. 837.

465

Q. A, an orphan, demands that his mother's husband, B,
give him money belonging to him. A claims that B admitted
having received money that belonged to A, and having recorded
it in A's name. B, on the other hand, either denies having ever
admitted having any of A's money, or claims that if he had
made such admission it was made for effect only, in order not
to appear wealthy.

A. B must take an oath in support of his denial.

SOURCES: Mord. Sanh. 703; *Mordecai Hagadol,* p. 354b; *Agudah* Sanh. 30.

466

Q. A says that B's mother before her death instructed B
to give A one *Mina* out of her possessions, since she had owed
money to A's mother and did not remember whether or not
she had repaid the entire sum. B denies having received such
instructions from his mother, and further claims that A's mother
owed him more than one *Mina*. But A has witnesses who
testify that after his mother's death B admitted having received
these instructions.

A. Since B's mother did not take the required oath regarding her *ketubah*, she had no property of her own; even
the clothes she wore on week-days belonged to the estate.
Consequently B is unable to carry out his mother's instructions.
B is under no moral obligation to repay his mother's debt since
the mother herself had not been pressed for payment.

SOURCES: Cr. 76.

467

Q. A demands from B rent for fifteen years, during which
period B lived in his house. B claims that he paid the rent,
and, in turn, demands payment for putting up, in A's house,
certain necessary structures. A, however, claims that he did
not ask B to put up such structures.

A. B should take an oath that he paid A the rent, and
be free from that obligation. If B can prove, or if A admits,
that he, B, put up the structures mentioned, B has a right
to remove them.

SOURCES: Pr. 962.

468

Q. A and B were joint owners of a house and they both
lived there. When A left town, B and his household remained
in the house for several years making full use of it. Now A
claims that B had promised to make improvements in the

house and build structures therein, in lieu of paying A rent for his half, and that B failed to keep his promise. A therefore demands his rent. B denies having promised to pay A any rent or to build any structures, and maintains that he offered no objections to A's renting his half of the house.

A. B must take an oath in support of his denial. If it were known that B did not promise any rent to A, we should not be justified in compelling B to pay for his use of A's half of the house, since, as long as the house was not partitioned among the partners, B could have claimed that whenever he used any part of the house he only used his own half. On the other hand, if B did promise rent to A, he is obliged to pay it to A even if he did not use A's half of the house, since A did not rent his half of the house to another because of B's promise of rent.

SOURCES: Sinai VII (1943) 1 nos. 503–4.

469

Q. A demands from B money (one *Mina*, Pr.) he owes him. B claims he paid the debt to A's wife. A says: "I gave you the money and I want you to pay it back to me".

A. If a depositary hands over his deposit to another watchman whom the owner of the deposit usually trusts with his valuables, that depositary is free from obligation. Therefore, if A permits his wife to take part in the management of his business, B must take an oath that he gave the money to A's wife, and be free from obligation.

SOURCES: Pr. 225; Mord. B. M. 272; Rashba I, 1096; Tesh. Maim. to *Mishpatim*, 3; *Agudah* B. M. 51.

470 (D)

Q. A charges that when he borrowed money from his uncle who sent it to him through B, B kept some of it for himself;

that he summoned B to court, and the court adjudicated in his favor; but, that B did not as yet comply with the decision of the court. B avers that the court freed him from obligation.

A. If B will take an oath to the effect that he owes nothing to A, he will be free from obligation.

SOURCES: Cr. 293.

471 (D)

Q. A says to B: "You owe me one *Minah*." B answers: "On the contrary, you owe me one *Minah*; either take an oath that I owe it to you or I will take an oath that you owe it to me."

A. If B meant to transfer his oath to A, A will swear that B owes him one *Minah*, and, again, that he owes nothing to B, and he may collect his money from B. But if B meant that he will allow A to take an oath and collect, on condition that A allow him to do the same, B's words are of no avail and the usual procedure [that the defendant takes the oath to free himself from obligation] is followed.

SOURCES: Pr. 276.

472

Q. A mortgaged his real estate to B in security of a loan with the proviso that should A fail to repay the loan by a certain date, title to the real estate should pass to B. The terms were put in writing. A, however, claims that B promised to pay him the difference between the value of the property and the amount of the loan, in case he failed to redeem his property. A maintains that he relied on B's verbal promise. B, however, denies having made such a promise.

A. If A demands that B should take an oath in support of his denial, B must take such an oath. Thus A's claim is not contradicted by the written agreement, and if B did promise

to pay the difference between the value of the property and
the amount of the loan to A, he must keep his promise. If A,
however, does not expressly demand that B take an oath, B
is free from obligation.

Sources: Sinai VII (1943) 1 no. 504.

473 (D)

Q. In the presence of witnesses, A gave merchandise to
B on credit. When the time for payment arrived, A claimed
that B owed him twenty-five shillings, but B claimed that the
amount due was twenty-four shillings. The witnesses supported
B's claim, but A claimed that they were mistaken, and demanded that either B take an oath and pay twenty-four shillings
or else he, A, would take an oath and collect twenty-five shillings.

A. Since witnesses support B's claim, he is under no obligation to take an oath.

Sources: Pr. 829.

474

Q. A pressed many claims against B. To one of his claims
B made no reply. Is B's silence to be considered an admission
of the truth of A's claim?

A. Silence is not considered admission even if the defendant
kept silent at court, unless the claimant summoned his listeners
to witness the fact that the defendant did not deny his claim,
and the latter still failed to reply.

Sources: Cr. 261; *Mordecai Hagadol*, p. 269c; Hag. Maim., *Toen* 7, 9.

475

Q. A demanded from B sixty pennies he owed him. B
admitted the indebtedness, but claimed that through A's wilful
neglect, he, B, was not able to collect a debt of four pounds

and sixty pennies. B, therefore, demanded that A pay him four pounds. The judges ordered A to swear that he did not willfully cause any damage to B, and ordered B to swear that A did willfully cause him a loss of at least sixty pennies. After the judges rendered this decision, B put forth his claim that, in partnership with A, he, B, loaned eight and one half pounds to Gentiles, and that, without his permission or consent, A relinquished that debt to the Gentiles. A, however, claimed that B gave him permission to do with B's share whatever he would do with his own. Moreover, A claims that B informed against him; a Jewish witness, the servants of the Bishop, and the burghers, support A's claim in this respect. The judges, however, demand that their former decision be carried out and that A and B present their new claims in another suit.

A. The decision of the judges that A must take an oath to the effect that he did not cause B to lose his investment by willful neglect, is correct. But if A released B's Gentile debtors (even though B gave A a blanket permission to do with his, B's, share whatever he, A, would do with his own), A must pay B as much as B's share was worth before A released the Gentiles. B must take an oath in the presence of the Gentile witnesses that he did not inform against A, in order to counteract the testimony of the single Jewish witness.

The question is signed by R. Yedidyah b. R. Israel.

SOURCES: Cr. 5 2; Pr. 699; L. 373–4; Mord. B. K. 96; Rashba I, 1096; *Mordecai Hagadol*, p. 258a. Cf. Moses Minz, *Responsa* 44; Isserlein, *Pesakim* 209.

476 (D)

Q. A demanded that B return the book he had lent him, but B averred that he held the book as security against four schillings A owed him. A protested that he had never borrowed anything from B, and that B had no right to hold his book as security against the four schillings B had won from him in a card game, since a person does not legally gain title to his winnings in a card game. B, however, refused to explain how A became indebted to him.

A. B is under no obligation to explain how A became indebted to him. He must merely take an oath to the effect that A legally owes him four schillings. A court does not investigate the manner in which a debt was allegedly contracted, nor the manner in which it was allegedly repaid.

SOURCES: Cr. 162.

477 (D)

I have heard that whenever a plaintiff, before formally relinquishing his claims against the defendant, registers his protest before witnesses and declares that the forthcoming relinquishing of his claims will be a mere pretense, the courts throughout these communities consider such relinquishing of claims null and void. They base such a decision on the talmudic statement that a protest registered against a forthcoming divorce or gift is "a mere clarification of the situation" (B. B. 40b), which they interpret to mean that a protest is valid in these two instances even though the person was not coerced into granting the divorce or the gift. This decision, however, is wrong and wicked, and is the greatest outrage practiced since the days of the Judges. Were this principle accepted in our law, life would be unbearable. A husband would grant a divorce to his wife in consideration of a substantial sum of money, and after pocketing the money would disclose that a protest preceded the granting of the divorce. Persons would do favors to others in consideration of gifts received from them and would later discover that protests preceded the deeds of gift. Why did Rabban Gamaliel the Elder (Git. 32a) decree that a divorce be not nullified unless the messenger or wife be notified of its nullification before the bill of divorcement reached the wife . . . .?

The concluding part of this Responsum is missing.

SOURCES: Am II, 239.

478 (D)

Q. Is the oath a partner takes at the request of the other partner(s) [that he did not retain anything belonging to the partnership], required by Biblical law, or is it a rabbinic enactment?

A. It is a rabbinic enactment.

SOURCES: Pr. 272.

479 (D)

Q. A was ready to take an oath denying B's claim. When he noticed, however, that B was going to insert in the oath a denial of a former claim B had had against him, A decided to pay B's present claim in order to avoid taking such an oath. Will A, upon such payment, be free from the obligation of taking an oath, or must he pay both claims before being free from this obligation?

A. Nowadays a person is required to take an oath whenever he denies any claims made against him, whether such denial is complete or partial, whether the claim involves immovables or movables. Therefore, the problem stated above does not exist nowadays. Let A pay B as much as he wants to pay. If B will put forth further claims against A, the latter must either pay such claims or take an oath. In former days, however, when certain claims if denied required no oath, the Rabbis differed in their opinions whether or not the defendant be required to take an oath regarding an earlier claim, in cases similar to the above.

SOURCES: Cr. 270; L. 238.

480

Q. If a litigant is proven to have lied in respect to one of his claims, is he considered untrustworthy in respect to his other claims so that he becomes disqualified from taking an oath?

A. He is still to be trusted under oath regarding his other claims.

SOURCES: Cr. 297; Am II, 235; Mord. B. M. 227.

481

Q. At first A denied that he had gone surety for C to B; but when it was proven that he had done so, he claimed that C had repaid his (C's) obligation to B. Is A free of his obligation to B?

A. We cannot apply to this case the talmudic principle that he who denies having contracted a loan from another thereby admits not having repaid that loan (Shebu. 41b), for when the debtor claims that he repaid his loan and is ready to take an oath in support of his claim, the surety is automatically freed from his obligation regardless of his own admissions or denials.

SOURCES: *Mordecai Hagadol*, p. 335 c; Hag. Maim. *Malveh,,* 22, 1; cf. Israel Bruno, *Responsa* 239.

482

Q. C, D, E, and F, went surety to A for B. B failed to repay his debt, and now A demands the entire sum from C and D. Moreover, the sureties claim that they have already paid five *marks* to A. The latter, however, avers that these five *marks* were paid to him in settlement of another debt.

A. If E and F have no money, A is entitled to collect the entire debt from C and D; otherwise, he may collect from the latter two only their share of the debt. Regarding the other claim of the sureties, if witnesses have heard A admit that he had received five *marks* from the sureties, he may not claim that such payment was made in settlement of another debt, for such a claim is upheld in court only when the claimant has had recourse to a *miggo* (Shebu. 42a).

SOURCES: Tesh. Maim. to *Mishpatim*, 63.

483

If three sureties guarantee a loan, they are severally responsible for the entire loan.

SOURCES: Cr. 110.

484 (D)

The surety may not press the creditor to demand his money from the debtor.

SOURCES: Cr. 113.

485

Q. A became B's surety to a Gentile. One of the stipulations of the surety agreement was that if B would not pay his debt before a specified date, B would have to pay for A's meals until B paid his debt. [This was the custom of the land with reference to sureties]. B did not pay his debt on time. Meanwhile A ate extravagantly in C's house at B's expense.

A. Jews who are sureties, are kind to their debtors and eat moderately at their expense. Moreover, A should have had pity on B who was just released from prison, and should not have dealt ruthlessly with him. Therefore, B must pay C the price of moderate meals, and the rest C is to collect from A. If A claims that C charged him exorbitant prices, he may summon C to court.

SOURCES: Pr. 83.

486

Q. A claims that he went surety to a Gentile for B, that B did not redeem him from his suretyship, and that he had to pay the Gentile more than three *marks*, since the latter hypothecated A's pledge with a third party and interest was accumulating on it.* B claims that he caused the Gentile to release A from his suretyship.

A. B must take an oath that he caused the Gentile to release A from his suretyship, and he will be free from any obligation to A.

SOURCES: Cr. 296; Pr. 496. Cf. *Agudah* B. K. 338. Weil, *Responsa* 110.

487

Q. A and B went surety to a Gentile for C, who could not repay his debt to the Gentile. A left the city. In accordance with the law of the land, the Gentile collected his debt from B. Now B demands that A share the loss with him.

A. Since according to the law of the land a creditor may collect the entire debt from one surety, even where there are other sureties, and since in such a case the law of the land must prevail, the Gentile was entitled to collect his debt from B. Therefore, since B was legally made to pay A's obligations, A must repay B's loss.

The question was sent by R. Asher b. Yehiel.

SOURCES: Pr. 116.

488

Q. A consented to go surety for B to a burgher. The bishop and the judge released A from his suretyship, but the burgher refused to release him, and pressed him for money by threats and false accusations, until A was forced to make a

* The Hebrew is not clear on this point.

money settlement with him. A, now, demands that B indemnify him for his loss.

A. B must indemnify A for all losses he suffered through his suretyship, even if the suretyship was used as a mere pretext for extortion. This is the law throughout our kingdom and is believed to be based on an ordinance of the communities. I believe, however, that it is sound talmudic law. But, A must prove the exact amount of his loss and can not collect by merely taking an oath. Even if witnesses testify that A gave a certain sum to the burgher and told him that the money was in final settlement of his suretyship for B, A must, nevertheless, swear that the money was given for that purpose only and that the burgher refused to accept a smaller amount in settlement of his claim. Only then may he collect that sum from B. If, however, A admits that the Gentile first released him from his suretyship and then returned with threats and accusations, B is free from any obligations to A.

SOURCES: Pr. 495; Mord. B. K. 160–161; Asher, *Responsa*, 18, 6. Cf. ibid. 18, 7; *Agudah* B. K. 138; Weil, *Responsa* 110; Moses Minz, *Responsa* 44; ibid. 74b.

489 (D)

Q. A went surety to B for a Gentile. When the Gentile returned* the pledge to him*, B said to A that he was relying on A unconditionally and would not demand from the Gentile the principal or the interest, for the Gentile was a violent man. Now, the Gentile threatens to kill B if he demands his money.

A. Since B told A that he would demand his money directly from him, A assumed unconditional responsibility for the debt and became a *Kablan* (B. B. 173b). Therefore, B is entitled to collect the debt directly from A.

SOURCES: Cr. 99.

*The Hebrew is not clear on this point.

490 (D)

Q. A claims that B took a valuable article of his, and, without his permission, gave it to a Gentile. B avers that the Gentile was A's creditor; that he had gone surety to the Gentile for A; and that he had to permit the Gentile to take A's article in order that he might free himself from this suretyship.

A. If B will take an oath in support of his claims, he will be free from obligation. Should A claim that he has paid his debt to the Gentile, such claim would be of no consequence. Since A did not repay the debt in B's presence, and since his creditor was a Gentile, who has held B directly responsible for such debt, and could still have collected it from B through the courts of the land, A was still under obligation to free B from his suretyship. Therefore, B acted within his rights.

SOURCES: Cr. 294.

491

Q. A's widow and son, through their representative, summoned B, A's brother, before us. The representative claimed that A had given wine to B for the purpose of transporting it to Magdeburg and selling it there, and that B bartered this wine for a horse. He demanded, therefore, that B return the horse either to the widow, in payment of her *ketubah*, or to the orphan who was the rightful heir. B claimed that he had become surety to a Gentile for a loan of five and one quarter *marks*, contracted by A, that A's wife had vowed to repay this debt and release him from his suretyship; that A had given him the wine for the purpose of selling it and buying his release with that money; that the horse was worth only three *marks*, and that the widow, therefore, still owed him two and one quarter *marks*. The representative, however, claimed that A had effected B's release from his suretyship. We decided, temporarily, that B should take an oath to the effect that he has as yet not been released from his suretyship and that he had received the wine for the purpose of buying such release; in which case he should be entitled to retain the horse. However, before B took the prescribed oath, he sold the horse for six pounds, which now had a value of four and one-quarter *marks*, and he made a settlement with the Gentile (A's creditor for the 5¼ *marks*) to pay him one *mark* per year for six years. B wanted to give the six pounds to his mother-in-law for investment purposes, she promising to pay the one *mark* per year for six years to the Gentile. The representative, however, claimed that B was in possession of an amount equal to the value of the horse only and that B must pay out of his own pocket the difference between this amount and the amount due the Gentile. He demanded that B return the six pounds to the widow and her son, who were willing to provide sureties to the Gentile guaranteeing the payment of one *mark* per year for six years. B, on the other hand, claimed that he was entitled to benefit from the advantageous settlement he negotiated with A's creditor; that being able to release himself completely from his suretyship by his shrewdness in the use of the four and one-quarter *marks*, he was entitled to do so; and that he was taking a risk since (the coins comprising) the six pounds were almost certain to be invalidated and be worth less than four and one quarter *marks*. Moreover, B claimed that A had promised to pay him for his efforts in selling the wine, and that he had guaranteed another debt of A which had not been paid. We shall follow your decision in this matter. Furthermore, please inform us whether or not B may exact an oath from the widow to the effect that she did not vow to release him from his suretyship.

A. B has no claim on the money he received for the horse if his complete release from his suretyship is effected in other ways, especially since he had as yet not taken the required oath. Since the widow and her son are willing to guarantee such a release, B must return that money to them. However, if B take an oath to the effect that A owed him a certain amount of money, either for his effort in selling the wine or for becoming surety for another debt, he will be entitled to retain such an amount. B may exact an oath from the widow (to the effect that she did not vow to pay the above debt of five and one-quarter *marks*) under the following conditions only: a) If it is an established fact that A did not effect the release of B from his suretyship; b) if B claims that the widow had made the vow mentioned above before he became surety for A. If the former condition is lacking, the widow is not required to take an oath when the claim against her is based on a doubtful premise; and if the latter condition is lacking, the widow never became responsible for that debt. If she made the vow referred to above, she is still under solemn obligation to keep her vow, but is not required to take an oath. However, the representative's claim that B was in possession of an amount equal to the value of the horse only, is baseless.

SOURCES: L. 218, 219; cf. Hag. Maim., *Shebuoth* 11, 3.

492

Q. A claimed that C owed him two denarii (Cr. reads: one pound), and that he refused to go to the Jewish court. When C wanted to leave the city, A complained to the judge,* who retained C's money until he would appear before the Jewish court and comply with its decision. B then interposed in C's behalf, became surety for him, took pledges from A (and, probably from C) and promised A by solemn hand-clasp that should C fail to appear in court and to comply with its decision, B would return the pledges to A. A believes he has witnesses to this effect, and demands the pledges from B. B, however, claims

---

* Probably a Gentile judge.

that he only guaranteed that C would return to the city before a certain date, that C did come to the city before that date, and that he (B) was thereby released from his obligation.

A. If A, through the testimony of his witnesses, can prove his claim regarding B's promise by solemn hand-clasp, then B must fulfill his promise, since promises made by solemn hand-clasp must be fulfilled. But, if A has no witnesses, B is free from obligation and does not even have to take an oath. Furthermore, B's suretyship was of no value, since a suretyship entered into after the original transaction had been completed, is not binding.

SOURCES: Cr. 187; Pr. 36; S. A. Wertheimer, *Ginzei Jerushalaim* 1; cf. Hag. Maim, *Shebuoth* 11,3.

493 (D)

Q. When B went out of town, the officer of the town stationed guards at his house in order to make sure that neither his wife, his children, nor his valuables would be removed from town. Three days later B's wife came to A and implored him to go surety for her to the officer, and to guaranty that neither she, her children, nor their valuables would be removed from town, until her husband returned and personally gave security to the officer that he would not move out of the overlord's territory. When subsequently B returned to town, A told him of his suretyship. B thanked A and commended him for having kept the guards out of his house. Then the overlord of the town, the king's highest officer, came and heaped accusations on B for having gone to dwell in another town — though this town was also a royal town and, therefore, under his jurisdiction — saying: "I know that you intend to flee from my territory". B, realizing that the officer had falsely accused him before the overlord, asked the dignitaries of two towns to induce the overlord to permit him to move into another town under his jurisdiction. When permission was granted, A's relative informed him that B was planning to move out of the overlord's territory. A protested to B's wife that he would be held responsible by the officer for such a move on B's part. B's wife reminded him that the overlord released B's sureties from obligation, but A pointed out that he had gone surety to the officer, and that the latter did not release him. B's wife, therefore, vowed and obligated herself by solemn hand clasp that in case the officer should inculpate A, and in case B should not compensate him for all ensuing losses, she would herself compensate him, up to twenty pounds, out of her clothes and jewels, without a court action. Subsequently B moved out of town, A was inculpated and incarcerated, and was forced to pay thirty pounds for his release. A, therefore, demands the thirty pounds from B.

A. A husband must redeem his wife even when the ransom asked is larger than her value (as a slave), and must pay his wife's debts which she contracted, for the purpose of buying her release. A person who goes surety for another must be compensated for all ensuing losses. Consequently, B must compensate A for his losses.

SOURCES: B. P. 286, no. 348. Cf. *Agudah* B. K. 138.

494

Q. [While B was out of town] B's wife was put under house arrest by the officer. The latter's servants kept constant watch over her not letting her take a single step outside of her house without their permission. She asked A to go surety for her to the officer. A complied with her wishes, and she was released. The officer, however, made unjust and extravagant demands on A, with which demands he was forced to comply. A now demands that B make good the losses he has suffered because of his suretyship.

A. B was under obligation to ransom his wife, for there was no practical difference between her being taken captive or her being placed under house arrest. When B's wife asked A to ransom her, she assumed responsibility for all damages A might suffer on this account. Since A is entitled to collect such damages from B's wife, and she is entitled to collect them from her husband B, A is entitled to collect such damages directly from B through "R. Nathan's lien" (garnishee proceedings).

SOURCES: Cr. 164. Cf. *Agudah* B. K. 138.

495

Q. L asked A why he was occupying her property, since her husband had inherited the property from his father and she was about to take it in payment of her *ketubah.* A averred that he had bought the property from L's father-in-law, that he could produce the deed as proof, and that he could prove through witnesses a long period of undisturbed possession. A was then asked to produce the deed. The deed showed, however, that after the death of L's father-in-law, A bought the property from L's mother-in-law to whom the court had adjudged such property in payment of her *ketubah.* When A was asked to explain the discrepancy between his statement and the deed, A answered that he had bought the property twenty-three years ago and did not remember the details.

A. A's statement did not invalidate the deed, for a person does not usually remember details that are of no particular importance to him.

SOURCES: Cr. 311; *Mordecai Hagadol,* p. 309a.

496

Q. A's window is narrow on the inside and wide on the outside. B, his neighbor, wants to build a wall alongside A's wall and extend it, as far as he is permitted, up to A's window. But, what is considered the window proper? Is it the narrow, inside, opening or the wide, outside, opening? We are inclined to the opinion that the wide, outside, opening is the window proper; some of our Rabbis (colleagues) disagree with us but their reasons for disagreeing are not convincing. Therefore, we want your opinion.

Signed: Eliezer b. Shlumiel, Mordecai b. Joseph, Simon Solomon b. Baruch.

A. The narrow part of the window is the window proper, for two reasons. First, anything a person can build in his house without his neighbor being able to object to it, can not be used as a restriction on such neighbor when he wants to build on his own property. Secondly, a person may increase his lights by beveling the outside border of his window as long as he does not touch the inside border of the window (or vice versa) without his neighbor being able to object to it. Surely one may make his wall very thin without his neighbor being able to object to it; the thinning of the wall has the same effect on the visibility of the window as the beveling of the border of the window. If one is permissible, so is the other. The neighbor, then, cannot be restrained from placing his wall exactly in the same position he could have placed it before the person widened the outside of his window. B, therefore, may extend his wall up to one *tefah* of the narrow part of A's window.

SOURCES: Cr. 11; Pr. 321; P. 528; Mord. B. B. 523; Hag. Maim., *Shekenim*, 7, 3. Cf. *Agudah* B. B. 49.

497

Q. B erected a building alongside of A's windows, thus shutting out the light from his windows. As soon as A learned about it, he protested vigorously. B, however, refuses to remove his building, claiming that A's protests are of no avail since the building had been completed long before A protested.

A. An abutter is not permitted to build a wall within four cubits of his neighbor's windows without the latter's permission. Therefore, B must remove the aforesaid building, for A protested as soon as he learned about its erection. Moreover, should B produce witnesses to the effect that A failed to protest immediately after he learned of the erection of B's building, it would avail B nothing as long as he does not claim to have bought, or to have received as a gift, the right to erect the building. Undisturbed possession in itself is of no legal consequence, unless it be accompanied by a claim of having once legally acquired the disputed right.

Sources: Cr. 237; Am II, 181; Tesh. Maim. to *Mishpatim* 71; *Mordecai Hagadol*, p. 314b; cf. Mord. B. B. 555.

498

Q. A constructed apertures for windows in his house which bordered on a Gentile's property. A had a right to construct these windows, while the Gentile had a right to build a wall immediately in front of these windows and obstruct their view, since according to the law of the country, a person may build anything he wants on his own property, regardless of his neighbor's conveniences. Some years later, the Gentile sold his property to a Jew, B, and specified in the bill of sale, which bore the burghers' seal, that B had a right to build a wall and obstruct the view of A's windows. Now B demands that A board up his windows, while A claims the right to these window lights because of the law of usucapion.

A. B could not buy from the Gentile any rights the Gentile himself did not possess. Therefore, since according to the law of the country one may build on his property whatever he pleases, B may build a wall on his property and obstruct the view of A's windows; but he can not compel A to board up his windows. However, if A claims that he bought the right to construct the apertures for the windows, he must produce documentary evidence or witnesses to support his claim, no matter how many years expired since the construction of his windows, since the law of usucapion is not valid when the original possessor of the right is a Gentile.

SOURCES: Cr. 63; Pr. 28; L. 338; Mord. B. B. 553; Hag. Maim., *Toen* 14.7; Tesh. Maim., *Mishpatim.* 70; *Agudah* B. B. 75.

499

Q. B bought property from a Gentile which bordered on A's property. Before paying for it, B, to acquire possession, did some digging in the Gentile's yard in the presence of witnesses. After B did so, but before he had paid the money to the Gentile, A constructed apertures for windows in his wall facing the property. Did A acquire rights to window lights?

A. In city property digging is not considered a valid act of possession. Likewise A did not acquire any rights to window lights since a Gentile does not renounce his rights to his property before he receives the money, and the Gentile's property was, therefore, not (*res nullis*) ownerless. However, before paying money to the Gentile, let B perform a valid act of possession (such as locking a door, fixing or breaking part of the fence, etc.); otherwise A will acquire rights to window lights during the interval between the paying of the money and B's taking formal possession, since during such interval the Gentile's property will be *res nullis*.

SOURCES: Cr. 63–64; Pr. 28–29; L. 338; Mord. ibid.

500

Q. Rabbi A (a relative of Rabbi Meir) at first admitted that a certain wall (which bordered on his property) belonged to his neighbor. Subsequently, however, he said that he had been informed that this wall had been built by his grandfather from whom he had inherited his property.

A. Since A first admitted that the wall belonged to his neighbor, his admission carried more weight than the subsequent testimony of witnesses. Since A had already reached his majority when his grandfather died, and thus should have known all the particulars regarding his inheritance, his admission regarding the ownership of the wall was valid, and he may no longer retract it.

SOURCES: Tesh. Maim. to *Mishpatim* 50; Mord. Sanh. 706.

501

Q. B's building was contiguous to A's property. The foundation of this building extended two hand-breadths beyond the wall itself. B wanted to build another wall in line with the edge of this foundation, the wall to extend two hand-breadths beyond the existing wall. A protested vigorously claiming that B's property ended at the edge of the wall of the building mentioned above, and that the foundation of such building extended two hand-breadths in his (A's) property.

A. Since B was in undisturbed possession of the width of the foundation, he was thus in possession of the disputed two hand-breadths of ground along the whole length of the property, and upwards reaching into the sky. Therefore, if B will take an oath to the effect that he did not remove his neighbor's landmark [when the foundation was built], the disputed two hand-breadths of ground will belong to him. Although according to Biblical law no oath is administered in disputes involving real property, such an oath is required by Rabbinic enactment.

SOURCES: Cr. 239; Am II, 184; Mord. B. B. 558; *Agudah* B. B. 109.

502

Q. A erected a building (of three walls) attaching it to a wall built exclusively by B on the latter's ground.

A. A must remove his building.

SOURCES: Cr. 238; Am II, 182.

503

Q. A well is situated on the boundary line between A's and B's properties, so that one half of the well is situated inside of A's property, and the other half inside of B's property. A erected a partition in the well (to separate the two parts) but placed the partition inside of B's property.

A. As expressly stipulated in the deed, the partition must be moved to the middle of the well.

SOURCES: Cr. 238; Am II, 183.

504

Q. B claims that A stopped off a conduit that used to drain off the water from the roofs through A's own property. A denies that such a conduit ever existed, and points out that B himself built a ledge intercepting the alleged route of such conduit.

A. Since B himself built a ledge blocking off the alleged conduit, he has no cause for action against A, and the latter need take no oath. A person who completely walls up his door leading into an alley and even removes the door posts may no longer reopen such entrance without the consent of the other dwellers in the alley.

SOURCES: Cr. 240; Am II, 185; Mord. B. B. 504.

505

Q. B constructed a stone duct near A's wooden house. A objected and B made a written promise to compensate him for any damage the duct might cause to his house. A now demands that B remove his duct because it occasionally permits water and sewage to flow into his house, and he objects to being forced to sue for damages every time it occurs. B claims that water flows into A's house only when the duct breaks. He promises to keep the duct in good condition, but refuses to remove it.

A. B must remove his duct from A's wall for a distance of 3 *tefahim* (hand-breadths). If the water should, nevertheless, continue to flow into A's house, it is for A to protect his wall by whatever means he sees fit, but he can demand nothing of B.

SOURCES: Cr. 3, 4; Pr. 92; L. 357; Mord. B. B. 520.

506

Q. A drained the water in his yard by means of a ditch which was adjacent to B's stone wall. B claimed that when the ditch was full, the water had flooded his house. He, therefore, demanded that A fill up his ditch. A claimed that the ditch had been in his yard for a period of twenty-four years and that B had never protested before. B, however, contended that the ditch had not previously caused him any damage. A's father bought the property with the ditch from a Jew who, in turn, had bought it from a Gentile.

A. If A removes his ditch one *tefah* from B's wall, he is free from further obligation. But even if A does not do so, he is free from any obligation since he inherited the ditch from his father, who, if alive, could claim that he bought the right to maintain the ditch from B. Moreover, A is not required to take an oath to the effect that he never heard his father say that he did not buy from B (or B's father) the right to maintain the ditch for the following reasons: *a*) Orphans are not required to take an oath in order to free themselves from a money obligation; b) the oath of orphans is a rabbinical decree and the Rabbis did not decree anything disadvantageous to the interests of the orphans.

The fact that A's yard originally belonged to a Gentile, has nothing to do with the case since B does not claim that the Gentile dug the ditch illegally. If B does put forth the claim that the Gentile dug the ditch illegally, it will avail him nothing, since, again, the court will have to put forth the claim, for A's benefit, that A's father bought the right to maintain the ditch from B or B's predecessors.

This Responsum was sent to R. Manahem b. David and R. Hillel b. Azriel of Würzburg (Cr. 23).

SOURCES: Cr. 23; Pr. 143; L. 388; Mord. B. B. 548; *Agudah* B. M. 180.

507

Q. A house belongs to several partners. One of the partners permits many persons to use his share of the house. May the other partners object to such use of the house by strangers?

A. The partners may object thereto.

SOURCES: Mord. B. B. 558.

508

Q. When the brothers A, B, and C divided among themselves the house they formerly held in common, a certain wall upon which heavy beams were resting crosswise, fell to A's portion. These beams extended beyond the wall into B's and C's portions on one side, and into A's portion on the other side. A cut off those parts of the beams which extended into his rooms. B and C objected to this act on A's part.

A. Those parts of the beams which extended into A's portion belonged to him exclusively, and he had a right to cut them off, especially since the intervening wall belonged to him. Although the act of sawing and chopping weakened B's and C's structures, since the extension of the beams into A's room served no useful purpose to B and C, and because of their unnecessary weight were even detrimental, A had a right to cut them off. In any event, B and C are not entitled to any compensation for their loss, now that the act has been done.

SOURCES: Am II, 198.

509

1) Q. A father left a house and a yard to his many children, so that his children A, B, and C were each entitled to one-eighth of this property. His son, A, bought one-third of his brother B's part, and C bought another third. One-eighth of the property is large enough to form a "usable unit."* A demands that it be partitioned in such a manner that he, A, receive his own part and the part he bought, as one unit. This division would be in accord with the rabbinical ordinance that upon division of property held in partnership, a partner should receive his part as one unit. C, however, desiring to block the partition of the property, is determined to waive the rabbinical ordinance originally intended in his favor, and demands that the part he bought from his brother be given to him separately. This would make the partition impossible, since one twenty-fourth of the property is too small a part to be used separately.

2. Q. The house is situated near the public thoroughfare and its northern door opens into the thoroughfare; while the yard extends south of the house, away from the thoroughfare. Upon partitioning this house among the heirs, one heir would

---

* According to R. Isaac b. Samuel, a "usable unit" is an area of four cubits by six cubits. The law requires that property held in partnership can be partitioned (against the will of one or more partners) only if every partner is able to receive a usable part.

receive the more valuable front entrance, while the other would
have to open up a door into the alley on the western side.
Moreover, a square cubit of ground in the northern part of the
yard, near the public thoroughfare, has double the value of a
square cubit in the southern part of the yard, away from the
thoroughfare. How, then, can this house be properly partitioned
among the heirs?

3. *Q*. Is the thickness of a wall, which can not be reduced
without weakening the entire building, to be considered as space
when the house is partitioned among heirs?

4) *Q*. What is the length of a *tefah*, six of which make a
cubit?

1) *A.* C can not refuse to abide by a rabbinical ordinance,
even though it was made in his favor, when such refusal inconveniences the other heirs.

2) *A.* To answer this question one must know exactly the
plan of the property. However, one must keep in mind the
following rule: The advantages that some parts of said property
have over other parts can be divided into two classes: a) posi-
tional advantages that can not be changed, i.e., some parts are
near the street, others are away from it; b) artificial advantages
caused by the presence of buildings, rooms, and doors in some
parts, and their absence in others. Therefore, regarding the
greater value of some parts of said property because of posi-
tional advantages, the size of each part should be, upon partitioning, inversely proportional to its value, thus equalizing the
value of each part. As regard the greater value of some parts
because of artificial advantages, the heir receiving the more
valuable part should pay the difference, in money, to the heir
receiving the less valuable part, for with the money he receives
the latter may so improve his part so as to have all the advantages the former has in his part.

3) *A.* No, the thickness of the above wall is not to be considered as space.

4) *A.* A *tefah* is the size of four thumbs measured at the middle.

SOURCES: Cr. 208; Pr. 237, 238, 239; Tesh. Maim. to *Kinyan*, 14; *Agudah* B. B. 25. Cf. *Terumat Hadeshen* 336.

510 (D)

Q. Upon dividing, among themselves, the land left by their father, A and B formally agreed (by means of a *Kinyan*) that the western part of that land shall belong to A and the eastern part to B. Upon B's portion was situated an unfinished stone structure. A demanded that it be torn down and the stones and gravel be divided between B and himself. B refused to tear the building down and wanted to pay A for his share of the value of the stones and the gravel. A, however, demanded that B also pay him half the amount it would cost to construct such a building.

A. As soon as A agreed to take the western part of the estate he relinquished his right to the building in the eastern part, excepting the value of the stones and the gravel of such building. Therefore, A is entitled to half the value of the stones and gravel only.

SOURCES: Pr. 836.

511

a) *Q.* Seven partners jointly own a house and a courtyard. Three eighths thereof belongs to A, one sixth to B, one-eighth to C, five forty-eighths to D, five forty-eighths to E, one-sixteenth to F, and one-sixteenth to G. A and B demand that the property be divided among the partners. Should the property be so divided, some of the partners would receive parts that are not "usable" [i.e., an area smaller than six cubits by four cubits].

A. Those partners who are to receive a "usable" part may

divide the house and courtyard in such a way that each of them receives his individual part, while the other partners hold the remaining parts jointly. Thus if F and G, are each to receive a part that is not "usable", they may be forced to hold jointly one eighth of the house and courtyard. F may not demand that he be given his part separately, even though such part be not "usable." Such a demand, if heeded, would leave G with a part that is not "usable" thus making the entire division impossible; we may use force in the case of a vicious (lit. Sodom-like) act of this kind.

b) *Q.* Who has charge over the division, the partners or the court?

A. The evaluation of the various parts is to be made by the court.

c) *Q.* If one partner is to receive, by a division, a part three cubits in width, and another partner a part five cubits in width, may the latter force the former to accept from him one extra cubit in width so that the first partner also receives a "usable" part, thus making the division possible?

A. The Talmud records a difference of opinion on this subject between the Rabbis who decided in the affirmative and Rabban Simeon b. Gamaliel who decided in the negative. Some post-talmudic authorities accept the former opinion, while others accept the latter. The talmudic discussion of the opinion of R. Simeon b. Gamaliel, however, leads us to accept the opinion of the Rabbis.

d) The thickness of a wall which cannot be reduced without weakening the building, is not to be considered as space. If thinning of such wall, however, would not seriously weaken the building, and the extra space thus gained would provide each partner with a "usable" unit, thus making a division possible, such a wall ought to be thinned accordingly, since peo' customarily thin walls for purposes of utility.

e) *Q.* Should the partner, who owns one-sixteenth of the property, receive his portion at the extreme end of the court-yard, away from the public thoroughfare, he would receive a "usable" unit. Should he receive part of the house near the public thoroughfare as his portion, he would not receive a "usable" unit. If said partner objects to a division of the property, may the other partners nevertheless divide the property in the hope that the extreme end of the courtyard would fall to his lot?

A. If upon receiving his portion midway between the house and the extreme end of the courtyard, the protesting partner would receive a "usable" unit, the partners may divide the property.

Sources: Cr. 208; Am II, 194–7; Tesh. Maim to *Kinyan,* 14–5; *Mordecai Hagadol,* p. 302a; *Agudah* B. B. 26; ibid. 28.

512

Q. A sold a half interest in his house to B. Subsequently A sold the other half to C and D. May C and D insist that the house be partitioned into four equal parts and that these parts be distributed among the partners by lot, so that B might by chance either receive his two parts adjacent to each other, or separated from each other, according to his luck?

A. C and D could not buy from A any right that A himself did not possess. Since A could not have insisted that the house be partitioned into four parts for distributing purposes, C and D can not insist on it. The house, therefore, must be partitioned by experts into two parts in either of the following two ways: a) The house may be divided into two parts equal in size, and the person or persons who would receive the more valuable half would have to pay the difference in value to the other persons or person; b) the house may be divided into two unequal parts inversely proportional in size to their intrinsic value, so that the smaller part is equal in value to the larger part.

SOURCES: *Mordecai Hagadol*, p. 301d.

513

Q. Jacob bought half an interest in a room from Noah. Subsequently Noah sold his remaining share to A and B; and later Jacob sold his half to C, D, and E. A now seeks to divide this room among the partners.

A. If the size of the room is ten cubits by ten cubits, A may force the other partners to agree to a partition since he, A, owning one quarter of the room, would receive a "usable unit" upon a partition even according to Ri who sets the minimum for such "usable unit" at six cubits by four cubits. For these measurements, the talmudic cubit of twenty-four thumb-breadths should be used. Even though such partition might leave C, D and E with parts smaller than this minimum, A would still be entitled to effect a partition of the property since before Jacob sold his share to C, D, and E each partner (A, B and Jacob) would have been entitled to a "usable unit." Moreover, A could have forced Jacob to agree to a partition even if he, A, would not have received a "usable unit." The restriction upon partners not to partition a house unless each partner receives a "usable unit", was decreed by the Rabbis for the benefit of those partners who were to receive the smaller parts. Therefore, A would have been entitled to waive this rabbinic decree that had been designed for his personal benefit.

SOURCES: Cr. 234: Am II, 178; Mord. B. B. 569; cf. Mord. B. M. 384; *Agudah* B. M. 158.

514

Q. A, B and C jointly owned a house, A owning a half interest therein and B and C, one quarter each. B died leaving his share to four sons. Now A wants to divide the house among the partners. B's heirs, however, object to such division since each of them would be left with a part too small for use as living quarters. A, however, avers that he wants to take half of the house for his exclusive use, and that if B's sons refuse to subdivide their father's share, they may hold that share jointly.

A. Since, while B was alive, the house was large enough to be divided among the three partners, and if A had then demanded a division, B's objection thereto would have been of no avail, B's sons may not now restrain A from effecting such a division. They can inherit no rights from B that he himself did not possess. The division of a house among partners should be executed by experts in one of two ways. a) Each partner should receive a part of the house proportional, in size, to his share while the difference between the value of such part and the money value of his share should be adjusted by the payment or receipt of money. b) Each partner should receive an appropriate part of the house inversely proportional, in size, to its intrinsic value, so that the estimated value of such part be exactly equal to the money value of his share.

This Responsum was addressed to Rabbi Hillel and Rabbi Menahem of Würzburg.

Sources: Cr. 234; Am II, 177; Mord. B. M. 384; *Mordecai Hagadol*, p. 301b.

515

Q. While pressed for money, A agreed to sell his house to C for one hundred twenty-five pounds, and promised him by solemn hand-clasp that if his neighbors (who owned the adjoining property) refused to buy the house for the stated sum, he would sell it only to C. Complying with C's demand A deposited a pledge of ten pounds with B to be delivered to C in case A did not keep his promise. A's neighbors agreed to buy the house for the price mentioned above. Meanwhile, A received money from a different source and after a conference with his relatives, he refused to sell the house altogether. A's neighbors summoned him to court claiming that he tricked them and that he used them as a means to free himself from his obligation to C. A, therefore, had to take an oath (in the form of a *herem*) that he had no intentions of trickery. Subsequently, with his pledge still in the hands of the trustee, B, A went to the Rabbis of a certain community and explained the situation to them. The Rabbis informed him that he did not lose his pledge since the consent of the neighbors to buy his house automatically voided his agreement with C. A, therefore, now demands his pledge from B. B, however, claims that A's agreement with C was that if A's neighbors did not buy his house by a certain date, A would sell it to C or forfeit the pledge. A single witness supports B's claim. B further claims that after the appointed time passed he delivered the pledge to C as instructed. Signed: Judah b. Rabbi Meshulam.

A. A's agreement to give C ten pounds in case he, A, does not keep his promise, is considered an *Asmakta*; and since the agreement was not made in the presence of an authoritative court, and was not accompanied by a *Kinyan*, it is not binding. A promised C by solemn hand-clasp to sell him the house, but no such hand-clasp accompanied A's agreement to pay the fine of ten pounds; therefore, A is under no obligation to pay ten pounds to C. And, since according to A's report of his agreement with C such agreement was voided by the neighbor's consent to buy the house, A is under no obligation to C, and B must return to A his ten pounds. The testimony of the single witness — that A promised by solemn hand-clasp to sell his house to C if his neighbors would not buy it by a certain date — does not oblige A to take an oath denying the truth of such testimony. For a solemn hand-clasp is equivalent to an oath; thus, if the testimony of the witness is true, A is already under a solemn obligation to sell his house to C and an oath is unnecessary.

SOURCES: Pr. 996; *Mordecai Hagadol* p. 265 b; ibid. 277d.

516

Q. A house belonged to three or four partners, one of whom was Leah. An abutting house was sold to Rachel. Leah wanted to buy the latter house and asserted her priority rights as an abutter. Indeed the Talmud rules (B.M. 108b) that an abutter may not assert priority rights, if the buyer is a woman. This law may not apply, however, when the abutter is also a woman.

A. The talmudic law cited above applies even when the abutter is a woman.

SOURCES: P. 285; Mord. B. M. 394. Cf. *Agudah* B. M. 170.

517

Q. A sold his ground, which bordered on B's property, to C for a sum of money plus C's share in a piece of ground C held in partnership with D in another part of town. After the sale was completed and the title conveyed, B pressed his rights as an abutter. Since Maimonides rules that the law of pre-emption does not apply to the case where a person exchanges his immovables for the immovables of another, C was advised to persuade A to refuse to accept from B, in payment of A's ground, anything but the particular piece of ground A was to receive from C. Accordingly A claimed that C's piece of ground was very precious to him and that he valued it like the "estate of Bar Marion" (B.B. 12b). B, therefore, bought from D his share of the particular ground he held in partnership with C, and offered it to A in lieu of C's share of the same ground. C, however, objected to D's sale claiming that upon the voiding of his transaction with A he would return to his former status as D's partner, and, having the right of preemption on D's share, he would buy such share leaving nothing to A. A and C employed many other tricks and artifices in order to void B's right of preemption.

A. Since C bought A's ground and gave away his own ground in partial payment thereof, he no longer owns the latter ground. Since a person who buys real property desired by an abutter, merely acts as the agent of such abutter (B.B. 108a), C must deliver to B the ground he bought from A, receiving in exchange the ground B bought from D plus a refund of his money. Were B unable to acquire such ground from D, he would have repaid C with money for the ground C gave to A; the value of such ground would have been determined by experts and not by C. C would not have been able to claim that his ground was very precious to him having for him the value of the "estate of Bar Marion", for such claim is valid only when a person is seeking to take away the property of another (in exchange of his own) against the will of the latter who may plead that his property is very precious to him. But in our case C has sold his property to A, and is only entitled to its market price. Moreover, even if the aforementioned sale were not concluded as yet, and an understanding merely existed between A and C that C convey his ground to A on condition that the conveyance of A's ground be without any interference on the part of the abutters, A could not have insisted on exchanging his ground for ground exactly similar to that of C. A could not have attached special importance to C's ground as having the value for him of the "estate of Bar Marion", for the reason already stated. Therefore, B would have been able to pay A with other ground, located in the same town, of equal value as that of C. Many persons have the erroneous notion that the preemptive right of an abutter is void whenever an exchange or real property is involved. Were this true, the parties to a sale of immovables would always add a small piece of ground to the purchasing price in order to place the transaction in the category of exchange of real property, thus turning into a hollow mockery the ordinance of the Rabbis who created the law of preemption for humane reasons. Therefore, whenever we suspect that the circumstances of a sale of real property were specially arranged in order to circumvent the law of preemption, we sustain the preemptive right of the abutter.

SOURCES: Cr. 193; Am II, 199, 200.

518

𝒬. A sold his house to his son-in-law, B, and to the latter's small children of a previous marriage. The actual sale, however, was concluded between A and C, since C acted as agent for B and B's children. At the conclusion of the sale, C delivered pledges to A. Thereupon, A's neighbors, D and E, summoned A to court asserting their priority rights as abutters, and demanded that A sell the house to them at the same price he was to receive from B and that he take the necessary steps to convey title to them in the courts of the land. E further claimed that the above house was mortgaged to him for over a year, and that he thus asserted his priority rights thereto both as a mortgagor and as an abutter. A averred that he had sold the house to B on condition that should the abutters assert their priority rights, the sale would be void. The witnesses to the sale, however, testified that no such condition was stipulated by A. A, however, claimed that he had sold the house to B at a low price, because B was his son-in-law; that when he learned that the abutters were anxious to buy the house, he refused to sell it altogether; and that he returned the pledges to C and thus annulled the sale. The abutters asserted, however, that when C took back the pledges, he warned A that he did not thus intend to annul the sale proper; and that A answered that he did not attach much importance to C's intentions in the matter, since C merely acted as a deputy. The abutters further claimed that by his cunning moves A merely intended to gain a higher price for his house. We ruled, therefore, that the abutters have no claim against A. The abutters do have a claim against B; but since they did not summon B before us, we dismissed the case.

Signed: Isaac b. Prigores, Ephraim b. Judah.

I am sending you this decision because I believe that the judges have erred. I showed Rabbi Isaac b. Prigores your Responsum in connection with the case of R. S. haLevi, his sons, and his son-in-law R. Isaac Gabbi, to the effect that a buyer merely acts as the abutter's deputy, and that the formal transfer (*kinyan*) of the real property from the seller to the buyer in reality transfers the property to the abutter. Rabbi Isaac, however, gave me unsatisfactory answers. Therefore, please let me know your opinion in the matter, for no deed is more worthy than establishing truth and justice in this world. Please explain to us the law in all its details, and write your answer on the reverse of this sheet. The court's decision was written by the judges at the order of the *parnasim* (community leaders) who were interested in dispensing justice and righteousness. You need not hesitate [therefore], for your decision will be accepted and enforced. The Lord will soon release you from captivity. Your servant, Abraham b. Eliezer haLevi.

A. The evasions of both A and the judges, are to no avail. The buyer merely acted as the abutters' deputy, and the aforesaid *kinyan* conveyed the house to the abutters. Therefore the latter have a claim against anyone now holding the house, whether seller or buyer, and may force A to take all necessary steps in conveying title to them in the courts of the land; for this is an implied obligation on the part of a seller. The fact that part of the house was sold to B's children, who were minors, was also of no consequence, since the minors took no active part in the formal transfer of ownership. As to your question regarding the priority rights of a mortgagor as against those of an abutter, a mortgagor of more than one year's standing has priority rights as against an abutter.

SOURCES: Tesh. Maim. to *Kinyan*, 32.

519

1) *Q.* May a person bestow, as a gift, on his son or son-in-law part of a certain piece of real estate, a part worth ten *marks* out of a piece of real estate worth one hundred and sixty *marks*, and subsequently sell to this son or son-in-law, who would thus be a partner to the property, the remainder of the real estate for a higher price than its actual worth (namely for the original one hundred and sixty *marks*) in order to evade intervention by the abutter?

A. If the donor sold the remainder of the real estate to the donee for less than the actual value of the entire piece of real estate (for less than 160 *marks*), the donee was thus in reality a partner in the property, and, therefore, had priority rights over the abutter. Otherwise, the donation was a mere fraud, and did not give the donee any priority rights to the property.

2) *Q.* Which clause in a deed of gift renders the gift a "donation with guaranteed title", the clause: "and I will compensate thee ...", or the final clause: "and I assume full responsibility for this deed of gift ..."? Is the presence of the latter clause by itself sufficient? Does the fact that the witnesses to the deed of gift claim to have written the final clause of their own accord, without having consulted the donor, affect its validity?

A. The final clause mentioned above is in itself sufficient to render the gift a "donation with guaranteed title." Under the circumstances, we lend no credence to the statement of the witnesses, for a verbal statement of the witnesses does not discredit the bond which bears their signatures.

3) *Q.* A owns a quarter interest in a piece of real estate which abuts his property. The other three quarters belong to C. The latter seeks to sell one quarter of the real estate to a woman, or to orphans. One quarter of such real estate, however, does not form a "usable part." May A object to the sale on the ground that, although he can now force C to partition the real estate between them even though he, A, is entitled to receive a "non-usable part", he will not be able to force a division later when the woman or the orphans will be entitled to receive a "non-usable part"?

A. C cannot sell to another any right he does not possess himself. Since C may not restrain A from dividing the property, those who buy any part thereof from C may not do so either. Incidentally, you specified that the buyer in the above transaction was to be a woman or orphans. You probably thought that against such buyers A would not be able to assert his priority rights as a partner. However, this is not so; for, unlike an abutter, a partner may assert his priority rights even when the buyer is a woman or an orphan.

4) *Q.* The shape of a piece of ground held by partners is such that if it should be divided in one way, each partner would receive a "usable part"; but if it should be divided in another way, one partner would not receive a "usable part", and thus no division would be possible. May a partner insist on the first method of division, in order to force the division of the property among the partners?

A. Yes, he may.

5) *Q.* If buildings obstruct the proper division of real estate among partners, are the buildings to be disregarded?

A. Walls must be thinned or completely removed, if necessary, in order to effect a proper division among partners while,
at the same time, damage to the property should be held to a
minimum. The difference in value between parts, however,
should be adjusted by having the partner who received the
more valuable part, pay the difference to the partner who received the less valuable part.

6) *Q.* When the property is divided among the partners, may
A demand that he be given a part adjacent to his own property?

A. Authorities hold conflicting opinions regarding this law.
Therefore, A may not insist on receiving a part adjacent to
his property.

7) *Q.* What constitutes a "usable part"?

A. A "usable part" is a piece of real estate four cubits
by six cubits.

8) *Q.* If two partners own a house that has only a single
door opening into the street and cannot have another, how
may such a house be divided among the partners?

A. The partner who receives the front part of the house
must allow the other partner to use the front door.

9) *Q.* May A, who owns a quarter interest in the house,
rent out a quarter of each room to a different lodger?

A. If A and C can come to no agreement regarding a
proper division of the house, they may use it in one of the
following ways: a) A may use the entire house for one year
out of each four years, and C may use it for the remaining
three years. b) The house may be rented to a tenant, one
quarter of its rent will go to A, and the rest will go to C; (c) one
partner may force the other either to pay him a certain amount
for his share, or receive a proportionate payment for his own
share.

This Responsum is addressed to R. Abraham b. Eliezer.

SOURCES: Tesh. Maim. to *Kinyan*, 32–40. Cf. *Agudah* B. M. 170.

520

Q. One part of a room is held in partnership by B, C, and D, and the other part belongs solely to A. B and C own estates which border on the east side of the room. When the partners are ready to partition the room with A, can they compel A to take the west part of the room so that B and C may have their own part, which they intend to continue to hold in partnership, contiguous to their estates?

A. According to the opinion of Rashi, the partners may compel A to take the west part of the room; R. Tam, however, thinks that they cannot do so. Since we cannot decide whose opinion should prevail, we must order A and the partners to cast lots; if the east part of the room falls to the partners, they shall gain title to it; but if the east part falls to A, he shall not gain title to it immediately, but whatever person or persons can by force succeed in taking possession of the east part that person or persons shall gain title to it. .

This Responsum was addressed to R. Meir's relative, Rabbi Joel.

The latter objected to R. Meir's ruling that the use of force be invoked in settling the above dispute, on the ground that this procedure would lead to serious quarrels.

R. Meir answered: In order to obviate the necessity of leaving the matter to be settled by force, I searched for a more practical solution and found that Maimonides in his code ruled that upon the partitioning of a field held in partnership, a partner may insist on receiving his part of the field adjoining his own property, provided that both parts of the field are exactly equal [in fertility or arrangement of irrigation facilities]. Therefore, if B, C, and D, agree to equalize the two parts of the room by adding structures to the western side of the room similar to the ones in the eastern side, they will be entitled to receive as their share the eastern part of the room. This ruling is in accordance with the views of both Rashi and Maimonides. In the present case we may disregard the view of R. Tam since it is contradicted by the two authorities, and since their interpretation of the pertinent talmudic source is more acceptable to our way of thinking.

SOURCES: Cr. 235; Pr. 948; Mord. B. B. 507; *Mordecai Hagadol*, p. 367a; *Agudah* B. B. 24. Cf. *Terumat Hadeshen* 352.

521

Q. The community pronounced the ban against anyone who would buy the house of a certain Gentile. Is one permitted to exchange houses with that Gentile? Signed: R. Menahem.

A. Exchange is equivalent to buying, and is included in the above ban.

SOURCES: Mord. B. M. 395; *Agudah* B. M. 170.

522

Q. B bought from a Gentile woman a house bordering on A's property. B agreed that the woman could remain in the house till the month of *Heshvan* (October). A and C claim that they were negotiating to buy the house before B appeared on the scene; that A has a partnership in the house since the beams of his house project into the wall of the Gentile's house; that the Gentile owed money to A; that B promised them not to buy the house; that the arbitrators reported to A and C, B's statement to the effect that A and C need not be concerned, and could rely on his word as a Jew that he would not buy the house; that the Gentile gave A and C the keys to her house, and that they opened it, measured the size and noted the arrangement of the rooms, the exits, and the entrances, and locked it, before B bought the house. They, therefore, demand that B transfer the house to them. B avers that he never promised A and C not to buy the house; and that he had negotiated to buy the house long before they did. The Gentile woman claims that A inserted his beams into her wall illegally.

A. A and C cannot force B to transfer the house to them, for the following reasons: a) B denies having promised A and C not to buy the house; b) if B did make such a promise to A and C, and then broke it he might be called *Rasha* (wicked) or *Abaryana* (renegade), but we can not force him to transfer the house to A and C; therefore, no useful purpose will be served by imposing an oath on B regarding such promise; c) although locking a house is considered a valid act of possession, and one may gain title to the property of a Gentile by taking possession thereof (Bechorot 13a), this rule applies only when such an act is accompanied by proper intention by both parties. However, before the two parties agree on the terms of the sale no such intention is possible; therefore, A's locking of the Gentile's house was of no consequence; d) the fact that the Gentile owed money to A does not vest in him the priority rights of an abutter, for, only a creditor who has a mortgage on a house, lives therein, and has a lease thereon so that he cannot be made to move before the year is up has the right of an abutter. Moreover, since A's property borders on that of the Gentile, B may assert: "I have driven away a lion from your neighborhood", and such assertion annuls the priority rights A could have claimed as an abutter, as a creditor, or as a partner; e) B's statement to the arbitrators constituted neither an oath nor a vow, but a mere assurance. Even if we agree with A, who has construed that statement to mean an oath, B may not be forced to transfer his house to A merely because he disregarded his oath. Thus A is not entitled to indemnity. Indeed, B should be fined for his sinful act (breaking his oath), but we do not have the authority to impose penalties. However, you, my teacher, and your community, if you find that a disgraceful breach of conduct was committed, you may impose a proper fine upon B, the money to go to charity. Finally, half of B's wall, upon which the ends of A's beams are resting, belongs to A; for, the presence of such beams is ample proof that the wall was held in partnership by the two neighbors.

The question was again referred to Rabbi Meir who answered: Since the judges did not clearly understand my last statement, I shall explain. If A claims that half of the wall and half of the ground it rests on belongs to him, we uphold his claim since the fact that his beams rest on the wall corroborates his statement, and no witness or witnesses contradict him. A is not required to take an oath, not even a *gilgul shebuah* (oath of implication) in support of his claim. If A, however, admits that the Gentile woman had built the entire wall on her grounds, but that he subsequently persuaded her to permit his placing of his beams on her wall, no part of the wall belongs to him; for the Gentile merely permitted him to place his beams on her wall, but she gave him no part of the wall itself.

I have considered your inquiry regarding a proper punishment for B who, you claim, is a righteous, reputable and blameless person. He, indeed, must suffer severe punishment in order duly to atone for his sin; for when a person of his character commits a shameful act, he profanes the name of the Lord. However, if B is a scholar, he should not be put under the ban, but should be required to give a certain sum to the charity chest, or for the support of your students, the amount of the fine to be determined by the leaders (of the community).

These Responsa are addressed to "our teacher Rabbi Eliezer."

Sources: Cr. 241–2; Am II, 123; *Agudah* 21.

523

Q. A sold his house, which bordered on B's property, to a Gentile. A claimed that B had refused to buy his house at the price the Gentile had offered.

A. If A can produce no witnesses, nor take an oath, in support of his claim, we place him under the ban until he undertakes to compensate B for all damages the latter may suffer from his Gentile neighbor.

SOURCES: Cr. 158.

524

Q. One quarter of a house belongs to A, and the other three quarters to B. A, needing money, negotiated a loan from a Gentile, who was willing to put up a mortgage of fifteen *marks* on A's part of the house on the following conditions: 1) That A pay the Gentile one *mark* per annum in perpetuity; 2) that in case A fails to pay the one *mark* per annum, the mortgaged part of the house is to belong to the Gentile; 3) that in case the house burns down, the ground shall be mortgaged to the Gentile on the same condition; and 4) that in case A wants to sell his part of the house, the Gentile is to have the privilege of buying it at twelve (?) *marks* less than the offer of the highest bidder. Before concluding this transaction, A informed B of his intentions and of the Gentile's terms, and offered to borrow the amount from B on the same terms. B vigorously protested against A's mortgaging part of the house to a Gentile who might cause B trouble; but, at the same time, he refused to lend fifteen *marks* to A on the ground that it would be considered a taxable loan, and that the one *mark* per annum would be considered usury from a fellow Jew.

A. If A sells his part of the house to B on condition that it be rented to A in perpetuity at one *mark* per annum, the sale will be legal and B will be permitted to collect the one *mark* per annum. If, however, B refuses to buy A's part on such terms, A may mortgage it to a Gentile.

SOURCES: Pr. 970.

525 (D)

Q. When the fence, which separates A's yard from that of his Gentile neighbor, broke down, the Gentile rebuilt the fence on A's property and wrested from A a piece of ground two yards wide and twenty yards long. A was afraid to protest as the Gentile was a violent man. Subsequently, B bought the Gentile's property without A's knowledge or consent. A, therefore, demands that B return to him the piece of property which the Gentile wrongfully acquired from him since title to real property cannot be acquired by violence, and that property, therefore, still belongs to A. B refuses to do so. Furthermore, he is about to rent the property to Gentile occupants.

A. The principle that title to real property cannot be acquired by violence refers only to the realm of *Mitzvot* (religious acts) but not to the realm of commerce. Therefore, though the Gentile took A's ground by force and violence, he, nevertheless, gained title to it by taking possession and building a fence on it. The sale of such property to B was valid and B is under no obligation to A. B, however, should not rent the property to Gentile occupants.

(2). *Q.* B claims that A constructed apertures for window lights facing his (B's) yard after he (B) bought the yard from the Gentile. A claims that those windows were always in their present place, but that they were closed by wooden boards because he did not want the Gentile to look into his house. He wants to keep those windows open now that he has a Jewish neighbor.

A. A cannot reopen his windows, since B does not want A to be able to look into his (B's) yard.

SOURCES: Pr. 674–675.

526

Q. The burghers built the city tower on the foundation of A's wall. Subsequently the burghers gave B certain rights in that tower, and he erected buildings therein. A, however, claimed that the burghers had wronged him, had misappropriated some of his ground, and that B's buildings were partly standing on his (A's) ground.

A. As I have already explained in my other letter, the fact that the tower is built on A's foundations shows that the ground also belongs to A. B can not claim undisturbed possession as evidence of title since, deriving his rights from Gentiles, he is in the same category as a Gentile and has no presumptive right of title. B's sons also lack such right, nor do we claim in their favor that perhaps their father bought from A the right to erect his buildings, since they are in the category of "sons of a robber." Since B's sons do not claim that B bought from A in their presence the right to erect his buildings, but merely state that the burghers claimed to have built the tower legally, B's sons must either remove their buildings from the ground in question or come to terms with A.

SOURCES: Cr. 236; Am II, 180; *Mordecai Hagadol*, p. 314c; ibid. p. 366d.

527

1) *Q.* Ten Jewish adult males were inhabitants of the town of T. One of them wanted to leave [temporarily for the holidays]. His leaving would disrupt congregational prayers. Could the other members compel him to remain?

A. It is an accepted custom throughout the Diaspora for small communities to hire one or two adult males whenever it is necessary to complete a *minyan* (quorum) for the high holidays. Therefore, if there are exactly ten adult males in the community, the other remaining members can compel the member seeking to leave either to remain in town or to hire somebody else in his stead. But, if there are eleven adult males in the community, no single member can be restrained from leaving; for he does not have to provide for the possibility of another member becoming sick or indisposed. However, if two out of the eleven want to leave, both have to share the expenses of hiring a person to complete the *minyan*.

2) *Q*. When nine Jews have to hire a tenth in order to complete the *minyan* (quorum), or when they have to hire a cantor for the holidays, do the members share equally in expenses, or do they pay in proportion to their wealth?

A. Since the members do not join a large community for the high-holyday prayers because they do not want to leave their homes, their possessions, and their investments, the forming of the local *minyan* is dependent upon monetary considerations, and the expenses thereof should be shared by the members in proportion to their wealth.

SOURCES: Pr. 1016; Mord. B. B. 878-9; Hag. Maim. to *Tefilah*, 11, 1. Cf. *Agudah* B. B. 15; Maharil, *Responsa* 107b; Israel Bruno, *Responsa* 163; Isserlein, *Pesakim* 243; Judah Minz, *Responsa* 7.

528

Q. A, who owns a share in the synagogue, is a quarrelsome and factious person. May the community expel him from its membership and demand that he either receive a certain amount for his share in the synagogue, or pay the community a proportionate amount for its share therein?

A. I hold a tradition that Rabbenu Gershom, the light of the exile, instituted an ordinance that no Jew should be permanently expelled from the synagogue nor "be driven from cleaving unto the inheritance of the Lord" (Sam. I 26, 19) except for a period of a week, two weeks, or a month. If a person is habitually quarrelsome he should be made to pay a fine, and in case he proves disobedient or altogether rebellious, the community should have a right to get Gentiles to flog him till he become submissive. Your community, therefore, cannot expel A from the synagogue. Many violent and powerful Jews in our midst, if given an opportunity, would seek to evade payment of taxes, but they are coerced into obedience through Gentiles or our resorting to threats of excommunication. A should be dealt with in the same manner.

SOURCES: Sinai V (1942) 10–12 no. 303.

529

Q. Dissension runs high in our community; our members can come to no agreement and cannot unanimously elect their leaders. One says one thing, another says another. Because of this disagreement the daily service is interrupted; justice cannot be carried out; neither truth, nor judgment, nor peace prevails in this town or throughout the kingdom that is dependent on it. What shall we do?

A. All members who pay taxes shall come together to form an assembly. Each member must first take an oath to the effect that whatever he shall say or do shall be motivated solely by a desire to sanctify God's name and to further the interests of the community. Thereafter, a majority vote of this assembly shall be binding on the whole community. This shall apply to the election of officers, appointment of cantors, or the creation of a charity chest and selection of its officers. It shall likewise be decided by majority vote whether to build or destroy aught in the synagogue, to buy a community wedding-hall or bakery, or to provide all other community needs. Should the minority refuse to heed the decision of the majority, this majority, or its appointed officers, shall use coercive force, whether through Jewish law or the law of the land, to compel the minority to abide by its rulings. Should an expense of money be involved therein, the minority shall have to defray its part of the expenses. Should some members refuse to express their opinions under the aforesaid oath, such persons shall be ignored, while a majority vote by those who have taken the oath shall decide the above matters, for the dwellers of a town, the Tosephta decides (B. M. 11, 23), may force one another to provide for the public needs of their town.

This Responsum was addressed to Rabbi Abraham haLevi.

Sources: B. p. 320 no. 865; Tesh. Maim. to *Kinyan*, 27; Hag. Maim. to *Hil. Tefilah*, 11, 2. Cf. Hayyim Or Zarua, *Responsa* 65; Maharil, *Responsa* 62; Menahem of Merseburg, *Nimmukim* (48). Moses Minz, *Responsa* 6; ibid. 67b; Judah Minz, *Respnosa* 7.

530

Q. A group of Jews of town T, without the knowledge or consent of the other Jewish inhabitants of T, formed a community organization and elected a single governing body with the power of apportioning taxes and managing all other communal and religious affairs. This organization assumed the authority to exercise these powers on all the inhabitants of T. Rabbi Meir Kohen, however, protested denying their authority, and refused to pay the taxes levied on him. He was willing to become a member of the community and share in the carrying of the community burden, provided he be permitted such rights in the election of leaders as were held by the other members of the community, or that the taxes be levied equitably, i.e., in exact proportion to a person's wealth. The elected leaders refused to accede to R. Meir's wishes and, with the help of Gentiles, forced their way into R. Meir's house and seized some of his valuables as pledges for the unpaid taxes.

R. Meir retaliated by hiring other Gentiles who took back his valuables by force.

A. The Jews of T who have banded together in electing leaders and giving them authority to manage all communal affairs, had no right to do so even though they represented a majority of the Jewish inhabitants of T, as long as a minority took no part in the reorganization, for no new custom or institution can be established in a community without the knowledge and consent of all its inhabitants. The talmudic statement: "The inhabitants of a city are permitted to enforce their rulings" (B.B. 8b), means: a) If the people of a city unanimously agree to enact a certain ruling, they are permitted to punish and fine anyone who subsequently disregards that ruling; or, b) the seven leaders of a community, originally elected with the knowledge and consent of all the members of the community to manage community affairs and to punish offenders, have the right to enforce their rulings and decrees. But, no majority of city dwellers can force a minority to be governed by a ruling to the original passing of which they have not consented, or to accept the authority of leaders whom they have not consented to elect.

Moreover, any ordinance passed by the inhabitants of a city without the knowledge or consent of a great man (a scholar) residing in their midst, is void and is not binding even upon those who passed the ordinance (B.B. 9a). There can be no doubt, therefore, that no community can pass an ordinance to be binding upon the scholar himself, unless he agrees to its enactment. Thus, an organization established against the express wishes of R. Meir Kohen, a person of high standing and scholarship, has no right to force its authority on all the inhabitants of T. Therefore, R. Meir had the right to resort to the help of Gentiles in order to recover his valuables.

Sources: Pr. 968; *Mordecai Hagadol*, p. 299c; ibid. p. 363b.

531

Q. Some members of the community seek to pronounce a *herem*, a community ban, for a certain purpose; while other members of the community openly protest against it. Are the former permitted to pronounce the ban, and when pronounced will the ban be binding on the latter group?

A. If the purpose for which the pronouncement of the ban is sought, is designed for the public benefit or to fill a great need in the community, while without the innovation the existence of the community would be jeopardized, the members of the community are permitted to coerce one another to adopt the required resolution and to abide by it once it is adopted. A *herem*, however, cannot be effectively invoked upon those who protest against its being pronounced, since a *herem* [being in the nature of an oath or a vow] must first be accepted voluntarily by a person before it becomes binding on him.

Sources: *Semak*, ed. Constantinople no. 79 end; ed. Cremona, 82 end.

532

Q. The community of T passed a certain ordinance and stipulated that whenever there would be sufficient indication that any member of the community violated the ordinance, he should be punished. It subsequently became known by circumstantial evidence that A violated the ordinance, although no one actually saw him do so. Moreover, when A was questioned about it, he equivocated and contradicted his own statements. The community leaders became convinced, therefore, that A had violated the ordinance.

A. The wording of the ordinance requires that whenever the judges become convinced that a person violated the ordinance, even though actual proof is lacking, he should be deserving of punishment. Since there is sufficient reason to believe that A violated the ordinance and since the members of the community know that he did so, the court has a right to punish him.

SOURCES: Sinai VI (1942) 4-5 no. 394.

533

Q. A gave a sum of money to a community to be used as an endowment fund for the maintenance of a Rabbi to be chosen by the community. After A's death, the people of the community chose their relative, B, as their Rabbi. A's daughter was married to a Rabbi who was the equal in scholarship to Rabbi B. Is the community obligated to accept as their Rabbi A's son-in-law in preference to Rabbi B? Moreover should some of A's children become poor, must the income from the endowment fund be used for their support rather than for the maintenance of the Rabbi, since it is to be assumed, in accordance with the principle of R. Simon b. Menassia (B.B. 132a) that A, while giving the money, intended that his own relatives be preferred to a stranger?

A. After the money was given over to the community, neither A nor his family had greater rights to it than any other member of the community. The community, therefore, is not obligated to appoint A's son-in-law as their Rabbi. Moreover, it is to be presumed that A made a nobly charitable gift to the community without attaching any reservations or conditions. The law of R. Simon (B.B. 132a) deals with a charitable gift made under an erroneous assumption, while in our case no such condition existed.

SOURCES: Pr. 942; Mord. B. B. 486; *Agudah* B. B. 20.

534

Q. The members of the community wanted to engage A as their cantor but encountered the opposition of a few members.

A asked the Duke for help, and the latter brought about A's election by asking the opposition to withdraw its objections.

A. A did wrong in procuring his election as cantor — a deputy of the community before the Almighty — with the help of the Duke. In our country a matter like that would be very sternly dealt with. A similar case happened in Cologne in the time of R. Eliezer b. Joel. A Jew wanting to honor a newly elected cantor, arranged that the bishop should invite the cantor to his house. Then the bishop removed his miter and gave it to the Rabbi [cantor] and said: "I give you herewith the office of cantor." The cantor became very much incensed and said to the bishop: "Sir, our law does not permit me to receive the right to serve our Lord from your hands." The cantor resigned his post and I believe that he fined the Jew who was responsible for the bishop's act. Therefore, A, too, should act accordingly.

SOURCES: Cr. 190; Pr. 137; Mord. B. K. 107.

535

R. Jacob, the cantor of Magdeburg, died and left a son, Hizkiyahu, who was worthy to succeed his father as cantor of Magdeburg, though inferior to him in some qualities. A majority of the membership of the Magdeburg community wanted the son to succeed his father, but a minority of possibly one or more strongly objected to the son. R. Moses b. Hisdai was asked for his opinion in the matter. He advised Hizkiyahu to try any measure in his power to ingratiate himself with the objectors. He asked the leaders of the community to direct their efforts toward effecting a reconciliation with the opposing faction, and expressed his opinion that a single person could not defy the will of the entire community. R. Isaac b. Moses (of Vienna) stated that according to Biblical Law a community could not hire a cantor to whom there was objection even by a single person. R. Meir stated his opinion that a cantor might officiate throughout the year even though not acceptable to a few congregants, but that he was not permitted to officiate on *Rosh Hashanah* and *Yom Kippur* or on fast days, if even a single congregant found him objectionable.

SOURCES: L. 109–11; *Or Zarua* I, 21a.

536 (D)

Q. The community of T engaged A as cantor for a three years' period, but soon retracted, discharging A and hiring B in his place. Now A institutes suit against B.

Q. A has no legal claim against B though he does have a claim against the community. Not having been asked regarding A's case against the community, I shall refrain from passing judgment thereon. Should the discussion that follows reveal any just claims A may have against the community, I rely on you not to disclose them to A, lest the community accuse me of encouraging claimants and inciting them against the community thus damaging its interests. It seems, however, that if A could have obtained another position, had he not been engaged by the community of T, and now can no longer obtain that, or a similar, position, the community ought to pay A the wages of an "idle laborer" (i. e. the wages a cantor would be willing to accept for abstaining from practicing his profession for a given period). But, if A is able to obtain another position even now, he has no legal claim against the community, though he has cause for reproof. Should the latter position require more effort than the position with the community of T, if there be also an increase in remuneration commensurate with the increase in effort, the community of T would be free from obligation to A; otherwise, the community of T would have to compensate A for the increase in effort. In any event, A has no legal claim against B, though he has cause for reproof, and the latter may perhaps be called "wicked".

SOURCES: Cr. 292; Am II, 234; B. p. 298 no. 392.

537

Q. A community employed A as cantor, ritual slaughterer and examiner (שוחט ובודק). The butchers, however, refused to allow A to perform his duties as examiner on the ground that he was a slow worker, and that the Gentile butchers resented his slowness.

A. If Gentile butchers are generally dissatisfied with ritual examiners as slow as A, he must appease the butchers or forfeit his wages as an examiner. If, however, Gentile butchers do not generally resent the slowness of an examiner, and it happens that only the Gentile butchers of that particular town do, A is entitled to the wages of an idle laborer [פועל בטל, i. e., the minimum wages a laborer of A's category would be willing to receive in order to abstain from work] since he was not informed of this condition at the time he was hired.

SOURCES: Pr. 90.

538

Q. The community wedding-hall borders on an alley into which the back doors of many houses open. The leaders of the community desire to open a door leading into the alley. They claim that part of the alley belongs to the community and that a door once led from the wedding-hall into the alley. The inhabitants of the alley, through their representative, deny that the community has any rights there, and introduce as evidence a bill of sale, countersigned by the leaders of the community, which reads: "A (a former resident there) sold to B his house and his part of the alley which borders on the community wedding-hall." Thus the leaders of the community admitted, by countersigning the bill of sale, that the alley belongs to the people who live in the houses around it, and that even though the wedding-hall borders on it, the community possesses no rights in the alley.*

A. The leaders of the community may not open any doors in the wedding-hall leading into the alley, even though they certainly have rights there, since a door that had been completely closed may not be reopened; and no new door may be opened in an alley without the permission of the inhabitants there. On the other hand, the evidence produced by the inhabitants of the alley is worthless; for leaders of a community sign a bill of sale as judges and not as witnesses; and according to the Talmud (Ket. 109a), judges sign a document without reading it and, therefore, are not responsible for its contents.

SOURCES: Pr. 118.

539

Q. A built a bath-house near the synagogue. The members of the community claim that the odor and smoke of the bath-house inconveniences them, and therefore, demand that A close the bath-house.

A. If A claims that the leaders of the community sold or gave to him the right to build the bath-house and if he has proof that they did not object to it for a while, after its construction and operation, he may continue to operate it, since the inconvenience is not so great, as it is being operated only once a week and the odor is mild.

SOURCES: Pr. 233.

* The wording of this Responsum is quite obscure and it is difficult to reconstruct the question. The interpretation given above seems to me to be near the truth; it is based on the readings of the old Prague edition.

540

Q. The people of the community complain that A constructed the cavity of his privy so that it extends under public domain (street).

A. A must fill up (with stones and sand) the part of the cavity under the public domain.

SOURCES: Pr. 234.

541

Q. A put a stone in front of his door which opens into the yard of the synagogue. The members of the community object to it, on the ground that it is a stumbling block and a nuisance.

A. One is not permitted to put anything in the public domain, without permission from the proper authorities. Therefore, A must remove the stone from the public property, unless he had received permission [from the community] to put it there.

SOURCES: Pr. 235.

542

Q. Some of the water from A's roofs used to drain into the Synagogue courtyard. Subsequently, A opened a spout, for the purpose of draining the water off his roof, which spout extended into the synagogue courtyard and thus all the water from A's roof was poured into the courtyard. The members of the community objected to this.

A. A must remove his spout.

SOURCES: Pr. 236.

543 (D)

(1) *Q.* A demanded that B saw off the beams extending from his house into the street. The court decided in A's favor. Are the other members of the community entitled to the benefits of the court's decision?

A. All the members of the community, even those who were absent from the town at the time of the trial, are entitled to the benefit of the court's decision, even though A did not act as their representative. But, had the court decided against A, such decision would be binding only on A and on all those who knew about the trial, while all those who were out of town at the time, or who were in town but did not know about the trial, would not be bound by such decision and would still be able to press suit against B.

(2) *Q.* The court did not specify in its written decision (see above) the name of the plaintiff nor the location of the beams that were to be sawed off.

A. The decision states that B must saw off his beams; therefore, the identity of the plaintiff is not important. The judges are permitted to testify as to the beams to which their decision refers.

SOURCES: Pr. 527–528.

544

Our masters, the community of Nuremberg, take notice that my relative, R. Abraham, came to me as a representative of his community. The latter complains against members of your community who came to their town (the town of R. Abraham) and are doing business there. You have the power to stop this evil practice, but you do nothing about it. You know that such practice is prohibited by the Torah as evidenced by the talmudic decision (B. B. 21b) that an inhabitant of one city may restrain inhabitants of other cities from competing with him within his city limits, and other similar decisions (ibid. 22a, 21b). Furthermore, were we unable to prove that the Talmud forbids the practice mentioned above, we should have adduced such prohibition by simple logic, as we positively cannot imagine that it be permitted; for otherwise life would be unbearable. The rich would do business outside their own community, in all the settlements, and would thus increase the volume of business there without helping the Jews of those settlements to carry the burden of increased taxation directly resulting from such increase in business. You, the community of Nuremberg, must correct this injustice and must save the distressed from their oppressors. No one but you can comfort them, for no one else can mete out justice within your sphere of influence. Therefore, you should use all the power of coercion you command to prevent your members from going into other towns and competing with the Jewish inhabitants there; by so doing you would serve as a good example to other communities.

SOURCES: Pr. 983; *Mordecai Hagadol*, p. 306a.

545 (D)

At all times, with the exception of public market days, the Jewish community of T may restrain all Jews who do not dwell under the rule of the overlord of T from lending money on interest in T. Even on market days the community may exact a tax from strangers for the right of doing business in T, and may demand that the latter pay their "tithe" (from the profits earned in T) to the community charity chest.

Regarding the legality of the community ordinances I can not answer you until I know what these ordinances are about; but a person is enjoined to listen to and obey the resolutions of his brothers, and to live with his brothers in harmony, friendship, and love.

SOURCES: Pr. 359.

546

Q. For many years the Jews of the entire kingdom paid their taxes to the king collectively. Then the king gave part of his kingdom to his son, and stated that henceforth the taxes of the Jews in that territory should be paid to his son. But the communities of the rest of the kingdom still demand the regular taxes from the Jews of the territory presented to the king's son.

A. The Jews of the entire kingdom became partners in the collective payment of their taxes for the reason that they were all the king's subjects and under obligation to pay their taxes to him. But, as soon as the Jews of the ceded territory ceased to be under the obligation of paying taxes to the king, the condition for the forming of the partnership no longer existed for them, and they could withdraw from the partnership (without the consent of the Jews of the rest of the kingdom). Therefore, if the king has given the entire income of the territory to his son, the Jews of that territory are under no obligation to their former associates. If, however, the king gave the territory itself to his son, but reserved the income to himself for a certain period of time, those Jews should continue to pay the taxes together with the Jews of the rest of the kingdom for that period of time.

This Responsum is addressed to R. Abraham.

SOURCES: Pr. 131; Mord. B. K. 183. Cf. Weil, *Responsa* 81; Moses Minz, *Responsa* 1; ibid. 22.

547

Q. The king held the Jews of the community responsible for A's failing to return to the city at an appointed time, and imposed a fine on them. The community, therefore, demanded that A reimburse them for the penalties they suffered on his account. A, however, claimed that the community did not guarantee his return at the specified date, and that the king used his failure to return as a mere pretext for extortion.

A. Since A claims that the community did not guarantee

his return, he can not be held responsible for the king's extortionate action. The king has no right to hold a community responsible for the whereabouts of an individual. Such action on the part of the king is not considered governmental law, but is to be put in the category of outright robbery.

SOURCES: Pr. 943.

548

Q. The king's deputy made unjust demands on the community of T in the name of the king. The Jews answered him brazenly and thus aroused his ire to the extent that he sought means of coercing them and of punishing them, and he even attempted to kill them. Thereupon the members of the community incarcerated the deputy, thus preventing him from carrying out his evil design. One member of the community even struck the Gentile (?). The king became enraged, arrested the Jews of T, brought false accusations against them, and forced them to pay ransom. Now A, a resident of T, charges that the community, by its rash acts, caused him a loss of money. He demands that the community make good this loss.

A. The community was not at fault. The king had no right to make unjust demands upon it, for his deputy was in the wrong, not the community. The king, most certainly, had no right to punish the Jews of T for the sin of a single Jew who struck the Gentile. The acts of the community leaders, and the misdemeanor of the Jew were mere excuses for the extortion but not the cause thereof. Therefore, A is not entitled to collect any damages from the community.

SOURCES: Tesh. Maim. to *Kinyan*, 2.

549 (D)

Q. A, B, and C were the only Jewish residents of the town T. A was much richer than either B or C. Their overlord often made loans from A, which at times he repaid together with the interest, and on other occasions he withheld the interest. When the lord put a tax of two or three *marks* on the Jews, he sometimes exempted A from the payment of such tax. He once put a tax of two *marks* on A, B, and C. A week or two later he sent to A for a loan of two *marks*. When A complained that both paying taxes and making free loans were too burdensome for him, the overlord sent him to his treasurer with an order to the latter to refund A for his share of the tax, with wheat. Must A share the wheat with B and C?

A. A, B, and C were partners in so far as paying the tax was concerned. Therefore, whatever A received from the lord, he must share with his partners, B and C.

SOURCES: Pr. 944. Cf. Pr. 134; *Terumat Hadeshen* 341.

550

Q. A is heavily encumbered by his overlord with taxes and forced loans. He originally came to settle in T because he had made a settlement with the overlord to pay a certain amount of taxes directly to the latter, and not in partnership with the rest of the community. The community, however, demands that A pay his share of the tax on the community.

A. If A had originally separated himself from the community with the latter's full knowledge and consent, he need not cooperate with the community in the payment of its taxes; but, if he did not obtain the consent of the community, he had no right to make a separate agreement with the overlord since the custom of the community provides that all Jews be partners in the payment of the taxes. A community has a right to force a rebellious minority in its midst, to obey its customs. Furthermore, the overlord had no right to make a separate agreement with A in violation of the custom he himself had established among the Jews of his town. Such an act on the part of the overlord is not considered "law of the land", but rather constitutes downright robbery. Although according to the Talmud a king may change the customary taxation arrangements of his subjects (B. B. 143a), he is permitted to do so only when he is acting of his own accord, but not when he is urged to do so by some of his subjects. A's objection that it will be prohibitive for him to pay taxes both to the overlord and to the community, is not very serious, for he may explain to the overlord that separating oneself from the community in the payment of taxes is prohibited by our laws, that on this account one becomes involved in quarrels with the Jews of the kingdom, and that henceforth he will refuse to pay his taxes independently of the community. In such matters we are permitted to act with severity even when not directly empowered by the Talmud, as long as we conform to the spirit of the Talmud; for, were a Jew permitted to separate himself from his community, great calamities would often ensue.

SOURCES: Cr. 222; Am II, 122; Rashba I, 841; Tesh. Maim. to *Kinyan*, 29b. Cf. *Agudah* B. K. 144; Maharil, *Responsa* 71; Weil, *Responsa* 38; Menahem of Merseburg, *Nimmukim* (25); Moses Minz, *Responsa* 61d; *Terumat Hadeshen* 341, Isserlein, *Pesakim* 144.

551

Q. a) A decided to remove from his province and from the jurisdiction of his overlord, and to settle in a town where B and his friends lived. Before taking up his residence under the new overlord he came to an agreement with him regarding the amount of taxes he was to pay, and further arranged to pay such taxes to him directly. A, therefore, refused to participate with the other members of the community whenever they jointly paid their taxes to the overlord. Hence they with B invoked against A the ban proclaimed by the communities against any one who refused to pay his taxes jointly with his community. Did A have the right to pay his taxes independently of the community?

b) For many years C resided in a locality where he paid his taxes jointly with D and the other Jews of the surrounding territory. He finally decided to sever his connections with them and made a separate agreement with the overlord to pay him a certain sum as a yearly tax. D and the other taxpayers strongly objected to this and therefore C came to an agreement with D and some of his friends. Others, however, still continued to raise objections to the course undertaken by C. Furthermore, whenever the ban (for nonpayment of taxes) was pronounced, it was couched in general terms which did not exclude C from it. Was C justified in his act?

c) Our overlord granted a release from taxation for the first year, to all Jews coming to settle in his territory. This release was granted against the wishes of the Jews already settled there. The new settlers paid no taxes during their first year of settlement in accordance with the above-mentioned release. But when payment of the taxes for the second year fell due, the old settlers, refusing to recognize the release granted by the overlord, forced the new settlers to pay taxes for both the current and the preceding years. Subsequently the overlord died and was succeeded by his son. The new and old settlers paid their taxes regularly without a complaint for many years. This year, however, quarrelsome persons came to settle here and they refused to pay their taxes for the first year because of the release granted by the father of the present overlord. Were they justified in their refusal?

A. A person settling in a town has no right to isolate himself from the rest of the community and pay his taxes independently. All (Jewish) dwellers in a town are partners in the expenses of maintaining the townwall, the horse guard, the armory and the city gates (B. B. 8a), and must share in paying the town safety tax, in maintaining the free kitchen and the charity chest, and in contributing to similar town expenses, such as a tax to the overlord who is responsible for the safety of the town. Since every town dweller is a partner in these expenses, no partner is permitted (according to talmudic law) to withdraw from a partnership without the consent of the other partners. Moreover, were paying of taxes independently of the community not forbidden by talmudic law, such practice would be proscribed by custom; for throughout the kingdom the custom of considering all taxpayers of a community as partners, and of not allowing anyone to pay his taxes independently, is well established. If not for this rule, equitable distribution of the burden of taxation would be impossible and endless quarrels would ensue, endangering the position of the Jew among his neighbors. Therefore, the community has a right to restrain A (and C) from paying taxes independently, even if only a single member of the community objects to such independent payment of taxes. The community has a right to use persuasion or force upon A and C, by flagellation, ban, or edict of excommunication. You have my full consent to resort to these coercive measures. The same rule applies to the quarrelsome new settlers (referred to in the third query). They must pay their full share of the taxes, even for the first year of their settlement.

These queries were sent to R. Meir by the Jews of Stendal. The following statements are appended.

I subscribe to the opinion of my teacher and relative, R. Meir, that they can not separate themselves from the community without its permission; for the goods of one town dweller may be mortgaged for the unpaid taxes of another town dweller (B. K. 113b). Moreover, even an idle man must help maintain the town's institutions (B. B. 55a)... signed: Menahem B. Natronai; Menahem b. David.

I agree to the above statements of my teachers.... signed: Ephraim b. Nathan; Isaac b. Judah.

I also agree with my teachers. . . . signed: Asher b. Yehiel haLevi.

We also agree with our great teachers to ban and anathematize all those who come to settle in a territory where Jews live unless they share the burden of taxes paid to the king and overlords. Signed: The community of Erfurt.

Whatever the new settler agreed to pay to the overlord and whatever the community agreed to pay, must be lumped together, and each member of the community must pay his share of this sum in proportion to his wealth and means. Signed: David b. Abraham; Baruch b. Yehiel.

SOURCES: L. 108 Cf. *Agudah* B. K. 144; Menahem of Merseburg *Nimmukim* (23); Moses Minz, *Responsa* 61d; Isserlein, *Pesakim* 144.

552

Q. A refused to contribute to the community charity fund or to pay his taxes together with the community. He insisted on paying his taxes directly to the authorities and on distributing his charity funds as he saw fit.

A. If there is an established custom in the community, of which A is a member, that every member pays his taxes directly to the authorities and distributes his charity as he sees fit, the community can not force A to abandon this practice unless A agrees to the change. But if the custom was that all the members were to pay their taxes and distribute their charities collectively, A must abide by this custom. Where the community is new and no custom exists, talmudic law prevails which provides that the majority may force the minority to pay their taxes collectively and to establish a community charity fund to which every member must contribute.

SOURCES: Cr. 10; Pr. 918; Tesh. Maim. to *Kinyan.* 29; *Mordecai Hagadol*, p. 297, d. Cf. *Agudah* B. B. 15; Menahem of Merseburg, *Nimmukim* (23); Israel Bruno, *Responsa* 163; Isserlein, *Pesakim* 144.

553

Q. A, a wealthy person, pays his taxes directly to the lord and not together with the community. He lent money to his friends B and C, who invested it for profit. The volume of business in that locality with Jewish money, however, was not enlarged through B's and C's transactions with A's money, since A would have invested the money himself had he not lent it to B and C. The lord, therefore, will not make any greater demands for taxes because of C's and B's investments. Must B and C pay taxes to the community for the money they borrowed from A?

A. The community can rightly claim that had A not lent the money to B and C he would not have invested that money but would have kept it in reserve. Therefore, the transactions by B and C with A's money do increase the volume of Jewish business and the overlord may demand more taxes because of this increase. Moreover, it is a custom in our kingdom that those who borrow money from wealthy individuals who pay their taxes independently of the community, must pay taxes to the community from the borrowed money.

SOURCES: Pr. 331. Cf. Menahem of Merseburg, *Nimmukim* (4).

554

A person who moved out of town before the authorities have levied a tax, even a regular tax, is not required to pay any share of such tax. This law is accepted by all communities.

SOURCES: Cr. 111.

555

Q. The community of T, with the consent of (R. Meir's relative) Kohen Zedek, decreed: a) that anyone who moves out of T may not return to it in order to lend additional funds to his debtors, for the purpose of fortifying his investments with them, without the knowledge and consent of the community, the latter having to determine whether or not such debts can be collected without lending additional funds to the debtors; b) that if the debts can be so collected, the non-resident creditor be not permitted to lend additional funds to the his debtors; c) that in case a member of the community will be willing to take over the investments of such creditor, the latter be forced to transfer such investments to the former; and d) that if anyone is found transgressing this decree and lending additional funds to his debtors without the knowledge and consent of the community, he should pay on all of his money that can be found a tax of six Cologne pennies per *mark*. A was discovered to have transgressed this decree.

A. If A was a resident of T when the aforesaid ordinance was passed, whether he supported the measure, accepted it tacitly, or openly protested against it, he is bound by it even though he subsequently moved out of T. For a person's protests against an ordinance designed for the public benefit and passed by a majority vote of the worthy members of the community are of no avail. Thus the ordinance of Rabbenu Gershom reads as follows: "If the residents of a city have established an ordinance for the benefit of the community, for the benefit of the poor, or for any other useful purpose, and most of the worthy ones have agreed to it, the others may not void such ordinance and may not demand to take the matter to court, for no court may sit in such a case, because everything depends on the opinion of the prominent men of the city, in accordance with the custom of the ancients, or as an emergency measure."

If A, however, moved out of T before the ordinance was passed, he is to be governed only by talmudic law and by customs generally accepted by the communities, while any restrictive measure adopted by the community of T after A moved

out is not binding on him. A community may force a dissenting minority and all those who subsequently come to
settle in the town, to accept its decrees and ordinances. But
a community possesses no authority over a person who moved
out of town before the decrees and ordinances were passed,
and who does not live there any longer. Therefore, if A had
had ample opportunity, since he left T, to force his debtors
to replay their debts to him, and failed to do so, he must pay
the community taxes on such debts. But if he was unable
to collect these debts, the custom is well established in all
communities not to tax such debts. Any local ordinance
in opposition to such custom is not binding on a non-resident
who was a non-resident at the time the ordinance was passed.
But, if the community representatives claim that A has had
ample opportunity to force collection of his debts, and A denies
such claim, the latter must take an oath to bolster his denial.

This responsum is addressed to "my relative Kohen Zedek."

SOURCES: Am II, 140; *Mordecai Hagadol*, p. 300a.

556

Q. Before A settled in T, the community borrowed money
on interest in order to pay a tax that had been levied on it.
A died before this debt fell due. Before his death, however,
A paid other taxes to the community on the twelve hundred
[*marks*?] he did business with, of which some was his own money
and some belonged to others. A's estate fell to several heirs
some of whom lived outside of T. An ordinance of the community of T required that anyone who moved from T had to
pay his share of all the debts the community had contracted
for the purpose of paying its taxes, even though such debts
did not yet fall due at the time the person moved from T. Does
this ordinance obligate A's heirs, who live outside of T, to pay

their share of the above mentioned debt before they remove the funds from T which they inherited from A?

A. The ordinance applies only to residents of T who seek to leave town, but not to outsiders who inherit money from residents. Since the ordinance does not explicitly include such inheriting outsiders, we cannot include them by any logical inference. Since A's heirs who live outside of T are not required by talmudic law to pay any share of the above mentioned debt [as it was contracted in order to pay a tax which was levied before A came to live in T], they cannot be required to pay anything because of the ordinance. They must pay, however, on the money they inherited from A, their proportionate share of all the taxes the community of T has paid during A's residence in T. A himself became obligated to pay such taxes on the twelve hundred [*marks?*] he did business with, even though part of this money did not belong to him; and his heirs must pay this obligation of A in full. The claim of the heirs, therefore, that the debts of the estate should be paid first, and that only the remainder of the estate should be assessed for the above-mentioned taxes, must be denied. On the other hand, although the ordinance mentioned above does not apply to A's heirs who live outside of T, those ordinances of the community of T which grant to heirs special exemptions from taxes, do apply even to the heirs who live out of T.

This Responsum is addressed to Rabbi Asher.

SOURCES: *Mordecai Hagadol,* p. 256d.

557

Q. Leah claims that she settled in the town T subsequent to the demand of a tax from the Jews by the burghers of the town, and after they had instructed the Jews to pay the tax to a Jew, A; that she was, therefore, not subject to this tax, even though A gave the community an extension of the time for payment; and that the community had no right to collect any money from her in payment therefor. The community claims that Leah sent her money to T for investment before the burghers demanded the tax; that her sister rented a house for her, which indicates that Leah had decided to reside in T before she actually came there; that it is a custom of the community to collect taxes from all those resident at the time of collection even though they were not residents at the time the tax was demanded; and that the tax was paid in order to save their lives, since the burghers threatened "to do what they did on the Rhine." Leah denied the claims that she sent her money to T, that it had been invested before her arrival and that her sister had rented a house for her. She stated that the Jews always paid a tax to the burghers whenever the latter demanded it; and that she did not intend to settle in T at all, but that being her sister's surety she had to follow her sister when the latter fled from her former settlement.

A. Matters of taxation depend on local custom. It is needless to ask me the custom of our community, for you may have a different custom. Anyone who settles in a new place is bound by the custom prevailing there. But since the community has completely settled its obligations to the burghers, by consenting to pay the tax to A, before Leah settled in T, the representatives of the community must prove through witnesses who are not residents of T, that according to their custom Leah was obliged to pay the amount the community demanded, before they could deprive her of any of her property. If Leah, however, rented a house in T before the tax was levied, she is bound to pay her share of the tax, despite the fact that the community may not be able to prove any prevailing custom to that effect.

SOURCES: Pr. 995. Cf. Menahem of Merseburg, *Nimmukim* (8).

558

Q. B informed the community of T that he wished to move out of town. He did move out of town, but settled within one mile of T. He continued to lend money to the nobles, his customers, asserting that he was unable to collect his debts from them unless he lent them additional funds. Subsequently, a heavy tax was imposed on the community by the overlord of T. The community protested to the overlord that B, the man who formerly used to defray half of the taxes imposed on the community, had moved out of town [outside of the overlord's jurisdiction], but their protests were of no avail. The community, therefore, demands that B pay his share of the tax.

A. If it is true that B left town before the overlord demanded the tax, he is under no obligation to pay it, since he lived outside of the city limits, even though within one mile of T. I have known many instances where men who have left their town and moved to places scarcely half a mile away, no longer paid their taxes to the community. Formerly, when the country had a king, the Jews of the surrounding territory — even those who lived eight miles away from town, in fact those who lived in the entire bishopric — would pay their taxes to the king collectively with the community. [But this is no longer done.] However, if, while B was still living in T, the community passed a ruling [regarding the payment of taxes, or the lending of additional funds to debtors, by the Jews who move to the surrounding territory], he is still bound by such a ruling. The community, on the other hand, did an improper thing by informing the overlord that B used to bear half the burden of the community taxes. They should merely have informed the overlord that B had moved out of town, and should have been satisfied with whatever reduction the overlord would have granted to them on this account. Regarding

B's business transactions, however, if B could not have collected his debts from the nobles unless he lent them additional funds, he is under no obligation to pay taxes on such investments.

SOURCES: Cr. 121. Cf. Hayyim Or Zarua, *Responsa* 226.

559 (D)

Q. A [moved out of T but nevertheless] lent money to his customers there. The community of T, therefore, forced him to pay taxes. He now claims that the community had no right to collect these taxes from him since he had made no new investments in T but merely had lent additional funds to his customers in order to be able to collect his old debts from them. The community representatives aver that A could have collected his debts without lending additional funds to his debtors.

A. If A could not have collected his debts unless he had lent additional funds to his debtors, he had a right to lend them such funds, and these transactions should have been tax-free. The members of the community, as interested parties, are not qualified to serve as witnesses in this matter. Therefore, either every member of the community must take an oath to support the claim of its representatives, or the community must permit A to take an oath in support of his contention. However, if the community can produce even a single, independent, witness — one who has no financial interest in this trial, or one from whom the community shall agree to take a certain specified amount as his share of the tax regardless of the outcome of this trial — in support of the claims of the representatives, or to the effect that A freed the community from the obligation of taking an oath, no oath will be required.

SOURCES: Cr. 156.

560

Q. A promised under oath to move out of T before the
first of *Iyyar* or pay one *mark* to charity. The inhabitants of
T claimed that A did not faithfully fulfill his promise, and they
gave the following reasons: a) A did not move out of T since he
had settled within the Sabbath limits (2000 cubits) of the town;
b) he did not pay any taxes to the Cologne community,
probably because he contended that he was still an inhabitant
of T; c) he occasionally returned to T to collect his debts.
Thus, A never intended to keep his promise; he was only trying
to evade his oath; he, therefore, was obligated to pay one
mark to charity. A, on the other hand, claimed that he had
moved outside of the Sabbath limits of T into the jurisdiction
of another overlord; that he had asked the tax collectors of
Cologne to free him from the tax, because he had as yet not
decided where to settle; that R. Jacob had told him that he, A,
had fulfilled his promise properly; and that R. Jacob had, therefore, freed him from his obligation.

A. Even though A settled only within two thousand cubits
of T, he had really moved out of T proper and had thus fulfilled
his promise; for the outskirts of a town are not part of the town
(as far as oaths or vows are concerned, cf. Ned. 56b). Moreover,
it was just A's good fortune that he did not have to pay taxes
to the Cologne community, because he was regarded as an inhabitant of T. We are in no position to determine whether or not
A intended to keep his promise; and we have no right to fine A
because of our suspicions or because we question his true intentions. However, in order to allay all suspicion, I advised A to
make a statement, accompanied by a solemn hand-clasp, to
the effect that he intended to fulfill his promise faithfully.

SOURCES: L. 217. Cf. Menahem of Merseburg, *Nimmukim* (2).

561

Q. When community leaders claim that a member of their community owes a certain amount of taxes to the community and the member denies owing anything and refuses to pay, the leaders usually break into his house, often with the help of Gentiles, and forcefully take away valuables as pledges to secure the payment of the taxes demanded. Where do the community leaders get that right?

A. Taxes levied by the secular government are considered to be in the possession of the government even before actual collection of same. The community [the collecting agency of the government's taxes] possesses the same rights as the government and is, therefore, allowed to impound a person's valuables in order to have actual possession of the tax money. Moreover, this procedure is followed by all communities and is an accepted custom, having the strength of a law.

Sources: Pr. 943; 915; 708; Cr. 48; L. 371. Cf. *Agudah* B. M. 108; Weil, *Responsa* 124; *Terumat Hadeshen* 341.

562

The custom is well established throughout the kingdom that when an individual has a complaint against the community regarding the tax he was assessed with, he must first pay that tax and, then, may summon the community to court, for the community prefers to be in possession of such tax-money. As corroborative evidence of the legality of this procedure I cite the talmudic ruling that those who pay the capitation tax for others are justified in forcing the latter in their service (B. M. 73b), since "the law of the land prevails". Moreover, since the members of the community are partners in the payment of the taxes, no individual may willfully withdraw from the partnership. Since the majority (of the members of a community) may force the minority to abide by its rulings (B. B. 8b), it may certainly force an individual to pay his taxes. The burden

of proof to the contrary rests upon the person who seeks to
deviate from this rule.

Since the overlord customarily collects his taxes collectively
from the entire community, the exact obligation of each member
of the community regarding such tax becomes determined as
if already collected (the very moment the overlord demands
the collective tax); and if the overlord subsequently desires to
free or relieve one member at the expense of the others, he has
no right to do so. Such an act on his part is not considered
"law of the land," but rather constitutes outright robbery,
and is, therefore, not valid.

SOURCES: Cr. 49; Pr. 708, 915; L. 371; Am II, 130. Cf. *Agudah* B. M. 108;
Weil, *Responsa* 124; ibid. 133; ibid. 147; Menahem of Merseburg,
Nimmukim (36); *Terumat Hadeshen* 341.

563

Q. A claims that his assets, equal to forty *marks*, for which
the community demands a tax, are not taxable.

A. The decisions on questions of taxation are dependent
more on custom than on talmudic law. The following rule is
generally accepted by the communities: In any tax dispute
between an individual and the community, the latter first
collects the tax and then goes to court. Therefore, even before
the tax is collected, the community is considered to be in possession of the tax-money, and the burden of proof falls upon the
individual. This is not only an accepted custom, but also good
talmudic law, and is operative even in a new community where
there are no established customs. But if the community in
question has a different custom, that custom prevails, though
it be at variance with talmudic law.

This Responsum is addressed to R. Eliakim ha-Kohen.

SOURCES: Pr. 106; Mord. B. B. 522; cf. also Cr. 49; Pr. 708, 915; L. 371;
Am II, 130. *Agudah* B.M. 108; Moses Minz, *Responsa* 72; *Terumat
Hadeshen* 341.

564

Q. C gave a pledge to the community treasurers, the collectors of the tax, as security for his share of that tax. The treasurers, however, later lost that pledge (apparently through no fault of theirs). Must C pay his share of the tax?

A. Since the overlord keeps the community responsible for the deficiency caused by the loss of C's pledge, the community is collectively held responsible for the entire tax (each individual, therefore, is responsible to the community and not to the overlord). Since C gave the pledge to the representative of the community, and it was lost while in the latter's possession, C is free from obligation. Therefore, the whole community must make up the deficiency. We can not compare this case to that of the man who betrothed a woman with a pledge (Kidd. 8b), and conclude that since the pledge was given as security only and did not constitute actual payment, that C did not as yet discharge his obligation; for the community is not obliged to pay the overlord actual cash, but may pay its tax in valuables as well as in cash. Thus the custom is that when a person gives a pledge to the community treasurer (and then fails to redeem it) the pledge is not sold but is handed over intact to the overlord's messenger, when the latter comes to demand the tax-money, in payment of that person's share of the tax, whether the pledge be worth much more than, or exactly as much as, that share of the tax. Therefore, whether a person pays cash or gives a pledge, makes no difference to the community. The second case you ask about, is exactly similar to the first. As soon as a person hands over his payment to the treasurer of the community, he is free from obligation. However, such payment must actually be made to the treasurer; mere setting aside of valuables as payment for taxes, is not sufficient.

SOURCES: Am II, 139.

565 (D)

A community may not force one of its members, who claims to have given up hope of ever collecting a certain debt, to take an oath to bolster such a claim. If such member by the use of bribery subsequently succeeds in collecting the debt, he shall be entitled to deduct the full cost of the bribe before he divides the balance with the community.

SOURCES: Cr. 105. Cf. Menahem of Merseburg, *Nimmukim* (7).

566

Q. At the time the tax was collected B did not pay any tax on an apparently bad debt. Shortly thereafter, A helped B to settle with the debtor for part payment of this debt. A, then, said to B that he would not be expected to pay taxes on the original value of the debt. Subsequently some members of the community summoned B to court regarding the tax on the debt, and the court reached a certain decision. A, however, was not satisfied and, as a member of the community, summoned B to court again. The latter claims that A's statement mentioned above proves that A had no case against him. A, on the other hand, contends that B swore to pay a tax on the value of the debt at the time the tax was collected. B denies this claim, while A has no disinterested witnesses to support his contention.

A. If A was in town when B was first summoned to court, he should have appeared in court at that time to press his claims. Even if A was out of town at the time, if B has complied with the court's decision in the matter, he is under no obligation to A. B is not required to take an oath denying A's claim, since no oath is imposed for the purpose of forcing compliance with an alleged former oath. On the other hand, A's statement to B did not, in itself, absolve B from obligation to A, since a person, sometimes, does not reveal his real arguments and claims to his opponent until they both appear at court.

SOURCES: Cr. 167; Am II, 136.

567

Q. The overlord incarcerated the Jews of his province for purposes of extortion. Among them was A, who did not possess sufficient funds to cover his ransom. He gave as part of his ransom, therefore, ten *marks* which B had lent him for investment purposes, the profits of which were to be shared equally by A and B. Must A return the ten *marks* to B?

A. You failed to explain the custom of your community governing the payment of taxes from profit-sharing investments. I have learned from your countryman, however, that taxes on such investments are paid in your town by both partners, the silent partner paying one half and the active partner paying the other half. The same procedure is followed by our community. Therefore, A can not be released from repaying half of the loan since his responsibility in regard to that half was that of a debtor responsible for losses caused through unavoidable accidents. He is under no obligation, however, to repay the entire other half of the above investment, since B has had to pay half of the taxes on the investment. B may not successfully claim that the money paid to the overlord was not a tax but a ransom, and that he is under no obligation to pay for A's ransom, for, in these days, we have no regular taxes. Whatever the overlord demands, must be paid. Those who refuse to pay, are imprisoned, shorn of their possessions, and even murdered. Yet, B had undertaken to pay half of such taxes. Although, in our case, the overlord had incarcerated his Jews, we know that he merely wanted to collect from them an extraordinarily heavy tax and was afraid that they might flee his domain to escape payment. Were he certain that they would not have fled, he would not have incarcerated them and would have collected the same amount in a normal manner. Therefore, the money paid to the overlord was paid as a tax, and not as a ransom; especially so, since A alone was not arrested but together with the rest of the community, and no false charges were brought against him. The overlord had intended that each Jew pay the tax according to the amount of money he used in business; therefore, all investments became liable to such tax. Moreover, B must pay his share of the tax, or his transaction with A would be a usurious one, for A would not have been arrested, had he not dealt with B's money. Had there been an understanding between A and B that the latter would not have to pay A's ransom money (should A be incarcerated for purposes of extortion), such understanding would imply that B expected to share in the profits but not in the losses; and this would constitute a usurious transaction.

SOURCES: Mord. B. K. 190–1; Tesh. Maim. to *Nezikin*, 2. Cf. Maharil, *Responsa* 71; ibid. 89; ibid. 121; Weil, *Responsa* 133.

568

Q. A and B were incarcerated by the overlord for purposes of extortion. They made a joint settlement with the overlord. A's wife possesses money of her own, which she obtained through selling her jewelry; and A has never used that money. Since A and B must contribute toward their ransom in proportion to their wealth, is the money of A's wife to be considered part of A's wealth?

A. The overlord had intended that A and B pay their ransom out of the money held by them and their wives, for an overlord's greed is directed toward all the money in active circulation. Moreover, the custom of our kingdom requires that a person pay taxes even out of the money belonging to his unmarried sons and daughters. Therefore, the money of A's wife became subject to the tax.

SOURCES: Mord. B. K. 191; Tesh. Maim. to *Nezikin*, 2; *Agudah* B. K. 146. Cf. Weil, *Responsa* 133; *Terumat Hadeshen* 342.

569

Q. A and B extended a loan and received a pledge as security. The pledge remained in A's possession. A was arrested by his lord who seized his property, including the pledge. He finally agreed to pay his lord a certain sum, in consideration of which he was set free and the pledge was returned to him. He demands that B pay him part of the redemption price. B, however, says: "My lord exercises authority over your lord, and if you had waited a little, my lord would have compelled your lord to return the pledge."

A. B must pay A as much as he (B) benefited by A's redeeming the pledge; i. e., as much as B would have paid to obtain the pledge immediately without necessitating the intervention of his lord.

This Responsum is addressed to R. Haim Paltiel.

SOURCES: Cr. 221; Pr. 226; Mord. B. K. 167; *Agudah* B. K. 141; Tesh. Maim. to *Nezikin*, 3. Cf. Moses Mintz, *Responsa* 1; ibid. 74a.

570

Q. A claims that when the overlord seized his valuables he also seized L(eah)'s valuables which were in the same room; and that when he finally settled with the overlord to pay him a fixed sum of money, and the latter returned all of the valuables to him, he pledged them with the persons who went surety for him to the overlord. L demands her valuables, and A demands that L pay part of the tax he promised to pay to the overlord.

A. If A's claim regarding the seizure of L's valuables is true, it is presumed that L abandoned all hope of recovering them. Although in the case of an ordinary robber no such presumption exists (B. K. 114a), at present every overlord is king in his domain; no one exercises any restraint upon him, and we presume that owners of movables seized by an overlord have abandoned all hope of recovery. Therefore, L's seized valuables belong to A since he acquired them through abandonment (*yeush*) and change of possession (*shinui reshut*), although the principle "the law of the land prevails" does not apply in this case of robbery and extortion. However, A is not entitled to collect any additional tax-money from L, since she was not personally included by the overlord in his extortionist act on A. Although all persons earning money in a town or locality must share the burden of taxation of such a town or locality, this ruling applies only to regular taxes of a fixed amount annually collected by the king (or overlord) from the entire community in one lump sum. The robbery and extortion of an overlord, however, on pretext or false accusation, is to be borne only by the person unfortunately caught in his toils, but not by those who, probably by the grace of God, have escaped them.

R. Meir adds the obscure statement: L must pay the rent for the house but would be permitted to deduct therefrom whatever she will assert under oath that he failed to spend on wood and illumination.

This Responsum is addressed to R. Isaac, R. Samuel, and R. Yehiel.

SOURCES: L. 381; Rashba I, 1105.

571

1) *Q.* Two brothers, A and B, owned a house and other valuables and investments in partnership. They always paid their taxes and levies out of the profit from their investments

before they divided the balance among themselves. A died and left a widow and a daughter. Subsequently B was arrested together with other Jews from his town for purposes of extortion, and was forced to pay a heavy ransom. B, therefore, sought to pay his ransom from the money of the partnership; the widow and her daughter objected to this insisting that since they were not arrested, they should be under no obligation to pay part of B's ransom.

A. Although A and B have paid their taxes from the money of the partnership, since there had been no formal agreement between them on this matter, each was entitled to dissolve the partnership at any time without giving previous notice to the other. Since A died and his estate went to his heirs, the latter are under no obligation to pay B's ransom. Since not all the Jews of the town were arrested, and those who were not arrested did not pay any part of the extortionate levy, the widow and her daughter did not become personally obligated to pay any part of this levy. Nor can they be made to pay part of the levy because of A's partnership with B. The widow is entitled to collect her *ketubah* from the money already collected from the debtors of A and B.

2) *Q.* Since A's widow did not receive payment of her *ketubah* immediately upon demand, but her case was unduly delayed, was she entitled to her sustenance during this period of protraction and delay?

A. As soon as a widow demands her *ketubah*, she forfeits her right to have her sustenance provided from the estate, no matter how long a time the collection of the *ketubah* will take.

These Responsa are addressed to Rabbi Samuel and Rabbi Shemariah.

SOURCES: Sinai V (1942) 10–12, 304–5.

572

1) ℒ. A paid his taxes directly to the overlord of his town, independently of the rest of the community. The overlord, suspecting that A possessed much greater wealth than he usually professed to have, and being driven by a greed for money, arrested him without cause and later arrested his wife L. Before her arrest, however, and before the reason for these arrests became manifest, L helped Gershom, A's son by a previous marriage, to flee the domain of the overlord and thus escape from his clutches. Meanwhile, A was put to death in prison. The overlord posted guards in the town to make sure that A's children did not escape, and demanded a large sum of money from L. He further proposed that L merge her taxes with those of the community and that the latter jointly with L negotiate the new tax. When the community representatives asked as to the identity of the persons who would be expected to pay this tax, the overlord answered that everybody would pay it, the young and the old, the rich and the poor. The community representatives, then, strongly objected to the merger with L; whereupon the overlord agreed to negotiate with them separately. He levied a very heavy tax on the community, but this tax did not exceed the estimated value of the wealth of the community members. L was warned that should she prove to be stubborn and unyielding, she and A's children would be made to suffer the same fate as A. Finally the overlord came to terms with L and agreed to release her, and to return to her A's impounded valuables, for a ransom of six hundred and twenty pounds. To insure the payment of this ransom the overlord demanded as hostages one of L's children and one of A's children by his former marriage. Now Gershom, and A's other children by his former marriage, refuse to pay their part of the ransom money, and instead, wish to pay their part of the assessment on the community.

A. Gershom is not obliged to pay any part of the ransom money since he escaped before the overlord asked for such money. Although L engineered his escape, he is under no monetary obligation to her, since she merely did him a favor. However, if Gershom is to claim, as his share of the inheritance, part of A's valuables that have remained in town within the grasp of the overlord, he must pay a proportionate part of the ransom for such valuables. A's children by his former marriage must pay their part of the ransom money in proportion to their wealth. Even though they were not imprisoned, there is sufficient indication that the overlord intended to include them in the extortion. Thus, guards had been posted in town to watch them, and their lives had been explicitly threatened upon L's refusal to come to terms with the overlord. Moreover, had the overlord negotiated with L regarding only her personal possessions, he would not have demanded 620 pounds from her, knowing full well that she was entitled to receive from A's estate only her *ketubah*, and that such a sum was well beyond her means. The overlord did not demand from the community a sum greater than the value of all their wealth; therefore, it stands to reason that he was not entirely unreasonable in his demands upon L. We may assume with certainty that had L refused to pay the ransom, A's children would have been seized, and would have been killed or forcibly baptized. Had A's children protested against being ransomed, we would have paid no attention to them and would have effected their release even against their will, and then, we would have collected the ransom money from them; for we are obliged to ransom a Jew even against his will. Now, that A's children have not protested against the ransom, they must certainly contribute thereto in proportion to their wealth. Although their lives were threatened, and the talmudic law (B.B. 116b) would thus require that the amount of the ransom money should be calculated, one half equally for each person, and the other half in proportion to the individual's wealth, this law does not apply to our case. We know that the overlord was interested only in their money, not in taking their lives, as the whole trouble started because the overlord thought A to be very wealthy.

2) *Q.* L seized some of A's movables claiming that she seized them for the purpose of paying for her sustenance. Some of these movables were originally impounded by the overlord and were later returned to L. May A's heirs force L to render under oath an account of such valuables?

A. Movables impounded by an overlord are considered abandoned property (*hefker*), title thereto, passing to the first person who seizes them, since the original owner must have given up hope of retrieving them. Although owners do not usually abandon movables taken away by Gentile robbers (B.K. 114a), they do abandon these when impounded by the overlord of the town, since he is the undisputed master of the town and no one can restrain him. This was especially true in our case, since his claim was bolstered by false accusations. Therefore, L is under no obligation to give an account of the movables returned to her by the overlord. However, those movables which the overlord had returned to her, and which she gave to the overlord in partial payment of the ransom, should be credited *pro rata* to all those who are obliged to pay the ransom, since the valuables had been given to her in order to decrease the ransom for all parties involved. Furthermore, L is under no obligation to give an accounting of the other movables she seized (the movables that were not impounded by the overlord) as long as it is known that the value of such movables does not exceed the value of her *ketubah*. For whenever L demands her *ketubah*, she will have to take an oath regarding these movables; as long as she does not demand her *ketubah*, no oath can be imposed on her.

3) *Q.* Rabbi Kuzlan, a relative of R. Meir, declared that A had deposited money with him and had told him to give the money, after A's death, to R. Mushlin, A's brother, who had received instructions regarding its disposal. Rabbi Kuzlan, therefore, gave the money to R. Mushlin. The latter claims that he was instructed by A to give all the money to A's children by his former marriage. R. Liber Shamash, another relative of R. Meir, testified that A made the following declaration in his presence: "Half of all the ready cash I have here, and in the house of Rabbi Kuzlan, and in the settlement, was given to Gershom my son, and the other half to his two older sisters, and I have empowered my brother Mushlin thus to dispose of the deposit that is in the house." L, on the other hand, produced a document wherein it was written that A had obligated himself not to alienate any of his property and thus put it beyond his wife's reach. L, therefore, demands that R. Mushlin take an oath to support his assertions.

A. The testimony of R. Liber Shamash is of no consequence since a verbal admission of having given valuables to a certain person, is no proof that title to such valuables was actually transferred to that person. Therefore, R. Mushlin has no witness to support his assertions. Although heirs may not exact an oath from a trustee appointed by their father (Gitt. 52a), this rule applies only to the heirs, who are to inherit the property managed by the trustee; but, the heirs who, according to the assertions of the trustee, are not to receive any part of such property, may exact an oath from the trustee even though they are not positive in their claim that the trustee had wronged them. Therefore, L and her children may exact the oath from R. Mushlin. Moreover, even if R. Mushlin's assertions were true, A's gift to his children by his former marriage would be considered a gift *causa mortis*, since it was to be given to them after A's death. Since a widow and orphaned daughters are entitled to draw their sustenance from all *causa mortis* gifts, L and her daughters would be entitled to draw their sustenance, and L would be entitled to collect her *ketubah*, from the money in the hands of R. Mushlin, if no unencumbered assets remain of A's estate. L's daughters are entitled to receive their sustenance till their marriage, the expense to be born proportionately by A's heirs (out of their inheritance). At the time of their marriage they will be entitled to a dowry of one tenth the immovables of A's estate. L's son, however, must derive his sustenance from his own portion of the inheritance, and when it will all be consumed he will have to resort to charity.

4) *Q.* L, at the time of her arrest, hired an agent to manage A's estate, to collect debts and sell valuables, in order to raise money for the ransom. She agreed to pay the agent a large sum of money for his efforts. Furthermore, R. Mushlin claims to have incurred expenses in his efforts to save L and A's children.

A. Since L had a right to hire an agent (Gitt. 52a) and since she was in urgent need of help, the agent is entitled to receive adequate compensation for his efforts; the court is to determine what constitutes adequate compensation. The agent, however, is not entitled to receive anything above such amount, even though L had promised him much more, for wages and hire are subject to reassessment. If R. Mushlin's claim is disputed, he must take an oath to support it. L had no right to sell any part of A's estate unless such sale was made in the presence of a lay court. Therefore, the articles sold must be reevaluated by such a court. If the articles had been sold below such evaluation, the difference should be deducted from L's *ketubah*; but if the articles were sold above the estimated value, the difference should revert to the heirs.

5) *Q.* Upon her marriage, A's daughter by a former marriage was given by R. Mushlin, as part of her dowry, her

share (one quarter) of the money originally deposited with Rabbi Kuzlan (see part 3).

A. L was entitled to collect a proportionate part of her *ketubah* exclusively from this money; now that this money had been given to the husband of A's daughter, L may no longer collect that part of her *ketubah*. Therefore, R. Mushlin has directly damaged L's interests and must make good, out of his own pocket, the loss thus sustained by L.

6) *Q.* Are the heirs permitted to pay L her *ketubah* by transferring to her debts due from Gentiles, if she objects to such manner of payment?

A. Debts due from Gentiles can not be directly assigned to a third person. Even though there is an indirect method of assigning such debts, a woman may refuse such manner of payment since even a creditor or one who has suffered damage may refuse to receive payment in such manner. Moreover, a woman is not expected to suffer the hardships and indignities entailed in collecting debts from Gentiles. Therefore, L may insist on being paid only in nonencumbered valuables.

7) *Q.* During the perilous period of the persecution by the overlord, a Gentile who owed ten *marks* to A came to L and asked her to release him from this debt. L, fearing lest refusal would aggravate the situation, said to the Gentile: "I shall never demand this money from you". A's heirs claim that this release caused them an unnecessary loss of ten *marks*.

A. Neither according to Jewish law nor according to the law of the land does L's statement release the debtor from his obligation to A's heirs. But, if according to the law of your particular town this debt is considered cancelled, L is to be held responsible for the amount the debt was worth at the time of the release. Surely the debt was not worth very much at a time when the creditor was in mortal danger! However, if L released the aforementioned debtor, as a safety measure, and

as a contributing factor to gain relief, the loss must be born
by L, and the heirs that were in town at the time, *pro rata*.

8) *Q*. A had deposited one pound with a burgher. After
L came to terms with the overlord, the burgher returned the
pound. L and the heirs who were in town during the period of
danger, claim that it would have been impossible to collect the
pound from the burgher if the settlement had not been effected
with the overlord, while the other heirs claim that the burgher
would have returned the money in any event.

A. If L is not able to take an oath to the effect, that
(she is certain that) the deposit would in all probability have
been lost if not for the settlement with the overlord, no ransom
money can be collected from this deposit.

9) *Q*. The youngest heir received for his share debts due
to the estate. The market value of these debts was much less
than their face value. Since every heir must contribute to the
payment of L's *ketubah* in proportion to the amount of money,
he or she, inherited from A's estate, what amount is the youngest
heir to contribute?

A. He must contribute in proportion to the market value
of the debts.

10) *Q*. Two notes of indebtedness were held in A's room
which had been sealed up by the overlord (at the time of the
extortion). Are the investments attested to by these notes, subject to the payment of the ransom money?

A. These investments are in the same category as the
money and the valuables that were held in the room; for had
no agreement been reached with the overlord, he would have
taken away the notes of indebtedness, and the investments
would have been lost. Even when the notes are presented to
(Gentile) debtors, they are often unwilling to repay their debts;
when such notes are lost, one can not expect repayment.

Moreover, the overlord would have collected these debts for himself.

11) *Q.* L took from Gershom's share debts to the value of one hundred and seventy pounds. Now that Gershom is not required to pay any ransom money, how can he collect his money?

A. Gershom may charge this amount to his sisters' shares of the ransom money and collect it from them, or he may charge it to the payment of L's *ketubah*. L does not have to collect her *ketubah*, or the ransom money, directly from the orphan girls; she may collect it from their money in the hands of R. Mushlin. The latter has no right to give the money he holds, to anyone until L receives all that is due her from the heirs, both male and female, each one according to his share.

If R. Mushlin has already given this money to the heirs, or should he in the future give it to them in order to put obstacles in L's way, and thus make it difficult for her to collect her money, then R. Mushlin is to be held responsible for such payments, and is to pay L out of his own pocket.

R. Meir adds: "You have protracted your case and have burdened me beyond endurance. I cannot bear your sending me any further inquiries regarding this case. It is obvious that the trustees are only interested in causing annoyance, vexation and protraction. From now on judge any case that may come before you, yourselves!" R. Meir further adds: "At last it has become apparent, it is sad to reflect, that all these cunning machinations are employed only to harass the widow, to procrastinate, and to deprive her of her *ketubah*; but you are merely succeeding in troubling and harassing me to no purpose."

These Responsa are addressed to "My relatives Rabbi Elijah and Rabbi David".

Sources: Am II, 19, 20, 21, 22, 23.

573

Q. The bishop imprisoned B in order to extort money from him. B said to A: "You owe me eight *marks*, give five *marks* to the bishop". Meanwhile a rich Jew promised to speak to the bishop on B's behalf and assured B that he would thus effect his release. A, however, gave five *marks* to the bishop and B was released. Now B demands that A repay him the full eight *marks*.

A. A is under no obligation to repay the five *marks* to B since he carried out a direct order to pay this amount to the bishop. Moreover, had A acted on his own initiative and ransomed B without being requested to do so, he would still have been entitled to reimbursement, for a Jew should be ransomed even against his express will, and may be charged with the expenses thus incurred. The promise of the rich man to speak to the bishop was of no consequence, since he did not offer to spend money on B's behalf. We know that mere words are of no avail. The Gentiles are not moved by words, only money affects them. Those who fall into their hands have no hope for deliverance save through the payment of ransom.

This Responsum is addressed to Rabbi Haim Paltiel b. Jacob.

SOURCES: Cr. 32–3; Tesh. Maim. to *Nezikin*, 17. Cf. Maharil, *Responsa* 78.

574

Q. A demands that B repay him the one pound B owes him. B admits that he owed one pound to A, but maintains that when the duke brought false accusations upon A and took away all his possessions, the duke's officer learned that he, B, owed money to A, and demanded that money. The officer threatened B with both bodily injury and confiscation of his property should he discover that B lied to him. Moreover, the officer forced B to take an oath as to the truth of his assertions; and because of this oath B was forced to admit that he owed money to A, and finally had to pay fifteen pounds to the officer. B, therefore, demands that A compensate him for the loss he suffered because of A.

A. If originally B borrowed the one pound from A, his responsibility thereto was that of a borrower, and he must now repay this amount to A. If A, however, had originally deposited this pound with B for safekeeping, and B kept this money intact and did not use it, he is now under no obligation to A since the officer specifically demanded that money from B. If B can produce no witnesses to testify to the fact that he was forced to deliver A's money to the officer, he must take an oath to that effect. In any event, B has no claim against A.

SOURCES: *Mordecai Hagadol*, p. 259d.

575

Q. A is held a prisoner by the overlord who promised to release him if he should marry a certain woman. A's wife, however, had died only recently, before *Rosh Hashanah*. Are *Rosh Hashanah*, *Yom Kippur*, and *Succoth*, considered to be in the same category as *Pesach*, *Shabuoth*, and *Succoth*, the intervening of which holidays permits a person to remarry? And, if the former three holidays are not in the same category as the latter three, is the above situation considered as serious as when a person is left with small children, and is permitted to remarry immediately after his wife's death? A suffers miserably being fettered in iron chains.

A. The intervening of *Pesach*, *Shabuoth*, and *Succoth*, only, permits a person to remarry. Regarding your second question, we put no trust in the promises of a perfidious overlord. Moreover, a person who is left with small children is permitted to remarry only because the life of the children is in danger, but not because of his discomfort. Therefore, even if the overlord releases A (on condition that he marry the woman) he will not be permitted to remarry till after the third holiday.

SOURCES: Mord. M. K. 936.

576

Q. A and B were captured and held for ransom. The former was rich and the latter, poor. A spent money with the help of his mother and effected the release of both A and B. A claims that B asked to be ransomed, and therefore demands that B pay his share of the expenses. B denies having asked to be ransomed.

A. A Jew should be ransomed even against his express will, and be charged with the expenses incurred. A captive in the hands of Gentiles is exposed to ruthless treatment and incessant flogging, and his very life is in danger. Therefore, anyone who effects the ransom of a Jew is praiseworthy and is entitled to the expenses incurred. Moreover, Jews threatened by a common danger may force one another to contribute of their means to the measures that will free them of that danger. A and B have to share the expenses in proportion to their wealth, since they were captured for the purpose of extorting money from them.

R. Meir adds that this question had already been sent to him from Magdeburg. He had also been asked concerning a tutor who was arrested because of a false accusation, and who requested his former employer not to ransom him. R. Meir's answer was the same.

SOURCES: Pr. 39; L. 345, cf. Mord. B. K. 58–59; Cr. 32–33; Am. II, 128; Tesh-Maim. *Nezikin*, 17. Weil, *Responsa* 148; ibid. 149; Moses Minz, *Responsa* 1.

577

Q. The leaders of the community demanded that the tutors and scribes who do business in their town, with their own money or with that belonging to others in their hands, pay taxes from such moneys. The scribes and tutors refused to pay the taxes and summoned the leaders to court. The latter refused to appear, claiming that[1] according to the regulations of the community, anyone who is asked to pay a tax must do so, otherwise the community leaders have a right to pawn his property. They see no reason, therefore, why they should answer a summons to court.

A. The scribes and tutors must first pay the levied tax; for the community is considered to be in possession of the tax money and the burden of proof lies on the individual. But, if the scribes and tutors later summon the leaders of the community to court, the latter must appear and present their claims before that body; for a community is not outside the pale of justice any more than an individual.

SOURCES: Pr. 716.

578

Q. At first all able-bodied men among the Jews, whether rich or poor, took their turn in guarding the gates and walls of the town in which they lived. A rich Jew would often be exempted from the duty by the town officials. Later, the Jewish community and the town officials agreed that the community pay a certain amount of money yearly to take the place of personal service. Must the rich and poor be taxed equally for this purpose?

A. Although the payment of money takes the place of personal service, the burden of which was shared equally by the poor and the rich, the community should apportion the taxes (to pay for this service) among its members in proportion to their wealth. For the personal service was administered by Gentile town-officials whose acts did not conform to talmudic law, and who often released the rich altogether and put the burden on the poor. Now that the Jewish community has to pay in money for the guarding of the gates, the cost must be distributed justly, i. e. in accordance with talmudic law. Moreover, it became an accepted custom in all communities (tantamount to a law) that when the guarding of the gates is done by the Jews themselves, then every Jew must take his turn regardless of his financial standing. But when, occasionally, a community comes to an agreement with its city officials to pay a special tax in place of the personal service, this tax is apportioned among the members of the community in proportion to their wealth.

SOURCES: Pr. 104; Mord. B. B. 475; *Agudah* B. B. 14. Cf. Moses Minz, *Responsa* 67b; *Terumat Hadeshen* 345.

579

Q. The leaders of a community decided to introduce a new method of taxation whereby real property was to be taxed at the same rate as money. Prior thereto, real property was not so taxed. Are leaders of a community empowered to introduce such a change in the method of taxation?

A. No; a change in an accepted custom, which will benefit some members of the community at the expense of others, can be introduced only by unanimous consent of the members.

R. Meir adds that throughout the kingdom, no taxes on real property are levied by the Jewish communities; that those whose wealth consisted mostly of money, attempted several times to introduce a change and tax real property; and that he, R. Meir, did not permit the enforcement of the change, for the reason quoted above.

SOURCES: Pr. 941; Mord. B. B. 481; *Agudah* B. B. 20. Cf. Weil, *Responsa* 84; Menahem of Merseburg, *Nimmukim* (44); Moses Minz, *Responsa* 63a; *Terumat Hadeshen* 342.

580

Q. Are houses to be assessed as capital for the purpose of taxation?

A. The method of allocating taxes is governed by local custom. This rule is explicitly and repeatedly stated in the Talmud (B. K. 116b). In the absence of a local custom, however, one must resort to talmudic law which provides: a) If the tax levied on the town is for the purpose of building a wall, a tower, or a gate, or for other purposes of protection, houses should be assessed as well as capital; b) the houses that attract attention and display opulence by their height, should be assessed accordingly (each house should be assessed in proportion to its effect upon an estimate of the wealth of the community); c) ordinary taxes that are paid yearly to the overlord or the burghers of a town are so paid because of the profits earned in that town; for which reason, houses are exempt from such taxes, while income derived from rent is similar to, and is to be taxed as, any other income (one, however, needs pay no taxes on the house he occupies as his dwelling); d) when the overlord demands an enormous tax of the Jews of the town, such as half their capital, or all their possessions, then houses must be assessed as well as capital.

SOURCES: B. p. 276, no. 57, 58; Mord. B. B. 475; *Mordecai Hagadol*, p. 297c. Cf. Hayyim Or Zarua, *Responsa* 110; Weil, *Responsa* 84; Menahem of Merseburg, *Nimmukim* (11); Moses Minz, *Responsa* 1; *Terumat Hadeshen* 342.

581

Q. A summoned the Community of Friedberg to court and put forth his claims as follows: Long* before the arrest (of the Jews of Friedberg) the members of the community were called upon to pay the (yearly) tax, and each one declared,

---

* The phrase השבעות לפני התפיסה might mean: ה' שבועות לפני התפיסה five weeks before the general arrest

under sanction of excommunication, the value of his assets.
A told the registrars of the declarations that he possessed
seventy *marks*, thirty-seven of his own, and thirty-three that
he owed to Gentiles and that were to be repaid immediately;
that all his neighbors knew of his obligation immediately to
repay that debt; and that he refused to pay taxes for these
thirty-three *marks*. The registrars told A that it was not worth
his while to argue about the matter since the tax was so small,
only three pennies per *mark*. A answered that he feared lest the
tax-rate later would be increased; but the registrars assured him
of their positive conviction that, with God's help, no increase of
the tax-rate would be necessary. A, therefore, agreed to pay
the tax on the whole amount. Subsequently the community,
including A's wife, was arrested. A, however, was in Frankfort
at the time, and he escaped to a place called Hunburg. As
soon as he arrived there he was seized by the knights, his creditors, for the purpose of collecting the money due them from
him before he became penniless. In order to pay off his creditors,
A had to call in his investments immediately and thus had to
settle with his debtors for much less than what they owed him.
A sent his nephew to the fortress, where the Jews of Friedberg
were held in custody, to inform them that he was forced to
repay his debts and consequently would be able to contribute
toward the ransom of the community only from the money he
still had left. The community leaders, however, paid no attention to him, taxed him an amount double the value of his present assets, and delivered his wife into the hands of the king's
servants with instructions to detain her and punish her till she
pay this amount. A was willing to pay the same tax-rate on
the money he now possessed, as the other members of the community had paid, but the amount he had been assessed was
well beyond his means. He contended that he should not be
expected to pay tax on the money he had owed to others, since
he had repaid that money before the amount of the ransom

(for the community) was agreed upon. Moreover, Rabbi Meborak, the trustee of the community, admitted to A that the custom of the Friedberg community always was for the members to declare their assets yearly under sanction of excommunication and to pay on the feast of *Hanukkah*, on the basis of such declaration, only the taxes already demanded by that date; while any unforeseen expenses or taxes demanded during the remainder of the year were paid with money borrowed on account of the next year's taxes.

The trustee averred: It is a custom long established in Friedberg, a community where great scholars and *parnasim* (community leaders) have dwelt, that a person pay taxes on the capital he does business with even though a great part of that capital is not his own. A himself has complied with this custom for many years. Now that we have been arrested, wise and discerning men have advised us to use the declarations made before the arrest as a basis for the apportioning of the ransom demanded from us; for, were we to rely on new declarations, since the tax is so excessively high, a few of our members might (by making false declarations) cunningly evade paying their due share.

A rejoined: The custom of paying taxes on capital invested with one by other people, applied only as far as ordinary taxes were concerned. But in the case of ruinous robbery such as the present one, when a person is expected to give away everything he has, how can one give that which is not his! Moreover, your decision, to use the former declaration as a basis for levying this tax, was reached without my consent and in spite of my protests. For the purpose of this tax you have evaluated your immovables and your books at half its actual value; an object evaluated at two *marks* was later sold for four *marks*. Who gave you the right to make such evaluation?

The trustee averred: Immovables and books are customarily exempt from taxation. But, for the advantage of the community, the wealthy among us have consented to pay taxes on immovables and books. They have decided, with the knowledge and consent of the whole community, to assess books at their actual cost, i.e. the cost of the parchment plus the scribe's wages. If this arrangement is displeasing to A, they are willing to revert to the generally accepted custom of paying no taxes on such valuables.

A replied: No custom can apply to the present case of ruinous robbery. Moreover, the rich have brought this calamity upon us by their high houses; why, then, should these houses be exempt? A further claimed that when one member of the community was discovered to have transgressed the ban and to have possessed more capital than what he had originally declared, the community confiscated that excess and distributed it proportionately among the tax-payers; and that one rich tax-payer promised to give his part of that excess to A in order to help him ransom his wife. That part amounted to sixteen *marks*, and A demanded that sum. The trustee answered that he did not consult the tax-payer referred to, but that he was sure that the latter would either deny having made such a promise, or would say that he had changed his mind.

Signed: Asher b. Rabbi Yehiel; Yehiel b. Isaak; Joseph b. Nathan.

A further claims that the community leaders have foregone part of the tax of some members, which in some cases amounted to as much as one hundred *marks* and in others to sixty *marks*, in order that these members might agree to the manner of apportioning the tax, while from A they demand that which he does not possess. Also, please instruct us regarding the laws governing the taxation of immovables and books; for I remember what you told us regarding the Mishna, Peah, 8, 9, and the *Yerushalmi* thereto, that you derived from these sources the rule that immovables be assessed at one quarter their value. Books, I believe, should not be taxed at all; if those who study the books are exempt from taxation, the books themselves ought to be similarly exempt. The Torah is termed "freedom" and ought to be free from the yoke of government. Moreover, house utensils are not taxed. Sometimes a person has many sets of such utensils, which are used only on rare occasions, yet he pays no taxes thereon. How much more reason to exempt books that are used daily by a person or by his sons and sons-in-law, or are lent to others for the purpose of study.

A. Why did you inquire of me concerning matters of taxation which are rooted in local custom, each community being governed by its own customs? The Talmud states that a person may withdraw from a partnership without the consent of the other partners when each person is attacked by a band of robbers and thus may suffer a loss of money (B. K. 116b). Therefore, if the Jews of Friedberg were accustomed to be partners in payment of normal taxes only, A had a right to withdraw from the partnership with reference to the exorbitant tax which constituted outright robbery. The rule, "the law of the land prevails", does not apply to extraordinary taxation, the latter being considered outright robbery. Therefore, since A warned the community to include him in their settlement with the authorities only if he was to bear the burden of the ensuing tax in proportion to the money he had left after paying his debts, the leaders of the community had no right to include him in their settlement unless they agreed to his terms. They should have excluded A's wife from their settlement with the authorities. However if such exclusion of A's wife might have led to her being abused and defiled by the uncircumcised — for a report reached us of the Jews of Friedberg having been threatened that unless they speedily come to terms with their captors their wives would be outraged and defiled — the leaders of the community were justified in including her in the general settlement in spite of A's protests. A Jew should be ransomed and delivered out of the hands of Gentiles even against his express will, and should be charged with the expenses incurred. Moreover, if the Jews of Friedberg were accustomed to be partners even in the payment of exorbitant taxes — for the custom in these kingdoms has been for a long time that there were no normal taxes, and every overlord levied taxes to his heart's content — the mere fact that the tax was more exorbitant than the others did not give A the right to withdraw from the partnership. Every tax levied by the overlord must be borne proportionately by all the Jews of the community. Even though A warned the leaders not to include him in the general agreement, except on his terms, his warning was of no avail as long as· the leaders did what they thought the right thing. Since in the opinion of the latter it was better to come to terms with the government instead of passively revolting against it, A was bound by the act of these leaders and must contribute his share in proportion to the capital he possessed at the time of the arrest. The fact that he was later forced to repay his debts did not diminish his obligation; for this obligation was not created at the time the agreement was reached with the authorities, but it was created at the time of the arrest, and at that time he still possessed seventy *marks*. A's complaint that some of the members of the community evaluated their immovables and books at less than their actual value, is irrelevant, for the community members have done him a favor by paying a tax on such valuables. Had they refused to pay such tax, no court would have compelled them to pay it. Already in former generations, many persons had complained bitterly before the courts and had demanded that immovables and books be taxed, especially when exorbitant taxes were demanded by the authorities — taxes that took away nine tenths of one's capital — but the owners of immovables and books were always acquitted in accordance with a long established custom instituted by the "ancients" [early settlers of Germany and France]. Since many good reasons, as well as the interests of public welfare, support the decision that immovables are not taxable, no court can override the decision of the other courts in this matter, unless the people of your community originally unanimously adopted a different ruling, for a community may change an established custom by a unanimous vote only. Regarding the alleged promise of the rich tax-payer to A, I have little to say as long as the promisor keeps silent. In any case, since the promise was not made formally, the promisor has a right to change his mind at any time. However, A's complaint that the community leaders have foregone certain obligations of some members, is a serious complaint since the leaders have no right to forego A's part of such tax obligations without his consent. But if these leaders were originally unanimously elected freely to manage the affairs of the community, and were thus vested with the power to forego obligations to the community whenever they would see fit to do so, they have acted well within their rights.

R. Meir adds: It is true that I was inclined to derive from the aforementioned talmudic sources the rule that immovables be assessed at one quarter their value, but the long established custom of not taxing such property prevails even in the face of talmudic law. Your arguments for not taxing books are conclusive.

SOURCES: Am II, 127–8. Cf. Mord. B. B. 480; *Agudah* B. B. 20; Israel Bruno, *Responsa* 123; *Terumat Hadeshen* 341; ibid. 342.

582

Q. A and B, former residents of T, escaped from the prison (where the other Jews of T were held), but their investments have remained in the hands of residents of T. Are A and B obliged to participate in the payment of the ransom money levied on the Jews of T?

A. If the Jews of T were accustomed to be partners in the payment of exorbitant taxes, A and B must pay their share of the aforementioned tax. The obligation to pay that tax was created at the time they were all cast into prison, and after that A and B could no longer free themselves from such obligation.

Sources: Am II, 130.

583

Q. Some members of the community made statements before the bishop [probably regarding their financial status] and swore to the truth of these statements. Subsequently they denied having made such statements. The bishop became enraged and threw some of them into prison. A and his mother-in-law, who had no part in this affair, asked the community to ransom the prisoners and offered to pay their part of the ransom money. The community tried to rescue the unfortunates, but the bishop would not free them. Finally they were freed by the grace of God. The bishop then became reconciled by receiving a certain amount of money, as a fine from the community. The community demanded that A and his mother-in-law contribute their share of the fine. A and his mother-in-law complained to the bishop, who, in his anger, increased the fine. The community now demands that A pay his share of the original fine plus the entire increase of which he was the cause. A claims that the community committed the first wrong by asking the bishop to put the tax on the entire community, after the bishop explicitly imposed the fine only on those members who were guilty of the perjury.

A. If the bishop originally imposed the fine only on those members who took the false oath, those who did not take such an oath are not obliged to pay any part of the fine. As to the increased fine, if A's claim is true, he is not to be held responsible for it. If, however, his claim is false, the community may collect from him any losses it has suffered on his account. The

amount of the loss must be established by witnesses. If, however, the community cannot produce any witnesses, and A
claims that he caused it no losses, he may take an oath and
be free from obligation. But if he admits having caused it
some loss, the community may take an oath as to the amount
of the loss, and collect that amount from A. A, however, is
free only from contributing to the additional tax which was
imposed as a fine, but he has to pay his share of the sixty *marks*
which is the yearly tax of the community to the bishop.

This Resp. is addressed to R. Isaac.

SOURCES: Cr. 53; Pr. 992; Rashba I, 1099. Cf. Hayyim Or Zarua, *Responsa*
253.

584

You ask too much of me in requesting me to arbitrate in
this matter. Heaven be my witness that I would not have
taken this case even for a large sum of money. But, since
you have adjured me, and have informed me that unless I
intervene a serious quarrel would break out, I shall go against
my inclination to comply with your wish. Briefly, therefore,
if you have been accustomed to be partners in the payment
of all kinds of taxes to the overlord, viz: normal taxes, exorbitant
taxes, poll taxes, tallages, penalties, and whatever other levies
came to his mind, you must assess each member, for the present
extortion, in the same manner and according to the same procedure as heretofore. If you have been accustomed either to
tax real property, or not to tax it, you must not deviate from
whatever was the custom except by unanimous consent. But
if up to the present you never paid any but normal taxes, if
heretofore your overlord never demanded any extraordinary
taxes, but was satisfied with collecting the regular, yearly tax,
you must search out and follow the custom of German communities. If the custom throughout Germany, when a com-

munity is arrested for the purpose of extortion, is to exempt
real property from taxation, you must not tax such property;
and if the custom is to assess such property at one half, one
third, or one quarter, its actual value, you must follow this
custom. This is required by strict law; but, I would prefer
that you voluntarily adjust your differences and reach some
compromise, if possible. You need not further inquire of me
regarding this case, for my answer will invariably be the same:
either you reach a compromise, follow your local custom, or,
in case no local custom exists, follow the custom of your country.

This responsum is addressed to: "My teacher Rabbi
Eliakum Kohen Zedek, and R. Meshulam".

SOURCES: Am II, 141.

585

Q. Some members of the community took an oath that
B is a proselyte. B was arrested as a result and was ransomed
for thirty *marks* to which amount A contributed his share.
A now demands that the members who caused B's arrest refund
him his money, since he was not among those who caused B's
arrest by their oath.

A. The members who took the oath are free from any
obligation to A since A paid his part voluntarily.

SOURCES: Cr. 54: Pr. 992: cf. Pr. 103.

586

Two Jews struck each other. Subsequently the authorities
came to the Synagogue and ordered the community to pronounce the ban [against anyone who witnessed the fight and
now refuses to testify]. . . .

If the community can pacify the authorities in any way,

it must do so. Otherwise let the witnesses testify against the culprits, and whatever damage the latter will suffer through such testimony, the community will have to make good, for no one is permitted to save himself through the use of another man's money.

SOURCES: B. p. 320 no. 792; *Mordecai Hagadol*, p. 260d; *Agudah* B. K. 137.

587 (D)

Q. A community summoned A to court and ordered that he answer the summons before a specified date, which date was extended to the first day of the (next) month, or be guilty of transgressing against a [community], solemn decree. Is the first day of the month included in the period given A to answer the summons of the community?

A. The community is entitled to consider the period given to A to answer its summons, as extending only up to, but not including, the first day of the month.

SOURCES: Pr. 825.

588

Q. The leaders of the community produced a promissory note signed by A, but bearing no signatures of witnesses, wherein was written that A owed a certain amount to the community, and wherein it was further stated that whenever the community leaders would present the note for collection, he would be obliged to honor it, and would not have the right to claim that it has been paid already. The community leaders now demand payment of the note from A's orphans.

A. A debtor may claim that the promissory note bearing his signature only, and produced by the creditor, had been honored already. The debtor, however, would have to take an oath in support of his claim. Although A himself could not have claimed to have repaid the debt but to have forgotten to retrieve the note, we do make such claim on behalf of A's orphans, since A might have forgotten that he had placed the community in a special position of trust and consequently did not bother to retrieve the note after he paid it. Therefore, A's orphans owe nothing to the community.

This Responsum is addressed to: "My teacher Rabbi Shemariah, and his companion".

SOURCES: Tesh. Maim. to *Mishpatim*, 38.

589 (D)

Q. A was pursuing his craft in town T when B began to pursue the same craft. A demanded that a ban be issued [in accordance with the talmudic law of competition] against any one besides himself who will engage in that craft. B, however, restrained him from such action until a decision, as to the legality of such a ban, be issued by a Rabbi. Subsequently A bribed the ruler of the town who issued a decree forbidding anyone, but A, to pursue that particular trade. A again demanded the issuance of a ban, claiming that the Jews are bound to abide by the law of the secular government. B, however, objected to the issuance of such a ban until a decision was rendered by a Rabbi.

A. If B is a resident of A's town,* A can not restrain him from pursuing his craft. The secular government, according to Jewish law, has no jursidiction over trade competition; therefore, the Jews are not bound to abide by their decree in such matters.

SOURCES: Pr. 677.

* The author uses the term *Bar-meboo*, a resident of A's alley, but he is only using the talmudic expression. The decision, however, is that in his own house B may pursue any craft he wants; while A may restrain B from settling next to A and pursuing A's craft.

590

Q. When the bishop, an officer of the king, came to redeem the king's pledges from A, the latter demanded his interest at the rate of four pennies per week per pound. The bishop became very angry, uttered many profanities against the Jews, and even threatened to have them driven out of France (?). Subsequently, the bishop demanded that the officers of the community (אמרכלים) obtain the king's pledge for him. The community officers took the pledge from A and delivered it to the bishop, who, thus appeased, paid them the same amount he had originally offered A. A now demands that the community officers pay him the amount they promised him by a solemn hand-clasp at the time they took the king's pledge from him. The community officers, on the other hand, claim that they did not intend to pay him more than they were to receive from the bishop. Moreover, there exists a community ordinance forbidding anyone to charge interest above two pennies per pound per week.

A. The people of a city have a right to enforce their regulations (B.B. 8b) and to punish and fine anyone not heeding them, especially in such cases where the regulations strengthen the position of the community and tend to ward off disaster. Therefore, the community officers had a right to force A to lower his demand for interest, and they did well even in misleading A, and thus avoiding a calamity.

The question is signed: Yedidyah b. R. Israel, probably of Nuremberg, cf. Cr. 12 end.

SOURCES: Pr. 980.

591

Q. Several Jews lent twenty-one pounds to the dean (*Dechant*), the overlord of the Jews of the city, on condition that he repay them thirty pounds. The dean asked the Jewish community to go surety from him and pay his creditors the thirty pounds, when the next payment of the taxes would be due. The community leaders agreed and gave a writ of indebtedness, bearing their signatures, for thirty pounds to A and B. The dean was deposed before the next payment of the taxes became due and the community was faced with the loss of this money. The community, therefore, refuses to pay the nine pounds interest to the creditors, claiming that since the community became responsible for the original debt contracted by the dean, the payment of the nine pounds, in addition to the twenty-one pounds borrowed by the dean, would constitute usury.

A. Since the creditors settled the interest on the dean as a loan, the dean became obligated to pay his creditors the full thirty pounds, which obligation was governed by the law of the country. The community leaders took over the dean's obligations in the presence of the three parties involved in the transaction, and became obligated to pay thirty pounds to the creditors. Moreover, the community is responsible for the full amount because its leaders went surety for the dean. The suretyship is binding in this case for two reasons: a) Although the suretyship was established after the debt was contracted (and should be invalid unless accompanied by a *kinyan*) the creditors did not free the dean from his obligations until the community leaders went surety for him; b) suretyship established by community leaders is comparable to one made before a Jewish court and is binding even without a *kinyan*.

SOURCES: Cr. 188; Pr. 38; Mord. B. M. 334. Weil, *Responsa* 30; ibid. 80; Moses Minz, *Responsa* 66d; *Terumat Hadeshen* 303; Ibid. 342

592 (D)

Q. A is seeking to sell his house of which he was the undisputed owner for many years. B, however, restrains A from selling the house by insisting that he has a claim on it. A is ready to answer B's claims in court immediately, but B refuses to proceed now, and says that he will press his case whenever he chooses to do so.

A. In order to obviate such abuses, we are accustomed throughout the kingdom, whenever a person sells his real property, to pronounce the ban in the synagogue against anyone who has any claim on such property and does not report it to the worthies of the community before he leaves the synagogue court. After all claims have been carefully examined and found to be baseless, a document is handed to the buyer wherein is written that on a specified date a ban was pronounced in the synagogue and said property was found to be clear of any encumbrance; consequently we have confirmed the buyer in the ownership of this proerty, and henceforth any claim against it that will be raised by a person who was present at the time the ban was pronounced, shall be null and void, and no one shall be permitted to attend such claim in a judicial capacity.

SOURCES: Cr. 262; Am II, 238.

593

a) *Q.* A was a *Gabbai* (officer) of a cemetery for twelve years. He lent two *marks* to the charity chest of the cemetery. When he took an oath as to his wealth from which he was to pay taxes, he included among his assets the two *marks* due him from the charity chest, and paid taxes for the whole amount. Subsequently he resigned his post as *Gabbai* and demanded that the community order the new *Gabbai* to pay him the two *marks*. When the case appeared at court, A said to the community representatives: "I do not ask anything from you." The judges construed this statement to mean that A relinquished his claim, in spite of A's protests that he meant to say that he demanded the money from the charity chest and not from the community.

A. It is customary for charity officers to advance their own money when the charity chest is empty and to collect it afterwards. Such officers' claims that money is due them from the chest are believed. Therefore, A is entitled to collect his two *marks*, and his subsequent explanation of his statement "I do not ask anything of you", should be accepted.

b) *Q.* Some members of the community are ready to testify in A's behalf. Is their testimony admissible as evidence?

A. The testimony of residents of a city is admitted as evidence in a case to which all the residents of the city are a party, if their testimony is against the interests of the city residents. Such testimony, however, is not admissible against the relatives of the witnesses.

SOURCES: Pr. 1012; *Mordecai Hagadol*, p. 301a; ibid. p. 350a; cf. Mord. B. B. 489; Weil, *Responsa* 124.

594

Q. Complying with A's request, the ruler of town T gave A the authority to admit as settlers only those persons of whom A would approve. A claims that B asked him for permission to remain in T for one year telling him that he had settling rights in another place, thus admitting that he possessed no settling-rights in T. B claims that he does possess such rights in T, that his father lived there before him, and denies having asked B for permission to stay there. Should both, B and A, be permitted to stay in T, it might lead to grave consequences, even to the spilling of blood, since B's conduct is known to be corrupt. Rabbi Moses asked what course he should take with respect to their claims.

A. If A produces witnesses to the effect that B asked permission to remain in T for a year, B will have to leave the town, since by his asking for permission he admitted that he either possessed no settling rights there, or had foregone any rights he might have had. If A can produce no such witnesses, B has a right to dwell in T. However, because of B's wicked conduct, you, Rabbi Moses, should deprive B of his settling rights in T and require A to pay adequate compensation to B. I have often seen communities deprive one of their members of his settling-rights because of misconduct; your court that has the right to confiscate a person's money, surely has the right to deprive one of his settling-rights. You should force, therefore, A and B to leave the case completely in your hands to be decided either by arbitration or according to strictly legal requirements, and then you will be able to decide as you see fit.

R. Meir adds:

Your opinion that B lost his settling-rights because of the legal principle "the law of the land prevails" is untenable. The ruler of T gave A the authority to pass on new settlers, but he gave A no authority to dislodge old residents. Had the ruler of T granted A the authority even to dislodge old residents, the validity of such a grant would depend on the reasons that prompted the ruler to grant such authority. If A asked the ruler for such authority, then A has no right to exercise his authority since by his request he directly injured B's interests. But, if the ruler of T, on his own accord, said that he does not want any Jew to live in T unless he receive A's permission, then A may dislodge B because of the legal principle: "The law of the land prevails".

The decision of R. Isaac (b. Samuel, the Tosafist) in the case of the Jews who fled from their town and whose real estate the ruler of the town confiscated and, then, sold to other Jews, has nothing to do with our decision. In this latter case, R. Isaac rightly decided that the purchasers must return the property to the original owners (as compensation, the purchasers were entitled to the amount the original owners would have spent to regain their property) for the ruler had no right

to confiscate real property that belonged to the Jews for generations. Such an act on the part of the ruler is not considered
"law of the land" but is rather outright robbery, and, therefore,
illegal. In our case, however, the ruler of T is the owner of T
and has a right to admit anyone into his town, and to keep
out of it anybody he wants to keep out. We cannot claim for
B's benefit that his father bought permanent settling rights
from the ruler of T and stipulated that he or his descendants
could never be dislodged from T, for such transactions were
very rare, even though such a stipulation if made would be
binding and would render the act of the ruler dislodging B
an illegal act.

The decision arrived at in the Talmud (B.B. 54b) accepting
as binding the Persian law that if the owner of a field defaults
in the taxes for that field, anyone who pays the taxes becomes
owner of the field, also, has nothing to do with our case; for
taxes on real property accumulate even when the owners are
away, while Jews are not required to pay taxes to their overlord, unless they actually live in the domain of these overlords.
For Jews are not subjugated to their overlords as the Gentiles
are, in the sense that they have to pay taxes to a particular
overlord even when they do not live in his domain. The status
of the Jew, in this land, is that of a free land owner who lost
his land but did not lose his personal liberty. This definition
of the status of the Jews is followed by the government in its
customary relations with the Jews.

SOURCES: Cr. 6; Pr. 101, 1001; L. 313; Mord. B. B. 559; *Mordecai Hagadol*,
p. 253b. Cf. *Agudah*, B. K. 144; ibid. B. B. 74; Maharil, *Responsa*
62; ibid. 77; *Terumat Hadeshen* 351.

595

ℚ. B claims that A's moving into his (B's) settlement forced
him (B) to move out and caused him a loss of 25 pounds. He
demands that A make good his loss.

A. It is an everyday occurrence that Jews move into places, where no ban against new settlers exists, without asking permission from the established inhabitants of such places. Therefore, A is free from any obligation to B.

SOURCES: Pr. 382.

596

Q. What is the custom of your locality regarding the admission of the testimony of a single witness as evidence, or of a witness reporting what he had heard from an eye-witness, in disputes involving settling rights?

A. We have no definite custom regarding these laws, for we never had a case of this nature. Were we confronted with such a problem, we would inquire of the communities as to the ruling accepted by them.

This Responsum was written by R. Meir in his youth, but in later life he decided that in disputes involving settling-rights, even the testimony of relatives or of witnesses reporting what they had heard from others, should be admitted in evidence; for, in such disputes, it is almost impossible to produce legitimate witnesses. The inhabitants of a town are the only ones who know whether or not a person possesses settling-rights, but such inhabitants are interested witnesses. Moreover, even they rarely remember what had happened years ago, and merely report vague memories, impressions, and hearsay. Therefore, when two groups of witnesses contradict each other, we admit the testimony of the group that has the most members. But usucapion is not a factor in proving settling-rights, since a person may have received permission to stay in town for a limited time only (Tesh. Maim.).

SOURCES: L. 214; Tesh. Maim. to *Shftim.* 13. Cf. *Agudah* B. B. 46; *Terumat Hadeshen* 342.

597

a) *Q.* M(eir) settled in the town T and lived there for many years buying houses and planting vineyards and groves. While he was alive certain persons contested his right to settle in T, but R. Judah ha-Kohen confirmed M's settling-rights. Now (after M's death) some inhabitants of T seek to oust M's son-in-law claiming that M possessed no settling rights in T.

A. Since R. Judah, my teacher and relative, acting in his official capacity as judge, confirmed M's settling-rights, no one is permitted to contest these rights of M. For, R. Judah deserves complete reliance on, and respect for his decisions. Therefore, you ought to silence all contestants by decree.

b) You state in your letter that two years ago you inquired of me regarding R. Isaac son of Rehabiah whose settling right was contested by the leading inhabitants of the town and that at that time we (?) had confirmed R. Isaac's right on the following grounds: a) witnesses testified that his father dwelt in this town for a year or two without disturbance; b) after his father's death he dwelt here for three years without disturbance; and c) in such cases the court puts forth the claim (for the heir) that had the father been alive he would have claimed to have bought (or obtained) settling-rights from the other dwellers of the town (and would have needed no further evidence under the circumstances). I have heard my teacher R. Judah ha-Kohen decide cases of settling-rights-disputes on the grounds quoted above; but I do not believe that such decisions are correct. According to talmudic law, undisturbed possession is not a factor in disputes involving settling-rights. Persons dwelling on their property during its occupancy by another, do not have to protest such occupancy since they are always in possession of their property (B.B. 29b). Therefore, the failure of the inhabitants of the town to protest against R. Isaac's settling in their midst, is of no consequence, and the decision given above is, indeed, faulty. However, it is possible that my teacher (R. Judah) arrived at such decision by following not talmudic law but community practice. Many communities accept, as legal, methods of proving a person's settling-rights that have no basis in, and that are entirely unacceptable to, talmudic law. For, settling rights are governed by the customs and practices of each particular community. The customs of the various communities differ from one another and are not at all dependent on strict talmudic law. R. Judah, therefore, finding a parallel in talmudic law, wanted to institute the custom of accepting undisturbed possession as a method of proving a person's settling rights. This custom ought to be followed in the communities where R. Judah instituted it (in deference to this scholar), and is in itself worthy to be followed in other communities as well.

Sources: L. 213.

598

Q. R. Moses maintained that he had settling-rights in the town of Quedlinburg. This claim was supported by the testimony of a single, qualified, witness, who subsequently died. R. Moses, therefore, demanded his rights. The members of the Q. community, however, disclaimed any knowledge of the existence of such settling-rights. Rabbi Isaac, of blessed memory, had instituted the custom of Q. of accepting the testimony of a single witness as evidence, in matters appertaining to settlingrights, and of disregarding testimony of disqualified witnesses.

A. Although the members of the Q. community are disqualified as witnesses in this case, they may take an oath (as litigants) to rebut the testimony of the single witness. Therefore, if the community will pronounce the ban (against anyone who will make false statements) and the inhabitants of Q. will declare in accordance with this ban that they had never heard that R. Moses had obtained settling-rights in Q., R. Moses will then have no right to settle there. If some of the inhabitants testify that they had heard, or had been told by their parents definitely, that R. Moses had no settling-rights in Q. — even if the rest of the inhabitants are silent on the matter — R. Moses will not be permitted to settle in Q. because it would constitute an infringement of the rights of these few. Statements of some of the inhabitants in R. Moses' favor, would, then, not affect the situation, since they are disqualified as witnesses.

SOURCES: P. 514; Pr. 231.

599

Q. R. Moses, the plaintiff, was not present when the defendants, the Jewish inhabitants of Quedlinburg, took an oath in order to nullify the testimony of R. Moses' single supporting witness; must they take the oath again in the presence of R. Moses?

A. If the oath has been legally administered by a proper person (who is related neither to R. Moses nor to the inhabitants of Quedlinburg) there is no need for another oath.

This Responsum is addressed to R. Shemariah, and is the second communication regarding this case.

SOURCES: Pr. 231; L. 382; Tesh. Maim. to *Haflaah*, 1. Cf. P. 514; Mord. Ket. 296–7.

600

Q. Has a *pardekat* (an idle or retired person) the right to evict from the town a person, A, who has no settling rights there?

A. The *pardekat* may claim that his opportunities of obtaining bargains or of finding, by chance, lost objects, have decreased since A came to settle in that town; that there has been a rise in house rents; and that he has suffered in many other ways from A's settling in this town. Therefore, he has a right to evict A.

SOURCES: L. 215; Mord. B. B. 552; Hag. Maim. to *Shekenim*, 6, 4. Cf. Weil, *Responsa* 106.

601

Q. A summoned B to court contesting his settling-rights in T. The court upheld B's rights. The other inhabitants of T now want to summon B to court again, on the ground that they have additional claims and arguments that would bolster their case against B. It is my opinion that they have forfeited their right to a retrial since they were in T during the first trial and failed to present their claims and arguments at the time.

A. Your opinion is correct. The inhabitants of T should have brought forth their claims and arguments at the original trial. For the same reason, a person summoned to court by a single inhabitant must not fail to answer the summons, on the ground that he wants to answer the claims of all the inhabitants at a single trial and does not wish to appear in court repeatedly with each individual inhabitant, since all claims against him should be brought forth during his trial when summoned by the single inhabitant or be permanently dismissed.

SOURCES: L. 216; B. p. 292, no. 367.

602

Q. A had lived undisturbed for more than three years in T when the community ordered him to leave the place because he had received no permission from it to establish a residence there. A claims that the settlement ban against new settlers had been waived for his benefit by all the members of

the community who lived in T at the time. The latter deny
A's claim.

A. The removal of the ban against settlement by waiver
is accepted by the communities as legally binding, although, in
talmudic law, rights in real property cannot be waived or
relinquished unless the waiver be accompanied by a formal act
of possession. But since the community denies A's claim, A
must produce proof that the ban against settlement had been
waived in his favor. A community is in complete possession
of its rights and does not have to protest any encroachments
on such rights. Therefore one can not claim usucapion as a
factor in obtaining possession of community rights. This law
is accepted throughout this Kingdom.

Sources: Pr. 46; L. 351; *Mordecai Hagadol,* p. 308a.

603

Q. A had no settling-rights in T, but lived there for a
number of years by permission successively granted to him by
the community for definite periods of time. Now, however,
a small number of the members of the community refuse to
grant him permission for a further stay in T. Your pupil is
inclined to think that A is entitled to stay in T long enough
to collect his debts. Thus the Talmud rules that bakers and
dyers are entitled to three years' notice because they usually
grant extensive credit, a person who lends money to Gentiles
on trust surely requires a great deal of time to collect such
debts. Meanwhile, A should be permitted to engage in lending
money on a limited scale, just enough to provide for his sustenance.

A. The talmudic law you quote (B.M. 101b) refers only
to a landlord who leased his premises to a baker, or a dyer,
for an indefinite period. One who leases his premises for a

definite period, however, need give no notice, and the tenant must vacate at the expiration of such period. The specification of a definite period, in itself, constitutes sufficient notice. Since A received permission to stay in T for a definite period of time, he must remove from T as soon as such period expires.

The query was sent by Rabbi Asher.

SOURCES: Am II, 244; *Mordecai Hagadol*, p. 300c.

604

Q. A had no settling-rights in T. Nevertheless, relying on the overlord's protection he moved to T and stayed there for over three years. He now claims to have acquired settling-rights in T, since B failed to voice his protests during this period.

A. Undisturbed possession is no proof of rightful ownership unless it be accompanied by a claim of rightful acquisition. Since A does not claim to have bought, or to have received as a gift, settling-rights from B, his undisturbed possession thereof is of no consequence. Moreover, if witnesses testify that A had originally settled in T by resort to violence, even a claim, by A, of rightful acquisition would be of no avail, for a person known to be a robber cannot claim undisturbed possession as proof of rightful acquisition.

This Responsum is addressed to R. Joshua.

SOURCES: Cr. 9.

605

Q. B and his sons claim to have received permission to settle in town T, and, they also show undisturbed settlement for more than three years. A claims that B and his sons received no such permission and that the only reason they were not disturbed was because they were informers and he was afraid of them.

A. Since B and his sons claim to have received permission to settle in T, and also show three years of undisturbed settlement, they have the right to dwell in T, and to prevent all newcomers from settling in T without their permission. If, however, A proves that B and his sons are informers, the latter cannot claim undisturbed settlement. If only B was proven to be an informer, his sons may still claim undisturbed settlement for themselves if their claim is entirely independent of that of their father.

SOURCES: Cr. 47; Pr. 100; L. 369; Mord. B. B. 532.

606

Q. In my efforts to collect the debts that were due to my departed father, which now belong to my orphaned niece and to myself, I have incurred expenses. Is my niece under obligation to pay her share of these expenses? Signed: R. Eleazar.

A. Your niece must not only pay her share of your expenses but must also pay you for your effort in collecting the debts, if you should insist on it, unless no extra effort was required by your acting on her behalf while acting on your own.

SOURCES: Sinai VI (1943) 13, no. 419.

607

Q. A and B, who lived in the territory of one lord, lent money on a partnership basis. Without the permission of his lord, A moved away into the territory of another lord. His former lord became angry and said to B: "I shall help you to collect your part of the loans, but not A's part." May B retain for himself the part of the loan which he will collect?

A. B has a right to dissolve the partnership without A's consent if the continuation of the partnership will cause him a loss of money. Therefore, if B, before he collected his part of the loans, expressly stated that he was going to collect only his share, then he may keep whatever he has collected. But, if he made no such statement, he must share the money he has collected with A.

This Responsum was addressed to R. Haim.

SOURCES: Pr. 105; Mord. B. K. 181; Hag. Maim. to *Sheluhim veShutfim*, 4, 5; *Mordecai Hagadol*, p. 256b; *Agudah* B. K. 143. Cf. Moses Minz, *Responsa* 22.

608 (D)

Q. A and his brothers were arrested by the bishop. They subsequently agreed to pay him a ransom of two thousand [white denarii?]. The brothers agreed among themselves that each one contribute an equal amount to the payment of the ransom. A, however, was short five hundred "white denarii" [and his brothers had to make up the difference]. Subsequently the bishop agreed to reduce the payment by five hundred [white denarii?]. A demands his share of the reduction.

A. Each brother is entitled to a share in the reduction proportionate to the amount he has paid.

SOURCES: Cr. 307.

609

1) *Q.* A's brothers were young when their father died, and A managed his father's estate together with his own business. One day A was arrested for purposes of extortion by the prefect of Ulrich and the overlord of Erstein. In order to extricate himself and be released by them, A cancelled a debt of three hundred and fifty *marks* that was due to the estate from the duke of Brunswick, and freed the sureties of this debt. There-

upon A was released. A's brothers now demand that he should compensate them for the loss of their share of the duke's debt.

A. A person is not permitted to buy his freedom with money belonging to others. The only exception to this rule is when a poor man hands over to robbers a valuable object deposited with him for safekeeping, in which case the poor man is free from obligation since we must assume that the robbers came expressly for the purpose of obtaining this valuable object (B.K. 117b). When the bailee himself is a wealthy man, however, we are not justified in making such an assumption. Since A is a wealthy man, he must pay to his brothers their share of the actual value of the duke's debt at the time it was cancelled. This law would apply even if it were known that the duke had plotted against A together with the overlords; the law, therefore, surely applies now when, according to the statement of the brothers, the duke was not associated with the overlords in their plot against A. A must also pay to his brothers their share of the interest that had accumulated on the debt before it was cancelled, even though the interest had not been made part of the principal by that time. A, however, must only pay their share of that interest which the duke would have definitely consented to add on to the principal; since the practice is for the debtor to promise a large rate of interest, but when the accumulated interest is to be added on to the principal, the debtor demands, and usually receives, a reduction of the amount of the accumulated interest. This reduction is an established custom and must be reckoned with.

2) *Q.* A deceived the overlord and paid him one hundred *marks* less than what the overlord thought he received. A now claims that these one hundred *marks* belong exclusively to him, and that he gave this money to his brothers by mistake. The brothers, however, aver that A paid them their rightful share of the money.

A. A may not claim that he paid the money to his brothers by mistake, especially so since according to talmudic law the brothers are fully entitled to their share of the money A saved by deception.

The case was then referred again to R. Meir thus: You, my illustrious teacher, have ruled that since A was a rich man he had to pay to his brothers their share of the actual value of the debt that had been due from the duke.

A, however, claims that with reference to the demands made on him by the overlords, he cannot be considered a rich man, for when he was arrested the lords demanded a ransom of thirty thousand* (schillings?). His captors enumerated all his investments in great detail in order to prove that he was in a position to pay such ransom. The investments thus enumerated included those that belonged to the estate. A claims that he was arrested because his managing of the estate made him appear a rich man, and because the duke was anxious to cancel the above debt; therefore, he should not be held responsible for the cancellation of this debt. Moreover, the duke died in the meantime. Had A not cancelled the debt, it would have been absolutely worthless anyway, now that the debtor was dead.

A. The fact that the overlords demanded one thousand *marks** from A does not prove that he was seeking the money of the estate, for when a person is thrown into prison for purposes of extortion, his rapacious captors first demand a huge sum as ransom, ten times his capital, without knowledge of the actual value of his assets. This is done in order to frighten him, force him to come to terms quickly, and pay a high ransom. Moreover, we must assume that A's captors would not commit such an outrage against the bishop and the burghers merely to cancel

---

*According to the question thirty thousand . . . was demanded from A, and according to the answer, one thousand *marks*.

a debt of a faithless debtor who had already lost his credit. Your contention that A's captors were intent on cancelling the above debt in order that the overlord should not be called a defaulter, is indeed untenable. The duke did not mind becoming known as a thief, a robber, a highwayman, and an extortionist; why should he object to the appellation defaulter? It is incredible. Therefore, A must pay his brothers their share of the actual value of the above debt at the time it was cancelled.

Regarding the deception A practiced on the overlord by having paid him a lesser amount than what the overlord thought he had received, I have written that A must share the amount thus saved with his partners. This decision I based on the ruling (of the Tosephta, B.M. 8, 25): "If publicans relinquish the tax of one partner, the other partners share the benefits thereof." You disagreed with my decision, however, and attempted to draw a distinction between the case of the publicans, who knowingly bestowed a benefit on the partner, and our case where the overlord was unconscious of the fact that the partner was deriving a benefit from him. However, your reasoning serves only to strengthen my ruling instead of weakening it. If a direct gift by the publicans to one partner must be shared by the other partners, then money which was not a gift to A and was not meant as a benefit directly and exclusively for him, must surely be shared with his partners. Moreover, a silent partner is entitled to an equal share in the profits earned by the industry and cunning of the active partner. Although A alone took the risk and braved the danger of severe punishment, he must share the benefits with his partners.

These Responsa were addressed to Rabbi Samuel and Rabbi Shemariah.

Sources: Sinai VI (1943) 13 no. 417; Cr. 305–6. Cf. *Terumat Hadeshen* 342; Isserlein, *Pesakim* 125.

610

Q. A and B jointly loaned money to a third party. The latter's friends went surety to A for the loan, since A was the active partner. Subsequently, A was arrested by his overlord and was forced to relinquish the debt and to release the sureties. B summoned A to court demanding his share of the loan. A claimed that his arrest was due to the loan and that he cancelled it under duress. B claims that A was arrested for other reasons, and that the investment was lost through A's own fault.

A. If A was arrested because of the aforesaid loan only and was forced simply to cancel the debt and release the sureties, he was free from obligation. Relinquishing another person's debts is a form of tort called *garmi* (damage done indirectly) for which the damager can not be held responsible if he acted under duress. This cancellation of the debt is similar to the burning of another person's notes of indebtedness, which latter act is considered *garmi*, for the debt itself is not cancelled by the burning of the notes of indebtedness; in our case similarly the obligations of the debtors and the sureties were not cancelled by A's act, even according to the law of the land, since A acted under duress. Were A able to summon the debtor and the sureties before a magistrate of another town, the latter would have held them responsible for the debt in spite of A's cancellation. Therefore, if A will take an oath to the effect that he was arrested solely for the purpose of being forced to cancel that debt, he will be free from obligation. R. Meir adds: You did not write A's answer to B's charge that when B tried to collect his share of the debt, A told the debtors they should not pay anything to B, since he, A, was the sole creditor and they owed nothing to B. The reason for this was that if B had been able to collect something on that debt, were it not for A's interference, A would be held responsible for B's loss, unless A was also forced thus to interfere.

SOURCES: Cr. 223; Am II, 157; Mord. B. K. 189; Tesh. Maim, to *Nezikin*, I; *Agudah* B. K. 146.

611

Q. A father left to his four sons a girdle and other objects which were pledged by the *landgraf** as security for a loan of one hundred and ten *marks*. One son, A, who owns a house but has no income, demands that the pledges be divided among the brothers since he and his family are starving for want of bread. The other brothers refuse to do so for the following reasons: 1) The pledges can not be divided among the brothers unless the girdle and the other objects be cut into pieces; 2) the debtor is powerful throughout the kingdom and if his pledges were damaged he would persecute the brothers and the entire community; 3) the pledges are worth less than the debt due. They, therefore, believe that it would pay to wait till peace is established in the country, at which time they might be able to induce the lord, through bribery, to pay his debt together with the accrued interest thereon. A, on the other hand, claims that in the last three years interest of more than four (hundred) *marks** has accrued; that the interest is four times the value of the pledges; that consequently the lord can have no reason for persecution even if the pledges be cut; and that he, A, can wait no longer since he must feed his children.

A. Under the circumstances, A cannot force his brothers to divide the pledges among themselves. If he is pressed for money, he may sell his interest in the pledges and the loan

* The *Mordecai Hagadol* reads: הלנטגרווא instead of the הלנט נרינא of Pr. Therefore it must mean *landgraf*, or landgrave. For a discussion of the identity of the *landgraf* and the amount of accrued interest, see Zimmels, *Beiträge zur Geschichte der Juden in Deutschland*, p. 113 foot note 389.

either to his brothers or to a stranger. Moreover, if A will receive the lord's consent to the division of the pledges or a guarantee from him (which the community will consider sufficient) that he will not persecute the brothers for such divison, A will be entitled to his part of the pledges.

SOURCES: Pr. 1005; *Mordecai Hagadol*, p. 258b.

612

Q. A and B jointly loaned money to a Gentile. When the Gentile repaid part of his obligation, A wanted to keep the entire sum for himself, and told B to collect his part from the Gentile.

A. A loan in the hands of a Gentile is very insecure. Therefore, A cannot dissolve the partnership until the entire loan is collected; and B is entitled to his share of the money already paid by the Gentile.

Thi, Responsum is addressed to R. Isaac.

SOURCES: Cr. 49; Pr. 916; L. 372; Mord. B. M. 392; Rashba I, 869; *Mordecai Hagadol*, p. 293d.

613 (D)

Q, R. Eliezer contributed thirteen *marks* to a loan extended to a Gentile. He offered to assign his interest in that loan to his brother A for thirteen *marks*. A accepted his offer and subsequently collected one *mark* as interest for his part of the loan. Is not the *mark* A received considered usury for the thirteen *marks* he gave to R. Eliezer, since a loan to a Gentile cannot be sold to a third party?

A. Since R. Eliezer did not guarantee the loan against default, the thirteen *marks* he received from A in payment therefor does not constitute a loan, and where there is no loan there can be no usury. Therefore, B is entitled to the *mark* profit. The law that a debt cannot be sold to a third party, means that the seller may later retract and may demand the accrued interest; but if the seller foregoes his right to the interest, the buyer may collect it lawfully.

SOURCES: Pr. 1008.

614 (D)

Q. A lent money to a Gentile. Part of this money belonged to B, but the Gentile was unaware of it. A collected the loan but refused to give any part of it to B saying: "Go and demand your money from the Gentile."

A. A must pay B the money coming to B from the Gentile for the following reasons: a) We assume that A became a trustee for B's part of the loan and, therefore, must collect it for B, for how else did B expect to get his money back?; b) A caused a definite loss of money to B and must compensate him for such loss; c) the Gentile became obligated to pay money to B, even though he did not know that part of the money loaned to him belonged to B. Therefore, when the Gentile paid off his debt to A, he gave to A the money he owed to B, and A must give that money to B.

SOURCES: Pr. 254.

615

Q. A says he is entitled to receive more than half of the interest due him and B from a Gentile, but B says he himself is entitled to an equal share with A.

A. Each one is entitled to receive the amount the other admits is coming to him; as to the remainder, it belongs to the one who will seize it first.

SOURCES: Am II, 155.

616 (D)

Q. A prominent burgher, a violent man, told A and B that he would take over the obligation of a debtor of theirs, since he himself owed money to this debtor. He invited them to his house in order to give them pledges as security for such debt. When they came to his house he placed pieces of cloth before them. A picked out one piece of cloth, twelve cubits in length, and said that he would like to have it for a Sabbath outfit. The Gentile sold it to him for two *marks* and deducted that sum from the debt. B then told A that he thus owed him one *mark*; but A objected to this claim saying that he took the cloth only because he wanted to withdraw his money from the Gentile, that he intended to keep the two *marks* for himself, and to even the score, he advised B also to buy a similar garment from the Gentile. B refused to buy it. The Gentile, then, gave them the rest of the cloth as security and they departed. Subsequently they returned the cloth in exchange for other pledges; they also held the Gentile's pledges for other debts contracted at various times. All in all, however, the pledges were worth much less than the debts and were never redeemed. Four years later the Gentile died and the pledges lapsed. Now, B demands that he be permitted to take two *marks* out of the pledges, and the remainder be equally divided between the partners; while A demands that the two partners bear the loss in proportion to the money that was due each.

A. Since the burgher was a violent man, A had a right to collect part of his debt independently of B. A had bought the garment for himself, had taken legal possession thereof from the Gentile, therefore, it belonged exclusively to him. Thus his share in the partnership was diminished by two *marks*, and he must now bear a smaller share of the loss; for the loss must be borne by each partner in proportion to his investment.

Sources: B. p. 277, no. 60.

617

Q. A Gentile asked A and B for a loan of 30 *marks*. C asked A and B to permit him to join their partnership, and they consented. A, B, and C, arranged the terms of the loan with the Gentile, calculated the amount of the interest, added the interest to the principal, and received the Gentile's sureties for the combined amount. A gave the Gentile four and one half *marks* before the other partners gave him anything. Subsequently, the Gentile informed the partners that he did not need to borrow any more money. Thereupon, A said to B and C that if they wanted to be partners in the above loan, they should each give him one and one half *marks*. B gave his share to A, but C died before he gave anything to A. Subsequently, B collected the principal plus the interest from the Gentile. He gave A one-third of the profit saying that he intended to give the other third to C's heirs. A, however, demanded two-thirds of the profit. I believe that A is entitled to two-thirds of the profit, since the Talmud rules that partners collect profit in proportion to the amount each partner invested (Ket. 93b).

Signed: Rabbi Solomon.

A. As long as the above partnership was not dissolved, A has acted on behalf of the partnership. Thus, both according to our law and according to the law of the land, the Gentile became indebted, and his sureties became responsible, to the partnership and not to A individually. Therefore, C's heirs are entitled to one third of the profits. The talmudic ruling you quote, however, deals with a partnership that was originally formed on an unequal basis.

SOURCES: Mord. Ket. 237–8.

618

Q. B, C and D with the help of D's father, A, lent money to a Gentile on a pledge that was worth less than the amount of the loan. The Gentile, therefore, put up Gentile sureties for the entire loan. A, originally, agreed to negotiate with the Gentile on condition that he (A) be free from any responsibility should B, C and D sustain a loss through his intervention even though it be as a result of his wilful neglect. Subsequently, A wrote to B and C to return the pledge, and the latter did so. Meanwhile, one of the sureties showed A and D a letter signed by B and C instructing them to release the sureties. Thereupon, they released the sureties. B and C claim that the letter was forged and demand their money from D.

A. D had no right to release the sureties until he was absolutely certain of B's and C's instructions. He was not to rely on a letter nor on any signature. Although the sureties were still legally responsible for the payment of the debt until released by B and C, D's release afforded the Gentiles an excuse to evade payment. Since A cannot be held responsible, D must make good B's and C's losses, the amount of which is to be evaluated by the court (not the face value of the loan since it was a bad debt and not worth its face value). If, however, B and C returned the pledge to the Gentile after the release of the sureties by D, though they had no knowledge of such release, the loss of the pledge is to be borne by them *pro rata.* Any additional loss, over and above the pledge, is to be borne by D alone.

SOURCES: Cr. 7; Pr. 93; L. 314; Tesh. Maim. to *Nezikin*, 12.

619

Q. A, B, and Leah, jointly lent 108 pounds to a Gentile. When the latter came to repay part of his debt in wine, as he used to do in former years, A and Leah, in B's presence, offered to take five wagons of wine at six pounds per wagon, which offer the Gentile rejected. Subsequently the Gentile met A's son, C, and complained to him about the ill treatment he received at the hands of his creditors. He also told the people in the street, that A, B, and Leah had already collected from him a thousand pounds in interest. To appease him, C agreed to take six wagons of wine for thirty-seven pounds. When A and Leah heard of it, they consented to take the wine, and ordered its delivery. Now, B refuses to accept his part of the wine claiming that he did not consent to the bargain, and that he would seek to collect cash from the Gentile. A claims that B angered the Gentile, who, consequently, repaid almost the entire debt, and thus caused them a considerable loss of money.

A. Whatever one partner does is binding on all other partners unless they openly protest against that partner's acts. Since B did not protest at the time of the first negotiations, he is bound by the subsequent agreement.

Sources: Pr. 961.

620

Q. A, B and Leah jointly lent money to one person. The debtor gave them the right to collect the annual produce of a certain village. A claims that B and Leah collected a certain amount of his share of the produce and gave it to farmers on condition that [at harvest time] they repay to B and Leah double the amount advanced. A, therefore, demands whatever B and Leah collected from these debtors. B, on the other hand, claims that he owes nothing to A, and that A collected part of his (B's) share of the produce. Leah claims that she is ready to return to A whatever he will state under oath she has taken from him. She further claims that she did not advance the produce for profit, but that she sold it when the prevailing market price was low.

A. Each partner must take an oath that he owes nothing to the others. Whoever admits that he took produce belonging

to the other, must return it in kind, unless he swears that
every year he sold the entire amount of the produce he collected,
in which case he may pay by money. The partner who admits
to have taken produce belonging to the other partner (or partners) is obliged to return the principal only, but is under no
obligation to return any income or interest earned with such
produce, for "robbers make retribution according to the value
of the object at the time it was robbed (B.K. 98b)."

SOURCES: Pr. 997; *Mordecai Hagadol*, p. 363d.

621

Q. A, B and C live in the same house. A Gentile came
to the house and sold to A and B an article at a bargain price,
on which they (A and B) made one *mark* profit. C claims that
since part of the house belongs to him, and since he was present
at the time the article was bought from the Gentile and he was
one of the buyers, he is entitled to one-third of the profits.
A and B deny C's claim that he was present at the time the
article was bought; they admit that they once bought an article
in partnership with C, but say that on that purchase they
earned no profit.

A. If A, B and C had made an agreement that they be
partners in all good business transactions that come to the house,
C is entitled to his share even though he was not present at
the time the article was bought; for, although a person cannot sell to another anything that is not yet in existence, people
may enter into a partnership to divide future gains (not yet in
existence) as in such a partnership each partner merely becomes
a hired worker to work for the benefit of the other partners.
But if no such agreement exists, A and B must take an oath
that C was not one of the buyers of the article, and that he
was not present at the time the transaction took place and did

not say: "I want to be a partner to this transaction." If, however, C was present at the time and expressed his desire to be
a partner, he is entitled to his share of the profits; for, if one
person tells another to lift up for him an article which has no
owner, and this person picks it up, the former gains title to it;
especially so if the second person is also to gain part ownership
in the article, as in the present case.

SOURCES: Pr. 325.

622 (D)

Q. A and B bought merchandise in partnership and sold
it in B's house. When they came to divide the profits, A demanded that B take the usual "partner's" oath, since the merchandise was sold in B's house. B claimed that A took part
in the selling of the merchandise and should, therefore, also
take a "partner's" oath. A, however, denied having taken any
part in the transaction of the sale. Furthermore, A claimed
that B owed him one Mina, which claim B denied. A demanded
that B take an oath and be free from obligation, and B demanded
that A take an oath and collect.

A. Since B admits that he had taken part in selling the
merchandise, and, therefore, must take a partner's oath, he is
also charged with the oath on A's second claim. However, if
B will take an oath that A took part in the selling of the merchandise, A will also have to take a partner's oath.

SOURCES: Pr. 839.

623

Q. Before A and B entered, as equal partners, into a business transaction wherein B was to be the active partner, A
said to B: "Give me your faithful word as a religious Jew that
you will not deny me my share of the profits." B complied
with A's request. When they came to divide the profits, A

demanded that B take an oath to the effect that there were no other profits except those he had admitted. B claimed that he had already given his word to A, which is equivalent to an oath.

A. B must take the oath usually taken by all partners, which is administered by the *hazzan* holding the Scroll of the law. Although giving one's faithful word is also considered an oath, it is not as solemn as the oath administered while holding the scroll of the Law, and can not take its place.

SOURCES: Cr. 171; Pr. 606; L. 379; Mord. Shebu. 765; cf. Hag. Maim. *Shebuoth* 11, 3; Moses, Minz, *Responsa* 17.

624

Q. A and B formed a partnership for the purpose of buying (and selling) silver, and minting coins. Subsequently A admitted C into the partnership. The affairs of the partners became highly complicated giving rise to litigation, each partner pressing various claims and counterclaims against the other. a) B who lent some of the partnership money on interest, and refused to share the profit on this investment with A, claimed that when he formed the partnership he agreed to share the profit arising out of his buying silver and minting coins, but not out of his money-lending transactions. b) A claimed that he had lent forty pounds to B out of the partnership money, and that B did not repay that debt; B averred that he did repay the forty pounds. c) A claimed that B owed fifteen *marks* to the partnership, and that the profits that flowed in from Enns, from Neustadt, and from the minters, were included in the fifteen *marks*. B denied this claim of A. d) A had sent a messenger to Enns to collect ten pounds. The messenger had collected the money but subsequently had lost it. B claimed that A was responsible for this loss since he had appointed the messenger without consulting him. A averred that he had consulted B about it. e) Sixty-one *marks* were found to be missing

from the partnership money. B claimed that the money had
been lost while in A's possession, and that the latter was responsible for the loss since he had put the partnership money in
the custody of his children who were minors.

A. a)   Since B lent money belonging to the partnership on
interest, he must share the profit from these investments with
the other partners, even though the partnership was originally
formed for other purposes than lending money on interest,
unless B had expressly stipulated the condition, at the time
the partnership was formed, that he would retain all profits
he might earn from money lending; for an agent who employs
his principal's money in his own business transactions must
share his profits with the principal even though he is fully held
responsible for all losses.   b) and c) Regarding the other claims
and counterclaims of the partners, each partner must take an
oath to support his claims and be free from obligation to the
partnership.   d) A is not responsible for the loss caused by his
messenger, since he gave nothing to the messenger, but merely
spoke to him.   But, if A did give money to the messenger, he
must take an oath to support his claim (that he consulted B
about appointing the messenger) or to the effect that his partners
allowed him a free hand in the management of their affairs,
and be free from obligation; otherwise he is to be held responsible for appointing an unreliable messenger.   e) If B is positive
in his claim that the sixty-one *marks* were lost while the partnership money was in A's possession, A will have to take an oath
denying that the money was lost at that time, or be held responsible for that loss; for putting money in the custody of
young children is considered wilful neglect; and a partner, being
in the category of a gratuitous bailee, is responsible for wilful
neglect. A is to be held responsible for the loss of the ten pounds
through his messenger and the loss of the sixty-one *marks*,
only if such losses had occurred before B joined A "in his work";
otherwise A can not be held responsible even for wilful neglect,

since a bailee is not responsible for losses caused by wilful neglect, if such losses occurred while the owner was with him
"in his work."

The matter was again sent to R. Meir for his opinion on
other problems that arose. f) Regarding the forty pounds lent
to B and demanded by A, which B claimed to have repaid, you
wrote that both, A and B, were required to take an oath to
support their claims. Will A, upon taking such oath, be entitled
to collect the forty pounds from B? g) B claimed that A had
admitted C into the partnership without his permission. If
not for this act of A, he, B, would have earned thirty pounds.
A denied B's claim. h) B claimed that towards the end [of
their business venture] they had been offered six pounds for
the coin [probably the coin-matrix], but that A did not permit
him to sell it for that price, while refusing to buy it himself,
and thus they lost the six pounds. i) B claimed that C and the
"officers" [probably the officers of the mint] owed money to
the partnership, but that A refused to collect this money. j) A
claimed that the sixty-one *marks* allegedly missing from the
partnership money, really represented the payment he had
made to the "treasurers" in order to free his partners from
their obligations to them. He demanded, therefore, that B pay
his share of this payment. B stating that the "treasurers" depended on him for the repayment of his obligation, denied A's
claim and said that A did not go surety for him and was, therefore, not required to pay B's obligation. B further claimed that
the above-mentioned money was actually lost because A put
it in the custody of his young children. A's youngest child,
however, is fifteen years of age.

A. f) If B takes an oath to the effect that he repaid the
forty pounds to A, the partners may hold A responsible for
these forty pounds. But if A subsequently takes an oath to
the effect that B did not repay the forty pounds, A will be free

from obligation to his partners regarding that sum. g) A must take an oath to support his claim. However, if at any time B had shown satisfaction with C's being admitted to the partnership, A's oath is unnecessary. h) Since A did not allow B to sell the coin [matrix] for six pounds hoping to sell it later for more, he can not be held responsible merely because his expectations were not realized. j) Since the money belongs to the partnership, B can sue C and the "officers" directly because of the "lien of R. Nathan" (garnishment). But, if the "officers" are Gentiles and the law of the land does not recognize the validity of the law of garnishment, A must institute proceedings against the "officers." k) I have already written to you that A is not to be held responsible even for losses occasioned by wilful neglect since B was with him "in his work." Moreover, since A's youngest child is fifteen years of age, the putting of money in the custody of his wife and children cannot be considered wilful neglect, since a bailee is expected to deliver his bailment into the hands of his wife and grown up children (B.M. 36a). If the partners, however, have not as yet divided the partnership money among themselves, B may exact an oath from A's children (but not from his wife until she be widowed or divorced) to the effect that they have not misappropriated any of the partnership money. He may exact this oath because of "the lien of R. Nathan." Regarding A's claim to have paid B's obligations to the "treasurers", B is free from obligation for that sum; for a person who repays the debt of another has no claim on the latter. However, if A claims that he went surety to the "treasurers" for B, the latter must take an oath denying this claim of A, or asserting that he owed nothing to the "treasurers."

These Responsa were sent to Vienna, the residence of Rabbi Abigdor haKohen.

SOURCES: Cr. 12, 15, 16; Pr. 102; ibid. 490; Am II, 162; Mord. B. K. 214.

625

Q. A, B, C, and D, were partners in a loan made by them. In repayment they received a quantity of silver which they divided among themselves by lot. Subsequently, A bought B's silver and sold it to merchants [probably Gentile merchants]. The latter broke up the silver and found it mixed with base metal. A averted a calamity by pacifying the merchants with gifts of money, thus preventing their bringing false accusations against him. A demands that B reimburse him with the price of the silver, and also compensate him for the money he had spent in pacifying the merchants.

A. The sale of the silver to A is void, since it was made in error. Similarly, the division of the silver among the partners is void, even though made by lot, since that too was made in error. However, B is not required to compensate A for the money he spent in pacifying the merchants, since B did not know, at the time of the sale, that his silver contained base metal. Moreover, even if B knew the contents of his silver, he would still be absolved from paying A the money he had given to the merchants, since he was only an indirect cause of A's loss, though he would be liable to punishment by the Heavenly Court.

SOURCES: P. 48, 49.

626 (D)

1) *Q.* A claims that B misappropriated money from their partnership. B denies A's claim.

A. If B will take the "partners' oath", he will be free from obligation. Although after a partnership is dissolved, an ex-partner is no longer required to take the "partners' oath", in this case, since B must take oaths in support of his other claims as against A, he must include an "entailed oath" regarding the above claim.

2) *Q.* B's former partners claim that the Gentile who seized from B valuables that belonged to the partnership, has seized them, as the Gentile claimed, in payment of money B owed him. B denies having owed anything to the Gentile.

A. Although Gentiles are robbers, and their excuses for seizing property from Jews are not to be taken seriously — ordinarily such a claim would not require an oath of denial on the part of B — in this case, however, B must take an "entailed oath". On the other hand, if B should admit that he owed money to the Gentile, he would have to pay this money to his former partners.

SOURCES: Cr. 302–3.

627 (D)

Q. A sent jewelry to C through B. A claims that he told B not to give the jewelry to C unless the latter gave him two *marks*. A, therefore, demands his two *marks* from B. B, however, denies A's claim.

A. A neutral party is believed without an oath. We cannot require an oath of B; for if we do, no one will do a favor for a friend lest he claim to have stipulated conditions for such a favor and the benefactor would be required to take an oath. Therefore, B is free from any obligation to A unless the latter claims that B received the two *marks* from C, in which case B has to take an oath to the effect that he did not receive anything from C.

SOURCES: Pr. 277.

628

Q. When A was imprisoned the community delegated B to endeavor to release him. A claims that he sent books to B, which were valued at twelve *marks*, so that B, using the books as security, might procure a loan from the charity-chest at its regular rate of interest; and that he, thus, owes B nine pounds Nürnburg coins, which he is ready to repay. He demands that B permit him to redeem his books. B claims: a) that when A gave him the books, he, A, undertook to make good all damages incurred in securing the loan; b) that he, B, suffered damages because of his endeavors on A's behalf; c) that A sent word to R. Yedidyah and to B, to sell two books; d) that he, B, gave the two books to Rabbi Yedidyah who sold them, but who now refuses to give the money to B. A, however, claims that he only advised B to secure the aid of Rabbi Yedidyah in selling the books, since R. Yedidyah knew their value and how to sell them, but that he did not permit B to give the books to R. Yedidyah. Moreover, A claims that R. Yedidyah retains the money he received for the two books, for a debt B owes him. B denies that he owes money to R. Yedidyah.

A.   If B admits that he received A's books, he is responsible for them. If, however, B claims that A gave him permission to give the books to R. Yedidyah, he must take an oath to that effect and then be free from obligation. Moreover, if A usually entrusted his valuables to R. Yedidyah, B is free from obligation without taking an oath. As to the damages B claims to have suffered on A's accounts because he went surety for A to Gentiles, if he has in his possession money belonging to A, he may take an oath as to the amount of damages he suffered, and be entitled to retain that sum. For if one Jew goes surety to a Gentile for another Jew, the latter must make good all damages suffered by the surety because of his suretyship, excepting damages caused by his wilful neglect. At first I was told that this law was an ordinance enacted by the communities, but now I realize that it is sound talmudic law (based on B. K. 114a: "thou hast placed a lion next to my field"). If, however, B has in his possession no money belonging to A, A may take an oath

that he expressly undertook to be responsible only for the
interest of a loan secured from the charity-chest, and be obligated to pay B only such interest.

SOURCES: Pr. 977.

629

Q. A received money from B for the purpose of buying for
him garments from a Gentile. He paid the Gentile only part
of the price of the garments. The Gentile forgot the balance
due him, and did not ask for it for two years. A wants to retain
the balance for himself.

A. B gave money to A for the express purpose of paying
the Gentile. As long as A does not pay the Gentile, the money
belongs to B and A has no right to keep it. Moreover A has
no right to give the money to the Gentile after the latter forgot
about it; for, if A wants to sanctify the name of the Lord by
paying the Gentile money the latter forgot about, let him (A)
do so with his own money, as he cannot use another person's
money for such a purpose.

SOURCES: Cr. 50; Pr. 326, 953; L. 335; Mord. B. K. 168, 169; ibid. Ket. 258;
Tesh. Maim. to *Kinyan* 20; Asheri B. K. 10, 21; *Tur Hoshen Mishpat*, 183; Isserlein, *Pesakim* 166.

630

Q. A claims that B released his (A's) debtor and sureties
without his knowledge or permission. B avers that A had
instructed him to release them.

A. If witnesses testify that the debtor owed money to A
at the time B released him, B must reimburse A with the amount
the debt was worth before the debtor and the sureties were
released by B. If there are no witnesses to determine the value
of the debt, B must state under oath the extent of the damage
he has caused to A, and must compensate him for this damage.

But, if A can produce no witnesses to testify that the debtor owed him money, B is free from obligation. We must be satisfied with B's explanation of his act, since he could have denied his act altogether, and since A might have instructed B to release his debtor for the simple reason that the debtor had repaid his debt.

This Responsum is addressed to Rabbi Yedidyah.

SOURCES: Cr. 13; Mord. B. K. 96; Tesh. Maim, to *Nezikin*, 12. Cf. *Agudah* B. K. 110; Moses Minz, *Responsa* 44; ibid. 74a.

631

Q. A gave B a power of attorney to sue C. May C refuse to answer B's summons to court?

A. C must answer B's summons to court. Should the court grant a judgment to B, C could refuse to abide by this judgment till A personally answers his summons to court.

SOURCES: *Tashbetz*, 511; *Mordecai Hagadol*, p. 251a.

632 (D)

Q. What laws govern those transactions which fall in the category of *asmakta*?

A. Such transactions are valid if accompanied by a *kinyan* and concluded before an authoritative court. However, some *asmakta* transactions are valid even when not accompanied by a *kinyan* and not concluded before an authoritative court. Thus the Talmud rules that if a person lends money to another against a field, and the debtor says that in case he does not repay the debt within three years title to the field shall have vested in the creditor from now on, the transaction is valid (B.M. 65b, 66b). An earnest deposited in connection with a marriage engagement becomes forfeited upon the breaking of the engagement, even

though the original transaction was not made before an authoritative court and was not accompanied by a *kinyan*. A mere
promise to pay a fine to charity, as when a person promises to
give a certain amount to charity in case he plays cards, is also
binding. Regarding this law I wrote at length in a Responsum,
which you will find in the possession of our friend R. Isaac of
Straubing, and is too long to be repeated here. A decision by a
court of arbitration is not binding unless the acceptance of the
judges by the litigants was accompanied by a *kinyan*. Search
further in the sources and you will learn the details of these
laws.

SOURCES: B. p. 291, no. 364.

633

Q. (1) A made a contract with B and gave him a pledge as
security that he would fulfill the contract and said, "If I do not
carry out the terms of the contract the pledge shall be yours."

(2) C went surety for A to B promising to pay him a
certain amount if A should break the terms of the contract.*
Do such transactions fall under the rule of *asmakta* (אסמכתא)?

A. Both cases fall under the rule of *asmakta* and are, therefore, not binding.

SOURCES: Cr. 34, Pr. 130; L. 356; Asher, *Responsa* 108, 27.

634 (D)

Q. B bought an article from A. Having no money, B
delivered a pledge to A as security for the price of the article,

---

*That two questions were asked of R. Meir, one regarding security, and another regard-
ing a surety, is seen from the fact that towards the end of this Responsum (in the Pr.
130 version which deals with a pledge) R. Meir uses the phrase וכ"ש ערב לא משתעבד,
מק"ו המשכון עצמו פטור כ"ש הערב, which seems to indicate that the question was also about
a surety. Furthermore, Responsum Cr. 34, gives exactly the same answer as Pr. 130,
regarding a surety.

with the understanding that should B not repay his debt to A by a specified date, A should have the right to rehypothecate B's pledge through a Gentile, and B would be responsible for the principal and the interest of that loan. Is such a transaction considered *asmakta* and, therefore, invalid?

A. A became B's agent to procure a loan for him; the transaction is, therefore, valid.

SOURCES: Pr. 817.

635

Q. A agreed to buy a house from B. They deposited five *marks* (each) with C as liquidation damages in case of a breach of contract. B bound himself to reconcile all persons who might protest against the sale. B's neighbor protested, claiming that he wanted to buy the house and demanding his priority rights. When the case came to our court, we (the judges) decided that the agreement between A and B was an *asmakta*, and therefore, void. Moreover, even if B's promise to reconcile all those who might protest against the sale, were made before an authoritative court and strengthened by a *kinyan*, it would be void, since it is incumbent upon the buyer to do "what is just and good in the eyes of the Lord," (namely, to deliver the house to the owner of the adjoining premises), and the seller has nothing to do with it. Subsequently, the neighbor refused to buy B's house. Neither A nor anyone else was willing to pay for the house the amount A had originally offered. B, therefore, sued his neighbor for damages. We (the judges) decided that the neighbor is under no obligation to B since he did not cause B any damage directly.

A. Your decisions are correct. But your statement: "even if the above promise were made before an authoritative court . . .

etc." is wrong, since it was in B's power to reconcile his neighbor by paying him a certain sum of money.

SOURCES: Pr. 1013. Cf. *Agudah* B. M. 89.

636

Q. A sold his house to B and undertook to settle with the abutter so that the latter would not take the house away from B. The abutter, also, told B that having no money he did not want to buy the house. B, however, failed to bind the abutter by a *kinyan*. A borrowed jewelry from his wife and deposited it with C stating: take formal possession of this jewelry on condition that if I fail to settle with the abutter it will belong to B from now on. B, on the other hand, deposited twenty* *marks* with C as a guaranty that he would pay the price of the house and that he would not change his mind. After the transaction was concluded, however, the abutter obtained money, paid off B, and took away the house; B, therefore, demanded of C that he turn over to him the valuables A had deposited with him. C told A in the presence of witnesses of B's demand and A replied that he should give the valuables to B "since it is legally coming to him". Is B entitled to the valuables?

A. A gave the valuables to C in order that he deliver them to B should a certain condition not be fulfilled. Such a transaction is called *asmakhta* and is not binding since it was not made before an authoritative court. When A finally told C to deliver the valuables to B, he was acting under misapprehension that they were due him legally, as his statement indicates. His order, therefore, was not binding and B should return the valuables to A.

SOURCES: Cr. 290; L. 309; Mord. B. B. 324; Tesh. Maim to *Kinyan*, 3.

* Cr. reads: "two;" Mord. reads: "four;" L. and Tesh. Maim. read: "twenty."

637

Q. It is the custom of judges to consider as valid conditional transactions classified as *asmakhta,* and even to enforce
the collection of the money-fines stipulated in such transactions,
when they were accompanied by a *kinyan* made before an
authoritative court. How can the judges enforce the collection
of such money when R. Hai Gaon and R. Hananel ruled that
these transactions were invalid? Moreover, occasionally the
conditional transaction is not concluded before an authoritative
court, but the scribe inserts the phrases: "accompanied by a
kinyan, made before an authoritative court", as a mere formal-
ity. Why should the signature of two witnesses to such writ
suffice? Why not require the signatures of three persons, those
of the prominent men of the community?

A. The ruling that a conditional transaction accompanied
by a *kinyan* made before an authoritative court is valid, is based
on the weighty opinions of R. Zemah Gaon, Rashi, Rashbam,
R. Tam, and Ri, while the opinion of R. Hai Gaon is untenable.
As to your second objection, if the scribe was instructed by the
contracting party (or parties) to draw up the contract, we assume that he was thus instructed to draw up a valid contract
in accordance with accepted custom. Since it is customary to
insert the phrase cited above in a conditional contract, the
scribe was thus instructed to insert it in the contract, and we
interpret such instruction as an admission by the defendant that
the transaction had taken place before an authoritative court.
Were two other witnesses to testify before us that the writ
was drawn up by the undersigned witnesses who recorded an
ordinary *kinyan* made in their presence, as a *kinyan* made before
an authoritative court without their (the latter witnesses) having
been instructed to draw up a valid contract, the contract would
be void. Lacking such testimony we must rely on the signatures
of the two witnesses as proof that the transaction was concluded

before an authoritative court; the responsibility for any irregularity must rest upon such witnesses.

This responsum is addressed to "my teacher and relative
Rabbi Asher".

SOURCES: Pr. 976; Am II, 107; Tesh. Maim. to *kinyan*, 4. Cf. Moses Minz,
Responsa 11.

638 (D)

Q. A gave B an object to sell in Cologne; B sold it elsewhere. It was rumored that B received for it more than what
he disclosed to A. Thereupon A told B of the rumor; then B
demanded that A take an oath in support of his charge that he,
B, had obtained more money for the object than he admitted to
A.

A. B must take an oath that he did not sell the object for
a higher price than he admitted to A.

SOURCES: Pr. 747.

639 (D)

1) *Q.* A sold merchandise to B on credit. From this
merchandise B sold one article to C and D in A's presence and
told them to pay A for the article. After A left, B told C and
D not to pay anything to A but to give the price of the article
to himself. Whom should C and D pay for the article?

A. B could not have given the money for the article to A
before he received the money from C and D, for as yet he had
no possession of it. Therefore, B was entitled to change his
mind before payment was made to A; and now C and D must
pay the money to B.

2) *Q.* A sold merchandise to B on credit. Before payment
was due A asked B to give him back his merchandise since B
found difficulty in selling it and would therefore not be able to
pay on time. B refused to do so, and further refused A's second

demand to make a partial payment of one ounce of gold. A, then, allowed B to keep one article of clothing (צינבר"ש של בכרונ"ש) for himself on condition that he return the rest of the merchandise. B did so; but now A demands the article of clothing from B, claiming that he did not intend to give it to B as a gift but used it as a ruse in order to get his merchandise back.

A. B may keep the article of clothing.

SOURCES: Pr. 830.

640 (D)

Q. Prior to leaving for a large city, B said to A: "Buy six guldens from me, give me the price (in pennies) now and I shall give you the guldens upon my return from the trip." A agreed and paid over the money to B in the presence of one witness. B died while on the trip, and the community appointed a trustee for his property. A demands his money from the trustee.

A. On the order of the community, B's trustee should pay the six gulden to A. The latter is under no obligation to take an oath, in view of the fact that B died before the time for payment arrived.

SOURCES: Pr. 831.

641

Q. A claimed that B's wife had given him her solemn promise to resell a (marten?) fur-coat to him, which he needed for his son's wedding, at the price she had paid to a Gentile. Subsequently A learned that she had sold the coat to him (to A) at a profit of more than one pound. B denied that his wife had ever made such promise to A.

A. B's wife is free from obligation and is not required to take an oath to support her husband's claim. A solemn promise is equivalent to an oath, and we do not impose an oath, in order to establish the existence of another oath.

SOURCES: P. 302.

642 (D)

Q. A sought the price of two *marks* for his heavy cloak, but B offered only one *mark*. Three weeks later, B came to A, and without discussing the price, asked A for this cloak. A gave it to him. Now A demands that B either pay him two *marks* or return the cloak. B claims that, at the time he took the cloak, he construed A's silence about the price as proof that he agreed to accept one *mark*.

A. Since A and B had no clear understanding about the price, the sale was invalid [and B must either pay two *marks* for A's cloak or return it].

SOURCES: Pr. 809.

643

Q. In the controversy between Rav and Samuel (B. M. 51a) regarding a person who concluded a sale on the condition that there be no claim of redress for overreaching, whose opinion prevails?

A. The opinion of Rav is accepted by all authorities. Notwithstanding the agreement to the contrary, a claim of redress for overreaching would be upheld.

SOURCES: P. 50.

644 (D)

Q. A made an offer to buy manufactured articles from B at a certain price. B agreed to sell these at that price and delivered to A the key of the box in which the articles were placed. A now wants to withdraw his offer; may he still do so?

A. Accepting a key is not a formal act of possession, and A may, therefore, withdraw his offer. But, if after accepting the key of the box, A put the articles in the box and locked it, the sale is valid.

SOURCES: Pr. 835.

645

Q. A ate at B's table for a period of two weeks and then entered into an agreement with him to board with him for the price of three *marks* per year. To bind the agreement A and B ate three pennies' worth together, as is the usual form of concluding agreements, which form is called *einkauf*. Subsequently A changed his mind and sought to invalidate the agreement. Some persons wanted to prove that *einkauf* was a valid form of concluding a contract from the talmudic law (B. M. 74a) under which the putting of a seal on wine barrels is a valid form of concluding a sale in those cities where it is customary so to conclude a sale of wine.

A. Eating together as a form of concluding a bargain is a custom current among Gentiles but not among Jews. The agreement, therefore, was not valid and A may retract his offer.

SOURCES: Pr. 730.

646

Q. A bought silver from B. Having no money to pay for it, he gave B a quantity of gold on condition that should he fail to pay B within three days, B would have the right to raise money against such gold by using it as security on an interest-bearing loan, or by having the money-changers exchange it for money, or by resorting to any other possible manner of raising money. B, however, pledged the gold with C on condition that it become forfeited after two weeks shall have elapsed, should A fail to redeem it within that time. A did not redeem his gold within the stipulated time. Now A demands that B return his gold since he never intended to allow B to pledge his gold on such unusual, and extremely unfavorable, conditions. By the phrase "any other possible manner" he meant to permit the employment of customary methods of raising money against security, and no more. Moreover, B did not necessarily have to raise a loan. He could have taken off a piece of the gold commensurate in value with the money due him, and returned the remainder to A; since gold bullion lends itself to such treatment without the necessity of appraisal [by a court]. B, on the other hand, claims that knowing what a dilatory debtor A was, he refused to do business with him until A gave him the gold and specified that it could be used to raise money "in any possible manner", the last phrase to be taken literally. He further claims that he could not raise the money in any other way than on the terms made with C, and that he informed A about this transaction with C, and that A agreed to it. A, however, denies B's assertions and claims that he was informed of the transaction with C after he had mounted his horse and had been ready to ride on his way, and that he did not realize at the time the meaning of B's words.

A. Even assuming the truth of B's version of his agreement with A, such agreement is considered an *asmakhta* and is not valid unless accompanied by a *kinyan* and made before an authoritative court. Therefore, B must pay to A the difference between the value of A's gold and the amount due B. Moreover, B's agreement with C regarding the forfeiture of the pledge is also considered an *askmakhta* and is invalid.

SOURCES: Cr. 170; L. 331.

647

Q. B discovered that the horse he bought from A is injured. He claims that the horse must have been injured while in A's possession, that the purchase was a mistake and demands, therefore, that the contract be rescinded. A, on the other hand, claims that the horse was in perfect condition when he delivered it to B.

A. Even if B had not, as yet, paid for the horse, the burden is upon him to prove that the horse was injured while in A's possession. If he cannot produce such proof, A is to swear that when he sold the horse to B he did not know that the horse was injured. If he takes such an oath he is entitled to collect his money from B.

SOURCES: Pr. 575; L. 122; Mord. Ket. 200; Tesh. Maim. to *Kinyan*, 7; *Mordecai Hagadol*, p. 165d; cf. Sinai vol. VI (1942) p. 221.

648

Q. A claims that B sold him an article, which he (A) thought was made of gold and later discovered was made of silver. A, therefore, demands his money back. B, however, claims that originally A bid against him in buying that article from the Gentile, and that he (B) did not know the article was made of silver, when he sold it to A.

A. Whether or not B intended to deceive A is not important. The fact remains that B sold A a silver article for a golden one. The sale, therefore, was made in error, and A is entitled to his money.

SOURCES: Cr. 70; Pr. 32; Mord. B. B. 563; cf. Pr. 1010; Cr. 258; Mord. B. M. 291.

649

Q. A claims that he bought a vessel from B, that B told him it was made of gold, and that when he broke it he found it made partly of lead. B claims that he did not guarantee the vessel to be of gold, and that he sold it as it was when he bought it himself. He is ready to return A's money if the latter will swear that he, B, guaranteed the vessel to be of gold, or if A will return to him the vessel in the condition he received it. However, A cannot return the vessel in the same condition, since he had broken it.

A. If it is certain that the vessel B sold A was partly made of lead, the sale is void, since A intended to buy a gold vessel and not a lead one. A cannot be held responsible for breaking the vessel and thus diminishing its value, since he was not supposed to know that it contained lead. If, however, B refuses to believe A that the vessel was made partly of lead, he may take an oath that he did not know of what metal the vessel was made and be free from any obligation to A.

SOURCES: Cr. 258; Pr. 110; Mord. B. M. 291; cf. Cr. 70; Pr. 32; *Agudah* B. M. 76.

650

Q. A Gentile wanted to buy a certain silver vessel from A. A, who had no such vessel to sell, wanted to take the Gentile to another Jewish dealer, but the Gentile commissioned A to buy the vessel for him. A went to B who was willing to sell a vessel weighing three pounds. A said to B: "The Gentile is my friend and I do not want to deceive him; if the vessel is truly made of silver, I shall buy it, otherwise, I shall not." B assured A that the vessel was made of silver, and added that since the silver was alloyed with a little copper, he was willing to accept forty-seven shillings for it. A took the vessel at night and sold it for fifty shillings to the Gentile who carried it away the same night. The Gentile, subsequently, complained that A deceived him, as the vessel was really made of copper. He, therefore, returned the vessel and forced A to refund him the money. A demanded that B take back the vessel, but B claimed that A saw what he was buying and accepted it for the stipulated price.

A. Since B sold A a silver vessel and gave him a copper one, the sale is void and B must refund the money to A.

SOURCES: Pr. 842; *Mordecai Hagadol*, p. 275c.

651

Q. A traded his horse with B for wine, and B received the horse. Before B shipped the wine to A, a Gentile claimed that the horse had been stolen from him, and took it away from B. Now B refuses to ship the wine to A, claiming the transaction was made in error.

A. As soon as B received the horse, the wine became A's property, and B cannot retain it. If A claims that his horse was not a stolen horse and that the Gentile took it away unjustly, or that he (A) had no knowledge that it was a stolen horse, he is not responsible (since we cannot rely on the Gentiles' word). If, however, B can prove that at the time of the transaction A knew that it was a stolen horse and that the Gentile had a right to take it, B may keep his wine.

SOURCES: Cr. 186; Pr. 35; Tesh. Maim. to *Kinyan,* 6; Mord. B. M. 298.

652

Q. A was robbed of his books during a riot. The books were later recognized in B's possession. Must B return the books to A upon receiving the amount he paid to the robbers?

A. Since the books were taken by Gentile robbers, A did not lose hope of retrieving them (B. K. 114a) and thus legally retained title to his books. Therefore, B must return the books to A. B is not entitled to any compensation, since it was common knowledge that A was robbed of his books, and since B bought them from known robbers.

This Responsum is addressed to "my teacher Rabbi Eliakim."

SOURCES: Pr. 1009; Cr. 196–7; Mord. B. K. 163.

653

Q. A's house was robbed and he reported this in town. Subsequently, he recognized one of his books in B's possession B had bought the book from C who had bought it from a Gentile. Moreover, A does not usually sell his books. B, therefore, stated under oath the price he paid for the book; but A constantly deferred payment of that amount.

A. A owes that amount to B. Since the court has a right to distrain a debtor's article for the benefit of the creditor, the court may surely confirm B in the possession of the book after the latter pays to A the difference between its actual value and the price he had originally paid. If B paid C for the book more than the latter paid to the Gentile, C must return the difference to A.

SOURCES: Am II. 138.

654

Q. A book was stolen from A and sold to B for one *mark*. It was subsequently stolen from B and sold to C for the same price. Both A and B recognized the book in C's possession.

A. If at the time of the theft from A, the fact was reported in the town, and if A does not usually sell his books, then A is to pay one *mark* to C and reclaim his book. B may look for the man who sold him the book and sue him; if he cannot find him, his money is lost.

SOURCES: Pr 88.

655 (D)

Q. Gentiles robbed some merchants (also Gentiles) of wool which they had brought from Cologne. The robbers sold the wool to A and B. At B's request, A secretly transported the wool to Mayence on a boat and sold it to C. The latter paid A part of the price, and specified a date for the payment of the balance. The robbed merchants, discovering the whereabouts of their wool, came to Mayence and sued C. C, however, bribed the city and court officials and thus evaded prosecution by the merchants. When A came to collect from C the balance due him, the latter deducted, from that balance, the amount he was forced to pay in bribes, despite A's claim that he, A, had given no warrant that no claims would be made by the original owners. B, on the other hand, charged A with the blame for C's act and demanded his share of the full price.

A. A and B must make good the losses C suffered, since, in this case, the Gentile merchants had a just claim on the merchandise. C must, therefore, prove by oath or witnesses the amount he was forced to expend in the form of bribes, and deduct this from the balance due A and B. The latter two were to share these expenses equally.

SOURCES: Pr. 828.

656 (D)

Q. A negotiated to buy from a Gentile a house which bordered on B's property. After A agreed with the Gentile on the terms of the sale, he withdrew his offer so that the Gentile should lower his price. He warned B not to negotiate with the Gentile since he, A, was still negotiating with him. B, however, disregarded A's warning and bought the house from the Gentile. In defense B claims that he had sought to purchase the house from the Gentile before A began his negotiations. Should B be punished for his act as violating the talmudic injunction against "a poor man turning a cake, and another coming and taking it (Kidd. 59a)?" How long should one refrain from offering to purchase an article which another Jew is seeking to buy?

A. R. Jacob Tam applies the aforesaid talmudic injunction only to mercantile pursuits but not to cases where a person is about to pick up a lost or ownerless object and another snatches it away. For finding a lost object is a rare opportunity and the second person is just as much entitled to the ownerless object as the first person. Buying abutting property from a Gentile is also a rare opportunity and is in the same category as picking up lost objects. Therefore, B is free from any obligation to A. A Jew should not approach a seller where another Jew had already agreed with the seller for the sale of the article, and where the writing of the contract and the scrutiny and transfer of the deed in the Gentile courts are the only things lacking in order to complete the sale. But, the mere offer of a Jew to buy something without the seller's acceptance of the offer, does not restrain another Jew from buying it. If such were the case, it would be very unfair to the seller who would be forced to sell his possessions to the very first bidder, no matter how low the offer, since no other purchasers would dare to buy it. The Torah was very careful, however, not to jeopardize the rights and opportunities of the sellers.

The author claims that the same question was sent to him from Neustadt.

Sources: Cr. 276-7; Pr. 1011; Berl. p. 284 no. 334; B. p. 292, no. 366.

657

Q. Whence did Maimonides derive the law that one should not sell to a Gentile a *talith* unless its *Zizith* are cut off, lest the Gentile gain the confidence of a Jew thereby, and kill him while traveling with him?

A. This law is clearly stated in the Talmud, (Menachot 43a).

This Responsum is addressed to R. Asher.

Sources: Pr. 543.

658 (D)

Q. A promised to help B with a sum of money should B move out of T; or, A promised the money to B should he buy a certain article. After B moved out of T, or bought the article, A changed his mind.

A. If the article is worth the money B paid for it, A is free from obligation; otherwise A must compensate B for his loss. Similarly, in the former case, if B had intended to leave T in any event, A may now claim that he was joking when he made his promise.

SOURCES: Cr. 203; Sinai VII (1943), 5–6, 51.

659

Q. A gave a writ of bestowal of movable property to B, in which the clause "the movable property is thus transferred to B together with, and by dint of, real property", was missing. Is the gift binding?

A. I have examined the writ of bestowal and could find nothing wrong with it, for title to movable property can also be transferred by *halifin* (symbol of exchange).

SOURCES: Cr. 256; Pr. 344.

660

Q. C gave his house to his son B as an outright gift. In the deed of transfer C wrote that the gift was to be irrevocable, but stipulated the following conditions: a) During his lifetime he, C, reserves the power to dispose of his property in whatever manner he deems proper, to rent, exchange, and even sell it; b) the income from that house (for the aforementioned period) shall go to him; c) in case he loses all his other possessions, he shall have the right to sell this house. In conclusion, however, he added: d) that should he desire to grant dowries to his other daughters, similar to the one he has given to his first son-in-law, he would have no right to dispose of any part of the aforementioned house for that purpose. After C's death, his other son, A, demanded that B give him his share of his father's estate. In answer to B's assertions that the house

belonged to him exclusively, A stated that C had voided the
aforementioned deed of transfer and subsequently wrote another deed whereby he transferred the house to A and to A's
sisters, and that C had the right to do so since he had reserved
in the first deed during his lifetime the power to dispose of his
property in whatever manner he deem proper (stipulation a).

A. The house belongs to B since his father had given it
to him as an outright and irrevocable gift. Although some of
the added stipulations of the deed, seem to contradict and to
cancel the original provision of the deed that the gift be irrevocable, still whenever possible a deed must be interpreted in a
manner that will reconcile and explain away all apparent con-
tradictions. Thus, stipulation a of the above gift must be
interpreted to refer to the remainder of C's property, but not
to the house itself. A person does not write a deed and cancel
its purpose at the same time. Furthermore, after C had formally
given the house to B in the presence of witnesses, he no longer
could refer to it as "my property". Moreover, the final clause
of the aforementioned deed, stipulation d, proves that the father
did not revoke the gift. Consequently, C had no right subsequently to give the house to A and to his sisters.

Sources: Tesh. Maim. to *Mishpatim,* 69.

661

Q. A and L drew up a deed of gift whereby they conveyed
to their son B one-eighth of their house, the boundary lines of
which they clearly described in the deed. Subsequently it
became known that A and L themselves owned but one quarter
of the house. A claims that he has conveyed to B one-eighth
of such quarter, while B's heirs lay claim to one-eighth of
the house.

A. Instructions given to, and admissions made before,
witnesses, are interpreted in accordance with their meaning

in common parlance. Since a quarter of a house is not usually referred to as "a house", the deed of conveyance establishes the rights of B's heirs to one-eighth of the whole house.

Sources: Mord. B. B. 570.

662

Q. One of B's sons, A, is poor. B desires to give him an appropriate portion of his property on condition that A does not collect any portion of B's estate after his death. It is legally impossible, however, to sell one's right of inheritance.

A. If B should now divide the rest of his property among his other sons on condition that these gifts become effective after his death, these bequests would be considered *causa mortis* gifts and would be valid. B would thus have accomplished his purpose.

Sources: Mord. B. B. 591; *Agudah* B. B. 177; Moses Minz, *Responsa* 66.

663

Q. A had two sons and one daughter. He gave his daughter in marriage to B and promised him by a written document that after his (A's) death, B would receive a share of A's estate equal to that of an heir. After A's wife died, A remarried and had two sons by his second wife. After her death, he gave presents to her young sons and expressly stated that these were to be in addition to their share in his estate after he should die. Subsequently, A lost his mind and three years later, he died. B demanded one-third of A's estate since at the time the promise of the gift was made to him, A had only two heirs. The grandfather of the younger orphans, acting as their representative, claimed that only one-sixth of the estate was due B, since two parts were to go to A's first-born son. Moreover, the representative demanded the *ketubah* of A's second wife, for her children, as *ketubat benin dikrin*. Subsequently, B admitted in the presence of many witnesses, that he knew the place where A hid his valuables. In order that he disclose the place of the hidden valuables, the representative of the orphans entered into an agreement with B, which agreement was strengthened by a *herem*, whereby B was to receive one-fifth of A's estate. Now B refuses to live up to the agreement and demands one-third of the estate.

A. B is entitled to one-sixth of that property which he can prove A possessed at the time of making the promise of the gift to B. The agreement with B should, therefore, not bind the orphans since it was entered into to their disadvantage. Moreover, the sons are entitled to collect their mother's *ketubah* as *ketubat benin dikrin*, before the estate is divided among the heirs. Although many of the *Geonim* wrote that the *ketubat benin dikrin* is not collectible nowadays (the reason being that such an ordinance was originally instituted in order that fathers willingly give their daughters dowries equal to whatever they give to their sons, but nowadays fathers give more to their daughters than to their sons) R. Hai Gaon and the Tosaphists were of the opinion that it is collectible; and we follow the latter opinion. However, since the representative of the orphans entered into the agreement in order to recover A's hidden valuables, the agreement with B is valid. B will find it to his advantage to abide by the agreement and not break a *herem*, for he is really entitled to much less than what he is getting under the agreement. B, however, will have to state under oath the amount of A's valuables he has in his possession.

SOURCES: Pr. 1004: Mord. B. B. 599. Cf. *Agudah* B. B. 181.

664

Q. A, the oldest brother in the family, who is in possession of his father's land, claims to have received it as a gift from him. He says that he was in undisturbed possession of it for

many years before his father's death and for many years thereafter. Now his brothers want a share of the land. The local
court decided in A's favor.

A. Since his brothers were young when their father died,
A cannot claim undisturbed possession as proof of ownership
for the period since his father's death, and must furnish documentary proof or witnesses to the effect that he enjoyed undisturbed possession for three years before his father's death.

SOURCES: Pr. 119; cf. Asheri, *Sanhedrin* 3, 37.

665

Q. A and his wife drew up a document for the benefit of
her son (A's stepson), in which was written: "Give to our son. . ."
Does the expression "our son" invalidate the document since
the beneficiary is not A's son?

A. A person who brings up an orphan in his house is in
the same position as the orphan's father. Therefore, the phrase
"our son" is quite appropriate. Moreover, the phrase in the
document "to our mother so and so the daughter of so and
so". . . referring to A's mother-in-law, does not invalidate that
part of the document as long as the name of the mother-in-law
is given. For the term "son" or "mother" is an affectionate
expression correctly used in this sense even when such relationship does not exist.

SOURCES: L. 242; Tesh. Maim. to *Mishpatim* 48. Cf. Maharil, *Responsa* 81.

666

Q. In the presence of witnesses A conveyed movables
and immovables to his sons and daughters, as presents, giving
one-eighth of such property to each. Subsequently, however,
it was discovered that the witnesses were related to one of the

recipients. May the recipients who are not related to the witnesses, each collect his share on the strength of the testimony of these witnesses?

A. The judges of Worms also inquired of me regarding this matter. Those who have preceded us debated this problem at length. Rabiah, in an actual case, ruled that the witnesses were completely disqualified. He based his decision on the ruling of R. Yohanan, Yer. Makkot ch. 1, hal. 7.

This Responsum is addressed to "my teacher Rabbi Asher".

SOURCES: Am II, 246. Cf. Asher, *Responsa* 3, 13.

667 (D)

Q. Before his death, A disposed of his property to his children in the presence of two witnesses, one of whom was A's cousin, B. Is B's testimony to be accepted in the disposal of A's property?

A. Although B is in the category of a near-kin to A, he is not a near-kin to his sons; therefore, his testimony in regard to A's sons is admissible.

SOURCES: Pr. 834.

668

Q. Before his death, A ordered that twenty *marks* be given to his daughters out of his estate. Only the mother and one of the heirs, B, however, were present when A gave this order.

A. The testimony of the mother and B is invalid since they are related to the interested parties. B, because of his admission, however, may be forced to pay his proportionate share of the twenty *marks* out of his inheritance.

SOURCES: Cr. 122.

669 (D)

Q. Without the knowledge of his wife, A, a dying person, distributed his possessions, giving some to his son, some to his sister, and others to charity. When his wife learned about it, she protested against the gifts to the sister and to charity. Does her protest invalidate these gifts?

A. A woman's *ketubah* is a lien upon her husband's property. Since even the husband's consecration of his possessions is ineffective, as it does not remove the wife's lien upon them, his giving them away to charity is surely ineffective. Therefore, if A's wife will take an oath to the effect that A's possessions were not in excess of her *ketubah*, she will be entitled to retain them.

SOURCES: L. 232. Cf. Isserlein *Pesakim* 86.

670

1. *Q.* We are sorry to trouble you about a case that has already been decided upon by the authoritative court of Rabbi Aaron. But the litigants are stubborn and troublesome, and we are forced to solicit your opinion. Two witnesses testify that, before his death, A's father instructed his wife to give thirty pounds to each one of his sons. She did not protest although he left her only a small piece of ground. A demands his thirty pounds. He also claims that, upon his marriage, his mother promised his wife, by solemn hand-clasp, to help him financially as long as she has a penny left, and that his mother took ten pounds from him. A's mother, on the other hand, denies that her husband told her to give money to her sons; she further denies having taken the ten pounds from A, or having promised anything to A's wife. Moreover, she claims to have spent more than thirty pounds on A, since she reared him, and since she educated him up to the age of thirty. She, therefore,

demands her *ketubah* from the remainder of the money A's father left. Finally, the mother claims that she was sued by all the heirs in the court of R. Aaron, that the court decided in her favor, and that she still has the written decision.

A. No court is allowed to review the decisions of another court; therefore, the decision of R. Aaron must prevail. But, since A claims that at the time of the first trial the heirs had no reliable witnesses to support their claims, and that now he has found two reliable witnesses who support his claim, the testimony of these witnesses must be taken into consideration, and A's mother must take an oath that she spent at least thirty pounds on A's education and upbringing. The court cannot impose an oath on A's mother regarding the promise, accompanied by a solemn hand-clasp, that she is alleged to have made to A's wife, since the mother denies having made such a promise.

2. *Q.* A threatens to lodge a complaint before the Duke in case his mother is successful in the suit.

A. A ban should be placed on A for even expressing such a threat; and if A dares to appeal to a Gentile court, [he shall be excommunicated, and] you shall surely excommunicate him together with his helpers, advisors, and supporters.

SOURCES: Pr. 245, 246, 247; cf. *Agudah* B. M. 27; ibid. B. B. 168; Hag. Maim. *Shebuot* 11, 3; Isserlein, *Pesakim* 86.

671 (D)

Q. A gave his daughters *causa mortis* gifts, each gift consisted of three *marks*. Subsequently, L, one of his daughters, and her husband said to A that he still owed them three *marks* worth of gold which he had promised them before their wedding. A answered incoherently, for he was losing consciousness, that he thus intended to repay them, but died before finishing his words.

A. A's last words are of no consequence since he was not in his right mind while uttering them. Therefore, if A's daughters admit that A had promised L three *marks* as part of her dowry and had not paid it to her, L is entitled to collect three *marks* in addition to the *causa mortis* gift, for while A, on his death-bed, gave presents to his other daughters, he probably intended to make no exception in his dealing with L. But, if the other daughters disclaim any knowledge of A's debt, they must take an heir's oath. Although I have often contended that an heir's oath is imposed on a claimant only, but not a defendant, the custom is widely accepted to impose such an oath even on a defendant.

SOURCES: Cr. 97.

672

Q. A left his possessions to his sons on condition that they give a certain amount to his four daughters, and if they have no cash that they should pay the daughters with real property. One of the daughters died before A.

A. A's sons must pay their three sisters three quarters of the designated sum, and may keep the other quarter for themselves, even if the deceased daughter left heirs. The death of one daughter does not annul the gift to the other three.

SOURCES: Cr. 189; Pr. 136; L. 387; Mord. Git. 431.

673

Q. A demands from B the money his mother deposited with B, to be given to A after her death. B claims that A's mother gave him the money on condition that he return it to her, in case she needs it herself, or else give it to A after her death.

A. According to B's statement, A never gained title to the money since it was not given to him as a gift *causa mortis,* and he did not perform the formal act of possession necessary in order to gain title to an ordinary gift. His brothers, therefore inherited their share of the money. However, if A claims that he was present when his mother deposited the money with B, and that this money was thus deposited specifically for his benefit, as a gift *causa mortis,* B must swear that the facts are as he claims them to be.

This Responsum is addressed to R. Menahem ha-Levi.

SOURCES: Cr. 38; Pr. 420–421; Mord. B. B. 592; *Mordecai Hagadol,* p. 321c.

674 (D)

Q. A's wife pursued a handicraft in his house without his interference. She thus acquired some gold, rings, and ornaments which she gave, before her death, to their married daughters. After her death A learned about the gift and demanded that his daughters return whatever they received from their mother.

A. A woman is not permitted to make any gifts without her husband's consent. A's demand is justified, and the daughters must return everything they received from their mother to A.

SOURCES: Pr. 856.

675

Case. When A died he left to his widow, Leah, and to his young daughter, an estate of two pounds plus a few articles of clothing. Before Leah remarried, she entrusted the two pounds to her cousin, Rabbi Yẹdidyah, who was also A's brother, as a trust fund for her daughter. Her second marriage, to the son of R. Isaac of Coburg, was an unhappy one as she had to wander from town to town with her children on her shoulder to procure her daily sustenance, not receiving any support from her husband. She succeeded, however, in saving the sum of twenty-two schillings which she deposited with her mother in payment of a silken garment, valued at three pounds, which she bought for her daughter. When her husband learned about it, he went to Leah's mother and tricked her into giving him the garment. Leah then demanded her daughter's garment from her husband. The latter, however, claimed that, since whatever a wife possesses belongs to her husband, the silken garment belonged to him. He further demanded that Leah return to him all the garments and objects she had given to her daughter.

Rabbi Moses was the judge in the case and decided that Leah must take an oath that she did not give to her daughter directly or indirectly any money belonging to R. Isaac's son. Rabbi Yedidyah then wrote to R. Meir, and, enclosing a copy of R. Moses' decision, argued against it since he thought that R. Moses imposed an oath on Leah even though her husband was not positive she took his money and maintained only a possibility of it. R. Meir wrote his opinion that we can impose an oath on a wife only when the husband is positive that she misused his money, (which was in seeming contradiction to that of R. Moses). He sent this opinion to R. Yedidyah and adjured him to show it only to R. Moses who, R. Meir hoped, would retract his decision. R. Moses, however, felt humiliated, protested that Leah's husband was positive in his claim, and produced a statement from the local *Beth-din* which read: "Our teacher, Rabbi Meir: We let you know that the husband was positive in his claim and enumerated all the things he demanded of his wife. Since he was positive in his claim, and did not merely suggest a possibility of it, we have imposed an oath on the wife as advised by our teacher, Rabbi Moses." R. Moses further stated that R. Yedidyah made public R.

Meir's letter and caused him great shame and humiliation.
R. Meir, then, withdrew from the case, saying that he did
not want to be a party to the personal quarrel between R.
Yedidyah and R. Moses unless he could effect a reconciliation
between the two.

SOURCES: Pr. 982; *Mordecai Hagadol*, p. 172d.

676

Your statement is correct. The act of a married woman who
disposed of her clothes on her death-bed, is invalid. The
clothes must be returned to the husband. For a husband buys
raiment for his wife only for the purpose of her wearing them,
not for the purpose of her giving them away. Although the
husband was present at the time the gifts were made, and did
not protest, his silence did not indicate consent. It rather
showed a knowledge that his wife's act was invalid, and required no protest.

This Responsum is addressed to: "My teacher Rabbi Asher."

SOURCES: Am II, 34.

677

Q. Before her death, Leah, in the presence of witnesses,
said: "All my possessions shall go to B and C except what I
have already given' to charity." After her death, B and C
found some of her possessions in A's hands. They demanded
these possessions from A who, in turn, claimed that Leah gave
them to him as a gift *mortis causa* before she gave anything to
B and C.

A. If, while making the gift to A, Leah indicated that
she was making such a gift in fear of approaching death, then
her final words, giving everything to B and C, prevail, since
she probably changed her mind regarding her gift to A. A,

then, must return the property to B and C. But, if Leah made no mention of death when she gave some of her possessions to A, then such a gift is in the category of a "sick man's gift of part of his property" (Baba Batra 151b) which requires a *kinyan* (formal act of possession). Since in this case, there was a *kinyan* (the property was in A's possession at the time of the gift), the property belongs to A.

SOURCES: Cr. 206; Pr. 34; L. 344; Tesh. Maim to *Kinyan*, 12. Cf. *Tur Hoshen Mishpat* 250; ibid. *Beth Joseph* ad. l.

678

Q. While critically ill, Mrs. Maimona said to the representative of the community that after her death the following matters should be attended to at her expense: 1) That the oil-lamp which burns during the services in the memory of her departed daughter, should be made to burn continuously day and night; 2) that every Friday evening a half-pound waxen candle should be lit in the synagogue in her memory; and 3) that half a *mark* should be expended on a *kiddush*-cup for the synagogue. When the representative asked her as to the source of the money for these expenditures, she answered pointing at an adjoining room: "You will find sufficient valuables and money in that room." The following day, a Friday, she called her brother Zemah and told him, in the presence of witnesses, to take for himself and for his sisters everything he finds in the room mentioned above. On the following Sunday, the representatives of the community came and asked her the whereabouts of the money she promised for the synagogue, but she refused to reveal anything. The representatives, therefore, broke into the room and took everything they found there. They also pronounced the *herem* against anyone who would not return to the community valuables or money belonging to Mrs. M. which might be in his possession. R. Isaac ha-

Kohen admitted that Mrs. M. had deposited eight Cologne-
marks with him and had told him that after her death he
should do with the money "the proper thing."

A. Mrs. M. probably withdrew her promise to donate
something to the synagogue. A gift made *causa mortis* even to
a holy cause can be rescinded. The money and valuables found
in her room, therefore, belong half to R. Zemah and half to his
sisters. R. Isaac must return the eight *marks* to Mrs. M's
heirs, for the proper thing to do with money of a deceased
person, is to return it to the heirs.

This Resp. is addressed to R. Jacob and the community of
Linpurk.

SOURCES: Pr. 998: Mord. B. B. 624; *Mordecai Hagadol*, p. 326d; *Agudah* B. B.
202. Cf. Maharil, *Responsa* 75; Isserlein, *Pesakim* 73.

679

Q. Before her death L(eah) distributed her property in
the presence of witnesses and added that the residue should
go to her relative A, an orphan. R(achel), another relative of
L, took care of L during her sickness, and received from her the
keys to everything in the house. After L's death it was learned
that R appropriated some of L's money and articles. A summoned R to court where she claimed to have received said
valuables from L as a present. Must she return the valuables
to A?

A. If the valuables can be identified as having definitely
belonged to L, and if witnesses saw such valuables in R's possession, R must prove that L gave them to her as an outright
gift (not *causa mortis*) before she will be entitled to retain them.
But, if the articles can not be so identified, or, if no one saw
them in R's possession, R must take an oath that she received them as an outright gift. We would have to accept such

an oath because of the principle of *Miggo*, since, in the absence of witnesses, R could have denied the charge altogether. However, if witnesses testify, or R herself admits, that the gift was made to her *causa mortis* — R must return the valuables to A, since L's final statement before the witnesses voided all previous *causa mortis* gifts.

SOURCES: Cr. 180; L. 249; Mord. B. B. 628; *Agudah* B. B. 207.

680

Q. Witnesses testified that, before her death, B's wife asked B to give some of her clothes to her nephew A, and that B consented thereto. B, however, now refuses to give the clothes to A.

A. If A is not a poor man, i. e. if he possesses more than two hundred *zuzim*, B may withdraw his promise of gift (cf. B. M. 49a). If A is a poor man, however, B must keep his promise; for a promise to give charity is equivalent to a vow.

SOURCES: Mord. B. M. 312. Cf. Cr. 73; Pr. 726.

681

Q. Must a remission, when the remittor is in possession of the remitee's pledge, be accompanied by a *kinyan* in order to be valid?

A. Remission is valid even when not accompanied by a *kinyan*. Although a creditor acquires a pledge deposited with him to the extent that his responsibility therefor is that of a paid bailee, the pledge itself does not belong to him. Therefore, as soon as the creditor remits the debtor's obligation, the pledge reverts to the latter and becomes his exclusive property wherever it be.

SOURCES: Cr. 220; Am II, 232; Mord. Sanh. 681.

682

Q. A fire, a veritable conflagration, broke out in town and people fled in fear thereof. A, however, braved the fire and saved a book the owners of which had already fled.

A. A is under no obligation to return the book to its owners, for as soon as the latter gave up hope of saving the book, it became abandoned property.

SOURCES: Cr. 251; Mord. B. K. 171; *Mordecai Hagadol* p. 392d; Hag. Maim., *Gezelah* 12, 6; *Agudah* B. K. 140.

683 (D)

Q. Is a leper considered a dead person in the sense that he has no right of inheritance? The trustees of the estate say that he is not.

A. The trustees are right. A leper has the same rights as any other heir. It is indeed silly to ask such a question.

SOURCES: Cr. 115.

684

Q. A promised B's daughter a sum of money as a wedding gift. She died before the betrothal. B, her rightful heir, demands from A the promised gift.

A. A promise of a wedding gift becomes binding only if the wedding takes place. B, therefore, could not inherit that which his daughter never possessed.

SOURCES: Pr. 84.

685

Q. A was survived by his wife, a married daughter, and a single daughter. Subsequently the married daughter died and then her death was followed by that of her mother. The latter had not taken the required oath regarding her *ketubah*. The unmarried daughter took possession of A's entire estate; but,

A's son-in-law demanded half of the estate on the grounds that his wife had been entitled to it, and that he was her rightful heir.

A. As long as A's widow did not take an oath regarding her *ketubah*, A's entire estate belonged to his two daughters. A's son-in-law, being his wife's rightful heir, is, therefore, entitled to half of A's estate.

This Responsum was addressed to Rabbi Menahem.

SOURCES: L. 226; Mord. Sheb. 780. Cf. Israel Bruno, *Responsa* 21.

686 (D)

Q. During a riot and massacre A and his wife, L, were killed and their daughter apostatized. A's brother and L's brother have survived them. Who is the rightful heir to A's property?

A. An apostate forfeits his rights as an heir, although he has the power to transmit his property to his Jewish heirs. Since it is not known whether A's daughter apostatized after her parents were killed, and thus inherited the property from either parent and upon apostatizing transferred it to A's brother, or that she apostatized before they were killed, her survival does not change the status of the estate. Therefore, the estate should be divided in the following manner: The amount recorded in L's *ketubah* as dowry, shall be divided equally between her brother and A's brother; L's private property, if any, shall go to her brother, while the remaining property shall go to A's brother. However, if A's daughter is still a minor, the estate should not be divided until she reaches majority. Then, if she still persists in her apostasy for one hour, the estate must be divided between the brothers; for a minor does not forfeit her rights as an heir upon apostatizing, since the persuasion of a minor is tantamount to inexorable compulsion.

The author adds: For further details see the Responsum

appended therewith which I have sent long ago to Frankfort regarding a similar question.

SOURCES: Cr. 82.

687

Q. A, his four daughters, and his wife, were killed when the house they occupied collapsed. A's heirs claim that perhaps the wife died first and that therefore they now were the only heirs to A's estate. The wife's brothers, on the other hand, claim that perhaps the wife died last and that therefore they were entitled to her *ketubah*. Some Rabbis are of the opinion that the wife's heirs were entitled to one-twelfth of the estate; while other Rabbis, computing probabilities, believe that they were entitled to one thirty-second of the estate.

A. It is my humble opinion that the wife's heirs are entitled to one-half of the estate, because of the talmudic principle *Kol Kavua kemahaze al mahaze domi*, meaning: whenever an event is about to befall (or has befallen) one of a number of fixed persons or objects, each person or object has a fifty-fifty chance that the incident will befall (or has befallen) him or it. Therefore, legally, there is a fifty-fifty chance for each one of the six persons involved that he or she died last. Had the daughters been married and had their husbands appeared to demand their share, the estate would have had to be divided into six parts. But, since only two persons demand their share, the estate should be divided between the two. Although a woman has to take an oath before she is entitled to collect her *ketubah*, no such oath is required in this case since A died suddenly and we have no reason to suspect that before his death he had deposited with her valuables to be used in payment of her *ketubah*.

SOURCES: Cr. 172; L. 378; Mord. B. B. 638; Tesh. Maim. to *Mishpatim*, 5; *Agudah* B. B. 213; Asher, *Responsa* 84, 3. Cf. ibid. 85, 1; ibid. 86, 1; Maharil, *Responsa* 63; ibid. 169; Moses Minz, *Responsa* 96; *Terumat Hadeshen* 330.

688

Q. Before marrying his second wife, A stipulated, in the presence of witnesses, the following condition in his agreement with the sons of his first wife: The sons that will be born from the contemplated marriage shall share equally with the sons of his first marriage in the inheritance of his estate. Subsequently A married and his second wife bore him a daughter. Before his death A sought witnesses to attest to his will that his daughter should inherit part of his estate, but he was overtaken by sudden death. Are we to assume that in the agreement referred to above A intended to give to a daughter the status of a son?

A. The term "sons" when used in vows does not include daughters. Moreover, a person who has sons has no right to give his daughter the status of an heir. Therefore, A's daughter is not entitled to the share of an heir in A's estate.

SOURCES: L. 236; Mord. B. B. 603; *Agudah* B. B. 190; cf. Sinai IV (1941) 10, no. 88.

689

Q. A father stated before his death that his son A should inherit no part of his house.

A. As soon as a person dies his estate falls automatically to his heirs, except whatever he has given away before his death. Therefore, the father's words are of no avail, and A receives his share of his father's estate.

SOURCES: Pr. 475.

690

Q. A married off his grown up son, B, giving him money and a book as a wedding gift, and shortly thereafter A died. His heirs refuse to give B an equal share of A's property, claiming that B's wedding-gift was part of his share of the inheritance.

A. B is entitled to share equally in the property left by his father, over and above his wedding-gift.

Sources: Pr. 848; *Tashbetz,* 502.

691 (D)

Q. A married off his sons and gave them marriage gifts. Subsequently A died. Are the unmarried sons entitled to receive marriage gifts from A's estate, and is only the remainder of the estate to be equally divided among the sons?

A. A's unmarried sons are not entitled to marriage gifts. The estate is to be divided equally among the sons.

Sources: L. 181.

692

Q. According to talmudic law, after the death of a person who had children by two wives, the sons of each wife first collect (from the father's estate) the *ketubah* of their mother; whatever is left of the estate is, then, divided among the heirs. Is this collection of a mother's *ketubah,* called *ketubat benin dichrin,* enforced nowadays?

A. Many *Geonim* are of the opinion that the *ketubat benin dichrin* is not collectible nowadays. But R. Hai Gaon is of the opinion that it is collectible; and I am inclined to decide, in accordance with the opinion of R. Hai, that it is collectible even from movable property, unless a custom exists in a particular community that it is not collectible.

This decision is based on R. Meir's Responsum as recorded in Pr. 248; Am. II, 64, 65; Tesh. Maim. to Nashim 26; and the opinion expressed in Mord. Ket. 162. But Cr. 116 records the following decision: Since a difference of opinion exists between the *Geonim,* the burden of proof [to prove according to which authority the law is to be decided] lies on the person who wants to collect money from the other person.

Tesh. Maim. *ibid.* continues: The *ketubat benin dichrin* is collectible nowadays from both real property and from personal property. As the ordinance of R. Tam, providing that a woman's dowry be returned to her heirs if the woman dies within the first year of marriage, is enforced; surely the ordinance of talmudic scholars, of a similar nature, should be enforced. According to the custom of the communities, the dowry is thus returned to the woman's heirs if she died within two years after her marriage. But R. Meir is of the opinion that the dowry should not be returned to her heirs, but to those who have given it originally. Similarly, R. Meir gave a dowry to his granddaughter Rachel. When she died in the second year of her marriage, R. Meir demanded that the dowry be returned to him although she had other heirs. In some communities only half of the dowry is returned when the woman dies in the second year of her marriage. The ordinance of the communities, which bears the signature of R. David of Merseburg, also has a similar provision.

SOURCES: Cr. 116; Pr. 248; Am. II, 64, 65; Tesh. Maim. to *Nashim*, 26; Mord. Ket. 162. Cf. Asheri Ket. 4, 24.

693

1) *Q.* May the sons of A's second wife plead that A's first wife, at A's request, has waived her children's right to her *ketubah*? Thus, while a person may not claim to have repaid a debt before it fell due because the presumption is that people generally do not repay a debt before it falls due, no such presumption exists in regard to waiving a right or an obligation.

A. The claim that an olbigation has been waived in one's favor is weak and is valid only when the legal presumption of *Miggo* exists; as in the case where the person could have successfully denied the very existence of the obligation, or could have claimed to have already discharged such obligation. Therefore, the claim in our case is invalid. Moreover, had A's first wife actually waived such obligation in the presence of witnesses, her act would have been invalid since she had no right directly to waive the monetary rights of her children, while retaining her own rights.

2) *Q.* Since the court does not attend to claims against young orphans except when interest is accumulating on their obligations, or when the widow's *ketubah* is demanded, in which latter case the court attends only because of *hinnah* (in order to enhance happy marriages); and since in our case (where A's sons by his first wife demand the *ketubat benin dichrin*) the element of *hinnah* is absent, must these sons wait (with the collection of their mother's *ketubah*) until A's youngest sons grow up?

A. A's sons by his first wife do not have to collect the *ketubah* of their mother; for it fell to them as an inheritance and is theirs already. All of A's sons are partners in the estate, which must be divided among them to give each of them his due share. Therefore, if A left money, the sons of his first wife may take their share of the money without the supervision of a court since the dividing of money between heirs needs no such supervision. But, if A's estate consists of real property, the sons of his first wife will have to wait until A's youngest sons grow up, as R. Tam is of the opinion that a court should not attend to the division of such an estate unless the young orphans agree to the division.

SOURCES: Am II, 65.

694

Q. A, a levir, married the widow of his brother B and had children with her. B had died while his father was still alive, but subsequently the father also died. Before his death, however, the latter divided his property equally among his sons. While A was away his remaining three brothers divided the father's landed property into four equal parts, one for each brother. When A returned he did not object to the division; and after his death, when the brothers sold their parts, his widow and orphans did not protest against the sale for over three years. Now, however, the latter claim that the division was unjust and the sale, therefore, invalid since A was entitled to a double portion of the estate, his own and that of his brother B.

A. Both, the division of the property by the brothers, and its subsequent sale, would be void, according to Rashi, since A was entitled to a double portion out of his father's estate. The fact that both transactions were not protested for over three years, is of no consequence since the brothers, or their successors, do not claim that A officially forewent or sold his rights. Moreover, A died before the three years of undisturbed possession were over, and one cannot claim undisturbed possession as evidence of title to property belonging to young orphans even after they grow up. However, since A's father divided his property among his sons, A is not entitled to any more than what his father gave him; for he received his portion as a gift and not as an inheritance.

This Responsum is addressed to R. Eliezer haLevi.

SOURCES: L. 384; Tesh. Maim. to *Mishpatim*, 51.

695

Q. A died leaving an estate that consisted of loans and investments in the hands of Gentiles. His first-born demands a double portion of the debts.

A. A first-born is entitled to a single portion only out of the part of the estate that consists of loans in the hands of others, especially when the debtors are Gentiles, even if such loans are already repaid at the time the estate is divided among the heirs. If the loans, however, were secured by pledges, the first-born would be entitled to a double portion therefrom.

SOURCES: Cr. 67.

696

Q. An heir (not first-born) sold his share of his father's estate before the partition of the estate had taken place. Is such sale valid? Thus R. Samuel b. Meir, in his commentary to B. B. 126b, implies that such sale is invalid.

A. The opinion of the Tosaphot is accepted that a sale by an heir has greater validity than that by a first-born. Since the Talmud rules that the sale by a first-born is valid, the sale by an heir is certainly valid.

This Responsum is addressed to Rabbi Asher.

SOURCES: Cr. 25; Tesh. Maim. to *Mishpatim* 42; *Mordecai Hagadol*, p. 319a; ibid. p. 320b.

697

1) *Q.* A summoned his father-in-law, B, to court and claimed: 1) that B's father-in-law, C, (A's grandfather), bequeathed twenty-five *marks* to B's two daughters with the provision that if one daughter died childless, the other should inherit her part, and if the second daughter likewise died childless, the twenty-five *marks* were to go to C's male heirs; 2) that the money was deposited with B; and 3) that after he, A, had been married to B's daughter for two years, the other daughter died while still a minor. A, therefore, demanded the twenty-five *marks* from B. B, on the other hand, claimed that he had given the twenty-five *marks* to A as dowry upon the latter's marriage to his daughter. A, however, claimed that upon receiving his dowry he was not told about the twenty-five

marks and that B could not have given him that money since the younger daughter was still alive. To this claim B answered that he expected to give his own money to his younger daughter. He further claims that A's wife has no children yet and, therefore, he, B, cannot give anything to A since in case A's wife dies childless, C's heirs will keep him responsible for the money.

A. B is under no obligation to A for the following reasons: 1) We believe B's claim that he included the money of his departed daughter in A's dowry, since B could have claimed that his younger daughter gave him her money, and this latter claim would have been irrefutable; 2) the father is the rightful heir of the departed daughter since C's provision for the disposition of his gift in case the daughter die childless is void.

2) *Q.* A claims that he has witnesses who will testify that B took from his (A's) father thirty *marks*. B claims that he returned to A whatever he had taken from his father.

A. If the witnesses will testify that B robbed A's father, A should take an oath that B did not as yet return the money to him, and be entitled to collect the thirty *marks* from B. If, however, B received the money from A's father in a legitimate way, B should take an oath that he had paid all the money he owed to his father, and be free from obligation.

Sources: Cr. 283–4; Pr. 1017; *Mordecai Hagadol,* p. 227a.

698 (D)

B must return the money to the trustee of the orphans. Though B has paid for the orphans the taxes that were demanded of them in his town, he merely freed them from a nuisance, like the man who drove away a lion from his neighbor's property (B. K. 58a), and he was entitled to no compensation, especially because the orphans never became obligated to pay the tax, since they transacted no business in that town, and since their money was not there. Regarding the four *marks*, however, that B paid in order that the orphans be taken to France, it is a well known fact that two *marks* are required of each person before he is accepted. Moreover, B claims that witnesses are ready to testify on his behalf, this is a matter the truth of which can easily be ascertained.

SOURCES: Cr. 114.

699

Q. May one heir sue his father's debtors independently of the other heirs?

A. Each heir may sue and collect his share of the inheritance.

SOURCES: Cr. 85; Pr. 212; Tesh. Maim. to *Kinyan*, 13; Am II, 8.

700

Q. Must a bailee, or debtor, return to one heir, his share of the deposit or loan, even though the other heirs are not present to receive their shares?

A. Each heir may collect his share, otherwise the continued absence of the single heir would deprive the other heirs of their portions and thus leave the money in the hands of strangers.

SOURCES: P. 399; cf. Cr. 43.

701

Q. Leah died leaving two sons, A and C; the former is now here but the latter is away. A demands his share of a deposit Leah had left with B. Must the latter give A his share, or may he defer the return of the deposit till C appears?

A. A is to be given his share of the deposit by the order

and supervision of a court; while the other half is to be left, with B, for C.

This Responsum is addressed to Rabbi Menahem haLevi and Rabbi Joseph.

SOURCES: Cr. 43; Am II, 206; Mord. B. M. 283; Tesh. Maim. to *Mishpatim*, 26.

702 (D)

Q. A Gentile casually remarked that A was killed while he was on the road. Part of A's money was kept by his mother. A's son, therefore, demanded that she give it to him. The mother replied that since A owed her money she intended to retain A's deposit in payment of the debt. She admitted, however, that A gave her the money for safe-keeping and not in payment of his debt to her.

A. Since A's mother did not take possession of the money in payment of the debt while he was alive, A's son inherited this money. A creditor cannot appropriate chattels inherited by the orphans of the debtor as repayment of a verbal loan. Therefore, A's mother must return the money to A's son.

SOURCES: L. 479.

703

Q. A avers that he was appointed trustee of orphans' property by their deceased father. May the court exact an oath from A that he was so appointed?

A. A must produce evidence through witnesses that he was appointed trustee by the orphans' father. If he has no witnesses, his oath is of no avail, and the court must appoint a reliable trustee of its own choice.

SOURCES: Cr. 273; Pr. 592; L. 240; Mord. Git. 390; Hag. Maim. to *Nahlot*, 10, 7.

704 (D)

Q. Before his death A, a trustee of the orphan B, appointed other trustees for B and gave them the money that had been deposited with him. The trustees are not certain whether A meant that the money be given to B's mother, or, merely, that she be manager of the estate during her lifetime.

A. The trustees must carefully consider A's last words. If he told them to take good care of the money for B because it belonged to B, and that they do nothing therewith except with the consent of B's mother, he probably meant that they serve as trustees together with B's mother till B grow up, but he did not mean that the mother be a trustee indefinitely. Therefore, as soon as B grows up, the trustees and the mother will have to withdraw from the estate. Moreover, if B's mother displayed any intentions of retaining some of the money for herself, her trusteeship should be terminated immediately, for even a trustee appointed by the father of the orphans is to be dismissed as soon as it is discovered that he damages the interests of the orphans.

SOURCES: Cr. 212.

705 (D)

Q. A died leaving a young son. Each one of A's surviving brothers demands that the orphan be left in his care.

A. The choice of a proper guardian for A's son does not lie with the brothers but with the elders of the community who are the fathers of all orphans. Therefore, the elders of the community shall appoint a proper guardian for A's son.

SOURCES: Cr. 308.

706

Q. A admits that B, before his death, gave him money to distribute among B's children. May B's children exact an oath from A that he did not misappropriate any of their father's money?

A. If A gives to every one of B's sons a part of the money entrusted to him, B's sons cannot exact an oath from A. A is a trustee appointed by the father of the orphans, and no oath is exacted from such a trustee unless the orphans claim to know definitely that the trustee misused their father's funds. But if A claims that he was instructed by B to give all of the money to one or two of B's sons and nothing to the other sons, those sons who receive nothing from A and on whose behalf, therefore, A is not a trustee, may exact an oath from him that he did not misappropriate nor waste their money, and that he will distribute B's money exactly as B instructed him.

SOURCES: Pr. 593; Mord. Gitt. 391.

707 (D)

Q. Is a trustee of orphans, appointed to his trusteeship by their father, required to take an oath [to the effect that he did not retain anything belonging to the orphans and that he did not willfully damage their interests]?

A. A trustee appointed by the father of the orphans is not required to take an oath. However, some authorities (*Ittur*) believe that when such a trustee has been removed by court, because of witnesses testifying to his mismanagement of the affairs of the orphans, he is required to take an oath.

SOURCES: Cr. 272; L. 239. Cf. Mord. Gitt. 389; Pr. 592; L. 240.

708 (D)

Q. B demanded that his mother return to him the books, silver, and gold, that had belonged to his father.

A. Until the widow take the required oath regarding her *ketubah*, all the possessions of her deceased husband belong to the orphans. The assurance by solemn hand-clasp that the widow gave B that she retained nothing which had belonged to her husband, is not sufficient. She must take the required oath over the Scroll of the Law.

SOURCES: Cr. 213.

709

Q. A deposited valuables with B for safekeeping. B, in turn, deposited them with C. Is B to be held responsible for them?

A. A bailee who redeposited with another, valuables that had been entrusted to him, is responsible for them. However, if A was in the habit of depositing valuables with C, B is not to be held responsible for the valuables.

SOURCES: Mord. B. M. 271. Cf. Am II, 221; Moses Minz, *Responsa* 92; ibid. 107.

710

I greatly disapprove of Rabbi Samuel's efforts to find excuses and subterfuges in order to free himself from obligation. Nor is it easy for me to pass judgment against my teacher Rabbi Shemariah. In order that it might not be said, however, that the Rabbis are partial to one another, and because we have been commanded to pursue justice and shun fraud, I must express my opinion that Rabbi Shemariah ought to pay such an amount as Joshua will state under oath was the value of the articles and moneys found in his box, provided such articles and moneys are usually placed in a box of this kind. Rabbi Shemariah is considered a bailee who turned over valuables deposited with him to another bailee and thereupon became fully responsible for the deposit, for he had no right to turn over the box to the servants of the worthy R. Eleazar. He certainly had no right to instruct these servants to break open the box. Although he intended thereby to save the valuables

contained in the box, he was not justified in breaking the box
since he could have ordered that the locked box be carried
out intact, for its bulk was not greater than that of the other
objects and large books that were carried out. Moreover, he
should have appointed a member of his household or one of
his students to watch the box, and thus would not have been
guilty of turning over the deposit to another bailee. Even when
the box was carried into the yard of the Christian priest, Rabbi
Shemariah should have placed a guard over it there. Although
Rabbi Shemariah guarded the box in the same manner as he
guarded his own valuables, he is not to be excused, since he
had no right to leave highly desirable valuables unguarded.
Money deposited with a person must be guarded very carefully,
and merely keeping it in the same place where one keeps one's
own valuables is not sufficient, unless such a place is reasonably
secure. You are acquainted with the servants of R. Eleazar
and should be able to judge whether leaving the valuables in
their care is to be considered willful neglect or not. Moreover,
Rabbi Shemariah had no right to break open the box and then
leave it unguarded, for an open box invites thieves; especially
so since he took the box to a place that was swarming with
thieves and robbers. We cannot free him from obligation on
the ground that the box was in imminent danger of being lost
in any event (it was a matter of common knowledge that the
bishop was intent on seizing it) since the box could have been
saved with little trouble had it not been broken open, and had
he placed a guard to watch it in the same manner as one watched
the silver and the gold. In short, Rabbi Shemariah, must take
an oath to the effect that Joshua's valuables are not in his possession, before paying for them. Let him comply with the
requirements of the law, write off his loss as a bad investment,
and the Lord will fully compensate him for it.

SOURCES: Sinai VI (1943) 7–8, nos. 415–16.

711 (D)

Q. A claims that he and his friend gave B a horse to ride on, but that B unwarrantably gave the horse to a Gentile and the horse was lost. B avers that he does not recall the incident.

A. If A and B were partners, and A was engaged in managing some of the partnership money, even if the horse was lost through B's willful neglect, B would be free from obligation since the horse would thus have been lost "in the presence of its owner." Your letter indicates that A and B were partners. Nevertheless, if A suspects that B misappropriated the horse, he may demand that B deny such charge under oath. In general, A may demand at any time that B take the "partner's oath", and B may impose the same oath on A. However, if A and B are not partners, B must merely take an oath either to the effect that he did not take a horse from A, or that he does not recall having taken a horse from A, and be free from obligation.

SOURCES: Cr. 295.

712 (D)

Q. A sent ten pounds to B to deliver to A's Gentile creditor. The Gentile refused to accept the money. Subsequently, robbers broke into B's home and took away this money. A claims that B did not hide the money properly and, therefore, was guilty of willful neglect. B avers that he kept the money in a good hiding place in his room, in the same place where he usually kept his own money, but that it was taken from him by force.

A. If B will take an oath in support of his claim, he will be free from obligation, unless he admits having used the money. In the latter case he would be responsible for the loss of the money no matter under what circumstances it was lost. If B, however, did not use A's money for his own benefit, his manner of guarding it was sufficient. Although the only safe place in which to keep money is in the ground — money being unidentifiable, more thieves are after it, and they take greater chances in stealing it than any other valuables — B was not required to keep A's money in the ground, since it was not given to him for safekeeping, for he expected to hand it over to A any day upon demand.

SOURCES: Cr. 301.

713 (D)

Q. A asked his road companion B to keep some money (sixty schillings) for him. B refused to take the money saying he had no place where to keep it. A suggested that he put it in his sheet, and B did so. Subsequently, the money was stolen from B. A, however, demanded his money and claimed that B was guilty of negligence since he slept in the market place among thieves.

A. If B took reasonable care to watch his sheet, even though he slept in the market place, he is free from any obligation to A, since he complied with A's instructions.

SOURCES: Pr. 843.

714

Q. A deposited valuables with L for safekeeping. L stipulated the condition, at the time, that she should be permitted to guard these valuables in the same manner as she guarded her own. Thereupon L deposited A's valuables, together with her own, with R. A died and his estate went to his sister D. Subsequently A's valuables in R's possession were lost through unavoidable accident. D now demands these valuables from L.

A. The condition L had stipulated with A was not valid as against D. L must state under oath the value of the articles A deposited with her, and pay that amount to D, for a bailee who transfers valuables to a sub-bailee, is responsible for their loss even if caused by unavoidable accident.

SOURCES: *Mordecai Hagadol*, p. 174d; ibid., p. 288d.

715

Q. A claims that he deposited with B eleven and a quarter *marks*, and that B undertook to repay him that sum in Frankfort. B claims that A gave him the money on condition that he return it to A immediately after a meal they partook [and that meanwhile the money was stolen from him].

A. The only proper method to safeguard money is to bury it in the ground (B.M. 42a). Keeping another person's money in the same place one keeps one's own, is not sufficient, for, a person may be careless with his own money, but he has no right to be careless with that of another. However, if B was expected to return the money immediately after the meal, then he was not supposed to bury it in the ground for the short time he was to keep it. Therefore, B must take an oath that he was to return the money after the meal, that he kept the money in the same place he kept his own, and that he was not unduly careless in handling it — and he would then be free from obligation.

The names of the litigants are given as R. Meir and R. Eliezer. Our author agrees with the opinion of those who sent the query to him.

SOURCES: L. 207.

716

Q. While A and B were in Hungary, A gave to him ten gilded vessels and two copper ones for delivery in Mayence. The gilded were to be delivered to C, and the copper to D. B, however, failed to deliver the vessels as instructed. A long time afterwards, A's brother came to Mayence and asked B about the vessels. B said that he forgot to deliver them at the time; and that he lost them without knowing exactly where, either in Mayence or in Hungary. He was, therefore, willing to pay A for the value of such vessels in Hungary. A, however, demanded the price of such vessels in Mayence.

A. If the place where B lost the vessels were known, B would have to pay their price as of that place. However, since the place of the loss is not known, B must pay the amount the vessels cost in Mayence.

SOURCES: Pr. 935; *Mordecai Hagadol,* p. 152 b.

717

Q. A deposited with B for safe-keeping a strongbox well locked up. Subsequently, B broke open the box and left it open. When A came for his box and found it open, he charged that several silver vessels and other valuables were missing. B admitted having opened the box, but said that he abstracted therefrom a single silver vessel because he had gone surety for A and needed the money in order to extricate himself therewith from the entanglements of that obligation.

A. A is to be held responsible for all articles that, according to B's assertion under oath, are missing from the strongbox, provided such articles are usually kept in a strongbox of this type, for the ordinance for the benefit of the robbed person [that the latter take an oath as to the extent of the damage he has suffered, and collect full compensation therefor], applies also to other, similar, damagees. (B.K. 62a).

SOURCES: Cr. 201; *Mordecai Hagadol,* p. 268b; Sinai VII (1943), 5–6, 49.

718

1) *Q.* L, who managed her husband's business, deposited money with B and C. Her husband, A, demands this money from B and C claiming that the money was his.

A. If the money is in the hands of the depositaries, they

must return it to A, since the latter entrusted his business to his wife. If, however, the money was returned to L and she claims that the money belongs to her, since it had been originally given to her on condition that her husband have no rights thereto; or that the money belongs to a person, D, who lent it to her, she may take an oath to support her claim and retain the money. Although a husband may not exact an oath from his wife regarding her management of his business (Ket. 88a), this rule applies only to the case where the husband is not positive in his claim.

2) *Q.* A left his wife L; and while he was away, L borrowed money for the sustenance of herself and of her infant daughter. A now refuses to pay the debts she thus incurred.

A. If L will take an oath to the effect that these loans were made to her with the expectation that she would personally repay them and that now she is unable to do so, A will be obliged to pay these debts. For a husband must provide for the sustenance of his wife, and of his children until they reach the age of six.

3) *Q.* L contends that A beat her. A denies this charge, but admits having left her without her consent. She now refuses to live with him unless he make a solemn promise, obligating himself by a *herem*, and drawing up a document to the effect that . . . [reference is made to the details that were enumerated in the inquiry, which was written on the other side of the parchment].

A. A must comply with L's wishes or divorce her, and pay her the *ketubah*; for a husband must honor his wife and not degrade her.

Sources: Am II, 24.

719

Q. A demanded of B the silver girdle and golden stomacher he had deposited with him. B averred that A's wife, before her marriage to A, had deposited these jewels with him in order to withhold them from A and keep them for the children by her former marriage. Now that she had died, B wished to do her bidding and deliver the jewels to her children. We, therefore, decided that B take an oath as to the truth of his statement and deliver the jewels to the heirs of A's wife. Next day, however, when B was to take the oath, he declared that he had been reminded, by his wife, of the truth of A's claim, and that he was ready to take an oath to the effect that A deposited the jewels with him. The heirs of A's wife, however, who were present at the trial on the previous day, claimed that B had, then, admitted having in his possession jewels that belonged to them. They, therefore, demanded these jewels.

A. If B takes an oath to the effect that A deposited the jewels with him, and returns them to A, he will be free from obligation to the woman's heirs. We must be satisfied with such an oath since B had recourse to a *Miggo* (an alternative claim) that would only have imposed a different oath on him; for B could have claimed that he had returned the jewels to the heirs, or that the jewels had been stolen or lost, after the court had reached the above decision. Such claims by B would only have obligated him to take an oath. Although we usually do not accept a defendant's claim to have been mistaken in his original admission, even when such defendant had recourse to a *Miggo*, this case is different, since B is not a litigant and is to gain nothing from either alternative.

SOURCES: P. 301; Mord. B. B. 524; *Agudah* B. B. 64.

720

Q. A demands that Leah return to him the money he deposited with her. Leah claims that A deposited the money with her on condition that she do not return it to him without his wife's consent. [A's wife does not consent to the return of the deposit]. Are we to believe a trustee who was appointed by the two opposing parties regarding the terms of his trusteeship, or may we require him to take an oath? Moreover, Leah is a married woman. May her husband object to her being degraded by imposing an oath on her?

A. A trustee appointed by both parties is not required to take an oath regarding the terms of his trusteeship. But, Leah was not appointed trustee by both parties. She was only appointed by the husband, and, therefore, is required to take an oath. Leah's husband cannot object to imposing an oath on her. If the law requires that a woman take an oath, the husband has no right to protest against her being degraded in court. But, since Leah, as long as she is married, has no money of her own, and were she to claim that she had already returned the deposit, no oath would be imposed on her, we now lend credence to her words and require no oath. However, the court should give A a writ stating that after Leah will be divorced or widowed she will have to return the money to A or take an oath to the effect that A deposited the money with her on condition that she return it upon his wife's consent only.

SOURCES: L. 306–7; Mord. B. K. 89. Cf. Pr. 739; Tesh. Maim. to *Mishpatim*, 44.

721 (D)

Q. B discovered that A stole some silver from him. Accompanied by several men, B went to C's house and seized an article which A had entrusted to C for safekeeping. C, who owed money to B, refused to repay the debt unless B return to him A's article.

A. B had a right to summon A to court, but he had no cause for action against C. Therefore, C is justified in retaining

B's money until the latter returns the articles he took from him by force.

SOURCES: Pr. 834. Cf. *Agudah* B. M. 99.

722

Q. A deposited money with B. Subsequently, C seized this money in payment of the money B owed him. B admits that the money belongs to A. Now A demands it from C.

A. Since B admits that the money belongs to A, C must return it to the latter. The fact that B is responsible for A's deposit and would have to compensate him for its loss, does not make B the owner of the deposited money. Thus the Talmud (B.K. 115a) rules that a creditor who received, from a thief, stolen goods in payment of his debt must return the goods to its original owner.

This Responsum was addressed to Rabbi Asher who took exception to R. Meir's derivation of the law by conclusion *ad majus*, arguing that our case cannot be compared to that of a thief who repaid his debt with stolen goods, for a thief has acquired his ill-gotten gain sinfully and those who received the goods from him are dealt with severely; but C committed no sin in seizing A's money since "a person may execute judgment on his own behalf" (B.K. 27b). R. Meir, however, pointed out that C also committed a sin in seizing the property of another, for the talmudic dictum "a person may execute judgment on his own behalf" merely means that a person may retrieve his own valuables which he finds in the hands of others; but a creditor is not permitted to seize the valuables of his debtor without a court order.

SOURCES: Cr. 26–7; Mord. B. K. 170; ibid. B. M. 438; Hag. Maim., *Nahalot* 11, 2; Asher, *Responsa* 107, 1.

723

Q. B's books were in A's possession. A pawned them with C. Must C return the books to B?

A. The market ordinance (B.K. 115a) was made to protect the pawnee. Therefore, C is entitled to receive the amount he has lent to A before he returns the books to B. Thus, if A admits that the books belong to B, C must allow the latter to redeem them. But if A denies B's claim, or if A is out of town, C owes nothing to B.

SOURCES: Cr. 104; Mord. Sheb. 778.

724

Q. A deposited valuables with B for safekeeping. Subsequently C ordered B, with the court's permission, to hold the valuables for C in payment of money A owed C. May B seize these valuables for C's benefit?

A. If it has been proved that A owes money to C, and if B admits, or is not in a position to deny, that A's valuables are in his possession, C is entitled to collect these valuables because of the lien of R. Nathan. Moreover, if A is a violent and insubordinate man (who refuses to subordinate himself to the ruling of the court), B would do a meritorious act in seizing A's valuables for C's benefit and thus save the court a great deal of trouble.

SOURCES: *Tashbetz,* 509; *Mordecai hagadol,* p. 149a.

725 (D)

Q. What objects are considered "usually lent or rented out" (Sheb. 46b)?

A. Regarding most books as objects "usually lent or rented out" a difference of opinion exists between Rashi and Rabbenu

Tam. Other objects must be considered individually, each one on its own merits.

SOURCES: Cr. 269.

726

1) *Q.* A sent his valuables, through C, to be deposited with B. Subsequently, C left for a distant country without informing A whether or not he had carried out A's instructions. Are we to presume that a deputy generally carries out his commission, and that A therefore may claim to be positive that his valuables had been delivered to B, thus obligating the latter to take an oath in support of his denial?

A. In money matters we do not presume that a deputy has carried out his commission.

2) *Q.* B admits that C had delivered the valuables to him, but claims that he subsequently returned them to C.

A. B is to be held responsible for A's valuables, for, the fact that A trusted C to be his deputy in delivering the valuables to B, does not mean that he trusted C as a depositee for an extended period of time. Therefore, B had no right to redeposit A's valuables with C.

This Responsum was addressed to Rabbi Asher.

SOURCES: Cr. 26, 28; Am II, 221. Cf. Moses Minz, *Responsa* 92; ibid. 107.

727 (D)

Q. A and B deposited a bond with C with the stipulation that C return the bond to B, should A fail to pay one *mark* to B within a certain period of time. The stipulated date passed but C does not know whether or not A paid the *mark* to B. What should C do with the bond?

A. C should return the bond to B; for had A paid the *mark* to B he would have informed C about it.

SOURCES: Pr. 447.

728

Q. Leah rented a house for a period of time and died before the expiration of this period. Her heirs offer to pay only for the time she occupied the house, or demand the right to rent it to anyone they please.

A. If Leah did not pay the rent for the full period, her heirs are bound to pay only for the time she occupied the house; for Leah is not responsible for not fulfilling her part of the contract since she was prevented from doing so by death. But, if Leah paid the rent for the entire period, her heirs may either rent it to a tenant as considerate as (or more than) Leah, or demand from the landlord an amount which a landlord would generally be willing to pay in consideration of terminating the lease and thus make the premises available for tenancy. The heirs, however, are not permitted to rent the premises to a tenant more severe and less considerate than Leah.

SOURCES: Pr. 1002: Mord. B. M. 345; *Agudah* B. M. 118. Cf. Moses Minz, *Responsa* 22.

729

Q. A, B, and C, rented their houses to tenants for a certain period of time. Within that period, however, the houses burned down. The landlords demand that their tenants pay them the rent for the entire period.

A. The tenants must pay their rent up to the time when the houses burned down. They are not to pay for the remainder of the period, however, since they are not to be held responsible for the breach of contract, for they are ready to fullfil their part of the agreement, while the landlords are not in a position to fullfil their part.

SOURCES: Tesh. Maim. to *Mishpatim*, 47; *Agudah* B. M. 124.

730

Q. A rented from B a house part of which was without a roof. A asked B to roof it; but B told A to do it and deduct the expenses from his rent. A refuses to do so since he does not as yet owe rent to B.

A. If the above transaction was not accompanied by a proper *kinyan*, both A and B have a right to retract. Otherwise, B is under obligation to roof the house, for we presume that a person rents a house in order to dwell therein. Since this house is not habitable, B must make it so.

SOURCES: Cr. 265; Hag. Maim. *Sekirut* 6, 1.

731

Q. A, a widow's trustee, leased half of the widow's house, for a term of ten years, to C, who, in turn, leased it to B. After B moved into the house, A became greatly dissatisfied with him and demanded that B move out of the house immediately, on the ground that he had leased the house to C, and therefore was under no obligation to B. He told B, however, that should C have any claims against him on account of the eviction of B, he, A, would answer these charges in court. B, however, claimed: that C rented the house from A on condition that he (C) lease it to whomever he wants; that he, B, was willing to partition off the part of the house he occupies from the rest of the house; and that he would guarantee to pay the widow for any damages she may sustain as a result of his remaining on the premises. A, however, claimed that he feared that grave damages to the widow will result if B stays, and that the widow cannot dwell in one house with a snake (meaning B).

A. Since A admits that C had the right to lease the house to anyone he pleased, A cannot evict B from the widow's house.

SOURCES: Cr. 259; Pr. 680; Mord. B. M. 357; *Agudah* B. M. 125. Cf. Hag. Maim. to *Sekirut* 5, 20; Weil, *Responsa* 10.

732 (D)

Q. A rented two houses from a Gentile. He, subsequently, agreed to sublet one house to B on condition that B pay him the rent at the time the rent for both houses becomes due, even though it be before B lived in the house a year. When the time came for A to pay the rent for both houses to the Gentile, B refused to pay his share. A, therefore, demanded that B move out. B refused to do so, claiming that he rented the house for three years. A, however, claimed that he rented the house for one year only. An arbitrator decided that the rental period be set at two years. After B lived in A's house for sixteen months, he moved out leaving some of his furniture till the end of the second year. A, therefore, demands rent for two years.

A. A is entitled to the entire rent for two years. A would be entitled to such rent even though B had not left some of his furniture till the end of the second year; for, B failed to give sufficient notice to A, which notice would have enabled A to find another tenant for his house.

SOURCES: Pr. 833.

733

Q. A and his son-in-law B were partners in a house. A leased his half to B for an indefinite period till the latter's death, at a fixed annual rental. Subsequently, A wanted to sell his part, but B objected. The case was brought before R. Meir who sustained B's objection. Now B is seeking to sell his half and also his right to a fixed rental for the other half. A, however, objects to a sale by B of the right to a fixed rental claiming that he had originally leased his half to B for a low rental in order that B and his family live therein and enjoy it themselves, but not for the purpose of selling it to another.

Is A's objection valid? Also, please note that A's daughter, B's wife, was dead, but the children she bore to A are living; does the fact that B's wife is dead prejudice B's rights? Moreover, B claims, and witnesses support his claim, that the agreement of lease was reached between A and B after a sharp quarrel which followed their buying of the property. Thus the lease was not a gift of love [in which case the purpose of the gift must be taken into consideration], but was rather the outcome of litigation and compromise and was, therefore, of the nature of a sale. B further states that should A's objection be sustained in court, he would sell his own half of the house and would dwell in the other half, or would rent out the latter half and would use the rent for his sustenance. Please further inform me, on the other side of this sheet, as to what was done in the case of the widow from Spiers and her two Levite levirs. Signed: Asher b. Rabbi Yehiel.

A. We are not to take into consideration A's purpose in leasing his half of the house to B, for various reasons. a) When B sells his right to a fixed rental to a third party, he benefits from such sale as much as he would have benefited from living in the house himself. b) Since B has lived in the rented half of the house for a long time, the transaction of the lease is by now complete so that A's original purpose in leasing it is no longer of any consequence. c) A transaction of sale, lease, or even gift, is concluded by two parties, being the result of a meeting of both minds and, therefore, such transaction is not conditioned by the special purpose or intent of one party when such purpose or intent was not in the mind of the other party. Therefore, even if B had no surviving children from A's daughter, the validity of the lease would not have been affected. d) According to your letter, the lease was not motivated by feelings of kindliness, but was a purely business transaction. R. Meir adds: Regarding the widow mentioned above, I shall order that my Responsum pertaining thereto be copied for your benefit.

The answer bears the superscription: "To my teacher Rabbi Asher."

SOURCES: Cr. 315; Am II, 174. Cf. Asheri B. M. 8, 25.

734

Your reasoning and the fine distinctions you draw are correct, but they apply only to a case where the person who is seeking to sell the house that he has rented to another, is not forced to sell the house by dire necessity. When a person is thus forced to sell his house, we assume that originally when he rented the house to his tenant he did not intend to let it remain rented while he was dying from hunger. Therefore, if the landlord take an oath to the effect that he is forced by dire necessity to sell his house, his tenant will have to vacate the house. If the tenant has paid his rent in advance for a certain period, however, he may not be forced to vacate before the expiration of that term, since renting is a form of buying limited to the period for which the rent is paid. In our case, the tenant may not claim that his landlord is not in desperate need of money since he owns real estate on which his wife's *ketubah* is a lien, and he could sell to another the right to take title to such real estate in case his wife die before him, for we assume that at the time the landlord rented his house to the tenant he did not intend that the renting should cause him to jeopardize his property in such a manner.

This Responsum is addressed "to my teacher Rabbi Asher."

SOURCES: Am II, 241; cf. Mord. B. M. 383; Asheri B. M. 25.

735

Q. A erected a building on premises owned by a widow in spite of the latter's protests and warnings not to do so. She now demands that A remove his building and that he pay her rent for the time the building stood on her premises. A claims that he rented the space for his building, for ten years (at an annual rental of ten denarii, one-half pound*), from the widow's son and son-in-law; that the latter two informed the widow of the transaction, and that the widow sent them her written consent thereto. The widow denies that she ever gave her consent to lease her courtyard to A.

A. Even A's producing a written consent from the widow would be of no avail unless he can also prove through witnesses that the widow instructed and ordered the writing of the instrument. Should he not be able to do so, he will have to remove the building from the widow's premises and pay her rent for the time his building stood thereon. Should A produce such witnesses, his contract with the widow's son and son-in-law will be non-voidable even though A did not yet pay the rent for the full ten years. Although the widow did not personally instruct her son and son-in-law to rent her premises to A, but sent such instructions in writing — such manner of sending instructions not being acceptable in talmudic law — nevertheless the son and son-in-law became the widow's agents, since it is the usual custom of merchants to accept as valid written instruments, and since the custom of merchants prevails in business transactions.

This Resp. is addressed to R. Eliezer ha-Kohen, and R. Eliezer.

SOURCES: Pr. 698.

---

* The rental price given above is mentioned in the answer only, and may represent, therefore, a mere arbitrary sum assumed by R. Meir instead of the actual rental.

736

Q. A, a gratuitous bailee, claims that he undertook to watch B's article with the express condition that he be not obliged to take an oath in case it got lost. A, however, has no witnesses to support his contention.

A. A must take an "oath of inducement" (שבועת היסת).

SOURCES: Pr. 271.

737

Q. A gave to a broker a ring to sell. The broker lost the precious stone of the ring. The Rabbis of the town are of varied opinions. Some say that the broker is responsible for the loss, and others are of the opinion that he is not responsible.

A. The responsibility of the broker is that of a hired watchman since he took the ring in the anticipation of making a profit. The broker, therefore, must swear that the stone is not in his possession; he must also take an oath as to the value of the stone, and must repay that amount to A.

SOURCES: Pr. 547, 548; Mord. B. M. 359. Cf. *Agudah* B. M. 127.

738 (D)

Q. A lent a silver key to B's wife. She says that she has lost the key. Has A any claim upon B, or his wife, for the value of the key?

A. Most authorities agree that a person cannot collect from the husband the value of an object lent to, or deposited with, his wife, and lost by her, even in cases where she is a business woman conducting her husband's affairs with his full knowledge and consent. But a ban should be pronounced in the synagogue against those persons (including B's wife) who have the silver key in their possession and do not return it to A, and also against those persons who may receive such key in the future and will not return it to its owner. More-over, A should receive a court decision entitling him to collect from B's wife, should she become widowed or divorced, an amount equal to the value of the key. A clause should be included in the decision providing that in case of a dispute between A and B's wife regarding the value of the key, it will be incumbent upon her to take an oath as to the value of the key.

SOURCES: L. 206.

739

Q. A claims that certain commentaries to the tractate *Yebamot* were once lent to B's father, to A's brother, and to himself; that when these commetaries were lost (or stolen) the three borrowers were required to compensate the lender to the extent of one pound; that his brother and he, A, paid two thirds of this compensation; that after B's father died, B found (or recovered) the commentaries; and that in A's presence, B evaluated them at one pound upon delivering them to his creditor. A, therefore, demands from B two thirds of a pound, for his brother and himself. B avers that he has no knowledge of A's having paid anything for the commentaries; that he received them as part of his father's estate; that he was answerable for only half of their value since he shared the estate with his brother; that he kept them for a period of three years without any protest on A's part; and that even if he were forced by the court to pay A for his alleged share in the commentaries, he would pay such share of their present, depreciated, value only. A rejoins that he holds B responsible for the entire sum, since he found the commentaries in B's possession; and that he learned only recently that they were in B's possession. B further claims that in order to retrieve the commentaries he paid (the thief) more than their actual value; and that he gave them to his creditor in A's presence without any protest on A's part. A avers that he has no knowledge of B's having paid anything for the commentaries; that B should not have paid anything for them, since they would have been returned at no cost, and that the reason for his failing to protest àgainst B's delivering them to his creditor, was that he sought to discover at what price B would evaluate them. Signed: Nethanel b. Nahman, Ephraim b. Ephraim.

A. If A claims that B knows that A and his brother paid two thirds of a pound when the commentaries were lost, B must take an oath denying such knowledge and be free from obligation. But, if A is not positive in his claim, B is not required to take an oath. A general ban should be pronounced against anyone (including B) who knows anything about this matter and does not report it to the court. If, however, B admits A's claim, but claims to have spent money in retrieving the commentaries, he is entitled to a refund of his expenses. If, however, he paid such money to the thief himself, he is entitled to no refund. Thus, one who buys a stolen object from a person known to be a thief is not entitled to a refund of expenses; he who buys an object from a thief knowing definitely it to be a stolen object, is surely not entitled to a refund. A did not lose his rights by failing to protest against B's delivering the commentaries to his creditor; and he is entitled to receive his share of the amount they were evaluated at, when so delivered.

SOURCES: Am II, 209.

740

Q. Are we responsible for the books we borrowed, which had been burned in a fire?

A. You are fully responsible for such books, since a borrower is responsible even for a loss by unavoidable accident.

SOURCES: Cr. 119.

741

Q. A demanded from B the book of the order *Kodashim* which he lent him to copy from. B, in turn, demanded from A the book of the order *Moed* which he gave to A as security, and which was worth twice as much as A's book. At first A denied that he received B's book, but when confronted by a witness who supported B's claim, A retracted his denial, but alleged: 1) that B loaned him the book with the understanding that his (A's) children should be permitted to study therefrom; 2) that he loaned the book to his son-in-law; and 3) that the book was subsequently burned in the latter's house, and that hence the loss of the book was an unavoidable accident. B denied that he gave A permission to allow his sons to use the book.

A. Since A and B lent books to each other, their responsibilities regarding these books were those of hired watchmen who are not responsible for unavoidable accidents. The question revolves, then, about A's lending the book to his son-in-law. Therefore, upon A's taking an oath that B gave him permission to allow his sons to use B's book, A will be free from any obligation to B. B, on the other hand, may retain A's book, upon taking an oath that he did not permit A to give his book to A's sons for study, and B is further entitled to collect from A's son-in-law (the difference between the value of the lost book and the one B retained) since the responsibility of the son-in-law regarding the book was that of a borrower who is responsible even for unavoidable accidents. If, however, A's son-in-law is willing to take an oath that he did not borrow B's book from A, he will be free from obligation to B, and his oath will not subject his father-in-law to any further obligation.

The question was submitted by R. Moses Azriel b. R. Eliezer Darshan, whose opinion, appended to the question, coincided with that of R. Meir.

SOURCES: Pr. 963; Mord. B. M. 282. Cf. Isserlein *Pesakim* 200.

742

Q. A says that without his knowledge or consent B took a book from his house. B admits having taken the book, but claims to have done so because A had once borrowed a book from him, that was later stolen from A's house, but A had refused to pay him for it or even to go to court with him. A avers that at the time he borrowed B's book, he told B to call for it and take it from his garret and that he was not to be held responsible for it. B denies A's allegation. The judges called B's attention to the fact that he violated the ordinace of the communities against "retention" (cf. Finkelstein op. cit. p. 133). Thereupon B returned the book to A, excusing himself that he did not seize the book in payment of the money due him, but merely wanted to force A to go to court with him.

A. B did not transgress the ordinance of the communities against "retention", for this ordinance applies only to those who have borrowed, or received as deposits, valuables from other persons and later sought to retain them because of a claim against their owners. Seizure because of a claim, however, was not included in the ordinance of the communities. Moreover, when borrowed or deposited valuables are returned to their owners because of the aforesaid ordinance, the borrower or bailee does not thereby lose the legal advantage that goes with possession of the litigated money. Therefore, if witnesses did not see A's book in B's possession, B had recourse to *Miggo* (he could have claimed to have returned A's book) and we now believe B's statement under oath, up to the value of A's book. Although B admits that he did not seize A's book in payment of the money due him, but merely sought thereby to force A to go to court with him, nevertheless B is considered to be in possession of the litigated money. However if witnesses saw A's book in B's possession before the trial, B had no recourse to *Miggo*, and his possession of A's book was of no legal consequence.

SOURCES: Mord. B. M. 407.

743

Q. A borrowed a book from B for one hour with the understanding that after the hour B would send for it, and if not, he should bring the book back to B. A few hours later a fire broke out in A's house, as a result of which, A was compelled to flee for his life, as the Gentiles were accustomed to throw into the fire Jews in whose houses a fire broke out. A could not, therefore, save B's book.

A. After the period, for which A borrowed the book, had passed, A's responsibility for the book became that of a hired watchman. Therefore, if, before he fled, A could have hired somebody to save the book, and did not do so, he was liable for its loss. But if this was impossible, he was free from obligation.

SOURCES: Pr. 140; Mord. B. M. 376; *Agudah* B. M. 152.

744

Q. C and D lent books to A (of the Responsum given above) with the understanding that A, in turn, lend books to them, which he did. C and D's books were burned during the fire in A's house.

A. Since there was a mutual exchange of books, A's responsibility was that of a paid watchman. Therefore, the answer given above (no. 743) is applicable to this case also.

SOURCES: Pr. 141; Mord. B. M. 376; *Agudah* B. M. 152.

745

Q. A asked a tutor to teach his son, but did not stipulate any wage. After the term was over, A refused to pay the tutor for his efforts.

A. A must pay the tutor the wages the latter was accustomed to receive in other places.

SOURCES: Mord. B. M. 346; Hag. Mord. B. M. 456.

746

Q. A promised to pay a sum of money to his rich son-in-law, B, if the latter would teach his own son. B taught his son, but A now refuses to give B the amount promised.

A. Since B is not a poor man, and since he is under obligation to teach his son, A may claim to have made the promise in jest.

SOURCES: Mord. Sanh. 704; Tesh. Maim. to *Mishpatim*, 64; *Mordecai Hagadol*, p. 354b; *Agudah* Sanh. 31.

747

Q. B engaged A as tutor to his son. B said to A that since he, B, was unlearned and did not know whether or not A had sufficient knowledge to tutor his son, A must go to his (B's) relative C to be examined before entering upon his duties. A came to B's house and began to tutor B's son. Subsequently B discovered that A had never been examined by C. He, therefore, summoned A to court. A now declares himself ready to be examined, but B argues that A's present knowledge is no proof of his previous fitness for his position. Moreover, one witness testifies that at the time A undertook to teach B's son, he was not qualified to do so because of insufficient knowledge.

A. If A has now sufficient knowledge to teach B's son, the burden of proof lies on B that A did not have such knowledge at the time he was engaged. However, since B has one witness to support his claim, A must take an oath to the effect that he had sufficient knowledge at the time of the agreement. If A takes such oath, he will be entitled to collect his full wages from B.

SOURCES: Cr. 3; Pr. 488; Mord. B. B. 621. Cf. *Agudah* B. M. 172.

748 (D)

Q. A claims that a tutor did not teach his son properly, having wasted a number of weeks.

A. Since A is in possession of the money, he may take an oath as to the truth of his claim and be free from obligation; or, should he so desire, he may impose the oath on the tutor.

SOURCES: B. p. 276, no. 55.

749

Q. A hired a tutor for his son. He made a stipulation, however, that should the tutor play cards, he would forfeit his wages. After a certain period of time the tutor began to play cards.

A. A's stipulation is considered an *asmakhta* and is not binding, for the tutor's wages up to the time he began to play cards, became a definite obligation upon A which could no longer be cancelled by a subsequent act of the tutor.

SOURCES: Cr. 310; *Mordecai Hagadol*, p. 278b.

750

Q. A hired B to tutor his son. After teaching A's son for six days B resigned. Thereupon A was forced to hire another tutor at a higher wage. Some time previously, B had pledged a book with A. A now seeks to collect the increase he was forced to pay the second tutor, out of B's book which had been pledged with him.

A. A may not collect any compensation for his loss out of B's book.

SOURCES: Mord. B. M. 349. Cf. *Terumat Hadeshen* 329.

751

Q. A tutor agreed, by solemn hand-clasp, to teach A's son until Passover. This promise involved the tutor in family difficulties, and he sought to break the agreement. The inquirer (Rabbi Yedidyah) was of the opinion that the agreement was invalid on the ground that it was unlawfully contracted, since entering into service for a long period of time is under the same prohibition as selling oneself for a slave.

A. Entering into service for a period not exceeding three years, is not prohibited. Therefore, the tutor must live up to the agreement to which he bound himself by solemn hand-clasp.

SOURCES: Pr. 72; cf. *Hagahot Mordecai* B. M. 460.

752

Q. A engaged a tutor for his son for one year. After the tutor had entered upon his duties, he was requested by A to leave. When the tutor had gone, A changed his mind and demanded that the tutor return to fulfill the terms of his agreement. The tutor, however, refuses to return, and claims that A released him from all obligations when he ordered him to leave.

A. A verbal release is not binding when the obligation is personal [such as the obligation of a slave or a tutor]. Moreover, the tutor is under an obligation to A's son, and A had no right to release the tutor from such obligation. Therefore, the latter must resume his teaching of A's son.

SOURCES: Cr. 125; Pr. 77; L. 205; Rashba I, 873; Mord. B. M. 346; *Agudah* B. M. 118. Cf. Moses Minz, *Responsa* 98.

753

Q. A tutor was hired for a season. Owing to illness, he was kept from carrying out his duties part of the time. Is he entitled to payment for the entire season?

A. All laws and regulations that benefit the Hebrew slave also apply to a workman who was hired for a season. A Hebrew slave who was sick for part of his six years of servitude does not have to make up for the time of his illness. Therefore, the tutor is entitled to payment for the entire season and is under no obligation to make up for the duration of his illness.

SOURCES: Pr. 85; Mord. B. M. 346. cf. Tesh. Maim., to *Kinyan* 31; *Tashbetz* 530.

754

Q. B hired A as tutor for his son for one year. A taught B's son together with other students. After four months of study, B took his son on a journey to a foreign country, for a period of two months. B's son returned to his studies at which he continued for three more months until the time of vintage, and then B took his son to the country and kept him there till the end of the year. A demands his wages for the whole year.

A. Since B's son studied under A for the major part of the year, and since A taught other students the whole year [and thus the absence of B's son did not result in A's being free from his labors] A is entitled to be paid for the whole year.

SOURCES: Pr. 833.

755

Q. B was interrupted in carrying on his duties as tutor to A's son as a result of the son's illness. Must A pay B his full wages?

A. I learned this law from my teacher, R. Samuel b. Solomon, of France: The tutor must be paid in full; for a tutor is in a similar position as the public workers of Mahoza who are reported to become weakened by lack of work (B. M. 77a). However, the following distinction should be made: If A's son was a sickly child, and A failed to warn the tutor about it, the tutor should get his full pay; but if the boy was usually healthy, the tutor should not be paid for the period of his pupil's illness.

SOURCES: Cr. 191; Pr. 137; L. 157; Mord. B. M. 344. Cf. Tesh. Maim. to *Kinyan*, 31; *Agudah* B. M. 117.

756

Q. B was interrupted in carrying on his duties as tutor to A's son as a result of the son's illness. Is A permitted to deduct from B's wages for the period of the son's illness?

A. The law provides that when a tutor is prevented from carrying on his duties by his own illness, he is entitled to his pay; but if he is so prevented by the pupil's illness, he is not entitled to his pay, unless the pupil is a sickly child. Since a child is usually healthy, the burden lies with the tutor of stipulating at the time of the agreement that he is to receive his pay in the event the child is sick.

This Responsum was addressed to Rabbi Yekutiel.

SOURCES: Cr. 2.

757

Q. A and B hired a tutor for their sons [for several terms] and paid him for one term in advance. Five weeks after the term began, A's son died. Since the tutor had to continue to teach B's son, he demanded that A pay him for the remaining term (or terms). A, however, claimed that when the tutor came to console him, after his son's death, he told him that he forwent the balance of his fee and that he would even repay him whatever he had received in excess of the fee for five weeks. A, therefore, demanded that amount from the tutor. At first the tutor admitted that he had forgone the balance of his fee, but claimed that his act was not valid since it was merely a verbal statement without a formal act of transference. Later, however, he completely denied ever having relinquished his claim.

A. If the tutor definitely admitted A's claim, and later retracted his admission, A is free from obligation to the tutor. However, he cannot collect anything he has already paid, since the tutor's promise of a refund was not accompanied by a formal act of transference. But, if the tutor's denial followed immediately upon his admission, or if the denial merely explained that the admission was really no admission, or if the admission was only implied but not definitely stated, A must pay the tutor his fee for the whole year. A, however, may bring another pupil to the teachr to be taught in place of his son.

SOURCES: Pr. 434–435. Cf. *Agudah* B. M. 118.

758

Q. The tutor of A's children loaned money to certain persons, in A's house, securing such loans by pledges. He lost some of the pledges and went away from the city before he

settled with his Gentile debtors. He left some money with B.
Now A demands the tutor's money from B because he has to
settle with the tutor's debtors for their lost pledges.

A. A can sue the tutor if he has suffered a loss because
of him; but the court cannot order B to pay to A the tutor's
money, before the rights of A against the tutor have been
established.

SOURCES: Pr. 37; Mord. Ket. 232; B. B. 674. Cf. *Terumat Hadeshen* 305;
Isserlein, *Pesakim* 64.

759 (D)

Q. A hired B to teach him the gladiatorial art. After
learning for a day, however, A changed his mind and refused
to continue his studies.

A. A must pay B the wages of an "idle worker", for a
skill is as important as a handicraft. Moreover, this particular
skill may often save a person's life, as in case one is attacked
by robbers.

SOURCES: B. P. 285, no. 335.

760

Q. A scribe was hired to copy a complete book. Is such
a scribe permitted to resign before he has completed his task?

A. A contractor, a worker hired for the completion of a
certain task and not hired by the day or week, is not permitted
to resign before his task is completed. A scribe, however, is
not permitted to resign even though he was hired for a specific
period of time, and was thus not classified as a contractor;
for the resignation of a scribe involves a definite loss of money
to the person who hired him, as a book copied by two scribes
is not uniform in appearance and, thus, commands a low price.

SOURCES: Cr. 247; L. 123; Mord. B. M. 343.

761 (D)

Q. A claims that B had promised to pay him half a *mark* for accompanying him on his ride to a certain place. He rode with B to that place, and now demands his pay. B avers that the offer had been made in jest.

A. Since A acted upon B's offer, the latter cannot, now, dismiss such offer as a mere jest. However, A is not entitled to receive the full amount offered, if such amount exceeds the actual value of his services by more than one-sixth. If such is the case, A is entitled to the actual value of his services only.

This Responsum is addressed to "my relative R. Kalonymus."

SOURCES: B. p. 294 no. 372.

762

Q. Is a matchmaker entitled to collect his full fee [even if it is out of all proportion to the time and effort spent in consummating the match]?

A. A person who is not a professional matchmaker is entitled to compensation in accordance with the time and effort spent in concluding the match. But, a professional matchmaker is entitled to his full fee since he could have earned the same amount had he devoted his time and energy to another match. However, even the professional matchmaker is not entitled to his full fee unless it be almost certain that he could have earned the same amount from another match. Thus, the case came before me of a matchmaker whom a man promised a sum of money upon successfully concluding a match between himself and a certain woman. After the match was concluded and the man paid the promised sum to the matchmaker, the latter demanded a particular sum from the woman, claiming that she had also promised to pay him a fee. The woman denied his claim. I freed the woman from obligation for the following reason: Even if the woman promised a fee to the matchmaker he would not be entitled to collect it since he occupied himself with this match because of the money promised to him by her husband. The woman's promise of a fee to the matchmaker and the effort he spent as a consequence thereof, did not deprive him of any income, since his time had to be spent anyway on consummating this match.

SOURCES: L. 308. Cf. *Agudah* B. K. 140.

763 (D)

Q. A matchmaker was promised two *marks* should he succeed in concluding a certain match. He was successful in his efforts. Is he entitled to the full two *marks*?

A. The matchmaker is only entitled to reasonable compensation for the time and effort he has spent. However, if because of his preoccupation with this match, he was hindered from devoting himself to other matches (from which, it is reasonable to expect, he would have earned a similar amount), he is entitled to the two *marks*.

SOURCES: Cr. 123. Cf. Pr. 498; ibid. 708; ibid. 952; L. 308; Mord. B. K. 172; *Agudah* B. K. 140.

764

Q. R stole 100 *marks* from her husband, A, and lent them to L for investment purposes to share equally in the profits. L knew that R had stolen the money from her husband; nevertheless, she subsequently returned it to R. Now A demands his money from L.

A. Since L knew that R was a thief, she had no right to return A's money to R. Moreover, since L used A's money without his knowledge she became fully responsible for its safety, and could free herself, of this responsibility only by returning the money to A. Therefore, L must pay one hundred *marks* to A. L may not plead that she was ignorant of the law that required her to return the money to A, since ignorance of the law is no excuse. Nor can L be released from obligation because of "the market ordinance", since this ordinance does not apply to those who buy valuables which they know to be stolen property.

SOURCES: Mord. B. B. 564.

765 (D)

Q. A produced witnesses who testified to the effect that B had informed against A and had caused the latter to sustain a loss. A now demands that B's sons make good that loss.

A. Damages caused by an informer fall under the heading of *Garmi* (damages caused indirectly) for which one is not directly responsible, but is liable to be fined. The amount an informer is required to pay [usually he has to make good the damage he caused], therefore, is a mere fine for his misdeeds and does not constitute the payment of a real obligation. Since heirs are not required to pay a father's fine, B's children are free from any obligation to A. Moreover, the court should claim for B's heirs that had B been summoned to court before his death, he would have claimed that he had already made good A's losses.

SOURCES: Pr. 460.

766 (D)

Regarding C's claim that A informed against him and caused him a loss of eighteen schillings, which claim A denies, A must take an oath in support of his denial. If a Gentile witness supports C's claim, A must take the oath in the presence of the Gentile. A must also take an oath to the effect that he caused B no damage by informing against him. B, however, need take no oath since he caused A no damage by informing against him. However, if it is true that B spoke to the overlord in the manner described in your query on the opposite page, the community must duly punish B.

SOURCES: Cr. 231. Cf. Maharil, *Responsa* 86.

767 (D)

Q. A claims that Leah delivered him into the hands of Gentiles and caused him a loss of one pound and five pounds. [Leah denies his claim].

A. Leah must take an oath to the effect that she caused A no loss.

SOURCES: Am II, 142.

768

Q. How can married women who turned informers be punished?

A. All punishments for sin prescribed by the *Torah* are applicable to women as well as to men. Therefore, a ban of excommunication may be put upon women informers. If they possess property over which their husbands exercise no rights, the injured party may collect damages from such property. He may also collect damages from their *Niksei Melug* [a wife's property, the income of which belongs to the husband although he is not responsible for the loss of the property itself] which may immediately be transferred to the claimant. The husband, however, will continue to reap the income of such property until his death or the death of his wife (whichever comes first) or until they are divorced.

SOURCES: Pr. 599; Mord. B. K. 90-1; *Agudah* B. K. 105.

769

He who summoned his friend before a Gentile court without first receiving permission from the community or the Jewish court, even though he merely forced his friend to abide by Jewish law, is guilty of a misdemeanor and deserves to be flogged. However, if the defendant has retaliated by complaining before the Gentile court against the plaintiff and thus damaged the latter's interests, he is not guiltless. A Jewish court should determine which of the two litigants has caused the greater damage, and should force that litigant to pay the difference to the other.

Sources: B. p. 323 no. 978. Cf. *Agudah* Sheb. 22.

770

Q. A was ready to obey the decision of a Jewish court regarding his dispute with B; nevertheless, B informed against him before the overlord and, consequently, A was forced to pay one pound to the [Gentile] judge. B admitted having informed against A and having asked (the overlord) to retain A's valuables till A answer his summons to [a Jewish] court and abide by its decision.

A. B had no right to force A to abide by the decision of a Jewish court through the intervention of a Gentile, unless the community or the court instructed him to do so. No person is permitted to take the law into his own hands except when he seeks to retrieve his own particular article. Therefore, if witnesses testify to the amount A lost through B's unlawful act, B must make good such loss. But if no such witnesses exist, and B claims not to know of any loss sustained by A, he may take an oath in support of his claim and thus be free from obligation.

(R. Meir alludes in an obscure manner to various claims and counterclaims of the two parties, the exact meaning of which is hard to determine. I. A.)

SOURCES: Cr. 185 b; L. 334. Cf. Menahem of Merseburg, *Nimmukim* (58).

771

Q. A (R. Ephraim) brought a complaint against B (R. Joel) before a Gentile court in order to compel B to answer A's summons before a Jewish court and abide by its decision. The Gentile court released B from all obligation. B, however, angered at A's act, turned informer against him and was responsible for his losing some money. When the matter came before us, we decided that B must compensate A for the damage he caused him. However, some people believe that B ought to be free from obligation since he acted while in the heat of anger. They state that a *takkanah* of the communities frees from obligation a person who in the heat of anger against a friend turned informer, retaliates by informing against him. Is our decision correct? Signed: R. Isaac and his court.

A. Your decision is correct. Although A committed a wrong by summoning B to a Gentile court — it is true that A only wanted to force B to abide by the ruling of a Jewish court, but he had no right to do so through the intervention of a Gentile court without the consent of the community or of the foremost authorities of the land — and ought to be flogged or be fined, the amount of the fine to be determined by the Rabbis of this country, nevertheless B had no right to inform against A and, therefore, must compensate him for his loss. It is true that we deal harshly with an informer, that we are even permitted to kill him, and that A committed the first wrong by turning informer against his friend B.* But, a person is in the

---

* A person who summoned a Jew before a Gentile court was considered an informer.

status of an informer while he threatens, or is on his way, to inform against his fellow, and not after he has already done so; for, while a person is on his way to inform against his friend, the amount of damage he might cause by his act is unlimited; since after a Jew is delivered into the hands of Gentiles they bring false accusations upon him until his very life is in danger. Therefore, as a precautionary measure, we are permitted to damage, maim, and even kill, the informer in order to prevent him from carrying out his evil intentions. But after the informer has completed his work, the extent of the damage is known. While the informer is obliged to pay for the damage he has caused and may be punished or fined for his crime, we are not permitted to damage indiscriminately his property, his interests, or his person. The *takkanah* of the communities referred to, probably frees a person who informs (against an informer) in the heat of anger from the special fines which communities usually impose upon those who violate public policy, but does not free him from responsibility for the actual damage he has caused by his act.

SOURCES: L. 247–8; Mord. B. K. 195; Tesh. Maim. to *Nezikin*, 15. Cf. *Beth Joseph* to *Hoshen Mishpat* 388; Weil, *Responsa* 147; Moses Minz, *Responsa* 44; Isserlein, *Pesakim* 208.

772

Q. A, a convert to Judaism, was arrested. The Jews, B, C, D, and E, who were summoned to testify under oath as to A's identity, were threatened with confiscation of their property, if they refused to tell the truth. They, therefore, admitted that A was a convert, and avoided the taking of a false oath. Luckily, A escaped being burned at the stake (which is the fate of converts to Judaism whenever they are detected) and suffered only a financial loss. Now A demands that B, C, D, and E make good the loss that befell him owing to their testimony.

A. B, C, D, and E must repay A for his losses sustained because of their testimony. Their testimony involved A's life, and their duty was to disregard the possible monetary loss to themselves and save A's life, even though it would involve the taking of an apparently false oath. Under duress one is permitted to swear to a statement which is apparently false and, then, modify that statement in one's thoughts so that it is no longer false; or one may completely nullify the false oath by a whispered statement. Many Jews resort to this practice whenever they are forced by their overlords to take an oath that they will not move out of the overlord's town.

R. Meir expresses his astonishment that A escaped being burned at the stake, since not even one out of a thousand (in such circumstances) ever escapes such a fate.

SOURCES: Pr. 103; cf. Cr. 54.

773

A claimed that B, in having declared himself ready to help a Gentile, his antagonist, had caused him a loss of sixteen pounds; for A, fearing B, had to settle with the Gentile, thus sustaining the loss.

R. Meir absolved B from any obligation to A. Since B had not actually taken an oath on the Gentile's behalf, he was only a passive cause of A's loss, which is a lesser degree of responsibility even than that of an indirect cause.

R. Meir further decided that when a Gentile chooses two Jewish witnesses in his litigation with a Jew, and the latter agrees to admit in evidence the testimony of these two (in the court of the land), they may testify on the Gentile's behalf, even though the (other) Jews protest against such action. Once having been accepted by the two parties to the litigation, their oath would not add anything.

SOURCES: P. 311.

774 (D)

Q. A says that B, his father-in-law, informed A's Gentile creditors of A's intention to leave town stealthily and thus caused him a loss of twenty *marks*. B categorically denies A's charge.

A. A should clarify his use of the term "loss". If he means thereby that he was forced to repay the money he owed to his creditors, this cannot be termed a loss, for, although B should not have warned the Gentiles, since he was under no obligation to do so, A was under obligation to repay his debts to the Gentiles. Had he successfully evaded payment, he would have committed a sin. Therefore, B is free from obligation. But, if the Gentile creditors, upon learning of A's intention to abscond with their money, trumped up charges against him so that he was forced to pay more than what he owed them, and if A is positive that B informed the Gentiles, B must take an oath in the synagogue denying A's charge. If the Gentiles report that B informed them, B must take the oath in the presence of the Gentiles. But, if subsequently to his conflict with his creditors A gave B a writ of remission, B is now free from obligation since such writ includes all claims.

SOURCES: Cr. 35. Cf. Menahem of Merseburg, *Nimmukim* (65).

775

Q. A claims that B caused him a loss of twenty *marks* by accusing him before the authorities of having bitten B's finger. B claims that A bit his finger fifteen years ago; that he, B, did not complain to the authorities; that the case was reported to the authorities while he, B, was still in the heat of anger; and that he can prove, through witnesses, that A had previously released him of all obligation in this matter.

A. An opinion is prevalent among the people that a

takkanah of the communities frees one from any responsibility, if, after suffering bodily injury at the hand of his neighbor, and while still in the heat of anger, he retaliates with force, or even turns informer against him. If such *takkanah* exists, in order to punish severely the person who began the disturbance, or if B's claim is true that A released him from obligation in this matter, B owes nothing to A. But the *takkanah* of the communities probably frees the assaulted person, who retaliates in the heat of anger, from the special fines which communities usually impose upon offenders against public policy, but does not free him from responsibility for the injuries he inflicted upon the assailant. The judges, therefore, must evaluate the five compensations (prescribed to the injured person by the Talmud) for biting B's finger. If B caused A a greater loss than the amount estimated, the former must pay the difference to the latter.

Sources: Pr. 994; Tesh. Maim. to *Nezikin*, 15b; Hayyim Or Zarua, *Responsa* 142. Cf. Weil, *Responsa* 28.

776

Q. The father of A provoked a quarrel with B who vigorously defended himself and made the nose of his assailant bleed. A became infuriated upon seeing his father's blood and informed against B causing him a loss of money. Some are of the opinion that A should be freed from any obligation to B since he acted out of love and respect for his father. R. Samuel was supposed to be a judge in this case. But some are trying to disqualify R. Samuel for the reason that he is host, or landlord, to one of the litigants.

A. A must make good the loss he caused B, for A had no right to inform against B regardless of what B did to A's father. R. Samuel is permitted to act as judge in the case;

for the Talmud does not include the landlord of one of the litigants among those who are disqualified to act as judges.

Sources: Pr. 717.

777

Q. A struck B who became highly incensed and informed against A so that he sustained damages. Some persons maintain that B is free from obligation since he acted in the heat of righteous anger, and that this is in accordance with the custom of the communities.

A. The logic of those who maintain that B is free from obligation, is faulty. If a person should strike another and inflict very slight injury upon him and the victim would retaliate by informing against the aggressor and cause him a loss of a thousand *marks*, would anyone hold the informer guiltless? Indeed not; but we must estimate the damage caused by the aggressor and that caused by the informer, and make the one who caused the greater damage pay the difference to the other. In actual cases I always render decisions in accordance with this rule.

This Responsum is addressed to Rabbi Menahem of Würzburg.

Sources: *Mordecai Hagadol*, p. 258d.

778

Q. D invited A and his household to a meal. A's household included his servant and protégé N. During the meal a quarrel broke out between D and A and the latter's men belabored D. Whereupon D went to the magistrate and lodged a complaint against A and the members of A's household. The magistrate, however, was told that A was not at fault, but that the full blame was upon A's household. Consequently, the magistrate,

who owed A six pounds, dismissed A with a mere warning
that he would hold A responsible for the misdeeds of the members of his household, and would expect A to make amends
therefor. D and his relative, B, however, later returned to the
magistrate and placed the blame squarely on A's shoulders.
Thereupon, the magistrate brought false charges against A,
and, as a result, A was forced to cancel the magistrate's debt.
The fact that D and B lodged complaints with the magistrate
is attested to by witnesses. A, therefore, demands that B refund
him the six pounds he thus lost through B's informing against
him. B contends that one, C, too has informed against A, and
that a Gentile witness would bear out this contention.

A. If it is known that D had complained to the magistrate
before B informed against A, even though at that time the
magistrate dismissed A with a mild warning, B is free from
obligation, for the extent of the damage D had done to A, cannot be ascertained. The possibilities are that the magistrate
would already have found cause to cancel his debt to A. However, if D had not lodged his complaint with the magistrate
before he was accompanied by B, the latter would be responsible for half the damage. Even if D is poor and thus unable
to pay his share, B is responsible for only half the damage.
If in your community, however, D is not to be held responsible
for his deed — for he was hurt and sorely grieved, and "a man
is not taken to account for what he does in his distress (B.B.
16b)" — B is to be held responsible for the full damage. The
damage, however, is not the face value of the loan by A to the
magistrate, for some loans, improperly secured, are worth much
less than the amount originally lent. Therefore, we must ascer-
tain the actual value of the above loan before we can determine
the extent of the damage done by B. However, if the actual
value of the loan is not ascertainable, but witnesses have heard
the magistrate admit that he owed six pounds to A, the latter

should state under oath to what extent his interests were damaged by B, and collect such amount from B. Although this
procedure is irregular — the ordinance introduced against
a robber, does not apply to an informer (B. K. 62a) — it was
accepted for the sake of social order, since the amount of damage
caused by an informer could never have been proven by un-
impeachable evidence. B's contention regarding C's interference is of no consequence, since the damage was done by
the time C appeared before the magistrate.

SOURCES: Mord. B. K. 55. Cf. Weil, *Responsa* 28; ibid. 133; Moses Minz,
Responsa 44; *Terumat Hadeshen* 342.

779

Q. A young man, A, the son of a wealthy man became
impoverished. He sought, however, to gain power and influence
in community affairs by slander and sycophancy. After the
new king [Pedro III] ascended the throne, A increased his
nefarious activities. In spite of warnings and threats he refused
to abandon his criminal career. When [the leaders of] the
communities of the three kingdoms, Catalonia, Valencia, and
Aragon, were summoned before the king, they were truly convinced that A had lodged information against them. They
begged him to desist at least on this occasion, and though at
first he agreed to do so, he came running after them and stubbornly insisted on accompanying them [on their way to the
king]. The deputies of the communities realizing that A was
an "assailant" (רודף), took council with the noble brothers,
Joseph and Moses Abrabalia who held high office at the Royal
Court and together they told the king of A's criminal activities
and expressed their opinion that he was deserving of death.
The king, who loved justice, arrested A and put him in chains.
A royal judge took the depositions of the advocates and representatives of the communities. Yet, I remained aloof from

the whole affair until several communities, together with A's relatives, demanded that a royal mandate be obtained empowering the aged Rabbi Jonah of Girona, the nephew of Rabbi Jonah Gerundi, and myself to become the judges in this case. I refused to become involved in this affair and mete out strict justice, unless I could effect an amicable arrangement of the matter. I warned A's relatives not to apply for a royal mandate, for I wanted to act as conciliator rather than judge. They, however, rejected my plan, and without my knowledge obtained the royal mandate. It seems, therefore, that A's relatives themselves, because he had caused them a great deal of suffering, were anxious that he be put to death. Finally the king summoned Rabbi Jonah (and myself) and commanded us to gather the evidence. The king ordered the communities to pronounce the ban against anyone knowing anything about this matter who did not report it to the Jewish court of his town; he further ordered the courts to send the depositions thus taken to Rabbi Jonah and to myself, and that we in turn report our findings to him or to his appointed judge. We procrastinated and delayed for a whole year in an effort to bring about an amicable settlement with the communities, but our efforts met with no success, since the communities feared that A would bring misfortune upon them. We even asked the king for an audience, but were refused. The delay in the proceedings incensed the king and he ordered us sent to him in chains — the king was then in a distant part of his kingdom — if we did not announce our decision. A's brother also constantly urged us to comply with the king's demand and announce our decision, for it was better that A alone be executed rather than have the whole family die with him. After much labor and great suffering we were forced to give our opinion to the king that according to his [the king's?] own statement and the testimony gathered by the various Jewish courts, A was deserving of death. I am appending herewith the depositions of the various witnesses who testified at the Jewish courts in the presence of A's representatives and in the presence of the deputies of the various communities. The king, then, sent our opinion to the royal judge in order that he pass judgment on A in accordance with it. A, however, claimed to possess further evidence of his innocence. The royal judge permitted him to argue his case before the representatives of the various communities, and thereupon we withdrew from the case. Meanwhile, the royal judge died. A short time afterwards, however, the king sent his officer to execute A. He was taken to the square in front of the Jewish burial-ground in Barcelona, where the veins of his two arms were opened, and he bled to death. Three years have since elapsed. The noble *parnas* R. Joseph Abrabalia, the representative of his people at the Royal Court, meanwhile passed away. One of A's brothers, however, thinking that the communities would now find no protector nor advocate of their interests at Court, rose in his brother's place and complained before the king's judges that we had erred in our decision since according to Jewish law we had no right to pronounce the death sentence against anyone. He contended that the Jews had forfeited this right long ago according to their own law; that at the time they still excercised that right, only a court of twenty-three judges had the right to pronounce the death sentence, and such a court had to order the witnesses to testify in the presence of the accused. Indeed, this accuser was silenced. But in order that no other advocate for A's family may appear to press charges before the king's judges, I shall set forth the reasons that prompted us to give the opinion mentioned above to the king.

a) A was a "pursuer" with criminal intentions, and such a "pursuer" might be put to death summarily without a court trial. This law holds true today and is applicable even outside of the Holy Land.

b) An informer whose nefarious activities are "well known" may be put to death even after his work has been accomplished, and putting him to death, even without a trial, is considered a praiseworthy act. The term "well known" in such cases, is used to describe a fact when many persons are aware it is true, although proof has not been established before a court of twenty-three ordained judges. Thus our great scholars who compiled codes repeat the law that a person whose activity as an informer is "well known" should be put to death summarily, and that no mercy be shown him even in our times. If the term "well known" would mean "a truth established before a court of twenty-three ordained judges", it would have been meaningless when referring to the present age since we have no ordained judges, and the phrase could not thus be used by the codifiers.

c) The custom of summarily putting to death any "well-known" informer is firmly established in many countries of the diaspora. Maimonides testified to the fact that this custom was accepted throughout the cities of the west. It is daily practiced in Castile and originally became accepted in that country by the advice of great talmudic authorities. In the kingdom of Aragon, and in the previous generation and even in our own time in Catalonia itself, informers were put to death. Were we uncertain regarding the talmudic law governing such cases, we would be justified in putting informers to death because of the custom of the country.

d) A court may put a person to death as an emergency measure even when he is not deserving of death according to talmudic law. The danger involved in permitting sycophants to go unpunished is well known.

e) Even in criminal cases a court may admit into evidence testimony of witnesses in the absence of the accused. This may be done whenever it is impossible to have the witnesses face the accused.

f) Many of the witnesses testified in the presence of A's advocates, which should be equivalent to testifying in A's presence, since in legal matters a person's deputy takes the place of the person himself.

You, our Rabbis, should silence all those who cast aspersions upon our action in the aforementioned matter. You are not on trial yourselves, and therefore your opinion will carry weight and no one will dare oppose it. Signed: Solomon b. Adret.

A. Your decision is correct. A person who turned informer against his neighbor, and repeated this nefarious practice on three different occasions, according to the testimony of witnesses, should be put to death, and he who hastened to execute him is to be commended. Although Maimonides ruled that we might not put an informer to death after he has already committed his nefarious deed, this law applies to a person who turned informer only on a single occasion. A habitual informer, however, one who repeated his criminal practice on three different occasions, should unquestionably be put to death even after the criminal deed was committed. Your words, therefore, are correct in every respect.

SOURCES: J. Q. R. o. s. VIII (1895–6) pp. 228–38. Cf. Neuman vol. 1, p. 133 f.

780

Q. A lent money to a Gentile at a definite rate of interest. B, then, approached the Gentile and said: "I shall let you have the money and charge you a smaller rate of interest than A. Take my money and pay him off."

A. It is doubtful whether B caused A a loss of money, since A may find another borrower for his money as soon as he receives it from the Gentile. Even if B definitely caused A a loss of money, he did so indirectly; therefore, B is under no obligation to A. However, B acted unethically and should be denounced and called *rashah* (wicked).

SOURCES: Cr. 59; Pr. 148; L. 375.

781

Q. A Gentile pledged a horse with C. D lent money to the Gentile who redeemed the horse from C and gave it to D as a pledge. Is D to be called "a wicked person"?

A. D is not to be called "a wicked person" if he did not know for what purpose the Gentile was borrowing money from him; or even if the Gentile expressly told him the use to which this loan would be put. But, if D approached the Gentile first, offering him money to redeem his horse from C, D may be called "a wicked person", is disqualified as a witness, and is barred from taking an oath, until he repents.

SOURCES: L. 305.

782 (D)

Q. A thief came to A's house and sold him some gold. A, then, passed B's house and heard people say that the thief had money in his pocket. B said to his friends, that anyone who would rob the thief of his money would lose nothing since the latter was afraid of being caught. B further remarked that he would suggest to his Gentile customer, a chieftain, to rob the thief and then repay him (B) the three schillings the chieftain owed him. A warned B not to do so lest it become known that he, A, bought the stolen goods from the thief. A further warned B that he would hold him responsible for any loss he might suffer because of B's being involved in this matter. B, however, did not heed A's warning, saying that his Gentile customer, the chieftain, was his friend and that he would ask him not to demand from the thief any explanation after taking his money. After B's customer robbed the thief and released him, the latter was arrested by the authorities and was forced to confess to whom he sold the stolen gold, which caused A a heavy loss. A, therefore, demands that B make good that loss.

A. B's act was only an indirect cause of A's loss; therefore, B owes nothing to A.

SOURCES: Pr. 844.

783

Q. A had Gentiles arrest his opponents. One of his opponents resisted arrest; he fled, but was pursued and killed by the Gentiles. A claims that he merely intended to coerce his opponents into answering his summons to court.

A. A is fully responsible for the murder of his opponent, for when a Jew falls into the clutches of Gentiles, his life as well as his property is in jeopardy; he can expect from them neither pity, mercy, nor restraint. The Gentiles are happy to hold a Jew in their power; and, especially when commissioned by another Jew, their cruelty is boundless. They consider it entirely legitimate and even praiseworthy to rob, maim, and even murder a Jew. Therefore, a person who delivers a fellow Jew into the hands of Gentiles is directly responsible for all their cruelties. Thus A is to be considered as much a murderer as if he killed his opponent with his own hands. No punishment is too great for him, no penance too harsh, and no manner of self-torture too severe. Let him be flogged and publicly disgraced, let him wander as an exile in foreign lands, let his face become black through fasting and self-torture for a year or two, and seek atonement for his crime. I subscribe to any punishment you may impose upon him, no matter how severe; and I would agree to still sterner measures but not to milder ones.

SOURCES: Cr. 214; *Mordecai Hagadol,* p. 248, margin; Hayyim Or Zarua, *Responsa* 141; cf. ibid. 25; Mahril, *Responsa* 86; Weil, *Responsa* 28; ibid. 111, ibid. 147; Menahem of Merseburg, *Nimmukim* (61).

784

Q. During the massacre of the Jews of Koblenz, A's wife and four sons begged him to kill them before they fell into the hands of the enemies. A did so, and was ready to kill himself, but Gentiles saved his life. He inquired of Rabbi Meir whether he was required to do penance for his sin.

A. I find great difficulty in deciding this case. A person is indeed permitted to take his own life for the sanctification of God's name; but whether one is permitted to take the lives of others, even for a deeply pious reason, is questionable. However, such an act became widely accepted as permissible, and we have heard of many great authorities who martyrized their sons and daughters. Even Rabbi Kalonymus did so, as he later lamented in a dirge which begins with the words: "I say, look away from me [in abhorrence]. . . ," [recited in the synagogue on the ninth day of *Ab*]. Thus anyone who should require A to do penance, would thereby vilify the pious men of former days.

SOURCES: Berl. p. 346; Sinai VII (1943), 5–6, 54.

785 (D)

Q. The Torah prescribes that when a blasphemer is to be executed the witnesses must lay their hands on the head of the blasphemer before he is stoned. Why does not the Torah prescribe the same procedure for the execution of those who are punished for having committed other sins?

A. There are many laws and ceremonies connected with executions for which no logical reason is apparent. The laying of hands on the blasphemer's head serves to emphasize the fact that he alone is the cause of his death. Since he dared to stretch out his hand against God himself, the cause of his death is ceremonially emphasized.

SOURCES: Pr. 431.

786

Q. Rashi, in his interpretation of the talmudic statement of Menahot 6b (s. v. וכי תימא), implies that after Aaron was appointed to the priesthood non-priests were excluded from serving even at high-places. How, then, did Manoah and Samuel personally offer up sacrifices on high-places? Moreover, [Midrash] Shoher Tob states that Samuel was guilty of three transgressions in making his burnt offering: a) he had no right to act as priest, b) he made the offering at the wrong time, and c) he made the offering on a high-place. The last statement thus supports Rashi's opinion.

A. The aforesaid opinion of Rashi was refuted by the Tosaphot (Manahot 6b, s. v. וכי תימא) who cited as proof the priestly activities of Samuel and Saul, and the explicit talmudic statement in Zebahim 118a. However, although non-priests were permitted to act as priests in offering up sacrifices on high-places, Levites were never permitted to do the work of priests (Erekin, 11b). The transgression of Samuel, therefore, consisted in acting as priest though he was a Levite.

SOURCES: Am II, 218.

787

Q. What constitutes the merit of emigrating to the Holy Land?

A. My knowledge on this subject does not go beyond the talmudic statement (Ket. 111a) that a person who emigrates to the Holy Land is absolved from sin. This applies to a person who commits no sins in the Holy Land proper, and who fulfils all the commandments appertaining to the Holy

Land. However, the punishment for a sin committed there is more severe than that for a sin committed elsewhere; for the Lord watches over the Holy Land more diligently, and the land itself can bear no sinners. For this reason the Holy Land is now desolate and contains no walled cities. Therefore, it is to those who go to the Holy Land and intend to be reckless in their behavior and particularly to quarrel there that the verse applies: "But when ye entered ye defiled My land (Jer. 2, 7)." When, however, a person emigrates to the Holy Land with sincere intentions and conducts himself there in piety and saintliness, his reward is unlimited; provided, of course, that he possess sufficient means of support there.

2) *Q.* Does a person buried in Palestine escape the *hibbut hakkever* (agonies of the grave)?

A. I do not know.

3) *Q.* Why did the Amoraim fail to move to the Holy Land?

A. Such an act would have seriously interferred with their studies, since in the Holy Land they would have to spend much time in finding means of support. A person is permitted even to leave the Holy Land in order to study with his teacher (Erub. 47a); therefore, one is surely not enjoined to break off his uninterrupted studies in the Diaspora and emigrate to the Holy Land where he would find his means of support with great difficulty.

4) *Q.* What is the meaning of the talmudic statement (Ket. 110b): A person who dwells in the Diaspora is as one who has no God?

A. God's presence is primarily concentrated in the Holy Land. Therefore, a person's prayers there ascend directly to His throne.

SOURCES: P. 14–5; *Tashbetz*, 561–5; *Kol Bo*, 127; *Mordecai Hagadol* p. 183d; *Orhot Hayyim* II, pp. 611–12. Cf. Moses Minz, *Responsa* 79.

788

Q. We eat peeled eggs which are inscribed with Hebrew letters. Why do we not fear the evil spirit that attacks persons who eat peeled eggs (Niddah, 17a)? Is it because evil spirits are rare in these parts?

A. Evil spirits are probably very rare in these parts, or possibly the holy writing on the eggs wards off such spirits.

Sources: Mord. Shabb. 461.

ABBREVIATIONS AND ABBREVIATED TITLES

Agudah — R. Alexander ha-Kohen Süsslein, ספר אגודה.

Am I — R. Meir of Rothenburg, *Responsa*, ed. Berlin, pp. 117–137.

Am II — R. Meir of Rothenburg, *Responsa*, ed. Berlin, pp. 138–244.

Asher — R. Asher b. Yehiel, שאלות ותשובות.

Asheri — R. Asher b. Yehiel, ספר האשרי.

B. or Berl. — R. Meir of Rothenburg, *Responsa*, ed. Berlin, pp. 275–347.

Beth Joseph — R. Joseph b. Ephraim Karo, בית יוסף 'ס; commentary on the ארבעה טורים of R. Jacob b. Asher.

Cr. — R. Meir of Rothenburg, *Responsa*, ed. Cremona.

Hagah — Moses b. Israel Isserles הגהות מור"ם or מפה to the שולחן ערוך of R. Joseph Karo.

Hagahot Asheri — Glosses to ספר האשרי, by R. Israel of Krems.

Hag. Maim. — R. Meir ha-Kohen, הגהות מיימוניות, on Maimonides' משנה תורה.

Hag. Mord. — Glosses to ספר המרדכי.

HUCA — Hebrew Union College Annual.

Isserlein — R. Israel b. Pethahiah Isserlein, author of תרומת הדשן 'ס, and ספר פסקים וכתבים.

JJLG — Jahrbuch der jüdisch-literarischen Gesellschaft in Frankfurt a.M.

J.Q.R. — Jewish Quarterly Review, New Series.

J.Q.R.O.S. — Jewish Quarterly Review, Old Series.

Kol Bo — כל בו 'ס of unknown authorship.

L. — R. Meir of Rothenburg, *Responsa*, ed. Lemberg.

Maharil — Jacob b. Moses ha-Levi Molin, author of ספר מהרי"ל, and שאלות ותשובות מהרי"ל.

Mahariv — R. Jacob Weil, author of שאלות ותשובות ה"ר יעקב וייל.

MGWJ — Monatsschrift für Geschichte und Wissenschaft des Judentums.

Mord. — ספר המרדכי, by Mordecai b. Hillel Ashkenazi.

Mordecai Hagadol — מרדכי הגדול, Goldschmidt Manuscript, Jewish Theological Seminary.

683

Ohalot — R. Meir's commentary to *Ohalot*, printed in the Rom edition of the Talmud.

Or Zarua — אור זרוע 'ס, by R. Isaac b. Moses of Vienna.

Orchot Hayyim — ארחות חיים 'ס, by R. Aaron ha-Kohen of Lunel.

P. — R. Meir of Rothenburg, *Responsa*, ed. Berlin, pp. 1–72.

PR. — R. Meir of Rothenburg, *Responsa*, ed. Prague.

RABIAH — Rabbi Eliezer b. Joel ha-Levi.

RASHBA I — שאלות ותשובות הרשב"א, by R. Solomon b. Abraham ibn Adret, vol. I.

RASHBAM — Rabbi Samuel b. Meir.

REJ — Revue des étude juives.

RI — Rabbi Isaac b. Samuel the elder.

Sefer Haparnes — ספר הפרנס, by R. Moses Parnas of Rothenburg.

Sefer Haterumah — ספר התרומה, by R. Baruch b. Isaac of Worms.

SEMAK — ספר מצות קטן, by R. Isaac b. Joseph of Corbeil.

Tashbetz — ספר תשבץ, by R. Samaon b. Zadok.

Terumat Hadeshen — תרומת הדשן 'ס, by R. Israel b. Pethahiah Isserlein.

TESH. MAIM. — תשובות השייכות, by R. Meir ha-Kohen, to Maimonides' משנה תורה.

Text — The digest of the Responsa of R. Meir of Rothenburg, contained in the present work, pp. 169–682.

WEIL — R. Jacob Weil, author of שאלות ותשובות ה"ר יעקב וייל.

ZGJD — Zeitschrift für die Geschichte der Juden in Deutschland (New Series, unless otherwise stated).

GLOSSARY

A

AB — Name of eleventh month.*

ADAR — name of sixth month.*

ADRAKTA — Legal permission to a creditor to trace the debtor's property for the purpose of seizing it in payment of his debt.

ASMAKHTA — A conditional stipulation, in a verbal or written contract, providing for the payment of a fine in case of nonfulfillment of a promise.

B

BAR MARION, ESTATE OF — An improved and highly valued estate which the owner would not sell for any amount.

BET-DIN — court of justice.

C

CAHORSINS — Italian money-lenders.

CAUSA MORTIS GIFT — A donation or gift by a person expecting to die, which is to take effect after his death.

E

ELUL — Name of twelfth month.*

ERUB — The incorporation of several private domains, within a certain area, into a single domain belonging to several partners within the limits of which objects may be carried on the Sabbath; the gate-like structure symbolizing such incorporation.

ERUB TABSHILIN — A symbolic act which has the effect of permitting the preparation of meals for the Sabbath on a holiday occurring on a Friday.

* Counting *Tishre* as the first month.

685

G

GAON (GEONIM) — The title of the head of a Babylonian Jewish Academy.

H

HABDALAH — The benediction over a cup of wine at the conclusion of the Sabbath and festivals.

HALAKAH — The traditional Jewish law.

HALITZAH — Drawing off the shoe of the levir; a symbolic act which has the effect of allowing the childless widow to remarry.

HALLAH — The priest's share of the dough.

HANUKKAH — The festival commemorating the Maccabean rededication of the Temple.

HAZZAN — Cantor.

HELLER — Denarii of Halle, for their value and buying power see Irving A. Agus הכתובה בתור קנה מדה לעשרם של היהודים בימי הבינים. Horeb, 1939.

HEREM — Ban, excommunication.

HOL-HAMOED — The intermediate days of a holiday.

HUPPAH — The marriage canopy.

I

IKKAR KETUBAH — The 200 *zuzim* prescribed by the Rabbis as the minimum marriage portion of a wife (100 *zuzim* for the remarrying widow or divorcee).

IYYAR — The name of the eighth month.*

K

KABLAN — A person who assumes another man's obligation unconditionally.

KADDISH — A doxology recited at the conclusion of certain prayers or in memory of the dead.

KASHER — Ritually permitted, fit for eating purposes.

KEDUSHAH — A solemn proclamation of God's holiness, recited as part of the third benediction of the *Amidah*.

KETUBAH — The portion of her husband's estate a woman is entitled to receive when widowed or divorced.

KETUBAT BENIN DIKRIN — The *ketubah* of a woman, who died before her husband, collected from his estate by her sons (who are also his sons) before the rest of the estate is divided among the heirs.

KIDDUSH — Benediction of sanctification of the Sabbath and festivals recited (usually) over a cup of wine.

KINYAN — A symbolic act which makes an agreement binding.

KOHEN (KOHANIM) — A descendant from the priestly family of Aaron.

L

LUG (LUGIN) — A liquid measure.

M

MAFTIR — One who concludes the reading from the Law; the portion of the Prophets read after the portion of the Law.

MARK — A monetary unit containing eight ounces of silver; for its value and buying power see Irving A. Agus, ibid.

MEZUZAH — A rolled up piece of parchment containing a portion of the Shema and fixed on the door-post.

MIGGO — An alternative claim that the litigant could have put forth (if he wanted to lie), one that would have given him greater advantage than his present claim.

MINAH — An ancient weight or sum of money, of similar silver content as the medieval pound. Cf. Irving A. Agus, ibid.

MINHA — Evening service.

MINYAN — A quorum of ten adult males required for congregational services.

MITZVAH — A meritorious deed, a religious or charitable action.

N

NIDDAH — A menstruating woman, period of menstrual flow.

NIKSE MELUG — A wife's property, the income of which belongs to the husband although he is not responsible for the loss of, or damage to, the property itself.

NIKSE ZON BARZEL — A wife's property held by her husband who is fully responsible for its loss or deterioration.

NISSAN — Name of the seventh month.*

O

ORLAH — The fruit of trees of the first three years after planting.

P

PARNAS (IM) — An officer or leader of a community.
PIYYUT (IM) — Liturgic poem.
PROSBOL — A document nullifying the Sabbatical cancellation of debts.
PURIM — Feast of Esther.

R

RESPONSA — Written replies by great talmudic scholars to questions
   of Jewish Law.
ROSH HASHANAH — New Year's holiday.
ROSH HODESH — New Moon; first of the month.

S

SEAH — A dry measure.
SHABUOT — Feast of Weeks; Pentecost.
SIDDUR — Prayer-book.
SOLIDUS (SOLIDI) — A schilling.
SUCCOTH — Feast of Tabernacles.

T

TAKKANAH — An ordinance, an enactment, or a statute.
TALITH — Prayer-shawl.
TAMMUZ — Name of the tenth month.*
TEFAH — A handbreadth.
TEREFAH — Forbidden food.
TERUMAH — The priest's share of the produce.
TORAH — The Law.
TOSAPHOT — The glosses to the commentary of Rashi on the Talmud.

U

USUCAPION — Undisputed possession of real estate (for a period of
   three years) as proof of rightful acquisition.

Y

YAALE VEYABO — A special prayer included in the *Amidah* on holy days and *Rosh Hodesh*.

YOM KIPPUR — The Day of Atonement.

Z

ZIZITH — The four tassels or fringes on the prayer shawl.

ZUZ (IM) — An ancient coin. Cf. Irving A. Agus, ibid.

LIST OF CORRESPONDING NUMBERS OF THE VARIOUS PRINTED EDITIONS AND THE PRESENT TEXT

CREMONA

Responsum No.		Text No.	Responsum No.		Text No.
1	—	454	38	—	673
2	—	756	39	—	59
3	—	505, 747	40	—	2, 232
4	—	505	41	—	3, 16, 50
5	—	47	42	—	32
6	—	594	43	—	701
7	—	138, 448, 618	44	—	49
8	—	12, 135, 448	45	—	72
9	—	604	46	—	73, 107
10	—	552	47	—	605
11	—	496	48	—	420, 561
12	—	624	49	—	562, 612
13	—	630	50	—	629
14	—	106	51	—	58
15	—	624	52	—	475
16	—	624	53	—	583
20	—	48	54	—	585
21	—	11, 230	55	—	93
22	—	207	56	—	440
23	—	506	57	—	131
24	—	216	58	—	198
25	—	696	59	—	780
26	—	722, 726	60	—	196
27	—	722	61	—	145
28	—	726	62	—	177
29	—	392	63	—	498,499
30	—	342	64	—	499
31	—	258	65	—	384
32	—	573	66	—	26, 214
33	—	573	67	—	695
34	—	633	68	—	66
35	—	774	69	—	42
36	—	282	70	—	648
37	—	4	76	—	466

Responsum No.		Text No.	Responsum No.		Text No.
81	—	381	131	—	324
82	—	531, 686	140	—	349
84	—	442	141	—	14
85	—	354, 699	150	—	300
86	—	255	151	—	262
87	—	199	156	—	559
88	—	339	157	—	411
93	—	306	158	—	523
94	—	306	159	—	264
95	—	323	160	—	397
96	—	366	161	—	245
97	—	671	162	—	476
98	—	395	164	—	494
99	—	489	166	—	441
100	—	56	167	—	430, 566
101	—	203	171	—	623
102	—	413	172	—	687
103	—	404	175	—	434
104	—	723	176	—	434
105	—	565	178	—	43
106	—	277	179	—	43
107	—	275	180	—	679
108	—	213	183	—	46
109	—	204	185	—	319, 770
110	—	483	186	—	651
111	—	554	187	—	492
112	—	38	188	—	591
113	—	484	189	—	672
114	—	698	190	—	534
115	—	683	191	—	755
116	—	692	192	—	331
117	—	283	193	—	517
118	—	219	194	—	254
119	—	740	195	—	348
120	—	451	196	—	652
121	—	558	197	—	652
122	—	668	198	—	197
123	—	763	199	—	373
124	—	150, 165	200	—	51, 110
125	—	752	202	—	658
126	—	286	205	—	332
127	—	324	206	—	677
128	—	324	207	—	418
129	—	324	208	—	510
130	—	324	209	—	21

Responsum No.		Text No.	Responsum No.		Text No.
210	—	263	261	—	474
211	—	427	262	—	592
212	—	704	263	—	328
214	—	783	264	—	369
215	—	391	265	—	730
216	—	226	266	—	334
217	—	284	267	—	366
218	—	285	268	—	305
219	—	449	269	—	725
220	—	681	270	—	479
221	—	569	271	—	299
222	—	550	272	—	707
223	—	610	273	—	703
224	—	428	274	—	398
227	—	452	275	—	365
230	—	401	276	—	656
231	—	766	277	—	656
233	—	122	278	—	388
234	—	513, 514	279	—	388
235	—	520	280	—	402
236	—	526	281	—	403, 416
237	—	497	282	—	389
238	—	502, 503	283	—	697
239	—	501	284	—	697
240	—	504	285	—	183
241	—	521	286	—	380
242	—	521	287	—	368
243	—	358	288	—	363
244	—	383	289	—	390
245	—	421	290	—	636
246	—	410	291	—	298
247	—	760	292	—	536
248	—	289	293	—	470
249	—	10	294	—	490
250	—	327	295	—	711
251	—	682	296	—	486
252	—	318	297	—	480
253	—	148	298	—	182
254	—	148	299	—	166
255	—	148	300	—	166
256	—	659	301	—	712
257	—	139	302	—	626
258	—	649	303	—	626
259	—	731	304	—	310
260	—	340	305	—	609

Responsum No.		Text No.	Responsum No.		Text No.
306	—	609	312	—	222
308	—	705	313	—	223
309	—	149	314	—	237
310	—	749	315	—	733
311	—	495			

PRAGUE EDITION

Responsum No.		Text No.	Responsum No.		Text No.
8	—	530	66	—	82, 89
13	—	36	67	—	34
18	—	225	68	—	5
19	—	269	69	—	212
20	—	239	70	—	35
25	—	109	71	—	27
26	—	109	72	—	751
27	—	109	73	—	201
28	—	498, 499	74	—	193
29	—	499	75	—	194
30	—	384	76	—	80
31	—	42, 66	77	—	752
32	—	648	78	—	228
33	—	113	79	—	248
34	—	677	81	—	297
35	—	651	82	—	291
36	—	492	83	—	485
37	—	758	84	—	684
38	—	591	85	—	753
39	—	576	86	—	431
40	—	30	87	—	376
41	—	30	88	—	654
42	—	31	89	—	60
46	—	405, 602	90	—	537
49	—	46	91	—	454
50	—	258, 422	92	—	47, 505
57	—	81	93	—	618
58	—	112	94	—	38
59	—	17, 94	95	—	77
60	—	74	96	—	43
61	—	231	97	—	261, 363
65	—	45	98	—	242

Responsum No.		Text No.	Responsum No.		Text No.
99	—	362	225	—	469
100	—	73, 107, 605	227	—	569
101	—	594	228	—	303
102	—	624	229	—	458
103	—	772	230	—	307
104	—	578	231	—	598, 599
105	—	607	232	—	288
106	—	563	233	—	539
107	—	13	234	—	540
108	—	12	235	—	541
109	—	448	236	—	542
110	—	15, 649	237	—	509
115	—	422	238	—	509
116	—	487	239	—	509
117	—	333	242	—	411
118	—	538	243	—	342
119	—	664	244	—	342
121	—	103	245	—	670
130	—	633	247	—	670
131	—	546	248	—	692
132	—	183	250	—	280
133	—	270	251	—	280
136	—	672	254	—	614
137	—	534, 755	271	—	736
139	—	22	272	—	478
140	—	743	276	—	471
141	—	744	277	—	627
142	—	75, 132	284	—	325
143	—	506	285	—	255
145	—	440	286	—	199
146	—	131	294	—	86
147	—	198	295	—	57, 83
148	—	780	296	—	417
149	—	196	307	—	608
150	—	145	309	—	233
166	—	418	317	—	79
170	—	646	321	—	496
176	—	358	322	—	11, 230
201	—	717	324	—	207
204	—	179	325	—	621
210	—	442	326	—	629
211	—	354	327	—	452
212	—	699	330	—	28
213	—	708	331	—	553
224	—	368	332	—	406

Responsum No.		Text No.	Responsum No.		Text No.
333	—	407	500	—	167
334	—	350	519	—	269
342	—	187	520	—	269
343	—	187	521	—	414
344	—	659	522	—	415
351	—	214	523	—	402
352	—	26	524	—	403
354	—	142	525	—	416
359	—	545	526	—	389
371	—	250	527	—	543
382	—	595	528	—	543
420	—	673	529	—	7
421	—	673	530	—	8
422	—	59	531	—	100
423	—	232	532	—	39
424	—	3	541	—	197
425	—	2	543	—	657
426	—	16	544	—	396
427	—	50	547	—	737
429	—	115	548	—	737
430	—	237	562	—	382
431	—	785	569	—	380
432	—	274	574	—	302
434	—	757	575	—	647
435	—	757	586	—	273
436	—	238	592	—	703
437	—	235	593	—	706
438	—	63	595	—	173
439	—	118	599	—	768
404	—	119	604	—	229
441	—	65	605	—	181
442	—	313	606	—	623
443	—	313	612	—	254
444	—	1	614	—	97
447	—	727	615	—	101
460	—	765	617	—	95
475	—	689	620	—	116
488	—	747	621	—	117
490	—	624	622	—	152
491	—	387	625	—	159
492	—	383	630	—	153
493	—	166	635	—	9
494	—	166	637	—	48
495	—	488	638	—	46
496	—	486	674	—	525

Responsum No.		Text No.	Responsum No.		Text No.
675	—	525	868	—	160
676	—	424	915	—	420, 561, 562
677	—	589	916	—	612
680	—	731	918	—	552
692	—	186	919	—	422
693	—	735	925	—	24
694	—	459	926	—	359
699	—	475	934	—	370
708	—	420, 561, 562	935	—	716
715	—	399	938	—	173
716	—	577	939	—	258
717	—	776	941	—	579
718	—	412	942	—	533
728	—	455	943	—	547, 561
730	—	645	944	—	549
733	—	732	945	—	404
747	—	638	946	—	303, 312, 314,
795	—	144			315, 317, 330
809	—	642	947	—	299
817	—	634	948	—	520
825	—	587	949	—	209
827	—	425	950	—	413
828	—	655	953	—	629
829	—	473	960	—	393
830	—	639	961	—	619
831	—	640	962	—	467
833	—	754	963	—	741
834	—	667, 721	964	—	358
835	—	644	966	—	361
836	—	510	968	—	530
837	—	464	969	—	137
839	—	622	970	—	524
841	—	172	971	—	252
842	—	650	972	—	429
843	—	713	973	—	436
844	—	782	975	—	390
846	—	426	976	—	637
848	—	690	977	—	628
855	—	385	978	—	453
856	—	674	980	—	590
857	—	377	981	—	360
858	—	260	982	—	675
859	—	443	983	—	544
860	—	335	985	—	147
864	—	249	986	—	147

Responsum No.		Text No.	Responsum No.		Text No.
987	—	332	1004	—	663
988	—	332	1005	—	611
989	—	142	1006	—	438
992	—	93, 583, 585	1007	—	461
993	—	268	1008	—	146, 613
994	—	775	1009	—	652
995	—	557	1011	—	656
996	—	515	1012	—	593
997	—	620	1013	—	635
999	—	200	1015	—	273
1000	—	375	1016	—	527
1001	—	594	1017	—	697
1002	—	728			

LEMBERG EDITION

Responsum No.		Text No.	Responsum No.		Text No.
108	—	551	181	—	691
109	—	535	182	—	296, 322
111	—	535	183	—	215
122	—	647	184	—	85
123	—	760	185	—	157
124	—	327	186	—	37
125	—	69	187	—	222
126	—	410	188	—	227
127	—	410	193	—	114
128	—	402	194	—	120
138	—	217	195	—	84
139	—	40	196	—	218
140	—	111	197	—	133
141	—	279	198	—	429
142	—	210	202	—	7
143	—	105	205	—	752
144	—	41	206	—	738
145	—	127	207	—	715
146	—	44, 55	208	—	136
148	—	413	209	—	447
151	—	281	211	—	166
157	—	755	212	—	166
176	—	77	213	—	597

Responsum No.		Text No.	Responsum No.		Text No.
214	—	596	322	—	87
215	—	600	323	—	88
216	—	601	326	—	428
217	—	560	327	—	306
218	—	491	328	—	306
219	—	491	329	—	221
220	—	427	331	—	646
223	—	4	332	—	62
224	—	4	333	—	454
226	—	685	334	—	770
227	—	236	335	—	629
228	—	236	336	—	58
229	—	236	337	—	93
230	—	1	338	—	498, 499
231	—	130	339	—	384
232	—	669	340	—	66
233	—	175	341	—	42
234	—	205	342	—	113
235	—	138	343	—	423
236	—	688	344	—	677
237	—	295	345	—	576
238	—	479	346	—	30
239	—	707	347	—	31
241	—	703	349	—	43
241	—	398	351	—	602
242	—	665	352	—	405
243	—	326	355	—	258
244	—	365	356	—	633
245	—	374	357	—	505
246	—	174	359	—	442
247	—	771	360	—	448
248	—	771	363	—	11
249	—	679	364	—	207
267	—	409	366	—	230
268	—	6	367	—	73
269	—	19	368	—	107
305	—	781	369	—	605
306	—	720	370	—	420
307	—	720	371	—	561, 562
308	—	762	372	—	612
309	—	636	373	—	475
310	—	246	374	—	475
312	—	224	375	—	780
313	—	594	376	—	145
314	—	618	378	—	687

Responsum No.		Text No.	Responsum No.		Text No.
379	—	623	420	—	36
380	—	432	425	—	202
381	—	570	426	—	134
382	—	599	442	—	78
383	—	288	478	—	201
384	—	694	479	—	702
385	—	452	480	—	324
386	—	280	481	— .	324
387	—	672	482	—	324
388	—	506	483	—	324
389	—	380	488	—	29
393	—	319	490	—	435
394	—	364	500	—	101
398	—	33	503	—	147
403	—	153	507	—	162
404	—	142			

PARMA

Responsum No.		Text No.	Responsum No.		Text No.
10	—	383	289	—	163
13	—	195	290	—	394
14	—	787	291	—	64
15	—	787	292	—	91
48	—	625	293	—	278
49	—	625	297	—	409
50	—	643	298	—	6
125	—	69	299	—	19
219	—	310	300	—	19
220	—	310	301	—	719
225	—	232	302	—	641
241	—	314	304	—	436
242	—	303	311	—	775
281	—	367	399	—	700
282	—	353	476	—	202
283	—	349	477	—	134
284	—	421	494	—	316
285	—	516	514	—	598
286	—	445	515	—	104
287	—	340	528	—	496
288	—	162			

Responsum No.		Text No.	Responsum No.		Text No.
	AM. I		46	—	331
41	—	51	47	—	331
48	—	69	48	—	308
61	—	64	49	—	159
62	—	67	51	—	154
68	—	109	52	—	155
75	—	106	53	—	156
76	—	91	54	—	161
77	—	108	55	—	163
88	—	110	63	—	242
93	—	386	64	—	692
94	—	25, 386	65	—	692, 693
95	—	164	66	—	355
96	—	211	67	—	344
97	—	216	68	—	350
			69	—	352
			70	—	352
	AM. II		75	—	294
3	—	364	78	—	373
4	—	367	79	—	180
6	—	334	80	—	241
8	—	354, 699	81	—	280
14	—	347	82	—	284
15	—	357	83	—	285
16	—	346	97	—	254
17	—	341	99	—	185
18	—	342	101	—	422
19	—	572	107	—	637
20	—	572	108	—	378
21	—	572	119	—	452
22	—	572	122	—	550
23	—	572	123	—	521
24	—	718	127	—	581
25	—	439	128	—	581
27	—	439	129	—	259
28	—	180	130	—	562, 582
29	—	439	136	—	566
30	—	434	138	—	653
32	—	305	139	—	564
33	—	190	140	—	555
34	—	676	141	—	584
35	—	290	142	—	767
41	—	271	143	—	430
42	—	271	151	—	139
45	—	449	155	—	615

Responsum No.		Text No.	Responsum No.		Text No.
157	—	610	245	—	444
159	—	460	246	—	666
161	—	457			
162	—	624			
164	—	441		*Berlin*	
165	—	433	p. 276, no. 53	—	446
169	—	177	p. 276, no. 55	—	748
174	—	733	p. 276, no. 57	—	580
177	—	514	p. 276, no. 58	—	580
178	—	513	p. 277, no. 60	—	616
180	—	526	p. 281, no. 154	—	372
181	—	497	p. 284, no. 334	—	656
182	—	502	p. 285, no. 335	—	759
183	—	503	p. 285, no. 337	—	316
184	—	501	p. 285, no. 338	—	316
185	—	504	p. 285, no. 339	—	316
194	—	511	p. 286, no. 348	—	493
197	—	511	p. 291, no. 363	—	90
198	—	508	p. 291, no. 364	—	632
199	—	517	p. 292, no. 366	—	656
200	—	517	p. 292, no. 367	—	601
206	—	701	p. 292, no. 370	—	456
209	—	739	p. 293, no. 371	—	189
218	—	786	p. 294, no. 372	—	761
221	—	726	p. 294, no. 386	—	176
231	—	191	p. 295, no. 387	—	69
232	—	681	p. 295, no. 389	—	125
234	—	536	p. 296, no. 390	—	123
235	—	480	p. 298, no. 392	—	536
238	—	592	p. 319, no. 780	—	298
239	—	477	p. 320, no. 792	—	586
240	—	18	p. 320, no. 865	—	529
241	—	734	p. 323, no. 978	—	769
242	—	293	p. 346	—	784
244	—	293, 603			

BIBLIOGRAPHY

AARON HA-KOHEN of Lunel, ארחות חיים. vol. I, Florence, 1750; vol. II, ed. by M. Schlesinger, Berlin, 1902.

ABRAHAMS, ISRAEL, ed., Hebrew Ethical Wills. 2 vols., Philadelphia, 1926.

———, Jewish Life in the Middle Ages. 2d revised ed., London, 1932.

———, H. P. STOKES and HERBERT LOEWE, eds., Starrs and Jewish Charters Preserved in the British Museum. 3 vols., Cambridge, 1930–32.

ADLER, J. G. C., Sammlung von gerichtlichen Jüdischen Contracten. Hamburg and Bützow, 1773.

AGUS, IRVING A., "שיעור הכתובה בתור קנה מדה לעשרם של היהודים בימי הבינים". *Horeb*, 1939, 143–68.

———, "The Development of the Money Clause in the Ashkenazic Ketubah." *J. Q. R*, XXX (1940), 221–56.

AHAI, RAB, שאלתות. Venice, 1546; Wilna, 1867; and other editions.

ALEXANDER HA-KOHEN, SÜSSLEIN, ספר אגודה. Cracow, 1571; reprinted in part, Jerusalem, 1899.

ALFASI, ISAAC B. JACOB, שאלות ותשובות 'ס. Leghorn, 1781.

ALTMANN, BERTHOLD, "Studies in Medieval German Jewish History". *Proceedings of the American Academy for Jewish Research*, X (1940), 5–98.

APTOWIZER, VICTOR, מבוא לספר ראבי"ה. Jerusalem, 1938.

ARONIUS, JULIUS, Regesten zur Geschichte der Juden im fränkischen und deutschen Reiche bis zum Jahre 1273. Berlin, 1887-1902.

ASHER B. YEHIEL, ספר האשרי (a legal commentary on the Babylonian Talmud). Printed with most editions of the latter.

———, שאלות ותשובות. Constantinople, 1517; Venice, 1552–3; also 1607–8; and other editions.

ASSAF, SIMHA, העונשין אחרי חתימת התלמוד. Jerusalem, 1922.

———, בתי הדין וסדריהם אחרי חתימת התלמוד. Jerusalem, 1924.

———, לקורות הרבנות. Jerusalem, 1927.

———, מקורות לתולדות החנוך בישראל. 3 vols., Tel Aviv, 1925-36.

AUERBACH, B. H., Geschichte der israelitischen Gemeinde Halberstadt. Halberstadt, 1886.

AUERBACH, SELIG, Die rheinischen Rabbinerversammlungen im 13. Jahrhundert, Würzburg, 1932.

AZULAI, HAYYIM JOSEPH DAVID, שם הגדולים ועד לחכמים. Ed. by Ben Jacob, Vienna, 1864.

BACK, SAMUEL, R. Meir b. Baruch aus Rothenburg. Frankfurt a. M. 1895.

BAER, FRITZ (יצחק), "Gemeinde und Landjudenschaft". *Korrespondenzblatt des Vereins zur Gründung. . . einer Akademie für die Wissenschaft des Judentums*, II (1921).

——, Das Protokollbuch der Landjudenschaft des Herzogtums Kleve. Berlin, 1922.

BAMBERGER, MOSES LÖB, Ein Blick auf die Geschichte der Juden in Würzburg. Würzburg, 1903.

BAMBERGER, SIMON, and BAMBERGER, HERZ, Geschichte der Rabbiner der Stadt und des Bezirkes Würzburg. Würzburg, 1905.

BARBECK, HUGO, Geschichte der Juden in Nürnberg und Fürth. Nuremberg, 1878.

BARON, SALO W., The Jewish Community. 3 vols., Philadelphia, 1942.

——, A Social and Religious History of the Jews. 3 vols., New York, 1937.

BELOW, GEORGE VON, Territorium und Stadt. München and Leipzig, 1900.

——, Probleme der Wirtschaftsgeschichte; eine Einführung in das Studium der Wirtschaftsgeschichte. Tübingen, 1920.

BENJAMIN OF TUDELA, מסעות ר' בנימין מטודילא. The Itinerary of Rabbi Benjamin of Tudela. Transl. into English and ed. by A. Asher. Vols. I & II, London, 1840–1.

BERGL, JOSEPH, Geschichte der ungarischen Juden. Leipzig, 1879.

BERLINER, ABRAHAM, Aus dem inneren Leben der deutschen Juden im Mittelalter. 2d. ed., Berlin, 1900.

BEZALEL B. ABRAHAM ASHKENAZI, ספר שאלות ותשובות. Venice, 1595.

BLAU, LUDWIG, Das altjüdische zauberwesen. 2nd ed., Berlin, 1914.

BLOGG, S. E., ספר החיים. Hanover, 1848.

BODENHEIMER, R., "Beitrag zur Geschichte der Juden in Oberhessen von ihrer frühesten Erwähnung bis zur Emanzipation." *ZGJD*, II (1931); III, (1932).

Böhmer, Johann Friedrich, Fontes rerum Germanicarum. Geschichtsquellen Deutschlands, vols. 1–4, Berlin, 1843–68.

———, Regesta Imperii VI. Die Regesten des Kaiserreichs unter Heinrich Raspe, Wilhelm, Richard, Rudolf, Adolf, Albrecht und Heinrich VII, (1246–1313), Berlin, 1844.

———, Regesta Imperii (new edition) VI. Die Regesten des Kaiserreichs unter Rudolf, Adolf, Albrecht, Heinrich VII. (1273–1313). . . . . neu herausgegeben und ergänzt von Oswald Redlich. Innsbruck, 1898.

Bondy, Gottlieb, and F. Dworsky, eds., Zur Geschichte der Juden in Böhmen, Mähren und Schlesien von 906 bis 1620. 2 vols., Prague, 1906.

Boos, Heinrich, Urkundenbuch der Stadt Worms. 2 vols., Berlin, 1886.

———, Geschichte der rheinischen Städtekultur von ihren Anfängen bis zur Gegenwart. 2d ed., 4 vols., Berlin, 1897–1901.

Brann, M., Geschichte der Juden in Schlesien. Breslau, 1896–1916.

Bresslau, Harry, "Diplomatische Erläuterungen zu den Judenprivilegien Heinrichs IV". *ZGJD*, O. S. I (1887).

———, "Zur Geschichte der Juden in Rothenburg an der Taube". *ZGJD*, O. S. III (1889), 301–36; IV (1890), 1–17.

Bretholz, Berthold, Geschichte der Juden in Mähren im Mittelalter. Brünn, 1934.

———, Quellen zur Geschichte der Juden in Mähren vom XI. bis zum XV. Jahrhundert (1067–1411). Prague, 1935.

Brisch, Carl, Geschichte der Juden in Köln und Umgebung. 2 vols., Mühlheim a. Rh., 1879.

Bromberger, S., Die Juden in Regensburg bis zur Mitte des 14. Jahrhunderts. Berlin, 1933.

Brüll, Nehemias, "Synoden der deutschen Juden in Mittelalter". *Jahrbücher fur Jüdische Geschichte und Literatur*, VIII (1887).

———, "Zur Geschichte der Juden in Mähren". *Kalendar für Israeliten*, auf das Jahr 5628 (1868). Vienna 1867.

Cambridge Mediaeval History. Vol. VI, New York, 1929.

Carlebach, Ephraim, Die rechtliche und sociale Verhältnisse der Jüdischen Gemeinden Speyer, Worms und Mainz. Frankfurt a. M., 1900.

CARO, GEORGE, Sozial-und Wirtschaftsgeschichte der Juden im Mittelalter und in der Neuzeit. 2 vols., Frankfort and Leipzig, 1908–20.

CARO, J., "Die Rabbinersynode zu Erfurt 1391". *Jüdisches Literatur-Blatt* XI (1882), 110–5..

COHEN, BOAZ, קונטרס התשובות. Budapest, 1930.

COHEN, SAMUEL, "ר' מרדכי בן הלל האשכנזי". Sinai, VI (1943), (Translated from the German).

CONFORTE, DAVID, קורא הדורות. Venice, 1746: Lemberg, 1845; ed. Cassel, Berlin 1845.

CORONEL, NAHMAN NATHAN, חמשה קונטרסים. Vienna, 1864.

COULTON, GEORGE G. Life in the Middle Ages. Cambridge, 1928-30.

CRÉMIEUX, ADOLPHE, "Les Juifs de Marseille au moyen âge". *REJ*, XLVI (1903); XLVII (1903).

DEPPING, G. B., Les Juifs dans le Moyen Age. Paris 1834.

DINABURG, BENZION, תולדות ישראל בגולה. 2 vols., Jerusalem, 1926–31.

DONATH, L., Geschichte der Juden in Mecklenburg von ältesten Zeiten bis auf die Gegenwart. Leipzig, 1874.

DUBNOW, SIMON, Weltgeschichte des Jüdischen Volkes. 10 vols., Berlin, 1925–9.

ECKSTEIN, A., Geschichte der Juden im ehemaligen Fürstbistum Bamberg, Bamberg, 1898.

———, Geschichte der Juden im Markgrafentum Bayereuth. Bamberg, 1907.

EISENSTEIN, J. D., אוצר ויכוחים. New York, 1928.

ELBOGEN, I., FREIMANN, A., and TYKOCINSKI, H., Germania Judaica. Breslau, 1934.

ELEAZAR B. JUDAH OF WORMS, ספר הרוקח. Cremona, 1557; Warsaw, 1880.

ELFENBEIN, ISRAEL, ed., ספר מנהגים דבי מהר"ם ב"ר ברוך מרוטנבורג. New York, 1938.

ELIEZER B. JOEL HA-LEVI, ספר ראבי"ה. Ed. by Victor Aptowitzer. Vols. I–III, Berlin, 1913 — Jerusalem, 1935. With a volume of "Addenda et Emendationes". Jerusalem, 1936.

ELIEZER B. NATHAN OF MAYENCE, אבן העזר, ספר ראב"ן. Prague, 1610. First part was reprinted and edited by S. Albeck, Warsaw, 1905.

ELIEZER B. SAMUEL OF METZ, ספר יראים. Venice, 1566; Jerusalem, 1843; Wilna, 1892.

Encyclopaedia Judaica; das Judentum in Geschichte und Gegenwart. Ed. by Jacob Klatzkin, *et al.* Vols. I–X [A-L], Berlin, 1928–34.

Ennen and Eckertz, Quellenbuch zur Geschichte der Stadt Köln. Vol. 1, Cologne, 1860.

Ephraim, Max, "Histoire des Juifs d'Alsace et particulièrement de Strasbourg depuis le milieu du XIII⁽ᵉ⁾ jusqu' à la fin du XIV⁽ᵉ⁾ siècle." *REJ* LXXVII (1923); LXXVIII (1924).

Eppenstein, Simon, "Zur Frühgeschichte der deutschen Juden". *MGWJ*, XXVII (1919).

Epstein, Abraham, "ordination et autorisation." *REJ*, XLVI (1903).

Epstein, Isidore, The Responsa of Rabbi Solomon b. Adreth of Barcelona (1235–1310) as a Source of the History of the Jews in Spain. London, 1925.

———, The Responsa of R. Simon b. Zemah Duran as a Source of the History of the Jews in North Africa. London, 1930.

———, "Pre-Expulsion England in the Responsa." *Transactions of the Jewish Historical Society of England*, XIV (1940), 187–205.

Finke, Heinrich, Konzilienstudien zur Geschichte des 13ten Jahrhunderts. Münster, 1891.

Finkelstein, Louis, Jewish Self-Government in the Middle Ages. New York, 1924.

Fischer, Herbert, Die verfassungsrechtliche Stellung der Juden in den deutschen Städten während des dreizenten Jahrhunderts. Breslau, 1931.

Frank, Moses, קהלות אשכנז ובתי דיניהם. Tel-Aviv, 1938.

Frankel, Zechariah, Entwurf einer Geschichte der Literatur der nachtalmudischen Responsen. Breslau, 1865.

Freimann, Alfred, "Asher b. Jechiel, Sein Leben und Wirken." *JJLG*, XII (1918), 237–317.

Geiger, Ludwig, Geschichte der Juden in Berlin. 2 vols., Berlin, 1874.

Geyer, Rudolf, and Leopold Sailer, Urkunden aus Wiener Grundbüchern zur Geschichte der Wiener Juden im Mittelalter. Vienna, 1931.

Gierse, Albert, Geschichte der Juden in Westfalen während des Mittelalters. Naumburg a. S., n. d.

Ginsburger, M., "Die Juden in Basel". *Baseler Zeitschrift für Geschichte und Altertumskunde*, VIII (1909).

GINZBERG, LOUIS, גנזי שעכטער. Genizah studies in memory of Dr. Solomon Schecter. 2 vols., New York, 1928–9.

GLASER, A., Geschichte der Juden in Strassburg. vol. I, Frankfurt a. M., 1925.

GRAETZ, HEINRICH, Geschichte der Juden. 11 vols., Leipzig, 1853–76.

GRAYZEL, SOLOMON, The Church and the Jews in the XIIIth Century. Philadelphia, 1933.

GROSS, HEINRICH, Eliezer b. Joel ha-Levi. Krotoschin, 1885.

——, Gallia Judaica, Paris, 1897.

GÜDEMANN, MORITZ, "Zur Geschichte der Juden in Magdeburg." *MGWJ*, X (1866).

——, Geschichte des Erziehungswesen und der Kultur der abendländischen Juden während des Mittelalters und der neueren Zeit. 3 vols., Vienna, 1880–8.

——, Quellenschriften zur Geschichte des Unterrichts und der Frziehung bei den deutschen Juden. Berlin, 1891.

GUTTMANN, JACOB, Die Scholastik des 13ten Jahrhunderts. Breslau, 1902.

——, Das Verhältniss des Thomas von Aquino zum Judenthum und zur jüdischen Literatur. Göttingen, 1891.

GUTTMANN, JULIUS, "Die Wirtschaftliche und soziale Bedeutung der Juden im Mittelalter." *MGWJ*, LI (1907).

HAENLE, S., Geschichte der Juden im ehemaligen Fürstentum Ansbach, Ansbach, 1867.

HALEVY, ISAAC, דורות הראשונים. vol. 3, Berlin, 1920.

HALPERIN, YEHIEL, סדר הדורות. Lemberg, 1858,

HAMPE, KARL, Deutsche Kaisergeschichte im Zeitalter der Salier und Staufer. 6th ed., Leipzig, 1929.

HARKAVY, ABRAHAM, זכרון לראשונים וגם לאחרונים. Berlin, 1887.

HAYYIM B. ISAAC OR ZARUA, שאלות ותשובות. Leipzig, 1860.

HEFELE, CARL JOSEPH VON, Konziliengeschichte. vols. 3–6, Freiburg, 1886.

ס' חמדה גנוזה (Hemdah Genuzah). A collection of geonic Responsa. Jerusalem, 1863.

HILGARD, ALFRED, Urkunden zur Geschichte der Stadt Speyer. Strassburg, 1885.

HOENIGER, ROBERT, "Zur Geschichte der Juden Deutschlands im früheren Mittelalter." *ZGJD*, O. S., 1 (1887).

——, und Moritz Stern, eds., Das Judenschreinsbuch der Laurenzpfarre zu Köln. Berlin, 1888.

HOFFMAN, FRIEDRICH W., Geschichte der Stadt Magdeburg. Magdeburg, 1845.

HOFFMAN, MOSES, Der Geldhandel der deutschen Juden während des Mittelalters bis 1350. Leipzig, 1910.

HOROVITZ, MARCUS, Frankfurter Rabbiner. Ein Beitrag zur Geschichte der israelitischen Gemeinde in Frankfurt A. M. 4 vols. Frankfort, 1882–5.

———, Die Inschriften des alten Friedhofs der Israelitischen Gemeinde zu Frankfurt a. M. Frankfort, 1901.

HURTER, FR., Innocenz III und seine Zeitgenossen. 3 vols. Hamburg, 1838.

HYAMSON, ALBERT M., History of the Jews in England. London, 1908.

IBN YAHYA, GEDALIAH, שלשלת הקבלה ס'. Venice, 1587; Cracow, 1596; Amsterdam, 1697; Zalkow, 1802; and other editions.

ISAAC OF DUREN, שערי דורא. Venice, 1547; Lublin, 1599, and other editions.

ISAAC B. JOSEPH OF CORBEIL, עמודי גולה, or ספר מצות קטן (סמ"ק). Constantinople, ca. 1510; Cremona, 1556; Kapost, 1803; and other editions.

ISAAC B. MOSES OF VIENNA, אור זרוע. Vols. I and II, Zhitomir, 1862; vol. III, Jerusalem, 1887; vol. IV, Jerusalem, 1890. To tractate שבועות, in *Festschrift zu Israel Lewy's siebzigsten Geburtstag*, (1911), by A. Freimann.

ISAAC B. SHESHET, Profet, שאלות ותשובות ס'. Constantinople, 1547; Wilna, 1878; and other editions.

ISAIAH OF TRANI, ספר המכריע. Livorno, 1579; Munkacs, 1900; Lublin, 1897.

ISRAEL B. HAYYIM OF BRUNA, שאלות ותשובות ס'. Saloniki, 1798; Stettin, 1860.

ISRAEL B. PETHAHIAH, ISSERLEIN, תרומת הדשן. Printed together with his ספר פסקים וכתבים. Venice, 1519; and other editions.

ISSERLES, MOSES B. ISRAEL, דרכי משה ס'. Commentary on the טורים of Jacob b. Asher. Printed with many editions of the latter.

———, ההגהות ס'. Glosses to the *Shulhan Aruk*. Printed with many editions of the latter.

JACOB B. ASHER, ארבעה טורים. Venice, 1475; Venice, 1522; Cracow, 1615; and many other editions.

Jacob b. Gershom Hagozer, זכרון ברית לראשונים. Ed. by Jacob Glassberg, Cracow, 1892.

Jacob b. Meir, Rabbenu Tam, ספר הישר לרבנו תם. 2 parts, Vienna, 1811. Second part was reprinted and edited by F. Rosenthal, Berlin, 1898.

Jacob b. Moses haLevi, Molin, ספר מהרי"ל שחבר ותקן מנהגי ק"ק אשכנז מראשית השנה עד אחרית השנה. Cremona, 1558, Lublin, 1590, and other editions.

————, שאלות ותשובות ה"ר יעקב ב"ר משה מולין סג"ל. Cremona, 1556; Cracow, 1881; and other editions.

Jacob Weil, שאלות ותשובות ה"ר יעקב וייל. Venice, 1549; Cremona, 1556; and later editions.

Jaraczewsky, A., Die Geschichte der Juden in Erfurt. Erfurt, 1868.

Jellinek, Adolph, קונטרס וירמייזא וקהל ווינא. Vienna, 1880.

Jewish Encyclopedia. Ed. by Isidore Singer. 12 vols. New York, 1901–6.

Joseph, Kolon, שאלות ותשובות ה"ר יוסף קולון ב"ר שלמה צרפתי. Venice, 1519; Cremona, 1557; Warsaw, 1884, and other editions.

Joseph b. Mordecai gershon ha-Kohen, שארית יוסף, שו"ת וביאורים על המרדכי. Cracow, 1590.

Joseph b. Moses, ספר לקט יושר. Ed. Jacob Freimann, Berlin, 1903–4.

Jost, I. M., Geschichte der Israeliten seit der Maccabäer bis auf unseren Tag. Vols. I–IX, Berlin, 1820–8; Vol. X, Berlin, 1846–7.

Judah b. Asher, זכרון יהודה, שו"ת יהודה בן הרא"ש. Berlin, 1846.

————, and Jacob b. Asher, צואת הרב יהודה בן הרא"ש ואחיו הרב יעקב בעל הטורים. Ed. by Solomon Schechter, Pressburg, 1885.

Judah b. Barzilai of Barcelona, ספר השטרות. Ed. by S. J. Halberstamm, Berlin, 1898.

Judah he-Hasid, ספר חסידים. Ed. by J. Wistinetzki, Frankfort, 1924.

Judah Mintz, שאלות ותשובות ה"ר יהודה מינץ וה"ר מאיר בה"ר שמואל יצחק קאצינעלנבויגן. Venice, 1553; Fiorda, 1726; and other editions.

Jüdisches Lexikon; ein enzyklopädisches Handbuch des Jüdischen Wissens. Ed. by George Herlitz and Bruno Kirschner, 5 vols. Berlin, 1927–30.

Juster, Jean, Les Juifs dans l'empire romain. 2 vols., Paris, 1914.

Kahn, Leon, Les Juifs à Paris depuis le VIe siecle. Paris, 1889.

Kantorowitz, Ernst, Kaiser Friedrich der Zweite, Berlin, 1928.

Karo, Joseph b. Ephraim, ס' בית יוסף. Commentary on the טורים of Jacob b. Asher, and printed with many editions of the latter.

KATZ, SOLOMON, The Jews in the Visigothic and Frankish Kingdoms of Spain and Gaul. Cambridge, Mass., 1937.

KAUFMANN, DAVID, "Jewish Informers in the Middle Ages." *JQR*, O. S., VIII (1895–6), 217–38.

——, "Zur Geschichte der Khethubba". *MGWJ*, XLI (1897), 213–21.

KISCH, ALEXANDER, "Die Anklageartikel gegen den Talmud und ihre Verteidigung durch R. Yechiel b. Joseph vor Ludwig dem Heiligen in Paris." *MGWJ*, XXIII (1874).

KISCH, GUIDO, Die Rechtsstellung der Wormser Juden im Mittelalter. Halle a. d. Saale, 1934.

——, "Studien zur Geschichte des Judeneides im Mittelalter." *HUCA*, XIV (1939).

——, "Research in medieval Legal History of the Jews." *Proceedings of the American Academy for Jewish Research, VI* (1935), 229–76.

——, "The Jewry Law of the Medieval German Law-Books." *Proceedings of the Amercan Academy for Jewish Research*, VII (1936), 61–145; X (1940), 99–184.

——, "The Landshut Jewry Oath." *Historia Judaica*, I (1939); III, (1941).

KOBER, ADOLF, Studien zur mittelalterlichen Geschichte der Juden in Köln am Rhein, insbesondere ihres Grundbesitzes. Breslau, 1903.

——, Grundbuch des Kölner Judenviertels, 1135–1425. Cologne, 1920.

——, Cologne. Philadelphia, J. P. S. 1940.

——, "Die deutschen Kaiser und die Wormser Juden." *ZGJD*, V (1935).

KÖHNE, C., Der Ursprung der Städteverfassung in Worms, Speier und Mainz. Breslau, 1890.

כל בו (Kol Bo). Constantinople, 1519; Venice, 1547; Lemberg, 1860, and other editions.

KRACAUER, ISIDOR, Geschichte der Juden in Frankfurt a. M., 1150–1824. 2 vols., Frankfort, 1925–7.

——, ed., Urkundenbuch zur Geschichte der Juden in Frankfurt a. M. von 1150–1400. Frankfort, 1914.

KRAUSS, SAMUEL, and ISIDOR FISCHER, Geschichte der jüdischen Arzte vom frühesten Mittelalter bis zur Gleichberechtigung. Vienna, 1930.

LUNDSHUTH, LAZAR, עמודי עבודה. Berlin, 1857–62.

LANGLOIS, M. ERNST, Les registres de Nicolas IV. Paris, 1886.

LATTES, ISAAC B. JACOB, שערי ציון. Ed. by S. Buber, Jaroslaw, 1885.

LAUER, CHAIM, "R. Meir Halevy aus Wien und der Streit um das Grossrabbinat in Frankreich". *JJLG*, XVI (1924), 1–42.

LÉVI, ISRAEL, "La lutte entre Isaie, fils d'Abba Mari, et Yohanan, fils de Matatia, pour le rabbinat de France à la fin du XIVe siècle." *REJ*, XXXIX (1899).

———, "Les Juifs de France du milieu du IXe siècle au Croisades." *REJ*, LII (1906).

LEVI, SALI, Beiträge zur Geschichte der ältesten jüdischen Grabsteine in Mainz. Mayence, 1926.

———, "Die Verbundenheit Zwischen den Jüdischen Gemeinden Worms und Mainz im Mittelalter." *ZGJD*, V (1934), 187–91.

———, Magenza, ein Sammelheft über das jüdische Mainz. Berlin, 1927.

LEVY, MAX, Zur Geschichte der Wormser jüdischen Gemeinde. Worms, 1911.

LEWIN, A., "Die Religionsdisputation des R. Jechiel von Paris 1240 am Hofe Ludwigs des Heiligen, ihre Veranlassung und ihre Folgen." *MGWJ*, XVIII (1869).

LEWYSON, JUDAH L., נפשות צדיקים. Frankfort, 1855.

LIBER, MAURICE, "Un mot sur les consulatations de Hayyim Or Zaroua." *REJ*, LIII (1907). 267–9.

LIEBE, GEORGE, "Die rechtlichen und wirtschaftlichen Zustände der Juden im Erzstift Trier." *Westdeutsche Zeitschrift für Geschichte und Kunst*, XIII (1893).

LOEB, ISIDORE, "La controverse sur le Talmud sous Saint Louis." *REJ*, I–III (1880–1).

———, "Les expulsions des Juifs de France au XIVe, siècle." *Graetz-Jubelschrift*, 1887, 39–56..

LOWENSTEIN, LEOPOLD, Geschichte der Juden in der Kurpfalz. Frankfort, 1895.

LUCAS, P., "Innocent III et les Juifs". *REJ*, XXXV (1897), 247–55.

LUCE, SIMÉON, "Catalogue de documents du Trésor de Chartes relatifs aux Juifs sous le regne de Philippe le Bel.". *REJ*, II (1881), 15–72.

ס' מעשי הגאונים (Maase ha-Geonim). Ed. by Jacob Freimann, with an introduction by A. Epstein, Berlin, 1909.

MANN, H. K., The Lives of the Popes of the Middle Ages. Vol. XI–XIV, London, 1925–31.

MANN, JACOB, "The Responsa of the Babylonian Geonim as a Source of Jewish History." *JQR*, VII (1916–7); VIII (1917–8); IX (1918–9); X (1919–20); XI (1920–1).

MARGOLIOUTH, MOSES, The History of the Jews in Great Britain. 3 vols., London, 1851.

MARGULIES, MORDECAI, ed., חילוקים שבין אנשי מזרח ובני ארץ ישראל. Jerusalem, 1938.

MAULDE, M. DE, Les Juifs dans les états francais du Saint-Siège au moyen âge. Paris, 1886.

MAYER, O., Die Geschichte der Juden in Heilbronn. Heilbronn, 1927.

MEIR B. BARUCH OF ROTHENBURG, ברכות מהר"ם. Riva di Trento, 1559.

———, שאלות ותשובות. Cremona, 1557; Prague, 1608, reprinted without change, Sdilkow, 1835, and by M. Bloch in Budapest, 1895; Lemberg, 1860; Berlin, 1891–2.

———, תוספות. On יומא, printed with most editions of the Babylonian Talmud; on אהלות, printed in the Rom edition.

———, הלכות שמחות. With Judah b. Nathan's מחנה לויה, Livorno, 1819.

MEIR HA-KOHEN, הגהות מיימוניות, on Maimonides' *Mishneh Torah.* Printed with most editions of the latter. Important variations are found in the Constantinople edition, 1509.

———, תשובות השייכות, on Maimonides' *Mishneh Torah.* Printed with most editions of the latter, but in the Constantinople edition it is integrated with the הגהות מיימוניות.

MEIRI, MENAHEM B. SOLOMON, מגן אבות. Ed. by Isaac Last, London, 1909.

———, בית הבחירה. Vienna, 1934.

MENAHEM OF MERSEBURG, נימוקי ה"ר מנחם מירזבורק. Appended to the Responsa of R. Jacob Weil.

MICHAEL, EMIL, Geschichte des deutschen Volkes während des 13. Jahrhunderts. Freiburg, 1897–9.

MICHAEL, HEIMANN JOSEPH, אור החיים. Frankfort, 1891.

Mitteilungen des Gesamtarchive der deutschen Juden. Published by Eugen Täubler, 7 vols. 1–5, Leipzig, 1908–1915.

Monumenta Germaniae Historica. Berlin, 1826–1938.

MORDECAI B. HILLEL ASHKENAZI, ספר המרדכי. Riva di Trani, 1559; Cracow, 1598; printed with most editions of the Alfasi.

——, מרדכי הגדול. Goldschmidt Manuscript, Jewish Theological Seminary.

——, מרדכי דבי רינוס. Manuscript in the library of the Jewish Theological Seminary. See description of these manuscripts in "The Seminary Bulletin", 1939, p. 65.

MOSES B. JABOB OF COUCI, ספר מצות גדול (סמ"ג). Venice, 1547; Kapost, 1807; and other editions.

MOSES B. MAIMON, Maimonides, ס' משנה תורה. Constantinople, 1509; Venice, 1524; Amsterdam, 1702; and other editions.

MOSES MINTZ HA-LEVI, שאלות ותשובות ה"ר משה מינץ סג"ל. Cracow, 1717; Saloniki, 1802; Lemberg, 1851; and other editions.

MOSES PARNAS OF ROTHENBURG, ספר הפרנס. Vilna, 1891.

MÜLLER, JOEL, תשובות גאוני מזרח ומערב. Berlin, 1888.

——, תשובות חכמי צרפת ולותיר. Vienna, 1881.

——, "Die Responsen Rabbi Meshulams sohn Rabbi Kalonymos." *Jahresbericht der Hochschule für die Wissenschaft der Juden zur Berlin.* XI (1893).

MÜLLER, WALTHER, Zur Frage des Ursprungs der mittelalterlichen Zünfte. Leipzig, 1910.

NETTER, NATHAN, Vingt Siècles d'histoire d'une communauté juive (Metz et son grand passe). Paris, 1938.

NEUBAUER, ADOLF, "Documents inedits". *REJ*, XII (1886), 80–94.

——, Medieval Jewish Chronicles and Chronological Notes. 2 vols., Oxford, 1887–95.

——, and M. STERN, eds., Hebräische Berichte über die Juden-verfolgungen Während der Kreuzzüge. Berlin, 1892.

NEUFELD, SIEGBERT, Die Juden im thüringisch-sächsischen Gebiet während des Mittelalters. 2 vols., Berlin and Halle, 1917–27.

——, Geschichte der Juden in Halle. Berlin, 1915.

NEUMAN, ABRAHAM, The Jews in Spain. 2 vols., Philadelphia, 1942.

NISSIM B. REUBEN GERUNDI, שאלות ותשובות. Cremona, 1557; Metz, 1786; Koenigsberg, 1840; Warsaw, 1907; and other editions.

NÜBLING, EUGEN, Judengemeinden des Mittelalters, insbesondere die Gemeinde der Reichsstadt Ulm. Ulm, 1896.

OELSNER, O., Schlesische Urkunden zur Geschichte der Juden in Mittelalter. Vienna, 1864.

PARKES, JAMES, The Jew in the Medieval Community. London, 1938.

PEREZ B. ELIJAH, הגהות על הסמ"ק. A commentary on עמודי גולה of R. Isaac of Corbeil, and printed with most editions of the latter.

———, הגהות על התשב"ץ. Printed together with the *Tashbetz*.

POZNANSKI, SAMUEL, Babylonische Geonim im nachgaonäischen Zeitalter. Berlin, 1914.

PRIBRAM, A. F., Urkunden und Akten zur Geschichte der Juden in Wien. 2 vols., Vienna, 1918.

RABINOWITZ, The Social Life of the Jews of Northern France in the XII–XIV Centuries. London, 1938.

———, "The Medieval Jewish Counter-part to the Gild Merchant." *Economic History Review*, VIII (1937–8).

———, "The Talmudic Basis of the *Herem ha-yishub*." *JQR*, XXVIII (1937–8).

REDLICH, OSWALD, Rudolph von Habsburg. Breslau, 1903.

REMLING, FRANZ, Geschichte der Bischöfe zu Speyer. Mayence, 1852.

———, Urkundenbuch zur Geschichte der Bischöfe zu Speyer. Mayence, 1852.

RIGG, J. M., Select Pleas, Starrs, and other Records from the Rolls of the Exchequer of the Jews, A. D. 1220–1284. London, 1902.

———, and H. JENKINSON, eds., Calendar of the Plea Rolls of the Exchequer of the Jews Preserved in the Public Record Office. 3 vols., London, 1905–29.

ROSCHER, WILHELM, Die Juden im Mittelalter, in Ansicht der Volkswirtschaft. 2 vols., Leipzig, 1878.

RÖSEL, ISERT, "Die Reichssteuern der deutschen Judengemeinden von ihren Anfängen bis zur Mitte des 14. Jahrhunderts." *MGWJ*, LIII (1909); LIV (1910); also reprint.

ROSENTHAL, BERTHOLD, Heimatsgeschichte der badischen Juden. Bühl, 1927.

ROSENTHAL, FERDINAND, "Einiges über die Takonaus des Rabbenu Gershom." *Hildesheimer Jubelschrift*, Berlin, 1891.

———, "Einiges über Takonaus Shum". *MGWJ* XLVI (1902).

ROTH, ABRAHAM NAFTALI ZEVI, דינא דמלכותא דינא. *Ha-soker*, V (1937–8), 110–26.

ROTH, CECIL, "The Jews in the Middle Ages". *Cambridge Medieval History*, VII, Cambridge, 1932.

SAITCHIK, R, Beiträge zur Geschichte der rechtlichen Stellung der Juden. Frankfort, 1890.

SALFELD, SIEGMUND, Das Martyrologium des Nürnberger Memorbuches. Berlin, 1898.

——, Bilder aus der Vergangenheit der Jüdischen Gemeinde Mainz. Mayence, 1903.

SAMSON B. ZADOK, ספר תשב"ץ. Cremona, 1556; Cracow, 1559; Lemberg, 1858; and other editions.

SAMUEL B. MEIR, פירוש הרשב"ם על בבא בתרא. Completion of Rashi's commentary to tractate Baba Batra, printed with many editions of the Talmud.

SCHAAB, KARL, Diplomatische Geschichte der Juden zu Mainz. Mayence, 1855.

SCHERER, J. E., Die Rechtsverhältnisse der Juden in den deutschösterreichischen Ländern. Leipzig, 1901.

SCHIFFMANN, SARAH, Die Urkunden für die Juden von Speyer 1090, und Worms 1157. *ZGJD*, II (1930).

——, Heinrich IV und die Bischöfe in ihrem verhalten zu den deutschen Juden zur Zeit des ersten Kreuzzugs. Berlin, 1930.

SCHIPPER, IGNAZ, Anfänge des Kapitalismus bei den abendländischen Juden im früheren Mittelalter. Warsaw, 1907.

——, יידישע געשיכטע, 4 vols., Warsaw, 1930.

SCHRÖDER, RICHARD, Lehrbuch der deutschen Rechtsgeschichte. 6th ed., 2 vols., Leipzig, 1919–22.

SCHUNK, Codex Diplomaticus Mogunt. Mayence, 1797.

ס' שערי תשובה (*Shaare Teshubah*). A collection of geonic Responsa. Saloniki, 1802.

ס' שערי צדק (*Shaare Zedek*). A collection of geonic Responsa. Saloniki, 1792.

SHOHET, DAVID MENAHEM, The Jewish court in the Middle Ages. New York, 1931.

SIMHA OF VITRY, מחזור ויטרי. ed. by S. Hurwitz, Berlin, 1893.

SMITH, A. L., Church and State in the Middle Ages. Oxford, 1913.

SOLOMON B. ABRAHAM IBN ADRET, שאלות ותשובות הרשב"א. Vol. I, Bologna, 1539; Vol. II, Leghorn: 1657; Vol. III, Leghorn, 1778; vol. IV, Vilna, 1881; vol. V, Leghorn, 1825; vols. VI, VII, Warsaw, 1868.

——, תשובות הרשב"א המיוחסות להרמב"ן. Warsaw, 1883.

SOLOMON B. ISAAC (RASHI), תשובות רש"י. Ed. by Israel Elfenbein, New York, 1943.

————, פירוש. Commentary on Babylonian Talmud, printed with most editions of the latter.

————, ס' האורה. Ed. by S. Buber. Lemberg, 1905. Probably compiled by his students.

————, ס' הפרדס לרש"י. Ed. by Ehrenreich, Budapest, 1924. Probably compiled by his students.

————, לקוטי הפרדס לרש"י. Amsterdam, 1715. Probably compiled by his students.

————, סדור רש"י. Berlin, 1911–2. Probably compiled by his students.

SOLOMON B. YEHIEL LURIA, שאלות ותשובות ופסקים הנוהגים בגלילות אשכנז. Lublin, 1574; and other editions.

————, ים של שלמה. A commentary on individual tractates of the Babylonian Talmud, Prague, 1616; Lublin, 1636; Cracow, 1646; Berlin, 1766; and other editions.

SOMBART, WERNER, Die Juden und das Wirtschaftsleben. Munich, 1920. English translation with notes by M. Epstein. London, 1913.

STARR, JOSHUA, The Jews in the Byzantine Empire 641–1204. Athens, 1939.

STEINSCHNEIDER, MORITZ, Jewish Literature from the Eighth to the Eighteenth Century with an Introduction on Talmud and Midrash. London, 1857.

STEINTHAL, FRITZ LEOPOLD, Geschichte der Augsburger Juden im Mittelalter. Berlin, 1911.

STERN, M. and NEUBAUER, A., Hebräische Berichte über die Judenverfolgungen während der Kreuzzüge. Berlin, 1892.

STOBBE, OTTO, Die Juden in Deutschland während des Mittelalters. Braunschweig, 1866.

STRAUS, RAPHAEL, Die Judengemeinde Regensburg im ausgehenden Mittelalter auf grund der Quellen kritisch untersucht und neu dargestellt. Heidelberg, 1932.

SZULWAS, M., Die Juden in Würzburg während des Mittelalters. Berlin, 1934.

Talmud, Babylonian. References are to the standard text, especially to the edition Vilna, 1885.

TÄUBLER, EUGEN, Zur Handelsbedeutung der Juden im Mittelalter vor Beginn des Stadtewesens. *Philippson Festschrift*, Leipzig, 1916.

————, "Zur Geschichte der Kammerknechtschaft". *Mitteilungen des Gesamtarchivs der deutschen Juden*, IV (1913), 44–58.

TAYLOR, HENRY OSBORN, The Medieval Mind. 2 vols., London, 1938.

תשובות גאונים קדמונים (*Teshubot Geonim Kadmonim*). A collection of geonic Responsa ascribed to Joseph Bonfils, ed. by David Cassel. Berlin, 1848.

תשובות הגאונים (*Tesubot ha-Geonim*). A collection of geonic Respohsa, ed. by Abraham Y. Harkavy, Berlin, 1887.

THOMPSON, JAMES W., An economic and Social History of the Middle Ages (300–1300). New York, 1928.

תוספות (*Tosaphot*). Commentary on the Babylonian Talmud by the students and followers of Rashi. Printed with most editions of the Talmud.

תוספתא (*Tosephta*). Ed. by M. S. Zuckermandel. Pasewalk, 1881; reprinted with "supplement to the Tosephta" by Saul Lieberman, Jerusalem, 1937.

TYKOCINSKY, H., "Die Schüler des Isaac Or Zarua." *MGWJ*, LXIII (1919).

————, "Lebenszeit und Heimat des Isaak Or Zarua." *MGWJ*, LV (1911).

UNNA, ISAK, "Die Bedeutung der Gutachtenliteratur für die Jüdische Geschichte. *Jeshurun*, I (1914), 397–402; 426–434.

WAXMAN, M., A History of Jewish Literature from the Close of the Bible to Our Own Day. 4 vols. New York, 1930–41.

WEISS, ISAAC HIRSCH, דור דור ודורשיו. 5 vols. Vilna, 1904.

WELLESZ, J., "Meir b. Baruch de Rothenbourg". *REJ*, LVIII (1909), 226–40; LIX (1910), 42–58; LX (1910), 53–72; LXI (1911), 44–59.

————, "Ueber R. Isaak b. Moses 'Or Zarua' ". *JJLG*, IV (1906), 75–124.

————, "Hayyim b. Isaac Or Zarua", *REJ*, LIII (1907), 67–84; LIV (1907), 102–6.

————, "Die Dezisionen R. Isaak's aus Corbeil." *JJLG*, IX (1912), 490–7; Hebrew section, pp. 1–8.

WERTHEIMER, S. A., ספר גנזי ירושלים. 3 vols., Jerusalem, 1896–9.

WEYDEN, ERNEST, Geschichte der Juden in Köln. Cologne, 1897.

WIENER, MEIR, Regesten zur Geschichte der Juden in Deutschland während des Mittelalters. Hanover, 1862.

————, "Ueber den Gewinn den die Geschichtwissenschaft aus dem Studium der religionsgesetzlichen (halachischen) Teile der Neu-hebräischen Literatur des Mittelalters zu erwarten hat." *ZGJD*, XIX (1865), 507–21.

WOLF, GERSON, Zur Geschichte der Juden in Worms, Breslau, 1862.

————, Die alten Statuten der Jüdischen Gemeinden in Mähren samt den nachfolgenden synodalbeschlüssen. Vienna, 1880.

Yerushalmi, Palestinian Talmud. Edition Krotoshin, 1886.

YOM TOB LIPPMAN HELLER, תוספות יום טוב. Commentary to the Mishnah, printed with several editions of the latter.

ZEDEKIAH B. ABRAHAM ANAV, שבלי הלקט. Venice, 1546. A more complete edition, with introduction and notes, by Solomon Baber, Vilna, 1886.

ZEITLIN, SOLOMON, Religious and secular Leadership. Philadelphia, 1943.

————, Maimonides, a Biography. New York, 1935.

ZEUMER, KARL, Die deutschen Städtesteuern im 12. und 13. Jahr-hundert. Staats-und sozialwissenschaftliche Forschungen, her-ausgegeben von Gustav Smoller, Vol. I (1878).

ZIMMELS, H. J., Beiträge zur Geschichte der Juden in Deutschland im 13. Jahrhundert, insbesondere auf Grund der Gutachten des R. Meir Rothenburg. Vienna, 1926.

ZUCKER, HANS, Studien zur jüdischen Selbstverwaltung im Altertum. Berlin, 1936.

ZUNZ, LEOPOLD, Zur Geschichte und Literatur. Vol. I, Berlin, 1845.

————, Literaturgeschichte der synagogalen Poesie. Berlin, 1865.

————, Die Ritus des Synagogalen Gottesdienstes geschichtlich ent-wickelt. Berlin, 1859.

ZURI, JACOB SAMUEL, תולדות המשפט הצבורי העברי. 2 vols. Paris, 1931

ADDITIONAL BIBLIOGRAPHY

IRVING A. AGUS, תשובות בעלי התוספות. New York, 1954.

————, *Urban Civilization in Pre-Crusade Europe*, N. Y., 1965.

SALO W. BARON, *A Social and Religious History of the Jews*, 2nd ed. Vols. IX-XII, N. Y., 1965-7.

SOLOMON B. FREEHOF, *The Responsa Literature*, Philadelphia, 1955.

GUIDO KISCH, *The Jews in Medieval Germany*, Chicago, 1949; New York, 1969.

MEIR b. BARUCH of Rothenburg, ס' שאלות ותשובות edited by Yitz-chak Z. Cahana, Jerusalem, 1943.

MEIR b. BARUCH of Rothenburg, תשובות, פסקים ומנהגים, 3 Vols., Jerusalem, 1957-63.

LIST OF INQUIRERS[1]

A. Abraham, 251(R)*, 546.
    Abraham b. Eliezer ha-Levi, 518-9.
    Abraham ha-Levi, 529(R).
    Asher, 18(Rt)*, 216, 293(R), 378(R), 460(R), 556(R),
        603(R), 637(tr)*, 657, 666(Rt), 676(Rt), 696(R),
        722(R), 726(R), 734(Rt).
    Asher b. Moses, 12(R), 13(t), 448(R)
    Asher b. Yehiel, 211(R), 487, 581, 733(Rt)

B. Baruch, 226(R)
    Baruch ha-Kohen, 159(Rr)

D. Dan, 436(R)
    David, 572(Rr)
    David b. Kalonymus, 209

E. Eleazar, 6(t), 606
    Eleazar b. Yehiel, 246
    Eliakim, 652(Rt)
    Eliakim ha-Kohen, 563
    Eliezer, 64(Rt), 522(Rt), 735
    Eliezer b. Ephraim, 342(Rt)
    Eliezer ha-Kohen, 735
    Eliezer ha-Levi, 694
    Elijah, 572 (Rr)
    Ephraim, 302(Rr)
    Ephraim b. Ephraim, 739
    Ephraim b. Joel, 246
    Ephraim b. Judah, 518

---

[1] References are to the numbers of the Text.
*Please note: (R) = Rabbi; (t) = teacher; (r) = relative.

727

Menahem b. Natronai, 287 (R)
Menahem ha-Levi, 673, 701(R)
Menahem of Würzburg, 332(Rtr), 386(R), 423(Rtr), 514(R), 777(R)
Mordecai, 251(R)
Mordecai ha-Kohen, 267
Moses, 169(R), 368, 594(R)
Moses Azriel, 360
Moses Azriel b. Eleazar Hadarshan, 246, 741

N. Nahman b. Nathan, 190
Nathan, 48(r)
Nathan b. Jacob, 352
Nethanel b. Nahman, 739

P. Perez, 331 (R), 379(Rt)

S. Samuel, 23(R), 436(R), 570, 571(R), 609(R)
Samuel b. Eliezer ha-Kohen, 190
Shemariah, 435, 471(R), 588(Rt), 599, 609(R)
Shemariah ha-Kohen, 432
Shneor, 214
Solomon, 185(R of France), 432, 617(R)
Solomon b. Adret, 779

T. Tobiah, 108

Y. Yakar ha-Levi, 381(R), 397(Rtr)
Yedidyah, 147(R), 630(R), 675(R), 751(R)
Yedidyah b. Israel, 475, 590
Yehiel, 570
Yehiel b. Isaac, 581
Yekutiel, 248, 440, 756(R)
Yekutiel ha-Levi, 373(R)

INDEX TO TEXT

I.

J.

Jacob, 280, 513, 535, 560

Jacob (cited as an authority), 106

Jacob, Rabbi, of Cracow, 249

Jacob b. Joseph, Rabbi, 280

Jacob b. Mordecai, 251

Jacob of Orleans, Rabbi, 47

Jesus, 18, 176

Jewelry, 39–40, 190, 275–6, 310, 318, 438, 442, 493, 568, 611, 627, 636, 674, 719, 737

Jews and non-Jews relation, 18, 46–50, 61, 66–7, 74–5, 85, 90, 108, 112–5, 121–33, 135-6, 140–6, 148–9, 174–6, 220, 223–6, 228, 232, 240–1, 243, 246, 251–3, 310, 317, 356, 383, 421, 430, 432–3, 437–8, 444–5, 451–2, 455, 459–60, 463, 475, 485–91, 493–4, 498–9, 506, 521–6, 528, 530, 534, 561, 572, 576, 581, 583, 603, 612–19, 621, 624, 626, 628–9, 634, 641, 645, 648, 650–3, 655–7, 695, 702, 710–12, 732, 743, 758, 766–7, 770–6, 778, 780–4

Joel ha-Levi, Rabbi, 256, 271

Jointure, additional, 301–2, 313, 320–2, 344, 373

Jonah Gerundi, Rabbi, 779

Jonah of Gironah, 779

Joseph b. Simon (Isaac?), 177

Joshua, 710

Judah ha-Kohen, Rabbi, 29(t), 323(tr), 597(tr)

Judah of Düren, 280

Judah of Paris, 396

Judeans, custom of, 367

Judges and courts, 77, 137, 143, 147, 165, 171–2, 174–5, 182, 184–5, 189–90, 213, 242, 247, 253, 256, 258, 268, 271, 280, 287, 290, 308–10, 320, 331, 337, 339–40, 342, 351, 360, 371, 382–3, 389–404, 406–21, 427, 429, 432–4, 437, 446, 449–50, 453, 464, 470, 474–7, 482, 485, 492–3, 495, 506, 511, 515, 518, 532, 538, 543, 555, 562–3, 566, 572, 577, 581, 587, 589, 591–4, 597, 601, 611, 618, 631–2, 635–7, 646, 653, 666, 670, 675, 678, 693, 697, 701, 703, 707, 715, 719–22, 724, 731–3, 737–9, 741–2, 747, 758, 765, 769–71, 776, 779, 783

Judicial discretion, 398

K.

Kablan, 489

Kalonymus (cited as an authority), 271